THE FAILURE OF POPULAR CONSTITUTION MAKING IN TURKEY

This book offers an in-depth account of the failure of popular constitution making in Turkey from 2011 to 2013. The aim to include different segments of society and political parties in constitution making makes this process an anomaly in the otherwise authoritarian history of Turkish constitutional politics. In the end, however, long-standing societal divides regarding political, cultural and religious diversity that were amplified in the negotiations led to the failure of the process. Most notably, the ruling AKP's insistence on establishing a presidential system – supported by neither the other three political parties nor the public – destabilized the process and exacerbated distrust among the drafters. In addition, unfavorable procedures prevented consensus and allowed the AKP to hijack the process. The failure of popular constitution making in 2013 was a missed opportunity for democratization before Turkey plunged into full-fledged democratic backsliding.

Felix Petersen is the Minerva Post-Doctoral Fellow at the Richard Koebner Center for German History at the Hebrew University of Jerusalem. His research interests include modern political thought, constitutional politics, theory of democracy, and German and Turkish politics. He is a co-author of the forthcoming book *The Constitutional Court of Turkey: Judicial Politics between Authoritarianism and Democracy*.

Zeynep Yanaşmayan is senior research fellow and coordinator of the Max Planck Society-funded research initiative "The Challenges of Migration, Integration and Exclusion" at the Department of Law and Anthropology, Max Planck Institute for Social Anthropology. Her research interests include migration and citizenship studies, governance of religious diversity, law and society and Turkish politics. She is the author of *The Migration of Highly Educated Turkish Citizens to Europe: From Guestworkers to Global Talent* (2019), and co-editor of *Belief, Law and Politics: What Future for Secular Europe?* (2014).

COMPARATIVE CONSTITUTIONAL LAW AND POLICY

Series Editors

Tom Ginsburg *University of Chicago*
Zachary Elkins *The University of Texas at Austin*
Ran Hirschl *University of Toronto*

Comparative constitutional law is an intellectually vibrant field that encompasses an increasingly broad array of approaches and methodologies. This series collects analytically innovative and empirically grounded work from scholars of comparative constitutionalism across academic disciplines. Books in the series include theoretically informed studies of single constitutional jurisdictions, comparative studies of constitutional law and institutions, and edited collections of original essays that respond to challenging theoretical and empirical questions in the field.

Books in the Series

The Failure of Popular Constitution Making in Turkey: Regressing Towards Constitutional Autocracy
Edited by Felix Petersen and Zeynep Yanaşmayan

A Qualified Hope: The Indian Supreme Court and Progressive Social Change
Edited by Gerald N. Rosenberg, Sudhir Krishnaswamy, and Shishir Bail

Constitutions in Times of Financial Crisis
Edited by Tom Ginsburg, Mark D. Rosen, and Georg Vanberg

Reconstructing Rights: Courts, Parties, and Equality Rights in India, South Africa, and the United States
Stephan Stohler

Constitution Making and Transnational Legal Order
Edited by Tom Ginsburg, Terence C. Halliday, and Gregory Shaffer

Hybrid Constitutionalism
Eric C. Ip

The Politico-Legal Dynamics of Judicial Review
Theunis Roux

The Invisible Constitution in Comparative Perspective
Edited by Rosalind Dixon and Adrienne Stone

Constitutional Courts in Asia: A Comparative Perspective
Edited by Albert H. Y. Chen and Andrew Harding

Judicial Review in Norway
Anine Kierulf

Constituent Assemblies
Edited by Jon Elster, Roberto Gargarella, Vatsal Naresh, and Bjorn Erik Rasch

The DNA of Constitutional Justice in Latin America: Politics, Governance, and Judicial Design
Daniel M. Brinks and Abby Blass

The Adventures of the Constituent Power: Beyond Revolutions?
Andrew Arato

Constitutions, Religion and Politics in Asia: Indonesia, Malaysia and Sri Lanka
Dian A. H. Shah

Canada in the World: Comparative Perspectives on the Canadian Constitution
Edited by Richard Albert and David R. Cameron

Courts and Democracies in Asia
Po Jen Yap

Proportionality: New Frontiers, New Challenges
Edited by Vicki C. Jackson and Mark Tushnet

Constituents before Assembly: Participation, Deliberation, and Representation in the Crafting of New Constitutions
Todd A. Eisenstadt, A. Carl LeVan, and Tofigh Maboudi

Assessing Constitutional Performance
Edited by Tom Ginsburg and Aziz Huq

Buddhism, Politics and the Limits of Law: The Pyrrhic Constitutionalism of Sri Lanka
Benjamin Schonthal

Engaging with Social Rights: Procedure, Participation and Democracy in South Africa's Second Wave
Brian Ray

Constitutional Courts as Mediators: Armed Conflict, Civil-Military Relations, and the Rule of Law in Latin America
Julio Ríos-Figueroa

Perils of Judicial Self-Government in Transitional Societies
David Kosař

Making We the People: Democratic Constitutional Founding in Postwar Japan and South Korea
Chaihark Hahm and Sung Ho Kim

Radical Deprivation on Trial: The Impact of Judicial Activism on Socioeconomic Rights in the Global South
César Rodríguez-Garavito and Diana Rodríguez-Franco

Unstable Constitutionalism: Law and Politics in South Asia
Edited by Mark Tushnet and Madhav Khosla

Magna Carta and Its Modern Legacy
Edited by Robert Hazell and James Melton

Constitutions and Religious Freedom
Frank B. Cross

International Courts and the Performance of International Agreements: A General Theory with Evidence from the European Union
Clifford J. Carrubba and Matthew J. Gabel

Reputation and Judicial Tactics: A Theory of National and International Courts
Shai Dothan

Social Difference and Constitutionalism in Pan-Asia
Edited by Susan H. Williams

Constitutionalism in Asia in the Early Twenty-First Century
Edited by Albert H. Y. Chen

Constitutions in Authoritarian Regimes
Edited by Tom Ginsburg and Alberto Simpser

Presidential Legislation in India: The Law and Practice of Ordinances
Shubhankar Dam

Social and Political Foundations of Constitutions
Edited by Denis J. Galligan and Mila Versteeg

Consequential Courts: Judicial Roles in Global Perspective
Edited by Diana Kapiszewski, Gordon Silverstein, and Robert A. Kagan

Comparative Constitutional Design
Edited by Tom Ginsburg

The Failure of Popular Constitution Making in Turkey

REGRESSING TOWARD CONSTITUTIONAL AUTOCRACY

Edited by

FELIX PETERSEN

Hebrew University of Jerusalem

ZEYNEP YANAŞMAYAN

Max Planck Institute for Social Anthropology

CAMBRIDGE
UNIVERSITY PRESS

CAMBRIDGE
UNIVERSITY PRESS

University Printing House, Cambridge CB2 8BS, United Kingdom

One Liberty Plaza, 20th Floor, New York, NY 10006, USA

477 Williamstown Road, Port Melbourne, VIC 3207, Australia

314–321, 3rd Floor, Plot 3, Splendor Forum, Jasola District Centre, New Delhi – 110025, India

79 Anson Road, #06–04/06, Singapore 079906

Cambridge University Press is part of the University of Cambridge.

It furthers the University's mission by disseminating knowledge in the pursuit of education, learning, and research at the highest international levels of excellence.

www.cambridge.org
Information on this title: www.cambridge.org/9781108497626
DOI: 10.1017/9781108596459

First published 2020

Printed in the United Kingdom by TJ International Ltd, Padstow Cornwall

A catalogue record for this publication is available from the British Library.

ISBN 978-1-108-49762-6 Hardback

Contents

List of Figures *page* ix
List of Contributors x

PART I INTRODUCTION 1

Introduction 3
Felix Petersen and Zeynep Yanaşmayan

1 Explaining the Failure of Popular Constitution Making in Turkey (2011–2013) 21
Felix Petersen and Zeynep Yanaşmayan

PART II CONTEXTUALIZING CONSTITUTION MAKING IN TURKEY 57

2 The People and Its Embodiment: Authoritarian Foundations of Constitutions in Turkey 59
Ertuğ Tombuş

3 Regime Cycles, Constitution Making, and the Political System Question in Ottoman and Turkish Constitutional Developments 84
Şule Özsoy Boyunsuz

4 Illiberal Media and Popular Constitution Making in Turkey 118
Burcu Baykurt

PART III DEBATING AND DRAFTING THE CONSTITUTION IN 2011–2013 143

5 Debating State Organization Principles in the Constitutional Conciliation Commission 145
Gözde Böcü and Felix Petersen

6 Glass Half Full: Drafting Fundamental Rights in the Turkish Constitution-Making Process (2011–2013) 183
Oya Yegen and Zeynep Yanaşmayan

7 Countermajoritarian Institutions in Turkish Constitution Making 218
Maria Abad Andrade

8 Debating the Amendment-Making Rule: The Rigidity vs. Flexibility Debate in the Turkish Constitution-Making Process 249
Oya Yegen

Appendices 282
Index 404

Figures

1.1 The spectrum of popular constitution making *page* 32
7.1 Party positions on the High Council of Judges and Prosecutors 237
7.2 Results of the deliberations on the High Council of Judges and Prosecutors 240
7.3 Party positions on the Turkish Constitutional Court 242
8.1 Historical evolution of constitutional amendment-making procedure in Turkey 261
8.2 Party proposals on the amendment-making procedure 270
8.3 AUK draft amendment-making rule (Art. 146) 275
Appendix 1.1 AUK members and legal consultants 283

Contributors

MARIA ABAD ANDRADE is a researcher in the Department of Social Sciences at Humboldt University of Berlin.

BURCU BAYKURT is an assistant professor of urban futures and communication at the University of Massachusetts Amherst.

GÖZDE BÖCÜ is a doctoral candidate in the Political Science Department at the University of Toronto.

ŞULE ÖZSOY BOYUNSUZ is an associate professor in the Faculty of Law at Galatasaray University.

FELIX PETERSEN is a research fellow in the Richard Koebner Center for German History at the Hebrew University of Jerusalem.

ERTUĞ TOMBUŞ is a research associate in the Department of Social Sciences at Humboldt University of Berlin.

ZEYNEP YANAŞMAYAN is a senior research fellow in the Department of Law and Anthropology at the Max Planck Institute for Social Anthropology in Halle, Germany.

OYA YEGEN is an assistant professor of Political Science in the Faculty of Arts and Social Sciences at Sabancı University.

PART I

INTRODUCTION

Introduction

Felix Petersen and Zeynep Yanaşmayan

"Turkey is an unfinished symphony. We have been looking for a constitution for the last 150 years."[1]

1 APPROACH OF THE BOOK: STUDYING THE FAILURE OF CONSTITUTION MAKING

With the fall of the Iron Curtain and the dissolution of the Soviet Union, liberalism appeared to become the only game in town.[2] The political cataclysms of the late 1980s triggered a wave of scholarship in political science and constitutional law on the prospects of political change. In particular, constitutionalism, constitution making, and constitutional politics became dominant topics accompanying the debate on transformations in the socialist states of Eastern and Central Europe, and later South Africa and Latin American countries.[3] The enthusiasm of the historical moment made most contributions to this debate focus on the conditions that make transformation (i.e., constitutionalization or re-constitutionalization) successful. As most transitions were from some sort of authoritarianism or autocracy to democracy, the question at the heart of scholarship has been how to successfully

[1] Zühtü Arslan (current president of the Turkish Constitutional Court), as quoted in Gary J. Jacobsohn, *Constitutional Identity* (Cambridge, MA: Harvard University Press, 2010), 333.

[2] Francis Fukuyama, *The End of History and the Last Man* (New York: Free Press, 1992).

[3] The following are a few select contributions to this debate: Jon Elster and Rune Slagstad, eds., *Constitutionalism and Democracy* (Cambridge: Cambridge University Press, 1988); Bruce Ackermann, *We the People, Volume 1: Foundations* (Cambridge, MA: Harvard University Press, 1991); Jon Elster, "Constitution-Making in Eastern Europe: Rebuilding the Boat in the Open Sea," *Public Administration* 71, nos. 1–2 (1993): 169–217; Andrew Arato, "Forms of Constitution Making and Theories of Democracy," *Cardozo Law Review* 17, no. 1 (1995): 191–231.

constitutionalize a liberal democratic state. Today, constitutional politics remains a hot topic, but there is one significant difference. In the course of de-democratization processes and democratic backsliding in a variety of countries (e.g., Russia, Turkey, Hungary, United States, and Brazil), scholars have shifted their attention toward conditions that can prevent a liberal democratic state from becoming autocratic.[4] What brings these perspectives together is their explicit focus on conditions that facilitate the establishment or maintenance of a constitutional system.

This book shares the overall epistemological interests of scholarship on political transformation and constitutionalization. However, our focus is on conditions that facilitate failure. Why is it interesting to study failure in the first place? Although failure is typically assumed to be bad, the reality of it is more ambiguous. Amy C. Edmondson argues that for organizations, in her case economic companies, failure is "sometimes … even good," as it provides "valuable new knowledge that can help an organization."[5] As successful social and political processes depend on the knowledge of potential pitfalls and mistakes to be avoided, studying failed social and political processes is a promising avenue for social research in general, and for research on constitutional politics in particular. The knowledge gathered in this book will deepen and expand scholarship on constitution making. It may also serve constitution makers to establish strategies and procedures that increase the likelihood of successful constitution making.

In constitutional scholarship, the study of failure has thus far not played a prominent role. With respect to the question of why constitutions fail, two contributions stand out. On the basis of his study of state constitutions in the United States, Donald Lutz shows that longer constitutions are more likely to be quickly replaced.[6] He identifies at least three reasons why a constitution might be replaced: new elites might prefer different values, institutions, or norms; constitutions might be outdated and not in sync with the times; extensive amendments might have altered a constitution to an extent that re-

4 See Tom Ginsburg and Aziz A. Huq, "How to Lose a Constitutional Democracy," *UCLA Law Review* 65 (2018): 78–169; Steven Levitsky and Daniel Ziblatt, *How Democracies Die* (New York: Crown, 2018); David Waldner and Ellen Lust, "Unwelcome Change: Coming to Terms with Democratic Backsliding," *Annual Review of Political Science* 21 (2018): 93–113; Roberto Stefan Foa and Yascha Mounk, "The Danger of Deconsolidation: The Democratic Disconnect," *Journal of Democracy* 27, no. 3 (2016): 5–17.

5 Amy C. Edmondson, "Strategies for Learning from Failure," *Harvard Business Review* 89, no. 4 (2011): 48–55.

6 Donald S. Lutz, "Patterns in the Amending of American State Constitutions," in *Constitutional Politics in the States: Contemporary Controversies and Historical Patterns*, ed. G. A. Tarr (Westport, CT: Greenwood Press, 1996), 24–46.

constitutionalization is necessary.[7] In their expansive study on the endurance of national constitutions, Zachary Elkins, Tom Ginsburg, and James Melton find that the "average life expectancy" of constitutions is 19 years. Environmental factors and constitutional design choices are reasons that determine the longevity or endurance of constitutions.[8] Interestingly, economic crises do not have a significant impact on constitutional change, nor do "loss and gain of territory" or "defeat in war."[9] With regard to constitutional design choices, they elaborate on three significant traits that characterize enduring constitutions: (1) the flexibility of a constitution, or its "ability . . . to adjust over time,"[10] matters for its survival throughout various historical situations; (2) the more specific a constitution is, the more easily it can be enforced, which prevents contestation around the constitution and makes it more likely to endure; and (3) inclusion of "important groups in society in the design and maintenance of the constitution"[11] increases the number of stakeholders, which makes it more likely that a constitution lives on. Looking at their findings from the other side, we can conclude that constitutions are likely to fail when they are rather rigid and unable to adapt over time; when they are vague, difficult to enforce, and hence easily contested; and when the constitution-making process and constitutional politics exclude important social groups.

Failure in constitution making is also rarely studied, although exceptions exist: Stefan Köppl has published a comprehensive study of the failure of constitutional reform in Italy, showing that disagreement among political parties and the two chambers of Parliament led to the failure of three reform attempts between 1983 and 1998.[12] Hélène Landemore, Jon Ólafsson, Alexander Hudson, and Thorvaldur Gylfason have all analyzed the failure of constitution making in Iceland in the 2010–2013 period. All four contributions illustrate that the disagreement and lack of communication between the constitution-making body and political elites and parties obstructed the coalition building that would have been necessary to push the constitution through

7 Ibid., 30.

8 They explain: "Consider design factors as those having to do with the content and drafting process of the constitution itself and environmental ones as those pertaining to the international and national environments that host the constitution." See Zachary Elkins, Tom Ginsburg, and James Melton, *The Endurance of National Constitutions* (New York: Cambridge University Press, 2009), 2.

9 Ibid., 136.

10 Ibid., 207.

11 Ibid., 208.

12 Stefan Köppl, *Italien: Transition ohne Reform? Gescheiterte Anläufe zur Verfassungsreform 1983–1998 im Vergleich* (Stuttgart: ibidem, 2003).

Parliament, which eventually led to the failure of popular constitution making in Iceland.[13]

Hanna Lerner studies the failed constitution-making processes in Israel and India. She concludes that constitution making failed in Israel in 1949 because constitution makers from different camps were unable to reconcile their conflicting ideals about "state institutions and Jewish religious tradition."[14] In India, on the other hand, the constituent assembly was unable to draft a constitution for the united India in 1948 because the Congress Party and the Muslim League fundamentally disagreed on very general issues (e.g., national identity, role of religion). The conflict was "imported" into the constitution-making process, and debates were shaped by contestation between the two political rivals that was clothed in legal language, but only served "to push through [the two parties'] ideological agendas."[15] This ultimately led to the partition of the country and the founding of India and Pakistan. In a more recent contribution, Lerner also shows that constitution making in Indonesia and Egypt failed for similar reasons. In Indonesia (1955–1957), disagreement between agents aiming to constitutionalize an Islamic state and agents "who envisioned an all-inclusive Indonesian national identity rather than an exclusively Islamic identity" persisted throughout the constitution-making process. In Egypt (2012), the "Islamist and secular leadership [could not] achieve any kind of agreement concerning controversial fundamental issues such as the role of Islam and the secular identity of the state."[16] Mara Malagodi studies the failure of constitution making in Pakistan (1947–1954) and Nepal (2008–2012), showing that in "both countries, significant segments of the political establishment felt threatened" by constitution making and "the direction of constitutional restructuring." As constitution makers and "key political actors" could not agree on constitutionalization, the latter "mobilized against the

[13] Hélène Landemore, "Inclusive Constitution-Making: The Icelandic Experiment," *The Journal of Political Philosophy* 23, no. 2 (2015): 166–191; Jon Ólafsson, "The Constituent Assembly: A Study in Failure," in *Iceland's Financial Crisis: The Politics of Blame, Protest, and Reconstruction*, eds. V. Ingimundarson, P. Urfalino, and I. Erlingsdóttir (London: Routledge, 2017); Alexander Hudson, "When Does Public Participation Make a Difference? Evidence from Iceland's Crowdsourced Constitution," *Policy & Internet* 10, no. 2 (2017): 185–217; Thorvaldur Gylfason, "Chain of Legitimacy: Constitution Making in Iceland," in *Constituent Assemblies*, eds. J. Elster, R. Gargarella, V. Naresh, and B. E. Rasch (New York: Cambridge University Press, 2018).

[14] Hanna Lerner, *Making Constitutions in Deeply Divided Societies* (Cambridge: Cambridge University Press, 2011), 196.

[15] Ibid., 34.

[16] Hanna Lerner, "Constituent Assemblies and Political Continuity in Divided Societies," in *Constituent Assemblies*, eds. J. Elster, R. Gargarella, V. Naresh, and B. E. Rasch (New York: Cambridge University Press, 2018), 68–71.

assemblies, sought to obstruct their proceedings, and put an end to their constitution-making work."[17]

Summarizing the findings of these studies on failed constitution making, it can be concluded that, broadly speaking, deep disagreements over the content and form of projected constitutions and the incapacity of constitution makers to come up with strategies to overcome divisions and facilitate consensus usually lead to failed constitution-making processes. This book aims to contribute to the debate on failed constitutional engineering with an in-depth analysis of a largely understudied case, the failed popular constitution-making process in Turkey in the 2011–2013 period.[18]

1.1 *Popular Constitution Making in Turkey: Overcoming the Past or Back to the Future?*

In the fall of 2011 the Constitutional Conciliation Commission (*Anayasa Uzlaşma Komisyonu*, AUK) was established by the Turkish Grand National Assembly (*Türkiye Büyük Millet Meclisi*, TBMM) with the aim of drafting a new constitution for the country in consultation with civil society members and the participation of individual citizens. Hopes were high that through this process Turkish society could break with a largely undemocratic and exclusionary history of constitution making. In other words, in historical perspective this attempt at popular constitution making was an anomaly, and it seemed that the polarized Turkish society might finally find conciliation and re-constitutionalize the foundations of the Turkish state in a democratic manner. Divided by ideological predispositions and political preferences, however, delegates involved in the constitution-making process were

17 Mara Malagodi, "Constituent Assembly Failure in Pakistan and Nepal," in *Constituent Assemblies*, ed. J. Elster et al., 79–108, 106.

18 Exceptions include Ergun Özbudun, "Constitution Writing and Religious Divisions in Turkey," in *Constitution Writing, Religion and Democracy*, eds. A. Bali and H. Lerner (Cambridge: Cambridge University Press, 2016); Elif Gözler, "Turkey's New Constitution-Making Attempt and the Participation of Minority Organizations during the Public Consultation Process," in *Contemporary Turkey at a Glance II: Turkey Transformed? Power, History, Culture*, eds. M. Ersoy and E. Üzyürek (Wiesbaden: Springer, 2017); Bertil Emrah Oder, "The Much Awaited and Deeply Controversial Constitutional Process: Learning from Turkey's Failure in 2013," in *Themes of Conflict in Middle Eastern Democracies: A Comparative Perspective from Turkey and Israel*, ed. Friedrich Ebert Stiftung and Van Leer Jerusalem Institute (Istanbul and Jerusalem, 2014); Oğuz N. Babüroğlu and Gülru Z. Göker, "Going Large Scale: The Polling Conference Process for Participatory Constitution Making in Turkey," *Action Research* 12, no. 4 (2014): 374–391; Zeynep Yanaşmayan, "Oppositional Usages of Europeanization in Turkish Constitution-Making: Discussions on Religious Freedom," *Turkish Studies* 18, no. 4 (2017): 644–664.

eventually unable to agree on a significant number of constitutional provisions. Of 172 provisions initially slated for debate for the new constitution, the AUK reached agreement on only 60 articles. Consequently, in the fall of 2013 the constitution-making process was abandoned without a full draft having been agreed on, let alone a new democratic constitution having been enacted.

Following the turmoil of the violently repressed Gezi Park protests in 2013, the popular election of Recep Tayyip Erdoğan to the presidency in 2014, the collapse of the Kurdish peace process, and the snap elections of 2015, the political sphere became even more polarized. After the failed coup d'état in 2016, the ruling Justice and Development Party (*Adalet ve Kalkınma Partisi*, AKP), in coalition with the Nationalist Movement Party (*Milliyetçi Hareket Partisi*, MHP), adopted constitutional amendments in April 2017 that in effect transformed Turkey into a hyper-presidential political system in which checks and balances are significantly weakened. These amendments confirmed a "growing and unprecedented consensus" among scholars that Turkey is transitioning to a form of authoritarianism.[19] In other words, while in 2011 Turkish society was set to break with the legacy of undemocratic constitution making by organizing an inclusive and participatory constitution-making process, by 2017 the country had already returned to the established path of majoritarian imposition in constitution making.[20] But what happened in between? And why did the democratization effort initiated by the constitution-making process fail?

As expected by experts familiar with Turkish politics and Turkey's constitutional history, irreconcilable societal divides – or rather the ways in which they have been reflected in the "red lines" drawn by the various

[19] Zenonas Tziarras, "Erdoganist Authoritarianism and the 'New' Turkey," *Southeast European and Black Sea Studies* 18, no. 4 (2018): 593–598, 594; see also Murat Somer, "Understanding Turkey's Democratic Breakdown: Old vs. New and Indigenous vs. Global Authoritarianism," *Southeast European and Black Sea Studies* 16, no. 4 (2016): 481–503; Kerem Öktem and Karabekir Akkoyunlu, "Exit from Democracy: Illiberal Governance in Turkey and Beyond," *Southeast European and Black Sea Studies* 16, no. 4 (2016): 469–480; Berk Esen and Şebnem Gümüşçü, "Rising Competitive Authoritarianism in Turkey," *Third World Quarterly* 37, no. 9 (2016): 1581–1606; Bahar Başer and Ahmet Erdi Öztürk, *Authoritarian Politics in Turkey: Elections, Resistance and the AKP* (London: I.B. Tauris, 2017).

[20] Hanna Lerner (*Making Constitutions in Deeply Divided Societies*, 36) identifies the 1924 constitution-making process as an act of constitutional imposition through secular elites. Andrew Arato ("The Constitutional Reform Proposal of the Turkish Government: The Return of Majority Imposition," *Constellations* 17, no. 2 (2010): 345–350) defines the practice of constitutional amendment under the AKP since 2007 as a practice of majority imposition. For a general discussion of constitutional imposition, see Richard Albert, Xenophōn Kontiadēs, and Alkmēnē Phōtiadou, eds., *The Law and Legitimacy of Imposed Constitutions* (London: Routledge, 2019).

political parties involved in the process – have played a significant role in the failure of popular constitution making in 2011–2013.[21] "Red lines" became particularly resilient over time, not least due to the growing suspicion of the process, which deteriorated immensely after the AKP's presidentialism proposal was announced, and to then-Prime Minister Recep Tayyip Erdoğan's regular interference in the work of the AUK. Moreover, the lack of experience with inclusive constitution making meant that the AUK did not always establish the most favorable procedures for its functioning. The initial deadline (end of 2012) turned out to be too ambitious and short-sighted; the predetermined time frame only served to increase external pressure. The unanimity rule for decision-making effectively impeded any meaningful coalition building, allowing the AKP to hijack the process with its insistence on presidentalism, a political system that the other three parties were unwilling to accept.

In hindsight, the party that benefited the most from the failure of popular constitution making was the ruling AKP, which ended up finding a partner in crime, the MHP, to help fulfill its aspirations. The failure of the constitution-making process allowed the regime to further discredit democratic politics and to justify a return to the tradition of majority imposition in constitution making. Many commentators, including some of the contributors to this book, argue that the process was actually never meant to succeed.[22] Clearly, the motivations and the power to influence the process were different for each actor involved. However, an in-depth look into the process reveals it to have been a significant missed opportunity, not only because of its break with exclusionary methods of constitution making, but also because of its "potential" break with (some of the) old statist-authoritarian ideas of Turkish constitutionalism (as evidenced by, for example, the agreement to make the concept of human dignity the founding principle of the constitution; agreement on constitutive rule-of-law principles; agreement to remove the politicized Council of Higher Education (YÖK) as a constitutional institution).[23]

[21] Ergun Özbudun, "Turkey's Search for a New Constitution," *Insight Turkey* 14, no. 1 (2012): 39–50; Burak B. Özpek, "Constitution-Making in Turkey after the 2011 Elections," *Turkish Studies* 13, no. 2 (2012): 153–167.

[22] See Tombuş, Chapter 2 in this volume.

[23] Human dignity debates are analyzed in Yegen and Yanaşmayan, Chapter 6 in this volume; rule-of-law debates and provisions are discussed in Böcü and Petersen, Chapter 5 in this volume; and debates on the removal of YÖK are elaborated in Abad Andrade, Chapter 7 in this volume.

Through an exhaustive analysis of party proposals, minutes of the Constitutional Conciliation Commission, contributions of civil society organizations and citizens, as well as public media discourse, this book analyzes the failure of the 2011–2013 constitution-making process. It sets out to explain the anomaly of popular constitution making in the context of the predominantly authoritarian past, present, and future of Turkish constitutional politics. The book complements the already strong scholarship on authoritarian constitutionalism by critically examining the mimicry of principles and practices of popular constitutionalism under autocratization and/or democratic deconsolidation in this understudied case. It also contributes to the heretofore scant literature on the reasons for the failure of constitution-making processes. Last but not least, it offers a missing piece to the scholarship on Turkish constitutionalism by discussing a recent chapter in Turkey's constitutional history that has been, up to now, relatively neglected.

2 STRUCTURE AND ARGUMENTS OF THE BOOK

The chapters in this book analyze the failure of popular constitution making in Turkey through a multidisciplinary prism that integrates political theory, comparative politics, sociology, constitutional and comparative law, and media and area studies. While pursuing different perspectives and developing different themes and arguments, all chapters historically embed the 2011–2013 constitution-making process with reference to past constitutions and constitution-making processes in Turkey. Overall, the chapters offer competing and yet complementary accounts of the process, relying on original data and different methodologies.

The book is divided into three parts: *Part 1: Introduction* provides a systematic analysis of why the 2011–2013 constitution-making process failed; *Part 2: Contextualizing Constitution Making in Turkey* situates the 2011–2013 process within Turkey's constitutional history as well as within the public debate in the media at the time; and *Part 3: Debating and Drafting the Constitution in 2011–2013* provides an in-depth analysis of the AUK debates on state organization principles, fundamental rights and freedoms, countermajoritarian institutions, and the amendment-making rule. The appendix to the book includes a list of all AUK members (Appendix A) and lists of agreed and non-agreed articles produced by the AUK (Appendices B and C).

The first chapter provides a systematic analysis of the historical failing of democratic constitution making in Turkey and explains the failure of popular constitution making in 2011–2013. **Felix Petersen** and **Zeynep Yanaşmayan** reconstruct minimal and maximal conditions of popular constitution making from political theory and constitutional law. With respect to past constitution-making processes in 1876, 1921, 1924, 1961, and 1982, the chapter illustrates that none of the prior attempts met even minimal conditions of popular constitution making, that is, direct and free election of a constituent assembly by all citizens, irrespective of gender, property, race, or other criteria. Against this background, it is indeed surprising that the 2011–2013 process was designed to meet maximum conditions of popular constitution making (e.g., election of MPs as constitution makers, public consultation before and after drafting). The chapter discusses why popular constitution making was initiated in the first place. It explains the establishment of the Constitutional Conciliation Commission and its working principles, and it elaborates how public consultation was facilitated and how the commission proceeded in the drafting stage. Explaining the failure of popular constitution making, Petersen and Yanaşmayan argue that it did not live up to the promise of an inclusive and democratic process: public consultation did not include all segments of society; constitution makers did not draft a constitution entirely on the basis of public proposals; and the commission did not produce a full democratic draft constitution. The process was in the end organized in a top-down rather than a bottom-up manner, and party interests prevailed over the public interest. Irrespective of the question of whether or not the process was organized in the inclusive and participatory manner promised by political elites, the chapter emphasizes that constitution making failed because parties were unable to overcome deep disagreements over contested issues (e.g., state-religion relations, citizenship, government system). The procedures established by the commission (especially the unanimity requirement for agreement on provisions and the tight time frame for drafting) turned out to obstruct rather than facilitate consensus, as parties were seldom able to agree unanimously, and reaching consensus required long discussions. As such, the unanimity clause and the tight time frame clearly worked against each other. Petersen and Yanaşmayan conclude that if reaching consensus was the priority, then the AUK should have allocated more time to create an open, deliberative environment that would have allowed drafters to make decisions unanimously. If the urgency to adopt a new constitution was the priority, then a different decision-making mechanism should have been chosen. In the end, the incapacity or lack of will to overcome disagreements deprived Turkish citizens of a democratic constitution and accelerated the return to majority imposition in constitution making.

The first two chapters in the second part (Ertuğ Tombuş and Şule Özsoy Boyunsuz) trace authoritarian path dependencies that characterized constitution-making processes from the late Ottoman Empire and the early republican period, through the two military constitutions enacted in 1961 and 1982, to more recent constitutional changes adopted through constitutional amendments in 2017. Despite their different approaches and explanations, these chapters concur on the fact that the 2011–2013 process could have offered an opportunity to break with the authoritarian past of previous constitution-making processes. The third chapter in the second part (Burcu Baykurt), on the other hand, contextualizes the 2011–2013 process within the media landscape of Turkey, pointing out that the media were already highly politically polarized well before the work of the AUK began. Under such structural constraints, which granted the AKP tight control over all means for the dissemination of information, the media did not help in the promotion of a deliberative, participatory constitution-making process.

Employing Claude Lefort's work as a lens through which to study the four republican constitution-making processes of 1921, 1924, 1961, and 1982, **Ertuğ Tombuş** argues that the Turkish tradition of constitution making is pervaded by a hegemonic-totalitarian logic whereby one actor claims to be the embodiment of the sovereign people. Democratic politics, on the other hand, requires that the place of power remain empty. Consequently, for a process to be truly democratic, political actors should refrain from all-encompassing embodiment claims. However, as Tombuş shows, with the exception of the 1921 process, the exact opposite has occurred in Turkish constitutional politics. Instead of taking the representation of the people and its will as a promise that can never be truly fulfilled, hegemonic political actors presented themselves as the ultimate realization of the people's will. Whether it be the Kemalists in 1924 and the republican alliance in the following decades, the Democratic Party (*Demokrat Parti*, DP) in the late 1950s, or the military in 1961 and 1982, irrespective of who sought to permanently occupy the place of power, Turkish constitutional practice has been shaped by the hegemonic-totalitarian logic. In this way, the authoritarian foundation of Turkish constitutions has been reproduced throughout the republic's history. This logic has also been ingrained in the AKP's constitutional politics. Through what Tombuş calls "populist closure," the AKP has further advanced the embodiment claim in an extremely polarizing manner since 2007. While the 2011–2013 process is discussed here as a remarkably different approach to constitution making that could potentially have facilitated a democratic departure from the path-dependent authoritarian track, its failure had the reverse effect of legitimizing a return to majority imposition in 2017. Tombuş concludes that the AKP never intended to produce a new constitution based on consensus but made strategic use of the AUK as part of its populist closure.

Şule Özsoy Boyunsuz provides a different perspective on Turkish constitutional history. Rather than identifying the whole republican period from 1924 onward as reproducing the authoritarian foundation, she conceptualizes Turkish constitutional history in cycles that are marked by democratic openings and authoritarian closures. With a special emphasis on institutional and political system choices made in each democratic and authoritarian phase, Özsoy Boyunsuz follows constitutional developments from the first Ottoman Constitution of 1876 to the present day. While the 1876 Constitution pointed to the beginning of a democratic phase with the establishment of the first General Assembly, the immediate dismissal of Parliament by Sultan Abdülhamit led to a long authoritarian phase that was characterized by a concentration of power. This phase was brought to an end by the 1908 reinstatement and amendment of the 1876 Constitution, which made the regime move toward democracy until the hegemonic reign of the Union and Progress Party (*İttihat ve Terakki Partisi*, İTP) in 1913. The authoritarian regime of the İTP was overthrown through the Turkish Independence War (*Kurtuluş Savaşı*), and the fate of the Ottoman Empire was sealed with the enactment of the two first republican constitutions in 1921 and 1924. With the single-party rule of the Republican People's Party (*Cumhuriyet Halk Partisi*, CHP), another authoritarian phase began. This was briefly interrupted by a democratic phase after the transition to multiparty politics in 1950. But Turkey returned to an authoritarian phase in the last years of the Democratic Party's rule. While the 1960 coup d'état and the approach to constitution making were clearly authoritarian, the 1961 Constitution initiated another democratic opening that was broken off by another military coup in 1980, turning the regime cycle back to authoritarianism. The AKP's constitutional politics proceeds along the same cyclical movements. The constitutional amendments of 2004 were made consensually and further democratized state and society. However, the 2007 and 2010 amendments were the result of majority imposition and geared toward concentrating power in the hands of the AKP. The 2011–2013 constitution-making process was an opportunity to embark on a new democratic phase. Yet its failure initiated another authoritarian phase, providing for extreme centralization of power through the "hyper-presidentialism" enacted with the 2017 constitutional amendments. The cyclic approach to Turkish constitutional history allows Özsoy Boyunsuz to finish on a more optimistic note than Tombuş, claiming that the demands for democracy articulated by civil society organizations during the 2011–2013 process may yet turn the tide of cyclical movements again toward a democratic opening.

Based on a combination of newspaper content analysis and institutional history, **Burcu Baykurt's** analysis of the role of the media during the 2011–2013 process points to the conclusion that the silencing of all forms of opposition and strict control over what the public was allowed to know prevented a meaningful and critical debate over the constitution and the work of the AUK from taking place. Baykurt demonstrates how the AUK's work started against the background of a fast-degenerating media environment that had witnessed record numbers of journalists jailed and blatant cases of corruption and censorship. The AUK's initial approach to the media was, therefore, cautious, trying to keep a tight grip on the information flow. Baykurt reconstructs the changing relationship between the AUK and the media in three phases. In the first phase (October 2011 to May 2012), the AUK stood behind its own decision to make official statements only through the commission and not to publicize any of the views received from citizens and civil society. Baykurt contends that, given Turkey's polarized political environment at the time, the AUK's lack of trust of the media is to a certain degree understandable. The controlling approach they took to sharing information also enabled more informative and less polarized reporting of the AUK's work in the first phase. During the second phase (May to December 2012), the media continued to rely on the AUK as a source of information and reported in a rather balanced way on the content of debates. This neutral tone changed entirely in the last phase (January to November 2013), when reporting became more polarized as disagreements within the AUK became difficult to hide. Reporting also relied less on the information from the AUK. Instead, external actors (especially then-Prime Minister Recep Tayyip Erdoğan) became more vocal in disseminating information about the process and shaping the media discourse on the AUK. Media reports increasingly questioned the progress made, the timeline for constitution making, and the very existence of the commission. Baykurt's analysis shows that the media in effect followed the AKP's lead in derailing the process, with December 2012 being a critical juncture when the AKP's motivations clearly shifted and the external pressure it exerted increased.

The four chapters in the third part (Gözde Böcü and Felix Petersen, Oya Yegen and Zeynep Yanaşmayan, Maria Abad Andrade, Oya Yegen) focus on the actual debates in the Constitutional Conciliation Commission. All four chapters analyze paramount constitutional matters (state organization principles, fundamental rights and freedoms, countermajoritarian institutions, amendment-making rule) that mostly remained contested. The four chapters approach their respective themes from a variety of theoretical angles. Taken together they reveal important insights that help qualify the failure of the process. First, despite losing the numbers game (only 60 agreed articles out of 172 deliberated), the AUK achieved significant, albeit incomplete, consensus on contested articles. Agreement on specific clauses or partially agreed reforms of constitutional bodies ultimately ended up among the non-agreed articles and therefore became invisible success stories. Yegen and Yanaşmayan provide an example of the former (agreement on a clause), showing that despite the overall disagreement on the religious freedom article, the AUK draft extended protection to non-believers in the first clause of the article. Abad Andrade provides two examples of partially agreed reform of constitutional bodies: The AUK agreed to remove the Council of Higher Education (*Yükseköğretim Kurulu*, YÖK) as a constitutional institution, and the CHP, the MHP, and the Peace and Democracy Party (*Barış ve Demokrasi Partisi*, BDP) submitted a joint proposal to codify the functions and election procedure of the Constitutional Court. These invisible success stories reveal the potential of the 2011–2013 process for democratization in Turkey. Second, across the different provisions that were negotiated, shifting alliances dominated the deliberations. For instance, as Böcü and Petersen show in the debates on the principles of state organization, the MHP and the CHP were more often on the same side of the table, sticking more strictly to the existing constitutional tradition when it came to constitutive concepts such as national sovereignty. However, in the discussions of fundamental rights and freedoms, as illustrated by Yegen and Yanaşmayan, the CHP sided more often with the BDP when it came to "transplanting" new rights into the domestic constitutional framework. Although political parties were ready to negotiate their positions depending on the theme discussed, parties with antagonistic identities (the AKP versus the CHP, the BDP versus the MHP) were unlikely coalition partners.

Through a historically grounded analysis of the commission's debates on state organization principles, **Gözde Böcü** and **Felix Petersen** show that deep, long-standing disagreements over fundamental political concepts and a nonconsensual approach to the government system question made it impossible to constitutionalize the basic structure of the state in the 2011–2013 process. As past constitutions and constitutional jurisdiction have only vaguely determined constitutive concepts such as popular (here national) sovereignty, separation of powers, or rule of law, and have rather utilized the democratic constitutional order to justify rights limitations, the chapter first argues that Turkish constitutional history has prioritized raison d'état over citizen's interests. The 2011–2013 process was hence an opportunity to break with this authoritarian statist path dependence. This could have been achieved, to a certain extent, had the constitution-making process not been abruptly terminated in 2013. Most importantly, the AUK agreed on some rule-of-law principles (e.g., narrower grounds for rights limitations, no special courts to try dissent), which, compared to prior constitutions, would have significantly improved the constitutional state order. However, Böcü and Petersen also explain that the historically contested nature of certain state organization principles (e.g., laicism, national sovereignty), the unclear meaning of constitutive political concepts (e.g., democracy and separation of powers), and the abuse of both through state elites in the past had created a situation unfavorable for consensual constitution making. AUK delegates fought over the role of laicism and national sovereignty in the projected constitution. Democracy appeared in debates as an empty signifier inviting agents to apply their own subjective understandings of the concept. Depending on party positions, separation of powers was presented as more or less functional under presidentialism and parliamentarism. The chapter concludes that party "red lines" and historically acquired convictions and predispositions around these concepts impeded constitution making. In particular, disagreement over the political system question became a deal breaker and contributed significantly to the failure of the entire constitution-making process.

Oya Yegen and **Zeynep Yanaşmayan** offer a less gloomy picture, as the fundamental rights and freedoms chapter was the only part of the draft constitution on which AUK members managed to reach substantial agreement: 43 of the 60 agreed articles concerned fundamental rights and freedoms. Although some of the most controversial issues regarding fundamental rights remained contested (e.g., freedom of religion, freedom of association and assembly, freedom of education in one's mother tongue), Yegen's and Yanaşmayan's analysis demonstrates that agreed articles or clauses did produce important constitutional novelties and would have provided for considerably better protection of fundamental rights and freedoms than prior constitutions. The chapter explains this relative success through the concept of constitutional borrowing. Yegen and Yanaşmayan uncover how agreement on the article on human dignity, which was borrowed primarily from the German Basic Law, allowed the AUK to establish a new normative foundation for the understanding of fundamental rights in Turkish constitutional law. Had this article become the guiding norm of the new constitution, they argue, it would have ended the constitutional prioritization of state interests over individual rights. This chapter also demonstrates that international norms, most particularly the European Convention on Human Rights (the Convention), enjoyed considerable normative authority in the deliberations. Besides the fact that party proposals were at times verbatim translations of the Convention's articles, it also assisted in shaping and substantially improving the restrictive, rights-limiting stance of the 1982 Constitution. However, the analysis also demonstrates the limits of constitutional borrowing, particularly when the issue at stake is very polarizing. With regard to successful constitution drafting in the 2011–2013 process, Yegen and Yanaşmayan identify three drafting techniques that assisted the AUK in moving forward and overcoming deadlock, namely deferral to subcommissions and consultants, deferral to "by law" clauses, and reasoning-writing. Although these tactics were ultimately not enough to resolve issues of high political stakes, they nevertheless enabled drafters to make progress. This begs the question of the extent to which similar tactics could have been employed to resolve deadlock on other issues (e.g., state organization principles), and why the commission did not take recourse to this approach.

If gross violations and regular restrictions of human rights have been one of the cornerstones of illiberal periods in Turkey, the introduction of countermajoritarian institutions with the 1961 Constitution solidified such regime abuses. **Maria Abad Andrade's** chapter focuses on four of the most important countermajoritarian institutions, namely the Constitutional Court, the High Council of Judges and Prosecutors, the National Security Council, and the Council of Higher Education. She traces their development from 1961 to today, with a specific focus on the 2011–2013 debates on countermajoritarian institutions. Against the backdrop of the political and/or military tutelage of these institutions and their path dependency, Abad Andrade examines to what extent political parties genuinely aimed at strengthening the ability of these bodies to decide independently and to avoid being politicized. Although the regulation of most of these countermajoritarian institutions remained contested, Abad Andrade's chapter shows that significant improvement could have been achieved. There was consensus regarding removing the Council of Higher Education from the ranks of constitutionally entrenched institutions, and tripartite agreements were reached regarding stripping the constitutional status from the National Security Council (with the exception of the MHP) and regarding the functions and election procedure of the Constitutional Court (with the exception of the AKP). The AKP's majoritarian approach, which was geared toward maintaining executive power over these institutions, as well as the MHP's reluctance to move away from the status quo, eventually impeded agreement on these articles. As Abad Andrade also notes, it is revealing that the AKP and the MHP, both parties that prevented the removal of tutelary countermajoritarian institutions, partnered up in 2016–2017 to push through constitutional changes that increased the power of the executive over these institutions. It is impossible to know to what extent this was a calculated move, but it is clear that without the AKP and the MHP's obstruction, the 2011–2013 process could have significantly reformed counter-majoritarian institutions.

The most recent constitutional amendments enacted by the AKP and the MHP in 2017 are in line with the mode of constitutional imposition through amendments that has been characteristic of the AKP's rule since at least 2007. Against this background, **Oya Yegen** analyzes the AUK debates on the amendment-making rule for the projected constitution in 2011–2013. While Turkish constitutions from 1921 to 1924 and 1961 to 1982 had become incrementally more rigid with regard to amendment making, Yegen shows that the 1987 constitutional amendments made the amendment-making procedures relatively more flexible, which enabled majority imposition through constitutional amendments. The chapter demonstrates that in the 2011–2013 process, opposition parties' concerns over past experiences made them wary of constitutional imposition in the future. In that context, it was not surprising that the CHP proposed the most rigid amendment-making rule, providing for a higher parliamentary majority and a mandatory referendum, whereas the AKP proposed the most flexible rule, removing the president as a veto player and requiring reduced majorities. With regard to the actual drafting, Yegen's analysis shows how political parties came to a partial agreement on the amendment-making rule by relying very much on the existing method of constitutional revision, that is, a double track procedure that allows for either direct adoption of amendments by supermajorities or by reduced majorities in Parliament plus a public referendum. In contrast to the existing rule, the draft rule of the AUK would have empowered Parliament, and not the president, to decide to resort to a voluntary referendum. Yegen also illustrates how the expertise provided by legal consultants helped reach this partial agreement. Outsourcing the actual wording of the amendment-making rule to legal consultants helped the AUK establish expert coalitions that managed to cross party lines. With regard to other issues that remained contested in the 2011–2013 process, this conclusion implies that, had the political parties managed to set aside their long-standing (mis)trust of one another and relied on technical expertise in negotiations and in the drafting, they would have certainly made better progress with their list of agreed articles and may have eventually even been able to produce a complete draft constitution.

3 CONCLUSION

This book sheds light on a particular period of Turkish constitutional politics through an in-depth case study of the failure of popular constitution making in the 2011–2013 process. It allows us to draw valuable lessons about the reasons for the failure of constitution making more generally. The findings stress the significance of cooperation and sociopolitical alliances in offsetting authoritarian actors' control over such processes and successfully making a constitution. Since political parties' vested political interests are likely to undermine conciliatory constitution making rather than help overcome social division and political contestation, strategies and tactics for overcoming disagreement (e.g., predrafting agreements or guiding principles, deferring discussions on contested issues, omitting contested issues from the constitution) are significant. In the Turkish case, these were implemented only to a minimal extent. The disagreements were further exacerbated because, in addition to the well-known societal divides that were expected to cause disagreement, drafters were torn with regard to state organization. Without agreement on how to constitutionalize the state, as our analysis shows, it is very unlikely that a document will be drafted that opens room to renegotiate contested issues once the constitution-making process is concluded (i.e., incremental constitution making[24]). Had the AUK taken public opinion and civil society proposals into consideration, disagreement on the government system could have been resolved, and the result would have diminished the chances that a strong executive would be able to abuse power in an otherwise overall rather authoritarian political setting. Interestingly, then, the Turkish case suggests that public consultation and public polling could be employed strategically to help resolve deadlock on the government system and other highly contested issues.

With regard to constitution-making methods, the analysis suggests that although insistence on unanimity in the voting rules, as was decided by the AUK for the 2011–2013 process, may aspire for all the right normative reasons to guarantee inclusion, supermajority rules (three-fifths, two-thirds, three-fourths) appear to be more realistic for constitution making in divided societies. Such majorities force constitution makers to strive to reach consensus and prevent individuals or groups from obstructing the entire process by insisting on provisions that do not have majority appeal and that can ignore rather than promote the public interest. In addition, it is essential to allow enough time for drafting and deliberation of contested issues in order to reconcile different political interests and historical experiences. The desire to found or refound a state and its basic norms can initiate a democratization process, hence it should not be rushed, especially when the society entering such a process is characterized by social division and deep disagreements over the nature and essence of its common union. Last but not least, the book suggests that legal consultation and the import of expertise can help overcome deadlock on

[24] Lerner, *Making Constitutions in Deeply Divided Societies*.

contested issues. However, the sources of inspiration or "borrowing" should enjoy uncontested acceptance among all participating parties. Using too many templates in an unsystematic and strategic manner in the debating and drafting process may serve to solidify party positions and can thus diminish the chances of reaching consensus.

Although many issues remained contested and were eventually unresolved in the Turkish constitution-making process, our findings point to the conclusion that, whether under conditions of democratic deconsolidation or autocratization, constitution-making processes that bring together different stakeholders can lead to significant improvement of constitutional texts and regimes. Given the potential for change that such "constitutional moments" carry, the importance of the design and methods of constitution making is not to be underestimated.

1

Explaining the Failure of Popular Constitution Making in Turkey (2011–2013)

Felix Petersen and Zeynep Yanaşmayan

1 INTRODUCTION

Studying past constitution-making processes in Turkey, we note that in none of the prior processes (1876, 1921, 1924, 1961, and 1982) did participation play a defining role. As we explain in the following, none of the past processes met even minimal conditions of popular constitution making, that is, direct and free election of a constituent assembly through all citizens, irrespective of gender, property, race, or other criteria. Against this background, it is indeed surprising that the Turkish Parliament initiated a constitution-making process in 2011 that was designed to meet maximum conditions of popular constitution making (e.g., election of MPs as constitution makers, public consultation before and after drafting). At the time, the promise of a participatory and inclusive constitution-making process raised hopes among civil society actors and citizens that Turkey would be able to change tracks, from a statist-authoritarian to a liberal-democratic path. This would be unprecedented in Turkey's modern history.

In October 2011 the Constitutional Conciliation Commission (*Anayasa Uzlaşma Komisyonu*, AUK) was formed, and delegates established working principles and started public consultations with civil society organizations to gather information on public demands for the projected constitution. In spring 2012 AUK delegates began negotiations and drafting. From the very beginning, constitution making was characterized by deep disagreements over constitutive constitutional principles. Ultimately, the AUK was unable to draft a full constitution. In November 2013, the ruling Justice and Development Party (*Adalet ve Kalkınma Partisi*, AKP) pulled out of the negotiations and the experiment in popular constitution making collapsed thereafter. In this chapter, we seek to explain the failure of popular constitution making in Turkey.

We begin with a theoretical reconstruction of minimum and maximum conditions of popular constitution making on the basis of the literature and case studies. The first part develops the notion that, under minimum conditions of popular constitution making, delegates to a constitution-making body explicitly tasked with constitution writing are elected in direct and free elections open to citizens irrespective of gender, property, race, or other criteria. Under maximum conditions, citizens elect delegates for a constitution-making body, citizens and civil society organizations provide input through public consultation before and after drafting, and citizens adopt a draft constitution through public referendum. Operationalizing the theoretical framework established, the second part of the chapter sets out to explain why popular constitution making failed in Turkey in the past. While in the first two constitution-making processes (1921 and 1924) the minimum conditions of popular constitution making were not met because election to the respective constitution-making bodies did not include women in the electorate, the two most recent processes (1961 and 1982) were dominated by the military, which tightly controlled and regulated selection of the constitution makers.

Against the background of undemocratic and exclusionary constitution making in the past, the third and fourth parts of the chapter focus on the 2011–2013 constitution-making process. The third part elaborates on why popular constitution making was initiated in the first place. It explains the establishment of the Constitutional Conciliation Commission, its working principles, how public consultation was facilitated, and how the commission proceeded in the drafting stage. In the fourth part, we show that the process did not end up being as inclusive and democratic as promised: Public consultation did not include all segments of society, constitution makers did not draft a constitution entirely based on public proposals, and the commission did not produce a full democratic draft constitution. We furthermore explain that, irrespective of whether the process was organized in the inclusive and participatory manner promised by political elites, constitution making failed because parties were unable to overcome deep disagreements over contested issues (e.g., state-religion relations, citizenship, system of government). The procedures established by the commission (especially provisions requiring unanimity and establishing the tight time frame for drafting) turned out to obstruct rather than facilitate consensus, as parties were seldom able to agree unanimously, and reaching consensus therefore required long discussions. In the end, the incapacity or lack of will to overcome disagreements deprived Turkish citizens of a democratic constitution and accelerated the return to majority imposition in constitution making.

2 POPULAR CONSTITUTION MAKING: THEORETICAL PREMISES

From the classical paradigm of sovereign constitution making to concepts such as popular,[1] post-sovereign,[2] and inclusive[3] constitution making, political thinkers have argued that legitimate constitutions are drafted and/or adopted through direct or indirect participation of those affected by the fundamental law, that is, the people.[4] Modern constitution-making processes usually involve public participation of one kind or another at some stage. According to Karl Loewenstein, a "standardized" procedure of constitution making requires that "a national assembly or *constituante* is elected by the entire people for this specific task." In addition the people should have the final ratification power in adopting or rejecting a draft constitution.[5] Although election of a constitution-making body representing the entire people is essential in many cases, in some contexts such bodies can also be formed less formally and organized in a more corporatist manner as roundtables or conventions bringing together different stakeholders (e.g., organizations, parties, government, and opposition).[6] Tom Ginsburg, Zachary Elkins, and Justin Blount distinguish at least three different types of participation in constitution making: approval by referendum, (s)election of constitution makers, and direct participation of the public or representative groups in constitution making.[7] Overall, they "find a broad consensus in the literature about the importance of public involvement as well as an apparent trend in practice."

1 William Partlett, "The Dangers of Popular Constitution-Making," *Brooklyn Journal of International Law* 38, no. 1 (2012): 193–238.

2 Andrew Arato, *Post Sovereign Constitution Making: Learning and Legitimacy* (Oxford: Oxford University Press, 2016).

3 See, e.g., Hélène Landemore, "Inclusive Constitution-Making: The Icelandic Experiment," *The Journal of Political Philosophy* 23, no. 2 (2015): 166–191.

4 See Tom Ginsburg, Zachary Elkins, and Justin Blount, "Does the Process of Constitution-Making Matter?" *Annual Review of Law and Social Science* 5, no. 5 (2009): 201–223; Yash Ghai and Guido Galli, "Constitution Building Processes and Democratization," in *Democracy, Conflict, and Human Security: Further Readings*, ed. J. Large, R. Austin, and T. D. Sisk (Stockholm: IDEA, 2006); Justin Blount, "Participation in Constitutional Design," in *Comparative Constitutional Law*, ed. T. Ginsburg and R. Dixon (Cheltenham: Edward Elgar, 2011), 38–46.

5 Karl Loewenstein, *Political Power and the Governmental Process* (Chicago: The University of Chicago Press, 1957), 135.

6 On roundtables, see Andrew Arato, "Conventions, Constituent Assemblies, and Round Tables: Models, Principles and Elements of Democratic Constitution-Making," *Global Constitutionalism* 1, no. 1 (2012): 173–200; Arato, *Post Sovereign Constitution Making*, 107–161.

7 Ginsburg, Elkins, and Blount, "Does the Process of Constitution-Making Matter?," 206–208. Justin Blount ("Participation in Constitutional Design," 38) argues elsewhere that dominant forms of participation in constitution making are representation, public consultation, popular ratification, and public oversight.

But they also emphasize that "many of the assumptions of proponents of participation remain untested, and the precise relationships between participation and desirable outcomes of interest remain underspecified."[8]

In sum, public participation can be either included in framing and legitimizing constitution making at the beginning of the process (i.e., electing constitution makers), and/or at the end (i.e., ratification of constitution). The role of the people is reduced to selecting representatives and authorizing the constitution, and it follows the logic of representative democracy. However, public participation can also be included at different stages in a constitution-making process, not just at the beginning or the end. Its organization can combine the logic of representative democracy (i.e., elect constitution makers and ratify the constitution) and participatory democracy (i.e., propose relevant issues to be addressed, suggest constitutional provisions, comment on and contribute to revision of the draft constitution). Analyzing the literature on modern constitution making, we note that beyond the general question of how and when democratic participation should be included in constitution making, there are two other related questions: What body should draft the constitution? And how should the process of constitution making be structured?

2.1 *The Constitution-Making Body*

Comparing historical forms of constitution making, we argue that one of the central elements of modern constitution making is the collective character of the agent making a constitution, that is, the constitution-making body. Up to the eighteenth century, legislation and constitution making were usually acts carried out by individuals (e.g., prince, legislator) or small groups (e.g., royal councils, governments). With the political revolutions and constitution-making exercises in the United States and France, this has changed. Based on the institutional structure present in both prerevolutionary France and the British American colonies, that is, an assembly structure, in these first two modern constitution-making processes, the bodies producing constitutions were collective agencies specifically focused on the task of constitution making. These bodies were not legitimized by the entire population of the respective state (i.e., they were elected by male, property-holding citizens only), but they were nevertheless grounded in the ideas of popular sovereignty and political representation. The question of what body is to draft a constitution and to what extent the form of the body matters for the output produced has shaped the debate on constitution making since then.

[8] Ginsburg, Elkins, and Blount, "Does the Process of Constitution-Making Matter?," 219.

Jon Elster and Walter Murphy emphasize the superiority of special constituent assemblies over legislative constitution-making bodies. Elster distinguishes four different types of constitution-making bodies: conventions, mandated constituent legislatures, self-created constituent legislatures, and self-created legislating assemblies.[9] Following this distinction, he argues that conventions are superior as they "promote active aptitude, they prevent path dependence, and they reduce the impact of personal and institutional interest on the decisions."[10] In other words, conventions are superior because they are exclusively focused on the task of constitution making without being distracted by other tasks or everyday politics. Moreover, conventions do not have to overcome the problem of path dependency in the way that legislative constitution-making bodies may have to due to the dual identity as legislative organ and constitution-making body. Likewise, Walter Murphy argues that "unlike legislators," members of a convention "would operate behind what John Rawls might have called a *thin* veil of ignorance; they might aspire to public office but would lack the linkage between personal ambition and institutional status that even fair-minded legislators might have." Moreover, he emphasizes that such a body would be legitimate, as it is elected by the people for the special task of making a constitution, and it will be dissolved once this task is accomplished.[11] Elster also notes that mixed assemblies may not be the best solution for constitution making, as they may create "an excessively strong legislative branch with correspondingly weak executive and judicial branches."[12] Tom Ginsburg, on the other hand, argues against both Elster and Murphy, holding that, empirically speaking, it is difficult to find "evidence for legislative self-dealing because there [is] no correlation between legislative involvement in drafting and legislative power."[13]

While special conventions have been used to draft constitutions and described for most of modern history as superior, given that they conform to the ideal of higher lawmaking,[14] other formations have been used as well. In

9 Jon Elster, *Securities against Misrule: Juries, Assemblies, Elections* (Cambridge: Cambridge University Press, 2013), 206–209.

10 Ibid., 210.

11 Walter F. Murphy, *Constitutional Democracy: Creating and Maintaining a Just Political Order* (Baltimore: Johns Hopkins University Press, 2006), 196.

12 Elster, *Securities against Misrule*, 212.

13 Tom Ginsburg, "How to Study Constitution Making: Hirschl, Elster and the Seventh Inning Problem," *Boston University Law Review* 96, no. 4 (2016): 1347–1358, 1356.

14 For higher lawmaking, see Bruce Ackerman, *We the People. Vol. I: Foundations* (Cambridge, MA: Harvard University Press, 1991), 266–294; Sujit Choudhry, "Ackerman's Higher Lawmaking in Comparative Constitutional Perspective: Constitutional Moments as Constitutional Failures?," *International Journal of Constitutional Law* 6, no. 2 (2008): 193–230.

more recent constitution-making processes, roundtables, that is, gatherings of various relevant social and political stakeholders, have been the institutional choice. With regard to the institutional form of the constitution-making body, Andrew Arato argues that forms vary depending on the type of transition and the context of constitution making. He distinguishes four paths of constitution making associated with democratic transitions (reform or revolution) based on the criteria of legality/legitimacy and rupture/continuity. He finds cases with continuous legality but ruptured legitimacy (regime change with legal continuity, Hungary 1989); cases with continuous legitimacy but ruptured legality (revolutionary reform or coup with plebiscitary legitimacy, Philadelphia Convention 1787); cases with continuous legality and continuous legitimacy (major reforms and amendments, Turkey 1983–2010); and cases with ruptured legality and ruptured legitimacy (revolution, Weimar 1919). The constitution-making bodies chosen depended on the path. Conventions, like the Philadelphia Convention of 1787, are, according to Arato, characteristic of transitions within a regime (here the postrevolutionary United States) that reconstitute the legal order and create new legality. Roundtables, on the other hand, are associated with constitution-making processes where a regime has lost legitimacy, but the new regime is built on the legality of the prior order.[15] The roundtable and the associated path of incremental constitutionalization is, for Arato, superior "in the domain of legitimacy creation."[16]

In South Africa, constitution making was central to the transition from the racist Apartheid regime. Like other roundtable constitution-making processes of the 1980s and 1990s (e.g., Hungary, Poland), the South African process was, normatively speaking, illegitimate to some extent because the roundtable negotiations were carried out through "*unelected* elites" who were negotiating with representatives of the authoritarian, white nationalist government. Nonetheless, legitimacy-wise, the process in South Africa was saturated, as "democratic elections" to a constitution-making body were held after initial negotiations between different political groups in the early 1990s.[17] The South African government and the opposition (i.e., the African National Congress, ANC) drafted an interim constitution through the Multi-Party Negotiating Process (MPNP) in 1993. This document established fundamental principles that the new constitution had to protect and develop (e.g., multiparty democracy, regular elections, minority rights protection, nonracism, constitutional superiority, separation of powers, bicameral legislature acting as constituent

[15] Arato, *Post Sovereign Constitution Making*, 110.
[16] Arato, "Conventions, Constituent Assemblies, and Round Tables," 200.
[17] Ibid., 162 (emphasis in original).

assembly). National elections were held in 1994, and after formation of the Parliament, which was also the authorized constituent assembly, the constitution-making process entered another stage. Over two years, parties negotiated and drafted the constitution. During these two years, constitution makers invited public participation at different stages. The "three-phase work programme ... included a first phase of activities to elicit issues to be considered in preparing a draft, ... a second phase where the public would be invited to comment on the draft text, and a third phase when the Constitutional Assembly would finalize and adopt the new Constitution."[18] The constitution was eventually adopted in 1996 with 86 percent of Assembly members' votes, but rejected by the Constitutional Court for violating certain fundamental principles protected by the interim constitution (e.g., entrenchment of fundamental rights, protection of public prosecutor, judicial review of ordinary statutes).[19] After amendment of the constitution through the Assembly and final approval by the Constitutional Court, it was signed into law the same year.[20]

This process is characterized by various types of public involvement at different stages: It was initiated through organizations representing the excluded part of society and the ruling minority; constitution makers were elected by the people in an electoral system that did not discriminate on the basis of race, gender, or wealth; and citizens could participate in constitution making by proposing general ideas and by commenting on the draft constitution prepared by the constituent assembly. If the constitution had not been adopted with a two-thirds majority in Parliament, it could have been adopted with simple majority in the Assembly and put to ratification in a public referendum. Hence, the people were considered the last resort to legitimize the constitution if the political elites had been unable to build overarching consensus. In Arato's analysis, the multistage character, with different stages for public input and an overall procedural setup preventing single actors from claiming to exclusively represent the people, make roundtable constitution-making processes normatively superior to other processes.[21] The South Africa example and the disagreement over the best constitution-making body

18 Catherine Barnes and Eldred De Klerk, "South Africa's Multi-Party Constitutional Negotiation Process," *Accord* 13 (2002): 26–33, 32.

19 James Fowkes, *Building the Constitution: The Practice of Constitutional Interpretation in Post-Apartheid South Africa* (Cambridge: Cambridge University Press, 2016).

20 For an overview of the South African constitution-making effort, see Heinz Klug, "Participating in the Design: Constitution-Making in South Africa," *Review of Constitutional Studies* 3, no. 1 (1996): 18–59.

21 Andrew Arato, *The Adventures of the Constituent Power: Beyond Revolutions?* (Cambridge: Cambridge University Press, 2017), 112.

(constituent assembly versus roundtable) leads us from the question of what body drafts a constitution to the broader question of how to organize and structure a constitution-making process.

2.2 *The Constitution-Making Process*

Jon Elster states that "a good constitution-making process turns out to consist of mutually interlocking parts much in the way a good constitution does."[22] He identifies the criteria that structure an optimal constitution-making process. The process must be so designed that interests and passions are reduced while the epistemic quality of debates is maximized. In order to realize this, election to the assembly must be representative, but delegates should not be bound in their vote to party interests or anything other than the public interest. When the assembly does debate and draft a constitution with general principles that are rather neutral with regard to ideologies or political positions, conflict and interest politics will be further reduced. As constant public pressure may turn into a burden and inflame passions, secret debate and voting can further reduce the negative influence of interest politics. Elster adds that "an isolated location of the assembly" will have a similar effect.[23] Describing the optimal process, he uses the image of an hourglass, whereby the process is designed so that "upstream and downstream public consultations" take place at the beginning and at the end.[24] Hence, debate is broadened out twice, while delegates still discuss and draft the constitution in secrecy and in a rather narrow debate in between the two stages of public consultation. Transparency and secrecy, which are both valuable assets in establishing the legitimacy and improving the functionality of a constitution, can thus contribute equally to the shaping of a constitution. Finally, information has to be gathered and processed in an optimal manner, which is realized by composing the constitution-making body so that it encompasses "many epistemic perspectives and a variety of experiences" and by establishing a working practice that promotes genuine debate and open exchange of views rather than self-presentation and interest politics.[25]

In addition to these fundamental criteria that Elster deduces (i.e., reducing passions and interests; drafting general constitutional provisions; debating and

[22] Jon Elster, "The Optimal Design of a Constituent Assembly," in *Collective Wisdom: Principles and Mechanisms*, eds. H. Landemore and J. Elster (New York: Cambridge University Press, 2012), 149.

[23] Ibid., 170.

[24] Ibid., 169.

[25] Ibid., 170–171.

voting in secrecy; being transparent about the process, including upstream and downstream public consultation; integrating different epistemic perspectives), Walter Murphy argues that compromise is fundamental to constitution making: "Practical considerations force founders to tailor their visions of an ideal polity not only to what the electorate will accept but also to what their colleagues will approve."[26] This illustrates that, apart from including the public in constitution making through consultation, the success and legitimacy of a constitution-making process hinges on the overall configuration of the constitution making.

Ginsburg, Elkins, and Blount emphasize that the drafting stage is crucial because that is when the constitution is negotiated. However, with regard to participation, it has to be noted that this "phase is also likely to be the least participatory, given the challenges of writing-by-committee, much less writing-by-nation."[27] In other words, often constitutions are "*made by assemblies*," but "*prepared* by unelected bodies or informal groupings"; and debate does not necessarily take place in the full assembly but in committees.[28] Although the constitution-making body is a collective agent, it changes form throughout the process, alternating between the form of the whole assembly and the form of the subdivided assembly (e.g., committees). Notwithstanding the fact that the role of the public in the actual drafting process might have to be limited, for a constitution-making process to be participatory, inclusive, and democratic, the people must be involved to some extent. To be able to define popular constitution making, we have to return once again to the question of when and how to include the public in the process.

2.3 The Spectrum of Popular Constitution Making

Two constitution-making processes allow us to elaborate minimum and maximum conditions of democratic and inclusive constitution making. The constitution-making process following the German November Revolution of 1918 is the paradigmatic case of a modern popular constitution-making process under minimal conditions. Following the revolution, elections for a constituent assembly were held that were open to all female and male citizens. The Weimar National Assembly was explicitly tasked with writing a constitution. It deliberated, amended, and adopted a draft constitution

26 Murphy, *Constitutional Democracy*, 204.

27 Ginsburg, Elkins, and Blount, "Does the Process of Constitution-Making Matter?," 208.

28 Jon Elster, Roberto Gargarella, Vatsal Naresh, and Bjørn Erik Rasch, "Introduction," in *Constituent Assemblies*, eds. J. Elster, R. Gargarella, V. Naresh, and B. E. Rasch (New York: Cambridge University Press, 2018), 3 (emphasis in original).

between February and June 1919, after which the assembly dissolved itself. Although citizens did not have a say in the eventual adoption of the constitution (no ratification by popular referendum), as this remained the responsibility of the representatives commissioned with the drafting of the constitution, citizens were involved in selecting the constitution makers. Compared to the American and French revolutionary cases referred to above, the input legitimacy of constitution making in Weimar was considerably higher, as all German citizens, irrespective of gender or property qualifications, were entitled to elect and stand for election to the constitution-making body. Conceptualizing popular constitution making as an essentially bottom-up process, we argue that having free and fair elections for a constitution-making body, open to all citizens, is the absolute minimum condition for popular constitution making.

The inclusive, participatory constitution-making process that took place in Iceland from 2010 to 2013 is the paradigmatic case of popular constitution making under maximum conditions. This process is, therefore, exceptional, as "for the first time in human history, a country's foundational text (or at least a draft proposal for it) was written with the more or less direct participation of its people."[29] Both civil society and Parliament organized constitutional conventions bringing together randomly selected citizens in 2009 and 2010. In June 2010 the Icelandic Parliament adopted an act on the formation of a consultative constituent assembly that was to review and revise the 1944 Constitution.[30] This assembly was to consist of a minimum of twenty-five and a maximum of thirty-one members, and it was to be elected by direct personal election. A total of 522 people stood for election, and fifteen men and ten women were elected to the assembly. Although the Supreme Court of Iceland deemed the election and the assembly unconstitutional in 2011, Parliament responded by appointing the elected members to the constituent assembly. Thus the assembly was turned into a constitutional council, that is, a commission of Parliament appointed by resolution.[31] The council drafted a new constitution, involving the public midway through the process by posting the (twelve) different drafts they were working on online and inviting comments and feedback from the

[29] Landemore, "Inclusive Constitution-Making," 167.

[30] The Act on the Formation of the Constituent Assembly (*Act. No. 90/2010*) can be found at www.thjodfundur2010.is/other_files/2010/doc/Act-on-a-Constitutional-Assembly.pdf (accessed March 30, 2019).

[31] Jón Ólafsson emphasizes that, due to the messy procedure, "the status of the members was strangely undefined" and the council was contested from the start; see Jón Ólafsson, "The Constituent Assembly: A Study in Failure," in *Iceland's Financial Crisis: The Politics of Blame, Protest, and Reconstruction*, eds. V. Ingimundarson, P. Urfalino, and I. Erlingsdóttir (London: Routledge, 2017), 252–272, 252.

public.[32] The final draft was submitted to Parliament in July 2011.[33] In 2012, a national referendum was held; 50 percent of the electorate participated, with two-thirds voting in favor of the draft. In the end, however, the draft was not adopted by Parliament, and no new constitution was enacted. Accordingly, this exercise in popular constitution making can be said to have failed.[34]

The Icelandic constitution-making process was an outstanding example of political participation, as the people were not only involved in selecting constitution makers (upstream) and in ratifying the constitution (downstream), but also in determining provisions that should be included in the constitution, and in evaluating the progress made in the constitutional council through commenting and feedback loops in the drafting state (midstream).[35] It can thus be argued that *input legitimacy* and *throughput legitimacy* of the Icelandic case were superior to prior cases. However, it was less successful with regard to *output legitimacy*, as it ultimately did not lead to adoption of the constitution.[36]

In an effort to systematize the theoretical benchmarks of popular constitution making on the basis of the cases discussed, it seems reasonable to distinguish at least two ideal types of popular constitution making that differ with regard to the extent of public involvement. On one end of the spectrum we find minimal public participation, the *sine qua non* of which is that a constitution-making body be composed of delegates elected in free and fair elections that do not exclude citizens on the basis of race, gender, property, or other criteria. Constitution-making processes can move toward the other ideal, that is, maximal public

32 Landemore, "Inclusive Constitution-Making," 174.

33 The rules of procedure adopted by the assembly can be found at www.stjornlagarad.is/english/rules-of-procedure/ (accessed March 30, 2019). For the draft constitution, see www.stjornlagarad.is/other_fles/stjornlagarad/Frumvarp-enska.pdf (accessed March 30, 2019).

34 Thorvaldur Gylfason ("Chain of Legitimacy: Constitution Making in Iceland," in *Constituent Assemblies*, eds. J. Elster et al., 180) argues that Parliament is responsible for the failure of the constitution-making process, as it stalled the draft constitution that had been passed by popular referendum, thus serving only "the interests of the political class and connected special interests at the expense of the people." Jón Ólafsson ("The Constituent Assembly: A Study in Failure," 264–265) explains that the process failed for a number of reasons: the constitutional council did not have a clear mandate; the time frame was too tight, hence the council was unable to properly consult with specialists who could have helped make the draft constitution methodologically bullet-proof; and the council failed to build coalitions with political parties and state officials that could have helped push the document through Parliament.

35 Landemore, "Inclusive Constitution-Making," 170–179.

36 On input and output legitimacy, see Fritz W. Scharpf, "Interdependence and Democratic Legitimation," *MPIfG Working Paper* 98, no. 2 (1998): 1–19; Fritz Scharpf, *Governing in Europe: Effective and Democratic?* (Oxford: Oxford University Press, 1999). On throughput legitimacy, see Vivien A. Schmidt, "Democracy and Legitimacy in the European Union Revisited: Input, Output *and* Throughput," *Political Studies* 61, no. 1 (2013): 2–22.

participation, by including several additional steps. First, along with the election of the constituent body, public involvement can be increased through ratification procedures. Constitutions can be ratified in public referenda or through the legislative assembly (assemblies in the case of a federal state). Ratification can also combine different methods, increasing democratic legitimacy but also transaction costs. For example, assembly approval plus public referendum plus legislative approval produces high democratic legitimacy but has the highest transaction costs; assembly approval alone has the lowest democratic legitimacy and lowest transaction costs. A third step that would render the constitution-making process closer to the maximum end of popular input is public consultation prior to drafting. Here citizens, social and political organizations, and economic interest groups can submit proposals for the new constitution. Depending on the process design, the consultation stage can be organized offline and/or online. A final step that we identify is to include multiple feedback loops that would allow the process to incorporate public input during or after drafting. Debating the draft constitution with the broader (or selected) public(s) can increase the legitimacy of the draft constitution, as citizens can provide feedback to constitution makers and will be more likely to feel a sense of ownership of the constitution. Increasing the number of feedback loops between the public and constitution makers may increase the legitimacy of the constitution, but it will also increase transaction costs, as new veto players are added and the process is prolonged. To meet maximum conditions of popular constitution making, citizens have to elect delegates, provide proposals before drafting and debate the draft with constitution makers, and ratify the constitution.

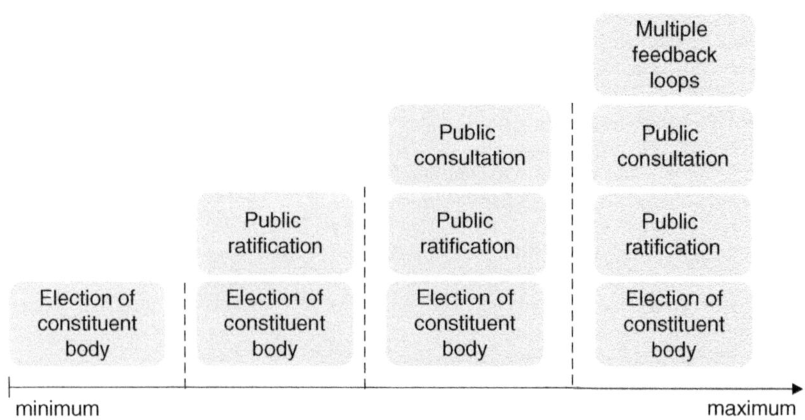

FIGURE 1.1: The spectrum of popular constitution making
Source: Own compilation.

3 THE ABSENCE OF POPULAR CONSTITUTION MAKING IN TURKEY

Turkey has a relatively long constitutional history. Considering the numerous Ottoman statutes and agreements between the royal family and the aristocracy, we can situate Turkey's earliest moves toward constitutional government in the early 1800s with adoption of the Charter of Alliance (*Sened-i İttifak*) in 1808. This treaty, which often goes by the misnomer "the Turkish [Ottoman] Magna Carta," aimed to regulate relations between the central Ottoman authority and provincial rulers. This earliest step of constitutionalism in the Ottoman era was followed by the two edicts of the Tanzimat period (1839–1876) and the short-lived 1876 Constitution, which for the first time allowed the creation of a legislative assembly. Counting the 1876 Ottoman Constitution, Turkey has seen five constitutions: one monarchist (OC-1876) and four republican (TC-1921, TC-1924, TC-1961, TC-1982). Despite this long tradition, it is generally accepted that Turkey has been a dysfunctional constitutional regime in which constitution making has never been democratic, popular, or inclusive.[37] While there are significant differences between the different constitution-making processes and the different constitutions, none of the five fundamental laws produced a fully consolidated democratic regime[38] nor did they provide room for minority views to be taken into account.[39] Consequently, they all had "weak political legitimacy."[40] Drawing on the framework for popular constitution making outlined above, the following provides a systematic overview of the historical failing of popular constitution making in Turkey.

The 1876 Ottoman constitution-making process lacked all conditions that would qualify it as democratic, participatory, or popular. The constitution-making body was hand-picked by the sultan and his bureaucrats. Ottoman citizens had no say in the drafting process or in the adoption of the Constitution. We know little about the deliberations on the Constitution

37 Ran Hirschl, *Towards Juristocracy: The Origins and Consequences of the New Constitutionalism* (Cambridge, MA: Harvard University Press, 2007); Gary J. Jacobsohn, *Constitutional Identity* (Cambridge, MA: Harvard University Press, 2010); Asli Bali and Hanna Lerner, eds., *Constitution Writing, Religion and Democracy* (Cambridge: Cambridge University Press, 2016).

38 Ergun Özbudun and Ömer Faruk Gençkaya, *Democratization and the Politics of Constitution-Making in Turkey* (Budapest: Central European University Press, 2009).

39 Burak B. Özpek, "Constitution-Making in Turkey after the 2011 Elections," *Turkish Studies* 13, no. 2 (2012): 153–167.

40 Ergun Özbudun, *Contemporary Turkish Politics: Challenges to Democratic Consolidation* (Boulder: Lynne Rienner Publishers, 2000), 52.

that was ultimately enacted, but it did not fulfill the conditions of a democratic constitution.[41] In other words, conditions of input, throughput, and output legitimacy were not met in the 1876 constitution-making process. As the people were not involved at all, the 1876 process falls outside the spectrum of popular constitution making.

Turning to the republican era, the 1921 and 1924 Constitutions were drafted by elected bodies. Hence, the criterion of input legitimacy was partially met. Elected by male citizens under circumstances of war, the Turkish Grand National Assembly (*Türkiye Büyük Millet Meclisi*, TBMM) drafted both constitutions. State building and constitution making were largely dominated in the founding years by the Association for the Defense of National Rights (*Müdafaa-i Hukuk Cemiyeti*) and after its establishment as a political party in 1923 by the Republican People's Party (*Cumhuriyet Halk Partisi*, CHP). As political pluralism was not one of the characteristics of the young Turkish Republic, constitution making and politics were dominated by a relatively homogeneous new elite. The first two constitutions were enacted through the Assembly, and not via public referendum.

About the actual process of constitution making in 1921 we know little, but it can be argued that the debates regarding the 1924 Constitution were relatively open and constructive. Delegates were able to overcome conflicts over different articles and succeeded in preparing draft constitutions to which the majority of the constitution makers could give their consent.[42] This does not come as a surprise, as the constitution makers represented a relatively homogeneous group. Thus, conflict was minimized from the very beginning due to the ideological and political proximity of the delegates involved. Ultimately, however, the public was not given a chance to have their interests and opinions taken into consideration. Hence, throughput legitimacy was quite limited in the making of the 1924 Constitution.

It can be argued that the first two constitutions were functional insofar as they realized the goal set by the Turkish Revolution, that is, to build a republican state order. The 1921 Constitution formalized the break from the Ottoman Empire, and the 1924 Constitution concluded the transformation from monarchy to republic. However, compared to other democratic constitutions established around the same time, neither of the two met contemporary standards of democratic regimes. The 1921 Constitution declared

41 See for an exception Aylin Koçunyan, *Negotiating the Ottoman Constitution, 1839–1876* (Leuven: Peeters, 2018).

42 Suna Kili, *Turkish Constitutional Developments and Assembly Debates on the Constitutions of 1924 and 1961* (Istanbul: Robert College Research Center, 1971), 30–63.

popular sovereignty to be the determining principle of political organization, and it established the Turkish Grand National Assembly as the supreme agency exercising national sovereignty, but it did not elaborate how the state or political contest were to be organized democratically. In contrast, the 1924 Constitution was more explicit in determining the organization of the republic, but it was no more democratic. Regarding political rights, for example, the Constitution excluded women from the right to vote and the right to run for office. Thus, the 1924 Constitution did not meet the standards of then–progressive democratic regimes such as the Weimar Constitution of 1919, which granted universal suffrage and gave women the right to stand for elected office. Likewise, it failed to institutionalize a strong separation of powers, one of the core principles of modern democratic state organization, and thereby facilitated and perpetuated the dominance of one political party and elite over society. It can therefore be concluded that the Constitution did not live up to the standards of other democratic constitutions of the era, and that the constitution-making process had little output legitimacy.

In conclusion, both the 1921 and the 1924 constitution-making processes fall outside the spectrum of popular constitution making, as neither of them meets the minimal condition of free and fair elections open to all citizens.

Like the first two republican constitution-making processes, the 1960–1961 and 1980–1982 processes did not at all feature direct elections for a constituent assembly. Strictly speaking, both constitutions were imposed by executive-appointed assemblies that were authorized by the military. In both processes the role of the people was reduced to ratification of constitutions prepared by bodies dominated by putschists and military leaders. Although the military junta did not ban campaigns against the referendum in 1961, it "consistently threatened potential opponents of the constitution. ... Therefore, nobody campaigned against the referendum."[43] In the 1982 referendum, the National Security Council issued a decree that prohibited negative campaigning against the Constitution. Moreover, ratification of the Constitution was tied to the election of the coup leader, General Kenan Evren, to the presidency.[44] Overall, we can hence conclude that these two constitution-making processes completely lacked input legitimacy.

The debates in the 1960–1961 constitution-making process were of consistently high quality, as constitution makers were able to overcome disagreement and draft a constitution. But the interests and views of the public did not

[43] Yunus Emre and Burak Cop, "The 1961 Constitutional Referendum in Turkey," *Sociology of Islam* 3, nos. 1–2 (2015): 49–75, 58.

[44] Özbudun and Gençkaya, *Democratization and the Politics of Constitution-Making*, 20.

play a role. Compared to 1924, the constitution-making body was less representative, as the military regulated who was able to participate in politics at the time. In the 1980–1982 process, the constitution-making body was even more dominated by the military, which reserved for itself the final word on the draft constitution. Although the consultative assembly participated in drafting, the draft was reviewed and revised by a small group of five military jurists appointed by the National Security Council. The military and hand-picked political leaders restructured the state in a top-down manner to serve specific hegemonic interests. A transparent and inclusive process of drafting, amending, and producing the Constitution was not part of the military's agenda. In sum, both constitution-making processes were deficient with regard to throughput legitimacy.

Often praised as the most liberal and democratic Turkish constitution, the 1961 Constitution comes closest to the standards of democratic principles of state organization as they were understood at the time.[45] It did include a bill of rights and broadened civil and political liberties. In addition, it was also the first Turkish constitution that explicitly established rule of law and separation of powers as defining principles of state organization. The commission that drafted the 1961 Constitution explained in a report that, in the future, all state activity would be subject to judicial review by the newly established Constitutional Court (*Anayasa Mahkemesi*, AYM). The 1961 Constitution nevertheless gave constitutional status to the National Security Council, an unelected body that has played a major role in ensuring military tutelage over politics in Turkey. Thus, while the 1961 Constitution was indeed the most liberal and democratic constitution of the modern republican era, it reserved a considerable amount of authority for unelected state officials and the military and therefore did not meet the standards of democratic constitutions. As such, the 1960–1961 constitution-making process lacked output legitimacy.

Overall, the 1982 Constitution has the poorest democracy score of all republican constitutions. "It is generally agreed that the basic philosophy of the 1982 Constitution was to protect the state and its authority against its citizens rather than to safeguard individuals against the encroachments of the state authority."[46] The preamble declares the Turkish state to be "sacred,"

[45] See Ergun Özbudun, "Democracy, Tutelarism and the Search for a New Constitution," in *Turkey's Democratization Process*, ed. C. Rodriguez, A. Avalos, H. Yilmaz, and A. I. Planet (London: Routledge, 2014), 296; Gülsen Seven and Lars Vinx, "The Hegemonic Preservation Thesis Revisited: The Example of Turkey," *Hague Journal on the Rule of Law* 9, no. 1 (2017): 45–82, 54.

[46] Ergun Özbudun, *The Constitutional System of Turkey: 1876 to the Present* (New York: Palgrave, 2011), 19.

and the norm hierarchy reveals the primacy of the state vis-à-vis its citizens: the Constitution defines first the state form with its various characteristics (Art. 1–3), and it protects this structure from amendment through an entrenchment clause (Art. 4). It then defines the fundamental organs of the state (Art. 5–11), and only afterwards elaborates fundamental rights and duties of citizens (Art. 12–74). Furthermore, the Constitution defines the circumstances under which rights and freedoms can be restricted and limited (Art. 13) before even elaborating the rights and freedoms themselves. Hence, the 1980–1982 constitution-making process also lacks output legitimacy.

Both the 1960–1961 and 1980–1982 constitution-making processes were dominated by the military, and the bodies drafting the two constitutions were not popularly elected. Thus, these two processes do not meet the minimal condition of free and fair elections open to all citizens and therefore also fall outside the spectrum of popular constitution making.

Analyzing Turkish constitution-making processes against the theoretical premises elaborated above, we can conclude that there was no systematic prior attempt at genuine popular constitution making. The historically rooted practice is one of constitutional imposition through homogeneous, hegemonic groups. In 1921 and 1924, constitution making was dominated by the new republican elites, while in 1960–1961 and 1980–1982, the military establishment and coup leaders dominated constitution making. As Turkey had no prior history or experience of democratic constitution making and given that past processes did not even meet minimal conditions of popular constitution making, it is indeed surprising that the 2011–2013 process was designed to meet maximum conditions of popular constitution making.

4 POPULAR CONSTITUTION MAKING IN TURKEY, 2011–2013

Turkey is still governed by the largely autocratic 1982 Constitution, which has been significantly amended over the years, notably in 2001, 2004, 2007, 2010, and, most recently, in 2017. Driven by the desire to facilitate the EU accession process, the constitutional amendments in 2001 and 2004 involved judicial reforms on issues ranging from gender equality to fair trial, and have sought to bring Turkish legislation in line with European standards as well as with the case law of the European Court of Human Rights (ECtHR).[47] From 2007 onward, constitutional amendments were more geared toward reflecting the

[47] Ergun Özbudun, "Democratization Reforms in Turkey, 1993–2004," *Turkish Studies* 8, no. 2 (2007): 179–196; Nathalie Tocci, "Europeanization in Turkey: Trigger or Anchor for Reform?" *South European Society & Politics* 10, no. 1 (2005): 73–83.

AKP's vision and interests. While the 2007 referendum allowed for the direct election of the republic's president, the 2010 referendum altered the judiciary appointments, thereby increasing government control. The latter amendments were so contested that Ergun Özbudun and Faruk Gençkaya describe the period as characterized by "constitutional battles" between secular state elites who dominated key institutions such as the Constitutional Court and a Parliament largely commanded by the conservative AKP.[48] These controversies demonstrated again the limited frame of the existing Constitution, which led to serious consideration of a complete overhaul. In April 2010 the Constitution Platform Initiative (*Anayasa Platformu*) had already declared that "the new Constitution should be established through a participatory process that targets the widest consensus possible."[49] A new constitution was promised in the election manifestos of nearly all political parties prior to the 2011 general elections. Soon after the 2011 elections, Parliament composed a special commission (the AUK) with the aim of drafting a new constitution. The intention was to write a democratic constitution in an inclusive process that would break with the past of exclusionary, undemocratic constitution making. The consensus-seeking approach sharply contrasted with previous processes, which, as described above, were characterized by the absence of popular participation. When the constitution-making process was launched on October 1, 2011, the hopes were high for a new constitution, drafted by democratically elected framers who represented the various segments of society.

4.1 *Establishment and Procedures of the AUK*

The Constitutional Conciliation Commission comprised delegates from all four parties represented in the TBMM at the time: the ruling conservative AKP, the Kemalist republican CHP, the Nationalist Movement Party (*Milliyetçi Hareket Partisi*, MHP), and the pro-Kurdish Peace and Democracy Party (*Barış ve Demokrasi Partisi*, BDP). The AKP sent the delegates Mehmet Ali Şahin, Ahmet Iyimaya, and Mustafa Şentop; the CHP sent Süheyl Batum, Atilla Kart, and Rıza Türmen; the MHP was represented by Tunca Toskay, Oktay Öztürk, and Faruk Bal; and the BDP

48 Özbudun and Gençkaya, *Democratization and the Politics of Constitution-Making*, 102.

49 Joint Statement by the Constitution Platform Initiative of April 9, 2010; see www.tepav.org.tr/upload/files/haber/1274359624–0.Constitution_Platform_Background_Note.pdf (accessed March 30, 2019).

sent as delegates Ayla Akat Ata,[50] Sırrı Süreyya Önder, and Altan Tan. All AUK members agreed that it was symbolically important to have the commission presided over by the president of the TBMM (then Cemil Çiçek, AKP) to highlight the priority of its work. However, in order to maintain the balance between the participating parties, Çiçek was granted no voting right. Prior to the kickoff of the process, Çiçek invited twenty-four constitutional lawyers to a brainstorming session, where the discussions revolved more around the methods of constitution making than the content of the projected constitutional text.[51] One of the key questions raised was whether or not Parliament was within its rights to make a new constitution. It was unequivocally affirmed that Parliament was the "primary constituent power."[52] Equipped with this legitimacy, in the first two meetings on October 19 and 25, 2011, the AUK established its working principles in fifteen articles.[53]

1) The name of the commission shall be the Turkish Grand National Assembly Constitutional Conciliation Commission.
2) The task of the commission is to govern the process of constitution drafting and to prepare a draft constitutional text.
3) The head of the commission is the president of the TBMM. In the absence of the president of the TBMM, the session shall be presided over by a commission member who is entrusted by him.
4) The commission shall meet at least twice a week. If necessary, the weekly meetings may be increased. The meetings shall be held on Tuesdays and Thursdays. The agenda, date, and time of the next meeting shall be determined at the end of the present meeting. The commission can also convene outside of Ankara.
5) The commission can convene with a minimum quorum of one member from at least three parties.
6) The commission shall make decisions on the basis of **unanimity** (consensus without voting) of all participating parties. Issues that cannot be agreed upon may be revisited at a time when the commission sees fit. The questions of whether the process has been completed and whether

50 Ayla Akat Ata was later replaced by Bengi Yildiz (see List of AUK Members, in this volume Appendix A).

51 TBMM Tutanak Müdürlüğü, "Anayasa Hukuku Hocalarıyla Toplantı," September 19, 2011. For an analysis of this meeting, see Yegen, Chapter 8 in this volume.

52 Ferhat Kentel, Levent Köker, and Özge Genç, *Making of a New Constitution in Turkey: Monitoring Report 1 (TESEV Report 1)* (Istanbul: TESEV, 2012), 4.

53 See *Anayasa Uzlasma Komisyonunun Çalisma Usulleri* ("Working Procedures of the Constitutional Conciliation Commission," translation by the authors); available at https://anayasa.tbmm.gov.tr/calismaesaslari.aspx (accessed March 30, 2019).

the final text (full draft) has reached maturity shall be decided by consensus.

7) Proceedings of the commission shall be recorded and transcribed. Under certain conditions, the commission may decide not to record the proceedings. The proceedings will be immediately distributed to the members in hard copy or electronic [CD] format. The proceedings may by no means be disclosed to the public prior to completion of the commission's work.
8) The commission shall be accompanied by three technical committees composed of experts suggested by each party and assigned by the Presidency of the Turkish Grand National Assembly. The allowances and expenses of the experts recommended by the political parties will be covered by the Presidency of the Turkish Grand National Assembly. The technical committees shall gather, sort, and analyze data and prepare an assessment report to be submitted to the commission. If necessary, the number of technical committees can be increased.
9) The commission members can be accompanied by a maximum of two consultants each in the commission meetings. Consultants shall not take part in the negotiations. The allowances and expenses of consultants will be covered by the Presidency of the Turkish Grand National Assembly. Depending on the conditions, different consultants may participate in different commission meetings.
10) The meetings of the commission are closed to the public. However, the commission shall take necessary measures to ensure transparency. The commission shall make a public statement, with the content that it sees fit, at the end of the meetings through its president. No one shall attend the meetings of the commission aside from its members, the persons invited, and the persons in charge.
11) The commission shall aim to complete its work by **the end of 2012.** The commission's work shall consist of the following stages:
    a. First stage: participation, data collection, and analysis.
    b. Second stage: identification of principles and drafting of the text.
    c. Third stage: presentation of the draft to the public and public discussion.
    d. Fourth stage: revision of the draft and turning it into a proposal on the basis of public opinion.
12) The commission shall ensure the participation of the public from all social strata in the constitution-drafting process.
13) The draft constitutional text cannot be altered or expanded in the conciliation commission, in legislative committees, or in the plenary

without the consensus of the participating political parties. If amendments are introduced to the draft constitutional text (the proposal) after its submission (by consensus) to the Presidency of the Assembly, the commission's opinion shall be sought.

14) The commission can review and change its own rules by unanimous consent. Moreover, when there are no provisions on a matter, the commission can establish norms. The law by which the adoption process of the draft constitutional text is bound shall be determined with the consensus of the political parties upon completion of the text.
15) The mandate of the commission shall be considered terminated when the constitution proposal is adopted or when a party withdraws or is deemed to have withdrawn from the process. A party that fails to participate in meetings three times in a row without prior excuse shall be deemed to have withdrawn.

Although the name of the commission may seem banal, it had the important function of differentiating the commission and its work from the Constitutional Commission (*Anayasa Komisyonu*), which is a regular working group under the TBMM that deals with constitutional amendments and the functioning of constitutional bodies. The name of the commission thereby also decisively signaled the ambition of making a new constitution rather than amending the old one. From the proceedings of the AUK, we understand that the process was not always perceived by all parties as leading to a new constitutional order. In deliberations of the AUK, the delegate Faruk Bal (MHP) argued that his party did not "think that the commission is qualified or has the right to change the political system because we are dealing with the constitution of an existing state. We are not making a new state."[54] In his view the AUK's power was limited to improvement of the old constitutional system, and he warned that the twelve delegates could not simply erase Turkey's constitutional identity. In this regard, it is not surprising that MHP proposals in the AUK were the least original and very often relied on the 1982 Constitution.

The procedures reveal the cautious – albeit hopeful – attitude of the AUK toward the process. Given the path-dependent constitutional tradition of imposition, as well as the largely majoritarian understanding of democracy dominant in Turkish society, AUK members had legitimate fears that their concerns and ideas would be swept under the carpet by majority rule. That is why they sought to put safeguards in place to ensure that a) the draft would be

54 AUK Proceedings, November 28, 2012.

adopted through consensus, and b) once consensus was reached on a given provision, it could not be easily altered. The relatively rigid unanimity clause could also be seen in keeping with the idea of higher lawmaking, but, as we discuss below, it is questionable whether this was the way forward for a divided society that cannot reconcile all its differences.

4.2 *Organization of Public Consultation and Drafting*

As stated in Article 11 of the working procedures of the commission, the constitution-making process was designed to include a consultation phase to gather and evaluate civil society proposals, a deliberation and constitution-writing phase where the AUK members would draft a constitution, a phase of public presentation and open discussion of the draft with representatives of civil society, and a rewriting phase to amend the draft on the basis of suggestions proposed during the public presentation phase. As the AUK was dissolved before it could reach the third and fourth phases, it is uncertain how it would have conceptualized and implemented public participation in the third phase.

The first phase of public input was organized around three subcommittees that together held more than 160 hearings with a variety of organizations. The AUK was represented in each subcommittee by at least one representative per political party. The first subcommittee, composed of Mehmet Ali Şahin (AKP), Ayla Akat Ata (BDP), Faruk Bal (MHP), and Süheyl Batum (CHP), was charged with listening to the proposals from political parties and constitutional bodies. In nineteen meetings, the first subcommittee met with forty-two organizations, including twenty universities and fourteen political parties that were not represented in Parliament. The second subcommittee was composed of Sırrı Süreyya Önder (BDP), Rıza Türmen (CHP), Tunca Toskay (MHP), and Mustafa Şentop (AKP), and dealt with proposals from professional groups and unions. In thirteen meetings, it met with thirty-nine professional associations and unions. The third subcommittee was composed of Ahmet Iyimaya (AKP), Atilla Kart (CHP), Altan Tan (BDP), and Oktay Öztürk (BDP), and was in charge of receiving input from NGOs and religious, cultural, and social foundations. In nineteen meetings, the third subcommittee met with seventy-nine foundations and civil society organizations.[55]

In addition to the hearings, the AUK continued to receive input from civil society actors in writing as well as from citizens through the new constitution

[55] It should be noted that these numbers reflect the authors' self-count of the meetings for which proceedings are available.

website. At the end of the consultation phase in April 2012, the AUK had received in total 114 proposals from civil society organizations and 64,000 opinions and suggestions from citizens.[56] With the notable exception of pro-Kurdish ideas and positions, a broad spectrum of views was included in the process (e.g., Sunni Muslim, non-Muslim, Alevi, secular, nationalist, environmentalist, LGBTI, and women's).[57] The AUK members also worked in close collaboration with roundtables organized by the Economic Policy Research Foundation of Turkey (*Türkiye Ekonomi Politikaları Araştırma Vakfı*, TEPAV), which held thirteen "Turkey Speaks" (*Türkiye Konuşuyor*) conventions attended by 500 to 1,000 people each.[58] The results of these conventions were also shared in commission meetings. Moreover, AUK members traveled to different cities and attended panel discussions to raise awareness of the new constitution.

When it comes to the second stage, namely identification of principles and drafting of the constitution, we note that the commission actually skipped the first step they set for themselves and moved immediately into the drafting phase, without prior agreement on the main principles. In the drafting phase, the AUK decided to reflect unanimity (or the lack thereof) by highlighting the text in different colors: green symbolized consensus while red implied disagreement on the article. When three of the four parties agreed on a provision, the text of the article would be inserted into the document, but it would nevertheless remain in red. When parties were able to form bipartite coalitions on articles, two different proposals would be inserted into the draft document. And when none of the parties could agree on a given article, four proposals – one from each party – would be presented. Practically speaking, this meant that the respective proposals would be projected on a screen, often alongside the equivalent article in the 1982 Constitution. Changes would then be introduced according to the different parties' proposals and discussed.

From May 2012 to mid-September 2012, the AUK functioned in a two-tiered fashion. Detailed discussions were being held in the writing commission, which worked more "informally." This meant that not just AUK members, but also their legal experts and consultants were deeply involved in negotiations and drafting. Subsequently, the draft provisions that they

56 Mehmet Uçum and Özge Genç, *Making of a New Constitution in Turkey: Monitoring Report 2 (TESEV Report 2)* (Istanbul: TESEV, 2012), 6–11.

57 Ibid., 7.

58 Oğuz N. Babüroğlu and Gülru Z. Göker, "Going Large Scale: The Polling Conference Process for Participatory Constitution Making in Turkey," *Action Research* 12, no. 4 (2014): 374–391.

produced were discussed again in the upper commission, which acted as the ultimate decision-making body. However, from mid-September 2012 onward, as worries about progressing too slowly increased, the two-tiered practice was halted, and the writing commission effectively became the AUK's main decision-making body until the dissolution of the process in December 2013. The upper commission, on the other hand, convened in a more ad hoc manner and became a platform to address more general, overarching issues such as reviewing the progress made, accelerating the pace of work, complaining about each other, and discussing whether to continue or not.

The AUK changed the composition of the writing commission several times. With the targeted deadline for producing a constitution (end of 2012) fast approaching, the AUK decided in mid-September 2012 to create two writing commissions. The first writing commission was in charge of negotiating contested issues about fundamental rights and freedoms and reviewing the extra catalog of fundamental rights suggested by the CHP and the BDP. It carried out this mission until mid-January 2013, when the AUK decided to go back to one writing commission. The second commission started its work in September 2012 with deliberations on economic and financial rights. In October 2012, it was supposed to move on to a new chapter, but the extremely contested legislation provisions that resulted from the AKP's presidentialism proposal obstructed the second writing commission and prevented it from convening until one month later. From November 2012 to mid-January 2013, the second commission was entrusted with the task of negotiating provisions relating to the legislative that were independent of the executive.

The AUK used the 1982 Constitution as a template not only for discussions of articles, but also to structure the draft constitution itself. The chapters of the draft constitution, therefore, drew heavily on the current constitutional framework, even though their order and contents were meant to be different. The AUK started its deliberations with the chapter on fundamental rights and freedoms in May 2012; moved on to the chapters on the legislative and the executive in November 2012; then on to public administration in January 2013; the judiciary in February 2013; and the chapters on financial, social, and economic provisions, the preamble, general provisions and fundamental principles, and final provisions after April 2013. While fundamental rights and freedoms were deliberated four times in the commission, following the change in the drafting rules, the chapter on the judiciary was negotiated three times and all the remaining parts only twice.

5 EXPLAINING THE FAILURE OF THE 2011–2013 CONSTITUTION-MAKING PROCESS

To explain the failure of popular constitution making in Turkey, two different subjects will be examined. First, we focus on the question of why the process ultimately failed to be popular and inclusive. Second, we examine why constitution making itself was unsuccessful.

5.1 *The Failure of Popular Constitution Making*

As noted above, the Turkish constitutional tradition has always been one that granted extreme discretion to the power-holding elites at the moment of constitution drafting and has fallen short of moving the country toward a stable democracy. The anomaly of the 2011–2013 process is even more intriguing against this background. Two broad and interrelated arguments can be made about why popular constitution making was initiated in the first place. First, despite the strong political will for a new constitution, no single party had accumulated sufficient power after the June 2011 election to forge its ideal constitution and impose it on the rest of the political landscape. Thus, those interested in developing a new constitution had to seek alternatives to the traditional mode of imposition. Second, most parties acted on the assumption that inclusive constitution making would help increase the legitimacy of political actors and the regime inside and outside of Turkey.

The 2011–2013 process was loudly and enthusiastically proclaimed to be participatory and inclusive. Then-Prime Minister Recep Tayyip Erdoğan declared before the press in January 2011 that a new constitution "will be prepared by civil society organizations, youth and women's associations, trade unions, economists, and social scientists," and he promised that the process would "ensure the broadest possible participation."[59] In the first public consultation phase starting in October 2011, many civil society organizations responded to the call to participate. Yet, despite the fact that the "Kurdish question" is one of the most divisive issues in Turkey's modern history, the consultation stage effectively excluded civil society organizations that promote Kurdish interests. The AUK only consulted with one additional political party, the Participatory Democracy Party (*Katılımcı Demokrasi Partisi*, KADEP), which at that time had only one delegate in Parliament.

[59] Quoted after Levent Gönenç, *Towards a Participatory Constitution Making Process in Turkey* (Istanbul: TEPAV, 2011), 2.

It is significant that although meetings with civil society organizations were held and the commission acquired input, the results of the public consultation phase were not made public. As elaborated above, among constitutional scholars it is common to argue that constitution making should take place out of the public eye, as negotiations might be more successful when shielded from public pressure.[60] Usually, however, the secrecy rule applies to the drafting process. In the Turkish case, political elites and constitution makers acted as gatekeepers with regard to the dissemination of information about civil society proposals that were gathered in the public consultation phase. Without a doubt, this impeded the development of a meaningful discussion in the media and in public on the broader interests of civil society.[61] Although public consultation initially followed a "political approach," that is, an approach enabling civil society, citizens, and political elites to "update their information about one another's expectations, preferences and likely outcomes,"[62] it did not in the end serve to reconcile diverging views about the constitution before the drafting phase. As such, this was not a bottom-up process, as promised by political agents, but yet another exercise in top-down constitution making, as might well have been anticipated in the context of Turkey's path-dependent history of exclusionary constitution making.

Overall, commission members did not make productive use of the proposals submitted in the public consultation stage. This was a major missed opportunity, especially with regard to the government system question, which was one of the most contested issues, with the AKP suggesting a transition to presidentialism and the other three parties conditionally (BDP) or completely (CHP, MHP) rejecting such a transition. It is inexplicable why the three opposition parties did not take recourse to public opinion or civil society proposals to convince the AKP to withdraw or amend its initial proposal. The majority of the population favored the government structure in place – that is, a presidential-parliamentary system with a prime minister elected by Parliament heading the government and a popularly elected president representing the Turkish Republic.[63] Among civil society actors, only two organizations, both with close ties to the AKP, proposed a presidential system. The

[60] See, e.g., Elster, "The Optimal Design of a Constituent Assembly," 170; Arato, *Post Sovereign Constitution Making*, 156; Jon Elster, ed., *Secrecy and Publicity in Votes and Debates* (New York: Cambridge University Press, 2015).

[61] *TESEV Report 1*, 7; *TESEV Report 2*, 7.

[62] Blount, "Participation in Constitutional Design," 46; see also Steven Haberfeld, "The Process of Constitutional Reform," in *American Indian Constitutional Reform and the Rebuilding of Native Nations*, ed. E. D. Lemont (Austin: University of Texas Press, 2006), 261–262.

[63] Babüroğlu and Göker, "Going Large Scale," 383.

majority of civil society organizations that submitted proposals on the government system suggested reducing presidential powers to a "symbolic level that is better suited to a parliamentary system."[64] Yet opposition parties did not even try to hold the AKP's feet to the fire regarding its claim to represent the will of the people. Therefore, in addition to the broader claim that constitution makers did not productively incorporate civil society and citizen proposals into the negotiation and drafting process (i.e., to realize what the public proposed), they also failed to strategically use public input to solve deadlock in the commission and convince other parties to amend their respective propositions.

Debates within the AUK reveal that AUK members across party lines were worried that the public would have the impression that they were too caught up in political controversy to make progress.[65] AKP delegates held that visible disagreements over issues important to the public would cast a shadow over the whole process.[66] Aside from discrediting the commission, political parties were afraid that the failure of the process would damage their political credibility. This scenario troubled the AKP in particular. Eager to keep their promise of giving the country a new constitution, AKP delegates threatened to search for alternative pathways to constitution making, pointing out that the AUK was only one way to achieve their goal.[67] The CHP, on the other hand, regularly complained about the public perception of the AUK as lazy and not putting enough effort into the process.

Throughout the drafting stage, and in particular toward the end of the process, the CHP and the BDP suggested submitting the draft to the public as it was (i.e., with non-agreed articles), and to use public input as a way to move forward.[68] The AKP and the MHP, on the other hand, did not support this idea, but nor could they agree among themselves on another strategy. The MHP delegates challenged the idea of simply submitting all articles – agreed and non-agreed – to the public, suggesting instead that they share only the agreed articles with the public through TV discussions.[69] AKP delegates disagreed, saying that TV discussions were not the appropriate forum for constitution making. In the final session of the AUK, the AKP proposed that

64 *TESEV Report* 2, 39.
65 AUK Proceedings, October 31, 2012; January 2, 2013.
66 AUK Proceedings, July 4, 2013.
67 AUK Proceedings, January 30, 2013.
68 AUK Proceedings, September 11, 2012 (BDP); January 2, 2013 (BDP); May 5, 2013 (CHP); May 7, 2013 (BDP); July 4, 2013 (CHP and BDP); November 14, 2013 (CHP and BDP); November 18, 2013 (CHP and BDP).
69 AUK Proceedings, July 4, 2013; November 11, 2013; November 18, 2013.

party proposals on contested issues should be made public and that the commission should be suspended.[70] In line with the strategy it had employed thus far, the AKP wanted to show the public that the deal breaker was not the debate on presidentialism, but that the AUK had failed to achieve consensus on several other issues as well. While the CHP and BDP propositions to submit all articles to the public may be interpreted as strategic interventions to make progress in the commission, the MHP's suggestion for a mediated TV discussion of the results confirms their top-down approach to public participation. Recall that the constitution-making process was designed to include two public consultation phases, one before drafting (the first stage of the AUK) and one after drafting (the third stage of the AUK). This setup was intended to boost the legitimacy of the process and the constitution so produced, and it would have moved the 2011–2013 process substantially toward the maximum end of the popular constitution-making spectrum. But the AUK never made it to the latter stage, and the reluctance of the AKP and the MHP to move to the third stage without a fully agreed draft shows that not all parties involved in the process genuinely meant to engage the public in it.

Regarding the minimal and maximal conditions of popular constitution making introduced above, we can conclude that the setup of the process aimed to meet the maximum conditions. According to the working principles of the commission, the public was to be included upstream (public consultation before drafting) and midstream (public consultation and presentation of draft constitution). Although downstream participation, i.e., a public referendum to adopt the constitution, was not explicitly stated in the working principles, the history of constitution making in Turkey suggests that this would have been a likely mode to adopt the projected constitution. Still, it is important to emphasize that only the setup of the process, and not the actual practice of constitution writing, came close to maximum conditions of popular constitution making. In practice, the work of the AUK did not live up to its promise to be an inclusive and participatory constitution-making process.

To begin with, the public did not elect a body exclusively tasked with constitution making. It elected a new Parliament, and the four largest parties represented in Parliament appointed delegates to the Constitutional Conciliation Commission. Moreover, constitution makers did not consult with civil society organizations representing all segments of Turkish society. Therefore, it can be argued that the input legitimacy of the process was at best moderate. Constitution makers received input from citizens and civil society, but they did not systematically include it in the drafting process. Public proposals were not

70 AUK Proceedings, November 18, 2013.

publicized, which forestalled any critical debate in the media and public sphere about the proposals submitted and the way in which they were incorporated or not incorporated in the drafting stage. At best, parties used public proposals to amplify their own arguments or ideas. They did not, however, exploit the consensus that existed among citizens and civil society to reach an agreement on issues contested in the AUK, such as the government system. The fact that the process was abandoned before the results were submitted to the public indicates that the actual process of constitution making was much less participatory and inclusive than initially announced. Hence, we can conclude that, overall, the throughput legitimacy of the process was between moderate and weak. As the commission was unable to draft a full constitution, and given that in the provisions they agreed on, public interests were not always prioritized, the output legitimacy of the constitution-making process was also weak.

The process was intended to guarantee participation through election and public consultation (and likely also through public ratification), so in theory it could have come close to meeting maximum conditions of popular constitution making. In practice, however, the analysis shows that it did not live up to this promise.

5.2 *The Failure of Constitution Making*

The constitution-making process was not a perfect exercise in popular constitution making, and its failure raises a lot of questions about what went wrong, particularly considering the overwhelming support that the idea of a new constitution enjoyed. Ahead of the process, some authors speculated that the commission's fate would depend on the accommodation of diverse interests, which could only be achieved through stringent interparty negotiations. Others declared the constitutional project stillborn relatively early due to irreconcilable disagreements between and demands from different political parties and segments of society.[71] As the ruling AKP did not have enough seats to impose its vision, the opposition parties saw the commission as a unique opportunity to make their voices heard, which was hardly the case in ordinary parliamentary proceedings. On the other hand, looking at the failure of popular constitution making in Turkey with the advantage of hindsight, the return to majority imposition that is expressed in the constitutional

[71] Ergun Özbudun, "Turkey's Search for a New Constitution," *Insight Turkey* 14, no. 1 (2012): 39–50; Michael M. Gunter "Turkey: The Politics of a New Democratic Constitution," *Middle East Policy* 19, no. 1 (2012): 119–126.

amendments realized by the AKP and the MHP in 2017 shows that the ultimate failure of an inclusive, participatory process allowed the regime to argue that participatory methods of constitution making were not adequate to solve the problems faced by Turkey.

But why did the AUK fail? The most evident and self-explanatory answer is that commission members were unable to overcome their disagreements and deeply rooted political cleavages. As state-religion relations have been historically contested throughout the republican era due to the importance of the laicism principle for the Atatürkist modernization movement, and given that the state has been keen on controlling and monopolizing the religious realm by incorporating Sunni Islam into its infrastructure,[72] it was clear from the very beginning that this issue would become a major problem in the constitution-making process. Although constitution makers debated religious freedom and the laicism principle in numerous sessions, they were unable to reach agreement.[73] Murat Akan's analysis of the debates on laicism in the 1961 constitution-making process proves that such political contestation has a long history, yet the drafters at that time could agree on leaving the main instrument regulating religion, the Presidency of Religious Affairs (*Diyanet İşleri Başkanlığı*, Diyanet), intact.[74] Within the AUK, the Diyanet remained highly contested. While the BDP wanted to strip it of its constitutional status and leave the religious field to civil society, the CHP suggested reorganizing so that it would include other religions and denominations.[75] The AKP and the MHP, on the other hand, favored keeping the Diyanet intact. Often, these deliberations quickly deteriorated into political bickering between the AKP and the CHP, with the CHP accusing the AKP of disregarding secularism and the AKP blaming the CHP for clinging to single-party-era secularist ideas.[76]

Due to the assimilatory definition of Turkish nationality prevalent in republican constitutions, which has historically refused to recognize differences among the people of Turkey under the pretense of "color blindness," citizenship was another issue that was destined to be contested in the constitution-making process. In his analysis of the genealogy of citizenship in Ottoman-Turkish

[72] See, e.g., Taha Parla and Andrew Davison, "Secularism and Laicism in Turkey," in *Secularisms*, eds. J. R. Jacobsen and A. Pellegrini (Durham, NC: Duke University Press, 2008).

[73] AUK Proceedings, September 6, 7, 11, 2012; AUK Proceedings, writing commission, August 6, 8, 2012; May 2, 8, 2013; August 13, 14, 2013.

[74] Murat Akan, "The Infrastructural Politics of *Laiklik* in the Writing of the 1961 Turkish Constitution," *Interventions: International Journal of Postcolonial Studies* 13, no. 2 (2011): 190–211.

[75] AUK Proceedings, writing commission, August 8, 2012.

[76] Ibid., August 6, 8, 2012; see also Böcü and Petersen, Chapter 5 in this volume.

constitutional texts, Mesut Yeğen shows how citizenship concepts are marked by inconsistent terminology.[77] It is not difficult to observe that these inconsistencies also characterized the deliberations of the AUK. Not surprisingly, the MHP was decidedly in favor of keeping current references to the "Turkish state" and "Turkish citizenship" in the constitution, phrases that are contested in Turkey. The debate on whether or not "Turkishness" is a civic or ethnic category has a long history and, despite proponents' claim that the category "Turkish" is color-blind, it has often been criticized for excluding non-Muslim and non-Turkish minorities.[78] The AKP chose more neutral terms, proposing "citizens of the Turkish Republic." The BDP sought explicit recognition for inclusive citizenship regardless of ethnicity, language, religion, or sexual orientation. The CHP epitomized the inconsistencies that Yeğen mentions, as it joined the BDP regarding acknowledgment of difference, but at the same time proposed using the term "Turkish citizenship." The CHP's contradictory proposal had in fact to do with an internal disagreement among its own delegates, which also led the CHP to suggest two different titles for the provision, one more and one less accommodating. Eventually, the draft ended up including all four proposals of the citizenship article (or even four and a half, if one counts the CHP's two titles). In contrast, civil society proposals revolved around more neutral terminology for citizenship such as "citizenship of Turkey" or "of the Turkish Republic." Although all of the parties acknowledged that disagreement over citizenship was one of the issues that prevented the commission from reaching consensus, they once again did not take recourse to public input to resolve the deadlock.[79] Moreover, they could have avoided regulating citizenship altogether, as many European constitutions do.

Last but not least, lack of consensus on constitutive principles of state organization can be identified as another central problem that led to the failure of constitution making. Disagreements over constitutive concepts such as national sovereignty, democracy, and separation of powers were amplified. Adherence to party positions and historically acquired convictions regarding the identity and nature of the state, or the function and role of the commission and the constitution-making process itself, impeded the actual

77 Mesut Yeğen, "Citizenship and Ethnicity in Turkey," *Middle Eastern Studies* 40, no. 6 (2004): 51–66.

78 Kemal Kirişci, "Disaggregating Turkish Citizenship and Immigration Practices," *Middle Eastern Studies* 36, no. 3 (2000): 1–22; Ahmet İçduygu, Yilmaz Çolak, and Nalan Soyarik, "What Is the Matter with Citizenship? A Turkish Citizenship," *Middle Eastern Studies* 35, no. 4 (1999): 187–208; Ioannis N. Grigoriadis, "Türk or Türkiyeli? The Reform of Turkey's Minority Legislation and the Rediscovery of Ottomanism," *Middle Eastern Studies* 43, no. 3 (2007): 423–438.

79 AUK Proceedings, May 3, 7, 2013; *TESEV Report* 2, 21.

constitution making. Most problematic and contested regarding state organization was the government system question. While the AKP proposed a transition to a presidential system, the other three parties rejected this idea. The BDP was open to popular election of the president but insisted that the political system guarantee strong checks and balances and constitutionalize a robust separation of powers between different bodies of the state. The CHP and the MHP, on the other hand, completely rejected the transition to presidentialism. The CHP aimed to constitutionalize a parliamentary system similar to the 1961 Constitution, while the MHP aimed to maintain the government system established with the 1982 Constitution but without the 2007 amendments, that is, without a directly elected president.

These three examples illustrate that constitution making failed because constitution makers were unable to put differences aside and overcome disagreement over contentious issues. Hanna Lerner argues that societies that are characterized by deep disagreements can only draft constitutions collectively when they remain merely procedural and leave symbolic definitions to future generations by deliberately using strategies of constitutional ambiguity, ambivalence, and vagueness. She suggests that constitution makers would be well-advised to establish in the constitution "clear institutional and procedural arrangements" while "definitive choices regarding the normative and symbolic basis of the state" should be left to future generations.[80] She calls this an "incrementalist constitution": "In deeply divided societies, incrementalist constitutions achieve legitimacy and consent by representing the identity of the people as it really is – a deeply divided one."[81] Lerner also emphasizes that "decisions regarding the structure of governmental institutions" cannot be "deferred to the future."[82] Our findings on the failure of popular constitution making in Turkey complement this argument, showing that when constitution makers are unable to codify a basic structure for the future state, it is impossible to create a procedural framework in which other contested issues can be solved in the future. With regard to constitution making in divided societies, the Turkish case shows that incrementalist constitution making only works when fundamental procedural issues and questions pertaining to the overall government structure do not have to be renegotiated alongside other contested issues of identity.

80 Hanna Lerner, *Making Constitutions in Deeply Divided Societies* (Cambridge: Cambridge University Press, 2011), 230.

81 Ibid., 231.

82 Ibid., 40.

The analysis reveals that constitution making was not approached in a way that would allow for the postponement of important, contested issues. From the beginning the process was symbolically overcharged, and all parties wanted to contribute on behalf of their constituencies (electorate and interest groups) to the best possible constitution with their respective proposals. Although Article 6 of the working principles would have allowed AUK members to leave contentious issues aside, they held tiresome discussions about them and amplified disagreement. The presidentialism debate in particular had an extremely destabilizing impact. Weeks passed before they could even discuss whether to negotiate it at all. The second writing commission remained without a task for more than a month because of these conflicts, and many discussions kept coming back to this issue. For instance, in a meeting called by AKP delegate Mustafa Şentop to discuss the note suggested by opposition parties (namely the CHP) stating that "the AKP's suggestions on the presidential system have not been negotiated," they held a very long discussion about what "negotiation" means.[83] Thus, rather than streamlining the process by postponing a contentious issue, the AUK got sidetracked and lost time.

If postponement did not work, what else could constitution makers have done to overcome disagreements? Roberto Gargarella suggests that "accumulation" is a possible strategy. When constitution makers "find it too difficult to reach a common agreement, and at the same time reject remaining silent about the topics that divide them," they can "decide to simply sum or put together (one on the top of the other) their different claims, leaving their demands in tension – leaving all those tensions or even contradictions, totally or almost totally intact."[84] In the drafting stage, the AUK followed a strategy resembling accumulation. On contested issues, they included different proposals in the draft. This, however, would have been difficult to enact in the final constitution. As parties in the AUK were deeply divided over constitutive parts that a constitution requires in order to be functional (e.g., government system), the accumulation strategy would have only helped to produce an incoherent constitution. For example, different proposals on the government system could not coexist in the final constitution, as this would make governing and electing a government impossible. The same can be said about citizenship. All this shows that disagreements prevalent in this constitution-

83 AUK Proceedings, January 30, 2013.

84 Roberto Gargarella, "Constitution Making in the Context of Plural Societies," in *Constituent Assemblies*, eds. J. Elster et al., 18.

making process concerned such fundamental issues that accumulation would not have been the appropriate strategy.

Hanna Lerner argues that constitution making in divided societies requires "predrafting agreements concerning controversial identity issues."[85] In other words, different stakeholders have to negotiate – prior to commencing constitution making – how to address or not address contested issues in the process. Indeed, this could have been a solution. Had the commission not skipped the projected first step in the drafting stage, that is, identifying constitutive principles, they may have been able to establish predrafting agreements. However, as such predrafting agreements did not exist, constitution makers were unable to take recourse to a strategy or route established prior to constitution making.

In practice, disagreements rendered coalition building impossible on many issues. On some issues, coalitions of three parties were formed – for example, the CHP, MHP, and BDP agreed that the constitution should constitutionalize strong checks and balances; the AKP, CHP, and MHP wanted to maintain the concept of Turkish nationalism. On other issues, coalitions of two parties opposed each other: The AKP and the BDP advocated for direct election of the president while the CHP and the MHP opposed this; the AKP and the MHP suggested a long list of grounds for restricting freedom of assembly, which was rejected by the CHP and the BDP; the CHP and the BDP suggested submitting the unfinished draft to public debate while the AKP and the MHP found this to be unnecessary. As the four parties were unable to bargain their way to full agreement on a number of contested issues, the unanimity rule established in Article 6 of the AUK's working principles became an insurmountable obstacle. In order to avoid deadlock, delegates could have pursued alternative strategies and amended the procedures when they found themselves unable to reach decisions. The working principles explicitly authorized the commission to amend its own rules (Article 14). Therefore, the unanimity principle could have been replaced by a supermajority principle (three-fifths, two-thirds, three-fourths). Delegates could have been explicitly encouraged to vote on the basis of their personal convictions rather than toeing their parties' lines. Alternatively, the commission could have identified crucial issues that required unanimity and less critical issues that required a lesser degree of consensus. As Parliament

85 Hanna Lerner, "Constituent Assemblies and Political Continuity in Divided Societies," in *Constituent Assemblies*, eds. J. Elster et al., 61. For a discussion of the predrafting stage, see Justin Blount, Zachary Elkins, and Tom Ginsburg, "Does the Process of Constitution-Making Matter?," in *Comparative Constitutional Design*, ed. T. Ginsburg (New York: Cambridge, 2012), 31–65.

would later vote on the constitution anyway, and the draft was likely to be submitted to public referendum, the commission could have justified less rigid voting procedures. This may have increased the chances for bargaining and consensus. Nevertheless, amending the strict procedures was never considered to make decision-making more effective. Toward the end of the process, AUK president Cemil Çiçek suggested that the commission should consider accepting articles on which three of the four parties could agree.[86] This, however, did not happen. All this shows that the procedural constraint to adopt provisions unanimously was not appropriate for the political setting.

Apart from the unanimity clause, another important obstacle was the targeted deadline for the end of 2012. Once the commission approached the deadline, more and more discussions were held about the need to speed up the process. Moving forward became more important than reaching consensus. AUK president Çiçek stated in October 2012: "Time is the biggest opportunity or impediment for us; it is clear to all of us that we need to move faster."[87] Passing the December 2012 deadline made the AUK vulnerable to external pressure, particularly from AKP circles. Then-Prime Minister Recep Tayyip Erdoğan publicly announced in January 2013: "If it is not finished [by March], the AKP will bring its own [proposal] to the agenda of the Parliament. We will, with God's will, have the chance to present our new constitution draft to our nation. The moment the draft receives the necessary support in Parliament, we will go to our nation for a referendum."[88] Within the commission, the hope for a complete draft began fading away, and some AKP members started presenting the very establishment of the AUK as a "favor" to the opposition. Mustafa Şentop declared in commission meetings that "the AKP made a promise to our nation about a new constitution. This commission is a means to achieve that, but if it fails, then the AKP will bring its own proposal before the Parliament in order to fulfill its promise."[89] Although the opposition parties vehemently criticized the time-pressure problem as a "fabricated issue,"[90] they could not prevent the AKP from changing its attitude toward the commission. The AKP statements show that the ruling party perceived the AUK as less useful for its aims, and the increasing external pressure after January 2013 was intended to discredit the commission's work and undermine the progress made.

86 AUK Proceedings, November 18, 2013.

87 Ibid., October 31, 2012.

88 "Uzlaşma Yerine Referandum mu?" *BİA Haber Merkezi*, January 31, 2013, https://m.bianet.org/bianet/siyaset/144007-uzlasma-yerine-referandum-mu (accessed July 8, 2019).

89 AUK Proceedings, January 30, 2013.

90 Ibid., December 26, 2012; January 15, 2013.

The procedures of the AUK that factored into the failure of the process, namely the unanimity rule and the unrealistic final deadline, also clearly worked against each other. If reaching a consensual agreement (without voting) was the priority, then the AUK should have allowed for more time to create an open, deliberative environment. If the urgency of a new constitution was the priority, then a different decision-making mechanism should have been chosen. All this points to the conclusion that the rigid procedure and the tight time frame complicated constitution making, as they obstructed rather than facilitated reaching consensus. Disagreements between constitution makers were amplified, and instead of conciliation between different political groups and segments of society, the failure of popular constitution making meant the return of majority imposition. Although Turkish society set out in 2011 to draft a democratic constitution with the participation of citizens and civil society, and notwithstanding the fact that significant progress was made with regard to some constitutive issues that a constitution should regulate, in the end social divisions, ideological predispositions, historical experiences, and party politics prevailed.

PART II

CONTEXTUALIZING CONSTITUTION MAKING IN TURKEY

2

The People and Its Embodiment: Authoritarian Foundations of Constitutions in Turkey

Ertuğ Tombuş

1 INTRODUCTION

The center-periphery cleavage, formulated by Şerif Mardin in his seminal 1973 article,[1] has a paradigmatic role in Turkish studies. Increasingly since the 1990s, scholars working on state-society relations have based their analyses on the center-periphery duality, which functions as a master narrative to explain modern Turkish politics.[2] From this perspective, in its simplest form, the clash between the modernizing secular center and the traditional and religious periphery determines the main cleavages in Turkish politics. The military, judicial institutions, and civil bureaucracy, as the so-called guardians of the Kemalist center, established an authoritarian governmentality to exclude and suppress the demands and challenges coming from the periphery. Since the transition to a multiparty system, the same binary has also determined political parties, electoral cleavages, and voting behavior.[3] According to this narrative, the Kemalist secular center, with its non-majoritarian institutions, and the military established a tutelage over democratic politics. The military interventions in the 1960s, 1970s, and 1980s are also considered episodes of this center-periphery struggle. Studies on constitutionalism in Turkey do not break away

[1] Şerif Mardin, "Center-Periphery Relations: A Key to Turkish Politics?" *Daedalus* 101, no. 1 (1973): 169–190.

[2] Ceren Lord, *Religious Politics in Turkey: From the Birth of the Republic to the AKP* (Cambridge: Cambridge University Press, 2018); Deniz Kandiyoti, "The Travails of the Secular: Puzzle and Paradox in Turkey," *Economy and Society* 41, no. 4 (2012): 515–531; F. Michael Wuthrich, "An Essential Center-Periphery Electoral Cleavage and the Turkish Party System," *International Journal of Middle East Studies* 45, no. 4 (2013): 751–773.

[3] Ali Çarkoğlu, "Economic Evaluations vs. Ideology: Diagnosing the Sources of Electoral Change in Turkey, 2002–2011," *Electoral Studies* 31 (2012): 513–521; Ali Çarkoğlu, "Voting Behavior," in *The Handbook of Modern Turkey*, eds. M. Heper and S. Sayari (London: Routledge, 2012), 160–171; Seda Demiralp, "The Odd Tango of the Islamic Right and Kurdish Left in Turkey," *Middle Eastern Studies* 48, no. 2 (2012): 287–302.

from the dominance of this explanatory model. Accordingly, constitutional politics has been portrayed as another venue for the struggle between center and periphery. The constitutions written after the military interventions in 1960 and 1980 in particular are considered to be the center's response to the increasing power the periphery gained through democratic elections. As the argument goes, the Kemalist center defended its hegemonic position through strong constitutional entrenchment and by establishing new constitutional institutions, such as the Constitutional Court of Turkey (*Anayasa Mahkemesi*, AYM) and the National Security Council (*Milli Güvenlik Kurulu*, MGK).[4]

Despite its paradigmatic status, the center-periphery model has significant shortcomings for explaining state-society relations, the politics of religion, sources of inequality and exclusion, and problems of democratization in Turkey. For one, the model is unable to register the co-optation, cooperation, and transition between the actors that it defines as center and periphery.[5] As a result, it cannot explain the role of the center-right parties, political Islam, and the Sunni majority in the institutionalization of a society antagonistic to differences, plurality, and heterogeneity. As Onur Bakıner underlines, Şerif Mardin "has offered a simple and politically appealing theoretical foundation ..., increasingly so in the context of the rise and consolidation" of the Justice and Development Party (*Adalet ve Kalkınma Partisi*, AKP).[6] His model provides the theoretical basis for the argument that the center, with its secular and elitist character, has been the source of authoritarian impulses, whereas the periphery is the source of pressure on the center to enforce a more democratic and liberal society. This misleading normative conclusion about the center-periphery duality played a critical discursive role in the AKP's drive to gain support from different social groups, especially during the first decade

4 Hootan Shambayati, "The Guardian of the Regime: The Turkish Constitutional Court in Comparative Perspective," in *Constitutional Politics in the Middle East: With Special Reference to Turkey, Iraq, Iran, and Afghanistan*, ed. S.A. Arjomand (Portland, OR: Hart Publications, 2008), 99–121; Ceren Belge, "Friends of Court: The Republican Alliance and Selective Activism of the Constitutional Court of Turkey," *Law and Society Review* 40, no. 3 (2006): 653–692. For an evaluation of the constitutional history of Turkey as an example of the hegemonic preservation thesis see, Ergun Özbudun, *The Constitutional System of Turkey: 1876 to the Present* (New York: Palgrave Macmillan, 2012), 122–129; Ran Hirschl, "The Fuzzy Boundaries of (Un)constitutionality: Two Tales of Political Jurisprudence (Pakistan, Turkey)," *University of Queensland Law Journal* 3, no. 31 (2012): 319–337.

5 For a critique of Şerif Mardin's approach, see Fethi Açıkel, "Entegratif Toplum ve Muarızları: Merkez – Çevre Paradigması Üzerine Eleştirel Notlar," *Toplum ve Bilim* 105, (2006): 30–69; Ali Rıza Güngen and Şafak Erten, "Approaches of Şerif Mardin and Metin Heper on State and Civil Society in Turkey," *Journal of Historical Studies* 3, (2005): 1–14.

6 Onur Bakıner, "A Key to Turkish Politics? The Center-Periphery Framework Revisited," *Turkish Studies* 19, no. 4 (2018): 503–552, 504.

of its rule, and in its efforts to justify its policies as democratizing reforms. Using a populist discourse based on the antagonistic duality between the people and the elite and a strong anti-establishment rhetoric, the AKP was able to claim that its policies had democratizing effects because they undermined the power of the Kemalist establishment and, most importantly, the tutelary power of the military. The debates on a new constitution in the 2000s epitomize the misleading conclusions that the center-periphery model has produced. Although from the day of its ratification the 1982 Constitution was a target of criticism, by the late 1990s and early 2000s recognition of the need for a new constitution had become virtually universal and was strongly and systematically emphasized by almost all political and civil society actors.[7] The 1982 Constitution was presented as one of the main obstacles to finding democratic solutions to endemic political problems related to individual rights and liberties, religious freedom, and ethnic conflict. Although it was amended many times with the aim of further democratizing state and society, the 1982 Constitution lacks democratic legitimacy because it is the outcome of a coup d'état and was written under the strict control of the junta leaders.[8]

The dominant narrative is that the military imposed a constitution in 1982 to establish its tutelage over civilian politics and to preserve the Kemalist center's hegemony. Therefore, its replacement with a new constitution is essential for the democratization of the political system. There is no dispute over the authoritarian origins and content of the 1982 Constitution, and nobody questions the need for a democratic constitution. The problem is that when the issue is framed exclusively in terms of its military authorship and within the center-periphery duality, the only remedy appears to be a constitution written by a civilian actor representing the periphery. The AKP has used this inference as the main justification for its constitutional agenda, presenting itself as the solution, as if *any* constitution made by a civilian political actor (i.e., the AKP) would be sufficient to solve the democratic deficits of the constitutional regime.

Civilian authorship, however, while a necessary condition, is not sufficient to guarantee the democratic quality of a constitution, as the AKP's constitutional changes over the last decade have proved time and again. Explaining the authoritarian character of constitutions in Turkey with reference to the

[7] Kemal Gözler, *Anayasa Değişikliği Gerekli mi 1982 Anayasası için bir Savunma* (Bursa: Ekin Kitabevi Yayınları, 2001), 2.

[8] For the amendments to the 1982 Constitution, see Ergun Özbudun, "Democratization Reforms in Turkey, 1993–2004," *Turkish Studies* 8, no. 2 (2007): 179–196; Levent Gönenç, "The 2001 Amendments to the 1982 Constitution of Turkey," *Ankara Law Review* 1, no. 1 (2004): 89–109.

center-periphery struggle or military tutelage has prevented us from seeing the authoritarian foundations that are reproduced by the center-right and political Islamist parties, which are regarded as the political actors representing the periphery. On the contrary, such a perspective leads to the misguided attribution of a direct causal relationship between civilianization and democratization.

This chapter locates the authoritarian foundations of Turkish constitutions from a perspective that is informed by Claude Lefort's understanding of modern democracy as a political regime where "the place of power is empty."[9] Lefort helps us detect a particular authoritarian logic that governs constitution-making processes in Turkey. This chapter draws a principal distinction between two logics that vie for domination in a constitution-making process. The first is the hegemonic-totalitarian logic, where one actor claims to be the embodiment of the sovereign people, which is understood as a monolithic, unitary entity. The second logic is the pluralist-democratic one, which is based on the acknowledgment that the people are unrepresentable as a totality and that its will is always indeterminate. In a nutshell, the main argument of this chapter is that the hegemonic-totalitarian logic undergirds the authoritarian foundation of Turkish constitutions, as it has been the modus operandi of all constitution-making processes, past and present. That is to say, the dominant constitution-making practice in Turkey has been the *performative closing of the empty place of power* by one actor who claims to exclusively represent the people's will. All republican constitution-making processes since 1924 were dominated by a single actor, assembly, or organ that claimed to embody the will of the people. This embodiment claim constitutes the authoritarian foundation of Turkish constitutions. The authoritarian logic that characterizes constitution-making processes is not merely the result of the Kemalist or military authorship of the constitutions. Neither Kemalists nor their main populist adversaries – the AKP and the Democratic

[9] Claude Lefort, *Democracy and Political Theory* (Minneapolis: University of Minnesota Press, 1988); Claude Lefort, *The Political Forms of Modern Society: Bureaucracy, Democracy, Totalitarianism* (Cambridge, MA: MIT Press, 1986); Bernard Flynn, *The Philosophy of Claude Lefort: Interpreting the Political* (Evanston, IL: Northwestern University Press, 2005); Carol C. Gould, "Claude Lefort on Modern Democracy," *Praxis International* 11, nos. 3–4 (1991): 337–345; Oliver Marchart, *Post-Foundational Political Thought: Political Difference in Nancy, Lefort, Badiou and Laclau* (Edinburgh: Edinburgh University Press, 2007): 85–108; Martin Plot, ed., *Claude Lefort: Thinker of the Political* (Basingstoke: Palgrave Macmillan, 2013); Raf Geenens, "Democracy, Human Rights and History," *European Journal of Political Theory* 7, no. 3 (2008): 269–286; Sofia Näsström, "Representative Democracy as Tautology: Ankersmit and Lefort on Representation," *European Journal of Political Theory* 5, no. 3 (2006): 321–342.

Party (*Demokrat Parti*, DP) – have ever come to terms with the constitutive feature of democracy, that is, the emptiness of the place of power. Instead, all major parties that have claimed to represent the periphery or the people against the Kemalist elite have understood politics and constitutional politics within the same hegemonic-totalitarian logic. Their political struggle has been about the identity of the actor who should occupy the place of power permanently; they thereby reproduce the authoritarian foundation. Whenever politics faces the facts of plurality, multiplicity, and heterogeneity, the fundamental wrong underpinning the embodiment claim is revealed. Whenever democratic politics in Turkey reveals that the embodiment claim is usurpation, and not legitimate representation, the political actor who is making that claim shuts down democratic politics by excluding or criminalizing political opponents.

In what follows, I first reconstruct Claude Lefort's theory of democracy. In the second part, I analyze the republican constitutions and the constitution-making processes from the viewpoint of the theoretical framework developed. In the final part, I show the 2011–2013 constitution-making process and the recent constitutional developments under AKP rule to be the populist reproduction of the embodiment claim and the hegemonic-totalitarian logic on which it is based.

2 CLAUDE LEFORT AND MODERN DEMOCRACY

In his writings on modern democracy and totalitarianism, Claude Lefort defines a typology of theologico-political, modern democratic, and totalitarian forms of society. He explains the peculiar characteristics of modern democracy through a comparison with the theologico-political forms of premodern monarchies, on the one hand, and with totalitarianism on the other. Both theologico-political and totalitarian forms are, for Lefort, mirror images of the democratic form. These two historical comparisons help Lefort define the radical nature of the democratic experience, its constitutive features, and the conditions of its survival and destruction.

Lefort explains the premodern theological character of monarchies with reference to Ernst Kantorowicz's notion of the king's two bodies: the real and the symbolic.[10] Through the mediation of the king, the symbolic unity of the political community finds a real body. The king, with his real body, is the visible embodiment of the symbolic unity of the body politic: "A carnal union

[10] Ernst H. Kantorowicz, *The King's Two Bodies: A Study in Mediaeval Political Theology* (Princeton: Princeton University Press, 1997).

was established between the great individual and his mass of servants, from the lowliest to the most important, and it was indissociable from the mystical union between the king and the kingdom."[11] The king, incarnating the theologico-political dimensionality of society, embodies the locus of power by uniting the real and the symbolic. For Lefort, modern democracy overturns the basic premises of premodern society by splitting the political from the theological. The symbolic unity of the political community loses its real body. Modern democratic revolutions create a condition where no figure can embody society's unity. The symbolic locus of power still exists, but it is an empty place. As Lefort explains:

> [M]odern democracy, of all the regimes of which we know, is the only one to have represented power in such a way as to show that power is an empty place and to have thereby maintained a gap between the symbolic and the real. It does so by virtue of a discourse which reveals that power belongs to no one; that those who exercise power do not possess it; that they do not, indeed, embody it.[12]

This void created by the gap between the symbolic and the real, between "the people as the legitimate sovereign, in its unity in principle, and the people as an existing society, in its actual complexity,"[13] is both constitutive of modern democracy and is the condition of its survival. What is critical to democracy is the permanent emptiness of the place of power. The people, as the democratic subject, symbolically occupy the place of power. However, this does not mean that the emptiness is filled. The people are the sovereign body in a democracy, yet this sovereign cannot speak for itself. Pierre Rosanvallon notes, "[T]he disincorporation of this theologico-political architecture signifies the collapse of unconditional rule – of an authority that can speak for itself."[14] Democracy, as the rule of the people, is instead a promise that is never fully achieved. The people and its representations are always subject to contestation. "Democracy inaugurates the experience of an ungraspable, uncontrollable society in which the people will be said to be sovereign, of course, but whose identity will constantly be open to question, whose identity will remain latent."[15] The sovereign people, or the people-as-principle, is an absent category that can only be present through representation. However, any representation will

11 Lefort, *Democracy and Political Theory*, 245.

12 Ibid., 225.

13 Pierre Rosanvallon, *Democracy Past and Future* (New York: Columbia University Press, 2007): 91.

14 Ibid.

15 Lefort, *The Political Forms of Modern Society*, 304.

always only be partial and temporary. The indeterminacy and the symbolic nature of the people resist any closure and provide guarantees for democratic contestation. However, these are also sources of the potential destruction of democracy. Any attempt to close the gap between the symbolic and the real by claiming to be the embodiment of the people is also a source of such destruction.

After modern democracy, the second mutation of the symbolic took place with totalitarianism, which also helps us understand the modern democratic experience as such. Understanding totalitarianism means for Lefort "thinking the question of democracy from its absolute negation."[16] The advent of totalitarianism, a political form that sprang from the goal of a reembodiment of power within the limits of the secular, has already ended democracy once. Under totalitarianism, power is reembodied and thus no longer designates an empty place. "[S]ociety is a unity in the gaze of an entity – only this time that entity is not God but the Party, which claims to possess total knowledge of the nature of the social."[17] Lefort explains the difference between democracy and totalitarianism as follows:

> The legitimacy of power is based on the people; but the image of popular sovereignty is linked to the image of an empty place, impossible to occupy, such that those who exercise public authority can never claim to appropriate it. Democracy combines these two apparently contradictory principles: on the one hand, power emanates from the people; on the other hand, it is the power of nobody. And democracy thrives on this contradiction. Whenever the latter risks being resolved or is resolved, democracy is either close to destruction or already destroyed. . . . If the image of the people is actualized, if a party claims to identify with it and to appropriate power under cover of this identification, then it is the very principle of the distinction between the state and society . . . which is denied. This phenomenon is characteristic of totalitarianism.[18]

Lefort does not discuss different forms of authoritarian closure between democracy and totalitarianism. However, as Andrew Arato points out, "Lefort's concepts allow us to make a distinction between occupying the empty place of symbolic power and obliterating the distance between the symbolic and the real."[19] Before reaching totalitarian obliteration, i.e., total

16 Pierre Rosanvallon, "The Test of the Political: A Conversation with Claude Lefort," *Constellations* 19, no. 1 (2012): 4–15, 4.

17 Martin Plot, *The Question of Democracy in Merleau-Ponty, Arendt, and Ranciere* (New York, NY: Bloomsbury, 2014), 6.

18 Lefort, *The Political Forms of Modern Society*, 279–280.

19 Andrew Arato, *Post-Sovereign Constitution-Making: Learning and Legitimacy* (Oxford: Oxford University Press, 2016), 282.

destruction of social plurality under the symbolic unity, a populist imaginary can also endanger a democratic regime through "a *pars pro toto* logic that necessarily involves the substitution of a segment of the people for the whole,"[20] in other words, when a part claims to represent the whole without allowing any room for contestation of this claim. Even if totalitarian closure will not always be the result, the embodiment claim has an affinity with totalitarianism. Francisco Panizza discusses populism in a similar vein: Populism always claims to occupy the empty place of power; therefore, it also endangers democracy. "If the uncertainty associated with a place of power which remains 'empty' is negated by a political discourse that claims to speak for the people as its unmediated representative – and which, under cover of this identification, seeks to appropriate the place of power – it is democracy itself, and not just liberalism, that is being denied. Taken to the extreme, populism descends into totalitarianism."[21]

Lefort helps us detect a particular hegemonic-totalitarian logic that may govern constitution making as well as other political processes in which a single political force is able to claim that it embodies the sovereign power of the people and has the authority to use the people's constituent power on its behalf. Arato develops his post-sovereign constitution-making paradigm by taking Lefort's warning as one of his starting points.[22] Under conditions of post-sovereign constitution making, no group, no institution, no leader is in a position to rightfully claim to use the constituent power of the people by itself. The form of representation in Arato's constitution-making model is plural and accountable rather than absolute and unitary. In Arato's model, in contrast to the sovereignty paradigm of the revolutionary or populist model of constitution making, which relies on the unitary idea of the people authorizing a body to embody its power, the process itself is organized by the acknowledgment of the emptiness of the place of power. The post-sovereign constitution-making paradigm is "the performative opening of the empty place of power."[23] Constitution making is organized in two or more distinct

20 Andrew Arato and Gábor Attila Tóth, "The Multifaceted Sovereign: Domestic and International Actors in Constitutional Regime Change," in *Constitutional Acceleration within the European Union and Beyond*, ed. P. Blokker (London: Routledge, 2016), 84.

21 Francisco Panizza, "Introduction: Populism and the Mirror of Democracy," in *Populism and the Mirror of Democracy*, ed. F. Panizza (London and New York: Verso, 2005), 1–32, 29.

22 Arato, *Post-Sovereign Constitution-Making*, 70.

23 Andrew Arato and Ertuğ Tombuş, "Learning from Success, Learning from Failure: South Africa, Hungary, Turkey, and Egypt," *Journal of Philosophy and Social Criticism* 39, nos. 4–5 (2013): 427–441, 428.

stages. It makes plurality, inclusion, compromise, publicity, free elections, self-limitation, and enforceable legality its main principles. The key issue this paradigm tries to avoid is the sovereignty problem, which organizes the constitution-making process on the basis of a hegemonic-totalitarian logic in which a single political actor dominates the process, without allowing any public input or pluralistic participation of multiple political and social actors. Arato's hypothesis is that "the post-sovereign process is likely to produce *constitutionalist* outcomes" and, "on logical normative grounds . . ., this constitution-making paradigm has at least an elective affinity with *democratic* constitutionalism."[24]

Constitutions in Turkey and the constitutional politics of the recent two decades under the AKP rule are based on the denial of the democratic paradox that informs Lefort's theory of modern democracy and Arato's post-sovereign constitution-making paradigm. Turkey's constitutions were the outcomes of processes that were not pluralistic, as they enabled instead of prevented the occupation of the empty place of power. In her analysis of the republican constitutions in Turkey, Ceren Lord shows that there is path dependency: "Religious majoritarianism, involving a focus on and concern with the Muslim Turkish majority, has been a persistent feature of the state and the fundamental logic of constitutional identity in Turkey."[25] What I argue in this chapter complements her analysis about the constitutions in Turkey. In addition to the majoritarianism of unitary and monolithic understandings of the people, the authoritarian foundation of Turkish constitutions is grounded in the undemocratic making of each constitution, in which one actor always claimed to embody the people as a unitary and monolithic entity.

3 REPUBLICAN CONSTITUTIONS IN TURKEY

3.1 *The 1921 Constitution*

Accepted by the first Grand National Assembly on January 20, 1921, the 1921 Constitution is the first Turkish republican constitution. Studies on Turkish

24 Andrew Arato, *The Adventures of the Constituent Power* (Cambridge: Cambridge University Press, 2017), 365 (emphasis in original). Although Arato emphasizes that there is no strong causality between post-sovereign constitution making and a democratic outcome, he argues that a two-track process based on a continuity of legality and democratic legitimacy is more likely to produce a constitution that establishes the rule of law, separation of powers, and democratic politics.

25 Lord, *Religious Politics in Turkey*, 38; on majoritarianism in Turkey, see also Ceren Lord, "The Persistence of Turkey's Majoritarian System of Government," *Government and Opposition* 47, no. 2 (2012): 228–255.

constitutional history generally disregard the 1921 Constitution on the grounds that it was "a constitution prepared and accepted in an emergency period – the period of National Struggle (1919–1922)–"[26] and, because it was a short constitution that was meant to be temporary to deal "only with the most urgent constitutional problems of the moment."[27] Although it is generally acknowledged to have been the first constitution based on national sovereignty, it is also noted that the monarchy was not abolished with the promulgation of this constitution. More importantly, because the principle of national sovereignty continued to be the constitutive principle of the 1924 Constitution, the first two republican constitutions are accepted as two steps in the incremental transition from monarchy to republic, without understanding the critical difference between these two constitutions. The difference, however, is important for the purpose of this chapter, that is, to explain the authoritarian foundation of Turkish republican constitutions. This foundation is laid with the 1924 Constitution, and not with its predecessor.

In a 2017 study, Dinçer Demirkent makes a detailed analysis of the two first republican constitutions.[28] Contrary to the established view, which underlines a continuity (i.e., the principle of national sovereignty) between the 1921 and 1924 Constitutions, Demirkent argues that each constitution represents a different founding moment, what he calls the first and second founding of the republic. These two founding moments led to two different and opposing understandings of political unity, representation, and the exercise of sovereign power. For Demirkent, what is critical to understand about the 1921 Constitution is not its length, duration, or the emergency nature of its context, but its exceptional quality compared to all republican constitutions following

[26] Suna Kili, *Turkish Constitutional Developments and Assembly Debates on the Constitutions of 1924 and 1961* (Istanbul: Robert College Research Center, 1971), 17.

[27] Ergun Özbudun and Faruk Gençkaya, *Democratization and the Politics of Constitution-Making in Turkey* (Budapest: Central European University Press, 2009), 10. Some of the studies on constitutional history in Turkey briefly mention the 1921 Constitution without recognizing the importance of decentralization and local autonomy in it; see Yavuz Abadan and Bahri Savcı, *Türkiye'de Anayasa Gelişmelerine Bir Bakış* (Ankara: Ajans Türk Matbaası, 1959); Tarık Zafer Tunaya, *Türkiye'de Siyasal Gelişmeler: 1876–1938*, vol. 2 (Istanbul: Bilgi Üniversitesi Yayınları, 2009); Taha Parla, *Türkiye'de Anayasalar: Tarih İdeoloji, Rejim 1921–2016* (Istanbul: Metis, 2016); Mustafa Erdoğan, *Anayasay Hukukuna Giriş* (Ankara: Liberte, 2004). Some other scholars have underlined the distinctively decentralized character of the 1921 Constitution, but have nevertheless dismissed it, claiming that it was never implemented; see Ilhan Arsel, *Türk Anayasa Hukukunun Umumi Esasları*, 1.cilt (Ankara; Mars Matbaası, 1965); Mümtaz Soysal, *Anayasa'ya Giriş* (Ankara: Sevinç Matbaası, 1969); Ergun Özbudun, *1921 Anayasası* (Atatürk: Araştırmaları Merkezi Yayınları, 1992).

[28] Dinçer Demirkent, *Bir Devlet İki Cumhuriyet* (Istanbul: Ayrıntı Yayınları, 2017).

it. The 1921 Constitution and its conception of political unity were the direct result of the Congress Government Period (*Kongreler Dönemi*, 1918–1920). In this period, the Ottoman state lost its power and control over the Ottoman territory and started to be replaced by local congresses. As Bülent Tanör notes, these multiple and local sources of power organized as congresses were not just local organizations with the aim of defense and independence, but they acted as public authorities in their respective localities. These local congresses were formed and functioned on the principles of representation, delegation, and participation.[29]

As Demirkent argues, the first founding of the republic, the drafting of the 1921 Constitution, was guided by an understanding of political unity that acknowledged the plural and conflictual character of the people. Instead of trying to impose a fictional unity and homogeneity onto the people, the political decision-making in this moment came to terms with the fact of plurality. Demirkent's main argument is that the different and more democratic nature of the 1921 Constitution was not the result of pragmatic and strategic reasoning on the part of the republican elite led by Mustafa Kemal. On the contrary, it was the result of an understanding reached through a period that was defined by the emergence of multiple local power sources in the form of congresses, which developed around the ideas of decentralized power and local autonomy.

According to the first article of the 1921 Constitution, "Sovereignty belongs unconditionally to the nation. The system of administration is based on the principle that the people personally and effectively direct their own destinies."[30] Demirkent points out that the first article consisted of two main principles. The first is national sovereignty, the principle that was maintained in all following republican constitutions. Although the 1921 Constitution did not abolish the monarchy, with the clear articulation of the principle of national sovereignty, it effectively replaced the monarchical principle with the republican principle. The second principle, embodied in the second part of the first article, stipulates that the state was to be grounded in political autonomy, practices of direct democracy organized at the local level, and a decentralized structure of political power. This principle was eliminated with the 1924 Constitution. In Demirkent's opinion, this elimination is neither accidental nor insignificant. On the contrary, he argues that it was the result of a fundamentally different political decision standing behind the 1924 Constitution.

29 Bülent Tanör, *Türkiye'de Kongre İktidarları* (1918–1920) (Istanbul: Yapı Kredi Yayınları, 2009).

30 Kili, *Turkish Constitutional Developments*, 160.

In addition to the second part of the first article, twelve articles of the total of twenty-three in the 1921 Constitution regulate administrative divisions and give autonomy to locally elected councils in the administration of education, health, agriculture, public works, and social aid.[31] This confirms that local autonomy was the main principle of the exercise of sovereignty in the 1921 Constitution.[32] As Levent Köker also underlines, "[D]rafters of the 1921 Constitution aimed at rendering 'power' into the hands of 'the people' by effectively localizing administrative units and at the same time, by establishing a mechanism to enable the people to directly elect their governors at all levels, from the smallest district through the province to the central government."[33] It was precisely the principle of local autonomy and a decentralized administrative structure that was its consequence that were excluded from the 1924 Constitution.

Ceren Lord treats the 1921 Constitution and what distinguishes it from ensuing republican constitutions with more caution than Demirkent. Lord emphasizes two rationales that governed the making of the 1921 Constitution. It had to bring different parties into a coalition during the war and, at the same time, it had to constitute a political unity against the Istanbul government. For both purposes, the 1921 Constitution had to be more pluralistic and remain silent on certain fundamental issues (e.g., the form of the political regime, the abolishment of the monarchy, state-religion relations, and the ethnic character of the nation), as these could become deal breakers separating the parties of the coalition.[34] Beyond these two strategic functions, Lord argues that there was no disagreement on the boundaries of the people; a pluralistic understanding of the people was not in question, and there was a "consensus on the people whom the constitution addressed,"[35] that is, the Muslim community. Given the exclusion of non-Muslims from the conception of the people, Lord argues that the 1921 Constitution, despite its relative plurality, was also

[31] Ibid., 160–161.

[32] Arsel, *Türk Anayasa Hukukunun Umumi Esasları*, 73. Arsel also notes that the 1921 Constitution is based on the idea that national sovereignty should be exercised not only by the Parliament but also by local administrative units.

[33] Levent Köker, "Local Politics and Democracy in Turkey: An Appraisal," *The Annals of the American Academy* 540, (July 1995): 51–62, 56 (emphasis in original); see also Köker, *Modernleşme, Kemalism ve Demokrasi* (İstanbul: İletişim Yayınları, 1993), 138–145.

[34] Lord, *Religious Politics in Turkey*, 48. Ergun Özbudun (*1924 Anayasasi*, 72) also argues that Atatürk and his close circle could not put forward a more centralized structure in the conditions of the independence war, despite the fact that it was their preference. The mobilization needed for the war could be possible only through local autonomy and a decentralized structure.

[35] Lord, *Religious Politics in Turkey*, 48.

essentially majoritarian. This interpretation differs from Demirkent's take on the radical nature of the 1921 Constitution, and it shows the limits of his account of the 1921 Constitution as representing a democratic beginning.

The 1920–1921 constitution-making process was shaped by the Congress Government Period, the emergence of local sources of power, and the heterogeneous character of the first Grand National Assembly (*Türkiye Büyük Millet Meclisi*, TBMM).[36] Even if the political community was understood along majoritarian lines in the 1921 Constitution, as it equated the Muslim majority with the people, from the perspective developed in this chapter, it is still noteworthy that, in contrast to following constitution-making processes, no single political actor – not one of the diversified parties of the war coalition – was in a position to make the embodiment claim in 1920–1921. Hence, the authoritarian foundation that I will reconstruct in the following pages had not yet emerged in the first republican constitution-making process.

3.2 *The 1924 Constitution*

The second Grand National Assembly elected in 1923 adopted the second republican constitution in 1924. This constitution was the outcome of a period that started with the establishment of the Republican People's Party (*Cumhuriyet Halk Partisi*, CHP) in 1923, the formation of the second Grand National Assembly in the same year, and the adoption of the constitution in 1924. In contrast to the composition of the first Assembly, the second TBMM was formed through an election the CHP "strongly controlled and dominated."[37] Although the principle of national sovereignty was retained in the 1924 Constitution, the second part of the first article of the 1921 Constitution, that is, the principle leading to the practices of local autonomy and direct democracy reconstructed in the foregoing section, was eliminated.

The political order established by the 1924 Constitution was based on the idea of a monolithic and homogeneous political unity – the nation – that denied the existence of plurality and internal conflict based on class or ethnic identities. The fiction of the people-as-one, to use Lefort's notion, had replaced the 1921 Constitution's political decision regarding the form of political unity. The essential component of such a monolithic conception of

36 For the heterogeneous and plural character of the first Grand National Assembly, see Özbudun, *1921 Anayasasi*; Niyazi Berkes, *Development of Secularism in Turkey* (New York: Routledge, 1998).

37 Özbudun and Gençkaya, *Democratization and the Politics of Constitution-Making in Turkey*, 10.

political unity, the principle of representation, was no longer meant to lead to practices of direct democracy and decentralized administration based on local autonomy. With the 1937 amendment, the six principles of Kemalism became part of the constitution.[38] Kemalism gave its name to the regime and the state. In other words, Kemalism succeeded in occupying the empty place of power. During the single-party period (1923–1945), the CHP treated all opposition to and dissent from its decisions, actions, and policies as threats against the state and the republic. The political sphere was substantially constrained, and all groups or identities disloyal to Kemalism were excluded and suppressed in the name of the national interest and will. The 1924 Constitution, with its "admirable assurances of popular sovereignty," did not give any "hint as to the real nature of the regime that claimed its sanction."[39] Özbudun also argues that it continued to be the constitutional foundation throughout the single-party as well as the multiparty period. For him, such a transition to a multiparty regime requires a new constitution. The paradox of the 1924 Constitution, Özbudun argues, is that without any changes, it served as the constitution of both an authoritarian and a democratic system.[40] However, from the perspective developed in this chapter, there is nothing paradoxical in the 1924 Constitution. It was the authoritarian foundation of the 1924 Constitution, the hegemonic-totalitarian logic, that continued to operate as the main political logic both in the minds of the Kemalist establishment and the DP. The CHP's single-party rule and the populism of the DP are two different versions of the same authoritarian logic. According to both, a single actor claims to embody the people/nation and considers other claimants to be enemies of the people/nation. Both the single-party regime and the populist challenge of the DP were based on the same principle of representation and political unity. One actor – whether the military, the CHP, or the DP, whether in a single-party or a multiparty system, in the form of an elitist or majoritarian/populist claim – professed to be the embodiment of the people or the agency symbolically uniting the nation. Hence, any other claim to represent the people and any form of plurality or heterogeneity challenging the monolithic conception of the nation faced suppression.

38 The six principles of Kemalism are republicanism, nationalism, statism, laicism, populism, and reformism; see Erik-Jan Zürcher, *Turkey: A Modern History* (New York: I.B. Tauris, 1993), 184–214.

39 Turkuler Isiksel, "Between Text and Context: Turkey's Tradition of Authoritarian Constitutionalism," *International Journal of Constitutional Law* 11, no. 3 (2013): 702–726, 712.

40 Özbudun, *1924 Anayasasi*, 12.

3.3 The 1961 Constitution

In the multiparty period, the DP styled itself as the new true representative of the people. Although the DP enjoyed significant election victories in the beginning, due to bad economic policies and a worsening economic situation, support for the party did decrease. It was able to remain in power by suppressing intraparty opposition and public protest until the 1960 coup d'état,[41] when the military purged the political system and reconstituted itself as the 'true representative' of the nation. Constituted as the National Unity Committee (*Milli Birlik Komitesi*, MBK), the military formed a constituent assembly to write a new constitution in 1961. The assembly was bicameral. The MBK reserved for itself the role as upper chamber of the constituent assembly while the lower chamber was composed of delegates appointed by the MBK.[42] Written under the strict control of the military, the Constitution was adopted in 1961, and is generally acknowledged to be the most liberal Turkish constitution.

Suna Kili notes that the main weakness of the 1924 Constitution was its failure to establish a system of checks and balances that could prevent the abuse of political power by the majority party. The majoritarian character of democracy that the constitution established did not envision tyranny of the majority as a possible danger to the regime and was, therefore, unable to guard against majoritarian abuses of power. According to Kili, the military saw the lack of an adequate system of checks and balances as the main reason behind the authoritarianism of the DP government and supported the introduction of a more liberal constitution in 1961.[43] "In short, by the year of 1960, Turkey had experienced one-man (Sultan Abdulhamit II) violation of the Constitution; the executive (The Union and Progress movement) violation of the Constitution; and after the transition to a multi-party system the majority party's (the DP) violation of the Constitution."[44] All these different violations of the constitution and abuses of political power, Kili concludes, are integral to the learning process of the Kemalist elite. The 1961 Constitution was the outcome of this learning process, which taught them that not only does the executive need limitations but the legislative branch does as well. For this

41 For a discussion of the DP rule, see Kemal Karpat, "Political Developments in Turkey, 1950–70," *Middle Eastern Studies* 8, no. 3 (1972): 349–375; Feroz Ahmad, "Politics and Islam in Modern Turkey," *Middle Eastern Studies* 27, no. 1 (1991): 11–13.

42 Özbudun and Gençkaya, *Democratization and the Politics of Constitution-Making in Turkey*, 14–17; Kemal Gözler, *Anayasa Hukukunun Genel Teorisi* (Bursa: Ekin Yayınevi, 2011).

43 Kili, *Turkish Constitutional Developments*, 6–7.

44 Ibid., 8.

reason, the 1961 Constitution approached a more liberal form of constitutionalism.

Bülent Tanör makes a similar argument when stating that the primary concern of the founders of the 1961 Constitution was "the moderation of the unrestrained majoritarianism of the political system founded by the 1924 Constitution through the introduction of separation of powers, judicial review, a proportional representation electoral system and a bicameral Parliament."[45] Likewise, Ergun Özbudun states that "the [CHP] and the military had developed a preference for a more liberal and pluralistic democracy based on a system of checks and balances, including constitutional review and strong guarantees for the independence of the judiciary."[46] Thus, according to many constitutional scholars in Turkey, the 1961 Constitution is the result of a learning process on the side of the Kemalist elite, foremost the military, which helped them understand and accept that the unity of power is open to abuse by any political party that gains the parliamentary majority. One problematic aspect of this argument is that these scholars assume that an effective system of checks and balances applied to the use of political power by elected governments necessarily indicates a change toward a more pluralistic democracy. However, it is important to recognize that there was no change in the conception of political unity as a monolithic entity in the 1961 Constitution. The constitution was still based on the idea of the people-as-one. It "did not mark a major departure from the majoritarian heart of the system."[47] As stated in the preamble of the 1961 Constitution, the military intervention of May 27, 1960, was considered a revolution from below exercised in the name of the nation:

> Having enjoyed freedom, and fought for her rights and liberties throughout her history, and having achieved the Revolution of May 27, 1960 by exercising her right to resist the oppression of a political power which had deteriorated into a state of illegitimacy through behavior and actions contrary to the rule of law and the Constitution, the Turkish Nation, prompted and inspired by the spirit of Turkish nationalism, which unites all individuals, be it in fate, pride or distress, in a common bond as an indivisible whole around national

[45] Lord, *Religious Politics in Turkey*, 61. Bülent Tanör, *Osmanlı Türk Anayasa Gelismeleri: 1789–1980* (Istanbul Der Yayınları, 1995): 309–313.

[46] Özbudun, *1924 Anayasasi*, 15. Ozan Varol makes a similar argument. He states that "the 1961 Constitution also established the legal and political foundations of a participatory democratic society and a pluralist social-political order that represented majority social groups." See Varol, "The Turkish 'Model' of Civil–Military Relations," *International Journal of Constitutional Law* 11, no. 3 (2013): 727–750, 739.

[47] Lord, *Religious Politics in Turkey*, 253.

consciousness and aspirations, and which has its aim always to exalt our nation in a spirit of national unity.[48]

As is evident from the preamble, the military considered its actions – intervention and constitution making – to be an exercise of the constituent power of the people. With the 1960 coup d'état, military interventions and constitution-making processes dominated by the military became the performative affirmation of the Kemalist claim that it occupied the place of power. Claude Lefort emphasizes that, in theory, principles and institutions of constitutionalism may help keep the place of power empty. However, the main aim behind the establishment of countermajoritarian institutions in the 1961 Constitution was to keep the Kemalist elite in the place of power, not to keep the place of power empty.[49] In fact, the authoritarian foundation was maintained with the 1961 Constitution, which is neither constitutionalist (i.e., aiming to limit state power) nor pluralist (acknowledging the impossibility of the people as a unitary and monolithic entity). The 1971 coup d'état and the following amendments[50] dictated by the military prove that the main aim of these institutions was to make sure that democratic politics would not reach the boundaries of the Kemalist regime and the embodiment claim of the military.[51] With the 1961 and 1982 Constitutions, the military reiterated the claim that it occupies the place of power, no matter who wins the election. From this perspective, the often-cited difference between the 1961 and 1982 Constitutions, that is to say, the more liberal nature of the 1961 Constitution when compared to the overtly authoritarian 1982 Constitution, does not matter much, as they are both founded on the same authoritarian logic.

48 Kili, *Turkish Constitutional Developments*, 172.

49 For a detailed discussion of countermajoritarian institutions in Turkish constitutional law, see Abad Andrade, Chapter 7 in this volume.

50 The 1961 Constitution was heavily amended in 1971 and 1973 (Law No. 1421 of June 30, 1971, in *Resmî Gazete*, July 2, 1971, Sayı: 13883; Law No. 1488 of Sept. 20, 1971, in *Resmî Gazete*, Sept. 22, 1971, Sayı: 13964; Law No. 1699 of March 15, 1973, in *Resmî Gazete*, March 20, 1973, Sayı: 14482).

51 Özbudun and Gençkaya (*Democratization and the Politics of Constitution-Making in Turkey*, 18) summarize the amendments as follows: "The amendments can be grouped into three categories: (1) curtailing certain civil liberties in conjunction with restrictions of the review power of the courts; (2) strengthening the executive, particularly by allowing the legislature to grant it law-making powers; and (3) increasing the institutional autonomy of the military by excluding it from review by civilian administrative courts and the Court of Account." Importantly, the 1973 amendments introduced state security courts, which were used to restrict political pluralism by prosecuting crimes against the state on rather broad grounds. (See William Hale, "Turkish Democracy in Travail: The Case of the State Security Courts," *The World Today* 33, no. 5 (1977): 186–194.)

3.4 The 1982 Constitution

The 1982 Constitution is the product of another military intervention. When the military seized power on September 12, 1980, the generals blamed the 1961 Constitution for the political unrest of the 1960s and 1970s. The political impasse in the TBMM and the turmoil in the streets showed that the political elite had failed to put the general interest of the nation before their particular interests. As a result, the 1982 Constitution established more limitations on rights and liberties and was more restrictive regarding democratic politics. Similar to the prior process, the junta took direct control over constitution making. The MGK formed a constituent assembly, which it controlled. The lower chamber was responsible for drafting the new constitution, but the MGK had the final say on the draft. The military itself appropriated the constituent power with the claim that it alone represented the real interests of the nation.

Similar to the 1961 Constitution, the second military-imposed constitution was also grounded in a narrative of national sovereignty and constituent power. The military justified the coup and the constitution it imposed, claiming that it was simply exercising the will of the people. The preamble of the 1982 Constitution demonstrates the tutelary role the military reserved for itself. In the original form (and after amendment in 1995), it includes a sentence stipulating that the constitution makers (identifying themselves with the Turkish nation) entrust the constitution "to the democracy-loving Turkish sons' and daughters' love for the motherland and nation." In other words, the military styled itself as the great legislator giving the people a democratic constitution that could help them realize the general will. Following the approval of the MGK, the final version of the constitution was ratified in a tightly controlled and monitored referendum.

However, it was not only the imposition of the constitution by the military and state elite that was authoritarian. The document itself reflects "the authoritarian, statist, and tutelary mentality of its military founders."[52] Considering the 1961 Constitution as one of the sources of the political turmoil of the 1970s, the military controlled the process and the content of the 1982 Constitution closer than before. As such, the 1982 Constitution imposed severe limitations on the bill of rights, diminished the autonomy of universities, and weakened judicial independence. What is important about the 1982 Constitution from

52 Ergun Özbudun, "Turkey's Search for a New Constitution," *Insight Turkey* 14, no. 1 (2012): 39–50, 39.

the perspective of this chapter is that it was the military's reiteration of its embodiment claim.

Toward the end of the 1990s, increasing demands for a democratic constitution and the European accession process came together in mutually reinforcing calls for change toward a more democratic society. As a condition for European accession, Turkey amended its constitution through a consensual parliamentary process. The All-Party Accord Commission (*Partiler Arasi Uyum Komisyonu*), as a semiofficial body, brought the parties in Parliament together to find common ground for amending the constitution in line with liberal democratic principles.[53] This, ideally, would lead to a new constitution, developed and written via a democratic process. Amendments were important, but they were not enough, and after a while, too many amendments led to an incoherent constitution with conflicting provisions. The All-Party Accord Commission was an important exception to the exclusionary practice of constitution making in Turkey. The consensual model itself was as crucial a step in the democratization process as the progressive reforms the amendments achieved. The AKP came to power at a time of increasing demands for a democratic society, with the EU accession process applying external pressure and the All-Party Accord Commission serving as a blueprint of a consensual model in constitutional politics. Turkey was in a position to take advantage of this constellation of factors and produce a democratic constitution with popular participation.

4 THE AKP AND THE POPULIST CLOSURE

With the exception of the 1921 Constitution, all republican constitutions were made under the control of a single organ that claimed to embody the sovereign (constituent) power of the people. This claim not only led to nondemocratic constitution making, but also constituted the authoritarian foundation that has endured in the political system throughout the course of the republican era. It is critical to underline that it is the embodiment claim that is the foundation of the hegemonic-totalitarian logic governing constitution making in Turkey, and not the fact that the Kemalist elite or the military made the embodiment claim. The same logic was reproduced by the DP government in the 1950s, and it has been the main characteristic of the populist constitutional politics of the AKP since 2007.

[53] Andrew Arato, "Democratic Constitution-Making and Unfreezing the Turkish Process," *Philosophy & Social Criticism* 36, nos. 3–4 (2010): 473–487.

When the AKP came to power in 2002, there was an agreement that the junta-imposed 1982 Constitution was one of the major obstacles to democratization and European integration. The amendments undertaken to fulfill certain EU conditions for full membership successfully brought a consensual model into constitutional politics that the AKP could have invested in. However, rather than building on such consensual measures, the AKP chose to take the established path of imposing amendments by majority party vote in all major constitutional amendment processes in 2007, 2010, and 2017.

The year 2007 was a year of constitutional crisis and struggle in Turkey. Starting with the presidential election, the AKP faced increasing resistance from the Kemalist establishment. After failing to prevent the election of Abdullah Gül as president of the republic, the CHP took the election to the Constitutional Court. The court, in a highly controversial decision, declared the election unconstitutional.[54] The AKP responded with a constitutional amendment providing for the popular election of the president. A referendum ratified the amendment. In 2008, the AKP amended Articles 10 and 42 of the 1982 Constitution. The amendments, known as the "headscarf amendments," aimed at abolishing the headscarf ban. As a controversial long-term issue in Turkey, the headscarf ban had been uncompromisingly defended by secularist groups. The CHP took the amendments to the Constitutional Court, and the court annulled the amendments. This decision started a debate about the authority of the court. Critics argued that the court was acting as a tutelary power over democratic politics.[55]

Since 2007, the AKP has adopted a populist political strategy based on an antagonistic divide between the people and its enemies. By assimilating political reality into this dichotomy, and by articulating the totality of society around this antagonism, the AKP has constructed a discursive framework within which it presents itself as the sole democratizing agent with an exclusive claim to represent the people. We see the populist logic at work especially in the 2010 referendum. The AKP presented the referendum as a choice between democracy and military tutelage. Then-Prime Minister Recep Tayyip Erdoğan asserted that only those who were against the people would reject the amendments. Instead of a democratic discussion on the merits of the amendments and their possible consequences, the AKP manipulated the discussion into an antagonistic divide between the "pure" people and

[54] *Parliamentary Procedure of Presidential Election* [E. 2007/45–K. 2007/54, May 1, 2007], in *Resmî Gazete*, June 27, 2007, Sayı: 26565. See also Özbudun and Gençkaya, *Democratization and the Politics of Constitution-Making*, 98.

[55] Aslı Bâli, "Courts and Constitutional Transition: Lessons from the Turkish Case," *International Journal of Constitutional Law* 11, no. 3 (2013): 666–701.

the "corrupted elite" in order to mobilize support and terrify opponents. Those who tried to discuss the amendments were immediately labeled defenders of military tutelage and enemies of the people. Erdoğan claimed that opposition to the amendments was coming from a "coalition of the evil." He said, "The gangs that hope to benefit from darkness oppose the amendments. The elite, who rely on the status quo, oppose a 'yes' vote, as does the terrorist."[56] In the 2010 referendum campaign, enemies of the people were no longer limited to the Kemalist establishment. Anyone who opposed the AKP was labeled as such. Moreover, the AKP presented the outcome of the referendum as more than simple approval of the amendments. Erdoğan himself declared the outcome as a "democracy feast" and an "end of the putschist and tutelary mentality."[57] It was framed as an acclamation of the party and its leader. The AKP turned the 2010 amendment referendum into a plebiscite, making any reasonable discussion impossible and riving society into two by deriding one of the choices almost as if it were a crime.

The populist claim to embody the will of the people cannot be made in nonexclusive terms. In other words, a populist cannot make this claim and at the same time accept or acknowledge that there are, or can be, other political actors who can also speak on behalf of the people, and that their ideas and views are legitimate expressions of the people as well. Once we understand that the populist claim of representation is essentially an exclusive claim, we also understand that the claim itself undermines the defining feature of modern democracy that Lefort underlines. The place of power must remain empty and no political actor can embody the symbolic unity of the people.

Although the general characteristic of constitutional politics under AKP rule has been majoritarian imposition of the AKP's preferences under the guise of "the will of the people," there was a missed opportunity that could have led to a democratic constitution. During the 2011 parliamentary elections, the AKP and almost all other parties promised in their election manifestos a new, democratic, and civilian constitution for Turkey.[58] After the elections, based on this consensus for a new constitution, the AKP brought up the idea of establishing a parliamentary committee to draft a new

56 "CHP-MHP-BDP-YARSAV ve Terör Örgütü Ittifak Yapıyor," *T24*, July 31, 2010, https://t24.com.tr/haber/chp-mhp-bdp-yarsav-ve-teror-orgutu-ittifak-yapiyor,88406 (assessed July 9, 2019); see also "Erdoğan Hatay'da Konuştu," *Takvim*, July 31, 2010, www.takvim.com.tr/guncel/2010/07/31/erdogan_konusuyor (accessed July 9, 2019).

57 "Erdoğan: 'Demokrasi bayramı . . . ,'" *CNN Turk*, Sept. 12, 2010; see www.cnnturk.com/2010/turkiye/09/12/erdogan.demokrasi.bayrami/589419.0/index.html (accessed March 15, 2019).

58 Canan Akman and Pınar Akçalı, "Changing the System through Instrumentalizing Weak Political Institutions: The Quest for a Presidential System Turkey in Historical and Comparative Perspective," *Turkish Studies* 18, no. 4 (2017): 577–600, 586.

constitution. The president of the Parliament initiated the process and formed an ad hoc parliamentary Constitutional Conciliation Commission (*Anayasa Uzlasma Komisyonu*, AUK) to work on a draft constitution. The commission was formed with equal participation of the four parties present in Parliament (AKP, CHP, MHP, and BDP). According to the rules of procedure that the commission gave itself, all decisions would have to be made unanimously. The commission would be dissolved if one party refused to participate.

When compared to the methods used for making previous constitutions, this was a remarkably different approach in constitution making that aimed at achieving consensus in society. The commission not only departed from the practice of majoritarian imposition by including all political parties present in Parliament, but it also sought input from civil society. As Yeşim Bayar underlines, "[W]riting a new constitution through the involvement of the political parties in the Parliament as well as the larger societal involvement marked a significant turning point."[59] The AUK could have achieved a democratic departure from the path-dependent authoritarian constitution-making approach established in 1924. This attempt could have furthermore contributed to a peaceful solution to the Kurdish conflict. A new constitution written with equal involvement of different social groups, without anyone making the embodiment claim, could have established a new social contract among the parties involved in this long-lasting conflict. But the attempt failed, and the commission dissolved itself in December 2013.

In retrospect, the failed 2011–2013 constitution-making process looks like a lost opportunity to depart from the established authoritarian constitutional practices. When we locate this process within the constitutional politics of the AKP since 2002, the failure of the popular constitution making of 2011–2013, I argue, was a failure by design. First, the design of the decision-making procedures of the AUK contributed to the failure. These procedures provided little incentive to seek compromise, especially on highly disputed matters. As the procedures required that all decisions be made unanimously, the individual parties were virtually invited to veto or stop the process when it came to party "red lines." Although the process seems to have been designed in such a way that no party was in a position to claim to represent the unitary will of the people, the absence of mechanisms that could have forced each party first to compromise on disputed matters, and second to take the extra-parliamentary input provided by civil society organizations, roundtable initiatives, experts, universities, and unions into account, turned out to be a significant problem.

[59] Yeşim Bayar, "Constitutional Debates and Nationalist Visions," *Nationalism and Ethnic Politics* 23, no. 3 (2017): 340–360, 341.

As Parliament made public participation an integral part of the drafting process, input was readily available to the AUK at the time.[60] However, not only did the working rules of the commission not create a mechanism to force parties to compromise, but also societal input and public expectations regarding a democratic constitution were not able to apply democratic pressure on the political parties. There is almost no evidence that members of the commission changed or modified their views on a contested issue on the basis of the input received from civil society.

The commission was a failure by design in a second sense. The AKP might have proposed and initiated the commission not with a sincere aim to produce a new constitution based on consensus, but with the strategic aim to make the commission fail in order to justify a return to majoritarian imposition. That is to say, the failure of the AUK may not have been merely a matter of disagreement on certain fundamental issues, but the projected outcome that the AKP needed to justify the imposition of the executive presidential system. The dissolution of the AUK became the grounds for the AKP to accuse the other parties of not being willing to compromise and reach agreement. The failure of popular constitution making left majoritarian imposition as the only option for constructing a new constitution. This interpretation would have been mere speculation at the time. However, after the 2017 amendments imposed by a coalition of the AKP and the Nationalist Movement Party (*Milliyetçi Hareket Partisi*, MHP), this view can be substantiated today.

Before the 2011–2013 process, the AKP followed the authoritarian constitution-making path established with the 1924 Constitution. The constitutional amendments of 2007 and 2010 were majoritarian-populist impositions that disregarded the importance of the broader participation of society in constitutional amendments. As mentioned above, the AKP capitalized on the center-periphery narrative and adopted rhetoric that identifies the party with the people. The AKP argued that it represents the people against the elite, the periphery against the center, and civilian politics against military tutelage. Moreover, the amendments were portrayed as democratic and legitimate, notwithstanding the undemocratic nature of the actual drafting processes producing them.

In 2017, the AKP substantially amended the constitution again. For some, the extent of the amendments led to a de facto regime change.[61] The 2017

60 Oya Yegen, "Debating Unamendability: Deadlock in Turkey's Constitution-Making Process," in *An Unamendable Constitution? Unamendability in Constitutional Democracies*, eds. Richard Albert and Bertil Emrah Oder (Wiesbaden: Springer, 2018), 281–311, 296.

61 Berk Esen and Şebnem Gümüşçü, "The Perils of 'Turkish Presidentialism,'" *Review of Middle East Studies* 52, no. 1 (2018): 43–53.

amendments replaced the parliamentary regime in Turkey with a presidential system. The office of prime minister and the Council of Ministers were eliminated, and executive power was transferred to the president of the republic. In the new system, the president has vast appointment powers, including the power to appoint vice presidents, cabinet members, and high bureaucrats. He or she can also issue executive decrees, declare a state of emergency, deploy the military, and shut down Parliament. Most importantly, the president can use all his unprecedented powers without parliamentary oversight.[62] The presidential system that Recep Tayyip Erdoğan asked the AUK to constitutionalize in 2011–2013 was achieved through the 2017 amendment process. In this process a conservative coalition of the AKP and the MHP imposed the changes by claiming to embody the sovereign will of the people. The same hegemonic-totalitarian logic that governed the AKP's constitutional politics before the AUK started its work in 2011 was utilized after the failure of popular constitution making in 2013. Ceren Lord argues with regard to the AKP approach to constitutional politics that the "constitutional changes ... represent not an overhaul of the 1982 constitution but the erosion of the relatively anti-majoritarian institutions established in 1961 and in some sense a return to the pure majoritarianism of the 1924 constitutional framework in removing any remaining checks on parliamentary sovereignty."[63] Evaluating the work of the AUK in relation to the AKP's approach in constitutional politics, there is no reason to think that it was ever meant to achieve its declared purpose of democratic and consensual constitution making.

5 CONCLUSION

In the history of the Turkish Republic, the norm has been constitutions and amendments that were prepared behind closed doors without any public input or the participation of political and social groups. In exceptional cases, such as the amendments of the early 2000s when at least parliamentary consensus was reached among different parties, the imposed character of constitutions was not in evidence. For a country with long-lasting political and social problems, a constitution made through an open, participatory process could have functioned as a social contract leading to conflict resolution and more inclusive

[62] Felix Petersen and Zeynep Yanaşmayan, "The Final Trick? Separation of Powers, Checks and Balances, and the Recomposition of the Turkish State," *Verfassungsblog* (Jan. 28, 2017); see https://verfassungsblog.de/the-final-trick-separation-of-powers-checks-and-balances-and-the-recomposition-of-the-turkish-state/ (accessed March 15, 2019).

[63] Lord, *The Persistence of Turkey's Majoritarian System*, 253–254.

and egalitarian politics. This was exactly the promise of the AKP when it came to power in 2002.

However, contrary to this promise, the AKP leadership took the established path of imposition in all major constitutional amendment processes (2007, 2010, 2017). In all these cases, the AKP claimed to have the democratic authority to impose changes as the sole representative of the people. The party made this claim not only on the basis of the parliamentary majority that it held at the time of these amendments, but also on the assumption that it represented the "pure" people as a whole against the corrupted elite. This claim was supported by a narrative that explains the history of the Turkish Republic through dualities such as center versus periphery, secular versus religious, black Turks versus white Turks, and civilian politics versus military tutelage.

Inspired by Claude Lefort, this chapter has developed a perspective on constitution making in Turkey. It resists the master narrative of the center-periphery duality, which explains the constitutional history of the republic as an imposition of the secular, elitist center over the religious (peripheral) majority. As such a narrative cannot explain the authoritarian foundations of constitutions in Turkey, which have been reproduced by political actors on all sides, the chapter suggests a different argument. Starting with the 1924 Constitution, constitutions and amendments have been made in processes in which a single actor claimed to embody the people. These embodiment claims were made by the Republican People's Party for the 1924 Constitution, by the military following coups for the 1961 and 1982 Constitutions, and by a populist party holding the parliamentary majority in the 2007, 2010, and 2017 amendment processes. All these agents acted as if they were entitled to assume the constituent power of the people and justified the imposition of their constitutional choices as the choice of the people. The authoritarian foundation of Turkish constitutions is the hegemonic-totalitarian logic, i.e., the performative closing of the empty place of power.

The AKP's constitutional politics has been another episode of the hegemonic-totalitarian logic in operation. The party made the embodiment claim by equating the voice of the people with its own voice. It has excluded other agents and parties and branded them the voice of the enemy, which must be suppressed. The fact that the AKP is a civilian political actor controlling a parliamentary majority does not make its constitutional changes any less of an imposition. The popular constitution-making process of 2011–2013 could have overcome the established practice of imposed constitutions; instead, its failure became another important step in the consolidation of the hegemonic-totalitarian logic in Turkish politics.

3

Regime Cycles, Constitution Making, and the Political System Question in Ottoman and Turkish Constitutional Developments

Şule Özsoy Boyunsuz

1 INTRODUCTION

In 2011–2013 a democratic constitution-making process was initiated in Turkey but failed to produce a new constitution. A few years later the ruling Justice and Development Party (*Adalet ve Kalkınma Partisi*, AKP) succeeded in amending the existing 1982 Constitution, imposing radical changes on the political system and introducing the so-called Turkish-style presidential system in 2017. This chapter argues that the latest constitutional changes and movements are part of a distinct and regular cycle of events, swinging toward and away from democracy, created by an intense power struggle between ideologically competing forces in Turkey.

In political science, cyclical movements have long been recognized as one possible mode of change over time.[1] Cycles are defined as "regular recurrences: fixed sequences of several phases that invariably return to their point of departure."[2] In some polities, scientists observe "regular and reasonably predictable cycles of movement both towards and away from democracy or autocracy."[3] With regard to Ottoman-Turkish constitutional history, regular cyclical movements between authoritarian and relatively democratic phases can be observed. Usually, these were motivated by intense power struggles between conservative forces opposing Westernization/modernization and/or secularization on the one hand and reformist/revolutionary forces favoring

[1] George Modelski, *Long Cycles in World Politics* (London: The Macmillan Press, 1987), 28.

[2] Ibid., 58.

[3] Henry E. Hale, "Regime Cycles: Democracy, Autocracy, and Revolution in Post-Soviet Eurasia," *World Politics* 58, no. 1 (2005): 133–165, 134; Samuel P. Huntington, *The Third Wave* (Norman: University of Oklahoma Press, 1991); Juan J. Linz and Alfred Stepan, *The Breakdown of Democratic Regimes: Crisis, Breakdown, and Reequilibration: An Introduction* (Baltimore: Johns Hopkins University Press, 1978).

secularization, democratization, and Westernization on the other. Authoritarian turns were instigated by one of the three following coalitions: civil forces that came to power in a relatively democratic environment but were not willing to hand over political power through free and fair elections; revolutionary civil forces aiming to design a new society, regime, and state based on their revolutionary ideas; or military forces that had no intention of establishing a long military rule, but wanted to design a constitution reflecting their vision of the state. Democratic turns, on the other hand, come with an alternation in political power (removal and replacement of government by a civil competitor) and are characterized by a return to relatively free and fair political competition. Each phase exhibits specific institutions, norms, and behaviors.

Authoritarian phases in Turkey involve institutional choices and practices typically associated with autocratic regimes: concentration of powers in the hands of the executive, weakened checks and balances, a weak assembly, strong executive power to dissolve the assembly, abuse of executive lawmaking authority, and weak or no protection of civil and political rights (especially to free speech, free association, free assembly, and a free press). Authoritarian cycles are also characterized by a certain style of constitution making. Constitution making is often the result of intense power struggles between competing classes or groups with different visions of the state. In Turkey, groups that manage to consolidate enough power to make or remake a constitution do so in a way that shapes state institutions according to their vision, promotes a single public identity, and enforces social uniformity. Constitution making in such cases is integrationist in that it rejects the participation as well as the visions of other groups or identities.[4] Authoritarian phases have produced the constitutions of 1924, 1961, and 1982. This does not imply that all constitutions produced during authoritarian phases promote authoritarian regimes. An integrationist process may also produce constitutions favoring democratic rule but as envisioned by a single group. In fact, the 1924, 1961, and 1982 Constitutions were all products of integrationist processes that promoted different forms of democratic rule. The 1924 Constitution promoted majority rule without checks and balances, an approach that is supported by a majoritarian electoral system that gives excessive representation to the majority. The 1961 Constitution was based on

[4] John McGarry, Brendon O'Leary, and Richard Simeon, "Integration or Accommodation? The Enduring Debate in Conflict Regulation," in *Constitutional Design for Divided Societies: Integration or Accommodation?* ed. S. Choudhry (New York: Oxford University Press, 2008), 41–87.

an idea of limited majority rule with constitutional checks and balances, supported by an electoral system of proportional representation. Finally, the 1982 Constitution weakened constitutional rights and checks and balances, thereby promoting a stronger majority rule that was further supported by an electoral system requiring a minimum of 10 percent of the national vote for a party to enter Parliament. All of this gave excessive representation to the majority.

In theory, democratic constitution making should be consensual and accommodationist. It aims to include different groups and identities in the process, and in the end it does not impose a single public identity on society; rather, it promotes pluralism and institutional respect for difference.[5] It also includes different stages of negotiation, bargaining, and consensus formation.[6] In Turkey, democratic phases have rarely produced new constitutions such as the 1921 document. But partial amendments, such as the 1995 and 2001 amendments promoting participatory democracy, are the result of consensual constitution-making processes.

This chapter explains how the different (democratic and authoritarian) cycles have appeared in past and present constitution-making processes and the institutions and behavioral traits that have accompanied each cycle. Beginning with the first and second constitutional periods in the Ottoman Empire, the next section revisits consecutive autocratic and democratic regime cycles in modern Turkey by focusing on the political system preferences at different historical stages. Exposing the cyclic regime changes, political forces, conflicts, and continuity of institutions and methods in past constitution-making processes helps us understand the most recent constitutional developments – the failed 2011–2013 process and the 2017 amendments – and their place in Turkish regime cycles.

2 REGIME CYCLES AND CONSTITUTIONAL DEVELOPMENTS

2.1 *The Ottoman Empire and the 1876 Constitution*

The Ottoman Empire was a theocratic sultanate ruled by a caliph sultan whose power depended upon maintaining harmony between certain internal forces, namely clerics (*ulema*) and the army (*yeniçeri*). In the eighteenth century, those institutions were corrupted and the harmony between them

[5] Ibid., 41.

[6] Andrew Arato, *Post Sovereign Constitution Making: Learning and Legitimacy* (New York: Oxford University Press, 2016), 95.

was disrupted.[7] In addition, economic difficulties, corrupt governance, and religious oppression induced uprisings among non-Muslim entities of the empire. Local feudal forces were emboldened by the weakness of the central authorities, and arbitrariness and injustice in public management became widespread. By the nineteenth century, the Ottoman Empire was losing internal and external power. A lack of legal security fueled a volatile social atmosphere characterized by ineffective economic production.

Throughout the nineteenth century, the bureaucratic elite and the sultan struggled over power, both calling on various external forces outside the political center for support. Military, legal, and technical reforms involving Western inventions were often implemented by both competing power segments to stop the decay of the empire.

However, the Westernization measures and the arbitrariness of governance triggered reactions from clergy and lower-ranking bureaucrats.[8] There were the reformists trying to save a decaying state by importing Western technical inventions and governing tools, and those who were disturbed by and critical of such reforms.[9] Both groups belonged to the state administration. In addition, Western capitalist forces were pushing for reforms to advance their economic and political interests, often in the name of non-Muslim subjects. Constitutional developments of the nineteenth century should therefore be seen as the result of such internal and external dynamics.

In 1876 the Ottoman Empire enacted its first written constitution. Lower-ranking bureaucrats, clergy, and military, with the help of external forces, gained command over the higher-ranking bureaucracy and imposed the first constitution as a limit to the power of the higher-ranking bureaucrats.[10] On the road to the constitution, one grand vizier, Sadrazam Mahmut Nedim Paşa, was forced out of power, and two sultans, Abdülaziz and Murad V, were dethroned. Although the "will of the nation" was used to legitimize all these events,[11] the constitution lacked social support, at least among the majority of Muslim subjects.[12]

With this first constitution, the cycle of regimes that will be reconstructed in the following – from authoritarian (whether civilian or military) to relatively

[7] Bülent Tanör, *Osmanlı-Türk Anayasal Gelişmeleri* (İstanbul: YKY, 1998), 22.

[8] Ibid.

[9] Taner Timur, *Türk Devrimi Tarihi Anlamı ve Felsefi Temeli* (Ankara: Sevinç Matbaası, 1968), 88.

[10] Akın Rıdvan, *TBMM Devleti (1920–1923) Birinci Meclis Döneminde Devlet Erkleri ve İdare* (İstanbul: İletişim Yayınları, 2001), 37.

[11] Tanör, *Osmanlı-Türk Anayasal Gelişmeleri*, 125–126.

[12] Timur, *Türk Devrimi*, 69.

democratic phases and back – starts. The 1876 Ottoman Constitution initiated the first democratic institution, the National Assembly (*Meclis-i Mebusân*, MM), but the movement toward democratization quickly turned into the first civilian authoritarian phase under a codified constitution. While this constitution instituted the first Ottoman Assembly, it did not create a constitutional parliamentary monarchy. The Assembly lacked real legislative powers; it could only exercise preventive authority in the legislative process. The sultan's authority was not really limited, and there was no separate cabinet that could be forced to resign by a vote of no confidence.[13] The sultan had absolute veto power, and he held the authority to convene, disperse, or dissolve the Assembly. Despite all its shortcomings, this first elected Assembly introduced the idea that the sultan was no longer the sole sovereign.[14] There was another power to be reckoned with, and that was the nation. Until then, the legitimacy of sultans derived from traditional and religious sources. With the first codified constitution, legislation gained legitimacy from the approval of the Assembly, which represented the will of the people.[15] This was a secular transformation of legitimacy in a theocratic establishment. The Assembly was able to convene for only five months before it was dispersed by Sultan Abdülhamit. He concentrated all state power in his hands and ruled oppressively for the next thirty years. As a response to Westernization measures, a type of political Islam became the leading ideology of Abdülhamit's autocratic reign of terror. Meanwhile, his pan-Islamist policy created political opposition and a desire for freedom among non-Muslim subjects as well as the Muslim educated classes. This accelerated the disintegration of the empire.[16]

2.2 *The Second Constitutional Period, 1908–1919*

Abdülhamit's reign of terror was brought to an end by an uprising of a large social alliance of different segments of the middle class.[17] The Ottoman Assembly was convened by the sultan once more in 1908. This time political power was to be transferred from the sultan to the elected Assembly. The "will of the nation" became the legitimizing imperative in the political discourse.[18]

[13] See Tanör, *Osmanlı-Türk Anayasal Gelişmeleri*, 136–141.
[14] Tanör, *Osmanlı-Türk Anayasal Gelişmeleri*, 149.
[15] Ibid., 136.
[16] Ibid., 71–72.
[17] Ibid., 177.
[18] The Decree of the Second Chamber of the Ottoman Assembly (*Ayan Kararnamesi*) announcing the constitutional amendments of 1909 declared that they were executing the "will of the nation" (*hakimiyeti milliyenin teeyüdü*). The members of the Ottoman Assembly collectively and individually expressed on many occasions that they saw the Assembly as the symbol of the

The parliamentary system began to emerge with this transformation in 1909.[19] The prime minister and his cabinet members became a separate council responsible before the elected Assembly.

With this transformation the first authoritarian period was over. The regime moved toward democracy, though it did not consolidate a democratic system. The slogan of the day was "freedom, equality, brotherhood, and justice," (*hürriyet, müsavat, uhuvvet, adalet*) much like during the French Revolution of 1789, but with the addition of justice.[20] As is typical of a democratic phase, an elected Assembly gained power at the expense of a strong executive (the sultan). In 1909, the Assembly changed the 1876 Constitution radically: Twenty-one articles were amended, three articles were added, and one article was abrogated. The main rationale was to reduce the power of the sultan in favor of the Assembly and to codify an early parliamentary system that was already emerging in political practice.[21] The Council of Ministers' political responsibility to the Assembly became a constitutional obligation. The countersignature rule was accepted, whereby the sultan's exercise of power was dependent on the initiative and signature of the prime minister (*sadrazam*) and the other relevant minister. The Assembly was given true legislative authority as well as powers to check the Council of Ministers. The conditions under which the Assembly could be dissolved made it very difficult for the sultan to abuse this power.

Unfortunately, after a few years of relative political freedom, another civilian autocratic episode began under the hegemonic rule of the Union and Progress Party (*İttihat ve Terakki Partisi*, İTP) that lasted until the end of World War I (1918). The İTP only checked and balanced the government in the beginning (1908), then took control of the government in 1909, and began turning authoritarian in 1912. In 1914, the İTP was the only party participating in elections. As a result, it won control over the Assembly and amended the

national will and that they worked for the formation and realization of this national will; see Cihan Osmanağaoğlu, *Tanzimat Dönemi İtibarıyla Osmanlı Vatandaşlığının Gelişimi* (İstanbul: Legal Yayınları, 2004), 304–305; Recai Galip Okandan, *Amme Hukukumuzun Ana hatları Türkiye'nin Siyasi Gelişmesi* (İstanbul: İ.Ü. Hukuk Fakültesi, 1977), 284–290; Hüseyin Nail Kubalı, *Türk Esas Teşkilat Hukuku Dersleri* (İstanbul: Tan Matbaası, 1960), 105–109.

19 Tarık Zafer Tunaya, *Devrim Hareketleri İçinde Atatürk Ve Atatürkçülük* (İstanbul: Bilgi Üniversitesi, 2nd ed., 2007), 87; Tarık Zafer Tunaya, *Türkiye'de Siyasal Partiler III: İttihat ve Terakki, Bir Çağın, Bir Kuşağın, Bir Partinin Tarihi* (İstanbul: İletişim Yayınları, 5th ed., 2011), 87; Kubalı, *Türk Esas Teşkilat Hukuku Dersleri*, 106.

20 Tanör, *Osmanlı-Türk Anayasal Gelişmeleri*, 178.

21 Ibid., 193; Kubalı, *Türk Esas Teşkilat Hukuku Dersleri*, 111; Orhan Aldıkaçtı, *Anayasa Hukukumuzun Gelişmesi ve 1961 Anayasası*, 3rd ed. (İstanbul: Fakülteler Matbaası, 1978), 71–72; Okandan, *Amme Hukukumuzun Ana hatları*, 328–330.

constitution to make it easier to dissolve the Assembly, but it did not need to exercise this power.[22]

The 1876 constitution granted temporary executive lawmaking power to the Council of Ministers at times when the Assembly was not convened. These decrees were called "temporary legislations" (*kanunu muvakkat*, Art. 36). Governments immensely abused this power, issuing more than a thousand such decrees in the ten years from 1908 to 1918, effectively transferring legislative power from Parliament into the hands of the executive, especially after 1913.[23] Thus, the first effort to transfer power to an elected Parliament ended with the consolidation of power in the hands of a single party, the İTP, which turned the state into an autocracy similar to the one it had overthrown.

The Ottoman Empire lost World War I, and its territory was consequently occupied by the Allied forces. The last Ottoman Assembly was convened following the 1919 election and declared the National Oath (*Missak-ı Milli*) just before the English forces occupying the capital raided the Assembly and arrested some members.[24] The remaining deputies decided in March 1920 not to convene under these circumstances. Sultan Vahdettin dissolved the last Ottoman Assembly in the same month, and the authoritarian İTP period ended with the convulsive breakdown of the Ottoman Empire. Once more, the cycle was about to swing toward democracy.

2.3 *The Revolutionary Era of the 1921 and 1924 Constitutions*

Following the occupation of Istanbul by Allied forces and the occupation of Anatolia by Greek troops, the national resistance movement started. The leader of the national resistance, Mustafa Kemal Pasha, united the national forces within the Association for the Defense of National Rights (*Müdafa-i Hukuk Cemiyeti*), declared Ankara the new political center, and assembled an elected Parliament, the Turkish Grand National Assembly (*Türkiye Büyük Millet Meclisi*, TBMM) in April 1920.

In terms of constitutional legitimacy, there was continuity between the Ottoman Assembly and the new Assembly.[25] Deputies of the last Ottoman Assembly were invited to join the TBMM, as their Assembly could not work

22 Tanör, *Osmanlı-Türk Anayasal Gelişmeleri*, 203.
23 Tunaya, *Türkiye'de Siyasal Partiler*, 466.
24 Based on the idea of self-determination and rejection of the occupation, the National Oath later became the main source of Turkish public law ideology. It formed the core principles of the secular nation-state founded after the revolution of 1921 (Akın, *TBMM Devleti*, 44).
25 Akın, *TBMM Devleti*, 47.

under the pressure of the Allied forces and was later dissolved by Sultan Vahdettin. A considerable number of deputies answered this historic call. From the beginning the TBMM was an assembly with extraordinary powers. It was in fact a constituent assembly.[26] The first TBMM enacted the first republican constitution (*Teşkilat-ı Esasiye Kanunu*, "Basic Establishment Law"), liberated the country from foreign occupation, and dissolved the sultanate.

The first TBMM was constituted by the Turkish national bourgeoisie of the time.[27] While women, peasants, and laborers were not represented in the first TBMM,[28] it can nevertheless be argued that the first TBMM represented the national will. The first TBMM comprised deputies elected in two different elections: the election for the Ottoman Assembly of 1919 and an election conducted under the national resistance movement in 1920.[29] In the 1919 election deputies were elected from Ottoman political party lists, and in the 1920 election, 337 deputies from diverse ethnic and ideological backgrounds (revolutionary nationalists, moderate nationalists, socialists/communists/Bolsheviks, moderate and stronger conservatives including Islamist monarchists) were elected from sixty-six districts.[30] Even though various political groups and a strong opposition were formed in the Assembly, the first TBMM denied the existence of political parties during the independence war.[31]

It is generally accepted that this was the most democratic constitution-making process in Turkish history.[32] The 1921 Constitution was made by an elected constituent assembly in which different groups and ideologies were

26 Tanör, *Osmanlı-Türk Anayasal Gelişmeleri*, 230.

27 Burak Çelik, *Ulusal Kurtuluş Savaşı Döneminde Anayasal Gelişmeler ve 1921 Anayasası* (İstanbul: GSÜ Yayınları, 2007), 41; Tanör, *Osmanlı-Türk Anayasal Gelişmeleri*, 232.

28 Tunaya mentions one deputy with a working-class background. See Tarık Zafer Tunaya, *Devrim Hareketleri İçinde Atatürk Ve Atatürkçülük* (Istanbul: Bilgi Üniversitesi, 2nd ed., 2007), 259.

29 Ibid., 258.

30 Bahar Bilgen, *Dönemin Basınına Göre 1919 Seçimleri ve Meclis-i Mebusan'in Oluşturulması*. Master's thesis, Trakya University Social Science Institute Department of History General Turkish History (2011); Niyazi Berkes, *Türkiye'de Çağdaşlaşma*, 17th ed. (İstanbul: YKY, 2012), 499; Ayşe Hür, "TBMM Hiç Çok Renkli Oldu Mu?" *Radikal*, June 28, 2015; Akın, *TBMM Devleti*, 49, 52–55; Enver Behnan Şapolyo, *Mustafa Kemal ve I. TBMM Tarihçesi* (Ülkemiz Matbaası: Ankara, 1969), 33; Salahi Sonyel, "Kurtuluş Savaşı Günlerinde İngilizlerin Eline Geçen TBMM Gizli Tutanakları," *Belleten* CXLV, no. 179 (1981): 215–301, 264–265, 277.

31 Tanör, *Osmanlı-Türk Anayasal Gelişmeleri*, 259–260.

32 Tanör calls it "the single constitution made by democratic and civil process, a model of harmony" (Bülent Tanör, "Cumhuriyet Anayasacılığımızda Üç Model," in *Cumhuriyet'in 75. Yıl Armağanı* (İstanbul: İstanbul University Press, 1999), 213–218; Çelik, *Ulusal Kurtuluş*

not only present, but also actively participated.[33] As such, it represents an exception in Ottoman-Turkish constitutional history.

The 1921 Constitution declared that the national will could only be represented by the TBMM. Constitutionally, this choice meant accepting the supremacy of Parliament (unity of powers) over the separation of powers doctrine.[34] The constitution concentrated constitutional powers in the Assembly. The Assembly held executive, legislative, and even judicial authority.[35] According to the theory of the assembly government system, ministers do not form a homogeneous body having a single political program and are bound by the directives of the Assembly.[36] There is also no need for a separate head of state,[37] and indeed, under the Assembly government system of the 1921 Constitution, there was no separate executive organ. Ministers were selected individually by the Assembly and were given the title Ministers of the Grand National Assembly.[38] The Assembly could always amend or annul decisions of ministers.[39] Executive

Savaşı Döneminde Anayasal Gelişmeler ve 1921 Anayasası, 67; Tanör, *Osmanlı-Türk Anayasal Gelişmeleri*, 250; Ergun Özbudun, *1921 Anayasası* (Ankara: Atatürk Araştırma Merkezi Yayınları, 1992), 2; İbrahim Kaboğlu and Eric Sales, *Darbe ve Demokrasi Sarkacında Türk Anayasa Hukuku* (İstanbul: Legal Yay., 2018), 18; Ahmet Demirel, "1920–1923 Arasında Türkiye Dünyanın En İleri Temsili Demokrasilerinden Birine Sahipti," *Türkiye Günlüğü Mart–Nisan* 60 (2000): 6; Kemal Gözler, *Türk Anayasa Hukuku* (Ekin Kitabevi Yayınları, 2nd ed., 2018), 67–68; Dinçer Demirkent, *Bir Devlet İki Cumhuriyet* (İstanbul: Ayrıntı Yayınları, 2017), 24–25.

33 Sonyel, *Kurtuluş Savaşı Günlerinde İngilizlerin*, 266–267, 272–273, 276–277, 293; Demirkent, *Bir Devlet İki Cumhuriyet*, 171–172; Berkes, *Türkiye'de Çağdaşlaşma*, 501–502. For the minutes of Assembly debates during the making of the 1921 Constitution, see Murat Sevinç and Dinçer Demirkent, *Kuruluşun İhmal Edilmiş İstisnası 1921 Anayasası ve Tutanakları* (İstanbul: İletişim Yayınevi, 2017).

34 This political system was based on Rousseau's theory of a single, undivided sovereignty represented only by the Assembly, similar to the French *gouvernement coventionnel* of the 1793 Constitution (Mehmet Turan, "Meclis Hükümeti (Konvansiyon Kuramı)," *Ankara Üniversitesi Siyasal Bilgiler Fakültesi Dergisi* 46, no. 1 (2015): 453–463, 455; Kemal Gözler, *Anayasa Hukukunun Genel Teorisi* (Bursa: Ekin Yay., 2011), 557–565; Mehmet Turhan, *Hükümet Sistemleri* (Ankara: Gündoğan Yay., 1993), 25–27.

35 Tunaya, *Devrim Hareketleri İçinde Atatürk ve Atatürkçülük*, 267–271.

36 Ibid., 221; Turan, *Meclis Hükümeti*, 457.

37 Turan, *Meclis Hükümeti*, 456–457.

38 The Selection of Ministers of the Grand National Assembly Act (*Büyük Millet Meclisi İcra Vekillerinin Sureti İntihabına Dair Kanun*) first regulated individual selection among the members, only to be altered seven months later. The amended Article 2 required nomination from the speaker of the Assembly. Yet in 1922 the Assembly restored the old formula. The method of selection of ministers was changed again, along with the declaration of the republic, on October 29, 1923. The president appointed the prime minister, who nominated the ministers, and then the Assembly approved the Council of Ministers (Turan, *Meclis Hükümeti*, 457).

39 Erdoğan Teziç, *Anayasa Hukuku*, 16. Bası (İstanbul: Beta Yayınları, 2013), 476.

authorities were considered agents who took orders from the Assembly.[40] There was no separate head of state until the declaration of the republic in 1923.

The Assembly was to be in session at all times (*istimrar*). No power to dissolve Parliament was constitutionally codified. These norms were accepted as a reaction to the past experience of the reign of Abdülhamit and the İTP. Whenever autocracy thrived in Turkey, assemblies were either dispersed or dissolved. The republican constitutional tradition flourished on the principle of the Assembly remaining convened. The typical institutional choices of authoritarian periods (executive powers to dissolve the assembly and issue decrees having the force of law, weakened assembly, weakened checks and balances) did not exist under the 1921 Constitution. In fact, the first TBMM was a strong assembly[41] – there were different political groups, views, and identities present, and deputies were able to check and balance ministers as well as the speaker, Mustafa Kemal Pasha.[42]

After the liberation of the country, the second TBMM was elected in 1923. It was dominated by the founding fathers of Kemalism, who were later gathered within the Republican People's Party (*Cumhuriyet Halk Partisi*, CHP). The first generation of Kemalists consisted of members of the petty bourgeoisie and the Anatolian gentry. They were mostly civil servants and officers from middle- or lower-income families who were well educated.[43]

After the second TBMM assembled, it was necessary to make a new constitution.[44] The 1921 Constitution was a short document that did not regulate the judiciary or codify basic rights. Therefore, in situations where there was no constitutional codification regarding a given subject, the 1876 Ottoman Constitution was still used. Turkey was in a confusing transitional state, especially after the declaration of the republic in 1923.

In the making of the 1924 Constitution, the TBMM acted in line with the principle of assembly sovereignty. The TBMM was presumed to be the sole representative of the national will, and it could act on behalf of the nation to make a new constitution. Since the 1921 Constitution did not require a qualified majority to change or replace the constitution and recognized the Assembly as the supreme constitutional organ, it was legally and politically

40 Tunaya, *Devrim Hareketleri İçinde Atatürk ve Atatürkçülük*, 267.

41 Akın (*TBMM Hükümeti*, 416) says that the first TBMM was a democratic, open to debate, forum-type assembly.

42 Ahmet N. Yücekök, *Siyaset Sosyolojisi Açısından Türkiye'de Parlamentonun Evrimi* (Ankara: A.Ü.S.B.F Yayınları, 1983), 101.

43 Taner Timur, *Türk Devrimi Ve Sonrası*, 7. Bası (Ankara: İmge Yayınları, 2013), 21–22, 65.

44 Ergun Özbudun, *Türk Anayasa Hukuku* (Ankara: Yetkin Yayınları, 2004), 31; Teziç, *Anayasa Hukuku*, 185.

sound to acknowledge the second TBMM as an elected constituent assembly.[45] It was not a pluralist constituent assembly in which different voices were present, even though different opinions regarding institutional choices were expressed and discussed.[46] Only two deputies were elected from outside the party lists that were designed by Mustafa Kemal Pasha.[47] In the end the collective choices of Kemalists became the constitution. There were many specialists, intellectuals, ministers, and deputies involved in the drafting process,[48] but there was no negotiation, bargaining, or compromise among different groups or identities.[49] The High Treason Act (*Hıyaneti Vataniye Kanunu*) was amended in 1923, making it very difficult for the opposition, especially Islamist monarchists, to challenge the choices of the majority or the constitution-making process.[50] Once again, the political majority formed through free and fair competition was turning authoritarian by erasing political opposition. However this cycle still has a unique place in Turkish political history, as it was the product of a revolutionary process following the collapse of an empire.

As core principles of state organization, the Assembly adopted the principles of unconditional national sovereignty and the supremacy of Parliament. As the sole representative of the national will, the TBMM was to exercise legislative power directly and executive power indirectly through the executive (i.e., the president of the republic and Council of Ministers). Judicial authority was to be exercised by independent courts.

Codifying the political system for the new republic, the deputies decided that the TBMM had to elect one of its members for a single legislative period as president. The president was to choose the prime minister. The prime minister would decide on the list of ministers, who were chosen from among the deputies and were to be approved by the president. The Council of Ministers had to present its program within a week to the Assembly and ask for a vote of confidence. Collective and individual responsibility was assigned to the Council of Ministers. The president, on the other hand, had no responsibility toward the Assembly, but his decisions were to be countersigned by the prime minister and cabinet members, who carried all responsibility. The formation of the executive organ, organic

45 Teziç, *Anayasa Hukuku*, 185; Burak Çelik, *Kurucu İktidar-Hükümet Sistemi-Vatandaşlık Ve idari Yapılanma Tartışması Çerçevesinde 1924 Anayasasının Yapım Süreci* (Ankara: Yetkin Yayınları, 2016), 61.

46 Çelik, *1924 Anayasasının Yapım Süreci*, 73–146.

47 Ibid., 56.

48 Ibid., 71.

49 Ergun Özbudun, *Türkiye'de Demokratikleşme Süreci Anayasa Yapımı ve Anayasa Yargısı* (İstanbul: Bilgi Üniversitesi Yayınları, 2014), 55.

50 Çelik, *1924 Anayasasının Yapım Süreci*, 40–47.

and functional fusion, the countersignature rule, as well as the chain of accountability and delegation,[51] are all disctinctive of the parliamentary system.[52]

With the 1924 Constitution, Turkey entered a revolutionary period in which elites built a secular nation-state. The power was in the hands of the revolutionary CHP, and other political groups were eliminated. The Progressive Republican Party (*Terkakkiperver Cumhuriyet Fırkası*, TCF) was dissolved in 1925. The Free Republican Party (*Serbest Cumhuriyet Fırkası*, SCF) was founded in 1930 and dissolved itself after a few months. Though the CHP dominated politics in the early republican era as a single ruling party, the 1924 Constitution was not written for single-party rule. On the contrary, it was open to competitive politics. Furthermore, there was no clear legislative rule preventing a competitive political system until 1938.[53]

2.4 *Competitive Politics under the 1924 Constitution*

The time of the CHP's single-party rule was a period of civilian authoritarianism that was not constitutionally codified. The typical institutional choices weakening the Assembly (e.g., executive powers of dissolution, decrees having the force of law) did not exist, but the constitution did not contain any effective checks and balances against the majority that could prevent abuse of power or an authoritarian turn.[54] The supremacy of Parliament was turned into the

[51] According to Kaare Strøm ("Delegation and Accountability in Parliamentary Democracies," *European Journal of Political Research* 37, no. 3 (2000): 261–289, 263), "The belief in the unfettered rule by the popularly elected majority lies at the heart of the tradition of parliamentary government." In this system, power has historically been delegated from Parliament to the majority and from the majority to the cabinet. Parliamentary supremacy turns into extensive delegation to the cabinet in certain parliamentary systems (see also Alan Siaroff, "Varieties of Parliamentarism in the Advanced Industrial Democracies," *International Political Science Review* 24, no. 4 (2003): 445–464, 447; Şule Özsoy Boyunsuz, *Başkanlı Parlamenter Sistem Cumhurbaşkanının Halk Tarafından Seçildiği Parlamenter Hükümet Modeli ve Türkiye İçin Tavsiye Edilebilirliği*, 2. Bası (İstanbul: 12 Levha Yayınları, 2014), 9–21).

[52] According to Mümtaz Sosyal (*Anayasaya Giriş* (Ankara: İmge Yayınları, 2011) 192), the political system merges the 1920 tradition with the parliamentary system tradition (see also Özbudun, *Türk Anayasa Hukuku*, 31; Kaboğlu and Sales, *Türk Anayasa Hukuku*, 31).

[53] The Associations Act (Law no. 3512 of June 28, 1938, in *Resmî Gazete*, July 14, 1938, Sayı: 3959) introduced a permission system for political parties. Parties had to submit documents required by the Ministry of Internal Affairs and could register once permission was granted. Furthermore, the act gave the government extensive powers to control and dissolve all parties and associations (Teziç, *Anayasa Hukuku*, 380).

[54] The absence of constitutional review or other independent institutions of checks and balances on the majority paved the way for the uncontrolled exercise of power through the majority in the Assembly; see Suna Kili, *Turkish Constitutional Developments and Assembly Debates on the Constitutions of 1924 and 1961* (Istanbul: Menteş Matbaası, 1971), 22; Özbudun, *Türk Anayasa Hukuku*, 33.

supremacy of the executive due to the parliamentary chain of delegation without checks and balances. The Assembly served as an enabling tool to alter the legal and social structure during the revolutionary secularist period of single-party rule.[55] Transitioning to competitive politics in 1945 did not require constitutional changes. Under the pressure of internal and external dynamics, the CHP itself led the way to competitive politics in 1945, and handed over power to the Democratic Party (*Demokrat Parti*, DP) in 1950.[56]

Turkey once again moved toward a democratic phase. The competitive period between 1950 and 1960 resembles the second constitutional period of the Ottoman era: starting off with the promise of greater democracy and then becoming authoritarian toward the end. The DP came to power inspiring great hopes and promising to run the country democratically with the support of both conservative voters and liberal intellectuals.[57] For the first few years, they delivered economic growth and relative prosperity, and consequently enlarged their political support.[58] However, their understanding of democracy was majoritarian. Once again, the idea that the majority could do everything without any control was readopted in political practice and impeded pluralist democracy. The parliamentary supremacy and fusion of powers caused the delegation of political power from the majority of the Assembly to the cabinet (Council of Ministers).[59] The prime minister became the strongest actor, as he controlled the administration and the political majority in the Assembly. Presidents were also selected by the majority of the Assembly and had affiliation with the majority party.[60]

The DP became the predominant party with the help of an extremely unfair election system[61] and went on to control the government for three consecutive

55 Özbudun, *Türk Anayasa Hukuku*, 21.

56 Bernard Lewis, *Modern Türkiye'nin Doğuşu* (Ankara: Arkadaş Yayınevi, 2011), 405–414.

57 Feroz Ahmad, *Bir Kimlik Peşinde Türkiye* (İstanbul: Bilgi Üniversitesi Yayınları, 2006), 131.

58 Ibid., 133.

59 Kili, *Turkish Constitutional Developments*, 22.

60 Presidents were a source of grievance starting in 1945, with the opposition often claiming that presidents should be impartial and not involved in daily politics if they were to unite the people (Rıdvan Akın, *Gaziden Günümüze Cumhurbaşkanlığı 1923–2007*, İstanbul: İş Bankası Yayınları, 2009, 55). The public demand for an impartial president standing above daily politics has echoes in more recent Turkish politics, becoming especially noticeable during the presidencies of Özal and Erdoğan (Şule Özsoy Boyunsuz, "Cumhuriyetin Kuruluşundan Bu Yana Türkiye'de Cumhurbaşkanlığı Seçimleri Meselesi," in *Prof. Dr. Erdal Onar'a Armağan*, vol. I, ed. M. Öden (Ankara: A.Ü. Yayınları, 2013), 367–432).

61 It was a system whereby electors voted for party lists in voting districts. The list receiving the majority of votes won, and all candidates on it were elected. In the 1950 election the DP gained 54.9 percent of the votes and 85.6 percent of the seats in the Assembly, whereas the main opposition party, the CHP, won 41 percent of the votes but only 14 percent of the seats (Soysal, *Anayasaya Giriş*, 208). In the 1957 election the DP got 47.9 percent of the votes and nearly

terms.[62] After having established dominance through reasonably free and fair elections, it then turned into a hegemonic party. Like all hegemonic parties, the DP did not allow fair, free, and equal competition for power and actively prevented challenges to its government.[63]

This authoritarian trend became apparent after the 1957 election, which showed declining support for the DP.[64] In 1958 economic growth was followed by an economic crisis that had a powerful negative effect on people. In this climate the coup in Iraq intimidated the DP leaders, who launched a fierce campaign of suppression against the opposition, accusing them of plotting a coup.[65] The DP also used the vast legislative and executive constitutional powers of the 1924 Constitution and state facilities to silence opposition and sustain its dominance.[66] The DP actively controlled the only radio station in the country and restricted opposition party representatives from appearing on radio shows. From 1958 until the end of its rule, the DP steadily increased pressure on the opposition and the free press. One opposition leader, Osman Bölükbaşı, was convicted of insulting the TBMM and imprisoned in 1959. Finally, the DP deputies created an ad hoc assembly commission to investigate the opposition and certain press organs in 1960.[67] The commission was invested with judicial authority to decide on the necessity of trial, ban news and publications, and prohibit political meetings.[68] The commission issued a general ban over political party conferences, meetings, all political activities, and news on activities of the commission.[69]

2.5 *The 1960 Coup and a Return to Democracy with the 1961 Constitution*

DP rule ended when a group of middle-ranking soldiers promised to hand over power quickly to a democratic civilian government in 1960. This coup was

70 percent of the seats in the Assembly, whereas the CHP got 41 percent of the votes and 29 percent of the seats (Tanör, *İki Anayasa 1961–1982*, 7).

62 Pelin Ayan Musil, "Emergence of a Dominant Party System after Multipartyism: Theoretical Implications from the Case of the AKP in Turkey," *South European Society and Politics* 20, no. 1 (2015): 71–92, 74, 77; Ahmad, *Bir Kimlik Peşinde Türkiye*, 137.

63 For a definition of "hegemonic party," see Giovanni Sartori, *Parties and Party Systems: A Framework for Analysis* (Colchester: ECPR Press, 2005), 173, 204–205.

64 Soysal, *Anayasaya Giriş*, 209; Sina Akşin, "Siyasi Tarih (1950–1960)," in *Türkiye Tarihi IV (Çağdaş Türkiye 1908–1980)*, ed. S. Akşin (İstanbul: Cem Yayınevi, 2008), 215, 218.

65 Akşin, "Siyasi Tarih," 218–220.

66 Kili, *Turkish Constitutional Developments*, 23; Tanör, *Osmanlı-Türk Anayasal Gelişmeleri*, 352–355.

67 Bülent Tanör, *İki Anayasa 1961–1982*, 4th ed. (İstanbul: 12 Levha Yayınları, 2012), 7–8.

68 Soysal, *Anayasaya Giriş*, 209.

69 Tanör, *Osmanlı-Türk Anayasal Gelişmeleri*, 353.

backed by university students, intellectuals, and civil servants from the middle and lower-middle classes who demanded freedom and democracy.[70] The 1960 military intervention echoed certain aspects of the 1908 uprising: They shared a similar social alliance (petite bourgeoisie, intellectuals, lower-/middle-ranking civil servants), a politicization of the military, and a demand for freedom.

The 1961 Constitution reflected the views of the groups behind the coup, whereas conservative political circles, capitalist bourgeoisie, big land owners, and feudal forces that had backed the DP opposed the new constitution.[71] Along with some intellectual circles, those groups described the constitution-making process as an imposition by the military and civil bureaucratic elite.[72] But this perception disguises an important class dimension: The coup supporters were middle-class employees of the state who were affected by the economic and social policies of DP rule.[73] They also ideologically opposed the conservative policies of the DP.

The 1961 Constitution was prepared by a constituent assembly made up of the National Unity Committee (*Milli Birlik Komitesi*, MBK) and the Assembly of Representatives (*Temsilciler Meclisi*, TM). There was no general election to form the constituent assembly.[74] The first body initially consisted of thirty-eight middle-ranking soldiers involved in the coup and therefore represented the leaders of the military coup.[75] The Assembly of Representatives was organized according to the principle of corporate representation. Representatives from the CHP; the Republican Rural Nation Party (*Cumhuriyetçi Köylü Millet Partisi*, CKMP); various associations (e.g., workers, artisans, lawyers, journalists, teachers, farmers); delegates representing economic, commercial, and industrial interests; the universities; the courts; and representatives of the younger generation were represented and participated in the constitution-making process.[76] Only former members of the dissolved DP were excluded.

70 Tanör, *İki Anayasa*, 5–9.

71 Ibid., 188.

72 Ibid., 185–187; Özbudun, *Türkiye'de Demokratikleşme Süreci*, 56.

73 Tanör, *İki Anayasa*, 192–193.

74 Tanör, *Osmanlı-Türk Anayasal Gelişmeleri*, 373.

75 One member withdrew from his position, and fourteen were dismissed by the committee due to their autocratic beliefs (Tanör, *Osmanlı-Türk Anayasal Gelişmeleri*, 369).

76 Taha Parla, *Türkiye'nin Siyasal Rejimi 1980–1989* (İstanbul: İletişim Yayınları, 2005), 51–52.

Immediately after adoption of the draft prepared by a smaller constitutional commission (*Anayasa Komisyonu*, AK) through the Assembly in 1961, the MBK conducted a referendum to gain democratic legitimacy for the new constitution. Even though there was no official prohibition against a "no campaign," the political climate made it difficult for the Justice Party (*Adalet Partisi*, AP), the new political party representing the social segments that formerly voted for the Democratic Party, to campaign against the new constitution.[77]

The style of constitution making was again integrationist, which is typical of authoritarian phases. The groups behind the coup made the constitution, imposing their views, choices, and demands. There was no negotiation, no bargaining, and no compromise procedure involving all political and social forces. Different identities or views on the state and its institutions were not accommodated in this constitution-making process. This made it difficult for the excluded to live with its result. The product of this integrationist process, the 1961 Constitution, was open to democracy. It reflected the idea of a democratic system checking and balancing the majority.[78] It accepted majority rule, yet limited it with constitutional and institutional boundaries to prevent the majority from turning authoritarian again.

The 1961 Constitution instituted a parliamentary democracy with a two-chamber system. It resembled the German limited parliamentary system of the 1949 Basic Law, checking and balancing the parliamentary majority through other constitutional organs.[79] This system differed greatly from the parliamentary system of the 1924 Constitution. The 1961 Constitution introduced constitutional review through the newly established and quite strong Turkish Constitutional Court (*Anayasa Mahkemesi*, AYM). Moreover, the constitution guaranteed separation of powers, judicial independence and impartiality, and autonomy of institutions such as universities and the Turkish Radio and Television Corporation (*Türkiye Radyo ve Televizyon Kurumu*, TRT). In addition to basic individual rights that had been codified in earlier constitutions (1876, 1924), social and political rights were constitutionally recognized and guaranteed for the first time. Under the new constitution, the executive was granted the prerogative to call for new parliamentary elections, but it was very difficult to exercise this power, and despite several political crises, it was never invoked. This demonstrates that while the 1961 Constitution did not acknowledge the

77 Ibid.

78 Tanör, *İki Anayasa*, 69.

79 Özsoy Boyunsuz, *Başkanlı Parlamenter Sistem*, 36–44.

republican tradition of parliamentary supremacy, it still carried its legacy.[80] In order to control the parliamentary majority, the 1961 Constitution not only introduced constitutional checks and balances, but also instituted military tutelage in the form of the National Security Council (*Milli Güvenlik Konseyi*, MGK), which gave army commanders a platform to channel the military's de facto influence over Parliament and to actively take part in decision-making.[81]

Turkey was back to competitive politics in 1961. The transition to democracy was led by three different coalition governments formed by the CHP from 1961 to 1965, which eliminated (mostly middle-ranked) officers backing the former coup and/or plotting new coups and reinstituted the chain of command in the military.[82] The Justice Party (AP) quickly replaced the DP's place in the polity by gaining the support of those segments of society holding socially conservative and economically liberal views.[83] Despite the proportional system, the AP managed to secure a simple majority in the Parliament (53 percent) in the 1965 elections and formed a single-party government.[84] Now the new constitution was in the hands of the political and social segments that had been excluded from the post-coup political scene.

The new constitution allowed for a strong opposition. Politics was organized through different political parties and associations as well as strong labor unions defending social and economic rights in a pluralistic but highly polarized political atmosphere.[85] In the 1969 election eight political parties won seats in the Assembly. From 1973 onward this pluralist atmosphere was strongly reflected in the Assembly, creating an "extreme and polarised" multiparty system functioning under pronounced political polarization with free and fair elections.[86] The difficulty of forming a functioning coalition government in such a system at a time of global

80 Tanör, *Osmanlı-Türk Anayasal Gelişmeleri*, 402.

81 Tanör,*İki Anayasa*, 69; Özbudun, *Türkiye'de Demokratikleşme Süreci*, 14; Aysegül Kars Kaynar, "Making of Military Tutelage in Turkey: The National Security Council in the 1961 and 1982 Constitutions," *Turkish Studies* 19, no. 3 (2018): 451–481, 459.

82 Hikmet Özdemir, "Siyasi Tarih (1960–1980)," in *Türkiye Tarihi IV (Çağdaş Türkiye 1908–1980)*, ed. Sina Akşin (İstanbul: Cem Yayınevi, 2008), 227, 249.

83 Ibid., 242–243.

84 Ibid., 250.

85 Ahmad, *Bir Kimlik Peşinde Türkiye*, 155–156, 163–165.

86 According to Giovanni Sartori (*Parties and Party Systems*, 116–117), an "extreme and polarised" party system consists of at least five or six parties (including anti-system parties) in the Assembly that have either coalition potential or the "power of intimidation" that can influence tactics of competition and functioning in a polarized polity.

and national economic difficulties frequently strained Turkey's political stability in the 1970s.[87]

Right-wing, conservative, capitalist, statist political circles blamed the constitution for weakening state authority and executive power.[88] The new military chain of command was among the critics of the constitution, sharing similar fears with the conservative right.[89] In 1971 the new military once again intervened and forced the Assembly to amend the constitution. Amendments introduced state security courts and executive decrees having the force of law for the first time since the Ottoman era. It implemented less liberal limitation standards for fundamental rights, weakened constitutional review and legislative control over the government, and gave more autonomy to military institutions.[90]

Criticism of the constitution, however, continued. It was argued that the two-chamber system was unnecessarily delaying the parliamentary decision-making process,[91] and no effective constitutional mechanisms existed to solve gridlock in the Parliament. Declaration of a state of emergency was impossible; only martial law could be declared, which gave greater control to the military but did not allow a stricter civilian executive emergency regime.[92]

Toward the end of the 1970s, critics of the 1961 Constitution sought to write another constitution implementing a presidential or semi-presidential political system with weak judicial review and weakened social rights protection.[93] In those days the right-wing Justice Party proposed direct public election of presidents.[94] The CHP, however, rejected the proposal on the grounds that it was not appropriate for a parliamentary system. Social democratic, liberal circles generally defended the 1961 Constitution, although they also agreed that decision-making processes had to be rationalized to make it easier to form a government and more difficult to propose a vote of no confidence.[95] Within this atmosphere of political instability, another democratic phase was ended by a military coup, turning the regime cycle back to authoritarianism.

87 Özdemir, "Siyasi Tarih (1960–1980)," 270–271, 273–278.
88 Şule Özsoy Boyunsuz, 1982 *Anyasası'nın Yapım Süreci* (İstanbul: 12 Levha Yay., 2009), 3–25.
89 Özdemir, "Siyasi Tarih (1960–1980)," 261.
90 Tanör, *İki Anayasa*, 44–49.
91 For technical defects of the system, see Tanör, *İki Anayasa*, 81–83.
92 Ibid.
93 Özsoy Boyunsuz, 1982 *Anayasası'nın Yapım Süreci*, 5, 8, 11, 14, 18, 24.
94 Ibid., 8–9.
95 Ibid., 28.

2.6 The 1980 Coup, the 1982 Constitution, and Swinging Back toward Democracy

The 1980 coup was carried out by the top commanders of the military, whose approach to the constitution was in line with the statist conservative critics of the 1961 Constitution. They believed that the constitution weakened state power and had to be replaced.[96] They also mistrusted political parties and accordingly dissolved them all. The 1980 coup leaders appointed a constituent assembly with 160 members, reserving the final word on the draft constitution for themselves.[97] The Constituent Assembly was only responsible for drafting the proposal and sending it to the military leadership, which declared itself the National Security Council (*Milli Güvenlik Konseyi*, MGK).

Most Assembly members were middle aged, university educated, and male.[98] The majority (78 percent) were paid by the state or indirectly benefited from the state. The Assembly was closed to social democratic or liberal views. The new constitution mirrored anti-liberal, authoritarian views and implemented a system of military tutelage.[99] As has been noted earlier, at the authoritarian end of the regime cycle, constitution making is typically integrationist, meaning that it promotes uniformity and a single public identity. Even though the constitution makers in 1980 did not reject democracy all together, the aim was to replace the constitution with a more majoritarian and less liberal version.[100] There were no negotiations, no participation of civil society, and no accommodation of different identities or political visions.

Before the referendum to adopt the constitution, it was impossible to call for a "no" vote. The National Security Council declared that only views aiming to improve the draft could be expressed in public. Unlike the 1961 constitutional referendum, during the 1982 campaign the process was completely controlled by the military.[101] The coup leaders deliberately created uncertainty regarding how the post-referendum period would unfold if the public were to reject the constitution. A "yes" vote would mean that new elections would be held shortly after the referendum, whereas rejection of the constitution would mean that the military regime could continue. This possibility encouraged people to vote "yes,"[102] and the constitution was accepted with 91.37 percent of

96 Ibid., 48.

97 Özbudun, *Türkiye'de Demokratikleşme Süreci*, 56.

98 Özsoy Boyunsuz, *1982 Anayasası'nın Yapım Süreci*, 77.

99 Özbudun, *Türkiye'de Demokratikleşme Süreci*, 56.

100 Ahmad, *Bir Kimlik Peşinde Türkiye*, 186–187.

101 Özbudun, *Türk Anayasa Hukuku*, 54.

102 In contrast, there was no uncertainty during the 1961 constitutional referendum campaign. A date for competitive elections was set which indicated that military rule was temporary from

the public vote. With the referendum General Kenan Evren was simultaneously elected president for seven years. He was given control over constitutional changes, as the TBMM needed three-fourths of the total votes to overturn his veto to constitutional amendments. Other members of the National Security Council also became members of the ad hoc Presidential Council for six years. Former politicians were banned from politics for five to ten years.

Despite proposals to change the political system to a presidential or semi-presidential system, the 1982 Constitution maintained the parliamentary system.[103] However, the constitution makers responded to the demands of statist circles for a stronger executive within the parliamentary system framework. The constitution empowered the president (giving him certain appointment powers to the judiciary and universities, the power to dissolve Parliament in times of political gridlock, and the power to file cases before the Constitutional Court), and it weakened Parliament and checks and balances.[104] Empowering the president at the expense of the Assembly was done on purpose. Assuming that presidents following Evren would also be military men, this would strengthen military tutelage over the political system.[105] The MGK also altered the former proportional electoral system to a system with double thresholds for winning seats in Parliament (parties had to pass both the 10 percent national threshold and district thresholds[106]), thereby creating excessive representation for the majority party.

Turkey returned to competitive politics with the government of the Motherland Party (*Anavatan Partisi*, ANAP) in 1983. It gradually transitioned to democracy, securing free and fair elections through which political power was altered. But the constitution and the majority of significant laws (e.g., political party and election laws) were made by the military. The political system was designed in accordance with the statist and illiberal views of the military. From enactment of the 1982 Constitution onward, demands to liberalize the country were continuously raised. The method chosen, however, was not to draft a completely new democratic constitution, but to amend the 1982 Constitution in piecemeal fashion.

To date, a total of nineteen amendments have altered almost the entire structure of the 1982 Constitution. Starting with political bans on former politicians and the constitutional amendment procedure in 1987, some of the

the beginning. If the 1961 Constitution had been rejected in the referendum, a new constituent assembly would have been elected to draft another constitution.

103 Özsoy Boyunsuz, *1982 Anayasası'nın Yapım Süreci*, 5.

104 Özbudun, *Türk Anayasa Hukuku*, 61–62.

105 Tanör, *İki Anayasa*, 112–113.

106 The Constitutional Court annulled the district threshold in 1995.

rules narrowing political participation and individual freedoms were gradually removed. After the 1987 amendment, political party leaders of the 1970s were back on the political scene. Their return and relatively free and fair competition created a multiparty system in a less polarized climate during the 1990s, despite the effect of the new election system (the D'hondt method of proportional allocation of parliamentary seats with double thresholds) and political party closures mostly targeting communists, Kurdish nationalists, and Islamists.

Amendments in 1987, 1995, 2001, and 2004 were important for political pluralism, democratization, and strengthening of fundamental rights. The most democratizing and liberalizing amendments were produced through consensus- and compromise-oriented negotiations among all political parties in Parliament in 1995 and 2001. Those reform packages reflected political agreement on the relevance of democracy and freedom and paved the way for a pluralist political climate.[107] But open and consensual constitutional reform processes through political parties gradually disappeared again, with the AKP coming to power in 2002.[108] It established dominance through reasonably free and fair elections and then turned authoritarian much like the İTP in 1908, the CHP in 1923, and the DP in 1950.[109]

The amendment package enacted in 2004 was created by the AKP with the consent of the CHP. It was a response to pressure from the European Union to further liberalize the political system as part of Turkey's EU accession process.[110] But the authoritarian spirit of the 1980 coup was not entirely erased from the constitutional structure. With the 2007 presidential election crisis, the method of majority imposition returned to Turkish constitutional politics.[111] Failing to elect its presidential candidate, Abdullah Gül, in 2007, the AKP significantly amended the constitution, introducing direct public election of the president.[112] Using the same majoritarian constitution-making strategy, the AKP specifically targeted the judiciary and the Constitutional Court in 2010.[113] This was a sophisticated act of court packing with the aim of changing the membership of the Constitutional

[107] Arato, *Post Sovereign Constitution Making*, 231.

[108] Ibid., 236.

[109] The CHP's authoritarian turn, however, occurred in a unique historical context that must be taken into consideration: It followed the 1923 election and was a revolutionary process aiming to form a secular republic and a nation-state after the collapse of the Ottoman Empire and the national liberation war.

[110] Arato, *Post Sovereign Constitution Making*, 233.

[111] Andrew Arato, "The Constitutional Reform Proposal of the Turkish Government: The Return of Majority Imposition," *Constellations* 17, no. 2 (2010): 345.

[112] Arato, *Post Sovereign Constitution Making*, 237.

[113] Berk Esen and Şebnem Gümüşcü, "Rising Competitive Authoritarianism in Turkey," *Third World Quarterly* 37, no. 9 (2016): 1581–1606, 1585.

Court, limiting the court's jurisdiction, and abolishing judicial checks and balances against majority rule.[114] With these amendments the last remaining constitutional actor that had the power to check the majority was tamed. According to Andrew Arato, this act of court packing was intended to neutralize the Constitutional Court (i.e., to avoid constitutional review of amendments) and to pave the way for a majoritarian constitution-making procedure that would constitutionalize hyper-presidentialism, concentrate constitutional powers in the hands of the president, and diminish checks and balances.[115] Turkey once again was about to move toward an authoritarian phase.

Winning the third consecutive general election in 2011, the AKP became a party seeking hegemony in order to render the possibility of changing governments merely a theoretical option,[116] but it lacked the necessary majority to amend the constitution alone. The AKP therefore formed a parliamentary commission in 2011 to draft a new constitution, although it seemed improbable that the AKP would seek real consensus.

3 CONSTITUTION-MAKING EFFORTS IN THE 2011–2013 PERIOD

The constitution-making process that lasted from 2011 until 2013 is worth studying because political actors tried to negotiate and bargain with the aim of making a new democratic constitution in a deeply divided[117] and polarized country that turned authoritarian shortly after these efforts failed in 2014. This process reflects the political actors' positions and preferences on democracy, the political system, and other institutions at the time. With regard to the work of the Constitutional Conciliation Commission (*Anayasa Uzlasma Komisyonu*, AUK), there are a number of questions to be answered in light of the theory of cyclical movements. Does the AUK's work mark a democratic phase? What institutions and political systems were proposed by the parties? And do these proposals fit with a democratic or an authoritarian logic?

In response to the first question, it can be argued that the work of the AUK marked a democratic phase. The process was open to democratic participation of different groups and identities.[118] There was a stage specifically designed for

114 Arato, *Post Sovereign Constitution Making*, 249.

115 Ibid., 254.

116 Galip Bashirov and Caroline Lancaster, "End of Moderation: The Radicalization of AKP in Turkey," *Democratization* 25, no. 7 (2018): 1210–1230, 1214; Ayan Musil, *Emergence of a Dominant Party System*, 74.

117 Hanna Lerner, *Constitution Making in Deeply Divided Societies* (New York: Cambridge University Press, 2011), 31.

118 See Petersen and Yanaşmayan, Chapter 1 in this volume.

negotiation and bargaining. However, it required unanimous consensus among the four major political parties in order to reach a decision. This turned out to be quite difficult to achieve in practice. The fact that the AKP needed the support of only one party to amend the constitution outside the AUK reduced the need to seek consensus, as expressed on numerous occasions by then-Prime Minister Erdoğan and other AKP representatives in 2011–2013.[119] According to Arato, the consensus requirement gave the AKP too much opportunity to block the process and create deadlock, which helped to demonstrate to the electorate that no consensus was possible before returning to the method of majority imposition.[120]

Ultimately the process failed to produce the required consensus and did not accommodate different identities and preferences regarding state institutions. Major topics of disagreement were the preamble, the first three unamendable articles of the 1982 Constitution, the definition of citizenship, the right to education in one's mother tongue, municipal authorities, and the political system.[121] The political system question, however, was the last straw that led to the eventual dissolution of the commission.[122]

Among the opinions and proposals submitted by civil society to the AUK, relatively few (around one hundred) dealt with the political system question.[123] Only two of them proposed the presidential system,[124] and none proposed the semi-presidential model. Despite the fact that direct presidential elections usually disturb the institutional balance in parliamentary systems, numerous proposals were in favor of a parliamentary system with a directly elected president.[125] However, the focus of these mixed institutional proposals was to render the office of the president symbolic and ceremonial.[126] A substantial number of civil society organizations agreed on a parliamentary system with effective parliamentary checks and balances. There is no evidence, however, that these proposals were taken into consideration when the parties formed their choices.

119 Arato, *Post Sovereign Constitution Making*, 257–258.

120 Ibid., 259, 265.

121 Selami Erdoğan and Eray Acar, "Türkiye'de Yeni Anayasa Yapım Süreci ve TBMM Anayasa Uzlaşma Komisyonu (2011–2013)," *Sosyal Bilimler Dergisi* 50 (2016): 180–190, 187.

122 See Petersen and Yanaşmayan, Chapter 1 in this volume, and Böcü and Petersen, Chapter 5 in this volume.

123 Mehmet Uçum, Ferhat Kentel, Levent Köker, and Özge Genç, *TESEV Yeni Anayasa Sürecini İzleme Raporu* 2, 2012, 38.

124 Adaleti Savunanlar Stratejik Araştırmalar Merkezi Derneği (ASSAM) and Birlik Vakfı. Both associations are known supporters of political Islam.

125 Özsoy Boyunsuz, *Başkanlı Parlamenter Sistem*, 57–70.

126 Ibid.

Proposals that political parties submitted were very explicit on the political system question. In line with the majority of civil society organizations, the three opposition parties (CHP, MHP, and BDP) suggested a parliamentary system with reduced presidential power. In particular, all opposition parties emphasized that the presidential power to appoint members of the judiciary had to be removed from the new constitution,[127] as creating an independent and impartial judiciary was a priority for all three parties. In general, their proposals stressed a strong parliament, rule of law, and checks and balances. The AKP, on the other hand, proposed Turkish-style presidentialism.

Debates on the presidential system and the AKP proposal were many and long. AKP representatives and legal experts defended the presidential system, saying it would contribute to political stability and government efficiency. Moreover, they claimed to have modified the pure presidential system to make it more suitable for Turkey by borrowing certain institutions from parliamentary systems (executive prerogative to call for new elections, concurrent elections) to reduce the risk of gridlock.[128]

The MHP and CHP in particular emphasized in those meetings that they would not support a presidential system that ran the risk of turning Turkey into an authoritarian regime.[129] They defended a parliamentary system with the necessary checks and balances. The Nationalist Movement Party (*Milliyetçi Hareket Partisi*, MHP) proposed and defended rationalized parliamentarianism with a constructive vote of no confidence (similar to the German and Spanish constitutions), through which a prime minister would be forced out of office only if a new prime minister was elected by Parliament.[130] The Peace and Democracy Party (*Barış ve Demokrasi Partisi*, BDP) was more open to bargaining regarding the political system, as long as the proposed system remained democratic with checks and balances.[131] The party representatives explicitly stated that they might consider the presidential system, but only if it came with federalism and other checks and balances.[132] Despite their general support for the parliamentary system, the BDP representatives advocated for popular presidential elections, arguing that it would not be appropriate to take the authority to elect the president away from the public because the majority

127 Mehmet Uçum and Özge Genç, *TESEV Yeni Anayasa Sürecini İzleme Raporu 3: Nasıl Bir Anayasaya Doğru Gidiyoruz?* March 5, 2013.

128 AUK Proceedings, writing commission, November 21 and 28, 2012.

129 Ibid.

130 Ibid., November 21, 2012.

131 Ibid., November 28, 2012.

132 Ibid.

of the public had expressed their desire for it.[133] The BDP proposal also demanded that the president's powers be reduced to symbolic and ceremonial functions. The BDP was the only party explicitly demanding the rejection of an integrationist approach in terms of imposing a single public/national identity, and it promoted the accommodation of diversity and the recognition of different ethnic identities.[134] The BDP also openly rejected executive decrees having the force of law. The CHP accepted the possibility of such decrees, but only in exceptional cases and with limited legislative permission, while the MHP seemed to have assumed that such executive decrees are necessary.

4 THE AKP'S 2011–2013 POLITICAL SYSTEM PROPOSAL

The AKP proposal bestowed executive authority upon the president, who was responsible for governing domestic and international politics.[135] As head of state, the president was proposed to oversee the implementation of the constitution and the harmonious functioning of all state organs. The presidential term of office was five years. A candidate could only be elected for two terms. The proposal also determined that concurrent parliamentary and presidential elections were to be held every five years. In the 2011–2013 proposal the president was given a wide range of legislative powers. He might veto legislative acts partially or wholly, and it required a three-fifths (60 percent) vote in Parliament to override the veto.

The president was also given the power to issue decrees having the force of law on every subject that was not regulated by legislation, including political, social, and economic rights, but not individual rights. The establishment, abolition, duties and powers, organizational structure of the ministries, and establishment of their central and provincial organizations would also be regulated by presidential decree. The president also had broad authority to issue emergency decrees without judicial review.

Presidential decrees gave supplementary legislative power to the president. The proposal also included a conflict clause, which gave priority to legislative acts over presidential decrees in case of possible conflicts. Presidential decrees could be brought before the Constitutional Court for review, but only by the majority party, the second largest political party group in the Assembly, or if

133 AUK Proceedings, writing commission, November 29, 2012.

134 Ibid., November 12, 2012.

135 For the draft, see http://ismetberkan.blogspot.com.tr/2012/11/ak-parti-baskanlk-sistemi-onerisi-tam.html (accessed February 25, 2019).

one-fifth (20 percent) of Assembly members formally filed for review. It must also be remembered that twelve of the fifteen members of the court were appointed by the president.

The AKP proposal also gave the president the power to submit legislative acts partially or wholly to referendum, seeking public approval to abolish them once a year. Parliament was given the same power. The power to propose a budget also fell in the domain of the executive branch. It had to be submitted to Parliament only for approval. Parliament did not have any power to change the budget plan.

As to nonlegislative powers, the AKP proposed that the president had unlimited power to select and dismiss ministers without Assembly approval. Similarly, without approval of another body, the president was able to appoint public authorities, university rectors, half of the members of the Constitutional Court, half the members of the Administrative Court of Appeals, the head public prosecutor of the Court of Cassation, and half the members of the Higher Council of Judges and Public Prosecutors (HSYK). This gave the president an incredible amount of control over judicial authorities as well as over the entire public sector.

The AKP proposed that the president and the Assembly should both have the power to call for new concurrent elections without any term or time limit attached. This gave the president the authority to remove an unfriendly Assembly majority at a suitable time. To grant the power to call for new elections defies the very logic of the separation of powers, hence it does not exist in any pure presidential (democratic) regime that is based on the separate origins and guaranteed survival of executive and legislative organs checking and balancing each other for a fixed term.[136]

Furthermore, the impeachment mechanism to hold the president accountable and remove him from office was highly difficult to activate under the AKP proposal. The Assembly needed a qualified majority (two-thirds) to open a criminal investigation against the president. Once an investigation was completed in the Assembly, three-fourths of the members of the Assembly would have to agree for the president to be tried before the Constitutional Court. The same holds for ministers.

In the AKP proposal the president enjoyed a central position with quite strong legislative and nonlegislative powers and without effective checks and

[136] Şule Özsoy Boyunsuz, *Dünyada Başkanlık Sistemleri* (Ankara: İmge Yayınları, 2017), 151–155; for definitions, see Matthew Soberg Shugart and John M. Carey, *Presidents and Assemblies: Constitutional Design and Electoral Dynamics* (New York: Cambridge University Press, 1995), 19–22.

balances. The Assembly's role as a counterweight (or veto player) was greatly weakened. The executive power to renew concurrent elections, to veto legislation, to propose referenda for legislation, and to issue decrees having the force of law curtailed the power of the TBMM even more than the political system created by the 1982 Constitution.

In all presidential systems, executive authority is bestowed upon popularly elected presidents who control the government, but the constitutional powers of these presidents, as well as the checks and balances on their power, differ greatly from constitution to constitution.[137] Pure presidential systems are structured through the separation of powers and institutional checks and balances supporting democratic regimes. Legislative powers given to presidents are especially important, as those powers may challenge the very logic of the separation of powers by delegating legislative power to the executive. According to Cheibub, Elkins, and Ginsburg, vast legislative powers (especially presidential decrees having the force of law) separate hyper-presidentialism from pure presidentialism.[138] The hyper-presidential system is an excessive type of presidentialism, with a strong emphasis on executive authority and an extraordinarily weak system of checks and balances, which is usually the result of an "overt action by the president to change the regime and centralize power in his hands."[139] In such regimes, presidents attempt and succeed in controlling or circumventing legislative and judicial organs.[140] Thus, it can be argued that the AKP proposal perfectly fits the hyper-presidential model.[141]

All opposition parties in the AUK vehemently disagreed with the AKP proposal, with some of them calling it the foundation of a "dictatorship with a constitution" and others referring to it as "a model for a sultan."[142] It became obvious that this political system could not win the approval of other parties. It is a logical imperative that consensual democratic processes cannot produce constitutional documents that do not support democracy. The process was,

137 Şule Özsoy Boyunsuz, "The AKP's Proposal for a 'Turkish Type of Presidentialism' in Comparative Context," *Turkish Studies* 17, no. 1 (2016): 68–90, 72.

138 José Cheibub, Zachary Elkins, and Tom Ginsburg, "Latin American Presidentialism in Comparative and Historical Perspective," *Texas Law Review* 89, no. 7 (2011): 1707–1739.

139 Christopher Larkin, *The Legacies of Hyper-presidentialism: Executive–Judicial Relations, Constitutional Cultures, and the Future of Democratic Governance in Argentina and Peru*. PhD thesis, University of Southern California (1998), 65.

140 Ibid., 64.

141 Christopher Larkin, "The Judiciary and Delegative Democracy in Argentina," *Comparative Politics* 30, no. 4 (1998): 423–442.

142 See www.aksam.com.tr/dunya/bbc-akp-baskanlik-sisteminde-yalniz-kaldi–159164h/haber-159 164 (accessed March 8, 2019).

therefore, predestined to fail. It also revealed that there was no common choice for a democratic political system among the major political actors. This split, aggravated by a high degree of polarization, indicated a political struggle that was about to trigger another cyclical movement toward authoritarianism.

5 THE POLITICAL SYSTEM UNDER THE 2017 AMENDMENTS

In 2012 Turkey's civil liberties score started to decline steadily.[143] Since 2014, the press and the Internet have been officially characterized as "not free."[144] The AKP had made concrete moves toward becoming a hegemonic party with clear authoritarian tendencies between 2012 and 2015.[145] The regime defied the minimal conditions for democracy (e.g., free and fair elections, the right to access alternative information sources, equal citizenship), and exhibited certain features of competitive authoritarian regimes (e.g., unfair elections and extensive violation of civil liberties).[146] Losing its dominant position briefly in June 2015, President Erdoğan called for snap elections, and the AKP regained its dominance in October 2015. After having survived the coup attempt in 2016, the AKP declared a state of emergency, and the authoritarian nature of the regime became apparent. The AKP turned into a hegemonic party, consolidated its authoritarian rule using emergency decrees as a tool to build a loyal judiciary and civil and military bureaucracy, and to control media and civil society.[147] In 2017, Turkey displayed all of the characteristics of unfair elections in competitive authoritarian settings during the referendum process:[148] (1) The leaders of the People's Democratic Party (*Halkların Demokratik Partisi*, HDP) were barred from campaigning (and jailed); (2) electoral abuse was centrally coordinated and tolerated; (3) the opposition was prevented from campaigning on equal conditions; and (4) there was systemic bias of electoral authorities that favored the AKP.

143 See https://freedomhouse.org/report/freedom-world/2012/turkey (accessed March 8, 2019).

144 See Freedom House Reports on Turkey, available at https://freedomhouse.org/report/freedom-press/2014/turkey; https://freedomhouse.org/report/freedom-press/2017/turkey (accessed March 8, 2019).

145 Kürşat Çınar, "Local Determinants of an Emerging Electoral Hegemony: The Case of Justice and Development Party (AKP) in Turkey," *Democratization* 23, no. 7 (2015): 1216–1235.

146 Esen and Gümüşcü, "Rising Competitive Authoritarianism in Turkey," 1586.

147 Hegemonic parties do not allow fair electoral competition and alternation of power; see Berk Esen and Şebnem Gümüşcü, "Turkey: How the Coup Failed," *Journal of Democracy* 28, no. 1 (2017): 59–73, 68–71.

148 Koray Çalışkan, "Toward a New Political Regime in Turkey: From Competitive toward Full Authoritarianism," *New Perspectives on Turkey* 58, (2018): 5–33, 25.

The constitutional amendments were authoritarian and integrationist. Even though the MHP participated in the process, it still reflected a single shared vision of state identity based on an ideological mix of political Islam and ultranationalism (conservative Sunni Turks). Forming an alliance does not mean that the power is truly shared with the hegemonic party in competitive authoritarian regimes. The MHP has been acting as a satellite party ever since the alliance was formed following the coup attempt in 2016. They were not given governmental positions as equal participants, but only access to neopatrimonial rewards controlled by the president.[149]

The 2017 amendments are the product of an authoritarian phase promoting a form of authoritarian rule. Confirming this conclusion, as of 2018 Turkey is considered "not free" by Freedom House measurements and is rapidly moving toward full authoritarianism.[150]

The 2017 amendment package introduced a presidential system similar to the 2012 AKP proposal. A single, directly elected executive authority has been created for the first time in Turkish history. The term of office, which is five years, and the two-term limit regulated in 2007 remain the same. However, it gives the president a longer office term if Parliament calls for new elections in the second term. The amendments do not introduce any transitional provision regarding the current president, who was directly elected in 2014 and again for a second term in early elections in 2018.

As in the 2012 AKP proposal, concurrent parliamentary and presidential elections are to be held every five years. The president and the Assembly (with a three-fifths majority vote) share the power to call for new elections at any time, but it is easier for the president to remove unfriendly assemblies.

The 2017 amendments give the president a wide range of legislative powers. He may veto legislative acts partially or wholly, and his vetoes can only be overridden with an absolute majority (out of 600 seats) of the Assembly. The MHP altered the AKP's original proposal and reduced the required majority to override the veto from a minimum of three-fifths (360) to an absolute majority (301).

The most important legislative power given to the president is the power to issue decrees. In addition to the emergency decrees having the force of law (to be issued on any subject without judicial review), the president may issue decrees under the new Article 104, "On matters regarding executive power." In

149 Fatih Çağatay Cengiz, "Proliferation of Neopatrimonial Domination in Turkey," *British Journal of Middle Eastern Studies* (2018): 1–19, 15–18.

150 Turkey's overall Freedom House score is 5.5 (7 being the least free). Civil liberties score 6/7, political liberties 5/7; see https://freedomhouse.org/report/freedom-world/2018/turkey (accessed March 8, 2019). See also Çalışkan, "Toward a New Political Regime in Turkey," 30.

addition to individual rights and matters explicitly regulated by law, presidential decrees cannot regulate "political rights" or "matters which are stipulated in the constitution to be regulated exclusively by legislation." Also, "a Presidential decree shall become null and void if the TBMM enacts a law on the same matter." In case of discrepancy between presidential decrees and legislation, the latter shall prevail.

The MHP claimed before the referendum in 2017 that, with these corrections inserted by the party, the TBMM's legislative authority as the sole lawmaker is not limited or harmed by the new decree power.[151] However, there are a number of issues that call this claim into question. First, most of the limitations are vague, and their effectiveness is doubtful. Until clarified by the Constitutional Court, it can be assumed that presidents will interpret those terms broadly or simply ignore them, as already happened in 2018.[152] These decrees supplement legislation when the Assembly is unable to legislate, and would be especially handy for presidents when there is no single party or coalition that can control the legislative agenda in a divided Assembly. Presidents have the power to veto legislation that is passed by simple majority of those present (minimum 151), and vetoes can be overruled with an absolute majority (minimum 301). Therefore, presidents have the power to at least delay or make it difficult for the Assembly to regulate a topic and, in the meantime, issue decrees overnight.

Second, in addition to the general rules under Article 104, other articles specify areas to be regulated by presidential decree (e.g., Art. 106: "the establishment, abolition, the duties and powers, the organizational structure of the ministries, and the establishment of their central and provincial organizations, procedures, and rules regarding appointments and dismissals of higher civil servants"; Art. 108: the "functioning and organization of the State Supervisory Council"; Art. 118: the State Security Council). The president may also establish public legal personalities by presidential decree (Art. 123). It is unclear if additional areas specified under Articles 106, 108, and 118 are exclusive to presidential decrees or whether the TBMM can still regulate such issues,[153] but even if the Constitutional Court rejects the notion that

[151] See www.amerikaninsesi.com/a/evet-diyen-mhp-18-maddeyi-nasil-yorumluyor/3786910.html (accessed March 8, 2019).

[152] Korkut Kanadoğlu, Ahmet Mert Duygun, and Deniz Bilgehan, "Anayasa ve İdare Hukuku Açısından 703 Sayılı KHK ve Cumhurbaşkanlığı Kararnameleri Devlet Yapısı Yeniden Düzenlenirken," *Güncel Hukuk* 173 (Eylül–Ekim 2018): 24–29.

[153] It has been argued that these specific areas are exclusive to presidential decrees and the TBMM cannot regulate them; see Özen Ülgen, "Cumhurbaşkanlığı Kararnamelerinin Niteliği ve Türleri," *Galatasaray Üniversitesi Hukuk Fakültesi* 69, no. 1 (2018): 3–39.

these areas are under the exclusive purview of presidential decrees, presidents are still given important new legislative power to challenge the TBMM's authority.

Third, following adoption of the 2017 amendments, President Erdoğan issued twenty-two decrees in five months that almost entirely reorganized the state structure, reducing the number of ministries from 26 to 16 and altering institutional structures, duties, and powers. As every president may now alter the organization of state and administration overnight without the approval or political oversight of the TBMM, it is hard to imagine that this will bring stability and certainty to public administration.

Under the original formula of the 1982 Constitution, decrees having the force of law were regulated by the Council of Ministers, countersigned by the president, and had to be based on an enabling law and presented before the TBMM to be reviewed on the same day that they were published in the *Official Gazette*. Now the president can issue such decrees without an enabling law and without presenting it before the TBMM. The new version abolishes the Assembly's control over executive lawmaking. Although presidential decrees can be reviewed by the Constitutional Court, those who can launch an application before the court are limited to the majority party, the second largest political party group in the Assembly, or one-fifth of the Assembly.

The 2017 amendments allow the president to reuse the previous year's budget (in accordance with the revaluation rate) until the Assembly approves the new budget under Article 161/4. Previously, the cabinet prepared and proposed the budget bill that was subject to parliamentary approval and control. In democratic presidential systems, participation of the Assembly in the process and approval of the budget assures significant checks and balances on executive powers. Under the new Turkish system, Assembly rejection cannot block the system and therefore cannot be considered an effective tool.

The president has unlimited power to select and dismiss vice presidents and ministers as well as to appoint members of the public sector without Assembly approval.[154] He or she appoints twelve members (out of fifteen) of the Constitutional Court, one-fourth of the members of the Administrative Court of Appeals, the head public prosecutor of the Court of Cassation, and six of thirteen members (four directly and two indirectly) of the Council of Judges and Public Prosecutors (HSK).[155] The TBMM, in contrast, appoints only three

[154] Presidential Decree no. 3, Art. 2 (in, Resmî Gazete, July 10, 2018, Sayı: 30474) regulates three types of appointment: Important appointments are made directly by presidential decision, less important ones with presidential approval, and others are delegated to inferior executive authorities.

[155] For further details on the judiciary, see Abad Andrade, Chapter 7 in this volume.

members of the Constitutional Court and seven of the HSK. The Assembly needs a simple majority for the Constitutional Court members, and a three-fifths majority for HSK members in the second ballot. In fact, the overall appointment procedure adopted with the 2017 amendments gives the president an incredible amount of control over judicial authorities as well as the whole public sector, at the expense of the TBMM.

The impeachment mechanism to hold presidents and ministers accountable and to remove them from office is highly difficult to activate under the 2017 amendments, even though the required majorities are less than in the 2012 AKP proposal because of MHP's involvement.[156] The absolute majority (301 of 600 instead of two-thirds) of the total number of members may request a motion to open a criminal investigation against the president or a minister. The TBMM may decide to launch an investigation with three-fifths (instead of two-thirds) of the total number of its members by secret ballot. Once an investigation is completed in the Assembly, two-thirds (instead of three-fourths) of the members of the Assembly are required to put the president or minister on trial before the Constitutional Court, which acts as the Supreme Criminal Tribunal.

The new political system strongly resembles the Turkish-style presidentialism proposed by the AKP in 2012. The few corrections made by the MHP do not alter the main character of the system. It is still a hyper-presidential system designed to be controlled by a single head. The amendments also reflect institutional features of authoritarian phases in Turkish history (e.g., weakened checks and balances, a weak assembly, strong executive lawmaking authority, executive power to dissolve the assembly and call new elections). Although the new "Turkish-style presidentialism" is a unique result of the current authoritarian cycle, it simply dresses old ideas in new clothes.

6 CONCLUSION

This chapter has argued that the Ottoman-Turkish constitutional developments clearly show regular cyclical movements between authoritarian and relatively democratic phases instigated by intense power struggles between competing political and social forces. Each cycle has its own characteristic institutions, practices, and political system preferences. In authoritarian phases the power of the Assembly is reduced, checks and balances and separation of powers are minimized or fully abolished, and executive decree

[156] For the AKP's original proposal, see https://erdalguven.wordpress.com/2013/04/01/ak-partinin-baskanlik-sistemi-teklifi-tam-metin/ (accessed March 27, 2019).

powers and the power to dissolve the Assembly and to call for new elections are strengthened. Political power is consolidated in a single hand, whether civilian or military. Fundamental freedoms, rule of law, judicial independence, and impartiality are curtailed. The judiciary is controlled by a political power. Constitution making, which has often coincided with authoritarian phases in Turkey, has an integrationist character that promotes a single vision of the state and a single public identity. The makings of the 1876, 1924, 1961, 1982 Constitutions and the 2017 amendments share this common feature.

Authoritarian cycles appear under the autocracy of Sultan Abdülhamit (1877–1908), the competitive authoritarian regimes under the İTP (1913–1918), the DP (1957–1960), the AKP (2014–), and under the revolutionary single-party rule of the CHP (1923–1945) and military coups (1960–1961, 1971–1973, and 1980–1983). Over time authoritarian phases are getting shorter. The longest authoritarian phase was the thirty-year rule of Sultan Abdülhamit; the shortest phase lasted for a year after the 1960 coup. The longest democratic period was the thirty-one years between 1983 and 2014.

This historical reconstruction reveals a pattern. Usually, a party manages to win the majority of seats in Parliament over time (more than three consecutive elections) in free and fair competition. Dominance is achieved by appealing to the majority social identity, and is sustained with the help of patronage, unfair electoral laws, and other factors diminishing free and fair competition. The party turns into a hegemonic agent dominating the political system and society. In the second stage, hegemony is maintained and the competitive nature of the system increasingly diminished. The rule of the İTP, the DP, and the AKP all share these characteristics. The single-party rule of CHP also bears certain similarities, but that regime was revolutionary and noncompetitive and handed over power voluntarily.

In contrast to authoritarian phases, democratic phases are characterized by support for a strong assembly, political participation, strong political and civil liberties (i.e., freedom of speech, association, and press), and constitutional checks and balances. In these periods we observe open and consensual constitution making grounded in compromise among political actors. Moreover, different visions of state and identity are accommodated, as was the case in 1921, 1995, and 2001. The constitutional products of such processes always promote participatory democracy.

In light of the abovementioned cyclical movements, the failed 2011–2013 process reveals that there was no common preference among major political actors for a democratic political system. Rather, the hegemonic desire of the majority triggered another cyclical turn toward an authoritarian phase. This constitution-making process was designed as a consensual and integrationist process in a semi-democratic climate. However, an integrative and consensual process produces neither a non-democratic political system similar to the one proposed by the AKP in 2012 nor a democratic system without a common desire and the willingness to work together to achieve it. Therefore, it can be argued that the process was predestined to fail from the beginning.

Although the AKP leadership succeeded in institutionalizing its hegemony and authoritarian rule through the 2017 amendments and 2018 elections, the demands for democracy and a democratic constitution articulated by civil society organizations during the 2011–2013 process may persist and turn the tide of cyclical movements once again in the direction of democracy at some point in the future.

4

Illiberal Media and Popular Constitution Making in Turkey

Burcu Baykurt

1 INTRODUCTION

Popular constitution making, a process that allows for public participation as opposed to a handful of elites writing a fundamental social contract behind closed doors and imposing it on the rest of society, is tricky. It sounds like a noble idea in theory, but it is difficult to execute effectively, efficiently, and, most importantly, democratically. Even trickier are the roles of publicity and media in popular constitution making. What are the consequences of reporting during the drafting of a new constitution? In what ways can the media lend legitimacy to the process by informing the public and incorporating public opinion into the drafting of a constitution? Coupled with the rise of new media technologies, an ideal of participatory constitution making (and an active role for the media) may seem desirable, not to mention attainable, but there are myriad ways to participate, and basing a constitution on popular opinion could easily devolve into a majority of 50 percent plus one that imposes its will on the rest. The bare minimum, ideally, is to expect journalists to report on facts without bowing to political or economic pressures, but even that is easier said than done. For which audiences are these journalistic facts intended? For those leaders drafting the new constitution or the public at large?

These are not easy questions to answer empirically, not only because media and communications are often neglected in studies of constitution making, but also because the relationship between the two is hard to ascertain precisely. Popular constitution making relies on the principle that the legitimacy of constitutions reflects the process by which they are drafted as much as their content. The media are expected to play a weighty and presumably unbiased role in linking and amplifying what happens during the process. But when some of the oldest and most resilient constitutions around the world were drafted, journalism was stridently partisan, and not at all an objective, even-handed intermediary.[1] The specific role of media in more contemporary examples of (popular) constitution making also varies significantly depending on the context in question.[2]

In liberal democracies, or those that aspire to become liberal democratic, the media are expected to report without bias, keep the public informed, and put pressure on decision makers.[3] In more autocratic regimes, the media usually function to signal the political power of elites to citizens while shaping the underlying belief structures and values of the public.[4] Normative theories aside, in any political system, the media constitute a semiautonomous institution whose positioning vis-à-vis the political and economic fields, not to mention their own internal dynamics, shape the news.[5] On the one hand, the state tries to constrain the voices and viewpoints presented in the media by providing official narratives, regulating speech, and controlling the political economy of the news industry. On the other hand, commercial pressure shapes and limits the range of content and views in the media considerably.[6] There are also historically established journalistic norms and practices that determine the autonomy of the profession and diversity of public narratives in a given country (e.g., the professionalization of journalism, public service orientation in reporting, limited interference from the state, and legal protections of speech, to name a few).[7]

What can we then learn about the media's role in popular constitution making from Turkey's 2011–2013 process? For one, this case demonstrates, yet again, how messy and complicated the role of media is in the process of democratization, especially when it comes to collectively agreeing upon the fundamental principles of a nationwide contract such as a constitution. Turkey has always been a so-called hybrid regime, one that combines

1 Sociologist Michael Schudson documents that during the ratification of the US Constitution in 1787–1788, federalists not only controlled the press but also forced the papers that strove to report views on both sides to end their coverage. See Michael Schudson, "The Objectivity Norm in American Journalism," *Journalism* 2, no. 2 (2001): 149–170.

2 Nicole Stremlau, "Media, Participation and Constitution-Making in Ethiopia," *Journal of African Law* 58, no. 2 (2014): 231–249.

3 Michael Schudson, "How to Think Normatively about News and Democracy," in *The Oxford Handbook of Political Communication*, eds. K. Kenski and K. Hall Jamieson (Oxford: Oxford University Press, 2014).

4 Haifeng Huang, "Propaganda as Signaling," *Comparative Politics* 47, no. 4 (2015): 419–437.

5 Pierre Bourdieu, *The Field of Cultural Production* (Cambridge: Polity, 1993).

6 Edwin Baker, *Advertising and a Democratic Press* (Princeton: Princeton University Press, 1994).

7 Daniel C. Hallin and Paolo Mancini, *Comparing Media Systems: Three Models of Media and Politics* (Cambridge: Cambridge University Press, 2004).

democratic and authoritarian elements,[8] but the regime of the Justice and Development Party (*Adalet ve Kalkınma Partisi*, AKP) represents a particular epoch in which political leaders not only have deliberately manipulated democratic institutions for their own gains, but also attempted to "create [their] own tutelage over democratic politics."[9] Even though Turkey's media system was far from perfect prior to the AKP's tenure, the consolidation of an illiberal media environment – one that purportedly has a plurality of news sources and viewpoints, but is also intimately tied to the government and restricted to binary narratives – distinguishes this era. The period from 2011 to 2013 substantiated, over and over again, the AKP's tight control over media and its overall autocratic inclinations. If the attempt at popular constitution making evidences an anomaly in what is otherwise a traditional case of constitutional imposition, as Petersen and Yanaşmayan suggest in this volume, the Turkish press mediated this anomaly against the background of a rapidly degenerating media system.[10]

Turkey's rare attempt to create an inclusive, participatory, consensus-driven political process with an illiberal media calls into question some of the taken-for-granted assumptions about the relationship between democracy and media, such as transparency is key to democratic decision-making, diversity of viewpoints leads to better public debates, and participatory processes are essentially more democratic. Rather than fundamentally challenging the significance of these principles (transparency, diversity, and participation), Turkey's experience serves as a reminder that autocrats can easily appropriate democratic discourses and practices for their own ends, and the media are not powerful enough to be a bulwark against creeping authoritarianism.

Based on a combination of newspaper content analysis and institutional history, I identify three distinct phases in the 2011–2013 period when journalists in Turkey, already quite limited in their capacity to report news, tried to cover this ambitious democratic experiment and its failure. First, in the early days of the Constitutional Conciliation Commission (*Anayasa Uzlaşma Komisyonu*, AUK), the AUK's tight control over the public narrative seems to have taken on an undemocratic tone (especially in contrast to their stated commitment to an inclusive procedure), yet it resulted in mostly neutral coverage that regularly

8 Larry Diamond, "Thinking about Hybrid Regimes," *Journal of Democracy* 13, no. 2 (2002): 21–35.

9 Ertuğ Tombuş, "Reluctant Democratization: The Case of Justice and Development Party in Turkey," *Constellations* 20, no. 2 (2013): 312–327, 314.

10 See Petersen and Yanaşmayan, Chapter 1 in this volume.

emphasized the values of a democratic process. Second, when the AUK began to negotiate how to draft the new constitution, the weakening of press control led to ostensibly more independent coverage of the new constitution, albeit in a way that simplified and polarized the debate over contested topics instead of inviting a multi-perspectival dialogue. Finally, as the AUK's work was derailed by failing to reach an agreement on key topics, the significance of which was the shift to a presidential system, the press coverage seemed to revert back to what it had already learned to do well in general, that is, to bifurcate the narrative as pro- or anti-AKP, or more precisely, as pro- or anti-the political leader, Recep Tayyip Erdoğan.[11]

In the following, I first present a brief overview of how the AKP government established a new media environment by suppressing liberal-critical voices, fortifying its own media bloc, and pushing its own narratives to shape the news agenda. Then I discuss how the AUK intended to break out of the polarized and repressed news cycles by instituting control over reporting on the new constitution. Finally, I examine how the press coverage less inhibited by the AUK ended up promoting simpler and more divisive narratives. Toward the end of the constitution-making process, the highly polarized, illiberal media amplified the impasse the commission was already experiencing and reduced the whole process to a debate over the AKP's proposal for a presidential system.

2 THE MAKING OF ILLIBERAL MEDIA IN TURKEY

Government pressure over media, self-censorship among journalists, tight alignment with state ideology, and political instrumentalization of the press have a long history in Turkey. During the AKP's single-party rule, however, not only have press-state relations, media ownership structures, and journalistic cultures transformed in myriad ways, but also the shift in political ideologies (from secular-nationalist to Islamist-nationalist) has challenged the existing rules and norms in the profession.[12] In this section, I first present a brief history of the media environment in Turkey prior to the AKP era, and then detail how the AKP government constructed a new, illiberal media system over the last fifteen years or so.

11 For a detailed discussion of the issues surrounding the AKP's presidentialism proposal, see Petersen and Yanaşmayan, Chapter 1 in this volume; Özsoy Boyunsuz, Chapter 3 in this volume; and Böcü and Petersen, Chapter 5 in this volume.

12 Ozan Aşık, "Politics, Power, and Performativity in the Newsroom: An Ethnography of Television Journalism in Turkey," *Media, Culture & Society* 41, no. 5 (2019): 587–603.

2.1 *Turkey's Media System Prior to 2002*

The active participation of Turkey's journalists in political life dates back to the late nineteenth century.[13] Such political engagement either resulted in highly intimate relations between the press and the government, or was repeatedly quashed if it was deemed too critical. Starting with the single-party years of the republican period (1923–1945), many journalists joined the ranks of the Republican People's Party (*Cumhuriyet Halk Partisi*, CHP).[14] *Cumhuriyet*, for example, now a left-of-center newspaper, was founded soon after the republic was established under the auspices of the CHP and Mustafa Kemal Atatürk. Journalists who were close to the party propagated the modernizing reforms of the regime in their newspapers. Some news outlets and journalists were critical of the government, especially during the attempts to form a multiparty regime in the years before 1945, but a critical press was either shut down or quite limited by the laws regulating political opposition.

The post-1945 multiparty regime, especially the era of the Democratic Party (*Demokrat Parti*, DP), offered "both the carrot and the stick" to the press.[15] On the one hand, a new Press Law was instituted in 1950 to recognize the freedom of the press and journalists' right to unionize. On the other hand, authoritarian clauses were added to enable the government to shut down publications and impose prison terms on journalists.[16] Party officials continued establishing clientelistic relationships with media owners and individual journalists. The DP government also transformed public radio into a political apparatus that was used both to spread party propaganda and to silence critics.[17]

Immediately after the 1960 coup d'état brought down the DP government, the military seized power over the press. Yunus Emre and Burak Cop report that the mass media played a critical role during the 1961 constitutional referendum. In order to increase voter turnout and encourage massive support for the new constitution, the press regularly covered declarations of "yes" votes.[18] In the 1960s and 1970s, Turkey's mass media started moving more toward television broadcasting, as the Turkish Radio and Broadcasting

[13] Metin Heper and Tanel Demirel, "The Press and the Consolidation of Democracy in Turkey," *Middle Eastern Studies* 32, no. 2 (1996): 109–123.

[14] Ibid.

[15] Raşit Kaya and Barış Çakmur, "Politics and the Mass Media in Turkey," *Turkish Studies* 11, no. 4 (2010): 521–537.

[16] Ibid.

[17] Cihat Göktepe, "1960 'Revolution' in Turkey and the British Policy towards Turkey," *The Turkish Yearbook of International Relations* 30 (2000): 140–189.

[18] Yunus Emre and Burak Cop, "The 1961 Constitutional Referendum in Turkey," *Sociology of Islam* 3 (2015): 49–75.

Corporation (*Türkiye Radyo Televizyon Kurumu*, TRT) quickly expanded across the country. Especially in the 1970s, every new government tried to seize control of TRT, and, eventually, the next coup in 1980 brought TRT under the control of the military.[19]

Turkey's media system has traditionally been identified as a "polarized pluralistic model," a category that also includes countries such as France, Greece, Spain, Italy, and Portugal. Polarized pluralist media systems, in general, tend to have limited newspaper circulation, politicized media organizations (with links to political parties or with clear political leanings), and an under-professionalized journalistic workforce.[20] The post-coup liberalization of Turkey's economy in the 1980s enabled a range of new commercial actors to emerge (especially in broadcast),[21] but journalism has been consistently influenced by political parties[22] and aligned with dominant state narratives.[23] As Ozan Aşık observes, "[T]he secularist consensus … served as the primary entity defining what should be perceived as the public interest and common good" in the press up until the early 2000s.[24] Despite a proliferation of publications with various political orientations in the 1990s, Turkey's mainstream media remained closely aligned with state ideology, a fact most significantly reflected in the coverage of Kurdish issues and the conflict with the Kurdistan Workers' Party (*Partiya Karkerên Kurdistan*, PKK) since 1983. Not only was the word "Kurdish" tacitly banned in the mainstream media until the 1990s, but many journalists who failed to follow this rule faced legal repercussions.[25] Even though the AKP's early years seemed to have increased the visibility of Kurds in the media via the government's official recognition of

[19] Esra Elmas and Dilek Kurban, "The Case of Turkey," in *Media Policies and Regulatory Practices in a Selected Set of European Countries, the EU and the Council of Europe* (European Commission Report, 2010), 412–444, available at www.eliamep.gr/wp-content/uploads/2010/10/BIR.pdf (accessed March 4, 2019).

[20] Hallin and Mancini, *Comparing Media Systems*; Esra Elmas and Dilek Kurban, "Communicating Democracy–Democratizing Communication: Media in Turkey: Legislation, Policies, Actors," in *TESEV Democratization Program Media Studies Series*, 1 (2011), available at www.fes-tuerkei.org/media/pdf/Publikationen%20Archiv/Ortak%20Yay%C4%B1nlar/2011/2011%20Communicating%20Democracy.pdf (accessed March 8, 2019).

[21] Kaya and Çakmur, "Politics and the Mass Media in Turkey."

[22] Salih Bayram, "Political Parallelism in the Turkish Press, a Historical Interpretation," *Turkish Studies* 11, no. 4 (2010): 579–611.

[23] Bilge Yeşil, "Press Censorship in Turkey: Networks of State Power, Commercial Pressures and Self-Censorship," *Communication, Culture and Critique* 7, no. 2 (2014): 154–173.

[24] Ozan Aşık, "The Fall of the Public and the Moral Contestation in the Journalistic Culture of Turkey," *Middle East Journal of Culture and Communication* 10, no.1 (2017): 69–85.

[25] Esra Ercan Bilgiç, *Vatan, Millet, Reyting: Televizyon Haberlerinde Milliyetçilik* (İstanbul: Evrensel Basım Yayın, 2008); Faik Bulut, *Türk Basınında Kürtler* (İstanbul: Evrensel Basım Yayın, 2010).

Kurdishness as a distinct identity and the opening of a Kurdish-language television channel, the AKP government has continued cracking down on Kurdish cultural and political expression throughout its tenure.

2.2 *The AKP Era (2002 Onward)*

After the liberalization wave in the industry, particularly in the 1990s, Turkey's mainstream media became overwhelmed by a combination of clientelism, in which media owners relied on state resources to become competitive in non-media fields, and a corporatist structure, in which companies needed to cater to multiple audiences.[26] This existing system enabled the AKP government to tame the media landscape and even create its own AKP-friendly media bloc (sometimes referred to as *yandaş* [partisan/advocate] media). Murat Akser and Banu Baybars-Hawks, for example, argue that the AKP government controls what they call "media autocracy" through neoliberal measures such as conglomerate pressure, judicial suppression, online banishment, surveillance defamation, and accreditation discrimination.[27] Bilge Yeşil suggests that the AKP exploited this historical and structural continuity in media-government relationships to cultivate the neoliberal authoritarian state of present-day Turkey.[28]

The AKP's early tenure, which overlapped with the aftermath of the 2001 economic crisis in the country, focused on realigning the extant corporatist-clientelist media environment with the interests of the party.[29] A couple of years after Recep Tayyip Erdoğan came to power, some of the bankrupt media companies were taken over by the Savings Deposit Insurance Fund (*Tasarruf Mevduatı Sigorta Fonu*, TMSF), a regulatory body under the prime minister's office. Existing media moguls – the Doğan Group, for example – jumped on this opportunity to acquire new outlets, thereby strengthening their dominance in the industry. It was not unusual for the TMSF, however, to take over a media company only to hand it over to an AKP-friendly bidder. In 2007, the

[26] Christian Christensen, "Breaking the News: Concentration of Ownership, the Fall of Unions and Government Legislation in Turkey," *Global Media and Communication* 3, no. 2 (2007): 179–199; Ali Çarkoğlu, Lemi Baruh, and Kerem Yıldırım, "Press-Party Parallelism and Polarization of News Media during an Election Campaign: The Case of the 2011 Turkish Elections," *International Journal of Press/Politics* 19, no. 3 (2014): 295–317.

[27] Murat Akser and Banu Baybars-Hawks, "Media and Democracy in Turkey: Toward a Model of Neoliberal Media Autocracy," *Middle East Journal of Culture and Communication* 5, no. 3 (2012): 302–321.

[28] Bilge Yeşil, *Media in New Turkey: The Origins of an Authoritarian Neoliberal State* (Urbana: University of Illinois Press, 2016).

[29] Çarkoğlu et al., "Press-Party Parallelism and Polarization"; Yeşil, *Media in New Turkey*.

Ciner Group, which included the popular newspapers *Sabah* and *Takvim* and one of the most popular national TV channels, ATV, was sold to the sole bidder, Turkuvaz Media, owned by the Çalık Group, which was then run by Erdoğan's son-in-law Berat Albayrak.[30] There were brand new players, such as the Çalık, İpek-Koza, and Sancak groups, which entered the field of media to cozy up to the government. They were not shy about it, either – Sancak Holding's CEO, Ethem Sancak, openly admitted that it was his support for the AKP that led him into the media industry.[31]

The confiscation and sale of financially challenged companies to pro-AKP enterprises in the 2004–2008 period were not the only steps toward the making of a pro-AKP media environment.[32] The incestuous ties between media companies and political elites were further solidified via public procurement contracts. Large holding companies with interests in construction, energy, transportation, finance, and tourism regarded media properties as "a levy that must be paid to ensure continued access to government contracts."[33] In order to continue benefiting from government bids and favors, media owners repeatedly interfered in editorial decisions and restricted criticism of the AKP government in the late 2000s.[34] In addition to these political-economic interventions, the early tenure of the AKP government also ushered in the appointment of new managers, editors, and pundits with clear pro-AKP views, despite the fact that most of them had no prior background in journalism.[35] It is important to note that all of these changes took place alongside the strengthening of a tightly networked group of media outlets following the Islamic preacher Fethullah Gülen, who at that time had a political-economic alliance with the AKP.

Media independence was further curtailed with the prosecution of several journalists under the Anti-Terror Law, part of two major political investigations known as Ergenekon (2007), a reference to an alleged shadow organization plotting against the government, and Balyoz ("Sledgehammer") (2010), after

30 Nina Ognianova, Jean-Paul Marthoz, Robert Mahoney, Joel Simon, Özgür Öğret, Şafak Timur, and Nebahat Kübra Akalın, *Turkey's Press Freedom Crisis: The Dark Days of Jailing Journalists and Criminalizing Dissent* (Committee to Protect Journalists, 2012), available at https://cpj.org/reports/Turkey2012.English.pdf (accessed March 8, 2019).

31 Yeşil, *Media in New Turkey*.

32 Ibid.

33 Susan Corke, Andrew Finkel, David J. Kramer, Carla Anne Robbins, and Nate Schenkkan, "Democracy in Crisis: Corruption, Media, and Power in Turkey," *Freedom House Special Report* (2014), available at https://freedomhouse.org/report/special-reports/democracy-crisis-corruption-media-and-power-turkey (accessed July 3, 2019).

34 Burcu Baykurt, "The Gezi Protests Have Shown the Rampant Institutional Bias in Turkey's Media Which Now Leaves Little Room for Facts," *LSE Europp Blog* (July 10, 2013), available at http://blogs.lse.ac.uk/europpblog/2013/07/10/gezi-protest-media (accessed March 8, 2019).

35 Yeşil, *Media in New Turkey*.

the code-name of a purported coup plot.[36] Some journalists, accused of "collaborating with the Ergenekon organization," were even imprisoned without trial. In addition to the chilling effect this had on reporters and media managers when it came to criticizing the AKP, the government's regular wiretapping and raiding of news organizations undermined the privacy of reporters and discredited their professional standing in society.[37] The use of the Anti-Terror Law to prosecute journalists was not limited to the cases of Ergenekon and Balyoz. Since 2009 dozens of journalists and editors from the Kurdish media have been arrested on the grounds of membership in the Kurdistan Communities Union (*Kürdistan Topluluklar Birliği*, KCK), thereby routinely criminalizing reporting on Kurdish rights and criticism of the Turkish military.[38]

In 2009 the AKP government struck an obvious blow against a critical media giant in the form of an exorbitant tax fine. After the Doğan Group's flagship newspapers *Hürriyet* and *Milliyet* covered a German court case in which several Turkish citizens with ties to the AKP leadership were accused of misappropriating tens of millions of dollars from Deniz Feneri, a Turkish charity, Erdoğan first called for a boycott of the media company. The Doğan Group was then hit with a $500 million tax fine, which was followed by an additional $2.5 billion fine a few months later. The combined tax levy nearly equalled the company's total assets, thereby posing an existential threat to its survival. The Doğan Group immediately appealed the charges, while also taking measures to appease then-Prime Minister Erdoğan. The chairman of the company, Aydin Doğan, stepped down, followed by the resignation of Ertuğrul Özkök, the editor-in-chief of its flagship daily newspaper *Hürriyet*.[39] In 2010 and 2011, the company sacked some of the critical columnists from the mainstream papers *Hürriyet* and *Radikal* and eventually sold two other newspapers, *Milliyet* and *Vatan*, to a holding company with strong ties to the government.[40]

Following the AKP's election victory in 2011, the intimate relationship between media owners and the government, which depended on complicity, censorship, and outright control, became so obvious that it simply could not be denied. As Yeşil evocatively notes, loyal businessmen who have entered the media industry since 2004 "were not simply motivated by prospects of receiving favors from the government, but they were also 'doing favors for the government.'"[41] Frequent defamation claims by politicians against journalists,

36 Yeşil, "Press Censorship in Turkey."
37 Yeşil, *Media in New Turkey*.
38 Ibid.
39 David O'Byrne, "Turkish Media Mogul Resigns," *Financial Times* (December 31, 2009), 16.
40 Corke et al., "Democracy in Crisis"; Yeşil, *Media in New Turkey*.
41 Yeşil, *Media in New Turkey*, 106.

along with increasing self-censorship or censorship by editors due to fears of repercussions, put major pressure on media coverage. A new wave of resignations and dismissals of critical voices from the mainstream media continued through 2011. Journalist Banu Güven, for example, was fired by the Doğuş-owned NTV in 2011 for her criticism of the AKP's stance on the Kurdish issue.[42] Following his dismissal from NTV in 2011, veteran journalist Can Dündar proclaimed the "dawn of a new era in Turkey's media field" that was marked by a "widespread purge, a cleanup."[43]

According to Turkey-based Bianet (Independent Communications Network), 104 journalists were in jail in 2011.[44] By way of contrast, according to the Committee to Protect Journalists, only 27 reporters were in jail at the end of 1998.[45] Reporters Without Borders (RSF) ranked Turkey 148th out of 179 countries on its World Press Freedom Index, and cited 2011 as the year of "unprecedented arrests, massive phone taps ... and escalating judicial harassment of journalists," all of which had created "a climate of intimidation in the media."[46] That was a significant drop from the country's ranking of 99th in 2002, the year RSF first published its index and the AKP came to power. As of 2018, Turkey had plummeted even further, ranking 157th in the World Press Freedom Index.[47]

In political journalism there is always a symbiotic relationship between journalists and politicians, but the terms and nature of this relationship vary across countries and time periods.[48] Ozan Aşık suggests that what distinguishes the AKP-era media environment is a significant departure from this "interest-

[42] Ayşe Buğra and Osman Savaşkan, *New Capitalism in Turkey: The Relationship between Politics, Religion and Business* (Cheltenham: Edward Elgar, 2014).

[43] Yeşil, "Press Censorship in Turkey."

[44] Emel Gülcan, "Press Freedom Day with 95 Journalists behind Bars!" *BIA Media Monitoring-News Center* (July 25, 2012), available at https://bianet.org/english/freedom-of-expression/139915-press-freedom-day-with-95-journalists-behind-bars (accessed March 8, 2019).

[45] "Turkey: Criminal Prosecutions of Journalists," *Committee to Protect Journalists* (1999), available at https://cpj.org/reports/1999/05/turkeyreport.php (accessed March 8, 2019).

[46] Reporters Without Borders, "World Press Freedom Index 2011/2012" (2012), available at https://rsf.org/en/world-press-freedom-index-20112012 (accessed March 8, 2019).

[47] According to the US-based Freedom House, Turkey's freedom rating did not shift significantly from the 1990s to the late 2000s. For example, Freedom House ranked Turkey "partly free" in 1999 (before the AKP came to power) with a 4.5 freedom rating (on a scale of 1=best and 7=worst), whereas the country received an improved 3.0 rating in 2011 and was marked as "partly free" again. Turkey's Freedom House ranking became significantly worse as of 2017, and the country was recognized as "not free" in 2018 with a 5.5 rating. See https://freedomhouse.org/report/freedom-world/2018/turkey (accessed March 26, 2019).

[48] Karin Wahl-Jorgensen, "The Production of Political Journalism: The Push and Pull of Power, Routines and Constraints," in *The Handbook of Communication Sciences – Political Communication*, ed. C. Reinemann (New York: DeGruyter Mouton, 2014), 305–324.

based" relationship, which has a long and asymmetrical history in Turkey, to one with "kinship-like ties and organic solidarity with the AKP."[49] Through political pressure, legal coercion, and economic incentives, the AKP has not only established several loyal media outlets, but also neutralized opposition media since the 2000s.[50] As the country became more polarized and the AKP tightened its control over the media starting in 2011, journalists in Turkey began displaying strong allegiance to the AKP's Islamist-nationalist narratives at the expense of fair and balanced reporting.[51]

3 PUBLICITY AND POPULAR CONSTITUTION MAKING

By mid-2011 the AKP had won a landslide victory in the general elections but lacked the constitutional mandate to unilaterally draft a new constitution. All political parties had pledged to a new constitution that should be democratic as well as civilian and had committed to joining the AKP in the new Parliament to write a new constitution. The media were to play a crucial role in this process of drafting a new constitution in an inclusive, pluralistic, and positive manner, which would mark a radical departure from the country's already divided and AKP-dominated sociocultural landscape.

At the time, the AKP was enjoying hegemony over the mainstream media, and the existing political criticism in Turkey's media environment was still orbiting around the narratives shaped by the party. As Ali Çarkoğlu and his colleagues demonstrate in the news coverage of the 2011 elections, opposition media failed to generate enough publicity for opposition political parties.[52] In other words, news outlets critical of the AKP were not able to provide wide-ranging and effective alternative coverage of Turkey's politics at the time. That is, of course, not entirely the media's fault. As the authors rightly acknowledge, the inability of the critical press to spotlight a more compelling opposition narrative was also due to the fact that no single opposition party was able to mobilize enough popular support to emerge as a viable alternative to the AKP. Nonetheless, this particular snapshot illustrates how ill equipped Turkey's critical media were in 2011 to cover such a complex and heated topic as the making of a new constitution.

In the following three sections, I explain how the media coverage of constitution making shifted from tightly controlled, yet relatively balanced and

49 Aşık, "The Fall of the Public," 81.

50 Bilge Yeşil, "Authoritarian Turn or Continuity? Governance of Media through Capture and Discipline in the AKP Era," *South European Society and Politics* 23, no. 2 (2018): 239–257.

51 Aşık, "The Fall of the Public."

52 Çarkoğlu et al., "Press-Party Parallelism and Polarization."

informative to less restrained but more partisan. In particular, the year 2013, which overlapped with the Gezi protests, corruption allegations against the AKP, and the dissolution of the AUK, marked a watershed in the history of Turkey's illiberal media. Not only did media control and censorship – and self-censorship – become undeniably visible post-2013, but they also took on outlandish proportions.

3.1 *The AUK and the Media (October 2011–May 2012)*

The AUK held its first meeting on October 19, 2011. The four political parties that were present in the Parliament at the time were each represented by three members, regardless of the seat distribution. Cemil Çiçek, then AKP MP and the president of the Parliament, was to chair the process. The AUK's decision-making process was based on the unanimity principle – a rare practice in a political system designed for majoritarianism. Çiçek echoed the value of seeking consensus on the opening day of the commission. "All of us may have a different constitution in mind," he said. "The tolerance and conciliation that a new constitution requires may help alleviate the cultural and political polarization that Turkey has long experienced."[53] Çiçek's emphasis on the significance of how the new constitution would be drafted (e.g., seeking consensus, based on tolerance and conciliation) was a welcome change in a country that was speeding toward an increasingly authoritarian state order. It also invited scrutiny from various actors, including the media, in order to hold the AUK accountable to these positive promises.

The AUK, however, began its tenure against the background of a new domestic crisis. A day before the first meeting, Kurdish militants clashed with the Turkish military, resulting in the killing of twenty-four soldiers.[54] In response, on October 20, 2011, Recep Tayyip Erdoğan convened a meeting with top media owners and editors to discuss the coverage of the Kurdish issue. Asking media executives not to "serve the aims of terror by knowingly or unknowingly propagandizing,"[55] Erdoğan practically issued a "quasi gag order" on the coverage of the armed conflict between the PKK and the

[53] "Anayasadan Dönmek Yok," *Milliyet* (October 20, 2011), available at www.milliyet.com.tr/-anayasadan-donmek-yok–siyaset-1452739/ (accessed March 8, 2019).

[54] Jonathon Burch, "Turkish Military Says Kills 49 Kurdish Militants" *Reuters* (October 22, 2011), available at www.reuters.com/article/us-turkey-pkk/turkish-military-says-kills-49-kurdish-militants-idUSTRE79LoSE20111022?feedType=RSS&feedName=worldNews&rpc=22&sp=true (accessed March 8, 2019).

[55] Jay Cassano, "Turkey: Media Bares Its Anti-Kurdish Bias," *Inter Press Service News Agency* (October 28, 2011), available at www.ipsnews.net/2011/10/turkey-media-bares-its-anti-kurdish-bias/ (accessed March 8, 2019).

Turkish military.[56] Erdoğan's message to the media might appear to be limited to this particular issue; however, his increased control over media, wrapped around a sensitive national security claim and an intimidating warning about "knowingly or unknowingly" spreading propaganda, had a chilling effect on editorial decisions beyond the issue of terror. In addition, it raised reasonable doubts about how sincere the AUK's promise to draft a new constitution in an inclusive manner was in the context of an ongoing armed conflict and limited freedom of political expression in the media.

Ahead of Erdoğan's meeting with the press, the AUK was already concerned with the extent of publicity about the commission's work. In their very first decision, the members unanimously decided that the media should not be privy to conversations inside the meetings. Calling on everyone, including the media, to act "responsibly" during this new process, Çiçek asked reporters not to write "background" stories about the closed meetings and added that he would be talking to the editors-in-chief of major newspapers about that. "The public should be informed about a constitution drafted in the name of the public," Çiçek then acknowledged, but nonetheless reiterated his instruction that the media should only cover the official statements of the commission.[57] Çiçek was adamant about the participation of regular citizens, along with members of civil society organizations, in the process. He just did not want the press to be mediating between the AUK and the public. Soon the AUK launched a website – www.yenianayasa.gov.tr – not only to showcase previous constitutional documents, examples from other countries, and press coverage but also to facilitate citizen feedback. The AUK also expressed the intention to use the website to poll public opinion regarding some of the articles of the new constitution once they were drafted.

Next, in early November 2011, the AUK convened a meeting at Dolmabahçe Palace with managers and editors from a wide range of news organizations. Cemil Çiçek, along with some AUK members from each party, asked the media to "support the work of the commission, encourage public participation, and advise in case of a deadlock."[58] There were reportedly thirty-three newspapers (including minority papers), five news agencies, three magazines, two foreign newspapers, and thirty-one broadcast channels from a variety of political positions in the room. There were also, however, some notable omissions, such as the leftist pro-Kurdish publication *Özgür Gündem*,

56 Yeşil, *Media in New Turkey*, 136.

57 Ayşe Sayın, "Komisyonda Ilk Uzlaşmazlık Başkanlıkta," *Cumhuriyet* (October 20, 2011).

58 "Anayasa için Basın Katkı Versin," *Radikal* (November 4, 2011), available at www.tbmm.gov.tr/develop/owa/gazete_haberleri.haber_detay?pkayit_no=1352773 (accessed March 8, 2019).

the Kurdish news sources *Dicle Press Agency* and *Azadiya Welat*, the Greek news source *İho*, and the Armenian outlet *Marmara*.[59]

After these initial meetings, the AUK kicked off a consultative process that lasted from October 2011 to April 2012 to capture the wide range of concerns and recommendations regarding the new constitution. They announced a series of meetings with a variety of organizations, including universities, unions, political parties, think tanks, and provincial bar associations. Nearly 10,000 citizens reportedly sent their recommendations to the AUK.[60] This rare process of listening to different interested parties by all members of the Parliament was perceived to be a positive step toward the making of a new constitution. Yet it was soon clouded by the AUK's decision not to publish the views and suggestions collected from different organizations. Dubbed the "secrecy rule" by some monitors of the process, the AUK members defended their decision on the basis of protecting these groups and preventing further conflict and polarization over the recommendations.[61]

The assumption motivating the virtue of publicity in any political process is not only to hold powerful institutions accountable, but also to create a more effective, responsive, and democratic regulatory process. In the case of political decision-making, however, sunlight may not always be the best disinfectant, pace US Supreme Court Justice Louis Brandeis. Jon Elster, for example, suggests that while public deliberations may help avoid "open logrolling or horsetrading" and encourage arguments in favor of the common good, they can also push decision makers to adopt "rigid, inflexible positions as a pre-commitment device," since it is harder to walk back public statements than those expressed in closed meetings.[62] In that sense, the AUK's effort to set limitations on the media, dictate what was newsworthy, and operate in outright secrecy seemed to be a genuine attempt to shield the commission from the potentially corrosive pressure of public opinion. The AUK tried to make up for this democratic deficit by using the website as a presumably open way to solicit citizen feedback. That was, however, a highly unsatisfactory substitute

[59] Ferhat Kentel, Levent Koker, Mehmet Ucum, and Özge Genç, "Yeni Anayasa Sürecini İzleme Raporu Şubat 2012–Haziran 2012," *Türkiye Ekonomik ve Sosyal Etüdler Vakfı Demokratikleşme Programı* (2012), available at http://t24.com.tr/media/editorials/files/Anayasaizleme2_08_10_12.pdf (accessed March 8, 2019).

[60] Ibid.

[61] Ibid.

[62] Jon Elster, "Constitution-Making in Eastern Europe: Rebuilding the Boat in the Open Sea," *Public Administration* 71, nos. 1–2 (1993): 169–217, 181. See also Jon Elster, "The Optimal Design of a Constituent Assembly," in *Collective Wisdom Principles and Mechanisms*, eds. H. Landemore and J. Elster (Cambridge: Cambridge University Press, 2012), 163–166.

for transparency, as the AUK was still at the helm, deciding what went online about the consultations and moderating the online discussions.

What did the news coverage look like when the AUK was tightly controlling the public narrative about the new constitution? A content analysis of newspaper reports from the period between October 19, 2011, and February 2012 shows that the coverage predominantly focused on Chairman Cemil Çiçek's statements and the day-to-day work of the AUK.[63] That is perhaps not surprising given the significance of a new constitution, the radical method of striving to draft it based on consensus and consultation with a wide range of organizations, and Çiçek's own commitment to making sure that the media acted "responsibly" in this process. The coverage was not always sympathetic. The opposition media criticized the AUK's decision to keep the meetings closed, with articles bearing titles such as "The Civilian Constitution Is behind Closed Doors" and "The Commission's First Disagreement Is about the Chairman" (both in *Cumhuriyet*) and "What Would Happen If Obama Convened Media Representatives?" (in *Habertürk*).[64] Nonetheless, most papers followed the instructions of the AUK, and there was little coverage of the organizations and groups that provided recommendations.

In hindsight, given Turkey's polarized political environment at the time and the already existing pressure on mainstream media, the AUK's aversion to full transparency makes sense. Even in more liberal democratic contexts, full transparency in government can sometimes do more harm than the democratic good it promises to deliver. More openness may expose decision makers to powerful and potentially malevolent authorities or interest groups, thereby inhibiting honest deliberations.[65] The glare of publicity may make it difficult for decision makers to negotiate with each other in candid and creative ways, especially in political climates marked by drastic partisanship. David Stasavage offers a game-theoretic justification for limiting transparency, suggesting that open deliberation has the potential to lead to mass polarization instead of consensus.[66] Restricting the work of the media through open

63 Kentel et al., "Yeni Anayasa Sürecini İzleme Raporu."

64 "Sivil Anayasa Kapalı Kapılar Ardında," *Cumhuriyet* (October 24, 2011), available at www.cumhuriyetarsivi.com/katalog/192/sayfa/2011/10/24/5.xhtml (accessed March 8, 2019); "Komisyonda İlk Uzlaşmazlık Başkanlıkta," *Cumhuriyet* (October 20, 2011), available at www.tbmm.gov.tr/develop/owa/gazete_haberleri.haber_detay?pkayit_no=1348251 (accessed March 8, 2019); "Obama Medya Temsilcilerini Toplasa Nasıl Olur?" *Habertürk* (October 27, 2011).

65 Michael Schudson, *The Rise of the Right to Know: Politics and the Culture of Transparency, 1945–1975* (Cambridge, MA: The Belknap Press of Harvard University Press, 2015).

66 David Stasavage, "Polarization and Publicity: Rethinking the Benefits of Deliberative Democracy," *Journal of Politics* 69, no. 1 (2007): 59–72.

warnings, one-on-one meetings, and withholding internal documents may appear somewhat overbearing even for Turkey, where some of those practices had become rather normalized by that time. Nonetheless, the early coverage of the AUK seemed to be more measured and informative, especially in contrast to the coverage of the commission's work in late 2012 and 2013. The limited autonomy of reporters resulted in relatively fewer and shorter stories about the new constitution, but the reports that were published gave the impression of a more consistent narrative across various media outlets. As the AUK professed a commitment to working with civil society organizations and soliciting citizen feedback, the mainstream media's regular reporting on the historical significance of making a democratic constitution and detailed information about the process were just the kind of publicity that the commission needed at the time.

3.2 *The AUK Starts Drafting a New Constitution (June–December 2012)*

The drafting of the new constitution began in May 2012. By June 2012 there was already not only more media coverage of the commission,[67] but also a change in the way the media covered the AUK.[68] While still driven by the work of the AUK and voices of the commission members (as opposed to civil society actors or minority voices), the media began to report on the progress of discussions in the commission. For example, the Gülen-affiliated *Zaman* newspaper, tightly aligned with the AKP government at the time, covered the AUK under the special rubric "Constitutional Diary."[69] In the beginning, the mainstream media remained loyal to the reporting conventions set out by the AUK, even when initial disagreements inside the commission flared up. Still reporting on the basis of the official statements put out by the AUK members, newspapers highlighted the content of debates rather than polarizing narratives, thereby providing "more neutral, informative, and even positive views."[70]

In July 2012, for example, the commission took a break from regular meetings due to a deadlock over two issues – the right to education in one's mother tongue and inclusion of sexual orientation in the text of the article on equality, both of which were proposed by the Peace and Democracy Party (*Barış ve*

67 Kentel et al., "Yeni Anayasa Sürecini İzleme Raporu."

68 Ceren Sözeri, "Yeni Anayasa Yapım Sürecinde Basın – Ocak 2013-Temmuz 2013" *Türkiye Ekonomik ve Sosyal Etüdler Vakfı Demokratikleşme Programı* (2013), available at http://tesev.org.tr/wp-content/uploads/2015/11/Yeni_Anayasa_Yapim_Surecinde_Basin_Ocak_Temmuz_2013.pdf (accessed March 8, 2019).

69 Sözeri, "Yeni Anayasa Yapım Sürecinde Basın."

70 Kentel et al., "Yeni Anayasa Sürecini İzleme Raporu," 25.

Demokrasi Partisi, BDP). The ideological orientations of newspapers shaped the headlines; nonetheless, all papers gave voice to political parties in equal measure in their stories. *Zaman*, for example, reported the impasse in an article titled "BDP Presses the Brake on Constitutional Drafting,"[71] but despite blaming the BDP for stalling the commission's work in the title, the story then extensively and soberly covered the BDP's complaint that the party's considerations were not taken into account during internal discussions. It also covered Cemil Çiçek's and other commission members' responses, along with updating the readers about the overall progress of the commission. *Cumhuriyet*, which is highly critical of the AKP, broke the same news under the headline "A Break on the Crisis of Mother Tongue,"[72] and led the story with a quote from BDP's Hasip Kaplan: "We will reveal who gets in the way of the process, but it will never be us who obstructs the process," thereby demonstrating that BDP's critical stance in the commission did not intend to hinder the process. Similar to *Zaman*'s story, *Cumhuriyet*'s version highlighted the critical voices on the commission, such as members of the CHP and BDP, as well as Cemil Çiçek. Despite the fact that the commission postponed its deliberations for a few weeks, newspapers did not escalate the severity of the situation. "A Break on the New Constitution," *Akşam* reported and highlighted quotes from each party representative.[73] "Mother Tongue Postponed in the Constitution," the liberal paper *Taraf* announced, while dedicating the rest of the story to the clauses that the commission had completed drafting to that point.[74]

This balanced and careful tone started shifting, however, as internal disagreements over specific articles continued into late 2012. At some point, reporters stopped following the AUK's earlier instruction not to cover the closed meetings or provide background stories. Even in countries where there is more press freedom, the media usually "patrol the boundaries of culture and keep discord within conventional bounds,"[75] and it is only when there is disagreement among elites that reporters deviate from dominant frames.[76] The Turkish media were much less experienced in taking a proactive, critical role that goes beyond the official frame of any story.

71 Habib Güler, "Anayasa Çalışmalarına 'BDP' Freni," *Zaman* (July 11, 2012).

72 "Anadil Krizine Mola," *Cumhuriyet* (July 11, 2012).

73 "Yeni Anayasada Mola," *Akşam* (July 11, 2012).

74 "Anayasada Anadil Ertelemede," *Taraf* (July 2, 2012).

75 Robert Entman, "Cascading Activation: Contesting the White House's Frame after 9/11," *Political Communication* 20, no. 4 (2003): 415–432, 428.

76 Daniel Hallin, *The "Uncensored War"* (New York: Oxford University Press, 1986); Lance Bennett, "Toward a Theory of Press-State Relations in the United States," *Journal of Communication* 40, no. 2 (1990): 103–125.

When the AUK stopped presenting a united front, media coverage started splintering and rendering the public narrative in line with the various outlets' ideological loyalties.[77] In other words, pro-government and opposition media chose which of the AUK's proceedings to cover on the basis of their political leanings, limited their sources to those who agreed with the views of the outlet, and framed the actual negotiations in a highly biased manner, again, in support of their political stance.[78]

Take what happened in September 2012, when the commission weathered another predicament over constitutional secularism, which secures freedom of religious expression and conscience.[79] *Cumhuriyet* chose to cover this debate with the exaggerated headline "Open Door for Sharia," and narrowed the overall discussion to the issue of state secularism, that is, the principle that a state does not govern according to religious laws.[80] Pro-AKP *Sabah*, in contrast, reported on the same day, "Atheists Are in the New Constitution," and summed up the complicated discussion about religious freedom with reference to only one of the settled terms among commission members, the one that recognized the right not to believe.[81] Relatively more moderate *Akşam* headlined their story "Agreement on the Constitutional Guarantee for Atheists," but then covered the whole debate over freedom of religion and conscience, especially regarding the impasse between the AKP and the CHP over the redefinition of secularism.[82]

Popular constitution making could have been a significant step toward democratization in Turkey, but it also offered a rare opportunity for Turkey's media, however repressed they were at the time, to report on a parliamentary commission that purportedly operated on the principle of consensus seeking and not one of deep polarization. Civil society organizations that monitored the constitution-making process expected this moment to be a "significant turning point" for the media to take on a more active role, and overall seemed disappointed with the fact that the press merely "reflect[ed] views, rather than endeavoring to provide guidance, contribute to the debate, and offer information."[83] Ideally, journalists should of course help people connect the

77 See Böcü and Petersen, Chapter 5 in this volume.

78 Sözeri, "Yeni Anayasa Yapım Sürecinde Basın."

79 Zeynep Yanaşmayan, "Oppositional Usages of Europeanization in Turkish Constitution-Making: Discussions on Religious Freedom," *Turkish Studies*. 18, no. 4 (2017): 644–664.

80 Ayşe Sayın, "Şeriata Açık Kapı," *Cumhuriyet* (September 12, 2012), available at www.tbmm.gov.tr/develop/owa/gazete_haberleri.haber_detay?pkayit_no=1433131 (accessed March 8, 2019).

81 Zübeyde Yalçın, "Ateistler Yeni Anayasada," *Sabah* (September 12, 2012).

82 Ebru Toktar Çekiç, "Ateistlere Anayasal Güvencede Uzlaşma," *Akşam* (September 12, 2012).

83 Kentel et al., "Yeni Anayasa Sürecini İzleme Raporu."

dots, offer explanations, and give voice to multiple perspectives. Informative, multi-perspectival, and critical media have the potential to expose the public to competing interpretations, thereby encouraging citizens to think about the political situation in more complex and original ways.[84]

Civil society's expectations of the media, however, may have been unrealistic. Not only did they overlook the immense pressure that was looming over Turkey's media industry, but also the fact that journalists, even in more liberal contexts, rarely attempt to influence outcomes. Rather, reporters try to protect and advance their careers in line with what they imagine to be the ideal role ascribed to them, whether as independent watchdogs in a relatively liberal context or as guardians of the unity of the country in a more illiberal environment.[85] Between 2011 and 2013, the ideal roles Turkey's media took upon themselves were in flux, and there was still some room for negotiation and editorial discretion inside newsrooms. The AUK's initial meetings with members of civil society and attempts to control coverage through official statements offered journalists an opportunity to practice the profession in a way they had not had much of a chance to do lately, that is, more independently. Most newspapers, in response, managed to cover only what was happening (as opposed to providing interpretations and background stories of events), give voice to each political party in equal measure, and report on conflicts in a balanced manner, albeit for a short period of time. Once the commission's unity began to shatter, journalists' accounts of the new constitution mirrored the news coverage of other subjects: conflicting, not to mention polarizing, stories.

Toward the end of 2012, media coverage of the AUK started to focus on the commission's timeline, along with a critical interrogation of the durability of the overall process as political disagreements persisted. In early November 2012, Recep Tayyip Erdoğan announced that he was losing hope for a new constitution. This not only received wide coverage, but also validated negative assessments of the odds of the commission's ultimate success in drafting a new constitution.[86] Erdoğan's statement also invited responses from leaders of other political parties, thereby shifting media attention from members of the AUK to outsiders. Once the AKP proposed drafting the clauses on the executive body in order to constitutionalize a presidential system, both

84 Herb Gans, *Deciding What's News: A Study of CSB Evening News, NBC Nightly News, Newsweek, and Time* (New York: Vintage Books, 1980); Mauro Porto, "Frame Diversity and Citizen Competence," *Critical Studies in Media Communication* 2, no. 4 (2007): 303–321, 312.

85 Scott L. Althaus, "When News Norms Collide, Follow the Lead: New Evidence for Press Independence," *Political Communication* 20, no. 4 (2003): 381–414.

86 Önder Yılmaz, "'Ümidim Azalıyor' Yankı Yarattı," *Milliyet* (November 3, 2012).

the inner dynamics of the commission and the overall coverage of the new constitution changed drastically.

3.3 *The AUK Fails as Turkey's Media Scene Further Deteriorates (January–December 2013)*

Starting in early 2013, when the AUK's internal unity continued to disintegrate from disagreements and quarrels, the readers of pro-AKP and opposition media were regaled with polarizing interpretations of the AUK's discussions and widely divergent expert opinions. One thing, however, united the coverage of the AKP-friendly and opposition press: Erdoğan's pronouncements, which became ever more prominent in the debate on the new constitution in early 2013. After he signaled the possibility of a constitutional referendum on the work of the AUK, which had already fallen behind schedule in completing a draft constitution, Erdoğan published an op-ed in AKP-friendly *Sabah* in February 2013. The title read "A New Constitution for a New Turkey," and the then-prime minister reiterated his party's commitment to a more democratic constitution and proclaimed that the AKP would not be "the party that leaves the table."[87] Despite this reassurance, word of the AKP's intention to unilaterally draft a new constitution began to spread (see, e.g., "Constitution Draft Will Be Rewritten"),[88] and the news media's focus soon shifted to openly questioning how much longer the AUK could survive, as signaled by headlines such as "Judgment Day for the Constitution," "The Ball Is in the Court of Political Parties," and "There Is No Point in Staying at the Table without Progress."[89]

In the following few months, while the commission's work slowed down, media coverage shifted to a variety of debates spurred by external actors – politicians, party leaders, and legal experts – with rare mention of commission members or of Cemil Çiçek. Speculation about what would happen if the AUK could not finish drafting the new constitution started circulating ("AKP's Plan B Is to 'Settle' with CHP," "A Transition Constitution Is on the Agenda," "Semi-Presidency with a Mini Package").[90] And even when the

87 Recep Tayyip Erdoğan, "Yeni Bir Türkiye için Yeni Bir Anayasa," *Sabah* (February 11, 2013).

88 "Anayasa Taslağı Yeniden Yazılacak," *Yeni Şafak* (February 11, 2013).

89 "Anayasada Kader Günü," *Radikal* (April 1, 2013); "Topu Partilere Attı," *Cumhuriyet* (April 2, 2013); Nevin Bilgin, "İlerleme Olmazsa Masada Oturmanın Anlamı Yok," *Star* (April 10, 2013).

90 Önder Yılmaz, "AKP'nin B Planı CHP İle 'Uzlaşmak,'" *Milliyet* (March 31, 2013); Erdem Gül, "Geçiş Anayasası Formülü Gündemde," *Cumhuriyet* (April 23, 2013); Zübeyde Yalçın, "Mini Paketle Yarı Başkanlık," *Sabah* (May 21, 2013).

AUK tried to pick up the pace of its work in May 2013, party representatives outside the commission openly expressed their doubts about its future in a manner intended to polarize. Media coverage, in line with the political leanings of the various newspapers, followed suit. "CHP Wants the Commission to Continue to Derail the New Constitution" headlined the pro-AKP, Gülen-affiliated *Zaman* in early May in a story about whether or not the AUK would continue its work.[91] "AKP Knocks Down the Table" announced the opposition paper *Cumhuriyet* in a story about how the parties were blaming each other for the delay in the drafting of the new constitution.[92]

As if the current political climate was not divisive enough, what started as a couple dozen activists occupying Istanbul's Gezi Park in late May 2013 turned into a wave of anti-government protests across the country. The Gezi protests became a critical moment in pushing Turkey's media into the spotlight. In its early days, the protests were either painted by pro-government media organizations as the work of a Western conspiracy or completely ignored by mainstream media. The now widely remembered breaking point was when the local CNN affiliate *CNN Türk* chose to show a documentary about penguins at the peak of the protests, while *CNN International* covered the protests as major breaking news from Turkey. The penguin thus became a symbol of media cowardice, while dozens of protestors organized sit-ins outside news organizations where they chanted "sell-out media," waved money at the media buildings, and circulated a popular hashtag on Twitter (*#korkakmedya* – "coward media") to express their discontent.[93]

Many reporters and editors lost their jobs in the wake of Gezi. The Turkish Journalists' Union revealed that fifty-nine journalists were sacked or forced to resign due to their coverage of the protests, while some reporters cited much higher numbers.[94] *NTV Tarih*, a history magazine owned by NTV, was shut down and its entire staff was fired after the magazine prepared to launch a special "Gezi" issue. Even after the protests waned, firings of journalists continued. In November 2013, TRT fired two employees who voiced their support for Gezi on Twitter.[95] In December 2013, leaks of telephone conversations of top AKP government officials resulted in a corruption scandal, with

91 "CHP, Anayasa Yaptırmamak İçin Komisyonun Devamını İstiyor," *Zaman* (May 7, 2013).

92 Erdem Gül, "AKP Masayı Dağıtıyor," *Cumhuriyet* (May 2, 2013).

93 Burcu Baykurt, "The Gezi Protests."

94 "59 Journalists Fired in the Wake of Gezi Protests, 40 Still behind Bars: CPJ," *Hurriyet Daily News* (February 13, 2014), available at www.hurriyetdailynews.com/59-journalists-fired-in-the-wake-of-gezi-protests-40-still-behind-bars-cpj-62430 (accessed March 8, 2019).

95 Mehmet Bilber, "TRT Gezi'ye Faturayı Kesti: 2 Kişi Kovuldu," *Radikal* (November 14, 2013), available at www.radikal.com.tr/turkiye/trt-geziye-faturayi-kesti-2-kisi-kovuldu-1160841/ (accessed March 8, 2019).

the arrests of several public officials and businesspeople. The investigations eventually caused the notorious fallout between the AKP and the Gülen movement, which was widely believed to have instigated the probe. The scandal not only stoked further polarization in media coverage but also revealed the bluntness of the government's control over the media. In one of the wiretapped leaks, then-Prime Minister Erdoğan was heard to order an executive of *Habertürk* to remove content at the height of the Gezi protests. In response, the editor-in-chief of *Habertürk* daily, Fatih Altaylı, acknowledged the intimidation reporters faced from government pressure. "The honor of journalism is being trampled on," he said. "Instructions rain down every day from various places. Can you write what you want? Everybody is afraid."[96] Between the Gezi Park protests and the December 2013 corruption scandal, the AUK, for all intents and purposes, collapsed, especially once the AKP members – including the Chairman Cemil Çiçek – stopped attending the meetings in November 2013.

The Gezi protests and corruption allegations not only demonstrated the AKP's heavy-handed control over the press but also pushed the government, especially then-Prime Minister Erdoğan, to declare an open war against critical journalism and social media. In the run-up to Turkey's local elections in 2014, he threatened at a rally to "wipe out Twitter." Immediately after his speech, Twitter was blocked for two weeks by a court order.[97] When the Constitutional Court ruled that the ban on Twitter violated freedom of expression, Erdoğan begrudgingly acknowledged that they had to follow the ruling, but he did not respect the court's decision. The following year AKP could not win a parliamentary majority in the June 2015 general elections, and a two-year-old ceasefire between Turkey and the PKK collapsed in July. Amid the intensifying political crisis, the censorship of news outlets reached a whole new level. Turkey's now-defunct Telecommunications and Communications Authority (*Telekomünikasyon İletişim Başkanlığı*, TİB) blocked nearly 100 Kurdish websites, most of which were news outlets, on the grounds that they were spreading terrorist propaganda.[98] The daily *Hürriyet* faced a legal investigation for publishing photos of dead soldiers and an interview with an

96 Nick Tattersall and Ece Toksabay, "Turkish Editor Hits Out at Media Coercion under Erdogan," *Reuters* (February 11, 2014), available at www.reuters.com/article/us-turkey/turkish-editor-hits-out-at-media-coercion-under-erdogan-idUSBREA1A1I120140211 (accessed March 8, 2019).

97 Burcu Baykurt, "Turkey's Twitter Ban Is Easily Bypassed, but There Are No Easy Answers to Erdoğan's Abuse of Power," *LSE Europp Blog* (March 24, 2014), available at http://blogs.lse.ac.uk/europpblog/2014/03/24/turkeys-twitter-ban-is-easily-sidestepped-but-there-are-no-easy-answers-to-erdogans-abuse-of-power/ (accessed March 8, 2019).

98 Burcu Baykurt, "Once a Safe Haven, Turkey Tightens Grip on Foreign Journalists," *Columbia Journalism Review* (September 23, 2015), available at www.cjr.org/analysis/once_a_safe_haven_turkey_tightens_grip_on_foreign_journalists.php (accessed March 8, 2019).

alleged PKK militant. An angry mob attacked the *Hürriyet* offices a couple of weeks later, accusing the paper of misquoting Erdoğan. The heightened nationalist sentiment afforded the AKP a clear majority in the snap elections of late 2015 and also enabled effective criminalization of journalism that did not toe the line of the government's narrative.

A failed coup attempt and a series of terror attacks in 2016 resulted in a massive purge of public employees, members of civil society, and academics accused of having connections to terror groups such as Fethullah Gülen's network and PKK. A total of 131 media outlets were shut down due to alleged links to the Fethullahist Terrorist Organization (*Fetullahçı Terör Örgütü*, FETÖ).[99] Instituting a state of emergency for two years after the coup attempt, the government was able to rule by decree and shut down newspapers, detain or charge critical journalists and media owners, restrict access to official meetings, and ban reporting of certain issues by official decree. Facebook, Twitter, YouTube, and other social media services were briefly blocked or throttled on multiple occasions.

It was against this backdrop that Turkey held a referendum in April 2017 on several proposed amendments to the 1982 Constitution, most of which granted sweeping new powers to the president, thereby changing the country from a parliamentary democracy to a hyper-presidential system. In the run-up to the referendum, the "yes" campaign received disproportionately wide and positive coverage across the media, while the "no" campaigners were repeatedly slandered and censored.[100]

In early 2018 one of the major media companies in the country, Doğan Media Group, which owned *Hürriyet*, was sold to the AKP-friendly Demirören Group.[101] According to Erol Önderoğlu, a Turkish representative of Reporters Without Borders, this sale ensured that the government would now control "more than 85 percent of national mainstream media."[102] While there is still

99 "Over 100 Media Outlets Shut Down over Turkey's Failed Coup Attempt," *Hürriyet Daily News* (July 26, 2016), available at www.hurriyetdailynews.com/over-100-media-outlets-shut-down-over-turkeys-failed-coup-attempt–102178 (accessed July 3, 2019).

100 Ece Algan, "Media in Turkey before, during and after the Referendum," *Open Democracy* (June 2, 2017), available at www.opendemocracy.net/ece-algan/media-in-turkey-before-during-and-after-referendum (accessed March 8, 2019).

101 Daren Butler and Ece Toksabay, "Sale of Dogan Set to Tighten Erdogan's Grip over Turkish Media," *Reuters* (March 22, 2018), available at www.reuters.com/article/us-dogan-holding-m-a-demiroren/sale-of-dogan-set-to-tighten-erdogans-grip-over-turkish-media-idUSKBN1GY0EL (accessed March 8, 2019).

102 Zia Weise, "How Did Things Get So Bad for Turkey's Journalists?" *The Atlantic* (August 23, 2018), available at www.theatlantic.com/international/archive/2018/08/destroying-free-press-erdogan-turkey/568402/ (accessed March 8, 2019).

a bit of space for critical voices, these few publications are struggling financially and reporting under the routine threat – and reality – of prosecution. Turkey has submitted more legal requests to remove content or withhold accounts on Twitter since 2014 than any other country, according to Twitter's annual transparency report.[103] The government also passed new laws in 2018 to control and curb content on the internet, to which many in the country now turn in order to follow critical reporting.[104]

4 CONCLUSION

"Journalists as a species, whether working in democracies or in autocratic states," suggests media sociologist Michael Schudson, "aspire to independent reporting and commentary on current affairs."[105] Reporters in Turkey's illiberal media environment – predicated upon clientelistic relations, political instrumentalization, and (self-) censorship – discovered a short-lived opportunity to enjoy somewhat independent reporting and commentary in late 2011 and early 2012, when the AUK embarked on writing a new constitution. Ironically, journalists were able briefly to indulge solely in documenting facts, covering all sides of a political disagreement, and offering an even-handed framing of events because the commission, chiefly its chairman Cemil Çiçek, firmly set the ground rules for covering this process from the outset. The limited transparency of the commission, along with its controlling attitude toward the press, may seem to contradict the original spirit of the AUK, which intended to be democratic and inclusive. Yet the commission's attempt to police the boundaries of journalistic work by putting together a media advisory council, routinely convening with editors and reporters, and sufficiently supplying the media with enough narratives about the terms of the debate inside the AUK enabled Turkey's mainstream media to offer the basic form of accountability in democratic politics: reporting on facts in a straightforward and balanced manner.

The significance of the AUK's check on media coverage became clearer when the narrative of popular constitution making drastically changed between the end of 2012 and November 2013, when the commission was effectively dissolved. The partisan fragmentation of the media landscape, along with increasing government pressure, resulted in highly polarizing

103 See https://transparency.twitter.com/en/countries/tr.html (accessed March 26, 2019).

104 "Turkey's Government Takes New Powers to Censor the Internet," *The Economist* (May 24, 2018), available at www.economist.com/europe/2018/05/24/turkeys-government-takes-new-powers-to-censor-the-internet (accessed March 8, 2019).

105 Michael Schudson, *Why Journalism Still Matters* (Cambridge: Polity Press, 2018), 6.

and, in some cases, conflicting news stories about the constitutional debates. As more political voices outside the AUK, especially top party officials and then-Prime Minister Erdoğan, began to comment on specific articles, the coverage became more divisive, and complex debates were reduced to ideologically driven sound bites. In more independent media environments, when government officials are less unified in their views on public issues, journalists use these disagreements to offer a variety of differentiated opinions and analyses of political decision-making processes. Yet in Turkey's illiberal media environment, which markedly deteriorated from 2013 onward, the inter-elite conflict over the new constitution greatly limited the work of journalists, who had to walk a very careful line as the AKP government's practices reached new levels of authoritarianism around the same time.

This analysis of Turkey's attempt at popular constitution making and the media's limited role in the process calls into question the inherent normative value of some of the deeply held assumptions about liberal democratic processes, transparency, the media, and publicity. First, as the AUK's control over the media narrative at the beginning of the constitution making indicates, limited transparency may lead to more informative and fair coverage of political discussions. Second, more voices in public debates do not automatically translate into multi-perspectival news coverage, especially when reporters operate in an illiberal, polarizing media environment. Third, attempts to include citizen feedback and civil society input in political processes, especially via media publicity, risk disintegrating into a series of opposing monologues motivated by different political agendas instead of generating a popular dialogue and a back-and-forth negotiation of competing ideas. Rather than rejecting the value of transparency, diversity, or participation in popular constitution making as mediated by journalism, Turkey's case underscores that, without the backing of formal, independent institutions and the rule of law, these ideals are not infallibly a democratizing influence. As Walter Lippmann famously asserted, "The press is no substitute for institutions."[106]

[106] Walter Lippmann, *Public Opinion* (New York: Free Press, 1922), 229.

PART III

DEBATING AND DRAFTING THE CONSTITUTION IN 2011–2013

5

Debating State Organization Principles in the Constitutional Conciliation Commission

Gözde Böcü and Felix Petersen

"This is unfortunately part of our political culture . . . . [W]hen it overlaps with presidentialism, since no one has a magic wand, things will result in what Montesquieu predicted, and the magic wand will open the door to a magical authoritarian order."[1]

1 INTRODUCTION

The Constitutional Conciliation Commission (*Anayasa Uzlaşma Komisyonu*, AUK) was established in 2011 with the hope of drafting a new constitution for the Turkish Republic in an unprecedented participatory process. This would have been a clear break from the deeply entrenched modern practice of elitist and exclusive constitution making. In the end, the attempt to draft a constitution failed due to the commission's inability to achieve consensus. In 2017, Turkey returned to the traditional path of majoritarian imposition in constitution making through constitutional amendments imposed by a coalition of the ruling Justice and Development Party (*Adalet ve Kalkınma Partisi*, AKP) and the Nationalist Movement Party (*Milliyetçi Hareket Partisi*, MHP), which were adopted in a public referendum.[2] The amendments not only eradicate the principle of separation of powers, but also rebuild the state according to the ruling groups' interests, without taking into consideration the overall integrity of the system and its long-term implications. Through these amendments the state has been progressively centralized and can be controlled without

[1] Faruk Bal (MHP), AUK Proceedings, November 21, 2012.

[2] For majority imposition in Turkish constitution-making processes, see Hanna Lerner, *Making Constitutions in Deeply Divided Societies* (Cambridge: Cambridge University Press, 2011), 36; Andrew Arato, "The Constitutional Reform Proposal of the Turkish Government: The Return of Majority Imposition," *Constellations* 17, no. 2 (2010): 345–350.

important constitutional counterweights.[3] In this context, the popular constitution-making process of 2011–2013, albeit unsuccessful, stands out as an anomaly in Turkish constitutional politics.

Alongside the official parliamentary commission that began its work in October 2011, civil society organizations and interest groups organized public events to generate input from citizens intended to inform the constitution-making process. This approach was meant to provide a setting where constitution making was accompanied by public participation and citizen deliberation. A variety of larger and smaller initiatives brought together simulated constituent assemblies.[4] At these assemblies, randomly and nonrandomly selected citizens met to discuss the constitutive principles to be taken into consideration by the AUK. Most participants of these assemblies supported the popular election of the president (77 percent), while a majority of participants also still preferred a parliamentary over a presidential system.[5] These statistics demonstrate that most citizens favored keeping the existing political system and retaining a separation of power between a popularly elected president on one side and the Parliament with the right to nominate a government and prime minister on the other. With regard to the question of who should hold the highest political authority in the country, 56 percent were in favor of the Turkish Grand National Assembly (*Türkiye Büyük Millet Meclisi*, TBMM), 23 percent opted for the president of the republic, and 20 percent were in favor of the prime minister or the cabinet/Council of Ministers.[6]

The expectations of citizens in this regard are important, as the political system question became the most contested issue in the AUK. Despite the public's clear preferences, the question of whether to constitutionalize a parliamentary or presidential system was one of the most hotly debated issues in the AUK's deliberations. Indeed, constitutionalizing a presidential system and expanding the executive powers already acquired with the 2007 amendments were the principal goals that the ruling AKP defended in deliberations, even though it was clear that this was going to cause deadlock.[7] The

[3] Felix Petersen and Zeynep Yanaşmayan, "The Final Trick? Separation of Powers, Checks and Balances, and the Recomposition of the Turkish State," *Verfassungsblog* (January 28, 2017), see https://tinyurl.com/yazd43tu (accessed April 2, 2019).

[4] For example, the Women's Constitutional Platform (*Anayasa Kadın Platformu*, AnKP), the Ecological Constitution Initiative (*Ekolojik Anayasa Girişimi*, EAG), and the Constitution Platform (*Anayasa Platformu*, AP).

[5] Oğuz N. Babüroğlu and Gülru Z. Göker, "Going Large Scale: The Polling Conference Process for Participatory Constitution Making in Turkey," *Action Research* 12, no. 4 (2014): 374–391.

[6] TESEV, *Definitions and Expectations Regarding the New Constitution* (Istanbul, 2012), 10.

[7] For a discussion of the 2007 amendments, see Ergun Özbudun and Ömer Faruk Gençkaya, *Democratization and the Politics of Constitution-Making in Turkey* (Budapest: Central

AKP's adherence to party policy over the interests of the people (which the AKP claimed to represent) obstructed the constitution-making process. Despite political leaders' statements about the significance of public input, the AUK did not take recourse to the input generated through public participation to resolve this issue.[8] This also illustrates that the participatory process accompanying the constitution-making process was more important for society than it was for the political parties and representatives entrusted with the task of drafting a new constitution.

As the AUK did not reach consensus on most of the constitutional provisions it debated and did not constitutionalize a government system,[9] our analysis focuses on the reasons that prevented it from doing so. Apart from the fact that the AKP was persistent in its aim to constitutionalize a presidential system, which was rejected by all other parties, and that this conflict contributed to deadlock in the commission, we argue that path dependencies regarding specific state organization principles prevented delegates in the AUK from achieving consensus. The historically contested nature of certain state organization principles, the unclear meaning of constitutive political concepts, and the strategic manipulation of both by state elites in the past created a situation unfavorable for consensual constitution making. As the failed 2011–2013 process shows, political agents lacked the will, competence, or means to overcome these deep disagreements.

The chapter begins with a historical reconstruction of the modern political and constitutional history of Turkey. Here the argument is organized around the idea that statism and raison d'état were far more important organization principles than popular sovereignty, democracy, checks and balances, separation of powers, or rule of law. The latter concepts are often used as vague and indeterminate *empty signifiers* that can be filled with varying content.[10] Following the historical reconstruction, the chapter turns to the debates on principles of state organization in the AUK. Disagreements over basic political

European University Press, 2009), 97–113; Vahap Coşkun, "Constitutional Amendments under the Justice and Development Party Rule," *Insight Turkey* 15, no. 4 (2013): 95–113.

8 For statements of Turkish politicians on the relevance of the constitution-making process, see TEPAV, *The Results of the Constitution Citizens' Assembly Meetings to Be Submitted to Parliament*, May 9, 2012; see https://tinyurl.com/yarh2hzw (accessed April 2, 2019).

9 The AUK did manage to reach consensus on a few general principles such as the republican state form, the primacy of the constitution, an impartial judiciary, and a few provisions regarding the Constitutional Court.

10 Ernesto Laclau (*Emancipations*, London: Verso, 1996, 44) defines an "empty signifier" as a concept that cannot be separated from its particular moments. Empty signifiers allow different social and political actors to present their own views, visions, opinions, and convictions to fill a concept with meaning without having to seek agreement with others.

concepts (e.g., laicism, democracy, national sovereignty, political representation), principles of state organization (e.g., constitutionalism, rule of law, separation of powers), and the question of how to organize the political system (parliamentarianism/semi-presidentialism versus presidentialism) caused insurmountable deadlock and resulted in the eventual failure of popular constitution making. The chapter concludes that the failure of popular constitution making and subsequent political developments can be seen as constituting a critical juncture that eventually allowed the ruling AKP, with the help of the kingmaker MHP, to reconstruct the state according to the ideals already advocated by the AKP in the 2011–2013 debates on state organization. After the implementation of the 2017 constitutional amendments, the Turkish state is now even more autocratic and centralized than it was under the 1982 Constitution.

2 PRINCIPLES OF STATE ORGANIZATION IN TURKISH CONSTITUTIONALISM

The politics of raison d'état has been central to modern Turkey from the beginning of the republican era.[11] After proclamation of the Turkish Republic in 1923, building a new state was the goal of the new elite surrounding Mustafa Kemal (Atatürk). While supporters of Atatürk struggled with supporters of the sultan over the form of state, religious conservatives and secularist factions of society quarreled over the role of religion in public life.[12] At the same time, Kurds, religious and political minorities, and a new elite aiming to build a coherent Turkish identity fought over the form of national identity. In this context, building a strong state was necessary to exercise sovereignty in the face of both internal and external disruptions. Hence, nationalism and statism became central features of the new Turkish Republic.

The literature on path dependency assumes that institutional choices made in the past put a society on a track from which it is difficult to deviate in the future.[13] With consolidation of a certain institutional structure and

[11] Cengiz Çağla, "Turkish Politics: Raison d'État versus Republic," *International Review of Sociology* 22, no. 3 (2012): 565–574; Banu Turnaoğlu, *The Formation of Turkish Republicanism* (Princeton: Princeton University Press, 2017).

[12] Feroz Ahmad, "Politics and Political Parties in Republican Turkey," in *Cambridge History of Turkey: Vol. 4*, ed. R. Kasaba (Cambridge: Cambridge University Press, 2008), 226; Banu Turnaoğlu, "Ideological Struggle during the Formative Years of the Turkish Republic," *Middle Eastern Studies* 52, no. 4 (2016): 677–693.

[13] On path dependency, see Giovanni Capoccia and Daniel Kelemen, "The Study of Critical Junctures: Theory, Narrative, and Counterfactuals in Historical Institutionalism," *World Politics* 59, no. 3 (2007): 341–369; James Mahoney, "Path Dependence in Historical

development of organizational logic and practices, a "path is even more firmly established, for organization tends to bring with it vested interests who will choose to maintain a path even when it is not optimal."[14] As the following historical analysis of Turkish constitutional law and constitution-making processes underlines, state authority and centralization of power were more relevant than concepts associated with democracy and limited government. This set the country on a path-dependent development that prioritized raison d'état over democracy, and statist power centralization over democratic power decentralization. Assuming that constitution-making processes are potentially critical junctures, that is, events that can reset a path-dependent trajectory,[15] the analysis shows that neither in past constitution-making processes nor in the most recent failed popular constitution-making process did Turkey succeed in changing tracks from a statist to a democratic path. The 2017 constitutional amendments entrenched centralized power even more firmly and consolidated an increasingly authoritarian statist path.

2.1 *National Sovereignty, Republicanism, and Representative Government*

While the Ottoman Constitution of 1876 determined that imperial sovereignty belonged to the eldest prince of the House of Osman (Art. 3), in the republican constitutions of 1921 and 1924 the actor possessing sovereignty is the nation. Article 1 of the 1921 Constitution declares that "sovereignty belongs unconditionally to the nation," which means that the whole "system of administration is based on the principle that the people personally and effectively direct their own destinies." The radical democratic language codified with the first republican constitution can be explained by the aims of the revolutionary action against the old system: The declaration of unrestricted popular sovereignty was meant to make it abundantly clear that sultanic sovereignty was over.[16] This narrative is developed in the 1924 Constitution, declaring that sovereignty belongs "without restriction" to the nation (Art. 3) and is exercised by the Grand National Assembly on behalf of the nation (Art. 4). Likewise, the 1961

Sociology," *Theory and Society* 29, no. 4 (2000): 507–548; Margaret Levi, "A Model, a Method, and a Map: Rational Choice in Comparative and Historical Analysis," in *Comparative Politics: Rationality, Culture, and Structure*, eds. M. I. Lichbach and A. S. Zuckerman (Cambridge: Cambridge University Press, 1997), 19–41.

14 Levi, "A Model, a Method, and a Map," 28.

15 Capoccia and Kelemen ("The Study of Critical Junctures," 341–342) define critical junctures as "brief phases of institutional flux … during which more dramatic change is possible."

16 Metin Heper, *The State Tradition in Turkey* (Walkington: Eothen Press, 1985), 49, 51.

Constitution (Art. 4) and the 1982 Constitution (Art. 6) reiterate the unrestricted sovereignty of the nation.

The two early republican constitutions stipulate that the Grand National Assembly is the sole and rightful body representing the Turkish nation and introduce the idea of representative government.[17] All four constitutions affirm that state organs exercise national sovereignty, and the 1961 Constitution even declares that judicial power is "exercised by independent courts on behalf of the nation" (Art. 7). Furthermore, all four constitutions contain a clause asserting that members of Parliament do not represent their constituencies or constituents, but the whole of the Turkish nation.[18] While the 1924 Constitution defines the president of the republic as an "intermediary" through which Parliament "exercises its executive authority" (Art. 7), the 1961 and 1982 Constitutions establish the president as another representative of the nation.[19]

Whereas the first two republican constitutions did not contain a clause on political parties, the 1961 and 1982 Constitutions define political parties as central to modern politics and determine their rights and limits in various articles.[20] None of the four constitutions explicitly defines political parties as relevant for representative government. More importantly, political practice shows that pluralist political representation has been curbed through the use of state power, which tightly regulates political contestation. Since its establishment in 1961, the Turkish Constitutional Court (*Anayasa Mahkemesi*, AYM) has banned a total of twenty-seven political parties.[21] The majority of parties banned by the AYM either advocated Kurdish emancipation and independence, thereby posing a threat to national and territorial integrity, or belonged to the broader spectrum of political Islam, thereby violating the laicist character of the republic.[22] This indicates that the court was serving political elites in power by helping them reduce the number of political parties and interests authorized to compete for office.

Furthermore, state elites sought other legal means to obstruct pluralist political representation. The coup d'état in 1980 and the introduction of

[17] TC-1921, Art. 2 and 4; TC-1924, Art. 4.

[18] TC-1921, Art. 5; TC-1924, Art. 13; TC-1961, Art. 76; TC-1982, Art. 80.

[19] TC-1961, Art. 97, 110; TC-1982, Art. 104, 117.

[20] TC-1961, Art. 19, 56–57, 84, 92, 94, 119–120, 148–149, 151; TC-1982, Art. 31, 33, 52–53, 68–69, 101, 106, 135, 149, 171.

[21] Ödel Celep, "The Political Causes of Party Closures in Turkey," *Parliamentary Affairs* 67, no. 2 (2014): 371–390.

[22] Ergun Özbudun, "Party Prohibition Cases: Different Approaches by the Turkish Constitutional Court and the European Court of Human Rights," *Democratization* 17, no. 1 (2010): 125–142.

a 10 percent electoral threshold for entry into Parliament shortly thereafter created a winner-takes-all electoral system.[23] Ever since, the electoral process has disproportionately served parties able to win majorities, reduced medium-sized parties to an insignificant oppositional role, and excluded small parties entirely from politics. In other words, political elites have sought to obstruct pluralist political participation by limiting political representation to organizations that are able to muster large majorities and that support the specific idea of the Turkish state with all its characteristics (e.g., laicism and Turkish nationalism). The restrictive and selective handling of political party organization under the 1961 and 1982 Constitutions reveals some of the democratic deficits in Turkey.

The central component of Turkey's modern constitutional tradition is republicanism, which, in political practice, has taken on a statist character. Particularly in the founding years, the republican state was identified as the instrument needed to transform and reorganize society. It was constructed as a sacred institution that demands submission and requires protection.[24] Part and parcel of this statist conception of republicanism are the principles of laicism and territorial integrity. Both of these principles have shaped modern Turkish politics over the course of the twentieth century. The prevalence of these two principles can be explained with reference to the fundamental challenges that religious and secessionist movements posed to the nascent Turkish state. Territorial integrity was from the beginning essential, as a state can only claim national sovereignty when it holds power over a territory and a population. With regard to the challenge from religious segments of society, a similar argument can be made. At the moment of the founding of the republic, at least two competing conceptions of sovereignty clashed: popular (national) and divine sovereignty. For clerical republicans, the new state was to be grounded in the Islamic tradition. Secular republicans strongly opposed this idea and feared that the continuing existence of the caliphate and the influence of religious leaders would diminish or destroy the accomplishments of the republican revolution.[25] With enactment of the 1924 Constitution, the

[23] The 10 percent threshold was introduced in 1983 (Law on Parliamentary Elections No. 2839 – *Milletvekili Seçimi Kanunu Nr.* 2839, in *Resmî Gazete*, October 6, 1983, Sayı: 18076). Among all member states of the Venice Commission, Turkey has the highest election threshold (Venice Commission, Compilation of Venice Commission Opinions and Reports concerning Thresholds Which Bar Parties from Access to Parliament, Strasbourg, 2018, 9).

[24] Suna Kili, *Turkish Constitutional Developments and Assembly Debates on the Constitutions of 1924 and 1961* (Istanbul: Robert College Research Center, 1971), 63; Heper, *The State Tradition in Turkey*, 48–52.

[25] Turnaoğlu, "Ideological Struggle during the Formative Years of the Turkish Republic," 681–683.

caliphate was abolished and secular republicanism triumphed over clerical Islamic republicanism. Laicism was introduced as a constitutional principle through an amendment in 1937. The amended Article 2 of the 1924 Constitution defined the Turkish state as republican, national, laicist, and revolutionary.[26] This amendment established the constitutional characteristics of the laicist Turkish Republic to which the 1961 and 1982 Constitutions continued to reference.

2.2 *Democracy*

Neither of the first two constitutions mentioned democracy or pluralism as foundations of the republican order. Democracy was conceptually introduced with the 1961 Constitution, paradoxically as a result of a military intervention. Article 2 does not straightforwardly define Turkey as a democracy but as a national democratic state (*millî, demokratik ... bir hukuk devleti*). With the 1982 Constitution, "democratic" (*demokratik*) becomes an unpaired characteristic of state organization. Analytically, we observe that in both the 1961 and 1982 Constitutions, concepts such as "democracy" and "democratic" are empty signifiers, that is, concepts that can be filled with varying content. At least four different types of reference to this conceptual field can be identified: 1) acclamatory references that summon the democratic spirit of the Turkish nation; 2) references that define the (democratic) state form; 3) references declaring (more or less explicitly) that the state has to act in accordance with "democratic principles"; and 4) references to democracy used to justify state action against agents opposing the state.

Acclamatory references to democracy characterize the 1982 Constitution. The preamble, for instance, refers to Turks as democracy-loving (*demokrasiye âşık*) people. The 1961 and 1982 Constitutions declare, in a rather acclamatory manner, that political parties are essential to democracy.[27] Moreover, both the 1961 and 1982 Constitutions refer to democracy in the oath members of Parliament and the president have to take at their inaugurations.[28]

To determine the state form of the republic, the preamble of the 1961 Constitution declares the establishment of a state based on the democratic rule of law (*demokratik hukuk devletini*); Article 2 defines the republic as a national state based on the democratic rule of law (*millî, demokratik, ... bir*

[26] Constitutional Amendment of Art. 2 through Law No. 3115 of February 2, 1937, in *Resmî Gazete*, February 13, 1937, Sayı: 3533.

[27] TC-1961, Art. 57; TC-1982, Art. 68.

[28] TC-1961, Art. 77, 96; TC-1982, Art. 81, 103.

hukuk devletidir); and provisional Article 4 proclaims that all legal measures undertaken as a result of the coup d'état aimed at building a normal democratic regime (*normal demokratik rejimi*). Likewise, the Constitution of 1982 declares in the preamble that it establishes the legal order of a free democracy (*hürriyetçi demokrasi*), and Article 2 mentions that the state has a "democratic, secular" nature based on the "social rule of law" (*demokratik, laik ve sosyal bir hukuk devletidir*).

The terms "democracy" and "democratic" appear in both constitutions as well to signify in a rather vague manner that the state should act in accordance with democratic principles. The 1982 Constitution postulates in Article 5 that the state has to protect the republic and democracy, and in Article 13 that measures limiting fundamental rights cannot contradict the principles of a democratic society. Article 41 of the 1961 Constitution entrusts the state with measures that are supposed to promote and support economic, social, and cultural developments in a democratic manner, and it explains under provisions related to the right to work and prohibition of slavery (Art. 42) that the citizen's duty to physical and mental labor is to be organized on the basis of democratic principles and through the law.

These three types of reference clearly employ terms related to the conceptual field of democracy in an ambiguous manner. In this regard, however, Turkey is not an exception to the rule. The constitutions of other countries also often codify the conceptual field of democracy in rather indeterminate terminology. Its more concrete meaning is generally developed through democratic politics and judicial review. In Turkey, judicial review did not contribute to further clarification of terms related to the conceptual field of democracy. Not even once has the Constitutional Court elaborated or specified the core principles of democracy or the free democratic order in a systematic manner.[29] In a number of rulings, the AYM has explained what democracy means by invoking other indeterminate concepts (e.g., constitutional state, state of law, requirements of liberal democracy). Aware of this problem, some judges noted in their dissenting opinions that separation of powers, equal entitlement to political rights, and gender equality are also

29 For different rulings elaborating the concept democracy, see "Constitutional Basis of Privatization Law" (E. 1994/49–K. 1994/45–2), July 7, 1994, in *Resmî Gazete*, September 10, 1994, Sayı: 22047; "Headscarf Decision I" (E. 1989/01–K. 1989/12), March 7, 1989, in *Resmî Gazete*, July 5, 1989, Sayı: 20216; "Immunity of Members of Parliament" (E. 1994/09–K. 1994/28), March 21, 1994, not published in the *Resmî Gazete*; "Right of Minorities to Choose a Non-Turkish Family Name" (E. 2009/47–K. 2011/51), March 17, 2011, in *Resmî Gazete*, July 12, 2011, Sayı: 27992. For English translations, see Silvia von Steinsdorff, Ece Göztepe, Maria Abad Andrade, and Felix Petersen, *The Constitutional Court of Turkey: Judicial Politics between Authoritarianism and Democracy* (Baden-Baden: Nomos, forthcoming).

constitutive of democracy.[30] Nonetheless, the court has not managed to overcome the indeterminacy around the conceptual field of democracy.

Focusing on the fourth type of reference, that is, references to democracy to justify state action against citizens and organizations opposing the state, we observe that democracy is employed in Turkish constitutional law to control society. Article 26 of the 1961 Constitution states that publications of political parties and organizations will be regulated according to democratic principles (*demokratik esaslarla*).[31] Article 57 obliges political parties to comply with the principles of a democratic and secular republic (*demokratik ve lâik Cumhuriyet*). Moreover, this clause stipulates that constitutional review of activities and financial matters of political parties will be regulated through laws that are based on democratic principles (*demokratik esaslara*). Articles 46 and 122 follow a similar rationale but address different sectors of society: The first addresses unions and labor organizations, and the second stipulates that professional groups cannot contradict democratic principles (*demokratik esaslara*). In the 1982 Constitution these provisions reemerge in almost the same wording but under different article numbers (Art. 51, 68, 69).

Two amendments that were added to the 1961 Constitution in 1971 and 1973 introduce the term "free democratic order" (*hür demokratik düzen*). Paradoxically, the concept is not employed to define the state form. Rather, it stipulates that a state of emergency may be declared in one or several regions when the "free democratic order" is under attack (amended Art. 124). It also stipulates that special state security courts (*Devlet Güvenlik Mahkemeleri*) have to be established to try crimes against the integrity of the country, the free democratic order, or the republican state (amended Art. 136).[32] The concept "free democratic order" resurfaces in state of emergency provisions of the 1982 Constitution (Art. 120, 122, 143). This illustrates that in Turkish constitutional law, democracy and related

30 See "Parliamentary Procedure of Presidential Election" (E. 2007/45–K. 2007/54), May 1, 2007, in *Resmî Gazete*, June 27, 2007, Sayı: 26565; "Annulment concerning Free Trade Area Law No. 3218" (E. 1985/21–K. 1986/23), October 6, 1986, in *Resmî Gazete*, March 14, 1987, Sayı: 19400; "Right of Female Spouses to Use Their Premarital Family Name II" (E. 2009/85–K. 2011/49), March 10, 2011, in *Resmî Gazete*, October 21, 2011, Sayı: 28091; English translations in Steinsdorff et al., *The Constitutional Court of Turkey*.

31 A 1971 amendment to Art. 22 of the 1961 Constitution determined that newspapers can be closed down upon a judicial decision declaring that the characteristics of the national, secular, and democratic republic have been violated; see Law No. 1488 of September 20, 1971, in *Resmî Gazete*, September 22, 1971, Sayı: 13964.

32 Constitutional amendment through Law No. 1488 of September 20, 1971; Constitutional Amendment through Law No. 1699 of March 15, 1973 (*Resmî Gazete*, March 20, 1973, Sayı: 14482). In addition, Law No. 1773 of June 26, 1973 (*Resmî Gazete*, July 11, 1973, Sayı: 14591) expansively defined the charges to be brought before state security courts.

concepts can be a means to control and regulate society instead of empowering individuals to freely organize.

2.3 *Organization of Government and Separation of Powers*

The first two republican constitutions codified an assembly government system (*meclis hükümeti sistemi*), that is, a system governed through an assembly that unites legislative and executive powers. Neither of the two constitutions sufficiently separates legislative and executive powers; they are, rather, concentrated in the Assembly, a situation that conforms to the "fusion of powers" doctrine as defined by Walter Bagehot.[33] In Turkish politics, fusion of powers has been problematic. Ergun Özbudun and Faruk Gençkaya remark that "[b]oth in the single-party (1925–1946) and multi-party (1946–1960) years, the authoritarian leadership of the chief executives and strong party discipline reduced the Assembly to a clearly secondary role."[34] While the (nominal or normative) 1924 Constitution established an assembly government system that centralized power in the legislative body, the political state was in fact dominated by the executive.

With the adoption of the 1961 Constitution, the assembly government system "was abandoned in favor of a parliamentary form of government based on a moderate separation of powers."[35] The term "separation of powers" (*kuvvetler ayrımı*) does not appear in the constitution, but the principle is entrenched in it. Although the basic government structure (i.e., the institutions) does not significantly change, its organization (i.e., relation of institutions) changes: Article 5 declares that the legislative prerogative (*yasama yetkisi*) belongs to the Turkish Grand National Assembly, while Article 6 establishes that the executive function (*yürütme görevi*) is carried out through the president of the republic and the Council of Ministers. Most interestingly is the change in wording – while the 1924 Constitution employs "legislative authority" (*teşri salâhiyeti*) and "executive power" (*icra kudreti*), the 1961 Constitution chooses the more formalistic "legislative prerogative" (*yasama yetkisi*) and "executive function" (*yürütme görevi*).

The constitutionalization of a second chamber of Parliament (the Senate) introduced a separation of powers in lawmaking. The 1961 Constitution

33 Walter Bagehot invented the term "fusion of powers" to describe the unclear separation of legislative and executive powers in the British parliamentary system; see Bagehot, *The English Constitution* (London: Chapman and Hall, 1867), 12–18.

34 Özbudun and Gençkaya, *Democratization and the Politics of Constitution-Making in Turkey*, 11.

35 Kili, *Turkish Constitutional Developments*, 70.

determines that the Senate can veto laws of the first chamber with an absolute or two-thirds majority (Art. 70). Such senate vetoes can only be overturned by the first chamber with the same (absolute or two-thirds) majority (Art. 92). As the president was to be elected by Parliament from among its members (Art. 95), this entanglement of legislative and executive branches provided additional checks and balances. The two chambers also had the authority to impeach the president (Art. 99). As a balance, the constitution granted the president veto powers in legislation (Art. 93) and a partial power to dissolve Parliament (Art. 108).

With regard to the judicial branch, the 1961 Constitution was also more explicit than its predecessor. The drafting commission explained in a report submitted to the 1960 constituent assembly that in the future all state activity would be subject to judicial review through the Constitutional Court. Establishing such a court was mentioned by many delegates in the 1960 debates as a significant improvement in the separation of powers.[36] The explicit powers, composition, and role of the newly established Constitutional Court were laid out in eight articles (Art. 145–152). Its role in controlling politics was emphasized and further elaborated in articles that concern the role of political parties (Art. 19, 57). Theoretically, this construction is not problematic, and other constitutional courts have similar powers. As indicated above, however, in practice the Turkish court, particularly in its approach to party prohibition, was an obstacle to free democratic government.[37] Even if the constitution drafters aimed to subject all state organs and their actions to judicial review, in practice the court often served powerful groups and government by preserving their hegemony.[38]

The 1982 Constitution is most explicit with regard to separation of powers. As the constitution is often framed as reflecting "the authoritarian, statist, and tutelary mentality of its military founders,"[39] this is indeed interesting. While

36 Ibid.

37 Celep, "The Political Causes of Party Closures in Turkey," 371.

38 Some scholars portray the Turkish Constitutional Court as a defender of raison d'état and of a specific political hegemony (e.g., Ceren Belge, "Friends of the Court: The Republican Alliance and Selective Activism of the Constitutional Court of Turkey," *Law & Society Review* 40, no. 3 (2006): 653–692; Esin Örücü, "The Constitutional Court of Turkey: The *Anayasa Mahkemesi* as the Protector of the System," *Journal of Comparative Law* 3, no. 2 (2008), 254–268). The president of the Constitutional Court, Zühtü Arslan, has argued that "the court has interpreted the Constitution in such a way that individual rights and liberties have been sacrificed for the sake of the state, that is, for the sake of *sacred authority*." See Zühtü Arslan, "Conflicting Paradigms: Political Rights in the Turkish Constitutional Court," *Critique: Critical Middle Eastern Studies* 11, no. 1 (2002): 9–25 (emphasis in original).

39 Ergun Özbudun, "Turkey's Search for a New Constitution," *Insight Turkey* 14, no. 1 (2012): 39–50, 39.

the term separation of powers (*kuvvetler ayrımı*) appears only in the preamble, separation of powers and checks and balances are codified in various provisions: Article 7 grants the Turkish Grand National Assembly the legislative prerogative (*yasama yetkisi*); Article 8 ascribes executive prerogative and function (*yürütme yetkisi ve görevi*) to the president of the republic and the Council of Ministers; and Article 9 attributes judicial power to independent courts. Formally, checks and balances also structure the organization of government. Although Parliament is authorized to legislate and to control (*denetlemek*) the Council of Ministers (Art. 87), the president has the right to return laws to Parliament that he refuses to countersign (Art. 89).

With respect to the judiciary, the 1982 Constitution explicitly codifies the extent to which the separation of powers principle applies to the organization of the republic. Article 138 stipulates that other organs of the state shall not interfere with the work of the judicial branch, and it prohibits the legislative Assembly from making statements "relating to the exercise of judicial power concerning a case under trial." The case law of the Constitutional Court sheds light on the separation of powers regime of the 1982 Constitution. For instance, the AYM declared excessive decree powers of the Council of Ministers unconstitutional, as the legislative power of the executive "unbalances the relation [of Parliament and government], which leads to superiority of the executive over the legislative organ."[40] Furthermore, it has declared that "the prosecution of civil servants should not fall under the responsibility of the executive," but must be carried out by the judiciary.[41] Perhaps motivated by sheer institutional interest, these rulings show that, in contrast to the case law on democracy, the court did contribute to some extent to specifying what separation of powers means. Nevertheless, it does not always systematically determine or develop its concepts. Although it highlights the necessity of separating legislative, executive, and judicial functions in the rulings mentioned, it does not always stick to those principles in later rulings.

2.4 Rule of Law

According to all constitutional texts, the Turkish Republic is formally a state based on the rule of law. All constitutions refer to the rule of law implicitly or

40 "Time Limits of Enabling Laws" (E. 1988/62–K. 1990/03), February 6, 1990, in *Resmî Gazete*, October 12, 1990, Sayı: 20663; English translation in Steinsdorff et al., *The Constitutional Court of Turkey*.

41 "Limits of Administrative Privilege in Prosecution" (E. 1991/26–K.1992/11), February 27, 1992, in *Resmî Gazete*, November 23, 1992, Sayı: 21414; English translation in Steinsdorff et al., *The Constitutional Court of Turkey*.

explicitly, and the Constitutional Court has elaborated what the rule of law entails. However, the selective application of the law (e.g., weak protection of minorities, prosecution on the basis of political interests) and some homegrown constitutional constructions (e.g., broad grounds for rights limitations, special courts to try crimes against the state) have significantly impeded the quality of the rule-of-law regime throughout the republican era.

The rule of law was not introduced as an individual characteristic of the state in the first two republican constitutions. But the 1921 Constitution stipulates in various articles that government should be organized on the basis of law (Art. 8, 11, 20). With the 1924 Constitution, the contours of a rule-of-law regime became more visible. Article 69 declares, "All Turks are equal before the law and are obliged to respect the law." Furthermore, this constitution enshrined the idea that fundamental rights are inalienable and can be restricted only by law (Art. 72). Similar to its predecessor, the 1924 Constitution also specified that the regulation of different aspects of government organization should be based on law (Art. 18, 43, 47, 48, 53, 55, 56).[42] Neither in its original form nor after amendment, however, did the 1924 Constitution define the republic explicitly as a state under the rule of law.

The objective of the 1961 Constitution was to establish a rule-of-law regime in order to enable the country to further modernize and democratize. Accordingly, it established the "supreme authority of the Constitution" (Art. 8) and defined Turkey as a "State governed by the rule of law, based on human rights, and the fundamental tenets set forth in the preamble" (Art. 2). The constitution also declared the independence of courts (Art. 132) and established the Constitutional Court (Art. 147–152). Likewise, the 1982 Constitution defined the state as governed by the rule of law (Art. 2, Art. 5). It proclaimed equality before the law (Art. 10), prohibited extraordinary tribunals and stated that individuals must be tried in designated courts (Art. 37), and declared the independence of the judiciary and the courts (Art. 138). Furthermore, it obliged political organizations to respect the rule-of-law principle. Article 68 states that members of Parliament have to swear in their oath "to remain loyal to the supremacy of law" (Art. 81) and that the president of the republic must abide by the rule of law (Art. 103).

42 The 1924 Constitution comprises a number of other relevant provisions to institutionalize a state under the rule of law, that is, organization of judicial power and courts by law (Art. 53), independence of judges who are "subject only to the law" (Art. 54), and the right to judicial assistance (Art. 59). Moreover, it stipulates that the border between one person's liberty and another person's liberty is determined only by law (Art. 68), that arrests can be made only based on law (Art. 72), and that expropriation/confiscation of private property must be determined by law and compensated for (Art. 74).

Judicial review was considered by constitution makers and observers of Turkish politics as one of the crucial elements established with the 1961 Constitution that would help realize the promise of a prospering democratic society. Yet the Turkish Constitutional Court was never designed to be a protector of fundamental rights but a guardian of the constitutional (state) order. In its first ruling, the court declared individual application by a single member of Parliament unconstitutional.[43] Thus, early on it deprived itself of the possibility to set precedent and open a loophole for future individual applications. Nonetheless, the case law of the AYM on the rule of law shows that the court contributed to an understanding of the rule of law. It established in 1965 that a state under the rule of law is a body that respects, promotes, and maintains human rights. In practice, the judges argued, the state had to stand in conformity with the constitution and the law, and its acts were subject to judicial review. Here, the AYM affirmed its own authority and declared the absolute superiority of the law, which was to stand even above the legislature.[44] In another relevant ruling in 1975, the AYM declared unconstitutional an amendment enacted under the state of emergency regime authorizing military judges in times of war to be chosen from among nonprofessional jurists. It held that this approach to the administration of justice violated Article 2 of the Constitution, which deems Turkey a state governed by the rule of law that protects and promotes human rights.[45] Both of these rulings show that in developing the concept of the rule of law, for strategic reasons the AYM provided an interpretation that affirms and elaborates its own authority and the boundaries of the judicial branch.

The Constitutional Court can, therefore, be considered an important actor in facilitating a legal understanding of the rule of law, as it drew the constitutional borders that state, government, political parties, and other entities should not trespass in the early years after its establishment. At the same time, the court has also participated, through party prohibition, in limiting political pluralism by banning parties that were supposedly a threat to relatively indeterminate characteristics of the republic – nationalism and territorial integrity (directed against Kurdish parties) and the laicist social

43 "Decision on Individual Petition to Constitutional Court" (E. 1962/2–K. 1962/1), September 5, 1962, in *Resmî Gazete*, October 3, 1962, Sayı: 11222.

44 "Annulment Case concerning Criminal Code Law No. 5844" (E. 1963/173–K. 1965/40), September 26, 1965, in *Resmî Gazete*, July 25, 1967, Sayı: 12656; see also Sait Güran, "Administrative Law," in *Introduction to Turkish Law*, eds. T. Ansay and D. Wallace (New York: Kluwer, 2011), 58.

45 "Annulment Case concerning Law No. 1602 on Military Courts" (E. 1975/159–K. 1975/216), December 18, 1975, in *Resmî Gazete*, April 12, 1976, Sayı: 15557.

and political order (directed against religious, Islamic parties). Similarly, in other human rights issues, it had adopted a statist approach. The AYM has consistently protected the headscarf ban.[46] Until recently, the court determined that a husband's legal prerogative to decide on his wife's family name did not violate gender equality. In one of these rulings judges argued on paternalistic lines that "public interest, public order, and some necessities prove" that it is preferable to prioritize the husband over the wife.[47] In a decision regarding the right to choose a non-Turkish family name, the court upheld the state's approach to naming practices against the right to self-determination of minorities.[48]

This ambiguity in the AYM's jurisprudence is related to the fact that the constitution itself, or more specifically the homegrown constitutional constructions, allow a restrictive approach to rights. In other words, "laws have ... allowed the interpretation of almost any act of opposition, advocacy of pluralism and diversity, demand for religious freedom, or criticism directed at the government or the military as a security threat, and permitted the criminalization of a wide range of thoughts and acts."[49] Turkuler Isiksel has argued that Turkey's tradition of authoritarian constitutionalism entails that human rights abuses are frequent even as constitutional discipline is upheld.[50] Hence, a major problem with regard to the rule of law is that constitutional provisions incorporate problematic clauses stipulating broad grounds to deny rights or prohibit organizations.

In the 1961 Constitution the right to demonstrate (Art. 28) and the right to form associations (Art. 29) can be restricted to maintain public order and morality. Article 19 on religious freedom states that religion and religious feelings must not be exploited for "political or personal benefit, or for gaining power," and that the state and social order cannot be based on "religious dogmas." Political parties violating this statute will be

46 "Headscarf Decision III" (E. 2008/16–K. 2008/116), June 5, 2008, in *Resmî Gazete*, October 22, 2008, Sayı: 27032; English translation in Steinsdorff et al., *The Constitutional Court of Turkey*.

47 "Right of Female Spouses to Use Their Premarital Family Name I" (E. 1997/61–K. 1998/59), September 29, 1998, in *Resmî Gazete*, November 15, 2002, Sayı: 24937; English translation in Steinsdorff et al., *The Constitutional Court of Turkey*. For a discussion of these rulings, see Felix Petersen, "Judicial Review and Social Construction: The Case of the Turkish Constitutional Court,"*Research and Policy on Turkey* 3, no. 1 (2018): 18–39.

48 "Right of Minorities to Choose a Non-Turkish Family Name" (E. 2009/47–K. 2011/51).

49 Zehra F. Kabasakal Arat, "Conclusion: Turkey's Prospects and Broader Implications," in *Human Rights in Turkey*, ed. Z. F. Kabasakal Arat (Philadelphia: University of Pennsylvania Press, 2007), 275–288, 282.

50 Turkuler Isiksel, "Between Text and Context: Turkey's Tradition of Authoritarian Constitutionalism," *International Journal of Constitutional Law* 11, no. 3 (2013): 702–726, 706.

"permanently closed down" by the Constitutional Court. Under the provisions spelling out rights and limits of political parties, Article 57 states that parties have to organize without violating "the principles of a democratic and secular republic, based on human rights and liberties, or the fundamental principles of the State's territorial and national integrity." The Constitutional Court is here again explicitly authorized to "permanently" ban parties that do not conform to this provision. In the 1982 Constitution the article on limitations of rights and freedoms (Art. 13) comprises a whole list of indeterminate legal concepts[51] that provide grounds for rights limitations, including "safeguarding the indivisible integrity of the State with its territory and nation, national sovereignty, the Republic, national security, public order, general peace, the public interest, public morals, and public health." In the face of these broad grounds to limit rights, the constitution provides only vague guarantees of the rights themselves, with Article 13 noting that rights restrictions "shall not conflict with the requirements of the democratic order of society." According to Articles 14 and 68, the Constitutional Court can ban political parties that do not conform to a variety of broad principles (e.g., indivisible integrity of the state with its territory and nation, existence of the Turkish state and republic, relevance of fundamental rights and freedoms) or that aim to replace the republic by empowering "an individual or a group of people" or by "establishing the hegemony of one social class over others."

Another problem of the rule-of-law regime is the existence and persistence of special security courts to try political dissenters. The tradition of special courts and practices of sentencing dissenters goes back to the Ottoman period. As early as the first state of emergency provisions enacted during the Ottoman Empire, a special court was established to prosecute and try actors standing in opposition to the regime.[52] The establishment of state security courts through amendment in 1973 thus marked the return to another problematic manifestation of path dependency in Turkish constitutional law. These courts were authorized to try crimes on broad allegations such as acting against the territory, the nation, the free democratic order, the republican state (with its specific characteristics), and state security (am. Art. 136). Although verdicts could be appealed before the Court of Cassation (*Yargıtay*), this court upheld

[51] On legal indeterminacy, see Brian Leiter, "Legal Indeterminacy," *Legal Theory* 1, no. 4 (1995): 481–492.

[52] Noémi Lévy-Aksu, "An Ottoman Variation on the State of Siege: The Invention of the Idare-I Örfiyye during the First Constitutional Period," *New Perspectives on Turkey* 55, no. 1 (2016): 5–28, 21.

most decisions of the state security courts (102 of 143).[53] In 1974 the AYM declared the law on state security courts unconstitutional on procedural grounds.[54] With enactment of the 1982 Constitution, state security courts were again formally established as part of the Turkish judicial system (Art. 143). They covered the same crimes and were equipped with the same powers as under the 1961 Constitution (as amended in 1973). Under the auspices of meeting the requirements for EU accession, state security courts were abolished and replaced by the so-called heavy penal courts of peace (*Ağır Ceza Mahkemeleri*, ACM) in 2004.[55] As the same judges who had presided over state security courts in the past presided over cases in the heavy penal courts, it was obvious after a few years that the changes promised by the AKP government were not fulfilled.[56] While the name of the courts had been changed, the institutional structure itself was largely maintained. In 2014, the law on heavy penal courts was again amended, although the change did not bring them more in line with the principles of the rule of law.[57] This shows that both the constitution and ordinary laws maintain, despite frequent amendment, the problematic institution of special courts to try offenses against the state, the territory, the nation, and the republic. This is a significant impediment to genuine implementation of the rule of law.

A comparison of the different elements of the rule of law in the four republican constitutions shows that the rule-of-law regime has developed incrementally – at least on the textual level. We can argue that the basic constitutional codification of the rule of law has improved over the course of the four constitutions. In the latter two constitutions, however, some constitutional constructions still contradict the rule-of-law principle. Moreover, the broad grounds on which rights can be limited and the weak protection of minority rights and political pluralism through state organs have further prevented the incremental textual improvements in the rule of law from being applied to political practice and government.

53 William Hale, "Turkish Democracy in Travail: The Case of the State Security Courts," *The World Today* 33, no. 5 (1977): 186–194, 188.

54 "Legal Basis of the Formation of State Security Courts" (E. 1974/35–K. 1975/126), May 6, 1975, in *Resmî Gazete*, October 11, 1975, Sayı: 15380; English translation in Steinsdorff et al., *The Constitutional Court of Turkey*.

55 Law No. 5170 of May 7, 2004 (*Resmî Gazete*, May 22, 2004, Sayı: 25469) abolished state security courts. Heavy Penal Courts of Peace were established by Law No. 5235 of September 26, 2004 (*Resmî Gazete*, October 7, 2004, Sayı: 25606).

56 Amnesty International, *Turkey: Justice Delayed and Denied*, EUR 44/013/2006 (September 2006), 5; see https://tinyurl.com/y6uu7gfj (accessed April 2, 2019).

57 Law No. 6545 of June 18, 2014 (*Resmî Gazete*, June 28, 2014, Sayı: 29044) amended Art. 10 of Law No. 5235.

3 DEBATING PRINCIPLES OF STATE ORGANIZATION IN THE AUK (2011–2013)

After several months of negotiation, the AUK was only able to agree on a limited number of articles concerning principles of state organization: the republican state form (Art. 157), the superiority and binding force of the constitution (Art. 161), and certain provisions regulating fundamental rights and the judiciary.[58] Democracy, rule of law, and laicism were also included in the separate party proposals for the provision on characteristics of the republic (Art. 149), but agreement was not reached on this article.[59] As AUK members disagreed on particular aspects to regulate and define these constitutive concepts and develop a government system from these fundamental principles, the commission remained deeply divided over most articles on state organization.

Overall, the debates were very much shaped by past experiences, which complicated the attempt to draft a new democratic constitution. The specter of restrictive application of characteristics of the republic (e.g., national sovereignty and laicism) turned debates on state organization principles emanating from the republican state form into extremely controversial discussions. The commission could not reach agreement on the meaning and role of national sovereignty and laicism. The lack of consensus on the meaning of democracy was also obvious. Democracy appeared in the AUK debates as an empty signifier, inviting different agents to apply their subjective understandings of the concept. With regard to democratic practice, the tendency of the AKP to assume the role of the exclusive representative of the people in the process became a central problem for the formation of a broad coalition to draft and adopt a new constitution.

Although separation of powers as a doctrine was clarified through judicial review in the past, its meaning, scope, and actual implementation remained contested in the AUK. In particular, debates on the government system show that past violations of the separation of powers principle, not least under the AKP government, made representatives of opposition parties wary that without clearly entrenching strong checks and balances in the new constitution,

58 The AUK agreed on articles limiting (Art. 41, 42) and protecting (Art. 43) fundamental rights and freedoms, independence and impartiality of the judiciary (Art. 112), security of tenure of judges and public prosecutors (Art. 114, 115), term of office and termination of membership of Constitutional Court judges (Art. 121), decisions of the Constitutional Court (Art. 126), and the right to claim unconstitutionality before courts (Art. 127). See List of Agreed Articles, in this volume Appendix B.

59 List of Non-Agreed Articles, in this volume Appendix C.

government would not be exercised according to democratic standards. In the end, the AKP's insistence on the presidential system, arguably in their view the system guaranteeing separation of powers to the greatest extent, and the rejection of this form of government by the other three parties – reflecting their view that under presidentialism power centralization and undermining of checks and balances are most likely to occur – caused such significant deadlock that this controversy marked the beginning of the end of the popular constitution-making process. Draft articles regulating the executive remained especially full of contradictory counterproposals.[60] Our analysis shows that the intensity of and reasons for disagreement played out differently for each state organization principle. Alliances between drafting parties shifted in accordance with political ideologies and calculus. Ultimately, it is not surprising that 47 of 112 non-agreed articles concern state organization principles.

3.1 *Republicanism and Its Characteristics: Laicism, National Sovereignty, Democracy*

Drafters had to address the crucial question of whether to maintain or change defining state organization principles. While they agreed on the republic as the state form, three key characteristics of Turkish republicanism – laicism, national sovereignty, and democracy – emerged as highly polarizing. Against the backdrop of the historical reconstruction provided above, this does not come as a surprise – as all three characteristics were applied to restrict rights and limit politics and society, they are (essentially) contested. Delegates of different political colors were unable to overcome past mistakes, choosing instead to embrace them. The path dependency of a rigid state order utilizing specific political principles to regulate and suppress certain identities thereby disrupted the prospects of constitutionalizing a democratic state.

Debates on Laicism

During meetings of the commission in August and September 2012, disagreement emerged over laicism, its role in the constitution, and its status as

60 The List of Non-Agreed Articles (in this volume Appendix C) shows that the commission disagreed on qualifications and impartiality of the president (Art. 161); presidential elections (Art. 162); the president's duties, powers (Art. 163), and responsibilities (Art. 164); presidential accountability, e.g., vote of confidence (Art. 167, 168); criminal liability and conditions that terminate a presidency (no article numbers assigned); acting for/substitution of the president (Art. 165); and the formation and composition of the Council of Ministers (Art. 166).

a principle protected by an eternity clause.[61] While the AKP and the Peace and Democracy Party (*Barış ve Demokrasi Partisi*, BDP) advocated the removal of laicism from the constitution, the MHP and the Republican People's Party (*Cumhuriyet Halk Partisi*, CHP) opposed this suggestion. In the end, laicism was adopted as a core characteristic of the state in the ultimately contested draft article on the characteristics of the republic (Art. 149). Delegates could not reach agreement on other articles to regulate laicism and suggested competing proposals on the Presidency of Religious Affairs (Art. 99), freedom of political parties (Art. 31), and freedom of religion and conscience (Art. 15).[62]

The CHP's efforts to emphasize the role of laicism in the constitutional article on religious freedom and to "fill the principle of laicism with meaning" were met with criticism. AKP legal expert Yavuz Atar criticized the inclusion of laicism in the article on religious freedom, arguing that it enforces a dangerous practice of "state interference on society through ... social and cultural methods."[63] With the AKP's concern about laicism's influence on politics and the CHP's insistence on keeping it in the constitution, drafters were unable to resolve the issue despite the conciliatory efforts of the BDP and the MHP:

MUSTAFA ŞENTOP (AKP): What have we done [to laicism]? Be concrete.

ATILLA KART (CHP): *All your actions and implementations. Simply, what you have done to it in the last 10 years is ....*

MUSTAFA ŞENTOP (AKP): You are misstating the truth!

ATILLA KART (CHP): *You have clearly destroyed laicism, you have ended laicism!*

MUSTAFA ŞENTOP (AKP): *What do you mean, tell me?*

ATILLA KART (CHP): You have completely ruined our legal regulations.

MUSTAFA ŞENTOP (AKP): *Your understanding of laicism needed to be changed anyway! You do not want laicism, you want your own CHP-style laicism!*[64]

61 For a detailed discussion of amendment making and eternity clauses in the 1982 Constitution, see Yegen, Chapter 8 in this volume.

62 Art. 15, 31, 99, 149, List of Non-Agreed Articles, in this volume Appendix C.

63 AUK Proceedings, writing commission, August 6, 2012.

64 Ibid.

According to Jon Elster, constitution making always involves passions and emotions. Their impact, however, should be minimized.[65] The mutual accusations between AKP and CHP drafters show that emotions had a negative impact on the debates. The above episode resulted in discussions over the whole purpose of the AUK. While Atilla Kart (CHP) argued that they were "trying to correct mistakes made in the past," Mustafa Şentop (AKP) claimed that popular constitution making was only "made possible by the AKP," and that "equal representation of all parties [in the drafting commission] was granted by the prime minister, although there was no necessity to do so." Expressing his frustration, BDP member Altan Tan argued that "political accusations and polemics . . . [were] exceeding the agenda [of the commission]."[66] Disagreement over laicism prevailed and reduced the chances for consensus.

Later debates on laicism also illustrate that at times the agents involved were able to put the public interest and the AUK mission before political red lines. In the agreed article on limitations of fundamental rights, the CHP initially insisted on including violations of the laicism principle as a reason for rights limitations.[67] For the sake of reaching consensus, CHP member Rıza Türmen announced that "they had thought through their position [and] decided that taking [laicism] out [of this article] would be appropriate." Nevertheless, prioritizing consensus over ideological beliefs remained an exception, and the above-mentioned episode did not decrease tensions in the commission. Regarding provisions on laicism, the AKP and the CHP were ultimately the agents hindering progress. Their antagonistic preferences created a hostile environment for consensus. As the AKP had suffered under the imposed secular order (e.g., the party prohibition case before the AYM in 2008), and the BDP strategically wanted to keep the religious Kurdish vote, their demands to break with the laicism principle were predictable. Likewise, the fact that the CHP and the MHP perceive themselves to be republican political parties obliged to protect the laicist state order made it unlikely that they would agree to give up this constitutive principle. While leaving this contested issue to be solved by future legislatures and government could have allowed the AUK to avoid exhausting, destructive debates, commission members did the opposite and embraced their disagreement.[68]

65 Jon Elster, "The Optimal Design of a Constituent Assembly," in *Collective Wisdom: Principles and Mechanisms*, eds. H. Landemore and J. Elster (New York: Cambridge University Press, 2012), 170.

66 AUK Proceedings, writing commission, August 6, 2012.

67 Art. 41, List of Agreed Articles, in this volume Appendix B.

68 For incremental constitution making, see Lerner, *Making Constitutions in Deeply Divided Societies*, 40.

Debates on National Sovereignty

Conflicting understandings of the exercise of national sovereignty by state organs were first revealed in discussions on the role and functions of Parliament in November 2012. The drafting parties were unable to agree where to locate national sovereignty, and which state organ was supposed to ultimately represent and exercise it. Secondly, drafters disagreed on the definition of "the people," which created a division between parties defining the people in ethnic terms (AKP, MHP, and CHP) and those applying a civic definition (BDP). In the draft article on sovereignty (Art. 153), the AUK only agreed on a clause stating that "sovereignty shall never be transferred to a person, a party, or a class," while all other issues remained open.[69] These debates illustrate that competing, ideologically grounded views on what national sovereignty means, which institutions should represent it, and who is part of the nation prevented agreement. Although at times converging points emerged between different parties, this did not reduce tensions in the commission.

Ahmet Iyimaya (AKP) suggested that Parliament should be the primary organ holding national sovereignty, arguing that it alone represents the will of the people. BDP legal consultant Meral Danış Beştaş supported this idea, arguing that "emphasizing the parliament as the highest organ representing the will of the people is very important . . . , [as] Turkey suffered from past coups, and military tutelage . . . ." CHP drafters opposed this framing and suggested an understanding that was in line with prior constitutions, which define all state organs as representing and exercising sovereignty on behalf of the nation. Rıza Türmen (CHP) expressed his party's concern that national sovereignty was being reduced to "the will of the people." He explained that democratic legitimacy is not only facilitated through elections, and that the rule of law and protection of human rights are equally important. Türmen suggested avoiding the term "will of the people" altogether in the constitution.[70]

Disagreement over this issue continued throughout meetings in March and April 2013. AKP drafters opposed nonelected bodies (countermajoritarian institutions) and their ability to exercise national sovereignty, which reflected their historical experience with constitutional organs repressing religious conservative parties in the name of national sovereignty.[71] Yavuz Atar (AKP legal expert) commented: "Personally, as an academic, I think that the powers

[69] Art. 153, List of Non-Agreed Articles, in this volume Appendix C.

[70] AUK Proceedings, November 29, 2012.

[71] For the debates on countermajoritarian institutions, see Abad Andrade, Chapter 7 in this volume.

used by the judiciary should not be understood as an act of sovereignty, because they are not elected. Sovereignty can only be exercised by elected organs."[72] In prior constitutions, Turkey had pronounced the state to be the holder and exerciser of national sovereignty through its different powers (i.e., executive, legislative, judiciary). This explains why CHP and MHP drafters were eager to protect the constitutional status quo. BDP legal consultant Meral Danış Beştaş supported the AKP's position, critically observing that in Turkish politics, "every organ understands itself as a representative and exercises sovereignty." Drafters from the CHP and the MHP, on the other hand, perceived this as a threat to the existing constitutional order and criticized the other two parties for promoting a populist (*halkçı*) understanding of national sovereignty.[73]

According to Hanna Lerner, in deeply divided societies no agreed notion of "the people" exists, but only a contested notion of "the divided people."[74] As Turkey is a divided society, a second dividing line emerged over the definition of "the people." In this context, BDP drafters signaled their disapproval of the term "national sovereignty" (*millet iradesi*), which they perceived as excluding Kurds and other ethnic groups, and tried to promote a pluralist notion of the Turkish people:

ALTAN TAN (BDP):	*We cannot accept claims that there is a right of national sovereignty for some people only .... From the perspective of the Kurds, Muslims, non-believers ... and our notion of citizenship, this is unacceptable. ... Kurds did not come to this land from the outside; it is their own authentic land, their own country and geography. ... Kurds even converted to Islam 200 years before the Turks.*
AHMET IYIMAYA (AKP):	What historical sources are you referring to?
ALTAN TAN (BDP):	*The Ulu Mosque in Diyarbakir was converted to a mosque in 639.*
FARUK BAL (MHP):	This is not true.[75]

[72] AUK Proceedings, April 18, 2013.

[73] Ibid. Later on, CHP drafters accused the AKP of promoting "a dangerous understanding of sovereignty" that jeopardized pluralist democracy (AUK Proceedings, April 22, 2013).

[74] Lerner, *Making Constitutions in Deeply Divided Societies*, 31.

[75] Ibid. For debates on alternatives to the term *millet* (nation), see AUK Proceedings, November 29, 2012.

The MHP in particular, who promoted a nationalist view of sovereignty, made clear their opposition to any changes that would diversify the concepts of nation and national sovereignty, arguing, "[I]n all previous constitutions … the founding people are the Turkish people" and "national sovereignty cannot be divided."[76] Hence, the BDP's attempts to explain that Turks have been sharing national sovereignty with Kurds and other groups were challenged.

Debates on Democracy

Disagreement over the meaning of democracy emerged between an electoral, majoritarian understanding of democracy (AKP) and a plural and substantive constitutional conceptualization of democracy (CHP, BDP). The diverging views on democracy came to the fore during debates on provisions concerning party closure,[77] the role of the opposition,[78] implementation of direct and participatory democracy,[79] and the role of civil society.[80] With regard to political rights constitutive of democracy, the AKP, the CHP, and the MHP agreed on a draft article on freedom of association (Art. 23), but the BDP rejected most of the drafted text and suggested a more liberal notion of freedom of association.

MUSTAFA ŞENTOP (AKP): *The meaning of democracy changes a little in accordance with the description …*

DOÇ. DR. SELIN ESEN (CHP LEGAL EXPERT): No, it does not change "a little." There is a basic definition of democracy.

MUSTAFA ŞENTOP (AKP): *It changes, it [democracy] has flexible meanings …*

RIZA TÜRMEN (CHP): By proposing a flexible definition of democracy, you are destroying democracy![81]

This brief exchange reveals the intensity of disagreement between drafters in debates on democracy. Throughout the meetings of the commission in August 2012, AKP drafters described democracy as the act of "respecting electoral results … expressed by the votes of the people."[82] They identified democracy with the dominance of an elected ruling party. Their majoritarian

76 AUK Proceedings, April 10, 2012.

77 AUK Proceedings, writing commission, August 16 and 29, 2012, September 4, 2012.

78 Ibid., August 15, 2012.

79 Ibid., August 6, 2012, September 13, 2012.

80 Ibid., November 28, 2012, January 10, 2013.

81 Ibid., March 28, 2013.

82 Ibid., August 6, 2012.

stance toward democracy stood in stark contrast to proposals by the CHP and the BDP, who stressed the necessity of explicitly protecting oppositional activities in the constitution. When the CHP's Rıza Türmen argued for protecting the rights of the opposition in order to change the "historically bad reputation of opposition activities in Turkey," the AKP and the MHP suggested that there was no need to protect the opposition because it is, generally speaking, insignificant in Turkish political culture. The AKP's Mustafa Şentop emphasized the role of leadership in Turkish politics, while the MHP's Mehmet Akyıldız pointed out that "Turkey still belongs to the Eastern cultures, where opposition is considered something bad."[83]

Competing views on democracy further emerged in debates on the role of civil society. Despite the efforts of the BDP and the CHP to stress civil society's role in constitutional provisions, the AKP refused to acknowledge civil society's importance for political life. The CHP's Rıza Türmen argued that "the government ought to share its power with civil society in modern states." In response, the AKP's Şentop argued that civic associations should not be granted power over the government.[84] The AKP expressed an outright statist understanding of democracy by rejecting the idea that public institutions should share power not only among themselves, but also with civil society. Portraying civil society as an agency that could, potentially, want to claim power over government, AKP delegates reflected the authoritarian sentiment guiding their past politics. All attempts to further substantiate the meaning of democracy beyond the traditional statist understanding were opposed by the AKP. The BDP's request to insert direct participatory decision-making procedures into the draft, which would have resulted in an expansion of positive political rights and could have enhanced democracy, was met with resistance by the AKP, as were suggestions that democratic rights (e.g., the right to unionize, economic and social rights) be expanded.

All efforts of the BDP and the CHP to give "substantive meaning to democracy"[85] were strongly opposed by AKP drafters, who, occasionally supported by the MHP, made it ultimately impossible to reach consensus on the meaning of democracy. A split between the CHP and the BDP on the one hand, and the AKP and the MHP on the other, continued to shape discussions on democracy. In discussions on the formation of the Constitutional Court in January–March 2013, drafters accused each other of promoting particularist notions of democracy. The AKP criticized previous governments for basing

[83] Ibid., August 15, 2012

[84] Ibid., January 10, 2013.

[85] Ibid., September 17, 2012.

their legitimacy on the constitution and unelected bodies rather than the will of the people, emphasizing the effects of the 1961 and 1982 Constitutions. The AKP demanded that the commission overcome the old order and prioritize the "will of the people." In response, the CHP and the BDP adopted an increasingly critical tone. CHP drafters criticized the AKP's winner-take-all notion of democracy, arguing that democracy is not only reflected in electoral shares held by the majority. They emphasized that "those who did not vote for the governing party should be protected under democracy, too." And the BDP even questioned the intentions underlying the AKP's promotion of a pluralist understanding of democracy.[86]

Overall, the AKP's much-criticized populist notion of democracy is captured in the following statement by Mustafa Şentop, who argued that the formation of the AUK shows the AKP's commitment to democracy: "What did we do? We took some of the vote that was given to us and sacrificed some of it [to form this commission]. This is something beyond democracy."[87] This not only shows how sensitive constitutionalizing democracy was for the drafters, but also reflects the AKP's self-conception within the process, namely, as absolute power holders who generously surrender some of their power to make a new constitution. Andrew Arato argues that for constitution making to yield democratic results, no actor can claim to exclusively represent the people.[88] In the AUK, the attempt to draft a new fundamental law reflecting the voices of all political and social forces was jeopardized by the unwillingness of the ruling AKP to abstain from any claims of exclusive representation of the "will of the people."

3.2 *Organization of Government and Separation of Powers*

The most substantial disagreement emerged over questions of government organization. While the AKP promoted a transition to a presidential system, which, they argued, would enhance democracy and the separation of powers, the CHP and the MHP expressed fears over executive dominance and concentration of powers.[89] Although the BDP sided with the CHP and the MHP regarding their demand for clear checks and balances and separation of powers, the BDP's preferences shifted when opportunities for the realization

86 AUK Proceedings, March 28, 2012.

87 Ibid., August 6, 2012.

88 Andrew Arato, *Post Sovereign Constitution Making: Learning and Legitimacy* (Oxford: Oxford University Press, 2016), 9, 69–72. See also Tombuş, Chapter 2 in this volume.

89 For a discussion of the political system question in Turkish constitutional history, see Özsoy Boyunsuz, Chapter 3 in this volume.

of regional autonomy emerged. Ultimately, the AKP and the BDP agreed that government organization should be changed irrespective of constitutional traditions. The AKP aimed for transition to a presidential system. The BDP was willing to consider such a transition, but only on the condition that it be accompanied by federalism and decentralization of political authority. While the MHP aimed to maintain the government system of the 1982 Constitution, the CHP sought to abolish the direct election of the president and return to a parliamentary system similar to the 1961 Constitution. These disagreements complicated consensus reaching and led to discussions over the general purpose of the commission. Of the 172 articles debated in the AUK, delegates could not agree on one single provision concerning the executive. The function and role of the legislative and the judiciary also remained contested: Consensus was reached only on five provisions regarding the legislative (TBMM) and nine provisions concerning the judiciary.

The AUK reached agreement on provisions regulating the activities incompatible with membership in Parliament, reasons to dismiss deputies, application to annul TBMM membership, the presidency of the TBMM, and the publicity and publication of TBMM debates.[90] On most articles determining the powers and functions of the legislative, the AUK could not reach agreement. There was little agreement on the general article establishing the legislative,[91] while absolute disagreement persisted throughout the process with regard to the oath that members of Parliament are obliged to take, authorization to issue decrees having the force of law, and public law proposals.[92] There was partial agreement on a number of other articles concerning the TBMM (e.g., eligibility to be a deputy, parliamentary immunity, convening and recess of the TBMM, rules of procedure and political party groups, quorums and majorities for decisions, duties and powers of the TBMM, introduction and deliberation of bills, promulgation of laws by the president of the republic, ratification of international treaties, declarations of state of war and deployment of the armed forces, election term of the TBMM, deferment of elections and by-elections, ways of obtaining information and supervision by the TBMM, questions directed to the government, parliamentary inquiries, interpellation, parliamentary investigations, request of reports on implementation of laws, and general administration and supervision of elections).[93]

[90] Art. 69, 70, 71, 72, 77, List of Agreed Articles, in this volume Appendix B.
[91] Art. 64, List of Non-Agreed Articles, in this volume Appendix C.
[92] Ibid., Art. 70, 83, 84.
[93] Ibid., Art. 65, 67, 71, 73–74, 76–79, 80–82, 85–91.

With regard to the judiciary, delegates were able to agree on provisions on independence and impartiality of the judiciary, security of tenure for judges and prosecutors, term of office and termination of membership of Constitutional Court judges, decisions of the Constitutional Court, and the right to claim unconstitutionality before the court.[94] On most provisions they did not agree (e.g., establishment of the Constitutional Court, its duties and powers, procedure of functioning and trial, annulment actions before and decision-making of the Constitutional Court, contention of unconstitutionality claims, military judiciary, the Court of Cassation, the Council of State, the Supreme Court, the High Council of Judges, and the High Council of Prosecutors).[95]

Overall, reorganization of government bodies and separation of powers were highly contested issues. The fact that AKP delegates declared the transition to presidentialism to be the main goal of the constitution-making process, while other parties generally (CHP, MHP) or conditionally (BDP) rejected the AKP proposal, made it impossible to agree on the basic government structure. The draft articles on the powers of the president show that the AKP proposal was in complete contradiction to the texts proposed by other parties and enforced their own vision of presidentialism.[96] Consequently, the CHP added to various articles notes stating that these were not negotiated because of the AKP's presidentialism proposal.[97]

Initially, the AKP's plan to extend the powers of the president faced resistance from all opposition parties (CHP, MHP, and BDP). Even MHP drafters, who agreed with the AKP that the existing system had to be fixed, opposed extending the powers of the president. The MHP's Faruk Bal argued that a parliamentary system would be appropriate as it is "less likely to turn into a dictatorship." Despite the attempt of the AKP's legal expert Yavuz Atar to defend presidentialism by invoking the example of the United States and arguing that it is the most democratic institutional design, both the CHP and the BDP continued to criticize the AKP's draft in subsequent discussions.[98] Dismissing Atar's US comparison, the CHP's Süheyl Batum pointed out "the lack of [institutional] requirements ... in Turkey" that are necessary to implement a presidential system (e.g., party discipline, federal structure, rule of law, bicameralism).[99] He accused the AKP of deliberately

94 Art. 112, 114–115, 121, 126–127, List of Agreed Articles, in this volume Appendix B.

95 Art. 117, 119–122, 114, 125–129, List of Non-Agreed Articles, in this volume Appendix C.

96 Ibid., Art. 161–168.

97 Ibid., Art. 76, 78, 80, 81, 100, 163–166, 171.

98 AUK Proceedings, writing commission, November 21, 2012.

99 Ibid., November 28, 2012.

eliminating checks and balances from the constitution. As the concerns of opposition parties were rooted in an ongoing drift toward authoritarianism under the AKP government, the question of separation of powers was a high priority for the CHP, the MHP, and the BDP.

Besides concerns over separation of powers and democracy, diverging preferences about state traditions also complicated consensus reaching, as drafters were unable to agree on whether it would be possible to break with the constitutional tradition of Turkish parliamentarianism. Eager to break with the legacy of the authoritarian 1982 Constitution, BDP legal consultant Özgür Sevgi Göral demanded a new constitution "which clearly disengages itself from a . . . monist and sexist state identity."[100] The BDP did not prioritize the shift to presidentialism, but did aim to change the existing order in one way or another. By supporting presidentialism they hoped to create a federal structure granting autonomy to provinces with Kurdish-majority populations. While former anti-system parties (AKP and BDP) advocated for a break with the past and its constitutional order, the two former system parties (CHP and MHP) argued for maintaining the status quo with regard to the political system. The MHP's Faruk Bal demanded that Turkey's history of state traditions be taken seriously and therefore that parliamentarianism be retained, despite its shortcomings. In response, the AKP's Ahmet Iyimaya acknowledged these concerns over state traditions, yet suggested that a "political system analysis" would help decide which system would be better for Turkey. CHP legal expert Selin Esen criticized the AKP's narrative of the superiority of presidentialism as a governance system: "All things considered, I do not believe that presidentialism will be as good for Turkey as Yavuz [Atar] implies; I also do not believe that it will be a better system of governance when we take our past as well as our cultural and societal characteristics into consideration."[101]

In AUK meetings in January 2013, disagreement over the potential effects of presidentialism was hard to overcome. The CHP and the MHP rejected presidentialism altogether. BDP delegates did not actively support the AKP, but were open to negotiation as they were seeking an opportunity to put federalism on the agenda. BDP delegates explained: "We told you from the beginning that we would discuss presidentialism if you would consider federalism. . . . This is why we did not side with the CHP and the MHP. . . . Ultimately, we suggested regional autonomy."[102] The seeming rapprochement between the AKP and the BDP over a possible transition to presidentialism in

[100] Ibid., November 21, 2012.
[101] Ibid.
[102] Ibid., January 28, 2013.

exchange for regional autonomy, which also coincided with the beginning of the so-called Kurdish peace process at the time, raised suspicions of an ongoing trade-off between the AKP and the BDP. The MHP's Bal accused the AKP and the BDP of having made "progress behind closed doors."[103] However, BDP drafters, who saw a political opportunity in presidentialism, made democracy and checks and balances conditional characteristics of the future constitution, ultimately revealing their preference for democracy. Given that the CHP and the MHP both favored the continuation of the unitary state tradition, the BDP's push for federalism still amplified divisions between drafting parties. Frictions between the MHP and the BDP persisted throughout March 2013, as MHP drafters contended that the BDP's demands jeopardized the task of the commission.[104] Ultimately, all issues revolving around the AKP's push for presidentialism remained unresolved.

3.3 *The Rule of Law*

Given that the rule of law was often in peril in Turkey's modern history, one would have expected rule-of-law debates to be at the center of the constitution-making process in 2011–2013. The AUK codified neither a draft article guaranteeing the rule of law nor a provision establishing the republic as a state under the rule of law. Among the agreed articles, not one mentions the term "rule of law," despite the fact that all parties suggested that the Turkish Republic should be a state based on the rule of law.[105] Likewise, all parties referred to the rule of law in their proposals for a preamble.[106] The CHP, the MHP, and the BDP proposed alternative versions of the provision regulating political parties, which all stipulated that party programs and statutes cannot stand in contradiction to the rule of law.[107] Both the AKP and the MHP included the rule of law in their proposals for the oath TBMM members have to swear upon inauguration.[108] The BDP proposed that in judicial review proceedings, the Constitutional Court should decide on the unconstitutionality of laws by evaluating whether or not the rule of law and the democratic state order were negatively affected.[109] As the BDP's suggestion to include sexual orientation in the equality before the law provision was found irrelevant

103 Ibid.
104 AUK Proceedings, writing commission, March 26, 2013.
105 Art. 149, List of Non-Agreed Articles, in this volume Appendix C.
106 Ibid., Preamble.
107 Ibid., Art. 31.
108 Ibid., Art. 70.
109 Ibid., Art. 122.

by the MHP and the AKP, the commission did not reach full consensus on the equality clause.[110] In the end, the AUK was only able to agree on the article declaring the supremacy and binding force of the constitution, which was largely a verbatim adoption of the provision in the 1982 Constitution.[111]

Regarding the problematic constitutional constructions that we observed in past constitutions and the question of the extent to which these would have been omitted from the projected constitution, it is clear that the draft constitution would not have reestablished state security courts. Delegates did not debate this issue at all, which shows that all members of the AUK agreed that these courts should not be reintroduced as state institutions enjoying constitutional status. Turning to the broad grounds that prior constitutions have recognized for limiting or restricting fundamental rights, we observe that some of the agreed articles still invoke the indeterminate legal term "public order" (*kamu düzeni*): The right to demonstrate (Art. 24) and the right to privacy (Art. 10) can be limited to "uphold the public order." Interestingly, the latter article includes a reasoning note which explains that public order is not a general limitation, but grounds that can only be applied in exceptional cases.[112] While the BDP approached the use of public order very critically in general, suggesting that public order should not be used to restrict fundamental rights (here religious freedom and freedom of association), the MHP included the term in its proposal for the articles on state of emergency (Art. 101) and prohibition of professional organizations (Art. 104).[113] Nevertheless, compared to the 1982 Constitution, the term appears less frequently in the draft articles. "Public morality" (*genel ahlak*) was suggested by AKP and MHP as grounds for limiting the right to privacy and family life and freedom of assembly.[114]

Article 14 of the 1982 Constitution, which elaborated a variety of vague grounds to prohibit political parties, was not reconsidered in AUK deliberations. But grounds for limiting fundamental rights were nevertheless agreed upon (Art. 41). While Article 13 of the 1982 Constitution had a long list of indeterminate concepts (e.g., "safeguarding the indivisible integrity of the State with its territory and nation, national sovereignty, the Republic, national security, public order, general peace, the public interest, public morals and

110 Ibid., Art. 3.

111 Art. 161, List of Agreed Articles, in this volume Appendix B.

112 Ibid. Art. 10. On reasoning-writing as a drafting strategy, see Yegen and Yanaşmayan, Chapter 6 in this volume.

113 Art. 15, 23 (BDP), Art. 101, 104 (MHP), List of Non-Agreed Articles, in this volume Appendix C.

114 AUK Proceedings, June 13, 2012; AUK Proceedings, July 4, 2012.

public health") that could be employed restrictively, the AUK draft article establishes in the first clause of Article 41 that "freedom is the norm, limitation is the exception." It furthermore declares that rights restrictions are only legitimate on the specific grounds listed in the individual articles.[115] Article 42 establishes that under a state of emergency, fundamental rights may be suspended. It reiterates the idea of Article 15 of the 1982 Constitution, but also names similar rights that cannot be suspended even under a state of emergency (e.g., the right to life). However, it is more protective in that it explicitly specifies that limitations of fundamental rights may not violate the basic principle of human dignity.[116]

Overall, this shows that principles and rights of the rule of law were among the articles on which AUK members could reach consensus. As the grounds to restrict fundamental rights were much less broad in the agreed articles, rights limitations would have been less likely under the projected constitution. Moreover, the AUK adopted the European Court of Human Rights (ECtHR) formula that rights limitations should be exceptional.[117] Nonetheless, the commission was deeply divided over the Constitutional Court and its role in politics. Guided by past experiences, drafters from the BDP and the AKP questioned the extent to which political parties should adhere to the democratic order based on the rule of law. As the rule of law was used by republican elites to enforce closures of conservative religious and Kurdish parties in the past, they argued that it was counterproductive for a democracy to make parties dependent on the good will of the state and the judiciary. Mustafa Şentop (AKP) held that "parties elected with 50, 60, 70 percent of the vote should not be reviewed by agents representing the rule of law [i.e., the judiciary and courts.]"[118] Ultimately, Şentop dismissed the debates about the compliance of political parties with democracy and rule of law, concluding that "parties supported by the votes of the people ... should not be subjected to such useless discussions."[119]

In subsequent AUK debates on judicial independence, differences evolved specifically regarding reorganization of articles that determine the role and function of the Constitutional Court as well as articles concerning the independence of judges and courts in general.[120] All drafting parties demanded

115 Art. 41, List of Agreed Articles, in this volume Appendix B.

116 Ibid., Art. 42.

117 See Yegen and Yanaşmayan, Chapter 6 in this volume.

118 AUK Proceedings, writing commission, August 16, 2012.

119 Ibid., September 4, 2012.

120 For a detailed discussion of debates on the Constitutional Court and other judicial bodies, see Abad Andrade, Chapter 7 in this volume.

that judicial independence be strengthened. Except for the CHP, all parties based their demands on Turkey's lack of judicial independence in the past and made demands to improve judicial independence in the future. Surprisingly, MHP drafters were at the forefront of those pushing for change. Faruk Bal criticized the politicization of the courts, arguing that Turkey "could not achieve rule of law and the supremacy of law because judges were influenced by their internal ideologies and lacked independence." He concluded that realizing the rule of law in Turkey was conditional on the success of constitutional conciliation.[121] The BDP and the AKP endorsed arguments raised by the MHP and further expressed their own preferences in this regard. BDP legal consultant Meral Danış Beştaş articulated concerns over the independence of the court and criticized it for "promoting statism and state ideologies instead of fundamental rights and freedoms through judicial activism."[122]

Likewise, the AKP demanded that judicial bodies refrain from promoting a particular ideology and questioned the ability of the court to make decisions on behalf of the people. This became evident in discussions on the characteristics of the republic in August 2013, in which Mustafa Şentop explained that "the power which the Constitutional Court uses does not come from constitutional law, but is rather political and ideological – to be frank, it's Atatürk's nationalism." The AKP was supported by BDP drafters, who suggested a de-ideologization of the court by adding a provision that guarantees "the independence of the state from ideologies, religion, beliefs, and lifestyles." CHP drafters were less concerned with the ideological orientation of the court in the past, but they did make an effort to advance the overall meaning and significance of the rule of law. Atilla Kart asked the commission "to fill the term [rule of law] with substance and meaning."[123]

This issue was picked up in subsequent meetings as frustration over the AUK's inability to reach consensus on this matter increased. While CHP drafters criticized the commission's inability to go beyond agreeing that "Turkey is a democratic state based on the rule of law," BDP drafters demanded "more clarity on these issues after all this time and work." AKP legal expert Yavuz Atar responded that "nobody has a problem with democracy, rule of law, laicism, social state, or human rights," but that the problem is caused by those who are "caught up in unamendability and Atatürk's nationalism," thus directly accusing the CHP of blocking the commission's work.[124]

121 AUK Proceedings, writing commission, March 19, 2013.

122 Ibid., March 25, 2013.

123 Ibid., August 21, 2013.

124 Ibid., August 26, 2013.

The AKP's expressions of frustration with the work of the commission can be understood as an attempt to shift attention from substantial debate on the rule of law to ideological differences.

In general, the basic conditions of the Turkish rule-of-law regime would have been improved had the AUK been able to produce a full constitution. Although commission members ultimately failed to agree on an article to specify what the rule of law means, they did agree on a number of important fundamental rights.[125] Grounds for rights restrictions were less broad and less vague. State security courts would not have been reintroduced. And the problematic role of the Constitutional Court in restricting political pluralism was at least addressed and discussed in the AUK. Overall, progress made with regard to improving the rule of law illustrates that the AUK constitution-making process was a missed opportunity to codify a more democratic constitution for the Turkish state.

4 CONCLUSION

Existing literature on constitution making in divided societies shows that, under conditions of deep social division, constitution making becomes an even more challenging task.[126] Hanna Lerner argues that, in such a setting, "the constitution's foundational aspects typically attract more political attention than its procedural ones, and the lack of shared norms becomes one of the central obstacles to the writing of the constitution."[127] Lerner refers to disagreements regarding symbolic politics or basic normative commitments, but she does not address a situation in which societies are deeply divided over the question of the form of the state, i.e., whether it should be federal or unitary, whether the government should be organized as a parliamentary or presidential system, etc. She explains, "The incrementalist approach does not mean that decisions regarding the structure of governmental institutions are deferred to the future. Rather, decisions on the institutions of government and regulation of power are clear, and they allow for the democratic order to function."[128]

125 See Yegen and Yanaşmayan, Chapter 6 in this volume.

126 For constitution making in divided societies, see Lerner, *Making Constitutions in Deeply Divided Societies*, 30–50; Arend Lijphart, "Constitutional Design for Divided Societies," *Journal of Democracy* 15, no. 2 (2004): 96–109; Sujit Choudhry, "Bridging Comparative Politics and Comparative Constitutional Law: Constitutional Design in Divided Societies," in *Constitutional Design for Divided Societies: Integration or Accommodation?*, ed. S. Choudhry (Oxford: Oxford University Press, 2008), 3–40.

127 Lerner, *Making Constitutions in Deeply Divided Societies*, 32.

128 Ibid., 40.

Relating Lerner's approach to the Turkish case, this chapter has shown that incrementalist constitution making becomes ineffective when state organization principles and basic political concepts are contested by constitution makers and in the absence of predrafting agreements regarding the fundamental structure of the state and political system.[129] In Turkey, the incapacity to agree on a basic structure for the future state made it impossible to constitutionalize a procedural framework in which other contested issues could have been solved in the future. With regard to constitution making in divided societies, the Turkish case shows that incrementalist constitution making only works when questions pertaining to the overall government structure do not have to be renegotiated alongside other contested issues of identity.

Deep disagreements over constitutive state organization principles were identified in AUK debates on national sovereignty, democracy, government organization, separation of powers, and rule of law. Although it was expected that drafters would come to the negotiating table with ideological differences and diverging preferences, the lack of consensus created a vacuum that was filled by political calculations. Rather than attempting to draft provisions in a formalist and functionalist manner, disagreements were amplified and embraced. AUK delegates fought over the meaning and role of laicism and national sovereignty in the new constitution. The concept of democracy was not used as a clear and concrete defining principle on which to ground state and government, but emerged instead as an empty signifier inviting agents to apply their subjective and often self-serving understandings to it. Depending on party positions, separation of powers was presented as more or less functional under presidentialism and parliamentarism. These party red lines and historically acquired convictions and predispositions impeded constitution making. The tendency of the AKP to assume the role of exclusive representative of the people became the nail in the coffin for consensus and the formation of a broad coalition in the AUK.

Different constitutional principles gave rise to different political coalitions. With regard to the characteristics of the republic, the CHP and the MHP advocated for maintaining the laicist character of the constitution and the

[129] With regard to predrafting agreements, Lerner explains, "[I]n deeply divided societies, external political factors – particularly the existence of predrafting agreements between the leading political parties concerning controversial identity issues – are crucial in facilitating the enactment of a democratic and inclusionary constitution." See Hanna Lerner, "Constituent Assemblies and Political Continuity in Divided Societies," in *Constituent Assemblies*, eds. J. Elster, R. Gargarella, V. Naresh, and B. E. Rasch (Cambridge: Cambridge University Press, 2018), 59.

state, while the AKP and the BDP argued from their historical experience that state organization principles that had caused harm in the past were to be omitted from a future constitution. Debates on national sovereignty illustrate that the CHP and the MHP aimed to maintain the traditional codification of national sovereignty as represented by the state and all its organs (executive, legislative, judiciary), while the AKP and the BDP argued that national sovereignty should be represented by the Parliament only. With regard to the constitutionalization of government and separation of powers, the CHP and the MHP argued that the parliamentary, or rather the historically homegrown semi-presidential structure of Turkish government, should be maintained but its recognized shortcomings were to be fixed. The AKP stated that its central goal was to constitutionalize a presidential system, while the CHP and the MHP were concerned that a further strengthening of the executive under presidentialism would cause centralization of power and increase the likelihood of autocratization in the future. The BDP was open to discussing presidentialism and changing the government structure, but only in exchange for federalization of the government system, which would have granted regions with a Kurdish majority a degree of political autonomy vis-à-vis the political center. As noted in the chapter's introduction, Turkish citizens favored maintaining the political system and the separation of powers between a popularly elected president and a popularly elected Parliament that would appoint the prime minister and cabinet. The public preference for a political system could have been utilized to overcome deadlock, but none of the drafting parties seriously considered this move. This ultimately left the commission without a strategy to overcome impasses in constitution making, and it deprived citizens of the prospects of a democratically drafted constitution.

While democratic constitution making failed with the dissolution of the AUK in 2013, the 1982 Constitution was significantly amended afterward. The AKP and the MHP proposed constitutional amendments in late 2016 that were adopted in a public referendum in early 2017.[130] Both with regard to the method of constitution making (majoritarian imposition) and to the constitution produced by the amendments (statist-authoritarian with strong executive powers), Turkey has returned to a statist-authoritarian path. Although majoritarian imposition in constitution making is well known from the past, the coalition imposing these amendments was rather unusual. Two parties that

[130] For a translation of the 2017 constitutional amendments, see *The 2017 Amendment Proposal to the Constitution*, translated by Zeynep Yanaşmayan and Canan Pour-Norouz, available at https://tinyurl.com/y7z7fmsw (accessed April 2, 2019).

are unlikely political allies, representing opposite ends of Turkish conservatism, joined forces.[131] The fact that both parties reject the Kurdish movement and its political representatives made this unexpected coalition possible. Linking the most recent constitutional amendments to the failed process in 2011–2013, it becomes clear that the MHP and the AKP were already articulating their disdain for political opposition and ignoring the need to recognize the opposition at the very beginning of the AUK deliberations. This shared anti-pluralist stance was another commonality facilitating cooperation between the AKP and the MHP.

Comparing the 2017 amendments to the proposals submitted to the AUK, we argue that the AKP was, after all, able to transform the constitutional regime and construct a hyper-presidential political system. To some extent the MHP also succeeded in its goals of maintaining territorial integrity and the laicist republican state order as well as preventing pluralization of the citizenship doctrine, as these provisions were not amended. Ultimately, the failure of popular constitution making opened the floodgates to constitutional and political autocratization. Viewed from this perspective, the 2011–2013 process was indeed a critical juncture in Turkey's recent political history – not a juncture leading the country toward democracy, but one consolidating and expanding the path dependency of statist-authoritarian constitutionalism.

[131] While the MHP represents the ultranationalist ideological spearhead of Kemalism, the AKP represents the religious-Islamist segment of Turkish society.

6

Glass Half Full: Drafting Fundamental Rights in the Turkish Constitution-Making Process (2011–2013)

Oya Yegen and Zeynep Yanaşmayan

1 INTRODUCTION

The 2011–2013 attempt to draft a new constitution for the Turkish Republic resulted in consensus on sixty articles, with most of them concerning fundamental rights and freedoms. Political parties' reluctance to move away from their initial narrow party positions and policy preferences prevented the Constitutional Conciliation Commission (*Anayasa Uzlaşma Komisyonu*, AUK) from achieving consensus on major political issues such as citizenship, the state organization, and the form of government. It is perhaps not surprising that out of the sixty articles that enjoyed consensus in the commission, forty-three belonged to the chapter on fundamental rights and freedoms.[1] Commission members decided to make this chapter the first item on the agenda; as a result, deliberations on fundamental rights and freedoms benefited from the initial momentum of the process.[2]

Twenty provisions that were supposed to be included in the draft constitution remained contested,[3] including freedom of religion and conscience, freedom of thought and opinion, freedom of residence and movement, freedom of the press, freedom of association, the right to collective agreement and strike, the right to and freedom of education, citizenship, the right to vote, the right to be elected and to engage in political activity, freedom of political

[1] The article on arbitration in sports was drafted under rights and freedoms but was supposed to be moved to the chapter on the judiciary.

[2] After the chapter on fundamental rights and freedoms, the AUK planned to tackle the drafting process in the following order: legislation; administration and public services; judiciary; financial, economic, and social provisions; final provisions; and preamble, general provisions, and fundamental principles.

[3] The final draft prepared by the AUK included 172 articles: Sixty met with consensus, while 112 articles were contested. The chapter on fundamental rights and freedoms was to include sixty-three articles and has the most agreed articles of the nine chapters of the draft constitution.

parties,[4] the right to enter public service, the right to enter national service, and the duty to pay taxes. These rights and freedoms not only include some of the most significant fundamental rights and freedoms in democratic constitutions, but they also touch upon the long-standing contested issues of Turkish (constitutional) politics (e.g., definition of citizenship, power of the central government, relations between state and religion, minority rights). On the surface, it may appear that the AUK only managed to reach agreement on noncontroversial issues. However, this chapter shows that debates leading to agreement on articles did produce important constitutional novelties. Even contested provisions that were not finalized show a much more liberal and progressive approach to fundamental rights and freedoms than the 1982 Constitution. The goal of this chapter is to shed light on the negotiations surrounding fundamental rights and freedoms and uncover the reasons why the AUK was able to produce consensus on these forty-three constitutional provisions.

This chapter relies on theories of constitutional borrowing to explain the relative success in drafting fundamental rights. It also demonstrates that constitution makers employed different drafting tactics to achieve consensus. While a certain degree of path dependence could be observed, particularly in the reliance on the 1982 Constitution as a drafting template, constitutional borrowing not only allowed for the introduction of constitutional novelties, but also lent the normative authority to forge consensus on a number of provisions. It also served as a negative model to determine what was to be rejected, albeit more rarely.

Constitutional borrowing, or the "migration of constitutional ideas," is a contested but widely reported phenomenon that is "emerging as one of the central features of contemporary constitutional practice."[5] Constitutional borrowing can occur in different forms, whether in the text of constitutions or in the jurisprudence of constitutional courts. This chapter focuses on the impact of borrowing during the AUK discussions, that is, in the constitution-making process. Focusing on the deliberations alongside the draft text produced by the AUK enables us to trace instances of borrowing as well as nonborrowing. Instances of explicit rejection of foreign norms

4 The 1982 Constitution addressed political parties under two articles (Art. 68 and 69) while the AUK intended to merge principles to be observed by political parties and their rights and freedoms in one article.

5 Sujit Choudhry, "Migration as a New Metaphor in Comparative Constitutional Law," in *The Migration of Constitutional Ideas*, ed. S. Choudhry (Cambridge: Cambridge University Press, 2007), 1–36, 16. It should be noted that despite the rich theoretical discussion on the use of "borrowing" and "migration" as metaphors, this chapter uses them interchangeably.

(nonborrowing) are as relevant as instances of borrowing when it comes to understanding the deep normative structure of a constitutional system.[6] Constitutional migration happens both vertically, between different jurisdictional levels, and horizontally, across equal jurisdictional levels. As the Turkish case shows, vertical migration often occurs from the supranational to the national level (e.g., implementation at the constitutional level of human rights obligations covered by an international law),[7] although there are exceptions.[8]

Tom Ginsburg, Svitlana Chernykh, and Zachary Elkins show that international treaties are more likely to be mentioned in constitutions than customary international law, not least due to their increased power to enforce the fulfillment of domestic actors' promises.[9] They also show significant diffusion effects in the appropriation of international treaties, particularly for newly democratizing states. While Ginsburg, Chernykh, and Elkins note that human rights treaties form a major part of the international treaties they cover, they do not specifically focus on the diffusion of rights. Benedikt Goderis and Mila Versteeg test precisely the hypothesis that there is a diffusion of constitutional rights.[10] Relying on a data set of post-1946 constitutions in 188 countries, they find evidence for three of the four mechanisms of diffusion that they postulate (coercion, competition, learning, and acculturation). Interestingly, acculturation, which posits that states adopt similar policies not because of social or rational learning but out of the desire to be part of the self-identified group of peers, is not supported by their data. This is all the more surprising as constitutional borrowing literature demonstrates the significance of

[6] Kim Lane Scheppele, "Aspirational and Adversative Constitutionalism: The Case for Studying Cross-Constitutional Influence through Negative Models," *International Journal of Constitutional Law* 1, no. 2 (2003): 296–324; Lee Epstein and Jack Knight, "Constitutional Borrowing and Nonborrowing," *International Journal of Constitutional Law* 1, no. 2 (2003): 196–223.

[7] Vlad Perju, "Constitutional Transplants, Borrowing and Migrations," in *Oxford Handbook of Comparative Constitutional Law*, eds. M. Rosenfeld and A. Sajo (Oxford: Oxford University Press, 2012), 1304–1318, 1319.

[8] For an exception of the diffusion of anti-constitutional ideas, see Kim Lane Scheppele, "The Migration of Anti-Constitutional Ideas: The Post-9/11 Globalization of Public Law and the International State of Emergency," in *The Migration of Constitutional Ideas*, ed. S. Choudry (Cambridge: Cambridge University Press, 2007), 347–333.

[9] Tom Ginsburg, Svitlana Chernykh, and Zachary Elkins, "Commitment and Diffusion: How and Why National Constitutions Incorporate International Law," *University of Illinois Law Review* 201, no. 1 (2008): 201–228.

[10] Benedikt Goderis and Mila Versteeg, "The Diffusion of Constitutional Rights," *International Review of Law and Economics* 39, Issue C (2014): 1–19.

"reputational effects" at both the drafting and the implementation stages.[11] The reputational effects underline how constitutional borrowing can be employed as a (selective) tool in order to generate legitimacy, to transplant norms that are thus far nonexistent in the domestic order, and to promote self-interest for political elites.[12] As Ginsburg, Chernykh, and Elkins also show, such reputational effects accrue more in newly democratizing states or new courts because they serve to boost external prestige.[13]

The Turkish case offers a prime example of such reputational effects. However, as is shown in this chapter, not all international norms enjoy a similar normative authority, which leads to a hierarchization of norms in the deliberations that influences whether or not a norm will be borrowed. While the AUK used the European Convention on Human Rights (the Convention) and, to a lesser extent, the judgments of the European Court of Human Rights (ECtHR) as guidelines in its discussions of fundamental rights, other international treaties were not mentioned as frequently nor were they given the same weight. To a certain extent such a hierarchization depends on the institutionalization of the international norm in question. Kenneth Abbot et al. assert that the Convention is in the category of highly institutionalized norms. The normative framework is further strengthened by the existence of the ECtHR, which has been empowered by governments to resolve disputes.[14] The fact that there was contestation regarding ECtHR judgments in the AUK deliberations shows that the hierarchization of norms was not a direct reflection of the degree of institutionalization, but was to a great extent influenced by parties' political preferences and their selective use of specific norms.

The literature recognizes that the process of borrowing changes the global norm in question. This process is usually called "vernacularization," and it includes local appropriations and uses of human rights frameworks.[15] Building on this actor-oriented scholarship on the norm-interpretation

[11] Perju, "Constitutional Transplants," 1319. For the impact of reputational effects at the drafting stage, see Epstein and Knight, "Constitutional Borrowing and Nonborrowing"; at the implementation stage, see Ran Hirschl, *Towards Juristocracy: The Origins and Consequences of the New Constitutionalism* (Cambridge, MA: Harvard University Press, 2004).

[12] Perju, "Constitutional Transplants,"1319–1320.

[13] Ginsburg, Chernykh, and Elkins, "Commitment and Diffusion."

[14] Kenneth W. Abbott, Robert O. Keohane, Andrew Moravcsik, Anne-Marie Slaughter, and Duncan Snidal, "The Concept of 'Legalization,'" *International Organization* 54, no. 3 (2000): 401–419.

[15] Peggy Levitt and Sally Engle Merry, "Vernacularization on the Ground: Local Uses of Global Women's Rights in Peru, China, India and the United States," *Global Networks* 9, no. 4 (2009): 441–461.

process[16] and translation practices[17] that occur when international norms are transplanted from one context to another, we show what is being borrowed by whom and why.

The chapter starts with a presentation of the shortcomings of the 1982 Constitution regarding the scope and exercise of fundamental rights and freedoms in order to highlight why, in the 2011–2013 constitution-making process, the chapter on fundamental rights and freedoms was vital for the legitimacy of the new constitution. Given the 1982 Constitution's reputation for being overly authoritarian, it is important to discuss to what extent the AUK used it as a template and to compare the agreed articles with the articles of the 1982 Constitution. We show that the AUK draft included articles that were completely new, articles that were considerably revamped (and therefore offered substantially more protection), and articles that were only minimally modified.

In a second step, we explain how such constitutional novelties and advances were achieved through horizontal and vertical constitutional borrowing. Starting with horizontal borrowing, the chapter shows how the concept of human dignity was imported from the German Basic Law. This was an attempt to provide a new normative foundation for the understanding of fundamental rights in Turkish constitutional law and to break the traditional predominance of state interests over individual rights. With regard to vertical constitutional borrowing, the chapter scrutinizes the AUK's selective recourse to international norms, illustrating particularly how technical and legalistic language and jargon from the European Convention on Human Rights were imported into the drafting process. Not all international norms enjoyed a similar level of normative authority among AUK members, however, which also led to instances of overt nonborrowing, that is, the explicit rejection of certain international norms. With regard to rights limitations, we demonstrate that the AUK adopted an approach that was in line with the Convention, which served as the minimal baseline for human rights. The principle "freedom is the norm, limitation is the exception," which is strongly established in ECtHR jurisprudence, was accepted as a main working principle.[18] Indeed,

16 Antje Wiener and Uwe Puetter, "The Quality of Norms Is What Actors Make of It Critical–Constructivist Research on Norms," *Journal of International Law and International Relations* 5, no. 1 (2009): 1–16.

17 Sally Engle Merry, "Legal Transplants and Cultural Translation: Making Human Rights in the Vernacular," in *Human Rights: An Anthropological Reader*, ed. M. Goodale (Malden and Oxford: Wiley-Blackwell, 2009), 265–303.

18 The norm is accepted as the first provision of the article on the limitations of fundamental rights and freedoms (Art. 41, List of Agreed Articles, in this volume Appendix B) and was

the AUK's effort to distance itself from the 1982 Constitution's infamous attitude toward fundamental rights and freedoms is nowhere more obvious than here. While constitutional borrowing was effective in forging agreement, it was insufficient for reaching consensus on most of the polarizing issues, such as religious freedom and the right to education in one's mother tongue.

We then go on to review the drafting techniques adopted to overcome differences and to resolve deadlock. Here we identify a number of strategies: deferral to subcommissions and consultants, deferral to by law clauses, and reasoning-writing. The chapter concludes by highlighting the important strides achieved in expanding rights, but also recognizes that the AUK failed to reach consensus on some of the most significant polarizing issues. In hindsight, the AUK process was a missed opportunity to put fundamental rights and freedoms in place before Turkey's ensuing backslide into authoritarianism, which considerably limits and violates all rights and freedoms.[19]

2 FUNDAMENTAL RIGHTS UNDER THE 1982 CONSTITUTION: BLACK SHEEP OR QUINTESSENTIAL TEMPLATE?

The significance attached to the fundamental rights chapter is partly related to the restrictive nature of the 1982 Constitution. While the 1961 Constitution is often remembered as a champion of rights and freedoms, the 1982 Constitution is recognized as being overly deferential to state authority.[20] Critics have argued that the wording of the unamendable provision that describes the Turkish Republic as "respecting human rights" is a weak formulation in comparison to the 1961 Constitution, which characterized the republic as "based on human rights."[21] Moreover, the duties and obligations of the individual listed in the 1982 Constitution are as expansive as the rights and freedoms accorded to the

a proposal of the AKP. As Rıza Türmen (CHP) explains, the norm that "limitation is the exception" is integral to the ECtHR (AUK Proceedings, writing commission, May 17, 2012). Moreover, the article on the limitations of fundamental rights and freedoms specifies that "[i]n case of uncertainty, interpretation is made in favor of freedom."

19 One important element of the democratic backsliding is the silencing and persecution of all opposition through the purge that the government initiated in the aftermath of the July 2016 military coup attempt. For a case study of purges, see Tom Ruys and Emre Turkut, "Turkey's Post-Coup 'Purification Process': Collective Dismissals of Public Servants under the European Convention on Human Rights," *Human Rights Law Review* 18, no. 3 (2018): 539–565.

20 Merih Öden and Selin Esen, "Fundamental Rights and Freedoms in Turkey and the Turkish Constitutional Court," in *The Convergence of the Fundamental Rights Protection in Europe*, ed. R. Arnold (Dordrecht: Springer, 2016), 127–162.

21 Although the 2001 constitutional amendments reintroduced the phrase "Turkish Republic based upon human rights" in another article (Art. 14 on the prohibition on the abuse of

individual. While these all already hint at the problematic normative structure of the 1982 Constitution, the main grievance against the document has been its approach to limitations on rights and freedoms.

In its original formulation, rather than including either a general limitations clause or right-specific clauses, the 1982 Constitution had both. The original Article 13 provided general grounds for limitations to function alongside the specific limitations imposed in each individual article. These general reasons for restrictions were also generously defined, and included safeguarding the indivisible integrity of the state, its territory, the nation, national sovereignty, the republic, national security, public order, general peace, the public interest, public morals, and public health.[22] The 2001 constitutional amendment removed the general grounds for restrictions, aligning its framework closer to the European Convention on Human Rights. It also strengthened the position of fundamental rights and freedoms by prohibiting infringement upon their essence. Furthermore, it set forth that restrictions cannot be in conflict with the letter and spirit of the constitution, the principle of proportionality, the requirements of the democratic order, or the secular republic.

The 2001 changes also modified Article 14 on the prohibition of abuse of fundamental rights and freedoms. The amendments shortened the list of legitimate aims for prohibition of abuse and removed sanctions against individuals who incite or provoke such aims. More importantly, the revised article included the state as an actor that could potentially abuse the rights granted by the constitution.[23] Although the reformulation eased the restrictive approach of the constitution and provided a stronger shield against the abuse of rights and freedoms, the article primarily safeguards "the indivisible integrity of the state" and "the democratic and secular order of the Republic based on human rights" against the exercise of rights and freedoms. These two are essentially meant as shields to protect the national and secular identity of the Turkish Republic against the challenges of Kurdish nationalism and political Islam.

Besides modifying these two articles (Art. 13 on restriction of fundamental rights and freedoms and Art. 14 on prohibition of abuse of fundamental rights and freedoms), the 2001 constitutional amendments also reformulated the specific grounds for restriction of several individual articles, thus harmonizing

fundamental rights and freedoms), it does not afford the same degree of protection as the 1961 Constitution because it is not embedded in an unamendable article; see Mümtaz Soysal, "İnsan Hakları Açısından Temel Hak ve Özgürlüklerin Niteliği," *Anayasa Yargısı* 3 (1986): 37–49.

22 Levent Gönenç, "The 2001 Amendments to the 1982 Constitution of Turkey," *Ankara Law Review* 1, no. 1 (2004): 89–109, 99.

23 Ibid., 101.

them more with relevant articles of the Convention. These are instances of constitutional borrowing prior to the AUK's work in 2011–2013.[24] However, the variety of restrictions listed under individual articles (e.g., national security, public order, and public morals) continued to provide lawmakers the legal leeway to tinker with rights, and it gave broader discretion to the Constitutional Court to interpret the scope of rights in a restrictive manner.

The record of the Turkish Constitutional Court (*Anayasa Mahkemesi*, AYM) on the interpretation of fundamental rights has also been mixed.[25] Some criticize it for failing to be a defender of fundamental rights and freedoms.[26] Others find that the AYM's interpretation of the constitution and international documents on human rights has generally gone in the direction of strengthening fundamental rights and freedoms.[27] Still others emphasize that it often adopted a conservative, restrictive attitude in areas such as gender equality and freedom to organize political parties.[28] When it

24 The 2001 constitutional amendments modified the specific grounds for limitation of these articles: privacy of individual life (Art. 20), inviolability of domicile (Art. 21), freedom of communication (Art. 22), freedom of residence and movement (Art. 23), freedom of expression and dissemination of thought (Art. 26), right to use media other than the press owned by public corporations (Art. 31), and the right to organize unions (Art. 51). Except for the article on freedom of expression and dissemination of thought, these changes narrowed the scope of limitations that could be placed on the rights listed and aligned the text with European standards (ibid., 102–106).

25 While this chapter does not attempt to examine the role of the AYM in rights protection, it should be noted that the court's role has altered significantly since the failure of the AUK process. In the course of increasing democratic backsliding in Turkey, specifically under the state of emergency (2016–2018), the AYM has become much more deferential to executive authority despite the introduction of the right to individual petition in 2012, which had raised hopes that the court could become a guarantor of individual rights. See Dilek Kurban, "Think Twice before Speaking of Constitutional Review in Turkey," Feb. 20, 2018, *Verfassungsblog*, https://verfassungsblog.de/think-twice-before-speaking-of-constitutional-review-in-turkey/ (accessed March 31, 2019). In a few instances, when the AYM attempted to claim its role in fundamental rights protection, it has faced backlash from the government and the local courts. See Başak Çalı, "Will Legalism Be the End of Constitutionalism in Turkey?" *Verfassungsblog*, Jan. 22, 2018, https://verfassungsblog.de/will-legalism-be-the-end-of-constitutionalism-in-turkey/ (accessed March 31, 2019). For a more comprehensive assessment of the court's transformation, see Bertil Emrah Oder, "Populism and the Turkish Constitutional Court: The Game Broker, the Populist and the Popular," *I-CONnect*, May 2, 2017, www.iconnectblog.com/2017/05/populism-and-the-turkish-constitutional-court-the-game-broker-the-populist-and-the-popular/ (accessed March 31, 2019).

26 Ceren Belge, "Friends of the Court: The Republican Alliance and Selective Activism of the Constitutional Court of Turkey," *Law & Society Review* 40, no. 3 (2006): 653–692; Levent Köker, "Turkey's Political-Constitutional Crisis: An Assessment of the Role of the Constitutional Court," *Constellations* 17, no. 2 (2010): 328–344.

27 Öden and Esen, "Fundamental Rights and Freedoms in Turkey," 158–159.

28 Felix Petersen, "Judicial Review and Social Construction: The Case of the Turkish Constitutional Court," *Research and Policy on Turkey* 3, no. 1 (2018): 18–39; Dicle Koğacıoğlu, "Progress, Unity,

comes to the exercise of rights, the AYM's recognition and protection of rights and the application of ordinary laws that regulate these rights demonstrate a considerable difference. Focusing on the right to freedom of assembly, Başak Çalı, for example, demonstrates the gap between the application of restrictive ordinary law by the executive and the overall protection of the right to assembly under constitutional and international human rights law.[29]

In general, the discrepancy between the guarantee of constitutional rights and their implementation has been one of the main grievances directed at the 1982 Constitution, a shortcoming often noted in other nondemocracies as well. This gap between constitutional text and practice was a driving force in the constitutional deliberations of 2011–2013. As one of the AUK members, Ayla Akat Ata (BDP), explained while discussing the nature of fundamental rights and freedoms, "Here is our concern: . . . despite the fact that fundamental rights and freedoms are guaranteed in the Constitution, the reality on the ground has not allowed the extension of their scope. Rather, they were sometimes suspended or limited. That is why we would like some points to be strengthened [in the new constitution]."[30]

Paradoxically, although it was the rights-related shortcomings of the 1982 Constitution that galvanized support for a new constitution, the textual frame of the 1982 Constitution nonetheless provided a general structure for debates in 2011–2013. During the deliberations in the writing commission, the text of articles of the 1982 Constitution and the respective proposals of the four parties were displayed next to each other on a screen.[31] Pleas to draft more liberal and progressive articles than those provided by the 1982 Constitution were generally shared among delegates involved in the AUK, but to some extent the ghost of this constitution still directed the contours of the draft articles. Ozan Varol calls this path dependency "constitutional stickiness"; he argues that constitutional change does not always mean change in substance, and that "during constitutional makeovers, existing provisions frequently 'stick,' even where they are arbitrary, suboptimal, or anachronistic."[32]

To argue that the writing commission did not depart from the 1982 Constitution would nonetheless be an egregious misstatement. Among the agreed articles on rights and freedoms, we can distinguish between three types: provisions that are in their entirety novel, provisions that are similar to the 1982

and Democracy: Dissolving Political Parties in Turkey," *Law and Society Review* 38, no. 3 (2004): 433–461.

29 Başak Çalı, "The Power of Ordinary Laws and the Feebleness of Constitutional Rights: The Right to Freedom of Assembly in Turkey," *Research and Policy on Turkey* 2, no. 2 (2017): 162–178.

30 AUK Proceedings, writing commission, May 17, 2012.

31 Authors' interview with Rıza Türmen on May 24, 2018, Berlin.

32 Ozan Varol, "Constitutional Stickiness," *UC Davis Law Review* 49, no. 3 (2016): 889–961.

text but have been significantly revamped, and provisions that introduce very limited changes.[33] There is only one article – on the protection of consumers – that remains completely unchanged from the 1982 Constitution.[34]

The first type comprises four articles that were completely novel to Turkish constitutional law: the provision on human honor and dignity, which is elaborated below; the right to live in peace and in a disarmed society; the right to lead a decent life; and the right to access to information and freedom of information technology.[35] These four provisions had no prior footprint in previous constitutional texts, were progressive, and responded to changing social circumstances; as such, they had to draw inspiration from other constitutional texts. Importantly, they aimed to define the role of the state around the primacy of human dignity, an imported norm that became the backbone of the projected fundamental rights chapter, which is discussed in more detail in Section 3.1.

The German Basic Law is clearly the source of the article on human dignity and honor.[36] The right to live in peace and in a disarmed society, as the CHP and the BDP explained to the rest of the writing commission, is a norm that is found in a new generation of constitutions and that falls under the category "third generation of rights."[37] With the overarching goal of developing

[33] In his report for SETA, Taylan Barın provides a comprehensive analysis of agreed articles by examining them under three headings: (1) 1982 Constitution provisions changed by the commission; (2) new provisions that were not regulated by the 1982 Constitution; and (3) provisions that do not require amendments to the 1982 Constitution (Taylan Barın, "Uzlaşma Yolunda Komisyon'un Uzlaştığı Maddeler ve Anayasa," *SETA Analiz* 71 (August 2013). The scheme adopted in this article follows a similar framework.

[34] The article regulating protection of consumers, which was listed under the chapter on economic provisions in the 1982 Constitution, was moved by the writing commission to the chapter on fundamental rights and freedoms.

[35] The right to information and freedom of information technology was initially formulated by the BDP as a right to the Internet and electronic communication. The other three agreed articles were both CHP and BDP proposals. There were also other proposals that were outside the scope of the 1982 Constitution and that did not receive the support of the AUK, including the right to cultural identity, the right to truth, the right to the use of one's mother tongue, the right to conscientious objection, animal rights, women's rights, the right to basic income, and the right to clean water and adequate food, which were all BDP proposals, some of which were addressed in weaker form under other social rights.

[36] Article 17 of the 1982 Constitution did include an individual's right to improve his or her corporeal and spiritual existence, but the AUK's formulation is different.

[37] AUK Proceedings, writing commission, November 7, 2012. Özgür Sevgi Göral (BDP legal consultant) also added the right to truth as a right that the BDP sought recognition for. Göral referenced the Argentine Constitution (1994) as the only constitution that regulates it as a separate article. Göral also explained that truth commissions were formed in forty-four countries, including Guatemala, Chile, South Africa, and several countries in Africa and Europe.

a culture of peace and tolerance, it intends to realize the right to peace by enlisting the state to take measures to make access to guns difficult (CHP proposal) and to counter hate speech and discriminatory activities (BDP proposal). While the source of the right to lead a decent life is not as obvious, the article puts flesh on the concept of human honor and dignity and provides for an umbrella social right that includes more concrete rights (e.g., rights to education, shelter, medical care, nutrition, clean water, social services) as well as protection against social exclusion and poverty. More importantly, it stipulates that those deprived of a decent life are entitled to a basic income and social welfare. The article on the right to information and freedom of information technology is a good example of how new developments in technology find reflection in constitutional norms. It extends the right to privacy to the digital domain, but also directs future legislators to take into consideration other constitutional principles (e.g., protection of private data, freedom of communication, freedom of expression, freedom of the press, and protection of children against sexual abuse) in regulating this right.

Articles in the second group refer to fundamental rights and freedoms that were previously recognized by the 1982 Constitution, but which were strengthened in scope and substance by the AUK. Seven articles fall in this category: the right to life, the status of aliens, the right to health, the right to environment, the right to protection of personal data and information, the right to housing and shelter, and the right to work, workplace safety, and fair pay. Even though some of the concepts and ideas may have been addressed in the 1982 Constitution in weaker form, the AUK articles are substantially different. For instance, Article 17 ("Personal inviolability, corporeal and spiritual existence of the individual") of the 1982 Constitution did include the right to life, but the title of the provision did not.[38] Although the protection of personal data and information was introduced into the 1982 Constitution with the 2010 amendment of Article 20 (privacy of private life), its scope is enhanced in the draft produced by the AUK.

The right to health and the right to environment were not previously defined in concrete terms under the 1982 Constitution, either. Instead, these were jointly addressed under one article (Art. 56 on health services and protection of the environment), which stated that "everyone has the right to live in a healthy and balanced environment" and obliged the state to regulate health services and protect the environment. The writing commission transformed the loose commitment to a healthy environment into a constitutional

[38] Article 17 of the 1982 Constitution is a broad article, so the writing commission decided to allocate its different provisions to separate articles.

provision that firmly provides for a right to health, including safeguards for patient rights and guarantees for women to free access to health services regarding reproduction and fertility. In the discussions of this article, BDP consultant Özgür Sevgi Göral often referred to the constitutions of Spain, Portugal, Bolivia, and South Africa in order to justify free access to health services, but ultimately domestic input, namely the proposal of the Women's Constitutional Platform (*Anayasa Kadın Platformu*), was important for codifying this provision.[39] The right to environment was also transformed into a separate, detailed, and progressive social right that includes a right to demand the protection of the environment and a corresponding obligation of the state and all persons to take responsibility for future generations. Moreover, the right to environment includes objectives (e.g., "food naturalness") and approaches (e.g., public participation in decision-making in matters related to the right to environment) that were absent from the 1982 Constitution. Likewise, the article titled "Right to housing" under the 1982 Constitution fails to provide a concrete right, but instead affirms the state's duty to support housing projects and respond to housing needs. The AUK writing commission transformed this vague right into a substantial right that is grounded in the concept of human dignity. The commission's agreed article on "the right to housing and shelter" also espoused a more holistic approach than the prior provision and dictated that historical and cultural characteristics and environmental values be taken into consideration when the state carries out its duty to provide housing and shelter. This latter emphasis on state duties came from the BDP and CHP proposals, which were admittedly inspired by the European Social Charter.[40]

The articles that fall under the third type do not significantly change the wording of the 1982 Constitution. Although none of the articles is an exact duplicate, their novelty is limited. For example, the article on the prohibition of slavery and forced labor included a further ban on human trafficking, and the article on privacy and protection of private and family life included a provision requiring consent to disseminate information in the media (including the Internet). Freedom of science and arts is strengthened by removing the restriction on the dissemination of ideas contrary to unamendable articles. The scope of the right to unionize was extended to include "home workers." And the right to social security orders the state to build a social security system and prohibits work without insurance. These examples illustrate that the 1982 Constitution may have served as a structure for drafting

[39] AUK Proceedings, writing commission, September 12, 2012.
[40] Ibid., September 17, 2012; European Social Charter, Art. 31.

these articles, but their contents were transformed to substantiate the constitution's claim to expand rights and freedoms.

3 FUNDAMENTAL RIGHTS IN THE 2011–2013 PROCESS: INSTANCES OF CONSTITUTIONAL BORROWING AND NONBORROWING

3.1 *Horizontal Borrowing: Human Dignity as the Normative Foundation*

A Practical Guide to Constitution-Making, edited by the Institute for Democracy and Electoral Assistance (IDEA), highlights the role of constitutional principles in constitutionalization processes. It argues that constitutional principles, which may be grounded in a particular country's history, its common values, or some international or regional standards, provide a normative foundation for the drafting of a constitutional text.[41] Pressing problems or post-conflict constitution building may necessitate that constitutional principles address the specific problems or conflicts and provide citizens a sense of unity and commitment to a higher principle. The experience of a two-stage constitution-making process in South Africa is the primary example of how constitutional principles can play a crucial role in post-conflict constitution building. Commitment to broad, pre-agreed principles may help craft the foundation on which future negotiations can be grounded, take some difficult-to-reconcile matters off the negotiating table, resolve an impasse when parties reach a political deadlock, and reduce distrust among the participants of the process.[42] Drawing on the experience of constitution making in divided societies, Hanna Lerner argues that "predrafting agreements" addressing contentious identity issues facilitate political compromise in the drafting process and allow the major political actors to produce an inclusionary and democratic constitution.[43]

The 2011–2013 process began without establishing a set of constitutive principles or a political declaration that would guide constitution making

[41] IDEA defines constitutional principles as "a set of principles that explain [the constitution's] purpose and normative foundation and guide the understanding of the constitution as a whole." See Markus Böckenförde, Nora Hedling, and Winluck Wahiu, *A Practical Guide to Constitution-Making* (Stockholm: International IDEA Resources on Constitution Building, 2011), 47.

[42] Ibid., 47–48.

[43] Hanna Lerner differentiates predrafting agreements from interim constitutions and political pacts; see Lerner, "Constituent Assemblies and Political Continuity in Divided Societies," in *Constituent Assemblies*, eds. J. Elster, R. Gargarella, V. Naresh, and B.E. Rasch (Cambridge: Cambridge University Press, 2018), 57–78.

and set the tone for the constitutional framework. Before the process took off, Cemil Çiçek (AKP), then-president of the Parliament and then-chair of the Constitutional Conciliation Commission, held a meeting in September 2011 that brought together constitutional and public lawyers to discuss the method that would be adopted when drafting the new constitution (i.e., constitutional amendment or replacement). A central issue of this debate was the question of whether Parliament possessed the constituent power to make a new constitution, or if it was merely in possession of a limited power to revise the constitution via amendment. Participants either supported the idea of an extraordinary constituent assembly or argued that the ordinary legislature, newly elected in 2011, was empowered to draft a new constitution. Only one of the twenty-four participants questioned the necessity of a new constitution. Eleven of the attendees called for preliminary legislation or a document of understanding that would strengthen the legal base of the ordinary Parliament's power to write a new constitution. The meeting ended without reaching a conclusion on the question of whether to keep the unamendable articles and substantially revise the 1982 Constitution or to replace the existing constitution altogether.[44]

The political parties establishing the AUK agreed on a fifteen-point working plan, which provided limited guidance on how to overcome possible deadlock in the commission and prescribed the unanimity rule for reaching consensus on contested issues.[45] Political parties avoided public discussion on what kind of procedure would follow after the first draft was finalized by the AUK.[46] Only the largest opposition party, the CHP, produced a document expressing its vision for the new constitution, but its proposal to first issue an understanding of "the new constitution's spirit and philosophy" was not embraced by other AUK members.[47] Political party proposals published before the 2011 elections only revealed the vague intentions of the parties involved in the process.[48]

44 During the meeting, Bertil Emrah Oder called for a "document of consensus" that would facilitate trust building among participants of the constitution-making process and ease the polarized political climate; see "Anayasa Hukuku Hocalarıyla Toplantı," *TBMM Tutanak Müdürlüğü*, September 19, 2011.

45 See Petersen and Yanaşmayan, Chapter 1 in this volume. See also Bertil Emrah Oder, "The Much-Awaited and Deeply Controversial Constitutional Process: Learning from Turkey's Failed Process in 2013," in *Themes of Conflict in Middle Eastern Democracies: A Comparative Perspective from Israel and Turkey*, eds. Friedrich Ebert Stiftung and Van Leer Jerusalem Institute (Istanbul & Jerusalem, 2014), 136–140.

46 Fırat Cengiz, "The Future of Democratic Reform in Turkey: Constitutional Moment or Constitutional Process?" *Government and Opposition* 49, no. 4 (2014): 682–703.

47 Burak Çelik, "Yeni CHP'nin Yeni Anayasa Vizyonu," *T24*, June 10, 2011, https://t24.com.tr/haber/yeni-chpnin-yeni-anayasa-vizyonu,150253 (accessed March 31, 2019).

48 Levent Gönenç, "Siyasal Partilerin Seçim Bildirgelerinde Anayasa Konusu: 'Yol Haritası' Değil, 'Niyet Beyanı,'" *TEPAV*, May 2011, www.tepav.org.tr/upload/files/1306232876-0.Siyasal_Partileri

With the exception of the nationalist MHP, which only identified the unitary state and national sovereignty as objectives of the new constitution, all other parties adopted the traditional values of modern constitutionalism and called for a "democratic, pluralist, and liberal" constitution, with the explicit proposals differing from one another only minimally.[49] The constitution-making process took off without any predrafting agreements, and even without a document of understanding that would express the significance or aspirations of the process and establish the legal basis for the new constitution.[50]

As the commission did not have a roadmap or general framework to make the constitution, the concept of "human dignity" served as a guiding principle for deliberations on fundamental rights and freedoms. After six months of public consultation and just a few days before the commission began the drafting process, the subcommission, presided over by Cemil Çiçek, met to discuss the general principles and put forward a catalog of fundamental rights and freedoms to be included in the new constitution.

At this meeting AKP members highlighted the need to eradicate the "philosophy" of the 1982 Constitution, with its emphasis on the "sanctity of the state," and establish instead a new "individual-oriented" philosophy. CHP members, who were already concerned about the social polarization they had witnessed firsthand during the town hall meetings organized in different regions of Turkey prior to the drafting, were keen for the AUK to make an explicit statement about the new constitution's contribution to social peace and reconciliation. Within this understanding of the urgency to mitigate growing polarization, Atilla Kart (CHP) called for drawing the framework under "guiding principles" or "legal principles" and suggested that the constitution begin with the concept of "human dignity."[51] The adoption of this concept, which was directly inspired by the German Basic Law, is a clear instance of horizontal borrowing. The AUK extensively debated the concept and its exact translation (*onur, haysiyet, şeref,* or *izzet*), and in the end the CHP's proposal to build the new constitution around the concept of human dignity was supported by the BDP and the AKP.[52] BDP commission member Ayla Akat Ata noted that while the source of the human dignity clause may be

n_Secim_Bildirgelerinde_Anayasa_Konusu_Yol_Haritasi_Degil__Niyet_Beyani.pdf (accessed March 31, 2019).

49 Ibid.

50 Oder, "The Much-Awaited and Deeply Controversial," 137–138.

51 AUK Proceedings, writing commission, May 8, 2012.

52 See Ayda Erbal, "Yeni Anayasa Sürecini İzleme Raporu: Biz, Türkiye'nin Haysiyetli İnsanları 'Anayasa'da Yeni Bir Temel Hak Olarak Haysiyet,'" *TESEV Demokratikleşme Programı*, February 2015, 23–31.

the German Constitution, it has been taken up by more than forty constitutions in the aftermath of 1947 and has become "a political symbol of the human-centric approach of post-conflict constitution-making."[53] The nationalist MHP acknowledged that the commission had received many proposals mentioning human dignity, but argued that the concept was vague and its incorporation could lead to judicial activism. However, after several days of deliberation, the subcommission agreed on the very first two articles of the new constitution, human dignity, and the nature and integrity of fundamental rights.[54]

Hanna Lerner argues that deeply divided societies face a unique challenge in constitution making – the absence of societal consensus on ideational issues. As a divided society, Turkey is challenged by three deep divisions related to "state-religion relations, a civic versus an ethnic conception of citizenship, and the statism that prioritizes a strong and centralized executive order over the protection of individual rights."[55] In this context, the deep social cleavages prevented the commission from achieving consensus on the common aspirations and norms for the future constitutional order, hence human dignity emerged as the minimal value-free foundation all parties could agree upon.[56]

During the drafting of other provisions, AUK members often referred to the concept of human dignity and recognized that incorporating it in the draft would give the new constitution a new frame to build upon. Rıza Türmen (CHP), former judge of the ECtHR, gave an account of international documents and constitutions that begin with this norm. According to Türmen, the fact that the new Turkish constitution would commence with this norm signified that it would fundamentally differ from the previous document, as it rested on the individual and not the person of the state. According to BDP member Sırrı Süreyya Önder, the norm was perceived as "a life ring and insurance" against fascism and had acquired a certain weight because it developed in response to the experience of authority. Mustafa Şentop (AKP) shared similar views but emphasized that natural rights derived from the status

53 AUK Proceedings, writing commission, May 17, 2012.

54 Ibid., May 18, 2012.

55 Aslı Bali and Hanna Lerner, "Constitutional Design without Constitutional Moments: Lessons from Religiously Divided Societies," *Cornell International Law Journal* 79, no. 2 (2016): 227–308, 283.

56 Ayda Erbal ("Yeni Anayasa Sürecini İzleme Raporu," 3) identifies education in one's mother tongue, freedom to wear a headscarf, freedom of religion and belief, and cultural and identity rights as some of the issues that the incorporation of the human dignity concept sought to address.

of being an individual (the term he used was *eşrefi mahlukat*, which can best be translated as "honorable creature" with religious connotations).[57]

The absence of a precommitment to a set of founding constitutional principles, the desire of opposition parties to mitigate growing social polarization, and the need to distinguish the work of the AUK from the approach of the 1982 Constitution led AUK members to borrow a guiding constitutional norm from the German Basic Law.[58] The AUK's decision to open the draft constitutional text with the article on human dignity also signaled a rupture with the architecture and organization of prior Turkish constitutions, which prioritized state interests over individual rights. It should be noted, however, that even though human dignity was enumerated as Article 1, there was no consensus that this would become the opening article of the new constitution, as the AUK could not reach an agreement on repealing or replacing the first three articles (the unamendable articles) of the 1982 Constitution.[59]

Consensus on framing human dignity as an overarching concept at times provided justification to those opposing further expansion of fundamental rights and freedoms. During deliberations of the article on the right to live in peace and in a disarmed society,[60] Faruk Bal (MHP) explained his party's reason for opposing the provision, saying that it would be stating the obvious: "How can we, as members of a political party that has said 'yes' to a process of constitution building based on human dignity and honor, defend arming?" Human dignity enabled AUK members to claim that they had altered the mindset of the constitution, even if specific articles are not new. Mustafa Şentop (AKP) explained his rejection of a provision that would explicitly allow freedom of the press in one's "preferred language" (i.e., Kurdish and other minority languages): "We [AKP] believe that the constitution's mentality has to be different. That has been achieved – we have drafted the first article on human dignity and its inviolability . . . . We think that is crucial."

57 AUK Proceedings, writing commission, May 10, 2012. Such an image of human rights as being mostly concerned with human dignity is in line with the argument that Islam has a tradition of human rights (see Jack Donnelly, "Human Rights and Human Dignity: An Analytic Critique of Non-Western Conceptions of Human Rights," *The American Political Science Review* 76, no. 2 (1982): 303–316). The 1943 Cairo Declaration on Human Rights in Islam also highlights human dignity in Article 1: "All men are equal in terms of basic human dignity and basic obligations and responsibilities, without any discrimination on the basis of race, color, language, belief, sex, religion, political affiliation, social status or other considerations."

58 Erbal ("Yeni Anayasa Sürecini İzleme Raporu," 2) notes that the decision to include human dignity is reminiscent of the transitional justice constitutions of South Africa and Germany.

59 Oya Yegen, "Debating Unamendability: Deadlock in Turkey's Constitution-Making Process," in *An Unamendable Constitution? Unamendability in Constitutional Democracies*, eds. R. Albert and B.E. Oder (Springer, 2018), 281–312.

60 Art. 44, List of Agreed Articles, in this volume Appendix B.

As illustrated with regard to human dignity, the drafting of fundamental rights and freedoms strongly relied on existing international norms. This is not surprising, as Turkey has previously engaged in significant legal import and constitutional borrowing. Esin Örücü describes the Turkish legal process as a product "constructed through a succession of imposed receptions, voluntary receptions, imitations and adjustments, the elements of chance, choice, historical accident and the prestige of the competing legal models all playing important roles."[61] In terms of constitutional law, there is precedent for borrowing. The 1961 Constitution bears the mark of the West German and Italian models, and, according to Örücü, borrows from India's constitutional provisions on economic development.[62] As Valentina Scotti argues, the type of judicial review adopted with the 1961 Constitution is influenced by the German model, and the individual complaint mechanism adopted in 2010 is a mix of the German and Spanish models.[63] This shows that in terms of constitutional borrowing, the AUK did follow in the footsteps of previous constitution makers. With regard to human dignity, the AUK used horizontal constitutional borrowing to compensate for the absence of any other normative foundation for the new constitution.

3.2 *Vertical Borrowing: International Human Rights Framework*

Hierarchization of Norms in the AUK: Superiority of the Convention

In the deliberations on fundamental rights, the AUK members made extensive reference to the international human rights regime. It was not only referred to as a broader framework with which Turkey should comply, but also used more

[61] Esin Örücü, "Comparatists and Extraordinary Places," in *Comparative Legal Studies: Traditions and Transitions*, eds. P. Legrand and R. Munday (Cambridge: Cambridge University Press, 2011), 467–493, 478. Örücü has produced most of the English-language scholarly work on legal imports in the Turkish case (Esin Örücü, "The Impact of European Law on the Ottoman Empire and Turkey," in *European Expansion and Law*, eds. W. J. Mommsen and J. de Moor (Oxford: Berg, 1992), 39–58; Esin Örücü, "A Theoretical Framework for Transfrontier Mobility of Law," in *Transfrontier Mobility of Law*, eds. R. Jagtenberg, E. Örücü, and A. J. de Roo (The Hague: Kluwer Law International, 1995), 5–18; Esin Örücü, "Turkey: Change under Pressure," in *Studies in Legal Systems: Mixed and Mixing*, eds. E. Örücü, E. Attwool, and S. Coyle (The Hague: Kluwer Law International, 1996), 89–111; Esin Örücü, "Turkey Facing the European Union – Old and New Harmonies," *European Law Review* 25 (2000): 57–71; Esin Örücü, "Law as Transposition," *International and Comparative Law Quarterly* 51, no. 2 (2002): 205–223.

[62] Örücü, "Turkey Facing the European Union," 57.

[63] Valentina Rita Scotti, "Constitutional Borrowing in Turkey: The Influences of Foreign Models from the 1924 Constitution to the New Constituent Attempts," IACL 2014 Conference, Panel 5, Oslo, June 16–20, 2014 (unpublished paper).

specifically to draw inspiration for the drafting of provisions. Particularly relevant was the European Convention on Human Rights. In several instances, the initial party proposals were verbatim translations of the Convention's provisions, which were considered minimal standards upon which they almost unanimously agreed. The instances in which citing the Convention led to successful argumentation are too many to cite, which shows that the Convention functioned as a significant source of consensus in the domain of fundamental rights.

This can be partially explained by the fact that representatives of the political parties predominantly had legal backgrounds (eight out of twelve), namely as lawyers, legal scholars, and judges (including a former judge of the European Court of Human Rights). Therefore, the AUK members and their consultants who were heavily involved in the drafting spoke the same technical and legalistic language and jargon that often made reference to the Convention. In other words, they can be likened to an "epistemic community," which is a network of professionals not only with recognized expertise and competence in a particular policy-relevant domain, but also with shared values, beliefs, and a common policy project with regard to that domain.[64] However, AUK members were not acting as a lobby group or an advisory body that promotes its shared values in order to influence policy making. They were representing political parties that stand at different ends of the political spectrum and were part and parcel of policymaking at the highest level possible, that of constitution making. Therefore, even though their socialization in the same epistemic community helped them move forward with constitution drafting, their allegiance to their political parties and commitment to "red lines" prevented them nonetheless from achieving full consensus on the fundamental rights chapter.

While the European Convention on Human Rights enjoyed enormous normative authority in the discussions, efforts to transplant norms from other human rights treaties or international norms were often met with resistance. This indicates a hierarchization of different international norms in the AUK discussions. As mentioned above, hierarchization had to a certain extent to do with the institutionalization of the respective norms. But in the end, it mostly depended on party preferences. For instance, Rıza Türmen (CHP), a former judge of the European Court of Human Rights, very often sought to make the

64 Peter M. Haas, "Do Regimes Matter? Epistemic Communities and Mediterranean Pollution Control," *International Organization* 4, no. 83 (1989): 377–405; Emanuel Adler and Peter M. Haas, "Conclusion: Epistemic Communities, World Order, and the Creation of a Reflective Research Program," *International Organization* 46, no. 1 (1992): 367–390.

case that the provisions of the Convention should be interpreted in light of the case law of the ECtHR. However, this did not always persuade other AUK members who had different party sensitivities on certain fundamental rights provisions that touched upon long-standing societal issues (e.g., state-religion relations, the Kurdish question, party closures).

Since its inception, the Turkish Constitutional Court has shut down twenty-seven political parties on the basis of the long list of grounds provided for party closure in the constitution, which have been interpreted by the court with extreme rigidity.[65] Most of these cases relate to alleged violations of constitutional provisions protecting the secular character or the indivisible national and territorial integrity of the state.[66] The BDP and the AKP were both born out of ideological movements – Kurdish and political Islamist, respectively – whose political parties have typically been banned by the Turkish Constitutional Court. This implies that members of some of the political parties represented in the AUK had been disproportionately affected by party closures in the past and had good reason to fear that it could happen again. A number of party closure cases were brought before the ECtHR, where Turkey was found to be in breach of the Convention in all but one case, which is the closure of the Welfare Party (*Refah Partisi*) in 1998. In its decision *Refah Partisi and Others v. Turkey* (2003), the ECtHR concluded that the Welfare Party's proposed changes to the system, particularly the desire to establish sharia, would be incompatible with democratic principles. It is precisely this point that Rıza Türmen (CHP) raised when explaining the CHP's formulation of the provision on party prohibition in reference to the case law of the ECtHR:[67]

> When you look at the judgments of the European Court of Human Rights, I have now in front of me the judgment on the HADEP case, but you have a series of decisions, you notice two principles that are reiterated. Political parties can propose to change the constitutional order or legislation; however, there are two conditions. First, the means used for bringing about such changes should be legal and democratic. That means you cannot resort to violence to change the system. And second, the proposed change should not be against the basic tenets of democracy. In other words, even if a political

[65] Ödül Celep, "The Political Causes of Party Closures in Turkey," *Parliamentary Affairs* 67, no. 2 (2014): 371–390; Ergun Özbudun, "Party Prohibition Cases: Different Approaches by the Turkish Constitutional Court and the European Court of Human Rights," *Democratization* 17, no. 1 (2010): 125–142.

[66] Ergun Özbudun and Füsun Türkmen, "Impact of the ECtHR Rulings on Turkey's Democratization: An Evaluation," *Human Rights Quarterly* 35, no. 4 (2013): 985–1008.

[67] AUK Proceedings, writing commission, August 16, 2012.

> party does not resort to violence but pursues goals that are incompatible with democracy, this cannot be protected under freedom of assembly and association.[68]

Even though CHP members did not specifically mention the Welfare Party case, the AKP legal consultant Yavuz Atar rejected this proposal and instead proposed using the Venice Commission recommendations as a benchmark:[69]

> Now, if we agree that the proposed change should be democratic, according to which criteria will the European Court of Human Rights make such a check? For instance, in the Welfare Party decision legal pluralism was considered to be incompatible with democracy. Is this really the case? We are of the opinion that the standard set by the Venice Commission is more appropriate than the ECtHR jurisprudence.

In a report titled "Guidelines on Prohibition and Dissolution of Political Parties and Analogous Measures," the Venice Commission mentions only incitement to or the use of violence as justifications for party prohibition.[70] This report and the Venice Commission's draft opinion on Turkey[71] were widely discussed by AUK members and their legal consultants, and in the end they served as the basis of the partially agreed clause on party closure, showing another instance of horizontal constitutional borrowing.

The deliberations also witnessed instances of reluctance to borrow, such as when Mustafa Şentop (AKP) stated that the ECtHR is a partial court that acts at times politically rather than "purely legally,"[72] particularly in its encounters with Islam, or when Süheyl Batum (CHP) strongly criticized the prioritization of Venice Commission recommendations over ECtHR judgments and called the former a "freak of an organization."[73] However, in general, there was strong consensus regarding the relevance of international norms and the need for Turkey to improve its human rights record. Initially, there was also great confidence that the AUK would be the most suitable body to achieve such an improvement. This is epitomized in the words of Ahmet İyimaya (AKP):

68 Ibid., August 16, 2012.

69 Özbudun and Türkmen, "Impact of the ECtHR Rulings," 10.

70 For the full report, see: www.venice.coe.int/webforms/documents/default.aspx?pdffile=CDL-INF(2000)001-e (accessed March 23, 2019).

71 See the draft opinion here: www.venice.coe.int/webforms/documents/default.aspx?pdffile=CDL(2009)014-e (accessed March 31, 2019).

72 AUK Proceedings, writing commission, August 8 and 16, 2012.

73 Ibid., September 4, 2012.

> Of course, we will make use of the European Court of Human Rights, but I think we are capable of building a regime of closure [of political parties] that would be exemplary to the European Court of Human Rights, to the European Convention on Human Rights, and to the world. Our experts are here, we are here, and our experience goes beyond Europe's.[74]

While in the discussions on party closure the Venice Commission criteria seem to have been prioritized over ECtHR judgments, there were also successful attempts, mostly from Rıza Türmen (CHP) but also from BDP legal consultant Meral Danış Beştaş, to transfer norms from ECtHR decisions into provisions. In the discussions on religious freedom (an article on which the AUK members did not agree), an unexpected agreement occurred regarding the first clause, which defined the meaning of this freedom. The Convention regulates freedom of religion under Article 9, on which the ECtHR has ruled in a considerable number of landmark decisions involving Turkey. For example, in the notorious *Leyla Sahin v. Turkey* decision (2004), the ECtHR found no violation of Article 9 and considered the ban on headscarves in universities a legitimate public measure that allowed the state to deviate from a rigid concept of religious freedom in order to uphold the secular structure of the state.[75] A great number of applications in similar cases from Turkey were almost automatically rendered inadmissible. In that sense, freedom of religion, as argued by Dilek Kurban, constitutes "a rare area where the ECtHR has by and large ruled in favour of the government."[76] Not surprisingly, these rulings were not positively evaluated by all AUK members. ECtHR judgments were nevertheless utilized in order to expand the first clause of the provision on religious freedom so as to include nonbelievers under its protection. Relying on the *Kokkinadis v. Greece* case, Rıza Türmen (CHP) stated that the contours of freedom of religion are defined to include agnostics, atheists, skeptics, and other types of beliefs.[77] Initially, this proposal was rejected by both the AKP and the MHP members, who insisted on a verbatim application of Article 9 of the European Convention on Human Rights, which does not explicitly mention the freedom not to hold any religious beliefs. Mustafa Şentop (AKP) further argued that the absence of an explicit reference is not an impediment to the freedom being inclusive of nonbelievers, nor to the

[74] AUK Proceedings, August 28, 2012.

[75] *Leyla Sahin v. Turkey*, Chamber judgment 2004, no. 44774/98.

[76] Dilek Kurban, "Protecting Marginalised Individuals and Minorities in the ECtHR: Litigation and Jurisprudence in Turkey," in *The European Court of Human Rights and the Rights of Marginalised Individuals and Minorities in National Context*, eds. D. Anagnostou and E. Psychogiopoulou (Leiden: Martinus Nijhoff Publishers, 2010), 159–183, 178.

[77] *Kokkinadis v. Greece*, Chamber judgment 1993, no. 14307/88.

article being read as such by the courts. This position was also backed by Faruk Bal (MHP), who contended that an explicit reference was not necessary and that the freedom not to believe was inherent in the formulation of the first clause.

This discussion is again a clear sign of the hierarchization of international norms, which prioritizes the Convention above all else. However, in this particular case, the interpretation of the Convention through the ECtHR was in the end accepted, that is to say, the parties agreed to include the freedom not to believe in the draft constitution in the last meeting of the AUK, where they had decided to postpone the negotiations on the article due to major disagreements.[78] Nevertheless, it shows again how horizontal borrowing has led to a striking constitutional novelty.

These examples from the deliberations on party closures and religious freedom show how ECtHR judgments and Venice Commission reports could be employed as legitimate sources for drafting fundamental rights. They helped the AUK reach consensus even on clauses of provisions that were not fully accepted. The examples also highlight the hierarchization of international norms among the actors involved in constitution making. While the Convention had clear authority, ECtHR judgments and Venice Commission recommendations, despite their different levels of legalization, were more contested. Such hierarchization became particularly clear in the discussions of the provision on nondiscrimination, during which efforts to draw attention to Turkey's international obligations under the Council of Europe Convention on preventing and combating violence against women and domestic violence (the Istanbul Convention) were categorically rejected by the AKP and the MHP.

The source of the conflict was the proposal to grant explicit protection to sexual identity as well as sexual orientation in the constitutional text. Not only were AUK members less acquainted with the content of the Istanbul Convention, they also did not perceive it as problematic to openly oppose and/or disregard it. Following Sırrı Süreyya Önder's (BDP) citation of Article 4 of the Istanbul Convention (Fundamental rights, equality, and nondiscrimination), and a summary of foreign constitutions that protect sexual orientation, an uninformed discussion ensued in the commission.[79] For instance, Mehmet Ali Şahin (AKP) stated that although he was not against protecting

[78] AUK Proceedings, writing commission, September 11, 2012. For more on the debates on religious freedom, see Zeynep Yanaşmayan, "Oppositional Usages of Europeanization in Turkish Constitution-Making: Discussions on Religious Freedom," *Turkish Studies* 18, no. 4 (2017): 644–664.

[79] AUK Proceedings, writing commission, May 15, 2012.

the fundamental right of persons with *such* orientations, he was strongly opposed to spelling out a protection clause:

> Different from you [he means the other BDP and CHP members], I consider such orientations to be an anomaly and a negative condition for society as a whole. I think it would be beneficial for society to take some measures. This is why I think it is sufficient to use the clause "everybody is equal in this regard without distinction as to sex." Otherwise, this would have a negative impact on public opinion about the constituting-making process.

Rıza Türmen (CHP) backed the suggestion of BDP members by clearly stating the paradoxical nature of the reluctance to codify protection of sexual identity and sexual orientation, given that Turkey is a party to the Istanbul Convention and also one of the first countries to have ratified it. However, such reminders of international obligations were rebutted very openly not only by AKP members, but also by MHP representatives. Oktay Öztürk (MHP), for instance, stated that not all the ECtHR decisions or EU regulations would have to find their way into the constitution, and that if they did, it would "blow up" the constitution. Therefore, following the hierarchization of norms that the AUK members had in mind, the deliberations also witnessed, albeit rarely, instances of nonborrowing. However, in general, horizontal constitutional borrowing allowed for substantial improvement of the 1982 Constitution, which is also evident in the discussions of the limitations on fundamental rights and freedoms.

Limitations on Fundamental Rights and Freedoms: Moving beyond the Convention?

The AUK's effort to distance itself from the 1982 Constitution's infamous attitude toward fundamental rights and freedoms is most obvious when it comes to limitations on rights. Deliberating limitations in the context of religious freedom (which ultimately remained contested), there was consensus that the 1982 Constitution could not possibly serve as a model for the AUK. Tunca Toskay (MHP) said that "it is a constitution that we are all allergic to." Rıza Türmen (CHP) agreed, stating, "Indeed. God forbid we take it as a model."[80] The Convention, then, played a double role in the discussions of the limitations on fundamental rights and freedoms. First, it allowed the AUK to structure the scheme of limitations (e.g., general clause or right-specific limitations). Second, it served as a template with regard to

[80] Ibid., August 8, 2012.

right-specific limitation clauses and enabled the AUK to claim that the draft went beyond the Convention.

Starting with the former usage of the Convention, limitations on rights and freedoms can be constitutionalized by either including a general limitation clause or by including right-specific limitation clauses.[81] The original text of the 1982 Constitution provided a general limitation clause in Article 13. This article was later amended with the 2001 constitutional amendments, which removed the grounds for a general limitation and introduced a prohibition against infringing on the essence of rights and freedoms. This brought the approach in line with the Convention. The agreed draft article on the restriction of fundamental rights and freedoms produced by the AUK does not alter this.[82] The drafted article establishes that rights and freedoms can be limited only by law or for reasons specified under the respective rights. The article also provides the conditions for these limitations. The limitations can only serve an objective defined by law and cannot go against the foreseen objective, the democratic public order, or the principle of proportionality. Furthermore, the revamped article on rights limitations stipulates firmly that "freedom is the norm, limitation is the exception," and, in case of uncertainty, it instructs future interpreters to side with an interpretation that expands freedoms.

The article on the prohibition of abuse of rights (Art. 14 of the 1982 Constitution) was removed from the draft text of the AUK, but its central provision, which prescribes that "[n]o provision of this Constitution shall be interpreted in a manner that enables the State or individuals to destroy the fundamental rights and freedoms recognized by the Constitution or to stage an activity with the aim of restricting them more extensively than stated in the Constitution," got absorbed in the article on the protection of fundamental rights and freedoms.[83] This provision is again an example of horizontal borrowing, as it repeats almost verbatim Article 17 of the Convention. Content-wise, it included the duty of the state to protect rights and freedoms and prevent their violation, established the liability of the state in cases of violation, and safeguarded against their destruction or limitation. It also opened the way for further horizontal constitutional borrowing by stipulating that, if international agreements and domestic law are in conflict, provisions of international agreements prevail as long as domestic law is not already broader in terms of freedoms. In short, this reconfigured draft article on protection of

81 It is also possible for a given constitution to have no limitations clause or for a general limitation clause to come with right-specific limitation clauses.

82 Art. 41, List of Agreed Articles, in this volume Appendix B.

83 Ibid., Art. 43.

fundamental rights and freedoms includes elements that were previously addressed elsewhere in the constitution, bringing together all elements that provide for the protection of rights and freedoms under one article.[84] Under the 1982 Constitution, there was no provision that called for effective implementation of fundamental rights and freedoms. Most significantly, the draft article provided that, in case of infringement, the state is liable and lawsuits could be brought against the state.

Regarding the temporary suspension of fundamental rights and freedoms, the draft article introduces some elements that were absent in previous constitutions.[85] In line with the new framework, the AUK draft text incorporates new grounds to consider when suspending fundamental rights: human dignity. Along with the individual's rights to life and integrity of his or her corporeal and spiritual existence, human dignity is recognized as another inviolable right that can never be suspended. Furthermore, the agreed article removed the distinction made by the 1982 Constitution between a state of exception and a state of siege. The BDP argued against including an article on the suspension of rights and freedoms by providing accounts of instances where the Turkish state has historically acted arbitrarily when it comes to suspending rights.[86] Limiting fundamental rights and freedoms under a state of emergency is well established in the Convention and in the 1982 Constitution, which made it easier for the AUK to achieve consensus on this matter.[87] In this instance, reference to the Convention served as a model that did not push for further protection of fundamental rights and freedoms, but instead allowed the AUK to maintain the suspension provision and, hence, a more restrictive approach.

When it came to specific limitations, the drafters were of the opinion that even the Convention was too broad in its recognition of limitations. All parties claimed to be more progressive than the Convention with regard to fundamental rights limitations. For instance, during the deliberations on the freedom of residence and movement, the AUK noted how it had narrowed down grounds for limitation from seven in the Convention to three in the draft text.[88] In cases where the Convention was invoked as a model by those who

84 The article has brought together provisions from Articles 14, 40, and 90 of the 1982 Constitution.

85 Art. 42, List of Agreed Articles, in this volume Appendix B. This article originates in Article 15 of the 1982 Constitution.

86 See Ayşe Kadıoğlu, "Necessity and the State of Exception: The Turkish State's Permanent War with Its Kurdish Citizens," in *Turkey between Nationalism and Globalization*, ed. R. Kastoryano (London: Routledge 2014), 142–161.

87 AUK Proceedings, writing commission, September 26, 2012.

88 Ibid., August 13, 2013.

championed broader grounds for limitation, supporters of enhancing fundamental rights pointed to the case law of the ECtHR. For instance, during the deliberations on the inviolability of one's domicile,[89] Selin Esen (CHP legal consultant) explained: "The ECHR is a contract made in 1950. The European Court of Human Rights interprets the grounds for limitations much more narrowly."[90] This idea that the Convention is outdated in some ways allowed the AUK to draft the article on protection of fundamental rights and freedoms, so that it takes into consideration scenarios in which an international treaty is outdated or the domestic laws are more specific.[91]

Now that we have shown the impact of both vertical and horizontal constitutional borrowing on introducing constitutional novelties and substantially improving the protection of fundamental rights, we turn to some of the different drafting tactics that the AUK employed to reach agreement on contested issues.

4 DRAFTING TACTICS

The AUK spent the great majority of its time on the chapter on fundamental rights and freedoms. This chapter was deliberated four times, while the chapter on the judiciary was discussed three times, and the remaining seven chapters were deliberated only twice. Initially, the AUK had agreed that each political party would prepare its own proposal for forty-two articles that were to be included in the catalog of fundamental rights and freedoms. Later proposals from the CHP and the BDP that attempted to expand the list were also discussed. Even though it would be difficult to claim that the AUK benefited from multiple deliberations, the sequence of debates, namely the initial momentum experienced when the AUK first began the deliberation process, gave the participants more impetus and incentive to achieve consensus early on in the process. They also made use of several drafting tactics to keep that momentum going. According to Hanna Lerner, in order to overcome internal ideational polarization, in deeply divided societies drafters may adopt such strategies as "avoiding clear-cut decisions, using ambiguous legal language, and inserting internally contradictory provisions into the

89 Art. 12, List of Agreed Articles, in this volume Appendix B.

90 AUK Proceedings, writing commission, January 8, 2013.

91 Art. 43, List of Agreed Articles, in this volume Appendix B.

constitution."[92] These strategies are intentional; they enable the constitution-making body to avoid having to make "unequivocal choices with respect to the most contested foundational issues" and allow it to defer controversial choices to the future and to the realm of ordinary politics.[93]

4.1 *Deferral to Subcommissions and Consultants*

In the case of the AUK, deferral did not necessarily entail deferral to future political institutions or legislatures. Opposition parties in particular were very wary of such deferral. Instead, to overcome immediate deadlocks and move forward, members of the AUK delegated controversial issues to subcommissions, the upper commission, or their consultants, or delayed contested issues until future deliberations.[94] This strategy, however, led drafters to defer compromise in anticipation that the upper commission could reformulate non-agreed provisions. Tuncay Toskay (MHP) conveyed this concern during the debates on freedom of residence and movement: "[W]hatever we do, my understanding from the work of the commission from yesterday, and previously as well, is that these articles will be discussed all over again."[95] Süheyl Batum (CHP) argued when deliberating freedom of association that, by virtue of not being the upper commission, they could put up a better "fight."[96] The upper commission's status and the fact that it was being presided over by Cemil Çiçek, the then-president of the Parliament, afforded additional civility and enhanced the possibility of compromise. In later stages, when the members of the writing commission were not able to resolve deadlock or had concerns regarding the procedure, calls for a meeting chaired by Çiçek were seen as a way out.[97]

92 Hanna Lerner, *Making Constitutions in Deeply Divided Societies* (Cambridge: Cambridge University Press, 2011), 39.

93 Ibid., 110.

94 During the early stages of drafting (covering the first round of deliberations on fundamental rights and freedoms), the commission worked in two subcommissions. According to the official note published on the website of the TBMM's Constitution and Rules of Procedure, the objective of working in two subcommittees was to achieve efficiency and productivity, but members' desire to take part in both committees and the difficulty of convening due to absences and scheduling constraints cut this experience short. From September 2012 to mid-January 2013, the two subcommittees held thirty-three and twenty-two separate meetings.

95 AUK Proceedings, writing commission, June 21, 2012.

96 Ibid., June 27, 2012.

97 During the deliberations on the possible incorporation of rights and freedoms that were initially left out of the pre-agreed catalog of rights and freedoms, AKP and CHP members agreed to make more of an effort to reach out to Cemil Çiçek (AUK Proceedings, September 20, 2012).

Another strategy regularly employed by the AUK was to delegate contested issues or the precise formulation of provisions to legal consultants. Such delegation of tasks provided the writing commission with several benefits. First, the meetings held by consultants were not recorded, and the secrecy may have made compromise easier and more likely.[98] For instance, in debating the right to health, Oktay Öztürk (MHP) suggested that the commission members step out of the meeting room and leave the experts alone so that they could craft consensus as they had previously done. The article on the right to health was ultimately one of the agreed articles. Second, although consultants were appointed by political parties, they had technical and legal expertise and were presumed to be less susceptible to deep disagreements based on party priorities. Continuing with the example of the right to health, Süheyl Batum (CHP) suggested moving on to the next clause of the article once a minimal consensus was established among the members and to leave the writing of the article to the experts.[99] Such delegation upon establishing minimum consensus among the four political parties was a common practice. In other instances where the AUK had achieved maximum consensus but differed with respect to the wording of a provision, they also appealed to consultants and legal experts because of their technical expertise and for the sake of time efficiency. For instance, in debating the right to housing, the members of the AUK could not agree on whether it should make reference to the right to shelter and the right to nourishment. Oktay Öztürk (MHP) and Ahmet İyimaya (AKP) suggested that, since they agreed on the content, the experts could "resolve the matter in terms of framing it."[100]

In addition, consultants were tasked with reviewing the proposals, analyzing constitutions of other countries and international documents, and sometimes also with conducting academic studies on certain unsettled concepts. Faruk Bal (MHP) instructed the consultants to do an academic study on concepts (e.g., national security, public order, preferred language, environmental) because the AUK needed "scientific and academic opinions":

> If political parties can ground their political will in scientific and academic values, once we proceed by articles, I believe a significant part of the matter [disagreement] will be resolved. If there is no consensus on a definition, each party understands it according to its own sensibilities – which is right from the

98 As Jon Elster ("Arguing and Bargaining in Two Constituent Assemblies," *Journal of Constitutional Law* 2, no. 2 (2000): 345–421, 414) argues, "secrecy tends to induce bargaining, and publicity to induce argument."

99 AUK Proceedings, September 12, 2012.

100 Ibid., September 17, 2012.

perspective of each party – and the natural result is that everyone defends their own opinion in case of disagreement.[101]

Relying on consultants did not always help achieve consensus, particularly when it came to the most polarizing issues. During the drafting of the article on freedom of religion and conscience, Tunca Toskay (MHP) recognized that there were some overlaps among three parties, and suggested that one consultant from each party study the proposals in order to come up with a working draft.[102] Even though this proposal "saved the day" and helped overcome the stalemate, it did not help the AUK reach consensus on an article that included "red lines" for all parties involved.

Deferral to future deliberations was also exercised by simply delaying the debate. This practice was most obvious with regard to articles that were proposed by political parties in addition to the catalog of rights and freedoms they had initially agreed on.[103] Debates over proposals that were outside the scope of the 1982 Constitution and the list of articles the AUK had agreed should be included in the rights framework were continuously deferred to future deliberations.

4.2 *Deferral through By Law Clauses*

Another deferral strategy was to delegate issues to future legislatures by explicitly including by law clauses. According to Rosalind Dixon and Tom Ginsburg, by law clauses may "either require the legislature to decide certain constitutional issues in the future, or explicitly empower it to decide such issues."[104] As a mechanism of constitutional deferral, by law clauses help respond to potential decision and error costs.[105] Constitution makers may agree that a certain issue demands to be regulated by the constitution, but they may not agree on how it should be regulated.[106] From the proceedings of

101 Ibid., December 20, 2012.

102 Ibid., August 8, 2012.

103 Fundamental rights and freedoms that were previously excluded from the catalog include the right to live in a peaceful and disarmed society, the right to access to information and freedom of the Internet, the right to lead a fair and decent life, the right to cultural identity, the right to truth, the right to use one's mother tongue, the right to conscientious objection, and animal rights.

104 Rosalind Dixon and Tom Ginsburg, "Deciding Not to Decide: Deferral in Constitutional Design," *International Journal of Constitutional Law* 9, nos. 3–4 (2011): 636–672, 640.

105 Decision costs refer to "the costs of deliberating, negotiating and finalizing an agreement," while the error costs refer to "the gap between the expected outcome of a policy and its actual outcome" (ibid., 642–643).

106 Ibid., 646.

the writing commission, we observe that on some occasions by law clauses had been utilized to break deadlock. A controversial issue for the AUK was how to reconcile the language rights demands of the pro-Kurdish BDP with the antagonistic attitudes of other parties regarding this issue. In one clause of the article on the freedom of the press, which ultimately remained contested, the AUK settled on the wording, "broadcasting in languages other than Turkish is regulated by law."[107]

By law clauses may also include certain procedural or substantive limits on how future legislatures should address a respective constitutional issue. An example of such an application of by law clauses is the article on the protection and utilization of the coasts. Based on the proposal of the CHP, the writing commission adopted a provision stipulating that the right to use the sea, lakes, waterways, and coasts was to be regulated by law, taking into account the public interest. Responding to a direct and current environmental issue of unregulated land reclamation, the article further stipulated that when land fill is necessitated by the public interest, methods and procedures for it shall be laid down in law. The issue of land filling therefore becomes constitutional, but taking into consideration potential environmental damage becomes a constraint placed on the ability of future governments to create new land from the sea. The 1982 Constitution did have an article on coasts (Art. 43), but it was not formulated as a right. Instead it stated that "the coasts are under the authority and disposal of the state." The new constitution would have included the identical provision, but it also stipulated that everyone has a right to the sea, lakes, rivers, and coasts. It went further in the protection of the environment by incorporating a by law clause limiting the choices of the legislature. In other words, the provision managed to achieve consensus on the centrality of the public interest regarding this issue without having to achieve consensus on the exact policy choices of the constitution-making body.[108]

[107] The provision on freedom of the press was not contested, but the MHP reserved the right to review it.

[108] Another example of a by law clause deferring a matter to future legislatures is the draft article on the right to information and freedom of information technology. This article also places constraints on how future laws ought to regulate the issue. The last paragraph of the draft article is a by law clause that lists a number of constitutional norms (including the right to privacy, freedom of speech, freedom of media, and protection of children against sexual abuse) that must be taken into consideration when future legislatures determine the scope of the right of access to the Internet and other electronic communication platforms. The decision to leave an issue to ordinary law, while at the same time determining its basic outlines, may also be a precaution against "vagaries of downstream change" (Dixon and Ginsburg, "Deciding Not to Decide: Deferral in Constitutional Design," 644). Information may be limited or subject to change, but at the same time drafters may wish to guarantee that future legislation follows the standards that they have established.

4.3 *Reasoning-Writing*

Another deadlock-breaking mechanism frequently employed during the drafting process was to resolve contention in the reasoning of a given article. During the several stages when AUK members debated the articles on fundamental rights and freedoms, some suggested that an explanation in the reasoning would help achieve consensus. This suggestion received a positive response from the majority of AUK members, and it enabled them to proceed with drafting. Rıza Türmen (CHP) explained that the rationale behind recourse to reasoning-writing was to find a compromise. Accordingly, if there is no consensus on whether the subject matter (here sexual orientation) is to be included in the text of the article, there is always the possibility of achieving consensus by including it in the reasoning.[109]

The strategy of pushing a specific issue out of the constitutional text and into the nonconstitutional text of reasoning, in the hope that future legislatures and courts would rely on the reasoning in order to interpret the constitutional text, only worked in a limited number of instances. Rıza Türmen's comment about rationale to recourse is from the deliberations on the draft article on equality, which remained contested despite efforts to include the reasoning text as a compromise between parties that demanded that different categories be included in the list of those protected from discrimination. The contentious categories were ethnic origin, sexual orientation, and sexual identity. While ethnic origin was incorporated into the article with a note in parenthesis that the MHP did not see the need to include it in the text, the other two – sexual orientation and sexual identity – were noted down not as an integral part of the article but in the reasoning.

The understanding of the role of the reasoning text also varied among members of the AUK. Faruk Bal (MHP) argued during the deliberations on freedom of the press that "shots are free" when it comes to the reasoning text, implying that drafters were free to incorporate their preferences as long as they were confined to the reasoning text.[110] Ahmet İyimaya (AKP), prudent with respect to the length of the constitution, suggested during the deliberations on the right to housing to address "homelessness" in the reasoning because otherwise "we drown the constitution in details."[111] As argued by CHP legal

[109] AUK Proceedings, writing commission, September 12, 2012.

[110] Ibid., August 2, 2012.

[111] Ibid., September 17, 2012. During the same meeting, Ahmet İyimaya contemplated constructing a constitutional norm about the interpretative significance of reasonings, which suggests a lack of consensus on the legal weight of reasonings.

consultant Bertil Emrah Oder, referring matters to the reasoning primarily served a political function, that is, to communicate to the public that certain issues were taken into consideration by the commission.[112]

Reasoning texts not only provide further explanation on the substance of an article; they also provide insight into the mindset of the constitution makers. This should help one arrive at a more precise interpretation of a constitutional provision. The draft article on the right to hold meetings and demonstrations stipulates that administrative authorities should decide on the time and place of these gatherings, but should take into consideration the democratic function of the right when doing so. The reasoning note indicates that the drafters would have liked it to be interpreted in a way that does not make authorization mandatory, thus conveying to future administrative authorities that this right should be interpreted in a manner that does not restrain its essence.

Using reasoning as a way to communicate with future interpreters of the constitution was deliberately chosen. According to Ayla Akat (BDP), however, past decisions of Turkish courts show that the judicial branch refuses to take such reasonings into account, to the detriment of the protection of fundamental rights and freedoms.[113] According to Rıza Türmen (CHP), the attitude of the Constitutional Court has been to ignore the reasoning and rely solely on the textual substance of an article.[114] In order to avoid such an effect, the article on the nature and integrity of fundamental rights and freedoms contains a general reasoning note that states that "the fact that a right is not listed in the constitution does not constitute an impediment for it to be recognized as a human right."[115]

While taking recourse to reasoning-writing was conceived as a mechanism to break deadlock in deliberations, it remained an ineffective measure in terms of leading to consensus on some of the most polarizing issues (e.g., the article on equality and its provision on protection against discrimination). Nevertheless, whether it was the initial momentum of drafting the first chapter, the availability of a catalog of rights and freedoms, or the multiple deliberations that these articles went through, the drafting tactics outlined above – deferral to subcommissions and consultants, deferral through by laws, and reasoning-writing – helped

112 AUK Proceedings, writing commission, August 2, 2012.

113 Ibid., May 17, 2012.

114 Ibid., May 24, 2012.

115 Art. 2, List of Agreed Articles, in this volume Appendix B.

produce consensus in the first chapter the AUK tackled, that is, the one regarding fundamental rights and freedoms.

5 CONCLUSION

The Turkish constitutional framework has traditionally prioritized state interests over individual rights and freedoms. The 1982 Constitution in particular, along with its restrictive interpretation by the Constitutional Court, has often been identified as the main culprit in the gross human rights violations in the country. Concerns over the statist nature of the 1982 Constitution largely account for the popular support for the 2011–2013 constitution-making process. And perhaps, not surprisingly, the fundamental rights and freedoms chapter enjoyed much more consensus than any other chapter debated by the AUK. Drawing on the theoretical framework of constitutional borrowing, this chapter has investigated the reasons behind the relatively successful deliberations on fundamental rights and freedoms and has made the case for the impact of vertical and horizontal borrowing.

While vertical borrowing, particularly of the concept of human dignity from the German Basic Law, played a crucial role in establishing a normative foundation upon which the entire fundamental rights and freedoms chapter was built, horizontal borrowing, particularly from the European Convention on Human Rights, served as the minimal ground of consensus for a number of provisions, including limitations of fundamental rights and freedoms. Both vertical and horizontal borrowing allowed for substantial modification of the existing constitutional framework, introducing not only constitutional novelties but also providing much more solid protection for established provisions. Even articles that were minimally revised were reformulated to substantiate the constitution's claim to be grounded in human dignity. Constitutional borrowing was supported by various drafting tactics (deferral to subcommissions and consultants, deferral to later regulation by law, and reasoning-writing) that the AUK employed in order to overcome deadlock.

At the same time, neither constitutional borrowing nor the drafting tactics were effective with regard to articles that touched upon polarizing issues (e.g., freedom of religion, definition of citizenship, equality). Therefore, the AUK members took selective recourse to international norms, eagerly so with regard to less sensitive topics but reluctant to do so with sensitive ones, as the blatant ignorance of the Istanbul Convention illustrates. Nor were they ready to delegate responsibility to legal consultants for issues that touched upon party "red lines."

The drafting of the chapter on fundamental rights and freedoms was neither an unequivocal success story nor a complete failure. Twenty articles, including very crucial and divisive issues (e.g., citizenship, freedom of religion, freedom of the press, freedom of association, freedom of opinion, and the right to fair trial), remained contested throughout the deliberations. Given that these fundamental rights and freedoms undeniably constitute the backbone of liberal democracy, it was not an entirely successful process. On the other hand, the AUK agreed on forty-three articles. This is significant as the commission managed to considerably improve the projected constitutional framework with regard to the protections that these articles would have offered.

Although it is difficult to estimate in hindsight whether more articles could have found consensus were it not for the other articles that remained contested, we nevertheless observe that the initial faith in the process had a catalyzing role. Had the process not been blocked elsewhere, the momentum might have been sustained, leading to more compromise rather than the saturation of partisan interests that ultimately ensued. Moreover, considering the erosion of rights, freedoms, and the rule of law that Turkey experienced following the failure of popular constitution making in 2013, as evidenced by the suppression of dissent during the Gezi Park protests in 2013, further crackdown after the failed coup d'état, the imposition of a state of emergency in 2016, and finally the centralization of power around the presidency and the weakening of the already frail judicial independence in 2017, the agreed articles on fundamental rights and freedoms present themselves as a missed opportunity in the moment just before Turkey plunged headlong into full-fledged democratic backsliding.

7

Countermajoritarian Institutions in Turkish Constitution Making[1]

Maria Abad Andrade

"We seek to eliminate the old mentality of September 12, the coup mentality."[2]

1 INTRODUCTION

Turkey has been defined as a military tutelary regime. This term refers to a political system that nonelected military officers dominate and elected officials rule: "borrowing institutions and practices from democracy and authoritarianism, tutelary regimes provide on-duty and retired officers with rights and devices to deploy political power when they deem it necessary."[3] Countermajoritarian institutions with significant supervisory powers over elected officials have been among the Turkish military's most important devices in their deployment of political power and have, therefore, been a (if not *the*) defining feature of the "coup mentality" that Faruk Bal, member of the Nationalist Movement Party (*Milliyetçi Hareket Partisi*, MHP), refers to in the above quotation. Most influential were the National Security Council (*Milli Güvenlik Kurulu*, MGK), the Council of Higher Education (*Yükseköğretim Kurulu*, YÖK), the Constitutional Court of Turkey (*Anayasa Mahkemesi*, AYM), and the High Council of Judges and Prosecutors (*Hâkimler ve Savcılar Yüksek Kurulu*, HSYK).

On the pretense of "saving the state," these institutions have intervened in politics whenever they saw their interests at stake. The MGK has determined security policies, vetoed government policies, and even ousted a coalition

[1] The author thanks Felix Petersen, Zeynep Yanaşmayan, and Ertuğ Tombuş for their helpful comments and remarks.

[2] Faruk Bal (MHP), AUK Proceedings, writing commission, April 1, 2013.

[3] Koray Çalişkan, "Explaining the End of Military Tutelary Regime and the July 15 Coup Attempt in Turkey," *Journal of Cultural Economy* 10, no. 1 (2017): 97–111, 97.

government from power.[4] The Constitutional Court has controlled the party system by repeatedly prohibiting Islamic and Kurdish parties.[5] Being responsible for appointments and dismissals of judges and prosecutors, the HSYK has served as an instrument for curtailing the judiciary.[6] The YÖK, acting as an ideological extension of the state apparatus, has controlled the universities by restricting academic freedom, canceling academic titles of dissenting academics, and banning the wearing of headscarves.[7] Under the impact of the EU accession process in the 2000s, these institutions underwent some minor reforms, but were not substantially democratized.[8] Thus, reform of these institutions and of the 1982 postcoup Constitution has remained high on the agenda of Turkish politics.[9]

In the campaign leading up to the 2011 parliamentary elections, all parties promised to prepare drafts of a new constitution that would, once and for all, end the illiberal legacy of the 1980 coup. After the elections, an all-party Constitutional Conciliation Commission (*Anayasa Uzlasma Komisyonu*, AUK) was established.[10] As we know today, this constitution-making attempt failed in 2013, and the post-2011 era has been defined as an era of rising authoritarianism.[11]

For the transformation of a political regime – whether toward democracy or autocracy – the role these countermajoritarian institutions play in a constitutional order is decisive. In this chapter, against the backdrop of the path dependency of political tutelage through countermajoritarian institutions, I examine the extent to which the proposals of different members of the AUK aimed at avoiding potential misuse of these institutions by the executive branch, by political majorities, or by powerful interest groups. In other words,

4 Yaprak Gürsoy, "The Changing Role of the Military in Turkish Politics: Democratization through Coup Plots?" *Democratization* 19, no. 4 (2012): 735–760, 742.

5 Dicle Koğacıoğlu, "Progress, Unity, and Democracy: Dissolving Political Parties in Turkey,"*Law and Society Review* 38, no. 3 (2004): 433–462.

6 Burak Gümüş, "Der Türkische Hohe Rat für Richter und Staatsanwälte HSYK als Politisches Instrument," in *Die Türkei im Spannungsfeld von Kollektivismus und Diversität*, eds. Burcu Doğramacı et al. (Wiesbaden, Germany: Springer, 2016), 63–96.

7 Bekir S. Gür and Zafer Çelik, "Three Decades of the Board of Higher Education of Turkey: Conflicts, Continuities, and Changes," *International Journal of Educational Reform* 25, no. 3 (2016): 299–318.

8 Meltem Müftüler Baç, "Turkey's Political Reforms and the Impact of the European Union," *South European Society and Politics* 10, no. 1 (2005): 17–31; Levent Gönenc, "The 2001 Amendments to the 1982 Constitution of Turkey," *Ankara Law Review* 1, no. 1 (2004): 89–109.

9 Burak B. Özpek, "Constitution-Making in Turkey after the 2011 Elections," *Turkish Studies* 13, no. 2 (2012): 153–167, 159.

10 See Petersen and Yanaşmayan, Chapter 1 in this volume.

11 Ziya Öniş, "Monopolising the Centre: The AKP and the Uncertain Path of Turkish Democracy," *The International Spectator* 50, no. 2 (2015): 22–41, 24–26.

to what extent were their proposals meant to strengthen the ability of these bodies to decide independently and to find appropriate solutions to the tasks delegated to them without systematically and unduly privileging certain groups and/or interests?

In what follows, I argue that countermajoritarian institutions in Turkey have always been dysfunctional from a liberal-democratic perspective, as they often acted as institutions of military tutelage. Astonishingly, party representatives of different ideological and political colors were close to codifying far-reaching constitutional changes with regard to countermajoritarian institutions in the constitution-making process of 2011–2013. In the end, however, MHP representatives obstructed the consensual constitution making by objecting to the proposed reform of the MGK, and delegates of the Justice and Development Party (*Adalet ve Kalkınma Partisi*, AKP) did the same with regard to the AYM and the HSYK. This indicates that these actors did not intend to substantially democratize these institutions, but rather wanted to (re-)shape them according to their own interests.

The first part of this chapter clarifies and defines the concept of the countermajoritarian institution. The second section reconstructs the historical emergence and development of these bodies in the Turkish case. Based on this historical assessment, criteria for possible reforms of these institutions are formulated. The empirical part of the chapter examines the proposals that the respective parties presented in the writing commission of the AUK, what results these discussions yielded, and how we can evaluate them. Finally, the results are contextualized within the broader picture of constitution making in Turkey up to 2017.

2 COUNTERMAJORITARIAN INSTITUTIONS BETWEEN DEMOCRACY AND AUTHORITARIANISM

2.1 *Countermajoritarian Institutions in Democratic Systems*

According to Mark Thatcher and Alec Stone Sweet, countermajoritarian institutions (also sometimes referred to as non-majoritarian institutions) can be defined as "those governmental entities that (a) possess and exercise some grant of specialized public authority, separate from that of other institutions, but (b) are neither directly elected by the people, nor directly managed by elected officials."[12] As the definition suggests, the term covers a wide range of

[12] Mark Thatcher and Alec Stone Sweet, "Theory and Practice of Delegation to Non-Majoritarian Institutions," *West European Politics* 25, no. 1 (2002): 1–22, 2.

institutions. Central banks, constitutional courts, regulatory agencies, and competition authorities all fall under the label of countermajoritarian institutions.[13]

The principal-agent approach helps to explain why these institutions might be established in the first place. Principals are officials who use their authority to delegate power. Agents are those who govern through the exercise of "delegated powers."[14] As principals can always point a finger at responsible agents, countermajoritarian institutions may help principals resolve commitment problems, overcome information asymmetries in technical governance areas, enhance the efficiency of rulemaking, and avoid taking blame for unpopular policies.[15] These potential gains explain why principals may be interested in delegating power to agents: "The superior performance of NMIs (nonmajoritarian institutions), relative to the result that would be likely if elected politicians were to perform the functions themselves, justifies their existence."[16]

However, as these institutions and their personnel are not directly elected, their legitimacy has been questioned. Illustrative of this problem is the debate on judicial review through high courts ("countermajoritarian difficulty"), which has been one of the most controversial issues in the theoretical-normative debate about constitutional courts.[17] This term, originally introduced by Alexander Bickel, captures the problem of unelected judges using the power of judicial review to nullify the actions of elected executives or legislators. In other words, they act counter to the "majority will" expressed by representative institutions: "(W)hen the Supreme Court declares unconstitutional a legislative act . . ., it thwarts the will of representatives of the actual people of the here and now."[18]

This criticism is usually refuted on the grounds that the will of the majority can be undemocratic as well, and the role of countermajoritarian institutions can therefore be crucial in protecting the interests of minorities against

[13] Ibid.; Frank Vibert, *The Rise of the Unelected: Democracy and the New Separation of Powers* (Cambridge: Cambridge University Press, 2007), 5.

[14] Thatcher and Sweet, "Theory and Practice of Delegation," 3–4.

[15] Ibid., 4.

[16] Ibid., 18.

[17] Ingeborg Maus, "Vom Rechtsstaat zum Verfassungsstaat. Zur Kritik Juridischer Demokratieverhinderung," *Blätter für deutsche und internationale Politik*, no. 7 (2004): 835–850; Mark Tushnet, *Taking the Constitution Away from the Courts* (Princeton: Princeton University Press, 1999); Jeremy Waldron, "The Core of the Case against Judicial Review," *The Yale Law Journal* 115, no. 6 (2006): 1346–1406.

[18] Alexander M. Bickel, *The Least Dangerous Branch: The Supreme Court at the Bar of Politics*, 2nd ed. (New Haven: Yale University Press, 1986), 16–17.

oppressive actions by majorities. That means courts can be important bulwarks against the "tyranny of the majority."[19] Critics of judicial review, on the other hand, have pointed out that the courts often decide on issues that actually should be decided by elected institutions, thus taking on tasks they were never intended to perform, such as those involving questions of political morality or the "very definition, the *raison d'être*, of the polity as such."[20]

Furthermore, the countermajoritarian difficulty rests on the assumption that a court does, in fact, act counter to political majorities. With regard to the US Supreme Court, some authors have argued that the assumption of such a counter-governmental body is inaccurate, as the US Supreme Court has rarely acted against the wishes of the dominant political faction.[21] This might lead to a different problem, namely that of a "majoritarian difficulty," which means that the US Supreme Court is insufficiently countermajoritarian insofar as it does not protect minority rights when they are really at risk.[22] Countermajoritarian institutions may also serve as "scapegoats" when politicians aim to avoid taking blame for unpopular policies.[23]

It can be concluded that countermajoritarian institutions are in principle Janus-faced: If they have a limited, specialized responsibility delegated to them and can decide independently, then they can be functional from a liberal-democratic perspective by producing results superior to those elected politicians would most likely produce if they were to perform the same tasks.[24] However, they may exceed their competencies, may unduly privilege certain groups or interests, and can be misused by powerful groups to achieve specific goals that do not benefit the larger public. Therefore, it is crucial to ensure that they are able to decide independently on the tasks delegated to them, and that they cannot be hijacked by other political agents in power struggles. One strategy to achieve this is to make sure that the composition of these institutions does not follow a political, majoritarian logic, but rather the rationale of representation and specialist knowledge. In addition, the tasks performed by these institutions should be explicitly delimited.

[19] Ronald Dworkin, *Freedom's Law: The Moral Reading of the American Constitution* (Cambridge, MA: Harvard University Press, 1996).

[20] Ran Hirschl, "The Judicialization of Politics," in *The Oxford Handbook of Law and Politics*, eds. K. E. Whittington, D. R. Kelemen, and G. A. Caldeira (Oxford: Oxford University Press, 2008), 119–141, 128.

[21] Robert A. Dahl, "Decision-Making in a Democracy: The Supreme Court as a National Policy-Maker," *Journal of Public Law* 6 (1957): 279–295.

[22] Michael C. Dorf, "The Majoritarian Difficulty and Theories of Constitutional Decision Making," *Journal of Constitutional Law* 13, no. 2 (2010): 283–304, 285.

[23] Thatcher and Sweet, "Theory and Practice of Delegation," 4.

[24] Ibid., 18.

2.2 *Countermajoritarian Institutions under Authoritarianism: The Turkish Case*

As sketched out above, Turkey has been defined as a military tutelary regime. The Turkish military has perceived itself as the guardian of the official state ideology and intervened in politics on numerous occasions. While the military has never stayed in power, it has always been careful to protect its prerogatives after each intervention. A key component of this strategy has been the delegation of constitutional powers to countermajoritarian institutions.[25] These institutions were designed to become "more reliable partners than the elected branches, particularly where the elected branches are dominated by the opponents of the military."[26] In many cases they have acted according to the interests and ideology of the military and its supporters (the "Republican alliance"[27]). As a consequence, these institutions have systematically and unduly disadvantaged certain groups.

While most authors agree on why countermajoritarian institutions were established in Turkey, they often use different terms for these institutions. Many use the term countermajoritarian and/or non-majoritarian.[28] Others avoid these general terms and speak of tutelary institutions[29] or unelected guardians.[30] I will use the term countermajoritarian, as it leaves open the possibility that all of these institutions can also work differently in a democratic system. In Turkish politics, the term countermajoritarian institutions generally refers to four specific institutions: the National Security Council, the Council of Higher Education, the Turkish Constitutional Court, and the High Council of Judges and Prosecutors.

25 Hootan Shambayati, "The Guardian of the Regime: The Turkish Constitutional Court in Comparative Perspective," *Constitutional Politics in the Middle East: With Special Reference to Turkey, Iraq, Iran, and Afghanistan*, ed. S. A. Arjomand (Oxford: Hart Publishing, 2008), 99–121, 99.

26 Ozan Varol, "Constitutional Performance in Transitions from Military to Civilian Rule," in *Assessing Constitutional Performance*, eds. T. Ginsburg and A. Z. Huq (New York: Cambridge University Press, 2016), 145–170, 151.

27 According to Ceren Belge, this alliance consisted of the military and civilian bureaucracies, the Republican People's Party (CHP), the intelligentsia (professionals, those working in universities, members of the media), and university students. "The glue of the Republican alliance was a shared Kemalist worldview, the ideological legacy of Mustafa Kemal Atatürk" (Ceren Belge, "Friends of the Court: The Republican Alliance and Selective Activism of the Constitutional Court of Turkey," *Law and Society Review* 40, no. 3 (2006): 652–692, 656).

28 Ibid., 656.

29 Ergun Özbudun, "Constitutions and Political System," in *The Routledge Handbook of Modern Turkey*, eds. M. Heper and S. Sayari (New York: Routledge, 2012), 194–204, 195.

30 Shambayati, "The Guardian of the Regime," 101.

3 COUNTERMAJORITARIAN INSTITUTIONS IN TURKISH CONSTITUTIONAL POLITICS PRIOR TO 2011

The following section reconstructs the historical emergence and development of countermajoritarian institutions in Turkey, with a focus on the 1982 Constitution and reforms of these institutions in the 2000s. This historical, contextual assessment enables us to specify criteria for reform of these institutions that would make them less likely to exceed their competencies, unduly privilege certain groups or interests, or be misused by powerful groups.

3.1 *The National Security Council (MGK)*

The National Security Council (MGK) was established with the 1961 Constitution.[31] Reestablished in 1982, the MGK was supposed to be presided over by the president, and it was to consist of the prime minister and ministers of national defense, foreign affairs, and internal affairs. Other ministers would be invited upon the prime minister's request. Military members of the MGK included the chief of the general staff and the commanders of the army, navy, and air force as well as the commander of the gendarmerie.[32] Thus, the five military members generally held the majority in the council (if no other ministers were invited).

Over the years, all governments complied with the decisions of the MGK.[33] The institutionalization of the military's participation in civilian politics through the MGK provided a regular means for the military leaders to convey their views to civilian policymakers, to veto government policies, and even to oust a coalition government from power, which it did in 1997.[34] It is for this reason that Ayşegül Kars Kaynar characterizes the MGK as a second ("shadow") cabinet, an alternative, illegitimate cabinet in addition to the Council of Ministers, transforming the two-headed executive into a three-headed one.[35]

Reforms of the MGK began in the course of Turkey's EU accession process and changed both the personnel composition and the competencies of the MGK. Beginning in 2001, the Turkish Parliament adopted constitutional amendments that would limit the military's role in the council. By adding

31 TC-1961, Art. 111.

32 TC-1982, Art. 118 (1).

33 Gönenc, "The 2001 Amendments," 107.

34 Gürsoy, "The Changing Role of the Military," 742.

35 Ayşegül Kars Kaynar, "Making of Military Tutelage in Turkey: The National Security Council in the 1961 and 1982 Constitutions," *Turkish Studies* 19, no. 3 (2017): 451–481, 472.

the minister of justice and the deputy prime minister(s) to the MGK, the number of civilian members increased (from four to six or more, depending on the number of deputy prime ministers) while the number of military members was kept at five. Furthermore, the MGK's competencies were limited by legally specifying its advisory nature: The original provision stated that the MGK should submit "its views on taking decisions and ensuring necessary coordination" to the Council of Ministers.[36] The amended provision specifies that the MGK was to submit "advisory decisions" to the president of the republic.[37] And while the original text stated that the Council of Ministers should give "priority consideration" to MGK decisions, the amended text states that these decisions should be "evaluated" by the Council of Ministers.[38]

Notwithstanding the amendments, Kars Kaynar points out that the central problem of the MGK was not solved. The body brings two executive heads together, the prime minister and the president. This indicates that the power of MGK decisions does not originate from its military members, but from its elected civilians. The Council of Ministers sees itself as politically bound by these decisions because they are already signed by civilian executives; yet it is not subject to a vote of confidence. This constellation contradicts provisions of the 1961 and the 1982 Constitutions, both of which state that the executive function shall be carried out by the president of the republic and the Council of Ministers.[39] Kars Kaynar therefore concludes that the council is not only problematic with regard to limited civilian control, but also for democracy in general. It is a "tutelary instrument over the legitimately assigned Council of Ministers. Its power is illegitimate and unacceptable irrespective of who exercises it."[40] From this point of view, we can argue that the reforms not only did not check the MGK's tutelary position and power as "an anti-democratic semi-military organ functioning in the hands of the civilian executives,"[41] but actually consolidated it.

3.2 *The Council of Higher Education (YÖK)*

The Council of Higher Education (YÖK) was established by law in the aftermath of the 1980 coup d'état.[42] The military junta accused universities

36 TC-1982, Art. 118 (3).
37 Ibid. (amended in 2001).
38 TC-1982, Art. 118 (3); TC-1982, Art. 118 (3) (amended in 2001).
39 TC-1961, Art. 6; TC-1982, Art. 8.
40 Kars Kaynar, "Making of Military Tutelage," 473.
41 Ibid., 474.
42 Law on Higher Education No. 2547–*Yüksek Öğretim Kanunu* Nr. 2547, in *Resmî Gazete*, November 6, 1981, Sayı: 17506.

of being a source of social unrest in the 1970s. During that time, universities had been sites of violent, at times armed conflict among student movements of different ideological leanings.[43] For this reason, the military deployed the council as an instrument to bring all higher education institutions under a single central authority that would limit their administrative autonomy.[44] With enactment of the 1982 Constitution, YÖK received constitutional status.[45]

The 1982 Constitution gave the president of the republic a decisive role in appointing members to YÖK.[46] He appointed seven of its members (selected from among rectors and professors), and the Council of Ministers likewise appointed seven members. The Inter-University Council (*Üniversitelerarası Kurul*, ÜAK), consisting of all rectors and a faculty member from each university, selected the remaining seven members. Until 2004, the MGK selected one additional member. The appointees of the Council of Ministers and the ÜAK had to be approved by the president, which bestowed much more power on him.[47]

Overall, YÖK functioned as a "tool for the re-imposition of official state ideology upon universities."[48] Especially during the 1980s and 1990s, it controlled universities, appointed university rectors and deans, and was responsible for the removal of hundreds of dissident faculty members from state universities. The council also assumed extensive supervisory powers over curriculum development. In the late 1990s, YÖK became the "guardian of the headscarf ban" in universities.[49] As Bekir Gür notes in a 2014 article, "during periods of considerable political and ideological differences between the government and the president, the BHE [YÖK] and sitting governments often disagreed and clashed."[50]

43 Ilter Turan, "University Governance in Turkey," in *Turkey's Engagement with Modernity: Conflict and Change in the Twentieth Century*, eds. C. Kerslake, K. Öktem, and P. Robins (Basingstoke, UK: Palgrave, 2010), 142–164, 149–152.

44 Ibid., 153.

45 TC-1982, Art. 131.

46 TC-1982, Art. 131 (2).

47 Art. 6 of the Law on Higher Education No. 2547.

48 Ioannis N. Grigoriadis and Antonis Kamaras, "Reform Paradoxes: Academic Freedom and Governance in Greek and Turkish Higher Education," *Southeast European and Black Sea Studies* 12, no. 1 (2012): 135–152, 137.

49 Ertuğ Tombuş, "Reluctant Democratization: The Case of the Justice and Development Party in Turkey," *Constellations* 20, no. 2 (2013): 312–327, 322.

50 Bekir S. Gür, "How to Abolish the Board of Higher Education," *University World News*, October 31, 2014, www.universityworldnews.com/article.php?story=20141028172430112 (accessed March 6, 2019).

Due to YÖK's links with the military coup and its repressive role, there were numerous debates and attempts to reform it, none of which was successful.[51] Only minor changes were adopted. For example, standardized curricula were dropped and departments were given more freedom to determine their academic programs. Moreover, the representative from the MGK was removed from YÖK in 2004.[52] But these reforms neither limited the executive branch's dominance in choosing members of YÖK nor curbed YÖK's ability to undermine the autonomy of universities.

3.3 *The High Council of Judges and Prosecutors (HSYK) and the Turkish Constitutional Court (AYM)*

The 1961 Constitution established the High Council of Judges. A constitutional amendment in 1971 established the High Council of Prosecutors. The 1982 Constitution merged the two bodies, institutionalizing the High Council of Judges and Prosecutors (HSYK). It consisted of seven members: the presiding minister of justice, the undersecretary of the Ministry of Justice, and five other members (plus five alternate members). The president appointed all these members, choosing from among three candidates for each vacant position that the high courts nominated: three regular and two alternate positions by the Court of Cassation (*Yargıtay*), and two regular and two alternate positions by the Council of State (*Danıştay*). All members were appointed for four years, and a second term was possible.[53]

The council had very broad competencies. It decided on the employment of judges and prosecutors in courts of first instance and administrative courts; it appointed, transferred, and promoted judges; and it had extensive powers to sanction judges and prosecutors. Decisions of the HSYK were not subject to judicial review.[54] Due to its broad competencies, the council could intervene in court cases and influence or dismiss judges and prosecutors.[55] The powers accorded to the executive branch in the HSYK were a particular target of criticism, most notably that the president appointed the members and that the council was able to convene only when the minister of justice participated in or initiated meetings. This enabled the minister and his or

51 Bekir S. Gür and Zafer Çelik, "Turkey's Education Policy during the AK Party Era (2002–2013)," *Insight Turkey* 15, no. 4 (2013): 151–176.

52 Turan, "University Governance in Turkey," 153.

53 TC-1982, Art. 159 (2).

54 TC-1982, Art. 159 (4).

55 Gümüş, "Der Türkische Hohe Rat," 64.

her undersecretary, as members of the executive, to impede the work of the council.[56]

The Turkish Constitutional Court (AYM) was also established by the 1961 Constitution.[57] After 1982 the court consisted of eleven regular and four alternate members. The president appointed all members: three members and one alternate were directly appointed from among senior civil service officials and lawyers. The president selected the remaining members from among three candidates nominated for each position: two regular and two alternate positions by the Court of Cassation; two regular and one alternate position by the Council of State; and one position each by the Military Court of Cassation (*Askeri Yargıtay*), the High Military Administrative Court (*Askeri Yüksek İdare Mahkemesi*, AYİM), the Court of Accounts (*Sayıştay*), and YÖK.[58]

This appointment procedure has been criticized for the disproportionately large amount of power and control it gives to the executive and the high judiciary. It has also been given as a reason for the trajectory the court has taken: The AYM has been dubbed the "guardian of the regime," an institution that has mainly represented and defended state interests while only selectively protecting basic rights and freedoms.[59]

In 2010 the AKP initiated an extensive constitutional reform process that also amended constitutional provisions regarding the HSYK as well as the AYM.[60] With these amendments the HSYK was restructured. The number of members was increased from seven (and five alternate members) to twenty-two (and twelve alternate members), and it was divided into three chambers. Appointment to a second term was not possible anymore. Dismissal decisions were now open to judicial review.[61] The minister of justice and the undersecretary remained members of the HSYK, but the minister, while still presiding over the council, was not supposed to take part in the work of the

56 Ece Göztepe, "Eine Analyse der Verfassungsänderungen in der Türkei vom 7. Mai 2010: Ein Schritt in Richtung Mehr Demokratie?" *Europäische Grundrechte-Zeitschrift* 37, nos. 22–23 (2010): 685–700, 695.

57 TC-1961, Art. 145. For a detailed analysis of the establishment, appointment procedure, and political role of the court prior to 1980, see Belge, "Friends of the Court," 659–674.

58 TC-1982, Art. 146.

59 Shambayati, "The Guardian of the Regime"; Belge, "Friends of the Court."

60 Belge, "Friends of the Court," 664–674. For a detailed analysis of the amendments, see, e.g., Andrew Arato, "The Constitutional Reform Proposal of the Turkish Government: The Return of Majority Imposition," *Constellations* 17, no. 2 (2010): 345–350; for a positive assessment of these reforms, see Aslı Bâli, "Courts and Constitutional Transition: Lessons from the Turkish Case," *International Journal of Constitutional Law* 11, no. 3 (2013): 666–701.

61 Göztepe, "Eine Analyse der Verfassungsänderungen," 696.

chambers.[62] The president appointed four members from among university faculty members and lawyers, thus maintaining the president's role and even extending his influence by giving him or her the authority to directly appoint members.[63] Other members were chosen directly by various courts: Three members (plus three alternate members) were elected by the plenary of the Court of Cassation, two (plus two alternate members) by the Council of State plenary, and one (plus one alternate member) by the plenary of the Justice Academy. Further, seven members (plus four alternates) were elected by ordinary judges and prosecutors, and three (plus two alternate members) by judges and prosecutors of the administrative justice system.[64] Thus, the majority of members came from judges and prosecutors of courts of first instance. This is misguided, according to Ece Göztepe, who asserts that the number of judges and prosecutors of courts of first instance should not exceed the number of judges from high courts because the former are at the beginning of their careers and are therefore potentially more open to manipulation and more dependent on the Ministry of Justice.[65] Göztepe is further critical of the fact that the powerful role of the minister of justice and the undersecretary survived the reform. She concludes that the 2010 amendments turned the HSYK into an institution subordinate to the Ministry of Justice.[66] It also strengthened the role of the president of the republic, thus even extending executive influence over the council.

When it comes to the AYM, the 2010 amendments increased the number of judges from eleven (plus four alternates) to seventeen (without alternate members). It grants the Turkish Parliament the authority to select three judges in total from among three candidates nominated for each seat by the Court of Accounts (two) and the presidents of bar associations (one). The president appoints the other fourteen members: He or she directly appoints four judges from among all judges, prosecutors, and rapporteurs of the AYM; practicing lawyers; and high-level public administrators. The other ten members appointed by the president are all nominated by other institutions. The president can choose from among three candidates for each of the ten vacancies proposed by the following institutions: the Council of Higher Education (three vacancies), the Court of Cassation (three vacancies), the Council of State (two vacancies), and

62 Ergun Özbudun, "Turkey's Judiciary and the Drift toward Competitive Authoritarianism," *The International Spectator* 50, no. 2 (2015): 42–55, 45.

63 Göztepe, "Eine Analyse der Verfassungsänderungen," 695.

64 TC-1982, Art. 159 (3).

65 Göztepe, "Eine Analyse der Verfassungsänderungen," 696.

66 Ibid., 697.

one vacancy each by the Military Court of Cassation and the High Military Administrative Court.

In other words, even following this reform the president still selects most of the judges, and the new procedure for appointing the three judges that the Turkish Parliament is entitled to select still does not meet the requirements of robust democratic legitimacy. Pursuant to amended Article 146 of the Constitution, judges are selected by a two-thirds majority of Parliament. If this majority is not obtained, an absolute majority of the total number of members is required for the second ballot. If this threshold is also not reached, a third ballot shall be held between the two candidates receiving the largest number of votes in the second ballot. The candidate who receives the majority of votes in the third ballot is then elected. This means that nonpartisan agreements are not necessary, as the majority party can select members of the AYM in the last round of voting. This voting procedure has raised reasonable fears that the president and the majority party can pack the court with like-minded judges.[67] Finally, the selection procedure of candidates appointed by the Turkish Grand National Assembly (*Türkiye Büyük Millet Meclisi*, TBMM) was also criticized because two members were supposed to be nominated from among members of the Court of Accounts. As Parliament elects the judges of the Court of Accounts, the election mode proved to be a closed circuit.[68]

3.4 *Reforming Countermajoritarian Institutions*

The different countermajoritarian institutions did in fact unduly privilege certain interests and acted as institutions of military tutelage. All of them were reformed to some extent in the 2000s, but the reforms did not substantially democratize these institutions. The 2011–2013 process provided an opportunity to try to tackle these remaining challenges. The historical assessment allows us to specify some criteria (with no claims to being exhaustive) for a potential reform of these institutions.

The core problem of the MGK is that it is part of the executive branch, along with the Council of Ministers and the president. Its power is therefore "illegitimate and unacceptable irrespective of who exercises it."[69] From this point of view it can be said that the MGK as an institution with constitutional status has to be abolished. It could be reestablished by law, but the executive

67 Andrew Arato, *Post Sovereign Constitution Making: Learning and Legitimacy* (Oxford: Oxford University Press, 2016), 247–254.

68 Göztepe, "Eine Analyse der Verfassungsänderungen," 691–692.

69 Kars Kaynar, "Making of Military Tutelage," 473.

would have to be excluded completely in order to avoid a situation in which the Council of Ministers sees itself bound by the decisions made by the MGK. To ensure that the new body provides expertise on defense and security policy only, without exceeding its competencies, it is crucial that it only consist of military experts and that its role as an advisory body be explicitly stated.

Similar suggestions can be formulated for YÖK. The Council of Ministers and the president both select seven members. In addition, all candidates selected by the ÜAK and the Council of Ministers have to be approved by the president. As such, this has always been in effect another executive body undermining the autonomy of universities. This suggests that in a future educational board, executive bodies have to be excluded. To ensure that the new body fulfills tasks in coordination and planning of higher education only, it is important that it only consist of representatives chosen by the universities themselves and other experts on higher education. It is not necessary that a reformed institution have constitutional status; it can be reestablished by law.

Regarding the HSYK, the 2010 reform did not tackle the problem of executive influence, but rather strengthened the influence of the Ministry of Justice and the president. It is important to limit executive influence by removing the minister of justice and his or her undersecretary from the council and by abolishing the president's role in appointments. As the judges and prosecutors of courts of first instance are generally at the beginning of their careers and are therefore more likely to be open to manipulation and to be dependent on the Ministry of Justice, it is also important to balance the number of judges from high courts and courts of first instance.

With regard to the AYM, it has been pointed out that the voting procedure raised reasonable fears that the president and the majority party could pack the court with like-minded judges, transforming it into a partisan court. To prevent this, a different voting procedure excluding the president has to be found. If members are to be elected to the TBMM, the procedure needs to avoid domination by slim political majorities. This can be ensured by introducing a two-thirds or three-fifths majority that is not reduced in further rounds. This would enforce a cross-party consensus. Furthermore, as two members were chosen by the TBMM from among nominees of the Court of Accounts, and judges of the Court of Accounts are elected by Parliament, the election mode proved to be a closed circuit.[70] This has to be changed by choosing another nominating institution.

70 Göztepe, "Eine Analyse der Verfassungsänderungen," 691–692.

4 COUNTERMAJORITARIAN INSTITUTIONS IN TURKISH CONSTITUTION MAKING (2011–2013)

4.1 *The National Security Council (MGK)*

Party Proposals on the National Security Council

The proposals of the Peace and Democracy Party (*Barış ve Demokrasi Partisi*, BDP), the Republican People's Party (*Cumhuriyet Halk Partisi*, CHP), and the AKP did not contain any provisions on a National Security Council.[71] This implies that the three parties wanted to abolish the MGK as an institution with constitutional status. In contrast, the MHP did foresee a National Security Council in its proposal. It suggested that the composition of the MGK be the exact same as after the 2001 amendments, with only one difference: It proposed removing the general commander of the Gendarmerie. This meant that the number of military members would be reduced (from five to four), and civilian members would hold the majority in the council (six or more, depending on the number of deputy prime ministers).[72]

Reducing military members is not a sufficient measure to democratize the MGK, as it does not tackle the core problem of this institution: its illegitimate role as a "shadow" cabinet to the Council of Ministers, scrutinizing the policies and actions of the government. Even worse, the proposal reversed the reforms of 2001 regarding the competencies of the MGK. The term "advisory decisions," which had been introduced in 2001 and emphasized the advisory nature of the MGK, was removed. The MHP proposal suggested that the MGK should "submit its views to the Council of Ministers to assist in taking and coordinating decisions related to national security,"[73] thus introducing a provision resembling the original one from the 1982 Constitution. To conclude, the MHP's proposal did not aim at democratizing this institution, but at maintaining it as an "anti-democratic semi-military organ . . . in the hands of the civilian executives."[74]

Deliberations on the National Security Council

In the deliberations on the National Security Council, starting in February 2013,[75] the BDP, the CHP, and the AKP had all decided that the

[71] CHP, "Cumhuriyet Halk Partisi Önerlileri" (CHP recommendations), 2012; AKP, "Adalet ve Kalkınma Partisinin Görüşleri" (AKP opinions), 2012; BDP, "Barış ve Demokrasi Partisinin Görüşleri" (BDP opinions), 2012.

[72] MHP, "Milliyetçi Hareket Partisi Önerlileri" (MHP recommendations), 2012, Art. 118.

[73] MHP, "MHP recommendations," Art. 118 (3).

[74] Kars Kaynar, "Making of Military Tutelage," 474.

[75] AUK Proceedings, writing commission, February 20, 2013.

National Security Council should not be a constitutional institution in the future and rejected the old provision in the 1982 Constitution. They noted that such an institution could eventually be established by law, solely functioning as an advisory institution. In subsequent discussions in June 2013,[76] MHP representatives acknowledged the dark history of the MGK. However, they stressed that such an institution was nevertheless necessary as an advisory board that has greater expertise and competencies than the Council of Ministers. MHP delegates justified the institution on the basis of its output, but did not problematize its "shadow" cabinet character. The other delegates refuted this argument. They acknowledged that there could be a National Security Council, but also stressed that this body should be accountable to elected bodies and regulated by law. This was especially emphasized by AKP delegate Ahmet İyimaya, who argued that Turkey's democratic "backwardness" was mainly related to the interventions of the National Security Council. The BDP's legal expert, Meral Daniş Beştaş, stressed that the National Security Council had not only influenced politics, but had even engaged in social engineering, making for example decisions on birth control methods.[77] Despite these objections, it was not possible to sway the opinion of the MHP delegates, and the MGK was inserted into the draft constitution as an MHP suggestion.[78]

It can be said that the legal experts involved in the constitution-making process agreed across party lines that it was important to strip a future security council of its constitutional status, yet MHP delegates were not willing to compromise. MGK had always functioned as a shadow cabinet. The abolishment of this relict of the former military tutelary regime could have ended this illegitimate interference, would have been a crucial step in democratizing the constitution and an important symbolic measure acknowledging the MGK's dark history in Turkish politics, and would have marked an end of the 1982 Constitution's tutelary philosophy. The consensus requirement, however, enabled the MHP to block majority agreement and perpetuate the status quo.

4.2 *The Council of Higher Education (YÖK)*

Party Proposals on the Council of Higher Education

All parties suggested abolishing the Council of Higher Education (YÖK) as an institution, but the proposals differed regarding the issue of autonomy of

76 Ibid., June 3, 2013.

77 Ibid.

78 Art. 172, List of Non-Agreed Articles, in this volume Appendix C.

universities, and whether and to what extent provisions on universities should be regulated in the constitution or by law.

The BDP explicitly included autonomy of universities in the first paragraph of the proposed article, emphasizing self-governance and stressing that universities should independently decide on personnel issues. To enable coordination among universities, the BDP suggested that a coordination committee consisting of university representatives be established by law, without further specifying its tasks or personnel composition.[79] The MHP's proposal resembled the provisions in the 1982 Constitution.[80] It only mentioned "scientific autonomy," emphasizing that this autonomy did not extend to actions against the independence and integrity of the Turkish state. This proposal did not foresee financial and administrative autonomy for universities, but it did explicitly regulate within the text of the constitution how university personnel were to be selected.[81] Instead of YÖK, the MHP foresaw having the ÜAK function as the main body responsible for the coordination of higher education. The composition of the ÜAK, which was not regulated in the 1982 Constitution, was specified in the MHP proposal: It was to be composed of university rectors and one faculty member holding the title of professor from every university, all selected by lot among the nominated faculty members.[82] In their proposal the AKP foresaw neither administrative nor financial autonomy, but it did explicitly state that administrative organs of the university and academic staff could not be removed from their duties by authorities other than the universities and the supreme councils authorized by law.[83] In contrast to past regulations and to the MHP proposal, the AKP suggested that all issues of university governance be governed by law; it did not mention a regulatory board.[84] Finally, the CHP stressed the importance of scientific, administrative, and financial autonomy. Similar to the MHP proposal, the ÜAK was suggested as the main body to enable coordination among universities but was explicitly barred from supervising universities. It also explicitly mentioned that the ÜAK should consist of elected university representatives only.[85]

79 BDP, "BDP opinions," 32–33.

80 TC-1982, Art. 130.

81 MHP, "MHP recommendations," 19–20.

82 Drawing lots as a method of selecting political officials has its origins in ancient Greece and can be considered a useful democratic selection method. See Hubertus Buchstein, *Demokratie und Lotterie: Das Los als Politisches Entscheidungsinstrument von der Antike bis zur EU* (Frankfurt/Main: Campus, 2009).

83 AKP, "AKP opinions," Art. 8 (2).

84 AKP, "AKP opinions."

85 CHP, "CHP recommendations."

Deliberations on the Council of Higher Education

Deliberations on the Council of Higher Education took place in February 2013.[86] The main arguments revolved around the issue of administrative and financial autonomy, that is, the central issue since the establishment of Turkey's university system. The nationalist MHP, and in parts also the ruling AKP, perceived the autonomy of universities as a threat. Again and again, MHP delegates reproduced an argument made by the military leaders responsible for the 1980 coup: autonomous university governance and political polarization created "social disorder." Repeatedly referring to those "chaotic times," they considered administrative autonomy impracticable. CHP and BDP representatives, on the other hand, stressed the problematic role YÖK had played in the past. They emphasized the importance of university autonomy for academic freedom. The CHP also underlined the need to regulate issues pertaining to university administration in the constitution, as regulation by law could endanger the independence of universities. Ultimately, the delegates agreed that a coordination body was necessary and managed to write an article on the function and role of a "Higher Education Coordination Council" (*Yükseköğretim Düzenleme Kurulu*, YDK).[87]

The duties and functions of the new board were similar to those of YÖK as codified in the 1982 Constitution. However, "supervision" and "administration" of universities were not included in the new text. Instead, the coordinating role of the new YDK was emphasized. The parties were not able to explicitly agree on administrative and financial autonomy of universities, as this was met with MHP resistance. Instead, they agreed on the lowest common denominator by inserting a vague provision that included the imprecise term "institutional autonomy" (***kurumsal özerklik***) only as a working principle of the board: The YDK would facilitate coordination "and take ... necessary measures on the basis of the principles of academic and scientific freedom, academic and institutional autonomy, transparency, accountability, and participation."[88] Finally, the newly established board would greatly differ from the existing institution in terms of its membership: The YDK was supposed to consist of fifteen members, of which nine were to be elected from among full professors by academic personnel currently working at institutions of higher education (according to the formula one person, one vote). The remaining six members were to be appointed following a vote in Parliament, with a minimum of three-fifths majority vote of those present. The

86 AUK Proceedings, writing commission, February 14, 15, 18, 25 and 26, 2013.

87 Art. 106, List of Agreed Articles, in this volume Appendix B.

88 Ibid.

president and the Council of Ministers were excluded from the selection process. However, in a note at the end of the article it was stressed that the proceedings regarding the election process in Parliament would have to be debated again, and that the MHP insisted on selection by lot, as suggested in its proposal.

The writing commission agreed to eliminate YÖK as an institution, and the new regulatory board was not conceptualized as a supervisory body, but as a coordinating and planning entity. Most importantly, the right of the executive branch (the president and the Council of Ministers) to select members was removed. Given that previous discussions on restructuring YÖK had always "turned into political power struggles and attempts made towards higher education reform fail(ed) every time,"[89] this can be defined as a success. The procedure to (s)elect members of this board was not finalized, and why the council was not abolished as a constitutional institution altogether remains an unanswered question. Furthermore, autonomy was only included as a working principle. This indicates that the idea that the state is exclusively responsible for higher education continued to shape the arguments of some actors (especially of MHP delegates) involved in the deliberations.

4.3 *The High Council of Judges and Prosecutors (HSYK) and the Turkish Constitutional Court (AYM)*

Party Proposals on the High Council of Judges and Prosecutors

In their proposals all parties ascribed the same competencies to the council(s), even though they widely disagreed on the appointment procedures and on whether the minister of justice and his or her undersecretary should remain members of the council or whether these executive representatives should be removed from the council.

As Figure 7.1 shows, the AKP suggested establishing a new Council of Judges and Prosecutors (*Hakimler ve Savcılar Kurulu*, HSK). Thus, it removed the adjective "high" (*yüksek*) from the original name, symbolically downgrading this institution. The proposal maintained the number of members at twenty-two and the structure of three different chambers: a judges' chamber, a public prosecutors' chamber, and a disciplinary chamber. In contrast to the procedure established with the 2010 amendments, the AKP proposed that Parliament would now take part in the appointment process, directly electing seven members with a two-thirds majority in the first round of voting and a simple majority in the second

[89] Gür and Çelik, "Three Decades of the Board," 199.

		AKP	CHP	MHP	BDP
APPOINTMENT	Basic Structure	Council of Judges and Prosecutors 22 members, (3 chambers)	High Council of Judges 11 members High Council of Prosecutors 11 members	High Council of Judges 15 members (2 chambers) High Council of Prosecutors 11 members (2 chambers)	High Judicial Council 20 members (3 chambers)
	Role of Ministry of Justice	Minister of Justice as President of the Council, Undersecretary as President of Prosecutor's Chamber	Minister of Justice is member, no voting right in Council of Judges, but President in High Council of Prosecutors	Minister of Justice as President of the Councils, Undersecretary as member	No role of Minister of Justice
	Selection	(7) TBMM (2nd round: simple majority) (7) President (6) lower courts	**High Council of Judges** (4) Court of Cassation (3) Council of State (1) Chief Prosecutor chosen by Court of Cassation (2) Interuniversity Council (2) TBMM (3/5 majority) from among nominees by Turkish Bar Association **High Council of Prosecutors** Next to Minister of Justice: (4) Court of Cassation (2) Council of State (1) Judge chosen by Court of Cassation (2) Interuniversity Council (2) TBMM (3/5 majority) from among nominees by Turkish Bar Association (Commissions screening High Court and TBMM candidates)	**High Council of Judges** Each chamber consists of: (3) Court of Cassation (2) Council of State (2) Turkish Bar Association (all elected by the respective General Assembly by lottery method); Minister of Justice does not take part in the meetings **High Council of Prosecutors** Minister of Justice as President Undersecretary of Minister of Justice (2) Court of Cassation (1) Bar Association (elected by the respective General Assembly by lottery method)	(6) TBMM (2/3 majority) (5) Court of Cassation (2) Council of State (5) Judges and prosecutors from first-instance courts (2) administrative courts
	Term Limits	4 years no reelection	6 years no reelection	4 years reelection is possible	4 years no reelection
COMPETENCES		appointment, promotion, supervision, dismissal, disciplinary punishment, suspension			

FIGURE 7.1: Party positions on the High Council of Judges and Prosecutors
Source: Author's own compilation based on party proposals by the AKP, the CHP, the MHP, and the BDP.

round of voting. The number of members selected by the president of the republic would be increased from four to seven, while the lower courts would be entitled to select only six members, down from ten according to the earlier constitution. High courts were fully excluded from the selection process. The minister of justice and the undersecretary remained on the board, as president of the council and president of the prosecutors' chamber.[90]

The CHP suggested establishing two councils, one for judges and one for prosecutors (as was the case following constitutional amendments in 1971). The president would no longer select any members of the two councils. The minister of justice, who would be the president of the Council of Prosecutors, would not have a voting right in either of the two councils. Higher courts would select the majority of members, while lower courts were to be excluded.

90 AKP, "AKP opinions."

The TBMM and the ÜAK also had the competence to nominate and select members.[91]

The MHP also suggested two councils. Similar to the AKP proposal, the minister of justice would become president of the two councils, but he or she was supposed to take part only in meetings of the Council of Prosecutors, and not in meetings of the High Council of Judges. The undersecretary of the Ministry of Justice would be a member of both councils. The MHP's proposal gave both the high courts and the Turkish Bar Association the mandate to select members, but they were supposed to be chosen by lot. The Turkish Grand National Assembly did not receive any appointment right, nor did the lower judiciary. Reelection of members was possible.[92]

The BDP suggested a High Judicial Council (*Yargı Yüksek Kurulu*, YYK). It was the only party that sought to completely exclude the minister of justice and his or her undersecretary from this institution. The proposal underscored the independence of the council not only in general, but also explicitly in terms of its budget. The BDP excluded the president of the republic from appointing members, and Parliament would be authorized to elect six out of twenty members with a two-thirds majority (not specifying what would happen in case of disagreement). Further, the BDP proposal diversified the composition of judicial members of the council, balancing the number of members from high courts and lower courts: seven members were to be chosen by high courts (five by *Yargıtay*, two by *Danıştay*), seven by lower courts (five by courts of first instance, two by administrative courts).[93]

Comparing all four proposals, we see that the AKP did not tackle the problem of executive influence over the council(s); rather, it exacerbated the problem by increasing the number of members appointed by the president. Further, instead of balancing the number of members from higher and lower courts, it excluded the former. In the proposal, Parliament would have the right to choose members, but the procedure would enable the majority in Parliament to determine the outcome instead of seeking an all-party agreement. The MHP did not address the problem of executive influence over the council either. It also failed to balance the number of members from high- and first-instance courts by excluding members of the latter completely. Furthermore, the MHP proposal provided for reelection of members, which could increase the likelihood of political interference. The CHP aimed to limit the influence of the executive by excluding the president and limiting

91 CHP, "CHP recommendations."

92 MHP, "MHP recommendations."

93 BDP, "BDP opinions."

the role of the minister of justice, and diversified the range of nominating institutions, but it excluded lower courts completely. The BDP balanced the number of members of high- and first-instance courts, and removed the minister of justice and his or her undersecretary from the council. The president would likewise not have any role in the council. Viewed from this end, it can be argued that the BDP proposal was aiming for substantial reform. The CHP proposal at least tackled some crucial issues. The MHP proposal sought to reestablish the selection procedure of the 1982 Constitution, and the AKP proposal aimed at strengthening the executive, majoritarian character of the council.

Deliberations on the High Council of Judges and Prosecutors

The deliberations on the HSYK began in April 2013.[94] On July 31, 2013, a partial agreement was reached: The parties agreed to reestablish the structure of the 1961 Constitution (including the constitutional amendments of 1971), replacing the HSYK of the 1982 Constitution with two different councils. They also agreed that the Council of Judges should consist of fifteen members and the Council of Prosecutors of seven. Moreover, the delegates jointly defined the institutions from which members of the two judicial councils were to be chosen (see Figure 7.2). These institutions were not to directly select members, however; Parliament should elect and appoint all members nominated by the various institutions. The agreed term of office was four years, and reelection of members was ruled out.

The delegates continued to disagree over the election procedures of the two bodies. The discussions reveal that the BDP, the CHP, and the MHP were close to reaching an agreement. According to their joint proposal, members of both councils were to be elected by a two-thirds majority in the first two rounds. If no candidate won a majority, members were supposed to be chosen by lot. This implies that these parties managed to reach an agreement by combining the different suggestions that the three parties initially brought to the table. The AKP undermined the prospects for consensus by rejecting the two-thirds majority proposal as well as the drawing of lots. It insisted on a three-fifths majority in the first two rounds of voting and a simple majority in the final round of voting, a procedure that clearly favors the majority party in Parliament.

The role of the minister of justice in these two councils remained contested as well. Under the 1982 Constitution, the minister of justice presided over the HSYK. With the 2010 amendments, he or she remained president of the

94 AUK Proceedings, writing commission, April 2, 2013.

		High Council of Judges	High Council of Prosecutors
APPOINTMENT	Number	15 members	7 members
	Role of Ministry of Justice	AKP/MHP: Voting right in disciplinary proceedings and exterior meetings <=> BDP/CHP: No voting right	
	Selection	(3) Court of Cassation (2) Council of State (2) Higher Education Institutions (2) Turkish Bar Association (6) First-Instance Court Judges	Next to Minister of Justice: (1) Court of Cassation (1) Council of State (2) Prosecutors (1) Higher Education Institutions (1) Turkish Bar Association
		All by TBMM, 2/3 in first two rounds, 3rd round drawing lots <=> AKP: 3/5	All by TBMM, 2/3 in first two rounds, 3rd round drawing lots <=> AKP: 3/5
	Term Limit	4 years, no reelection	4 years, no reelection

FIGURE 7.2: Results of the deliberations on the High Council of Judges and Prosecutors
Source: Author's own compilation based on deliberations in the writing commission.

council, being responsible for the "administration and the representation"[95] of the council, but was not allowed to "participate in the work of the two chambers."[96] The proposals of all four parties foresaw that the chair of the council ought to be elected by the council members. The AKP and the MHP suggested that the minister of justice could lead meetings except for disciplinary proceedings, and would have a voting right in both councils. The CHP and the BDP were committed to limiting the executive influence and opposed any voting rights for the minister of justice.

In summary we observe that the parties approached each other and were able to agree on the establishment of two councils and the diversification of nominating institutions. Even more important, the president of the republic was to be excluded from the selection procedure altogether. This agreement was therefore an important achievement. But the AKP insisted on a three-fifths majority in the first two rounds and a simple majority in the third round of voting in the TBMM, suggesting that the AKP did not want to give up its ability

95 TC-1982, Art. 159 (7) (amended in 2010).
96 Ibid.

to determine the final composition of the councils. Furthermore, the MHP and AKP wanted to retain the role of the minister of justice in both councils, thus leaving it under some executive control.

Party Proposals on the Turkish Constitutional Court

The party proposals for the Turkish Constitutional Court differed significantly (see Figure 7.3). The AKP suggested a process in which the president of the republic and the Turkish Parliament would have a say in selecting seventeen judges, while high courts were to be completely excluded from the appointment procedure. The president was supposed to choose from among professors, top executives, independent lawyers, judges, prosecutors, and rapporteurs of the AYM. Thus the high courts were no longer eligible to nominate their candidates, as they had been able to do after the 2010 amendments. Parliament was to elect from among faculty members in a confidential vote and by two-thirds majority. If this majority could not be reached in the first round, candidates obtaining a simple majority in the second round would become members of the AYM. This proposal would have given a greater role to Parliament in selecting members of the AYM (from three to nine), while leaving the influence of the president in the appointment process untouched. It would not have addressed the problematic voting procedure that enables the parliamentary majority to determine their candidate; in fact, it would have made it even worse: Under the 2010 provisions, the majority was able to select members in the third round of voting. In the AKP's proposal, this was already suggested for the second round of voting.

In backing the president and the ruling party's right to select AYM members without having to compromise, the AKP once again revealed its majoritarian approach to government and state organization. This interpretation gained further support when we consider the competencies suggested for the court. The AKP proposal provided for the abolishment of the court's competency to review constitutional amendments with regard to their form.[97] At the same time, the ruling party did not seek to broaden the right to appeal, which would have made it possible for other actors to challenge laws before the AYM, thereby strengthening checks and balances within the political system. In line with its proposal for a "presidential system," the AKP suggested that the Constitutional Court should act as a supreme court in presidential impeachment proceedings and should be able to review presidential decrees. In principle, this should increase the checks on executive power, but given the court's proposed composition, namely of candidates chosen by the executive

97 TC-1982, Art. 148 (1).

		AKP	CHP	MHP	BDP
APPOINTMENT	Number of Judges	17	17	34	21
	Procedure	(9) TBMM (2nd round: simple majority) (8) by President	(4) Court of Cassation (4) Council of State (1) Court of Accounts (1) High Council of Judges (7) TBMM (3/5 majority; prior public screening of candidates in parliamentary committee)	(7) Professors (7) Court of Cassation (6) Council of State (1) Court of Accounts (4) top executives (2) lawyers (1) financial consultants (6) TBMM (drawn by lottery in Constitutional Commission of the TBMM)	(9) TBMM (2/3 majority) (4) Court of Cassation (4) Council of State (2) Court of Accounts (2) lawyers (by bar presidency)
	Term and Age Limits	9 years 65 years	12 years 67 years	8 years no retirement age	12 years 65 years
COMPETENCES	Proposals for New Competences	Review of presidential decrees; acting as Supreme Court in presidential impeachment proceedings	Review of international agreements		Solving conflicts between state institutions and regional institutions in a federal system; temporary suspension of activity or financial punishment, but no competence to prohibit parties; financial auditing of party finances now competence of Court of Accounts*
	Review of Constitutional Amendments	No review	Review only with regard to their form		No review
	Right to Appeal	Abstract norm proceedings can be initiated by President and by 1/5 of the TBMM	Abstract norm proceedings can be initiated by President political parties in Parliament or 1/10 of the TBMM; High Council of Judges, High Council of Prosecutors, Supreme Court, Council of State, municipalities, universities, and public institutions can file a complaint if laws concern their assets and duties	Abstract norm proceedings can be initiated by President and party groups in the TBMM	Abstract norm proceedings can be initiated by President political parties in Parliament and Regional Parliaments having received 5 percent of votes; High Council of Judges, Supreme Court, Council of State, Court of Accounts, bar associations, and universities can file a complaint if laws concern their assets and duties
	Individual Complaint	yes			

* in the BDP proposal regulated under Rights of Political Parties, not under articles establishing the Constitutional Court

FIGURE 7.3: Party positions on the Turkish Constitutional Court
Source: Author's own compilation based on party proposals by the AKP, the CHP, the MHP, and the BDP.

and parliamentary majority, these control mechanisms were unlikely to actually function.

The CHP suggested keeping the number of judges at seventeen, as under amended Article 146 of the 1982 Constitution. Seven judges were to be elected by Parliament by a three-fifths majority that would not be reduced in further rounds of voting. That would have introduced a procedure making cross-party consensus necessary. Furthermore, both *Yargıtay* and *Danıştay* would directly elect four members, and *Sayıştay* and the High Council of Judges one member each. Thus, the president's power of appointment was completely abolished.

The CHP also aimed at broadening the right to appeal to the court to enable more actors to challenge laws in front of the court. In addition to the president, political parties in Parliament had the right to appeal. Moreover, an appeal could be initiated if one-tenth of all members of the TBMM supported it (compared to one-fifth in the 1982 Constitution).[98] The High Council of Judges, the High Council of Prosecutors, the Supreme Court, the Council of State, municipalities, universities, and public institutions would all also have been eligible to appeal laws concerning their specific assets and duties.[99] While the CHP's proposal did not abolish party prohibitions, it aimed at substantive reform of the court in terms of appointment procedure and the right to appeal.

The MHP's proposal increased the number of judges to thirty-four and suggested that it should work in three chambers. It proposed a broad range of candidates: seven professors working in faculties of public law or political science, seven members of the Court of Cassation, six members of the Council of State, one of the Court of Accounts, four senior executives, two lawyers, and one public accountant with at least fifteen years of service. Furthermore, it suggested that six former or current members of the TBMM with law degrees would be chosen by lot from a pool of candidates nominated by the political parties in Parliament. The number of nominations by each party was not specified in the proposal. Finally, it removed the power of the president to appoint judges. The wide range of professions from which candidates could be nominated and the large number of judges might be an indicator that the MHP aimed to keep the court as a countermajoritarian institution. Like the AKP, the MHP did not suggest broadening the right to appeal, and like both the CHP and the AKP, it did not suggest abolishing the Constitutional Court's competency to ban political parties.

Finally, according to the BDP proposal, the AYM would consist of twenty-one members. Nine judges were to be elected by Parliament with a two-thirds majority that would not be reduced in further voting rounds. That suggestion resembled the CHP's proposal for court members selected by the TBMM and would have introduced a procedure making cross-party consensus necessary. *Yargıtay* and *Danıştay* would both directly elect four members, and *Sayıştay* and the presidents of the bar associations two members each, thus abolishing the president's power to appoint judges. The BDP proposal also suggested broadening the right to appeal. In addition to the president, political parties in Parliament and regional parliaments having received five percent of votes, the

98 TC-1982, Art. 150.

99 CHP, "CHP recommendations."

right to appeal laws concerning their assets and duties would have been granted to the High Council of Judges, the Supreme Court, the Council of State, the Court of Accounts, bar associations, and universities.[100] The BDP was also the only party that did not include party prohibition as a competency of the Constitutional Court.[101] In line with its proposal to establish a federal political system, the BDP recommended giving the court the competency to solve conflicts among state and regional institutions.

The proposals of the BDP, the CHP, and the MHP differed from one another with regard to the number of judges and the exact (s)election procedure. All three proposals nonetheless shared two important features: They excluded the president from the (s)election procedure and broadened the range of actors involved in the appointment of judges. All proposals also tried to avoid a situation in which the candidates elected by Parliament could be chosen by a simple majority. All three proposals substantiated the intention to limit the power of the president and the ruling party, ensuring that the composition of the court would not follow a political, majoritarian logic, but rather the rationale of cross-party compromise. The AKP, on the other hand, increased the power of Parliament to select members of the AYM, while maintaining the provision that only a parliamentary majority would be necessary to elect a candidate in the second round of voting. While leaving the influence of the president in the appointment process untouched, the AKP proposal would have deprived high courts of their right to nominate candidates. The AKP sought to finally bring the AYM under full control of the ruling majority and a partisan president.

Deliberations on the Turkish Constitutional Court

The main deliberations on the AYM started on March 19, 2013. The parties reached a compromise on important parts of the provisions on the Constitutional Court. They agreed on a term of office of nine years, and a mandatory retirement age of sixty-seven years. They also concurred on the basic provisions on the decisions of the court, their finality, and their publication in the *Official Gazette*. There was as well consensus on the individual complaint procedure and on the working procedures of the court.[102] Because of the AKP's insistence on the "presidential system" and the suggestion that the AYM should have the authority to review executive decrees, major

[100] BDP, "BDP opinions."

[101] For a discussion of the debate revolving around party prohibition, see Yegen and Yanaşmayan, Chapter 6 in this volume.

[102] Art. 127, List of Agreed Articles, in this volume Appendix B.

disagreements regarding the duties and competencies remained unresolved. The other parties did not accept the AKP's proposal that the AYM serve as a supreme court in cases in which the president, the president of Parliament, and ministers were to be tried; they opposed the presidential system as such and did not want to agree on any such competencies.[103] Delegates also failed to agree on the court's competency to review constitutional amendments. While the CHP and the MHP perceived it as essential to keep this competency in order to avoid having constitutional amendments contradict constitutional norms or the rules of procedure of Parliament, the AKP argued that form and substance could not be separated and insisted on explicitly prohibiting the review of constitutional amendments with regard to their form.[104] The BDP opted for an explicit prohibition of the competency to review constitutional amendments, as this would impede constitutional change.

Most disagreement arose concerning the question of how members of the court should be appointed. Regarding this central question, the commission did not find a solution. Although it is not obvious from the final list of non-agreed articles (since this list contains separate provisions on the organization of the court by the four different parties), the discussions in the writing commission reveal that the BDP, the CHP, and the MHP were close to reaching an agreement.[105] After various rounds of discussion and meetings among the legal advisers of these three parties, a proposal was formulated on April 1, 2013. The appointment procedure suggested in this proposal combined the three parties' proposals. It suggested that a parliamentary commission screen candidates before their appointment; that six members be appointed by high courts (three by the Court of Cassation, two by the Council of State, one by the Court of Accounts); and that eleven be selected by Parliament from among lawyers, human rights lawyers, public lawyers, and public officials. The joint proposal recommended a two-thirds majority for the appointment process in Parliament. If this threshold were not reached in three rounds of voting, a candidate could be chosen by lot.[106]

Although the CHP, the BDP, and the MHP were able to put aside their differences and agree on a joint proposal to codify the functions and election procedure of the Constitutional Court, the majoritarian approach of the ruling AKP prevented a nonpartisan agreement between all four parties.

[103] Art. 119 (3), List of Non-Agreed Articles, in this volume Appendix C.
[104] AUK Proceedings, writing commission, March 26, 2013.
[105] Ibid.
[106] Ibid., April 1, 2013.

Party representatives and legal experts working on behalf of the AKP insisted on their proposal, which they deemed the most democratic proposal because it included both the president and Parliament in the appointment process. The three other parties vehemently criticized this approach, pointing out that, among other issues, if parliamentary and presidential elections were to be held on the same day – as the AKP had proposed – single party dominance was likely to be the result.

The AKP's insistence on the appointment procedure is indicative of a majoritarian approach. Their proposal showed (again) that the party wanted to retain executive influence over the Constitutional Court through the inclusion of the president in the appointment procedure. The BDP, the CHP, and the MHP were all willing to exclude the president from appointing Constitutional Court judges, thus abolishing a provision that had been criticized since the adoption of the 1982 Constitution. All three opposition parties furthermore suggested broadening the range of actors involved in the appointment process, aimed to limit executive influence over the court, and tried to implement a rationale of cross-party compromise. But the delegates of the three parties were not able to convince the AKP representatives. Ultimately, all parties inserted their own proposals in the final list of "non-agreed articles."[107] With regard to the crucial question of how to appoint Constitutional Court judges, disagreements between the ruling AKP and the other three parties were irreconcilable.

5 CONCLUSION

Analyzing the deliberations in the AUK, we observe that party representatives reached conciliation in some areas and were very close to reaching agreement in others. With the exception of the MHP, all parties concurred in removing the MGK from the constitution. This would have been a crucial step toward democratizing the constitution, as it would have ended the existence of this illegitimate "shadow" cabinet. All parties reached an agreement to eliminate YÖK as an institution with constitutional status. The new board was not conceptualized as a supervisory body, but as a coordinating and planning entity. In a reformed board of education, the executive (the president and the Council of Ministers) would not have been involved in selecting members. Regarding the HSYK and the Constitutional Court, the BDP, the CHP, and the MHP were close to reaching an agreement that would have excluded the president from appointing members to any of these bodies, diversified the

[107] Art. 119, List of Non-Agreed Articles, in this volume Appendix C.

range of potential candidates, and established a consensual parliamentary appointment procedure. If these near-agreements had been implemented, all this could have strengthened the ability of these bodies to decide independently and to find appropriate solutions to their delegated tasks. But the fact that consensus between all parties was required to adopt a constitutional provision enabled actors to obstruct final agreements: the MHP with regard to the MGK, and the AKP with regard to the HSYK and the AYM. This indicates that these actors did not intend to substantially democratize these institutions, but rather to (re)shape them according to their own interests.

Countermajoritarian institutions re-emerged on the political scene after July 15, 2016, serving – once again – as instruments to silence or punish political dissent and further entrench the hegemony of the ruling party. The MGK called for emergency rule and its repeated extension. Thousands of judges and prosecutors accused of having ties to the Gülen movement were dismissed by the HSYK. YÖK has been responsible for suspending university deans, sacking presidents, and suspending or firing academic and nonacademic staff at a number of institutes of higher education as well as many teachers in primary and secondary schools.

The 2017 amendments implemented by the AKP and the MHP were carved into the constitution by way of a highly controversial public referendum. The infamous National Security Council has not been abolished; in fact, its composition has hardly been changed, while more power has been centralized in the office of the president as the Council of Ministers was abolished.[108] Thus, the MGK continues to function as "an anti-democratic semi-military organ . . . in the hands of the civilian executives."[109] The constitutional provisions on YÖK were not amended, but as the 2017 amendments abolished the Council of Ministers, the power of the president has been strengthened even further. Now, fourteen of twenty-one members of YÖK are directly appointed by the president (compared to seven before 2017). The seven remaining members were nominated by the ÜAK and then appointed by the president as well.[110]

Finally, the HSYK remains a unitary body although a restructuring into two separate councils was suggested in the deliberations of the AUK. In line with the AKP's 2011–2013 proposal, this body has been renamed the Council of

108 Furthermore, vice presidents are included, and the general commander of the Gendarmerie has been removed from the MGK (TC-1982, Art. 118 (amended in 2017)).

109 Kars Kaynar, "Making of Military Tutelage," 474.

110 TC-1982, Art. 131 (amended in 2017); Art. 6 (1; 5) of the Law on Higher Education No. 2547 (amended in 2017).

Judges and Prosecutors, which symbolically downgrades the institution. With the 2017 amendments the president gains even more influence in appointing members to the judicial council. While the president was able to choose four out of twenty-two members under the 2010 provisions,[111] he or she can now appoint three out of thirteen. The minister of justice and his or her undersecretary remain members of the council. Since they are appointed by the president, they cannot be held accountable by Parliament anymore. The other seven members are now appointed by the TBMM, which did not have a role in this selection process before.[112] Making Parliament responsible for the selection of members of the Council of Judges and Prosecutors was suggested in the joint proposal of the CHP, the BDP, and the MHP in 2013, but the members of the writing commission were not able to finally agree on the voting procedure due to the AKP's intransigence. Under the 2017 amendments, the AKP accepted the MHP's suggestion to draw lots in a third round of voting if a two-thirds and a three-fifths majority cannot be attained in the first two rounds of voting. It also agreed to the MHP's proposal that reelection to the new council is possible. Surprisingly, the AYM was not changed profoundly by the 2017 amendments. Due to the abolishment of military courts, the number of AYM judges was reduced from seventeen to fifteen.[113] But the restructuring of the Council of Judges and Prosecutors and the immense political pressure on the highest judiciary make it unlikely that the Constitutional Court will be able to limit or control government and secure fundamental rights if "state interests" are at stake.

After the first substantially democratic constitution-making process in modern Turkish history failed in late 2013, the AKP and the MHP – the two parties that obstructed the consensual constitution-making process to a greater or lesser extent – now found an arrangement that serves both parties' power interests. Today countermajoritarian institutions are once again misused by those in power. In Turkish constitutional history these institutions were always dysfunctional from a liberal-democratic perspective, as they often acted as institutions of military tutelage. Today, they function as institutions of partisan, executive tutelage.

[111] The AKP had already introduced changes to the HSYK in 2014 (Özbudun, "Turkey's Judiciary and the Drift," 46–51).

[112] TC-1982, Art. 159 (amended in 2017).

[113] TC-1982, Art. 146 (amended in 2017).

8

Debating the Amendment-Making Rule: The Rigidity vs. Flexibility Debate in the Turkish Constitution-Making Process

Oya Yegen

1 INTRODUCTION

When the Constitutional Conciliation Commission (*Anayasa Uzlaşma Komisyonu*, AUK) finalized deliberations on the amendment-making rule for the draft constitution, Ahmet Iyimaya (AKP), one of the drafters involved in the 2011–2013 constitution-making process, argued: "Yes, dear friends . . ., we have drafted the article on how to amend the constitution for the constitution we have not yet produced."[1] The members of the AUK managed to draft the constitutional amendment procedure even though ultimately they failed to agree on most other provisions of the constitution. Based on the drafting process of the constitutional amendment rule, this chapter investigates the debate on the amendment-making rule with regard to the rigidity versus flexibility problem, and it contextualizes the dilemma that constitution makers faced in balancing the competing values of rigidity and flexibility in light of the recent Turkish experience with constitutional amendments (i.e., majoritarian imposition) in the 2011–2013 process. The availability of the proceedings of the AUK provides an opportunity to investigate how constitution makers approached the pros and cons of rigid and flexible constitutions and negotiated a balance.

Written constitutions often outline the means for their own amendment, and the provisions that determine its amendment are regarded as the most crucial part of any given constitution.[2] Amendment-making rules are what

[1] AUK Proceedings, July 8, 2013 (author's own translation).

[2] See John W. Burgess, *Political Science and Constitutional Law* (Charlotte: Baker & Taylor, 1890), 137; Richard Albert, "Amending Constitutional Amendment Rules," *International Journal of Constitutional Law* 13, no. 3 (2015): 655–685; Akhil Reed Amar, "The Consent of the Governed: Constitutional Amendment Outside Article V," *Columbia Law Review* 94, no. 2 (1994): 457–508.

Richard Albert calls "gatekeepers" to the constitutional document.[3] On the one hand, they may help determine the endurance of a constitution; on the other hand, they may be the reason it is resistant to change and prone to constitutional replacement rather than revision.[4] As amendment-making rules establish the basic rules that determine how the constitution can be modified, their significance is rather self-evident. In today's world, where elected officials are able to exploit democratic and legalistic procedures to achieve self-serving and nondemocratic ends, the role of amendment-making rules is gaining even more attention.[5] Amendment rules reflect the constitutional designers' trust that future political actors will, when necessary, change the constitution to remedy its defects, improve it, and generally keep it in sync with the existing political, social, and economic realities. Yet, amendment rules also reveal the constitutional designers' wariness of future political actors and therefore predetermine the requirements that they must fulfill in order to change the constitution.[6] Concerned about partisan attempts to overhaul the constitution in order to alter the political game hastily or on the basis of short-term considerations, constitution makers may seek to safeguard the established text.

In Turkish politics, constitutional change and amendments have been rather controversial in the last decade. Prior to the formation of the AUK in October 2011, the 2007 and 2010 amendments, as well as the annulled amendments of 2008, were polarizing, and constitutional change realized by the Justice and Development Party (*Adalet ve Kalkınma Partisi*, AKP) followed a confrontational approach and imposed changes without seeking consensus.[7] The 2017 constitutional amendments that transformed the parliamentary system into an executive presidential system were similarly mired in controversy. These amendments were drafted under a state of emergency and approved in a public referendum, also under a state of emergency. Rather than seeking reconciliation between parties represented in the Turkish Grand National Assembly (*Türkiye Büyük Millet Meclisi*, TBMM), the AKP

3 Richard Albert, "The Structure of Constitutional Amendment Rules," *Wake Forest Law Review* 49, no. 4 (2014): 913.

4 Zachary Elkins, Tom Ginsburg, and James Melton, *The Endurance of National Constitutions* (New York: Cambridge University Press, 2009), 99–103.

5 See David Landau, "Abusive Constitutionalism," *UC Davis Law Review* 47, no. 1 (2013): 189–260; David Landau, "Populist Constitutions," *The University of Chicago Law Review* 85, no. 2 (2018): 521–544; Ozan Varol, "Stealth Authoritarianism," *Iowa Law Review* 100, no. 4 (2015): 1673–1742; Kim Lane Scheppele, "Autocratic Legalism," *The University of Chicago Law Review* 85, no. 2 (2018): 545–583.

6 Albert, "The Structure of Constitutional Amendment Rules," 913–914.

7 The 2007 amendments introduced direct election of the president, and the 2010 amendments restructured, among other institutions, the high courts and the judicial system.

government decided to push these amendments through Parliament with the help of the Nationalist Movement Party (*Milliyetçi Hareket Partisi*, MHP) and the additional approval of a public referendum. On the one hand, the AUK experience was a return to the consensual approach that had characterized constitutional change in Turkey during the 1990s and early 2000s. On the other hand, the constitutional crises that were a hallmark of the AKP government, specifically over the 2007, 2008, and 2010 amendment processes, were examples of majoritarian imposition. The AUK's attempt to construct an amendment-making rule in light of these controversial experiences was an important effort to safeguard against future majoritarian imposition. This chapter shows that the 2011–2013 deliberations on the amendment-making rule were historically charged. Although we observe that delegates aimed to find a balance between constitutional rigidity and flexibility, they were constrained by the path dependency of the existing amendment-making rule and past practices of amendment making. The eventual partially agreed amendment-making rule (Art. 146) exhibits just about the same degree of flexibility and rigidity as the amended rule of the 1982 Constitution, although parties proposed more rigid and more flexible amendment-making rules before deliberations commenced.

Drawing on the literature on constitutional amendments, and specifically the debate on the merits of rigid versus flexible constitutions, this chapter first provides an overview of the different mechanisms that can be utilized by constitution makers in the formulation of the amendment procedure. Looking at the evolution of amendment-making rules in Turkish constitutional history and practice, it provides a synopsis of the rule and its transformation, with a special emphasis on the current procedure under the 1982 Constitution. Subsequently, we examine the proposals for a new amendment rule as presented to the AUK by participating political parties in the course of the 2011–2013 process. This chapter furthermore shows that the partial compromise reached before the process was abrogated in 2013 resembled the amended amendment-making rule of the 1982 Constitution much more than the proposals presented by political parties in the AUK.

2 AMENDMENT-MAKING RULES: THE THIN LINE BETWEEN RIGIDITY AND FLEXIBILITY

The constitution is the supreme law of the state, what Roger Congleton describes as a "law for making laws."[8] It is therefore unlikely to be amended

[8] Roger D. Congleton, *Improving Democracy through Constitutional Reform: Some Swedish Lessons* (Boston: Kluwer Academic Press, 2003), 11.

in the same fashion as other laws.[9] For this reason, amendment rules for constitutions usually require a more difficult legal and political process than ordinary laws.[10] Constitutions of today all have a provision for constitutional amendment, albeit with varying designs.[11] Unamendable articles that aim to protect the core characteristics of the constitutional order represent the most rigid arrangement to safeguard against repeal. Globally, unamendability provisions exist in 40 percent of the world's constitutions.[12] Rosalind Dixon provides two main reasons why constitutional stability is important. First, it promotes the process of democratic self-government, since a constitution serves the task of providing the rules of the polity. Second, constitutional stability fosters elements of "precommitment" that help ensure minority rights and maintain inclusionary policies.[13]

Constitutional flexibility/rigidity determines the conditions for constitutional stability.[14] The literature offers a variety of categorizations to measure a constitution's amendment stringency, but these are difficult to compare because they cannot be easily operationalized.[15] Moreover, each system of

9 Considering the American approach, Donald S. Lutz ("Toward a Theory of Constitutional Amendment," *American Political Science Review* 88, no. 2 (1994): 355–370, 356) notes the significance of the deliberative process. According to Lutz, a constitution is not simply a means to reach collective decisions in an efficient manner "but to make the best possible decisions in pursuit of the common good under a condition of popular sovereignty." The pursuit of "the common good" is a difficult one that requires a highly deliberative process. Constitutional matters are distinguished from normal legislation because the constitution is the higher law; it provides the blueprint for the limitations and content of normal legislation. Because of this distinction between normal legislation and constitutional matters, the amendment process for constitutional matters needs to be more rigorous and scrutinized than that which is used for normal legislation.

10 Albert, "Amending Constitutional Amendment Rules," 656.

11 Markus Böckenförde, *Constitutional Amendment Procedures* (Strömsborg: International IDEA, 2017).

12 See Yaniv Roznai, "Unconstitutional Constitutional Amendments—The Migration and Success of a Constitutional Idea," *The American Journal of Comparative Law* 61, no. 3 (2013): 657–720; Michael Hein, "Entrenchment Clauses in the History of Modern Constitutions," *Legal History Review* 86, nos. 3–4 (2018): 434–481.

13 Rosalind Dixon, "Constitutional Amendment Rules: A Comparative Perspective," in *Comparative Constitutional Law*, eds. T. Ginsburg and R. Dixon (Cheltenham: Edward Elgar, 2011).

14 Tom Ginsburg and James Melton, "Does the Constitutional Amendment Rule Matter at All?" *International Journal of Constitutional Law* 13, no. 3 (2015): 686–713, 687.

15 See Jan-Erik Lane, *Constitutions and Political Theory* (Manchester: Manchester University Press, 1996); Arend Lijphart, *Patterns of Democracy: Government Forms and Performance in Thirty-Six Democracies* (New Haven: Yale University Press, 1999); Bjørn Erik Rasch and Roger D. Congleton, "Amendment Procedures and Constitutional Stability," in *Democratic Constitutional Design and Public Policy: Analysis and Evidence*, eds. R. D. Congleton and B. Swedenborg (Cambridge, MA: MIT Press, 2006), 319–342.

measuring amendment difficulty has its own shortcomings.[16] Arend Lijphart considers four basic types of majority requirements: ordinary majorities, between two-thirds and ordinary majorities, two-thirds majorities or the equivalent, and supermajorities greater than two-thirds.[17] Procedural constraints for amendment vary immensely between constitutions. Many constitutions have hurdles beyond the majority voting threshold and involve nonvoting criteria such as referendums, delays, intervening elections, national or subnational ratifications, and constitutional review. Some provisions may be more forcibly entrenched, such as through higher supermajority requirements. Constitutions may distinguish between constitutional amendment and total revision of a given article, and may have different formulas on how to trigger the amendment process. Alternatively, amendment rules may offer multiple routes to constitutional change, meaning that different procedures or thresholds may be sought for different articles of the constitution.[18] Constitutions may choose to insulate certain provisions from change altogether, or restrict or prohibit amendments during states of emergency. Amendment rules serve an important corrective function that may override stability concerns; they provide the institutional means to alter the constitution to respond to deficiencies in its design and problems that appear as current needs and circumstances change, keeping it relevant for the times. Moreover, amendment-making rules provide new generations of citizens the possibility to consent to the constitutional order under which they are living.[19]

The first danger of excessive constitutional amendment flexibility is that the polity may become susceptible to endless debates about its basic functions and institutions. Such prolonged debates will only amount to the undermining of democratic action. In that sense, Stephen Holmes compares constitutional amendment rules to grammar rules: "Linguistic rules allow interlocutors to do many things they would not have been able to do or even thought of doing."[20] Constitutions perform a similar function. Just as having open rules of grammar would undermine communication, having an open constitution would also undermine a democracy's ability to formulate policy.[21] A stringent

16 Ginsburg and Melton, "Does the Constitutional Amendment Rule Matter at All?," 687.

17 Lijphart, *Patterns of Democracy*, 219.

18 Böckenförde, *Constitutional Amendment Procedures*, 19.

19 Ginsburg and Melton, "Does the Constitutional Amendment Rule Matter at All?," 678.

20 Stephen Holmes, *Passions and Constraint: On the Theory of Liberal Democracy* (Chicago: University of Chicago Press, 1995).

21 From a normative perspective, Donald Lutz ("Toward a Theory of Constitutional Amendment," 356) adds that an easy amendment procedure that cannot be differentiated from normal legislation devalues the principle of popular sovereignty and does not provide for the high level of deliberation that is expected of constitutional procedures.

amendment procedure is, therefore, necessary to ensure that constitutional commitments remain stable and credible. The second danger of excessive constitutional amendment flexibility is that it might erode the constitution's capacity to guarantee established rights and protections. When a temporary majority grasps power and makes significant constitutional changes to stay in control, such dangers become more likely to occur. By setting the structural framework for governance, the constitution assures that "momentary majorities attempting to lock themselves in power" do not succeed, and partisan efforts are curtailed.[22] Efforts to marginalize minorities, limit rights, or extend the terms of those in power can be preemptively addressed by procedural limitations on amendment making.

Jon Elster maintains that if the amending procedure is difficult, people tend to view the constitution "as a given framework for policy rather than as a tool for policy."[23] However, he contends that it also must not be too rigid, as people may find it like an "intolerable prison."[24] A highly difficult amendment procedure fails to take into account the fact that human beings are prone to mistakes. The possibility of correcting the ill-conceived commitments of their predecessors provides a way out for future generations.[25]

While the literature on amendments deals with the definitions of rigidity and flexibility, the jury is still out on the influence of constitutional amendment procedures on the difficulty and, ultimately, the rate of amendment. Regarding amendment procedures, the IDEA primer for constitutional designers reflects this view: "Not only must the amendment formula reflect the specific needs and circumstances of each jurisdiction, but similar amendment formulas may generate different results in different cases, depending on the political culture, the political system and the history of the country in question."[26]

22 Samuel Issacharoff, "The Enabling Role of Democratic Constitutionalism: Fixed Rules and Some Implications for Contested Presidential Elections," *University of Texas Law Review* 81, no. 7 (2003): 1985–2011, 1997.

23 Jon Elster, "Arguing and Bargaining in Two Constituent Assemblies," *Journal of Constitutional Law* 2, no. 2 (2000): 345–421.

24 Ibid., 353. However, Rasch and Congleton ("Amendment Procedures and Constitutional Stability," 540) warn that sometimes the only possible method of "amending" ultrarigid constitutions is a civil or revolutionary war.

25 Jon Elster, *Ulysses Unbound: Studies in Rationality, Precommitment, and Constraints* (Cambridge University Press, 2000), 95.

26 Böckenförde, *Constitutional Amendment Procedures*, 12. In addition to political culture, Ginsburg and Melton ("Does the Constitutional Amendment Rule Matter at All?," 686–713) point to the role of "amendment culture." The authors argue that institutional factors such as the amendment-making rule are not good predictors of constitutional change, claiming that "amendment culture" – that is, attitudes toward amendment – plays a much more important role.

From an empirical perspective, Donald Lutz's pivotal article finds that a more difficult amendment process leads to a lower amendment rate. The author considers a variety of complexities of amendment making such as legislative majorities, intervening election (double vote), and the threat or requirement of referendum.[27] John Ferejohn reconsiders Lutz's data and concludes that legislative complexities such as special majorities, separate majorities in different legislative sessions, and bicameralism help explain amendment rates. However, the author does not find the ratification requirement, whether it is through popular referendum or ratification at the state level, to be a crucial factor in explaining the amendment rate.[28] Bjørn Erik Rasch and Roger D. Congleton question the findings of Lutz and Ferejohn, as both have neglected to take into account whether the amendments result in major or minor revisions. For Rasch and Congleton, studying veto players and the number of veto points has stronger explanatory power. According to their definition, veto players are "actors whose agreement is necessary for amending the constitution."[29] Besides the legislative chamber, institutional veto players may include the voters in a referendum, the constitutional court, and the president, to the extent that their consent is necessary to achieve constitutional amendment.[30] In other words, institutional authorities can impose constraints on decision-making in the amendment-making procedure.

Among OECD (*Organisation for Economic Co-operation and Development*) countries, the authors find "that the number of veto players and veto points have systematic effects on the amendment rates," separating these variables from legislative supermajorities.[31] The key element determining procedural constraints, then, is the degree of consensus necessary. George Tsebelis applies his veto players theory to produce an index of constitutional rigidity for democracies. He finds that "high rigidity makes amendments rare" and provides an index that differentiates amendments according to their significance. In his model, significance is defined by whether or not amendments make consequential modifications to the constitution. Tsebelis

27 Lutz, "Toward a Theory of Constitutional Amendment," 362.

28 John Ferejohn, "The Politics of Imperfection: The Amendment of Constitutions," *Law and Social Inquiry* 22, no. 2 (1997): 501–530, 523.

29 Rasch and Congleton, "Amendment Procedures and Constitutional Stability," 543.

30 In countries where the constitutional court exercises a priori review of amendment initiatives, such as Romania, the court acts as a veto player within the amendment-making mechanism, reviewing initiatives for constitutional amendments before parliament begins the process. Alternatively, the constitutional court may exercise such a power during the processing of constitutional amendments or after amendment approval.

31 Rasch and Congleton, "Amendment Procedures and Constitutional Stability," 543.

concludes that a "lack of constitutional rigidity is a necessary but not sufficient condition for significant constitutional amendments."[32]

In a nutshell, the literature on amendment making addresses the question of how to strike the optimum balance between rigidity and flexibility and focuses on the effects of amendment procedures on the rate of constitutional change. The scholarship concludes that different mechanisms of constitutional change, including adding or removing veto players, as well as normative considerations regarding the role of the people, legislative majorities, and courts, affect constitutional rigidity and flexibility. These are important elements of procedural design that must be taken into consideration when constructing amendment-making rules in any given country, but it is difficult to isolate the procedural arrangements from their historical and social contexts.

3 EVOLUTION OF AMENDMENT-MAKING RULES IN TURKISH CONSTITUTIONAL LAW AND PRACTICE

The Ottoman Constitution of 1876, the *Kanun-i Esasî*, did include an amendment-making rule (Art. 116) stipulating that a two-thirds majority was required in both chambers (*Meclis-i Mebusân* and *Meclis-i Âyan*) in order to amend the constitution. Unlike the monarchist Ottoman Constitution, the republican 1921 Constitution did not stipulate the amending process, thus prompting observers to conclude that it could be amended, like ordinary laws, with a simple majority.[33] The 1921 Constitution can therefore be defined as flexible. It was first amended in 1923 in order to transform the newly founded state into a republic and to incorporate other related provisions (e.g., creating the office of the presidency and determining its powers, defining the process of government formation, establishing Islam as the official religion and Turkish as the official language).[34] For the 1923 amendment, no supermajority vote was required and, in fact, the 1921 Constitution itself was approved with a simple majority. The challenges of the independence war had necessitated a flexible and short constitution that avoided adopting a rigid procedure, despite the fact that the 1876 Ottoman Constitution, which was still in force, had set forth an example of bicameralism and required a supermajority for constitutional change.[35]

32 George Tsebelis, "Constitutional Rigidity Matters: A Veto Players Approach," (*unpublished manuscript*) (2018).

33 Kemal Gözler, *Türk Anayasa Hukuku Dersleri* (Bursa: Ekin Basım Yayın Dağıtım, 2013), 24.

34 Turkish Constitution of 1921 (Law No. 85), in S. Kili, *Turkish Constitutional Developments and Assembly Debates on the Constitutions of 1924 and 1961* (Istanbul: Robert College Research Center, 1971), 160–162.

35 The 1924 Constitution formally abolished the 1876 Ottoman Constitution.

The short-lived 1921 Constitution was deemed insufficient for state-building and was replaced by a two-thirds majority vote in 1924.[36] The amendment-making rule of the 1924 Constitution (Art. 102)[37] stipulates that to initiate an amendment, one-third of the members of Parliament must sign the proposal, and in order to approve the amendment, two-thirds must vote in its favor.[38] The 1924 Constitution did not grant any role in the amendment-making process to the president. It was, moreover, the first constitution to include an unamendable article, which entrenched the republican state form.[39] The 1945 amendment added an additional restriction establishing a complete prohibition against even proposing amendments modifying the republican form of government.

The 1961 Constitution followed a similar formula, except that Parliament was now composed of two chambers – the National Assembly (*Millet Meclisi*) and the Senate of the Republic (*Cumhuriyet Senatosu*) – and the amendment procedure required a two-thirds majority in both chambers (Art. 155).[40] Similar to the previous constitution, the only irrevocable provision was the republican form of the state (Art. 9), and amendment making was a strictly parliamentary undertaking in which the president played no part.[41] The adoption of the 1961 Constitution marks the first time that Turkish citizens went to the polls to ratify a constitution.[42] The introduction of the referendum as a tool for constitutional change entered into Turkish constitutional practice to provide popular legitimacy to reconstitutionalization under military rule.

36 The 1924 Constitution was drafted by an ordinary legislature, but for the purposes of constitution making, the Parliament adopted a higher threshold; see Kili, *Turkish Constitutional Developments and Assembly Debates*.

37 Gözler (*Türk Anayasa Hukuku Dersleri*, 28) defines it as a rigid constitution.

38 Ergun Özbudun (*1924 Anayasası* [İstanbul: İstanbul Bilgi Üniversitesi, 2012]) reports that in the reasoning section of the constitution, a two-thirds qualified majority was considered sufficient, and the drafters did not consider the formation of a constituent assembly necessary for constitutional change.

39 According to Özbudun (ibid., 74), during the parliamentary debates, some members had suggested expanding the number of unamendable articles.

40 See Erdal Onar, *1982 Anayasası'nda Anayasayı Değiştirme Sorunu* (Ankara: Ankara Üniversitesi, 1993).

41 It was with the 1961 Constitution that a constitutional court was established in Turkey, but it did not include a provision on the judicial review of constitutional amendments. However, the Constitutional Court did assume such authority and reviewed the 1969 and 1970 amendments with respect to both form and substance. An amendment passed in 1971 explicitly prohibited the Constitutional Court from reviewing the substantial constitutionality of constitutional amendments. Despite the explicit restriction to form, the high court did make five decisions that reviewed the constitutionality of amendments with respect to substance, while claiming that they were exercising procedural review.

42 The constitution was approved in the referendum with the support of 61.8 percent of the votes; see Walter F. Weiker, *The Turkish Revolution 1960–1961: Aspects of Military Politics* (Washington: Brookings Institution, 1963), 65–72.

The 1982 Constitution was drafted under the absolute influence of the orchestrators of the 1980 coup d'état, and it was also approved in a nationwide referendum.[43] The revised amendment-making rule was more rigid, and it included the president in amendment making, granting him the competence to veto amendments and the authority to take amendment proposals to public referendum (Art. 175). Accordingly, the president could return an amendment proposal for reconsideration to Parliament (under the 1982 Constitution again with only one chamber). In the event that Parliament adopted it again without changes, the president had the prerogative to submit it to a referendum. In fact, after the transition to electoral democracy for an interim period of six years (1983–1989), Parliament had to have a three-fourths majority to override a presidential veto.[44]

The most rigid aspect of the 1982 Constitution is the expanded list of unamendable articles. The first three articles of the Constitution establish the republican form of government, stipulate its characteristics, and provide its symbols. Article 4 protects the first three articles from amendment.[45] In theory, the long and vague list of characteristics of the state was a "legal device" to control possible "despotic tendencies of the parliamentarian majority."[46] In practice, it provided a "back door" for the Turkish Constitutional Court to engage in substantial review of constitutional amendments despite an explicit prohibition on substantial review.[47]

Comparing all four republican constitutions, we observe incrementally increasing rigidity in Turkish constitutional law. While the 1921

[43] Held under the extraordinary conditions imposed by the military regime, the referendum also confirmed the presidency of the coup leader, General Kenan Evren. In addition to the one-sided campaign by the military rulers, the referendum was marked by other controversies, such as the use of transparent envelopes. The Constitution was approved with 91.5 percent of the votes.

[44] Provisional Art. 9.

[45] Tarık Olcay, "The Unamendability of Amendable Clauses: The Case of the Turkish Constitution," in *An Unamendable Constitution? Unamendability in Constitutional Democracies*, eds. R. Albert and B.E. Oder (Cham, Switzerland: Springer International Publishing, 2018); Serkan Köybaşı, *Anayasalarda Değişmez Maddelerin Teorisi ve Pratiği* (DPhil thesis, Galatasaray Üniversitesi, 2013): 334–335.

[46] See Bertil Emrah Oder, "Chapter 12: Turkey," in *The "Militant Democracy" Principle in Modern Democracies*, ed. M. Thiel (Farnham, England: Ashgate, 2009): 263–310, 268.

[47] Yaniv Roznai and Serkan Yolcu, "An Unconstitutional Constitutional Amendment. The Turkish Perspective: A Comment on the Turkish Constitutional Court's Headscarf Decision," *International Journal of Constitutional Law* 10, no. 1 (2013): 175–207. For the AUK's debate on unamendability and its contribution to the failure of the 2011–2013 constitution-making process, see Oya Yegen, "Debating Amendability: Deadlock in Turkey's Constitution-Making Process," in *An Unamendable Constitution? Unamendability in Constitutional Democracies*, eds. R. Albert and B.E. Oder (Cham, Switzerland: Springer International Publishing, 2018).

Constitution did not even have an amendment-making clause, the 1924 Constitution introduced such a provision and the first unamendable clause to protect the republican state form (Art. 102). The 1961 Constitution included an amendment-making rule that constitutionalized the additional restriction introduced with the 1945 amendments, i.e., that amendments to the republican state form cannot even be proposed (Art. 155). Finally, the 1982 Constitution maintained the majority requirement of the 1961 Constitution (Art. 175), but stipulated approval in the now unicameral legislature. Moreover, it broadened the state organization principles that cannot be amended (e.g., republican state form, Turkish language, integrity of the country, secularism principle, Art. 1–3). Another aspect of increased rigidity under the 1982 Constitution was the introduction of the president of the republic's veto power, which can force a delay on amendments by sending the proposal back to Parliament and referring it to public referendum.[48]

The original amendment-making rule of the 1982 Constitution was amended in 1987 as part of the first amendment package proposed after the transition from military rule in 1983. The reform package addressed four issues: increasing the size of the assembly, decreasing the voting age, relaxing the rigid amendment-making rules, and lifting the sanctions on political leaders of the precoup era. While all other provisions would directly enter into force, the provision regarding the removal of the ban on politicians of the old regime would be conditioned on approval by plebiscite.[49]

According to the then-governing Motherland Party (*Anavatan Partisi*, ANAP), it was consequential to alter the amendment-making rule because it could potentially lead to political deadlock. Turkey had applied for European Economic Community (EEC) membership in 1987, and ANAP leader and then-Prime Minister Turgut Özal had argued that an easier amendment-making procedure would make it possible for Turkey to implement constitutional reforms more swiftly.[50] Originally, the constitution required a two-thirds supermajority and allowed for a referendum in the event that Parliament

[48] Bülent Tanör, *İki Anayasa: 1961–1982* (İstanbul: XII Levha, 2012), 154–155.

[49] Bertil Emrah Oder ("Turkish Constitutional Transformation and the EU: Europeanisation towards Constitutionalism," in *Turkey and the European Union: Processes of Europeanisation*, eds. Çiğdem Nas and Yonca Özer (Farnham: Ashgate, 2012), 74) emphasizes that even though the original constitutional amendment procedure of the 1982 Constitution included only voluntary referendum, the 1987 amendment regarding the abolishment of political bans forced a "compulsory referendum" on the voters. The Constitutional Court dismissed the argument that a compulsory referendum was unconstitutional.

[50] See Ali R. Usul, *Democracy in Turkey: The Impact of EU Political Conditionality* (London: Routledge, 2011), 91.

insisted on a constitutional amendment proposal overturned by the president. If Parliament insisted against the president's objections, the president could utilize his or her "super-veto" power and submit amendment proposals to referendum on his or her own initiative.[51] The amendment provided an additional mechanism for constitutional change that reduced the threshold to a three-fifths majority, but the referendum became obligatory (see Figure 8.1).[52] According to Ergun Özbudun, Özal had argued that the two-thirds majority requirement was responsible for parliamentary deadlock over constitutional change and, as a result, constitutional change could only be achieved under military rule.[53]

The 1987 changes made the amendment-making rule relatively less rigid and offered two different methods with two qualified majority thresholds: either three-fifths or two-thirds. By utilizing the plebiscite mechanism, the amendments allowed the public a greater role in amendment making through mandatory or voluntary referendum.[54] Özal argued that, in case of deadlock in Parliament over proposed amendments, the public could settle the matter.[55] However, the new rule also made the procedure much more complicated,[56] as it provided two alternative paths of revision and invested three veto players (the Parliament, the president, and the people) with different roles under different parliamentary arithmetic.[57]

The opposition argued that the 1982 Constitution's original rule required cooperation and negotiation, while the proposed rule deviated from this

51 Taha Parla, *Türkiye'de Anayasalar* (İstanbul: İletişim Yayınları, 2007), 128.

52 The rule provided for two different procedures for constitutional change. The reduced majority course required a three-fifths majority of the Parliament to approve the proposal but required the president to submit it to referendum unless he decided to send it back to Parliament for reconsideration. The more stringent mechanism required a two-thirds majority of the Parliament to approve the proposal and empowered the president to submit the proposal to an optional referendum. Türkiye Cumhuriyeti Anayasası (Act No. 3361), in *Resmî Gazete*, May 17, 1987, Sayı: 2709.

53 Ergun Özbudun, *The Constitutional System of Turkey: 1876 to Present* (New York: Palgrave, 2011), 130.

54 Turkey has held five referendums thus far on constitutional amendments. The first was on September 6, 1987, regarding lifting the ban on precoup political leaders. The second one was held on September 25, 1988, regarding ANAP's proposal to change the timetable for local elections, and it was rejected. The rest were held under AKP governments on October 21, 2007, September 11, 2010, and April 16, 2017. These will be discussed later in the chapter.

55 Ergun Özbudun and Ömer Faruk Gençkaya, *Democratization and the Politics of Constitution-Making in Turkey* (Budapest: Central European University Press, 2009), 33.

56 The 1987 amendment also clarified the rule and stipulated that the constitutional amendment proposals are to be debated twice. Previously, the 1982 Constitution had prohibited the debate of amendments under conditions of "urgency," without defining what constitutes "urgency."

57 Parla, *Türkiye'de Anayasalar*, 128.

	1876 (Art. 116)	1924 (Art. 102)	1961 (Art. 155)	1982 (Art. 175)	1987 (Art. 175)
How to Initiate Amend-ments	Proposal by the Ministry or by either of the two chambers	Proposal by at least one-third of the members of the Assembly	Proposal by at least one-third of the members of the Assembly	Proposal by at least one-third of the members of the parliament	Proposal by at least one-third of the members of the parliament
Legislative Approval Quorum	Two-thirds majority in both chambers	Two-thirds majority	Two-thirds majority in both chambers	Two-thirds majority	A) Three-fifths majority (but less than two-thirds) B) Two-thirds majority
The Role of the President	Requirement of the sanction of His Majesty of the Sultan			Send the amendment back to the parliament for reconsideration. If parliament readopts (2/3) without any amendment, the President may submit it to referendum.	A) Send the bill back to the parliament for reconsideration OR Submit the bill to referendum (obligatory) B) Ratify the bill OR Send the bill back to the parliament for reconsideration OR Submit the bill to referendum (optional)
Referen-dum				Optional if the bill is vetoed by the president / Affirmative vote of more than half of the valid votes cast	A) Obligatory B) Optional Affirmative vote of more than half of the valid votes cast
Other Hurdles and Consi-derations		*Unamendable article: Art. 1 – The Turkish State is a Republic (stipulated in the amendment-making rule article)	*Not to be debated with urgency. *Unamendable article: Art. 1 – The Turkish State is a Republic (stipulated in Art. 9 on the irrevocability of the form of the state)	*Not to be considered under urgent procedure. *Unamendable articles: Art. 1, 2 and 3 (stipulated in Art. 4 on irrevocable provisions)	*Proposal debated twice on the plenary *Secret ballot *TBMM, in case of a referendum, takes a decision on which amendments will be voted together and which will be voted separately. *every measure including fines can be applied to ensure participation in the referendum. *Unamendable articles: Art. 1, 2 and 3 (stipulated in Art. 4 on irrevocable provisions)

FIGURE 8.1: Historical evolution of constitutional amendment-making procedure in Turkey

principle.[58] In order to buttress the proposed amendment-making rule against majority manipulation, the opposition suggested additional measures. These included a three-fifths affirmative vote for the plebiscite, the requirement that each article be put up for a separate vote, and the guarantee that the public be informed in case of a plebiscite. The opposition hoped to gain support for these measures by pointing out the manipulation inherent in ANAP's yoking together in the same reform package two very different issues – the amendment

58 This argument was made by opposition SHP member Cahit Tutum, *TBMM Tutanak Dergisi*, Period 17, Legislative Year 4, Vol. 40, Session 106, May 17, 1987, 552.

rule, which the opposition opposed, and the lifting of the ban on politicians of the precoup period, which the opposition supported. Ultimately, however, the opposition's motion to include the proposed measures was defeated.

Linking these two very separate issues under one decision was, in fact, a very calculated move by Özal. In order to amend the constitution for the first time, the ANAP government had to apply the original amendment-making rules of the 1982 Constitution rather than the proposed procedure. It remained as the only instance when the original amendment-making rule of the 1982 Constitution was utilized. The Özal government needed a two-thirds majority but only had enough seats to meet a three-fifths requirement, thus it had to secure the support of opposition parties. Incorporating the removal of the ban on party leaders of the precoup era was intended to ensure that the opposition would also be forced to support the amendment proposal.

ANAP wanted to avoid giving the impression that it was in favor of maintaining the ban on former leaders. Turkey had just applied for EEC membership and the ban was one of the most blatant undemocratic provisions of the 1982 Constitution, often highlighted by critics as an indication of the country's democratic deficit.[59] Yet, for political reasons ANAP did not want to remove the constitutional restraints on politicians, and made its support for elimination of the ban depend on approval of the measure in a public referendum.[60] It furthermore led a "no" campaign against removal of the ban.[61] The vote took place on September 6, 1987, and the ban was lifted by less than a one percent margin (50.1 percent).

The opposition's suspicion that the government had lowered the required threshold to make it easier for the ruling ANAP to pass constitutional amendments without being forced to compromise with other parties can be substantiated with reference to ANAP's constitutional amendment attempt in 1988, which was intended to allow early local elections. The ANAP government had suffered a decline in its popularity. It wanted to prepone the local elections while its support was still relatively high and sought a constitutional amendment to facilitate this move.[62] The maneuver failed when the proposal was

59 Itamar Rabinovich and Haim Shaked, eds., *Middle East Contemporary Survey 1987* (Boulder: Westview Press for Dayan Center for Middle Eastern and African Studies, Tel Aviv University, 1989), 664.

60 For the proposal on eliminating political bans, a specific requirement was added, stipulating a referendum. This was despite the fact that the existing 1982 Constitution's amendment-making rule did not include a referendum mechanism for constitutional change.

61 Feroz Ahmad, *The Making of Modern Turkey* (London: Routledge, 1993), 196.

62 The ANAP government proposed a constitutional amendment that would have modified Article 127 by providing that the Parliament could decide to hold local elections one year in advance, and it added a transitory provision to schedule an election for November 13, 1988 (Özbudun and Gençkaya, *Democratization and the Politics of Constitution-Making*, 33).

defeated, with 65 percent of voters casting "no" votes in another public referendum. To this day, this referendum remains the only one in which "no" votes prevailed.

This failed amendment attempt set a precedent for using constitutional amendments for antidemocratic ends, which has become a common practice under the AKP single-party government (2002–present).[63] The availability of two constitutional amendment routes, one via two-thirds majority (with optional referendum) and another via three-fifths majority (with obligatory referendum), represent what Richard Albert calls a "multi-track framework."[64] The availability of an alternative route with a reduced majority but the additional benefit of taking recourse to popular vote provided majority governments the institutional means to dismiss a consensual approach for constitutional change. The option to switch veto players led to majoritarian politics and polarizing referendums. In fact, the 2007, 2010, and 2017 constitutional amendments initiated by the AKP governments and submitted for public approval helped the party centralize power, shifting first to direct election of the president, and later transforming the presidency into "a very strong single executive with very little or no constitutional constraints"[65] and weakening the independence of the Constitutional Court.[66]

Following the 1987 amendments, Turkey experienced a constitutional transformation that was driven by the prospect of European Union membership. It aimed at democratizing the military-drafted 1982 Constitution by seeking a consensual approach of constitutional amendment through ad hoc committees deliberating and drafting amendments. The 1995 and 2001 amendment packages removed restrictions on political participation and fundamental rights and freedoms. The Inter-Party Constitutional Committee (*Partilerarası Uzlaşma Komisyonu*), which later became a model for the 2011–2013 Constitutional Conciliation Commission, performed an important function as a "prior consultation and deliberation body" that

63 The phrase "anti-democratic uses of constitutional amendment powers" is borrowed from Rosalind Dixon and David Landau, "Transnational Constitutionalism and a Limited Doctrine of Unconstitutional Constitutional Amendment," *International Journal of Constitutional Law* 13, no. 3 (2015): 606–638.

64 Albert, "The Structure of Constitutional Amendment Rules," 917.

65 Şule Özsoy Boyunsuz, "The AKP's Proposal for a 'Turkish Type of Presidentialism' in Comparative Context," *Turkish Studies* 17, no. 1 (2016), 68–90, 68.

66 The constitutional amendments initially helped the AKP undermine the influence of the military and the judiciary and, together with other institutional reforms, "pacified most of the veto players in the system and ended the era of tutelary democracy in Turkey"; see Berk Esen and Şebnem Gümüşçü, "Rising Competitive Authoritarianism in Turkey," *Third World Quarterly* 37, no. 9 (2016): 1581–1606.

adopted an inclusive and consensual approach.[67] However, the consensual amendment-making model was abandoned in favor of a confrontational approach in which amendments were approved primarily by the votes of the majority party, which could later claim democratic legitimacy because the amendment procedure included a referendum. This happened in 2007 and 2010.[68] In both of these processes, the AKP fell short of the two-thirds majority but did not want to seek compromise or consensus in the legislature, and hence pushed for constitutional amendments via referendum.[69] The most

67 Oder, "Turkish Constitutional Transformation and the EU," 82. Oder differentiates between three types of amendment-making models. The first is nonconsensual constitutional change achieved without prior consultation with other relevant actors. She argues that Turkey experienced this type of constitutional change in 2004, 2007, and 2010. The second type refers to amendments that were "initiated by a group of political actors from political parties who have implicitly reached consensus, but not deliberated the amendments explicitly and extensively." Such cases of constitutional change were realized in 2002 and 2008. Oder calls this a "pattern of alliance-building constitutionalism" (ibid., 137). The third type refers to the "consensus-building approach" Turkey experienced in 1995 and 2001. İbrahim Kaboğlu ("Constitutional Democracy through Referendum in Turkey?" *Revista Română de Drept Comparat*, no. 1 (2018): 242–261) differentiates between two types of constitutional change for the post-1987 period: "those carried out by the compromise of the Parliament and those approved by the referendum." Andrew Arato ("Democratic Constitution-Making and Unfreezing the Turkish Process," *Philosophy & Social Criticism* 34, nos. 3–4 (2010): 473–487, 476) also considers the 1995 and 2001 constitutional reform processes to be successful examples of the consensual procedure.

68 The 2007 constitutional amendment introduced the direct and popular election of the president; see Türkiye Cumhuriyeti Anayasasi (Act No. 5678), in *Resmî Gazete*, June 16, 2007, Sayı: 26554. The twenty-six amendments introduced in 2010 seemingly aimed at broadening the democratic content of the constitution, but in fact provided window-dressing for the controversial amendments that restructured the judiciary. These amendments addressed positive discrimination measures for children, women, and the disabled (Art. 10); children's rights (Art. 41); access to information (Art. 74); protection of personal data (Art. 20); freedom to travel abroad (Art. 23); collective bargaining for public servants (Art. 53); removal of certain restrictions for labor unions (Art. 51 and 54); repealing the loss of membership for deputies whose statements and actions led to dissolution of their parties (Art. 84); allowing judicial review for disciplinary sanctions given to public servants (Art. 129); introduction of an ombudsman to investigate complaints against state institutions (Art. 74); constitutionalizing the Economic and Social Council (Art. 166); establishing an individual constitutional complaint mechanism (Art. 148); increasing the quorum of the Constitutional Court in party prohibition and a review of the constitutionality of constitutional amendments; allowing judicial review of the Supreme Military Council's decisions (Art. 125); restricting jurisdiction of military courts (Art. 145); widening the scope of the Supreme Court's jurisdiction (Art. 148); and removing immunity for perpetrators of the 1980 coup (PA 15). Two controversial issues were amendments changing the composition of the Constitutional Court and the High Council of Judges and Prosecutors (HSYK). See Türkiye Cumhuriyeti Anayasasi (Act No. 5982), in *Resmî Gazete*, May 13, 2010, Sayı: 27580.

69 Ersin Kalaycıoğlu ("Kulturkampf in Turkey: The Constitutional Referendum of 12 September 2010," *South European Society and Politics* 17, no. 1 (2012): 1–22, 2) defines the 2007 and 2010 constitutional amendments as "examples of the enhanced partisanship and elite conflict in

recent referendum on constitutional amendments (April 2017) was held under a state of emergency, with severe restrictions on liberties. The AKP took full advantage of the uneven playing field and instituted an executive presidential system that constitutionalized the AKP leader's monopoly on power "through the dubious legality of a referendum."[70]

Andrew Arato argues that constitution-making models are path determined and illustrates this with Özal's exploitation of the "democratic potential" of the 1982 Constitution.[71] It should be pointed out that the two constitutions (1961 and 1982) drafted under the supervision of military rulers had utilized referendums as a stamp of popular legitimacy for constitutional replacement. Moreover, both instances of constitutional replacement took place under the extraordinary conditions of military rule following coups. All five constitutional amendments via referendum discussed above took place under a majority/single-party government, first under ANAP (in 1987 and 1988) and later under AKP (2007, 2010, and 2017). For the AKP period, the availability of a popular vote in the amendment-making procedure allowed for the rise of "populist constitutionalism," in which the parliamentary majority consolidates power and undermines checks on its power and authority by relying on the tools of formal constitutional change.[72]

The constitution-making attempt through the AUK in 2011 came after the AKP had successfully applied its majoritarian constitution-making strategy in

Turkey" because both of these amendments were approved in the legislature as a "partisan bill" that was put up to popular vote as a "partisan proposal." Ece Özlem Atikcan and Kerem Öge ("Referendum Campaigns in Polarized Societies: The Case of Turkey," *Turkish Studies* 13, no. 3 (2012): 449–480, 451) compare the 2007 and 2010 referendum campaigns and argue that both resulted from a "partisan battle," but the 2010 constitutional change campaign capitalized on social cleavages and as such was more polarizing.

70 Banu Bargu "Year One: Reflections on Turkey's Second Founding and the Politics of Division," *Critical Times* 1, no. 1 (2018): 23–48, 38. See also Peter Klimek, Raul Jimenez, Manuel Hidalgo, Abraham Hinteregger, and Stefan Thurner, "Forensic Analysis of Turkish Elections in 2017–2018," *PLoS ONE* 13, no. 10 (2018); Ahmet Erdi Öztürk and İştar Gözaydın, "Turkey's Constitutional Amendments: A Critical Perspective," *Research and Policy on Turkey* 2, no. 2 (2017): 210–224; Berk Esen and Şebnem Gümüşçü, "A Small Yes for Presidentialism: The Turkish Constitutional Referendum of April 2017," *South European Society and Politics* 22, no. 3 (2017): 303–326; Ertuğ Tombus, "The Fall of Turkish Democracy: Codifying Autocracy through Constitutional Amendments," *Public Seminar*, available at: www.publicseminar.org/2017/03/the-fall-of-turkish-democracy/# (accessed March 11, 2019); Hasret Dikici Bilgin and Emre Erdoğan, "Special Focus on Turkey: The Evolution of a Referendum: Obscurities of a Referendum Foretold: The 2017 Constitutional Amendments in Turkey," *Review of Middle East Studies* 52, no. 1 (2018): 29–42; S. Erdem Aytaç, Ali Carkoğlu, and Kerem Yıldırım, "Taking Sides: Determinants of Support for a Presidential System in Turkey," *South European Society and Politics* 22, no. 1 (2017): 1–20.

71 Arato, "Democratic Constitution-Making," 476.

72 Landau, "Populist Constitutions," 532.

2007 and 2010. As the AKP by that time had the necessary majorities in Parliament, it could rely on the plebiscitary legitimacy of a public referendum.[73] The failure of the constitution-making process in 2013 allowed the AKP again to rely on its majoritarian amendment making to introduce an executive presidency. Following the failed coup attempt in 2016, the AKP set aside the limited consensus achieved by the AUK and formed an alliance with the Nationalist Movement Party (*Milliyetçi Hareket Partisi*, MHP). It was thus able to introduce its single-handedly prepared draft, get it approved in a referendum following a traumatic coup attempt in 2016, and engineer in this way the transformation to an "executive" presidential system. Viewed against the history of constitutional imposition, the 2011–2013 process was a window of opportunity before the AKP adopted a full-scale autocratic legalist approach to constitution making.[74]

The evolution of amendment-making rules in Turkish constitutional law and practice illustrates that the procedure of constitutional change has been altered in response to political dynamics. With the exception of the wartime 1921 Constitution, majority thresholds have been either two-thirds (1876, 1924, 1961, 1982) or three-fifths (1982 Constitution as amended in 1987). The introduction of the president as an actor in constitutional amendment making was an invention of the military-drafted 1982 Constitution, which expanded the powers of the presidency. Introduction of the referendum into Turkish constitutional law and practice came with ratification of the 1961 and 1982 Constitutions, both produced under military rule. Therefore, prior to incorporating the referendum (whether voluntary or obligatory) as an additional procedure in the amendment-making process, the referendum device was employed in order to compensate for the democratic shortcomings of the constitution-making process. In retrospect, we observe that in the post-1982 period, rather than seeking parliamentary compromise, referendums have been utilized to bypass consensual constitutional change. Comparing all four constitutions in their original form, we can see an incremental increase in rigidity from the 1921 Constitution (flexible), to the 1924 Constitution (less flexible), to the 1961 Constitution (more rigid) and the 1982 Constitution (rigid). The 1987 constitutional amendments rendered the amendment-making procedures

[73] Andrew Arato calls it "the majoritarian-plebiscitary path"; see Arato, "Ten Theses on Constitutional Change in Turkey," *Public Seminar* (October 4, 2013).

[74] Kim Scheppele ("Autocratic Legalism," *The University of Chicago Law Review* 85, no. 2 (2018): 545–583) describes the amendments as fitting her model of autocratic legalism, and argues that Turkey's recent experiences under Erdoğan put it in the same camp as Hungary under Viktor Orbán, Poland under Jarsław Kaczyński, Russia under Vladimir Putin, and Venezuela under Hugo Chávez.

relatively less rigid, but they also cleared the path to dismissing consensual constitution making and allowed constitutional change by majority imposition.

4 DELIBERATING THE AMENDMENT-MAKING RULE: PROCEEDINGS OF THE AUK

As explained in the introduction to this volume, the Constitutional Conciliation Commission (AUK) was an ad hoc commission that developed its own working principles and was able to determine its own roadmap with the guidance of Cemil Çiçek (AKP), the head of Parliament and the chair of the constitution-making body.[75] According to the scheme that the AUK members agreed on, "Final Provisions" (which would have included the article on the amendment-making rule) were to be debated as the next-to-last issue.[76] All of the political parties prepared and presented their proposals. The article was debated in the writing commission in six different sessions, starting with the meeting on April 12, 2013.[77]

In the first stage of the process, the commission received proposals from political parties, universities, associations, unions, and foundations as well as suggestions from citizens and civil society organizations that were communicated through mail, email, and the website established for the constitution-making process. Citizens participated in semistructured town hall meetings, and the process was designed as an attempt at popular constitution making. But even after the commission began its actual deliberations, political actors and participants in the process refrained from settling the question of how the new constitution was to be made. The 1982 Constitution does not include a provision for its replacement. Moreover, it includes unamendable articles. Before the commission held its first meeting, Cemil Çiçek organized a structured session that brought together constitutional and public law experts to discuss the method of making a new constitution.[78]

The main debate focused on the question of whether Parliament possessed the constituent power to make a new constitution or if it was limited to an amending power authorizing revision of the constitution only. Participants of the meeting were divided into two camps: those who argued that Parliament

75 See Petersen and Yanaşmayan, Chapter 1 in this volume.

76 The other topics to be debated under "Final Provisions" were the constitutionality of the preamble and the headings of the articles.

77 Other meetings in which this article was debated and drafted were held on April 15, June 27, July 3, July 5, and July 8, 2013.

78 TBMM Tutanak Müdürlüğü, "Anayasa Hukuku Hocalarıyla Toplantı," September 19, 2011.

had the power to totally revise the constitution, and those who argued that only a constituent assembly could replace the whole constitution. Those arguing that an ordinary legislature lacks the power (derived power) to make a new constitution without there being a "legal (constitutional) loophole" were in the minority.[79] This minority, arguing in favor of a constitutional convention, stressed that only such an inclusive and pluralistic process could bring together different societal forces and provide the institutional setup for representative deliberations.[80] Those arguing that the ordinary assembly had the power to make a new constitution referred to the absence of a constitutional prohibition against such an endeavor.

Another controversial issue was the question of how an ordinary parliament that does not possess the constituent power can rely on an existing constitution's amendment procedure and at the same time remove or change the unamendable articles. For example, highlighting the importance of legal continuity, the legal expert Zafer Gören argued that it would be deceitful and legally problematic for the derived constituent power (Parliament) to change the unamendable articles. However, he argued that as long as their core remains intact, it could be possible to refine these articles.

Eleven of the twenty-four legal experts who attended the meeting called for preliminary legislation or a document of understanding that would strengthen the legal base of Parliament's ordinary power to draft and adopt a new constitution. Suggestions included: adding a provision to the article regulating the amendment-making process (Art. 175) in order to define the constituent power of the Parliament or allow for elections for a constituent assembly; and issuing legislation or a memorandum of understanding that would clarify the roadmap for making a new constitution.

Although the goals of the meeting with the legal experts were to define whether the process aimed at amendment or replacement (and how to approach the unamendable articles) and to define the legal framework that would enable it, the AUK began to work on drafting a new constitution. Thus, the issue of whether the process would lead to a new constitution or a thorough revision was not settled, and it remained unresolved throughout the deliberations. When the AUK finally moved on to the deliberations on the amendment-making procedure of the draft constitution, not only had the commission lost steam because it had failed to reach consensus on

79 For a discussion of main arguments, see Yegen, "Debating Amendability," 298–300.

80 Bertil Emrah Oder, "The Much-Awaited and Deeply Controversial Constitutional Process: Learning from Turkey's Failed Process in 2013," in *Themes of Conflict in Middle Eastern Democracies: A Comparative Perspective from Israel and Turkey*, eds. Friedrich Ebert Stiftung and Van Leer Jerusalem Institute (Istanbul & Jerusalem, 2014), 137.

fundamental pillars of state organization and other contested issues, but the members had also not settled among themselves how the 1982 Constitution could be amended or replaced.[81]

4.1 *Party Proposals: Individual Party Positions*

The proposals of all political parties reiterated the provision of the 1982 Constitution, namely that constitutional amendment proposals must be proposed in writing by at least one-third of the members of Parliament. None of the political parties proposed maintaining the last clause of the amendment-making rule in the amended 1987 form, which dictates that "every measure including fines shall be taken by law to secure participation in referendums, general elections, by-elections and local elections." All political parties agreed that compulsory voting, albeit not enforced since no one is actually fined for not participating in elections, be removed from the amendment-making rule in the future constitution.

With the exception of these two issues, the amendment-making rules proposed by the four political parties approached the issue of constitutional rigidity differently. The AKP and the Republican People's Party (*Cumhuriyet Halk Partisi*, CHP) proposals were on two different ends of the spectrum in terms of flexibility and rigidity, with the AKP proposal being highly flexible and the CHP proposal highly rigid. The MHP proposal remained more rigid than the AKP's, but less rigid than the CHP proposal. The proposal of the Peace and Democracy Party (*Barış ve Demokrasi Partisi*, BDP) was close to the MHP's on the rigidity-flexibility spectrum (and close to the 1982 Constitution), but left out the president's power to delay by veto.

The AKP Proposal

The AKP proposal sets the legislative majority threshold for constitutional amendment at three-fifths, in which case the president would have the authority to approve, veto, or submit amendment proposals to public referendum. The referendum is envisioned as a voluntary popular vote at the discretion of the president (see Figure 8.2). In the event that the president veto an amendment bill, Parliament has the power to take it to referendum, provided that the amendment proposal is able to receive three-fifths of the legislative votes. However, in the event that Parliament be able to muster a two-thirds majority against a presidential veto, the president is obligated to approve an amendment bill. Therefore, the AKP proposal removes the president as a veto player, as it is possible for Parliament to

81 AUK Proceedings, writing commission, April 12, 2013.

	AKP	CHP	MHP	BDP
How to Initiate Amendments	Proposal by at least one-third of the members of the parliament	Proposal by at least one-third of the members of the parliament	Proposal by at least one-third of the members of the parliament	Proposal by at least one-third of the members of the parliament
Legislative Approval Quorum	Three-fifths majority	Two-thirds majority	A) Three-fifths majority (but less than two-thirds) B) Two-thirds majority	A) Three-fifths majority (but less than two-thirds) B) Two-thirds majority
The Role of the President	A) Ratify the bill B) Veto the bill (To override the veto: 1. two-thirds majority to adopt the bill or 2. three-fifth majority decision to submit the bill to referendum) C) Submit the bill to referendum	A) Send the bill back to the parliament for reconsideration (To adopt the bill, two-thirds majority)	A) Send the bill back to the parliament for reconsideration OR Submit the bill to referendum (obligatory) B) Ratify the bill OR Send the bill back to the parliament for reconsideration OR Submit the bill to referendum (optional)	A) Submit the bill (approved by three-fifths but less than two-thirds) to referendum (obligatory) B) Ratify the bill OR submit the bill to referendum (optional)
Referendum	A) Can be submitted by the president if the bill is adopted by three-fifth majority B) Parliament with a three- majority can submit the bill to referendum in case it is vetoed by the president *Affirmative vote of more than half of the valid votes cast	Obligatory *Affirmative vote of two-thirds of the registered voters and votes cast	A) Obligatory B) Optional *Affirmative vote of more than half of the valid votes cast	A) Obligatory B) Optional *Affirmative vote of more than half of the valid votes cast
Other Hurdles and Considerations		*Proposal debated twice on the plenary *Secret ballot *Except when the constitution is replaced altogether, all amendments that are not issue-related are voted separately *no constitutional amendment can be made during state of emergency, martial law, mobilization and war time.	*Proposal debated twice on the plenary *Secret ballot *TBMM, in case of a referendum, takes a decision on which amendments will be voted together and which will be voted separately.	*Proposal debated twice on the plenary *TBMM, in case of a referendum, takes a decision on which amendments will be voted together and which will be voted separately

FIGURE 8.2: Party proposals on the amendment-making procedure

quash the presidential veto and take recourse to referendum with the same qualified majority.

The AKP's proposal is significant in many aspects. First, the proposal uses the word *Başkan* rather than *Cumhurbaşkanı*, which signals that it is meant for a presidential system rather than the parliamentary system of the 1982 Constitution. The shift to a presidential system was the main issue of contention between political parties in the AUK, with only AKP supporting such a transformation.[82] Second, as explained above, the president's role in the amendment-making procedure is weakened by the AKP proposal. It is Parliament, not the president, that can submit an amendment bill to referendum if the president vetoes a bill. Third, the AKP proposal does not require that constitutional amendment proposals be debated in the plenary. Fourth, the proposal does not require a secret ballot, another point for which the AKP received much criticism. Members of other parties argued that, because of strong party discipline, AKP deputies tend to vote along party lines and to reveal their vote, despite the instituted secret ballot. Without a secret ballot requirement, it was argued, AKP deputies would be even further pressured to vote along party lines rather than according to their own consciences.

This issue is politically significant, as the opposition had asked the Constitutional Court to annul the 2010 constitutional amendment bill because AKP deputies had violated the amendment-making procedure, including the provision for a secret ballot.[83] During the deliberations in 2013, the AKP argued against the secret ballot requirement, averring that for a constitutional amendment bill, an MP's vote must represent his constituents and the public interest, and that constitutional change is a political party's undertaking rather than an individual issue on which a deputy should vote based on his or her conscience. To support these arguments, AKP representatives (Ahmet İyimaya and legal consultant Yavuz Atar) mentioned other countries' constitutions (without specifying which cases they were referring to) and claimed that the secret ballot requirement was added during the 1987 amendments because Özal sought to protect Parliament and its members from military tutelage.[84]

Finally, the AKP proposal eliminates the provision in the 1982 amendment-making rule that stipulates that, if a proposal is to be put to a referendum, Parliament decides "which amendments will be voted on together and which will be voted on separately." This provision was a matter of contention during the 2010 amendment process, when the opposition criticized the AKP government for the decision to submit the whole amendment package to a public vote rather than allowing the public to vote on each amendment separately.

[82] See Böcü and Petersen, Chapter 5 in this volume.

[83] E. 2010/49–K. 2010/87, July 7, 2010 in *Resmî Gazete*, August 1, 2010, Sayı: 27659.

[84] AUK Proceedings, April 12, 2013. Additionally, the AKP defended open ballots on the basis of transparency and argued that secret ballots deprive voters of the right to know how their elected officials vote in Parliament. Furthermore, the AKP argued that if MPs vote differently under secret and open ballot, they do not have the mettle to be MPs.

One can argue that by removing this provision from the constitutional text, the AKP aimed to end the debate on whether constitutional amendments submitted to referendum had to be approved individually or as packages.

The CHP Proposal

The CHP proposed setting the voting threshold for constitutional amendments at two-thirds, and suggested eliminating the alternative scheme which prescribes further steps when a bill receives more than three-fifths but less than two-thirds of the vote (see Figure 8.2). With this proposal, the CHP returns to the original amendment-making rule of the 1982 Constitution and advocates increasing rigidity in amendment making. In the event that the president returns a bill for reconsideration, Parliament must have a two-thirds majority in support of an amendment to override the presidential veto. The CHP proposal also stipulates a mandatory public referendum that would require that two-thirds of registered voters participate in the referendum and two-thirds of the voters participating vote "yes" to approve the bill (see Figure 8.2).

In a nutshell, the CHP's proposal imposes a higher parliamentary majority for amendments, eliminates the alternative scheme with a lower threshold than under the 1987 amendments, and requires a mandatory referendum with a higher threshold than the original amendment-making rule of the 1982 Constitution. The CHP also suggested that proposals be debated twice in Parliament, and that votes on proposals be carried by secret ballot. In contrast to the amendment-making rule in the existing constitution (as amended in 1987), which stipulates that Parliament decides whether amendments submitted to referendum in packages are voted on individually or together, the CHP proposal dictates that unless the constitution is being replaced altogether, all amendments that are not issue related must be voted on separately. This proposal also specifies that no constitutional amendment can be made during a state of emergency, martial law, mobilization, or wartime.

The MHP Proposal

The amendment-making rule established in the 1982 Constitution and amended in 1987 remained a model for some of the constitutional drafters involved in the 2011–2013 process.[85] The nationalist MHP proposed the

[85] Ahmet İyimaya (AKP) identifies two challenges for reaching compromise: first, the existing amendment-making rule being used as the main model; and second, the wariness of changes because of the AKP's presidential system proposal (AUK Proceedings, writing commission, April 12, 2013).

existing constitutional amendment rule word for word (see Figure 8.2). Infamous for being resistant to change, the MHP did not add an extra barrier to alter the amendment-making mechanism or remove any of the required steps. On the flexibility-rigidity spectrum, the MHP proposal remains more rigid than the AKP proposal but less rigid than the CHP proposal.

The BDP Proposal

The BDP proposal also follows the blueprint of the existing amendment rule, but rather than literally applying the amendment-making rule (as amended in 1987), the BDP proposal simplifies the amendment-making process by eliminating the presidential veto and the qualified parliamentary majority to override it (see Figure 8.2). The proposal sets the voting threshold at three-fifths, but it requires that the president submit an amendment proposal to referendum. In the event that an amendment proposal receives a two-thirds majority in the Parliament, the president has the prerogative to submit it to a voluntary referendum. Thus the BDP's proposal provides for both mandatory and voluntary referendums, depending on the majority that a proposal receives. In brief, the BDP proposal maintains the multitrack framework established by the 1987 amendment but leaves out the president's role as a veto player. The president's authority is limited to submitting the proposal to referendum or to approving it. On the flexibility-rigidity spectrum, the BDP proposal remains less rigid than those of the CHP and the MHP, but more rigid than the AKP's.

The AUK Draft Amendment-Making Rule (Art. 146)

Although the proposals presented by the AKP and the CHP would have altered the amendment-making rule significantly, the rule that the members of the commission were able to agree on in the end does not deviate much from the existing norm. It maintains the one-third requirement to propose an amendment, the requirement that proposals be debated twice, and that they must be approved by secret ballot. The draft proposal preserves the two routes for amending the constitution with some alterations, depending on whether a bill receives three-fifths or two-thirds of the vote in Parliament. Accordingly, if an amendment proposal receives two-thirds of the vote, and if Parliament has not taken a decision with a two-thirds vote to submit the proposal to a public referendum, the president must approve the amendment.

In contrast to the rule of the existing constitution, the commission's draft rule empowers Parliament rather than the president to decide whether to submit a constitutional amendment that has received the support of two-thirds of Parliament to referendum. It is up to Parliament to decide whether or not to seek a voluntary referendum. In the event that an amendment proposal receives three-fifths of the vote in Parliament, the president may return the bill to Parliament for reconsideration or submit it to referendum. If Parliament readopts it with a three-fifths majority, Parliament may decide to submit it to referendum, again with a three-fifths majority. If Parliament is unable to muster the three-fifths majority to submit the vetoed proposal to a referendum, the bill is considered not approved. If Parliament is able to override the presidential veto with a two-thirds majority, the president must approve the bill unless Parliament decides to submit it to referendum (with a two-thirds majority decision). This formulation is close to the proposal for an amendment-making rule outlined in the 2007 constitutional draft prepared by a group of constitutional scholars, which was requested by AKP but sidelined quickly after the government went through a series of constitutional crises in 2007 and 2008.[86]

The provision stipulating that the public may have the option to vote individually on each amendment of a constitutional amendment package in a referendum is also preserved from the 1982 Constitution (as amended in 1987), except that the draft article provides an additional clause: Unless the entire constitution is being replaced, the public has the option to vote separately on unrelated articles.[87] The existing amendment-making rule does not consider a total revision of the constitution.

Overall, the drafted amendment-making rule empowers Parliament with the decision to take recourse to referendum (see Figure 8.3). The president only has a delaying veto power and the authority to seek a voluntary referendum if a proposal is adopted with a three-fifths majority. This latter authority she/he shares with Parliament, which can also decide to override the presidential veto. The draft amendment rule allows a three-fifths majority combined with public referendum to override a presidential veto.[88]

Neither the AKP's proposal to relax the amendment-making rule nor the CHP's proposal to make it more difficult to amend the constitution found its

86 Article 134 of the 2007 proposal also empowers Parliament to take the decision whether to submit the constitutional amendment bill to referendum when it has received two-thirds of the votes (voluntary referendum), and to submit the bill to referendum when it has received three-fifths of the votes (mandatory referendum). The 2007 amendment-making rule differs from the AUK's draft rule in that it does not provide any delaying veto power for the president and it does not stipulate majorities to override the presidential veto.

87 The MHP protested against this provision, as it foresees the possibility of constitutional replacement.

88 The existing amendment-making procedure (as amended in 1987) stipulates a two-thirds majority to override a presidential veto.

How to Initiate Amendments	Legislative Approval Quorum	The Role of the President	Referendum	Other Hurdles and Considerations
Proposal by at least one-third of the members of the parliament	A) Three-fifths majority B) Two-thirds majority	A) Send the bill back to TBMM for reconsideration or submit the bill to referendum B) Ratify the bill (unless TBMM by two-thirds vote decides to submit the bill to referendum) To override the presidential veto: A) Three-fifth majority (obligatory referendum with three-fifths majority decision of the TBMM) B) Two-thirds majority (optional referendum with two-thirds majority decision of the TBMM)	A) Obligatory (three-fifths majority decision of the parliament after overriding the presidential veto) A) Optional (two-thirds majority decision of the parliament after overriding the presidential veto) B) Optional (two-thirds majority decision of the parliament) *Affirmative vote of more than half of the valid votes cast	*Proposal debate twice on the plenary *Secret ballot *TBMM, in case of a referendum, takes a decision on which amendments will be voted together and which will be voted separately. TBMM provides opportunity to voters to vote separately for amendments that are not issue related

FIGURE 8.3: AUK draft amendment-making rule (Art. 146)

way into the draft proposal prepared by the commission. The draft rule is based on the existing arrangement but delegates slightly less authority to the president. The existing constitutional configuration, which is often criticized for its complexity, ultimately "sticks."[89] If we were to evaluate the amendment-making rule in terms of Arend Lijphart's majority scale, the draft rule does not change the type of legislative votes required.[90] However, in terms of veto players, the draft amendment-making rule alters the dynamics. Parliament can force the president to send an amendment proposal to referendum if it can muster a three-fifths majority; if it can produce a two-thirds majority, it can push for a public referendum to seek additional approval by the citizens.[91] Other configurations (such as a three-fifths majority with an optional referendum) that deny the president a delaying veto power were questioned by non-AKP members of the AUK: "Aren't we giving free rein to political power, the power that sees democracy as nothing more than a regime of numbers?"[92] Yet bargaining about the exact configurations ultimately led to partial

[89] On "constitutional stickiness," see Ozan Varol, "Constitutional Stickiness," *UC Davis Law Review* 49, no. 3 (2016): 899–962.

[90] Lijphart, *Patterns of Democracy*, 207.

[91] As Yavuz Atar (AKP legal consultant) explains, "[A] parliament that can muster the majority for constitutional change will have no problem finding the necessary majority for referendum" (AUK Proceedings, writing commission, July 8, 2013).

[92] AUK Proceedings, writing commission, July 3, 2013.

consensus on the formula. Only two issues remained contested: the MHP's concern over the incorporation of a provision that allows for constitutional replacement,[93] and the AKP's proposal to refer to the head of state as *başkan*. Due to the deadlock over these two issues, the drafted amendment-making rule (Art. 146) was not part of the sixty articles that were finalized by the AUK.

The discrepancy between the initial party proposals is resolved partly because the existing amendment-making procedure (as amended in 1987) provided a compromise with two routes for constitutional change involving two different majority requirements and two types of referendums: voluntary and obligatory. However, one major deviation from the procedure (as amended in 1987) was that Parliament is vested with the authority to submit the constitutional amendment bill to referendum. On the flexibility-rigidity spectrum, the drafted, partially agreed Article 146 remained close to the existing amendment-making rule, with minor changes regarding the roles of the president and Parliament in referring the proposal to popular referendum. In other words, the AUK-drafted rule maintained the method of constitutional revision of the existing rule, but empowered Parliament rather than the president in the decision to submit the amendment proposal to voluntary referendum.

4.2 *Bargaining and Negotiating: Debates on the Amendment-Making Rule*

The proceedings of the AUK offer a window into the process of designing constitutional amendment-making rules. The debates reveal that, with regard to reaching consensus, the question of which representatives from the various political parties attended meetings was decisive. The lack of procedural details in the workings of the AUK was furthermore responsible for the failure to achieve sustained deliberation. It can also be observed that the possibility of political actors to call upon the advice of legal experts allowed consensus reaching. But their own experience with the rules and practices of prior constitutions and future concerns still dominated the negotiations. Nevertheless, the informative role of deliberations for constitution making was made explicit when the AUK engaged in the rigidity versus flexibility debate and in debates over the role of veto players in amendment processes.

Regarding the negotiations of Article 146, no alliances between political parties were built. Depending on the issue, members from different parties

93 According to Oktay Öztürk (MHP), the incorporation of a provision that allows for a constitutional replacement "tacitly removes the first four articles (unamendable articles)"; see Yegen, "Debating Amendability," 305.

had no problem aligning with members they had had differences with earlier. For example, MHP representative Faruk Bal joined forces with AKP representative Ahmet İyimaya against the CHP's Rıza Türmen on the issue of amendments during a state of emergency.[94] However, on the issue of voting in secret ballot, the alliances shifted and the MHP and the CHP aligned against the AKP.[95] These shifting alliances were possible in part because there is not always cohesiveness among the members of a given political party. This was especially evident within the CHP, where the three representatives disagreed on particular issues (e.g., the rule to debate the constitutional amendment proposal twice in the plenary, the majority requirement).

Consensus at times appeared when a member who was absent from a previous meeting joined debates and his personal preference turned the tide. When Mustafa Şentop (AKP) participated in the meeting on June 27, 2013, the AKP's earlier resistance against the rule on debating the constitutional amendment proposal twice in the plenary disappeared. On the issue of turnout quorum for the referendum, the AKP made a convincing argument for the right to abstain from voting, while the opposition invoked the legitimacy issue in the case of a low turnout. Rıza Türmen (CHP) changed his opinion and eventually agreed that not participating in a referendum is also a political stance.[96] Such instances offer a glimpse of genuine debate. They also show that the debates did include significant theoretical constitutional considerations on the merits and problems of rigid amendment-making rules, the referendum as a tool of democratic participation, majoritarian tendencies inherent in the legislative voting majorities, and the presupposed limitations of the derived constituent power.

94 Ahmet İyimaya (AKP) argued that it might be necessary in the future to make amendments under a state of emergency, and there should be no constitutional obstacle to such a scenario. Faruk Bal (MHP) agreed with İyimaya, reminding the commission that the 1921 Constitution was made under a state of emergency (AUK Proceedings, April 15, 2013); Oya Yegen, "2011–2013 Tutanakları Işığında Bugünkü Anayasa Değişikliği Süreci," *Birikim*, January 17, 2017, available at: www.birikimdergisi.com/guncel-yazilar/8117/2011-2013-tutanaklari-isiginda-bugunku-anayasa-degisikligi-sureci#.XFGbuy2B3UJ (accessed March 1, 2019).

95 Arguing in favor of keeping the secret ballot requirement, the MHP and the CHP put forward several rationales: 1) 2010 constitutional amendments have demonstrated that even when secret ballot is constitutionally mandated, deputies tend to reveal their vote to prove their party loyalty, so the secret ballot rule should be maintained and observed; 2) considering that it is not political parties but individual members of Parliament that propose constitutional change, deputies should be able to decide individually whether to approve or reject the amendment proposal; 3) Turkey's clientelistic party system does not allow party members to go against party discipline and therefore, without the secret ballot rule, constitutional change would be a matter decided at the political party headquarters rather than in Parliament; and 4) if the national vote is secret, members of Parliament should also vote secretly.

96 AUK Proceedings, writing commission, July 8, 2013.

The debates show that although it was easy to make a deal, it was just as easy to break it. When Süheyl Batum (CHP), who was absent at all earlier debates on the amendment-making rule, joined the deliberations on July 3, 2013, the previously agreed formulation of the article once again became a matter of contestation.[97] The fact that not all members attended all meetings also forced the commission to repeat the debates. The overall inefficiency of the AUK stemmed from the shortcomings in its working methods, which required the participation of one representative from at least three political parties.[98]

The availability and active involvement of constitutional law experts provided additional ammunition for the commission members. The AUK members regularly outsourced the actual wording of the amendment-making rule to legal consultants. Not only did they provide much stronger theoretical arguments and examples, they were also, because of their extensive involvement in the process, invested in realizing the actual drafting of articles.[99] The shared interest among legal consultants in achieving consensus on the draft they had negotiated led rather surprisingly to occasional disagreement between commission members and their experts. For instance, regarding the optional referendum in the amendment-making process, Ahmet Iyimaya (AKP) argued that a simple majority was enough to decide whether to send an amendment proposal to a popular vote. However, the AKP-appointed legal consultant, Yavuz Atar, opposed Iyimaya, arguing that a two-thirds majority should be sought since the proposal itself would have been approved by Parliament with a two-thirds majority. Challenging Iyimaya's argument, Atar's position was supported by CHP legal consultant Selin Esen. The consultants showed solidarity with fellow constitutional law experts, who shared a common interest in achieving consensus and in making solid legal arguments.

Rather than being a genuine search for the right institutional balance between constitutional rigidity and flexibility, the deliberations over the amendment-making rule were dominated by arguments based on future concerns and past disappointments. The opposition invoked the 2010 constitutional amendments on multiple occasions in order to make a case for a rigid

97 Ibid., July 3, 2013.

98 See *Anayasa Uzlasma Komisyonunun Çalisma Usulleri* ("Working Procedures of the Constitutional Conciliation Commission,"), Art. 5. For a translation of the "Working Procedures," see Petersen and Yanaşmayan, Chapter 1 in this volume.

99 When Faruk Bal (MHP) protested that the commission constantly delegated the task of drafting the amendment-making rule to consultants, AKP legal expert Yavuz Atar defended the work of consultants, arguing that they worked hard to reach a consensus only to see the AUK break what they had achieved (AUK Proceedings, writing commission, July 5, 2013).

amendment procedure. In return, AKP members accused the rest of engaging in a reactionary constitution-making process. For instance, the opposition criticized the AKP for violating the spirit and principle of the secret ballot rule during the 2010 constitutional amendment process, and argued that in the absence of such a rule it would be impossible for deputies dissenting from the party line to cast their votes according to their own free will. The opposition parties' primary concerns were checks and balances and, related to this, the question of the role of the president in the amendment-making procedure. On the one hand, the opposition feared that the president might not be impartial, as they anticipated that in the near future the president and the parliamentary majority were likely to be from the current majority party, that is the AKP. This was expressed rather bluntly by Ali Akyildiz, legal consultant on behalf of the MHP. He argued, "The main thing is, let's not give this job [amendment-making power] to one political power, this is the clear situation."[100] AUK members of the three opposition parties insisted on institutionalizing a constitutional safety valve because they envisioned the unraveling of checks and balances if the president and the legislature are from the same party.

Another example of future concerns was the CHP proposal to provide a prohibition against constitutional change during a state of emergency. Selin Esen, legal consultant for the CHP, provided examples from Latin America to argue that constitutional amendments under states of emergency result in restriction of rights and freedoms and enable power grabs. But she later explained that legal consultants, despite spending hours finding a common ground, had failed to do so, and withdrew the proposal, "hoping that the Parliament will not abuse it during a state of emergency."[101]

The drafting of the amendment-making rule in the 2011–2013 period did involve meaningful theoretical debates on majority thresholds, the role of Parliament and president as veto players, citizen participation in referendums, secrecy of parliamentary voting, and constitutional amendments during states of emergency. However, the deliberations were constrained because they took place toward the end of the drafting process, when the AUK had already lost its steam and the likelihood of drafting a full constitution with consensus among all parties was already in doubt. Drafting an amendment-making rule for an unfinished constitutional draft was an elusive task. The recent experience of

100 AUK Proceedings, writing commission, July 5, 2013.

101 Riza Türmen argued, "It is necessary to release the will of the TBMM during a period of state of emergency rule. ... Additionally, maybe because it is an extraordinary situation, there might be need for constitutional change" (AUK Proceedings, writing commission, June 21, 2013).

AKP amendment practices and opposition party members' fear of abuse of amendment-making powers by future authorities defined the attitude of these agents toward veto players and majority requirements in amendment making. Similar to the drafting of other articles, the bargaining and negotiations that went into the amendment-making rule also attest to the important role of legal advice from consultants. The failure to agree on an eventual provision for amendment making reveals the shortcomings of the AUK's operational procedures.

5 CONCLUSION

The foregoing analysis of debates on the amendment-making rule in the Constitutional Conciliation Commission reveals that, although parties came to the negotiation table with very different proposals for constitutional amendments, in the end the form of the old amendment-making rule (as amended in 1987) served as a blueprint for the partially agreed draft Article 146. The new amendment-making rule maintained the two majority thresholds (two-thirds to adopt and three-fifths to submit it to referendum) and did not introduce additional barriers for amending. While several aspects of the rule (e.g., secret ballot, veto power forcing delays, referendum threshold, change under state of emergency) were debated, the final draft reflected the main scheme of the existing amendment-making rule, with some minor revisions. In terms of the flexibility-rigidity continuum, Article 146 remained less rigid than the 1961 and 1982 rules (before amendment). With the exception of Parliament's new role in deciding on submission of amendment proposals to voluntary referendum, the amendment-making rule maintains the same number of veto players and required majorities as the 1987 version did.

The deliberations over the amendment-making rule are a solid example of how the drafting process in the 2011–2013 period was marred by historical disputes and experiences. The 1987 constitutional amendment had provided a precedent for the use of constitutional amendments to achieve antidemocratic ends. The 2007–2008 constitutional crises and the 2010 constitutional amendments showed that the AKP's electoral majority allowed it to dismiss the need for consensus in constitutional change. In the AUK debates, opposition parties articulated the fear that a flexible amendment-making rule could empower strong majoritarian parties to use formal constitutional change via popular approval in plebiscites to avoid having to seek parliamentary consensus. The political and constitutional politics following the failed constitution-making process in 2013 confirm the concerns expressed in the AUK regarding a flexible constitutional amendment rule. The coup attempt in July 2016 hastened Turkey's move from electoral majoritarianism to a competitive authoritarian regime.[102] The 2017 constitutional amendments replaced the parliamentary system with a presidential one, which legalized Recep Tayyip Erdoğan's de facto executive presidency, transformed executive-legislative relations, and reduced checks and balances drastically. These amendments were realized under a state of emergency, when governing by decree and crackdowns on the opposition allowed President Erdoğan and the AKP government to restrict freedom of speech and assembly.[103] The 2017 constitutional amendments once again demonstrated how referendums can be utilized as a stamp of legitimacy, and how lower legislative majority requirements can allow majority governments to abuse amendment-making power. In retrospect, the AUK-drafted amendment-making rule, which did not prohibit constitutional change under a state of emergency and did not add additional barriers, could have allowed a similar outcome.

[102] Berk Esen and Şebnem Gümüşçü, "A Small Yes for Presidentialism: The Turkish Constitutional Referendum of April 2017," *South European Society and Politics* 22, no. 3 (2017): 303–326, 305.

[103] Ibid., 7–14. For more discussion of the 2017 constitutional amendments and how the process violated the secret ballot norm and took place under state of emergency conditions, see Yegen, "2011–2013 Tutanakları Işığında Bugünkü Anayasa Değişikliği Süreci."

Appendices

APPENDIX A

Members and Legal Experts of the Constitutional Conciliation Commission (*Anayasa Uzlaşma Komisyonu*, AUK)

TABLE APPENDIX 1.1 *AUK members and legal consultants*

	AKP	CHP	MHP	BDP
AUK Members	Ahmet İyimaya Mustafa Şentop Mehmet Ali Şahin	Bedii Süheyl Batum Rıza M. Türmen Atilla Kart	Faruk Bal Tunca Toskay Oktay Öztürk	Ayala Akat Ata/later replaced by Bengi Yildiz Sirri Süreyya Önder Altan Tan
Legal Experts	Prof. Dr. Yavuz Atar Prof. Dr. Yusuf Şevki Hakyemez Tarık Olcay Dr Mehmet Ali Zengin Taylan Barın	Ass. Prof. Selin Esen Prof. Dr. Necmi Yüzbaşıoğlu Prof. Dr. İbrahim Kaboğlu Bertil Emrah Oder Ali Ersoy Prof.Dr. İlter Turan Prof. Dr. Ömer Faruk Gençkaya Prof. Dr. Ali Çarkoğlu Dilek Kumcu Fatma Betül Damar Furkan Kararmaz Dr. Abdurrahman Saygılı Mustafa Kemal Çiçek	Prof. Dr. Hasan Tunç Prof. Dr. Ali Akyıldız Kürşat Türker Ercan Mehmet Parsak Oğuz Turhan	Özgür Sevgi Göral Meral Daniş Beştaş Ferhat Kabaiş Yusuf Uygar Neslihan Yıldırım Yusuf Buzgan

Source: Authors' own compilation.

Agreed and Non-Agreed Articles of the AUK: Note to the Reader

This part of the appendix provides the English translation of all agreed and non-agreed articles that the AUK produced between October 2011 and November 2013. Among the 172 articles (including an article about the nature of the preamble but not the preamble itself) the commission set out to negotiate, the AUK agreed on sixty full articles while 112 articles remained contested. Among the sixty articles that the AUK has reached agreement on ("agreed articles"), we find forty-three articles that regard fundamental rights and freedoms (e.g., human dignity and honor, right to life, inviolability of the domicile, freedom of communication, right to hold meetings and demonstration marches, right to health, right to environment, restriction of fundamental rights and freedoms, protection of fundamental rights and freedoms). The remaining seventeen articles concern the administration and public services (one article: higher education coordination council); the preamble; general provisions and basic principles (two articles: republic principle, primacy of the Constitution); the legislative power (five articles: activities incompatible with deputyship, loss of deputyship, application for annulment, Bureau of the Assembly, publicity and publication of debates); and the judiciary (nine articles: judicial independence, security of tenure of judges, public prosecutors and tenure of prosecutors, judicial law enforcement, supervision of the judicial services, court of jurisdictional disputes, term of office of Constitutional Court judges, decisions of the Constitutional Court, constitutional complaint).

Albeit being incomplete, the fundamental rights part of the projected Constitution is relatively liberal and progressive with regard to, for example, environmental rights and duties. Moreover, the human dignity article underlines that the Constitution would have governed rights and their limitation with a more democratic and human rights approach. The fact that some fundamental rights articles (e.g., the protection and the integrity of human material and spiritual well-being; prohibition of torture, inhuman treatment and degrading treatment; status of aliens; right to housing and shelter; the right to work, security at work and fair wage; the rights of the persons requiring special protection) include human dignity as a benchmark the state has to respect when limiting rights shows that this constitutional guideline was entrenched in more than one article.

Among the 112 contested ("non-agreed") articles, we find twenty articles that refer to fundamental rights and freedoms, twenty-three articles that refer to legislation or the legislative organ, twelve articles that refer to the executive power, sixteen articles that refer to administration and the public services, twelve articles that refer to the judiciary, sixteen articles that refer to financial, economic and social provisions, two articles that refer to final provisions, the preamble, and eleven articles that refer to general provisions and fundamental principles. Part of the non-agreed articles are provisions that found almost full agreement with only one party disagreeing (e.g., equality, rights of the child, freedom of residence and movement, freedom of thought and expression, freedom of association), articles that reached agreement among at least two parties (e.g., freedom of the press, attorneyship and the bar associations), and those that remained fully contested (e.g., citizenship, right and freedom of education and instruction, freedom of religion, conscience and belief, the composition of the Grand National Assembly of Turkey and representation of the nation, functions and powers of the Grand National Assembly of Turkey, declaration of state of war and authorization to deploy the armed forces, military justice, election of the president, duties and powers of the president). This part provides a good overview on the exact disagreement between parties and the language in which they framed their proposals for the projected Constitution. It shows, among others, that the most contested were issues pertaining either to Turkish identity (e.g., citizenship; freedom of religion, conscience and belief; official language; right and freedom of education and instruction) or the government system (e.g., election of the president, duties and powers of the president, functions and powers of the Grand National Assembly of Turkey).

In the list of non-agreed articles (Appendix C), we have visualized the different proposals of different political parties in the Constitutional Conciliation Commission by italicizing the respective part of the articles. The different proposals of the respective political parties are indicated by naming the party (e.g., Proposal of BDP). In both the list of agreed articles (Appendix B) and the list of non-agreed articles (Appendix C), the political parties included reasonings and notes. Reasonings were often used to explain how a certain concept (e.g., public order) that was formulated in the constitutional text should be interpreted. They also served to define the scope of the respective provisions. Notes, on the other hand, reflected more often the disagreements. A recurring note, for instance, was inserted by CHP announcing that the presidentialism proposal of the AKP had not been negotiated in the commission. They were also used as reminders for subsequent negotiations when, for instance, political parties agreed (or at least one party suggested) to place the provision in another chapter or article, or when a party made its consent dependent on the result of negotiations of another article. They were also used simply to express reservations and annotations.

APPENDIX B

Agreed Articles of the Constitutional Conciliation Commission (AUK)[1]

FUNDAMENTAL RIGHTS AND FREEDOMS

A) *Fundamental Principles*

Human Dignity and Honor

Article (1): (1) Human *dignity and honor* are inviolable. Human *dignity and honor* are the basis of human rights and the constitutional order.

(2) The state shall respect human *dignity and honor* and one's right to develop his or her material and spiritual well-being and protect these values and eliminate all obstacles to them.

Reasoning: (The note below is to be taken into consideration when the reasonings related to the fundamental rights and freedoms are drafted.)

Human *dignity and honor* encompass recognition, protection, and the development of the values that originate solely from being human.

The notion "the state" in its broad meaning contains all organs or institutions that exercise public authority or power.

The Nature and the Integrity of Fundamental Rights and Freedoms

Article (2): (1) Everyone possesses inherent fundamental rights and freedoms, which are inviolable and inalienable.

(2) Fundamental rights and freedoms form a whole and complete each other.

Reasoning: (The note below is to be taken into consideration when the reasonings related to the fundamental rights and freedoms are drafted.)

The fact that a right is not codified in the Constitution does not prevent it from being considered a human right.

[1] Translated by Hilal Sarbak, hereinafter TN.

B) Rights and Freedoms of the Individual

Right to Life

Article 4: (1) Everyone shall have the right to life.

(2) The situations of self-defense and use of force which may end or jeopardize the right to life in cases where it is absolutely necessary and prescribed by law are exceptions.

Reasoning: Although it is not included in the article, cases of "necessity" shall fall within the scope of the exceptions.

The acts of murder ... [incomplete in the original, TN].

The Protection and the Integrity of Human Material and Spiritual Well-Being

Article 5: (1) Everyone shall have the right to protect and develop his or her material and spiritual well-being and to demand those to be respected.

(2) The physical integrity of the body cannot be violated, including in scientific and medical tests, with the exception of medical necessities or when the informed consent is obtained, under circumstances clearly indicated by law.

(3) The body (physical integrity) and organs (and body parts and tissues) of the human cannot be commodified in contradiction with human dignity and honor.

Note: In case the article regarding the right to cultural identity is not accepted, the expression of "protection of his or her own culture and identity" shall be reintroduced.

Note: (MHP) If the article is restored, the MHP's reservation shall also be reintroduced to the article.

Prohibition of Torture, Inhuman Treatment, and Degrading Treatment

Article 7: (1) Torture, inhuman treatment, and degrading treatment are prohibited.

(2) No one shall be sentenced to a punishment and subjected to a treatment that is in contradiction with human dignity and honor, even in case of restriction of freedoms and execution of sentences.

Note: Judicial control and security measures fall within the scope of the expression "shall not be subjected to treatment."

Prohibition of Slavery and Forced Labor

Article 8: (1) No one shall be required to perform forced labor. Human trafficking and forced labor are prohibited.

(2) Principles regarding the citizenship duty envisaged in areas necessitated by the needs of the country and the work having the nature of national service or the work of a convicted individual shall be prescribed by law.

Reasoning: Alternative measures and sanctions shall be considered within the scope of "convicted."

In accordance with the requirements of the principles of a democratic society, proportionality and not infringing upon the essence of rights ... [incomplete in the original, TN].

Liberty and Security of the Individual

Article 9: (1) Everyone shall have the right to liberty and security of the person.

(2) No one shall be deprived of his or her liberty, save in the following cases:

a) Execution of sentences and implementation of security measures restricting liberty decided by courts,
b) Execution of court decisions of arrest and detention,
c) Execution of court decisions aimed at protecting the rights and freedoms of the individual himself or herself or others, or execution of administrative measures prescribed by law,
d) Arrest, custody, or detention of a person who enters irregularly into the country or for whom a deportation or extradition order has been issued.

(3) Arrest and detention shall be based upon the decision of a judge. Decisions of arrest may only be delivered for individuals against whom there is strong evidence of having committed an offense, solely for the purposes of preventing escape, or preventing the destruction or alteration of evidence, or other circumstances necessitating detention that are prescribed by law. The strong evidence of having committed an offense and the gravity of the accused crime in question cannot be considered alone as a reason for detention. Continuation of detention cannot be determined unless the reasons for detention are justified on grounds of concrete facts and the insufficiency of judicial control measures is clarified. Arrest of a person without a decision by a judge may be executed only when a person against whom there is strong evidence of crime is caught in flagrante delicto or in cases where delay is likely to thwart the course of justice. The principles and procedures regarding arrest and detention shall be prescribed by law.

(4) Individuals arrested or detained shall be promptly notified, in all cases in writing, or orally when the former is not immediately possible, of the grounds for their arrest or detention, the charges against them and the rights

granted to them by law; in cases of offenses committed collectively this notification shall be made, at the latest, before the individual is brought before a judge. Individuals shall be made to consult a defense counsel as soon as he or she is taken into custody. The defense counsel's competence to review the file during the investigation phase cannot be restricted in a manner that would invalidate the right to defense. The bar association shall appoint defense counsel for those who do not have defense counsel. The arrest or detention of an individual shall be immediately notified to one of his or her relatives.

Note: *(Proposal of BDP) The expression of "in a language that he or she prefers" has been proposed to be reincluded here in case there is no consensus on the articles regarding the right of using one's mother tongue and right to a fair trial.*

(5) The person arrested or detained shall be brought before a judge within at most twenty-four hours, and in case of offenses committed collectively within at most ninety-six hours, excluding the time required to send the individual to the court nearest to the place of arrest. No one can be deprived of his or her liberty without the decision of a judge after the expiry of the above-specified periods.

(6) Persons under detention shall have the right to request trial within a reasonable time and to be released during investigation or prosecution. Release may be conditioned by a guarantee to ensure the presence of the person at the trial proceedings or the execution of the court sentence or other duties.

(7) Persons whose liberties are restricted for any reason are entitled to apply to the competent judicial authority for timely conclusion of proceedings regarding their situation and for their immediate release if the restriction imposed upon them is not lawful. The judicial authority shall listen to the person whose liberties are restricted before it delivers its decision. The maximum detention time during investigation and prosecution shall be determined by law. Under no circumstances shall detention become a way of punishment.

Reasoning: The term "other circumstances . . ." in paragraph three intends to mean the reasons, such as unsound mind, that are laid down under Article 19(3) of the 1982 Constitution.

Protection of women, protection of family stipulated under Law No. 4320, prevention of violence.

Note: "The execution of the decision to keep a child in custody or bring a child before the competent authority" will be negotiated under the article concerning children's rights.

Note: (First proposal: The periods may be extended for offenses committed collectively, during a state of emergency, martial law, or in time of war, to the extent required by the conditions of these events.) (Second proposal: The periods may be extended during a state of emergency or in time of war up to three days.) (Third proposal: Such sentence should not be included.) This will be negotiated in the article concerning state of emergency.

Note: "Damage suffered by persons subjected to treatment other than these provisions shall be compensated by the state in accordance with the general principles of the compensation law." The violation of fundamental rights and freedoms will be negotiated in a separate article. The possibility of taking recourse not only to the state but also to the person who caused the damage shall be negotiated.

Privacy and Protection of Private and Family Life (Shall be reviewed.)
Article 10: (1) Privacy of private or family life shall not be violated. Everyone shall have the right of respect and protection of their private and family lives.

(2) Information concerning individuals' private and family life cannot be published either on audial or visual media nor on Internet and other platforms without their consent.

(3) Unless there exists a decision duly given by a judge on the grounds of public order, protection of public health or the rights and freedoms of others or prevention of crime where there is strong evidence for crime, as well as unless there exists a written order of a public prosecutor, in cases where delay is prejudicial, again on the above-mentioned grounds and due to the requirements of the judicial investigation, neither the person, nor the private papers, nor any belongings of an individual shall be searched nor shall they be seized. The decision of the competent authority shall be submitted for approval to a judge having jurisdiction within twenty-four hours. The judge shall announce his or her decision within forty-eight hours from the time of seizure; otherwise, seizure shall automatically be lifted.

Reasoning: The notion of "public order" referred in this article is not a generic reason for restriction and may apply only in exceptional cases. Hence, it shall be interpreted very narrowly as required by the general principles of law.

Protection of Personal Data and Information
Article 11: (1) Privacy of personal data and information is essential.

(2) Everyone shall have the right of protection of their personal data and information. This right includes being informed of, having access to, and

requesting the correction and deletion of his or her personal data and information, and to be informed whether these are used in consistency with the objectives envisaged.

(3) Personal data and information can only be collected, processed, and used in a nondiscriminatory manner on grounds of a person's explicit consent or legitimate reasons envisaged by law. Personal data and information cannot be automatically collected or processed.

(4) The principles and procedures regarding the protection of personal data and information shall be regulated by law in a manner that allows the effective exercise of this right.

Reasoning: Inconveniences that may arise from the exercise of this right to the freedom of press shall be referred to in the relevant article or reasoning.

The reasonable time and exceptions shall be explained in the reasoning.

The following proposal of the BDP shall be discussed as part of the reasoning: "Personal data regarding the person's race, ethnic origin, political opinion, philosophical belief, religion, sect or other beliefs, the membership to associations, foundations or unions, and health and private life shall not be collected or processed."

Inviolability of the Domicile (Shall be reviewed.)

Article 12: (1) The domicile and the nonpublic workplace of an individual shall not be violated. Everyone shall have the right to have protection against illegal interventions and attacks on their domicile or workplace.

(2) Unless there exists a decision duly given by a judge on the grounds of protection of public health or the rights and freedoms of others or prevention of a crime where there is strong evidence for a crime, and unless there exists a written order of a public prosecutor, in cases where delay is prejudicial, again on the above-mentioned grounds and due to the requirements of the judicial investigation, neither the domicile of a person could be entered and a search could be carried out nor could the belongings in the domicile be seized. The decision of the competent authority shall be submitted for approval to a judge having jurisdiction within twenty-four hours. The judge shall announce his or her decision within forty-eight hours from the time of seizure; otherwise, seizure shall automatically be lifted.

(3) Without prejudice to the powers of the administrative police regarding the protection of general health, no preventive search can be carried out in the domicile or nonpublic workplace of a person.

Note: (MHP) "Public order" shall be included as a reason for restriction if there is an example in which the reasons for limitation in the article are found to be insufficient.

Freedom of Communication

Article 13: (1) Everyone shall have the freedom of communication. Privacy and inviolability of communication are essential.

(2) Unless there exists a decision duly given by a judge on the grounds of protection of national security and/or the rights and freedoms of others or prevention of a crime where there is strong evidence for a crime, as well as unless there exists a written order of a public prosecutor, in cases where delay is prejudicial, again on the above-mentioned grounds and due to the requirements of the judicial investigation, communication shall not be impeded nor its privacy be violated. The written order of the public prosecutor shall be submitted for the approval of a judge having jurisdiction within twenty-four hours. The judge shall announce his or her decision within forty-eight hours from the time of intervention; otherwise, the decision (to impede or violate, TN) shall automatically be lifted.

(3) The principles and procedures to be applied in institutions where supervision of the communication is mandatory shall be regulated by law.

Reasoning: The expression of "the posts used in the communication" shall be referred to in the reasoning.

Freedom of Science and the Arts

Article 18: (1) Everyone shall have the right and freedom to study and teach, express, perform, and disseminate science and the arts, and to carry out all sorts of research in these fields.

(2) The state is under the duty to eliminate all obstacles against this right and freedom and to ensure the effective exercise of it.

(3) The state shall promote the arts and cultural activities and protect artists.

Note: Scientific autonomy shall be written down in another article.

Right of Rectification and Reply

Article 20: (1) Everyone whose personal reputation and honor is injured or against whom unfounded allegations are published shall have the right of rectification and reply.

(2) If a rectification or reply is not published, a judge decides within forty-eight hours of appeal by the individual involved whether this publication is required.

Right to Property and Inheritance

Article 21: (1) Everyone shall have the right to property and inheritance.

(2) The right to inheritance may be restricted for the purpose of public interest, the right to property may be restricted for the purpose of public interest, and for foreigners also for the purpose of national security.

Reasoning: The common opinion is to negotiate this paragraph (second, TN) within the "right to environment and natural life." Intellectual and industrial property shall be evaluated within the scope of the right to property.

Freedom of Work and Contract

Article 22: (1) Everyone shall have the freedom to work and conclude contracts in the field of his or her choice. Establishment of private enterprises is free.

(2) The state shall take measures to ensure the operation of private enterprises in accordance with national economic requirements and the principle of the social state, in security and stability, and to prevent the establishment of monopolies.

(3) The state is under the duty to ensure and supervise that all sorts of enterprises take necessary measures with respect to the exploitation of natural resources, environmental pollution, and the occupational health and security of employees.

Right to Hold Meetings and Demonstration Marches

Article 24: (1) Everyone shall have the right to hold unarmed and peaceful meetings and demonstration marches and participate in them without prior permission.

(2) The right to hold meetings and demonstration marches may be restricted for the purposes of protection of public order, public health, the rights and freedoms of others, and prevention of crime.

(3) The administrative authorities shall determine the place, route, and time of meetings as well as of demonstration marches by taking into consideration the democratic function and effect of the right.

Right to Appeal and Information

Article 26: (1) Everyone shall have the right to apply individually or collectively to the competent authorities and to the Turkish Grand National Assembly with regard to requests and complaints concerning themselves or the public. The competent authorities shall respond to the applications without delay.

(2) Everyone shall have the right to obtain information with regard to acts and actions concerning either themselves or the public.

(3) The state shall indicate in its proceedings the legal remedies and authorities the person concerned should apply to, and the time limits for application.

Note: Transferring this paragraph to a more suitable part will be considered.

(4) The foreigner's right to information shall be regulated by law in accordance with the principle of reciprocity.

Note: The paragraph regarding foreigners shall be evaluated within a general article concerning the rights and freedoms of foreigners.

Note: The right to access information, together with the freedom of information, shall be discussed separately as rights regarding the information society.

Note: The right to appeal to the ombudsperson shall be evaluated in the part on the legislative.

Note: The right to constitutional complaint shall be evaluated in the part on the Constitutional Court.

Principles Relating to Offenses and Penalties

Article 27: (1) Crimes, penalties, and security measures in lieu of penalties shall be prescribed only by law.

(2) No one shall be punished for any act that does not constitute a criminal offense under the law in force at the time committed, and no one shall be given a heavier penalty for an offense other than the penalty applicable at the time when the offense was committed.

(3) The provisions of the above paragraph shall apply also to the statute of limitations on offenses and penalties, and to the results of a conviction.

(4) No one shall be considered guilty until proven guilty in a court of law.

(5) No one shall be compelled to make a statement that would incriminate himself or herself or his or her legally prescribed relatives, or to present incriminating evidence to that end.

(6) Criminal responsibility shall be personal.

(7) No one shall be convicted more than once for the same crime.

(8) No one shall be deprived of his or her liberty merely on the ground of inability to fulfill a contractual obligation.

(9) Neither death penalty nor general confiscation shall be imposed as punishment.

(10) The state shall take administrative measures to ensure affirmative action for women in the execution of their sentences.

(11) Detainees and convicts cannot be subjected to torture and cruel, inhuman, and degrading treatment.

(12) The administration shall not impose any sanction resulting in restriction of personal liberty.

(13) No citizen shall be extradited to a foreign country because of an alleged offense, except under obligations resulting from international law.

Reasoning: The reasoning to paragraph eleven is as follows:

1) Refusing treatment to severely ill detainees and convicts outside of prison if their treatment is not possible in the prison falls within the scope of "torture and cruel treatment."

2) The state shall ensure that individuals can practice their beliefs, continue their cultural life, and talk in their own language while serving a sentence or during detention.

MHP objects to adding the second paragraph of the reasoning since the matters it touches upon will be regulated in the relevant articles.

Status of Aliens

Article 28: (1) The fundamental rights and freedoms with respect to aliens may be restricted by law in a way that is compatible with international law.

(2) The right of asylum shall be regulated by law in accordance with Turkey's obligations stemming from international treaties.

(3) No one shall be returned to a country where he or she is very likely to be subjected to the death penalty or treatment or punishment that contradicts human dignity.

d) Social and economic rights

Right to Health

Article 33: (1) Everyone shall have the right to health.

(2) No one can be deprived of basic medical services.

(3) The principles of the right to health, including patients' rights, shall be regulated by law in accordance with the right to life and protection of health.

(4) Every woman has the right to receive free of charge services regarding reproductive health and fertility rights.

(5) The state has the duty to take all measures to ensure the exercise of the right to health. The state shall carry out its duties in the field of health through establishing an efficient health service network by way of utilizing health and social institutions both from the public and private sector and by supervising them.

Note: Regarding the formulation of the second paragraph, BDP has expressed and insisted on the fact that providing health services free of charge is an indispensable element. CHP has declared this proposal to be acceptable.

Reasoning: It shall be indicated that fertility rights also include the right not to give birth. The issue of general health insurance has been left outside the scope of the Constitution as it is assumed to be regulated by the legislative authority.

Right to Social Security

Article 34: (1) Everyone shall have the right to social security.

(2) No one can be employed without being bound by the social security system.

(3) The state shall take necessary measures to ensure the exercise of the right to social security and shall establish the suitable/adequate social security system for this.

(4) The state shall take necessary special measures to ensure the enjoyment of the right to social security by socially weak groups, such as the widows and orphans of martyrs of war and duty, together with the disabled war veterans, disabled people, the elderly, and children in need of protection.

Note: BDP insists on regulating a specific provision with regard to housewives within the scope of this article.

Reasoning: The "right to social security" referred to in the last paragraph is not used in a narrow but in a broad sense. The efficient exercise of the right to social security will be emphasized.

Right to Environment

Article 35: (1) Everyone shall have the right to environment. This right includes living in a healthy, ecosystematically balanced environment that enables human development, and demanding the effective protection of the environment.

(2) Everyone and the state are under the obligation to develop the environment, to protect environmental values, to prevent environmental pollution, to increase the quality of the environment, and to ensure the naturalness of foods considering the responsibilities owed to future generations.

(3) All principles, including sanctions, regarding the right to environment and the principles and procedures of the public's right to participate in

decision-making mechanisms in case of plans and implementations that may have an adverse effect on the environment shall be regulated by law.

(4) The state shall protect natural life and animals. It shall take necessary measures for the purpose of preventing ill-treatment of animals.

Reasoning: 1) The right to demand effective protection of the environment includes rights to receive information regarding the environment, to participate, and to appeal.

2) It has been defended that the sentence, "The state shall promote and support the use of technologies that keep the environment clean and do not cause damage to it by both the public and private sectors" shall be included in the reasoning.

3) The right to property cannot be claimed on common natural, cultural, and historical wealth and assets in a manner that can cause the deprivation of their authenticity and that can prevent others from utilizing them for cultural purposes.

4) Water, air, genes, seeds, and other natural creatures, as other elements of nature, belong to all living organisms; they cannot be subject to property. They and their genetic codes cannot be patented.

Reasoning: 1) It will be written that the expression of employees encompasses all the employees, including the civil servants, without any distinction being made for public or private.

2) Judges and public prosecutors benefit from the freedom of association in order to protect and improve their professional and social rights and freedoms. The law shall not impose restrictions that hinder the exercise of this freedom. [This reasoning is misplaced in the original, it is the reasoning of Article 37, Right to Unionize, TN]

Right to Housing and Shelter

Article 36: (1) Everyone shall have the right to housing and shelter that meets the basic human needs of him or her, in accordance with human dignity.

(2) In order to ensure the exercise of these rights, the state shall take necessary measures within the framework of a plan that takes into account the historical and cultural characteristics of cities and other residence areas, as well as environmental values.

Note: The topic of recognizing constitutional assurances against illegal (forceful) evacuation and violations that infringe the essence of these rights will be worked on.

Right to Unionize (Shall be reviewed.)

Article 37: (1) Employees and employers shall have the right to form unions and higher organizations, without prior permission, and they possess the right to become a member of a union and to freely withdraw from membership. No one shall be forced to become a member of a union or to withdraw from membership.

(2) The establishment, administration, and operations of unions and higher organizations cannot be incompatible with the principles of equal representation and participation of women and men, and democratic principles.

(3) Unions and higher organizations may be dissolved with a court decision only under mandatory circumstances prescribed by law.

(4) Measures to be taken to encourage union membership in workplaces shall be prescribed by law.

(5) Economic, social, and union rights of employees cannot be restricted by implementing different forms of employment. The state shall take necessary measures to prevent such restrictive implementations.

(6) Provisions of the first paragraph shall not prevent imposing restrictions on the Turkish Armed Forces, security forces officials, and judges and public prosecutors to the extent that their duties so require.

Note: It will be considered prohibited for the Turkish Armed Forces and permitted for the others. (The right to association and to unionize shall be examined with respect to NATO law and other constitutions.)

(7) Houseworkers cannot be deprived of the right to unionize.

Reasoning: 1) It will be written that the term "employees" encompasses all employees, including civil servants, without any distinction being made for public or private.

2) Judges and public prosecutors benefit from the freedom of association in order to protect and improve their professional and social rights and freedoms. The law shall not impose restrictions that hinder the exercise of this freedom.

Right to Work, Security at Work, and Fair Wage

Article 39: (1) Everyone shall have the right to work, to security at work, and to a fair wage that enables them to live in accordance with human dignity and honor.

(2) No one shall be required to perform work unsuited to his or her age and capacity.

(3) The state shall take necessary measures to ensure a fair wage for employees in accordance with their jobs and utilization of social aids, to raise the standard of living of employees, to increase employment, to protect employees and the unemployed people, to promote labor, to create suitable economic conditions for prevention of unemployment, to eliminate the gender-based inequalities in work life, and to ensure security of work and labor peace [unclear meaning in Turkish, TN].

(4) In determining the minimum wage, the living conditions of employees shall be taken into account. Minimum wage shall not be taxed.

(5) The employees shall have the right to participate in procedures regarding the regulation and improvement of rest and leisure, annual leave, the rights of paid weekends and holidays, and the conditions relating to work and workplace.

(6) Pregnant women and women who recently gave birth, as well as minors and physically and mentally disabled persons, shall enjoy special protection with regard to working conditions. Such protective laws cannot include provisions that complicate or delay the participation of women and disabled people in economic and social life.

(7) The employer is obliged to undertake the liability insurance that is paid by himself or herself for compensations arising from work accidents and occupational diseases. The principles and procedures regarding this insurance shall be prescribed by law.

(8) The state shall promote employers to provide child care services.

Reasoning: The following sentence is to be included in the reasoning: "It is prohibited for minors to be employed in any kind of work that is not appropriate for their age, that may harm their safety, health or physical, spiritual, moral, or social development, or prevent their education."

Limits of Social and Economic Duties of the State

Article 40: (1) The state shall fulfill its duties in the social and economic field as laid down in the Constitution and within the capacity of its financial resources, taking into consideration the priorities appropriate for the aims of these duties.

(2) The limitation "capacity of its financial resources" shall not apply to the right to health, social security, and security at work. The duties of the state in relation to these rights shall not be deemed to be fulfilled unless the minimum guarantees are provided.

Restriction of Fundamental Rights and Freedoms

Article 41: (1) Freedom is the norm, limitation is the exception.

(2) Fundamental rights and freedoms may be restricted only by law, and in conformity with the reasons mentioned in the relevant articles of the Constitution. These restrictions cannot be contrary to intended purposes, the requirements of the democratic society, and the principle of proportionality, and they cannot infringe the essence of fundamental rights and freedoms.

Note: CHP's proposal to include the following paragraph, "The legislative, executive, judicial organs, and administrative authorities are obliged to comply with the principles established with regard to limitations of restrictions" shall be accepted in the article on the supremacy and binding force of the Constitution.

Note: There will be a separate provision regarding the prohibition of abuse of fundamental rights and freedoms. This can be either included in a new article or a separate paragraph may be added to Article 40.

Temporary Suspension of the Exercise of Fundamental Rights and Freedoms

Article 42: (1) In the event of declaration of state of emergency procedures prescribed by the Constitution, the exercise of fundamental rights and freedoms may be restricted or temporarily suspended to the extent required by the exigencies of the situation, as long as obligations under international law are not violated.

(2) Even under the circumstances indicated in the first paragraph, the individual's dignity and honor, the individual's right to life, and the integrity of his or her corporeal and spiritual existence shall be inviolable except where death occurs through acts in conformity with law of war; no one shall be compelled to reveal his or her religion, conscience, thought or opinion, nor be accused on account of them; offenses and penalties shall not be made retroactive; nor shall anyone be held guilty until so proven by a court ruling; and the right to claim rights shall not be withdrawn.

Protection of Fundamental Rights and Freedoms

Article 43: (1) The state organs are under the obligation to make all necessary regulations and take precautions in order to ensure the effective execution of fundamental rights and freedoms by all, and to prevent their violation.

(2) The state shall be responsible for the damages incurred from the violation of fundamental rights and freedoms and a lawsuit shall be filed against the state. The state shall notify the public officer who caused the violation about the lawsuit. The state shall immediately take recourse to the responsible officer if a sentence for compensation is issued.

(3) In case of a conflict between international agreements (duly put into effect) that concern fundamental rights and freedoms and ordinary laws, due to differences in provisions on the same matter, the provisions of international agreements shall prevail unless the law provides wider protection with regard to freedoms.

Reasoning: Legislative, executive, and judicial organs, in their proceedings and their interpretation, shall take into consideration the treaties concerning fundamental rights and freedoms to which Turkey is a party.

(4) None of the rights and freedoms in the Constitution may be interpreted in a way that would allow the state or any person to perform any act aimed at the destruction of the rights and freedoms or at their greater limitation than is provided for in the Constitution.

Right to Live in Peace and in a Disarmed Society

Article 44: (1) Everyone shall have the right to live in peace and to be protected from violence. In order to ensure this right, the state shall take measures to make access to weapons difficult.

(2) The state shall prevent any sort of discourse and activity that promotes or spreads hatred between social groups or hatred against a certain social group by making legal regulations and shall take effective and deterrent measures.

Reasoning: This article includes the prevention of discourses such as propaganda for war, militarism, racism, and all sorts of discrimination as well as the development of a culture of peace.

Protection and Utilization of the Coasts

Article 47: (1) The coasts are under the authority and disposal of the state; they cannot be subject to private property.

(2) Everyone shall have the right to utilize seacoasts, lake shores, or riverbanks.

(3) This right shall be regulated by law considering public interest.

(4) Principles and procedures regarding the acquisition of soil by filling and drying when necessitated by public interest shall be prescribed by law.

Protection of Historical, Cultural, and Natural Wealth and Assets

Article 48: (1) The state shall ensure the protection of the historical, cultural, and natural assets and wealth, and shall take supportive and promotive measures toward that end. The restrictions to be applied for the purposes of public interest to those that are subject to private property, and the financial assistance to be granted to the private property holders in this regard, as well as the exceptions to be recognized, shall be regulated by law.

Reasoning: The first paragraph includes all civilizations and the wealth and assets of different communities of culture and belief.

(2) The state shall take necessary measures to protect its historical and cultural inheritance outside of Turkey.

Reasoning: Adoption/reacquisition by Turkey and Turkey's right to restore.

Exploration and Exploitation of Natural Resources and Wealth

Article 49: (1) Natural wealth and resources shall be under the authority and at the disposal of the state. The right to explore and exploit them belongs to the state. The state may delegate this right to persons or corporate bodies for a certain period provided that environmental assets are protected. Of the natural wealth and resources, those to be explored and exploited by the state in partnership with persons or corporate bodies, and those to be directly explored and exploited by persons or corporate bodies, shall depend on the explicit permission of the law. The conditions to be observed by persons and corporate bodies in such cases, the procedures and principles governing supervision and control by the state, and the sanctions to be applied shall be prescribed by law.

Note: This article shall be included under duties and obligations of the state.

Protection and Development of Forests

Article 50: The state shall take the measures required for the protection and extension of forests. Burnt forest areas shall be reforested; other agricultural and stockbreeding activities shall not be allowed in such areas. All forests shall be under the supervision of the state.

The ownership of state forests shall not be transferred, and they shall be managed and exploited by the state in accordance with the law. Ownership of these forests shall not be acquired by prescription, nor shall servitude other than that in the public interest be imposed in respect to forests.

Acts and actions that might damage forests shall not be permitted. No amnesties or pardons for offenses against forests shall be granted exclusively.

To reduce the size of forest areas shall be prohibited, except in areas where preservation of forests is considered scientifically and technically useless but conversion into agricultural land has been found to be definitely advantageous; with respect to fields, vineyards, orchards, olive groves, or similar areas that technically and scientifically ceased to be forest before December 31, 1981, and whose use for agricultural or stockbreeding purposes has been found advantageous; and with respect to residential areas in the vicinity of cities, towns, or villages.

The state shall take necessary measures to protect the forests and biological diversity, to enlarge forest lands, to ensure the effective operation of the soil, to fight against erosion, and to develop the agricultural areas.

Rights of the Persons Requiring Special Protection

Article 52: (1) The state shall take necessary measures to protect the rights of the youth, the elderly, disabled persons, chronical patients, relatives of martyrs of war and duty, disabled war veterans, widows and orphans, and other groups in society that require special protection and to ensure that they live in accordance with human dignity and honor and participate effectively in social life. Taking measures to enable the participation in political life of persons requiring special protection is one of the duties of the state.

Reasoning: It will be clarified in the reasoning that the term "widow" includes both women and men.

Right of Access to Information and Freedom of Information

Article 55: (1) Everyone shall have the right to access information, Internet, and other electronic communication media. The state shall make the necessary regulations to ensure the effective and fair exercise of this right.

(2) Privacy of communication through the Internet is essential. Everyone has the right to demand protection of his or her personal data shared through the Internet and to demand respect for the privacy of his or her opinions.

(3) Right of access to Internet and other electronic communication media shall be regulated by law in accordance with the constitutional principles regarding the privacy of private and family life, protection of personal data, freedom of communication, right to access information, freedom of expression and press, freedom of contracts, and protection of children against sexual exploitation.

Reasoning: The expression "constitutional principles" in the third paragraph shall be considered together with the guarantees and restrictions of rights and freedoms in the relevant constitutional articles.

Right to Have a Decent Life

Article 56: (1) Everyone shall have the right to be protected from social exclusion and poverty, and the right to have a decent life including the rights of education, shelter, medical care, nutrition, access to clean water, and benefit from social services.

(2) Everyone who is deprived of the opportunity to have a decent life shall have the right to basic income.

(3) The state shall take necessary measures to ensure individuals' right to lead a decent life.

Expropriation

Article 61: (1) In case it is required by public interest, the state and public corporations shall be entitled to expropriate privately owned real estate wholly or in part, and to impose administrative easement on it, in accordance with the principles and procedures prescribed by law, provided that the actual compensation is paid in advance.

(2) The compensation for expropriation shall be paid in cash and in advance.

(3) The procedures to be applied to compensate for land expropriated for the purpose of carrying out agriculture reform, protection of environmental values, biological diversity and cultural assets, realizing of irrigation and housing projects, growing new forests and protecting the coasts shall be regulated by law, on the condition that the installment of compensation does not exceed five years.

(4) Payment in installments except for the cases laid down under the third paragraph and confiscation without compensation are prohibited.

Reasoning: The necessary regulations to ensure that the owner's rights are not harmed in the implementation of the payment procedure shall be regulated by law.

Nationalization and Privatization

Article 62: (1) Private enterprises carrying public nature may be nationalized by law, in case public interest so necessitates, on the basis of their real value.

(2) Principles and rules concerning the privatization of enterprises and assets owned by the state, state economic enterprises, and other public corporate bodies shall be prescribed by law to prevent monopolization and cartel building.

(3) The privatization of strategically important enterprises shall be based on the principle of public interest.

(4) The question of which investments and services carried out by the state, state economic enterprises, and other public corporate bodies and could be performed by or delegated to persons or corporate bodies through private law contracts shall be regulated by law.

(5) The measures to be taken to protect the rights of employees during nationalization and privatization shall be regulated by law.

Protection of Consumers

Article 63: (1) The state shall take measures to protect and inform consumers and shall encourage and support their initiatives to protect themselves.

Turkish Citizens Living Abroad

Article 64: (1) The state shall take the necessary measures to ensure family unity, the education of children, the cultural needs, and the social security of Turkish citizens living abroad, and to safeguard their ties with the home country.

Arbitration in Sports

Article 65: (1) The decisions of sport federations relating to administration and discipline of sportive activities may be challenged only through compulsory arbitration. The decisions of the Board of Arbitration are final and cannot be appealed to by any domestic judicial authority.

Note: This clause may be added to the chapter on the judiciary.

Protection of Agriculture, Livestock Breeding, and Persons Engaged in These Activities

Article 66: (1) The state supports farmers and livestock breeders particularly in order to prevent improper use and destruction of agricultural land, meadows, and pastures and to increase crop and livestock production in accordance with the principles of agricultural planning and protection of diversity of local species and to promote the methods of organic agriculture and livestock breeding. The state facilitates the acquisition of machinery, equipment, and other inputs for farmers and livestock breeders.

Note: It was agreed to negotiate in the upper commission whether Articles 64, 65, and 66, except for the one concerning arbitration in sports, should be added to the Constitution.

LEGISLATIVE POWER

Activities Incompatible with Deputyship

Article 69: (1) Members of the Turkish Grand National Assembly shall not hold office in state departments and other public corporate bodies and their subsidiaries; in the enterprises and corporations where the state or other public corporate bodies take part directly or indirectly; in executive and supervisory boards of public benefit associations whose private resources of revenues and privileges are provided by law; of foundations receiving subsidies from the state and enjoying tax exemption; and of professional organizations having the quality/nature of public institutions and trade unions and their higher bodies, as well as enterprises and corporations in which they hold shares. Nor shall they be representatives, accept any contracted engagement of the boards stated above directly or indirectly, or serve as a representative, meditator, and arbitrator therein.

(2) Deputies shall not be entrusted with any official or private duties involving proposal, recommendation, appointment, or approval by the executive organ. A deputy's acceptance of a temporary assignment, not exceeding a period of six months, given by the Council of Ministers on

a specific matter, is subject to the decision of the Turkish Grand National Assembly.

(3) Deputies cannot use their status and power arising from their deputyship capacities to derive personal interest and benefit, and cannot directly or indirectly conduct paid work with third parties.

(4) Other duties and activities incompatible with deputyship shall be regulated by law.

(5) A Political Ethics Commission shall be established with the participation of two, either most senior or oldest, members from each political party who are to be notified by the political party groups to determine the principles of political ethics that members of the Turkish Grand National Assembly shall comply with, and to examine appeals concerning the violation of ethical rules. Its duties and powers shall be prescribed by law and the Rules of Procedure of the Assembly. The commission shall carry out its duties in accordance with the principle of consensus and publicity. In case of failure to reach agreement, this shall be reported. When deemed necessary, the commission may issue a confidentiality order.

Reasoning: Seniority shall be evaluated with regard to parliamentary service. All reports and decisions of the commission shall be made public.

Loss of Deputyship

Article 70: (1) The loss of membership of a deputy who has resigned shall be decided upon by the Plenary of the Turkish Grand National Assembly after the Bureau of the Assembly attests to the validity of the resignation.

(2) The loss of membership, through a final judicial sentence that concerns a crime that impedes eligibility for deputyship, or deprivation of legal capacity, shall take effect after the Plenary has been notified of the final court decision on the matter.

(3) The loss of membership of a deputy who insists on holding a position, or carrying out a service incompatible with membership, shall be decided by the Plenary through secret ballot, and with the absolute majority of the total number of members, upon the submission of a report drawn up by the commission in charge of setting out the factual situation.

(4) The loss of membership of a deputy who does not participate in sessions in total five times in the period of one month without an excuse or permission shall be decided by the Plenary through secret ballot, and with the absolute majority of the total number of members, upon the detection of the situation by the Bureau of the Assembly.

Application for Annulment
Article 71: (1) If the parliamentary immunity of a deputy has been lifted, or if the loss of membership has been decided according to the first, third, or fourth paragraphs of the article above, the deputy in question or another deputy may, within seven days from the date of the decision of the Plenary, appeal to the Constitutional Court for the decision to be annulled on the grounds that it is contrary to the Constitution, law, or the Rules of Procedure. The Constitutional Court shall make the final decision on the appeal within fifteen days.

Bureau of the Assembly
Article 72: (1) The Bureau of the Assembly of the Turkish Grand National Assembly shall be composed of the speaker, vice speakers, clerks, and administrative managers elected from among the deputies. The principle of equal representation of genders shall be considered while the Bureau of the Assembly is established.

(2) The Bureau of the Assembly shall be so composed as to ensure proportionate representation of the number of members of each political party group in the Assembly. Political party groups cannot nominate candidates for the Office of the Speaker.

(3) In one legislative term, two elections to the Bureau of the Turkish Grand National Assembly shall be held.

(4) The candidates for the Office of the Speaker of the Turkish Grand National Assembly from among the members of the Assembly shall be announced within five days of the convening of the Assembly to the Bureau of the Assembly. Election of the speaker shall be held by secret ballot. In the first two ballots, a two-thirds majority of the total number of members, and in the third ballot the absolute majority of the total number of members, is required. If the absolute majority cannot be obtained in the third ballot, a fourth ballot shall be held between the two candidates who have received the majority of votes in the third ballot; the member who receives most votes in the fourth ballot shall be elected as speaker. The election of the speaker shall be completed within five days after the expiry of the period for the nomination of candidates.

(5) Impartiality of the speaker and the members of the Bureau of the Assembly who preside over the sessions is fundamental.

(6) Other issues that are not regulated under this article shall be prescribed by the Rules of Procedure.

Publicity and Publication of Debates

Article 77: (1) Debates held in the Plenary of the Turkish Grand National Assembly shall be public and shall be published verbatim in the Journal of Minutes.

(2) The Turkish Grand National Assembly may hold closed sessions with the absolute majority of the total number of members. The publication of debates of such sessions shall be subject to the decision of the Turkish Grand National Assembly.

(3) The live publication/broadcasting of open sessions in the Assembly by all means is fundamental. One of the channels of the Turkish Radio and Television Association shall be devoted to this purpose.

ADMINISTRATION AND PUBLIC SERVICES

The Higher Education Coordination Council

Article 106: (1) The Higher Education Coordination Council plans and expresses opinions on the needs of the country with regard to higher education; ensures coordination between higher education institutions; promotes cooperation between higher education institutions and the different groups in society and takes measures to increase its quality; determines the criteria regarding the establishment of universities, faculties, institutions of higher education, and institutes as well as opening and closing program by consulting the universities, and makes decisions in light of the reports of the competent institution to assess higher education; recognizes the equivalence of diplomas and academic titles received from foreign higher education institutions; expresses opinions regarding the establishment of new universities and regulations concerning higher education; determines the fundamental criteria for academic positions and the student quota of higher education institutions; and assesses the activities of higher education institutions and takes necessary measures on the basis of the principles of academic and scientific freedom, academic and institutional autonomy, transparency, accountability, and participation.

(2) The council plans, regulates, and supervises the activities and duties of higher education institutions.

(3) The council shall be composed of fifteen members. Nine members of the council shall be elected from among academic staff working in higher education institutions and holding the title professor. Every academic member shall have one vote in these elections. Six members of the council shall be elected by the Turkish Grand National Assembly with three-fifths of the total number of members.

(4) The organization, duties, powers, and working principles of the council, and other issues regarding the election of its members, shall be regulated by law.

Note: The election procedure of the members shall be reviewed. In case a general regulation is established with regard to the elections that the Turkish Grand National Assembly conducts for assignments, this same regulation shall also apply to this subject.

MHP proposes voting by lot in elections to the council, which is referred to also in the note regarding the article on universities.

Reasoning: It will be pointed out that the expression of "different groups in society" refers to civil society.

JUDICIARY

Impartiality and Independence of the Courts

Article 112: (1) Judges shall be independent and impartial in the discharge of their duties; they shall give judgment in accordance with the Constitution, laws, and their personal conviction conforming with the law. Judges shall comply with the ethical rules of the profession.

(2) No organ, authority, office, or individual may give orders or instructions to courts or judges relating to the exercise of judicial power, send them circulars, or make recommendations or suggestions. Recourse to legislative auditing remedies regarding the issues exclusively concerning the execution of judicial power, for the purpose of effecting a case under trial, shall not be allowed.

(3) State organs shall comply with court decisions. These organs shall neither alter the court decisions nor delay their execution.

(4) The establishment, duties and powers, functions, and judiciary procedures of the courts shall be regulated by law.

Note: BDP is of the opinion that the first sentence of the second paragraph is sufficient and hence finds it unnecessary to add the last sentence.

Reasoning: 1) The notion law shall include the general principles of international law.

2) The term "impartial" used in the first paragraph implies objective as well as subjective impartiality. The subjective impartiality shall be elaborated in the reasoning.

Judges and the Security of Tenure of Judges

Article 114: (1) Judges shall not be dismissed unless they request, shall not be retired before the age of sixty-seven, nor shall they be deprived of their salaries, allowances, or other rights relating to their status, even as a result of the abolition of a court, or a position. Exceptions indicated by law in relation to those convicted for an offense requiring dismissal from the profession, and those who are definitely established as unable to perform their duties because of ill-health are reserved.

(2) Judges and public prosecutors shall not assume any official or private occupation other than those prescribed by law.

(3) The qualifications, admission requirements, appointment and personal rights of judges, the temporary or permanent change in their posts or place of duty, the initiation of disciplinary proceedings against them and the imposition of disciplinary penalties, the conduct of investigation concerning them, and the subsequent decision to prosecute them on account of offenses committed in connection with, or in the course of, their duties, the conviction for offenses requiring their dismissal from the profession, their in-service training, and other matters relating to their personnel status shall be regulated by law in accordance with the principles of the independence of the courts and the security of tenure of judges.

(4) Judges function as civil and administrative judges.

Public Prosecutors and Security of Tenure of Prosecutors

Article 115: (1) The security of tenure of judges shall apply to the public prosecutors in their judiciary duties.

(2) Public prosecutors shall be attached to the Ministry of Justice with respect to their administrative functions.

Review Note: The commission shall negotiate later:

a) the framework of the functions outside the scope of the public prosecutors' judicial activities; and
b) the necessity of taking comparative law into account when introducing the institution of public prosecution (Spanish example).

Judicial Law Enforcement (Shall be reviewed.)

Article 116: (1) Judicial law enforcement shall be established in the provinces and districts to serve as a deputy of the public prosecutors in order to ensure that judicial authorities carry out their duties of investigation and prosecution consistent with the principle of judicial independence, and that they reach the accused persons and evidence in a timely and reliable manner. The establishment and the operation of the judicial law enforcement and their relationship with administrative law enforcement shall be regulated by law.

Supervision of the Judicial Services

Article 119: (1) The supervision of the judicial services shall be carried out by the Ministry of Justice. The principles and procedures with regard to this task shall be regulated by law.

Court of Jurisdictional Disputes

Article 120: (1) The Court of Jurisdictional Disputes shall be empowered to deliver the final judgments in disputes between administrative and judicial courts concerning their jurisdiction and judgments.

(2) The organization of the Court of Jurisdictional Disputes, the qualifications and electoral procedure of its members, and its functioning shall be regulated by law. The court shall elect one of its members as president for two years with the absolute majority of the total number of its members.

Term of Office of the Members and Termination of Membership

Article 121: (1) The members of the Constitutional Court shall be elected for one term only and for a term of nine years. The members shall retire when they are over the age of sixty-seven.

(2) Membership in the Constitutional Court shall terminate automatically in case a member is convicted of an offense requiring his or her dismissal from the judicial profession, and by a decision with two-thirds of the total number of members of the Constitutional Court if it is definitely established that he or she is unable to perform his or her duties on account of ill-health.

Decisions of the Constitutional Court

Article 126: (1) The decisions of the Constitutional Court are final. These decisions shall not be made public without a written justification by any means. The decisions of the court shall promptly be published in the Official Gazette.

(2) The Constitutional Court may decide, with the majority of three-fifths of the total number of its members, to suspend the execution of a provision under an annulment action, if its implementation would result in damages which are difficult or impossible to compensate for and if there is strong conviction that the provision is in violation of the Constitution.

(3) Provisions that are annulled by the Constitutional Court shall cease to have effect from the date of publication of the justified annulment decision in the Official Gazette. Where necessary, the Constitutional Court may also decide on the date on which the annulment decision shall come into effect. That duration shall not be more than one year from the date of publication of the decision in the Official Gazette.

(4) The Constitutional Court cannot act as the legislator and shall not establish a new application with its decisions.

(5) Annulment decisions cannot be applied retroactively.

(6) In the event of postponement of the date on which an annulment decision is to come into effect, the Turkish Grand National Assembly shall debate and decide with priority on the government bill or private members' bill, designed to fill the legal void arising from the annulment decision.

(7) Decisions of the Constitutional Court shall be binding on the legislative, executive, and judicial organs, on the administrative authorities, and on persons and corporate bodies.

Constitutional Complaint

Article 127: (1) Everyone may file a constitutional complaint to the Constitutional Court on grounds that his or her individual and political rights and social rights and freedoms, not imposing positive obligations on the state that are regulated under the Constitution, were violated by public authorities. In order to appeal, there has to be a violation of an actual and individual right and ordinary legal remedies should have been exhausted. Constitutional complaint shall be made within thirty days after the exhaustion of ordinary legal remedies. The issues that are considered as part of legal remedies shall not be reviewed in the constitutional complaint. The ombudsperson's application of a constitutional complaint, and other principles and procedures regarding the constitutional complaint, shall be regulated by law.

(2) Applications of constitutional complaints regarding the right to vote and to be elected shall be made within three days. These applications shall be finalized so as to prevent loss of the right and promptly as required by election law.

PREAMBLE, GENERAL PROVISIONS, AND FUNDAMENTAL PRINCIPLES

Form of the State

Article 152: (1) The state of Turkey is a Republic.

Supremacy and Binding Force of the Constitution

Article 161: (1) The provisions of the Constitution are binding upon legislative, executive, and judicial organs, administrative authorities and other institutions, and individuals.

(2) Laws shall not be contrary to the Constitution.

APPENDIX C

Non-Agreed Articles of the Constitutional Conciliation Commission[1]

FUNDAMENTAL RIGHTS AND FREEDOMS

A) *Fundamental Principles*

Equality

Article 3: (1) Everyone is equal before the law.

(2) No privileges shall be granted to any individual, family, group, or class.

(3) No one can be subjected to discrimination on grounds such as language, race, color, sex, political opinion, philosophical belief, religion, sect, or ethnic origin. *(The inclusion of the notion of "ethnic origin" in the article was considered unnecessary by* MHP.*)*

(4) Men and women have equal rights. Measures taken for this purpose cannot be interpreted as contrary to the principle of equality. The state is under the obligation to ensure the realization of this equality in practice and prevent any sorts of violence and ill-treatment against women.

(5) The state shall take all measures to eliminate the obstacles and all sorts of discrimination that hinders the utilization and exercise of civil, social, economic and cultural rights and freedoms of women.

(6) Special measures, including the application of quota, shall be taken in order to ensure the equal participation of women in the Turkish Grand National Assembly [abbreviated hereinafter as TBMM, TN], central and provincial organizations of the political parties, executive organs of the universities and the unions and higher organizations, duties, and positions that are determined by election such as provincial assemblies, municipal assemblies, and metropolitan municipal assemblies as well as the administrative and judicial organs and other professions.

(7) Measures taken for children, the elderly, persons with disabilities, widows and orphans of war, and duty martyrs and veterans shall not be considered as contrary to the principle of equality. The state shall take

[1] Translated by Hilal Sarbak, hereinafter TN.

special measures for these groups in order to provide equal opportunities.

(8) State organs and public officers shall ensure in their acts and procedures that everyone benefits from the fundamental rights and freedoms and public services in accordance with the principal of equality before the law and shall prevent social exclusion.

Reasoning: The state organs shall act together with relevant nongovernmental organizations and especially with women's organizations in order to realize the equality of men and women in all areas.

Note: (BDP) If the writing commission accepts the article on equality as a whole, the reservations and annotations which are attached to the other articles relating to the equality of men and women will be removed.

Note: The prohibition of discrimination on the grounds of sexual orientation and gender identity will be referred in the commentary.

B) Rights and Freedoms of the Individual

Rights of the Child

Article 6: (1) Every child has the right to benefit from the guardianship and the care that is required for his or her own well-being; to develop his or her moral and material values; *(Proposal of BDP: to benefit from its own culture and use its own language)*; to freely express his or her opinions; to be protected from sexual exploitation, violence, and all sorts of ill-treatment and abuse; to maintain his or her life within a family; to have an individual and direct relationship with his or her parents unless it is manifestly against the child's interests; to know his or her parents; to benefit from appropriate care in case the child is separated from his or her family; to benefit from adequate housing and shelter, basic health, and social services. The state shall take all measures regarding the exercise of all the rights laid down in this paragraph.

(2) The best interest of the child shall be considered in all circumstances concerning the child.

(3) The participation of the child shall be ensured regarding all decisions concerning the child.

(4) In principle, the child shall be tried without detention. In cases of detention and conviction, the child shall be detained in the institutions where he or she is separated from adults and that is convenient for his or her age.

Freedom of Residence and Movement

Article 14: (1) Everyone has the freedom of residence and movement.

(2) Freedom of residence may be restricted for the purposes of achieving a healthy and orderly urbanization and protection of the environment and cultural heritage while freedom of movement may be restricted for the purposes of protection of the public health, *(Proposal of CHP and BDP: where there is strong criminal suspicion)* prevention of crimes, and investigation and prosecution of an offense.

(3) No citizen shall be deported and deprived of the right of entry into his or her own country.

(4) The citizen's freedom to leave the country may only be restricted by the decision of a judge based on a criminal investigation or prosecution.

Freedom of Religion, Conscience, and Belief

Article 15: (1) Everyone has the freedom of religion, conscience, and belief; this freedom includes the freedom to believe or not believe and to change his or her belief.

(2) This freedom shall include the right, either individually or in community with others and in public or private, to worship, to enjoy, manifest, and disseminate his or her religion or belief by means of *(Proposal of AKP and BDP: education)* teaching *(CHP considers it more convenient to refer to "teaching" in the fifth paragraph)*, religious practice, rites, and ceremonies.

Note: MHP thinks that the notions of "teaching" and "practice" comprise the notion of education. Moreover, there is a separate article concerning education in the Constitution.

Note: CHP, on the other hand, thinks that the notion of "teaching" does not involve the notion of "education"; "teaching" includes the religious education given to a child by his or her family and not education provided by public institutions.

(3) No one shall be compelled to worship, to participate in religious rites and ceremonies, to reveal religious beliefs and convictions, or be prevented from doing so. No one shall be reprimanded, accused, or treated in a different manner *(Proposal of CHP: discriminated)* because of practicing or not practicing his or her religious beliefs and convictions.

(4) The state shall be impartial to all religions and beliefs in its acts and procedures; it shall respect the pluralist society based on the diversity of religion, conscience, and belief.

(5) The state shall respect the parents' right to educate and instruct their children in accordance with their own religious and philosophical beliefs while it carries out its duties with regard to education and instruction. Religious education and instruction shall be subject to the individual's

own desire and, in the case of minors, to the request of their legal representatives.

(6) *(Proposal of CHP and MHP: Religious and moral education and instruction shall be conducted under state supervision and control.) (Proposal of AKP and MHP: Education and instruction in religious culture and morals shall be one of the compulsory lessons in the curricula of primary and secondary schools.) (Proposal of CHP: Education and instruction in religious culture and morals shall be taught in a manner appropriate to the age of the children. Elective education and instruction of religious culture and morals shall be pluralist, objective, and critical.)*

Note: CHP and MHP are of the opinion that the provisions concerning education within this article shall be placed under the article regarding the "right of education and instruction."

(7) Worship and religious ceremonies may be restricted only for the purposes of the protection of public order *(Proposal of BDP: the term "public order" should not be included in the text)* and for the protection of the rights and freedoms of others.

(8) *(Proposal of CHP: The freedom of religion, conscience, belief, and worship shall not be exploited for the purpose of even partially basing the fundamental, social, economic, political, and legal order of the state on religious tenets or for the purposes of personal or political interest or influence. No one shall be allowed to exploit or abuse religion or religious feelings, or things held sacred by religion. The sanctions to be applied concerning this paragraph shall be prescribed by law.)*

(9) *(Proposal of CHP and BDP: The state shall provide a fair distribution of public resources in order to ensure religious services.) (Proposal of BDP: and affirmative action shall be applied in favor of different disadvantaged religious groups.)*

Freedom of Thought and Expression

Article 16: (1) Everyone has freedom of thought, opinion, and expression.

(2) No one shall be compelled to reveal his or her thoughts and opinions for any reason or purpose; nor shall anyone be reprimanded or accused because of his or her thoughts and opinions.

(3) Everyone has the right to express and disseminate his or her thoughts and opinions by speech, in writing, in pictures, or through other media, individually or collectively. This freedom includes the liberty of receiving or imparting information or ideas without interference by official authorities.

(4) The exercise of these freedoms may be restricted for the purposes of national security *(BDP objects to this term)*, the protection of the rights and

freedoms of others and preventing the praise and promotion of violence and hatred between the individuals and for maintaining the independency and impartiality of the judiciary.

(5) State secrets cannot be defined in ways that are not consistent with the requirements and purposes of service. Under the circumstances contravening these principles, neither the freedom of thought and opinion nor the right to access information and data shall be restricted on grounds of state secret.

Note: BDP reserves its right to decide to add the term "in a language which he or she prefers" to the third paragraph of this article, depending on the codification of language rights in the Constitution.

Right and Freedom of Education and Instruction

Article 17: (1) Everyone has the right and freedom of education and instruction. No one shall be deprived of the right of education and instruction.

(2) *(Proposal of CHP: The state shall take necessary measures to ensure the equal, effective, and uninterrupted enjoyment of the right of freedom of education and instruction for all.)*

(3) *(Proposal of CHP: Education and instruction shall be conducted under the supervision and control of the state, guided by pluralist and libertarian democratic values, equality of men and women, the principle of secularism, and based on contemporary scientific and educational principles. Educational institutions contravening these principles shall not be established.)*

(Proposal of BDP: Education and instruction shall be based on free thought, directed to the complete development of human dignity and of strengthening the respect for human rights, ensure effective participation of all to a free society, and aim at developing understanding, tolerance, and fraternity for all different groups. The supervision and control of the state over education and instruction shall be made in accordance with these principles.)

(4) Primary education is compulsory for all citizens and is free of charge in state schools. The state shall provide assistance and take appropriate measures for the students lacking financial means to continue their education and for those in need of special education.

(5) *(Proposal of CHP: Education shall not be conducted in a language other than Turkish in educational institutions. Everyone has the right to learn their mother tongue and engage in cultural activities in their mother tongue. In schools where there is a concentration of students whose mother tongue is not Turkish, the procedures and principles providing mother tongue education upon request shall be prescribed by law. Foreign languages to be taught in institutions*

of education and the rules to be followed by schools conducting education in a foreign language shall be determined by law. The provisions of international treaties are reserved.)

(Proposal of MHP: The language of education and instruction is Turkish. Foreign languages to be taught in institutions of education and lessons to be taught in foreign languages shall be determined by law. The provisions of international treaties are reserved.)

(Proposal of BDP: It is one of the primary duties of the state to provide qualified education and instruction to everyone in their own mother tongue.)

(6) *(Proposal of BDP: Principles regarding private schools shall be determined by law in accordance with the third paragraph of this article.)*

Note for the First Paragraph: In case there is a consensus on the first paragraph regarding the relationship between rights and freedoms, the paragraph will not be written in red.

Freedom of the Press

Article 19: (1) The press is free and one of the indispensable elements of democracy and shall not be censored in any manner.

(2) Periodical or nonperiodical broadcasting and establishment of a printing house for this purpose shall not be subject to limitations that restrain the freedom of the press such as prior permission or the deposit of a financial guarantee.

(3) The state shall take necessary measures to ensure the enjoyment of the freedom of the press and information, the free formation of public opinion, and provide pluralism in the media.

(4) The establishment and operation of radio and television stations and news agencies are free. Radio, television, cinema, and broadcasting institutions conducted by information technologies may be subject to prior permission. Broadcasting in languages other than Turkish shall be prescribed by law.

Note: MHP will review the last sentence of this paragraph.

(5) The freedom of the press may be restricted for the purposes of national security *(BDP: the term "national security" is unnecessary) (Proposal of AKP and MHP: public morals)*, the protection of the rights and freedoms of others, and the prevention of praise and promotion of violence and hatred between individuals.

(6) No ban shall be placed on the reporting of events to ensure the proper functioning of the judiciary, except by the decision of a judge issued within the limits specified by law.

(7) Media institutions shall not report in a manner that would impair the independency of the judiciary and the principle of presumption of innocence. Related procedures and principles shall be determined by law.

(8) Periodical and nonperiodical publications may be seized only by a decision of a judge in cases where there are reasons laid down under the fifth paragraph specified by law or in cases of crimes regarding the prevention of abuse of children specified by law. They may be seized by the decision of the public prosecutor in situations where delay may constitute prejudice. This decision shall be submitted to the judge having jurisdiction within twenty-four hours at the latest. The order to seize shall become null and void unless upheld by the judge within forty-eight hours at the latest.

(9) Distribution of publications may be prevented only by a decision of a judge, or by decision of the public prosecutor, in situations where delay may constitute prejudice. This decision shall be submitted to the judge having jurisdiction within twenty-four hours at the latest. The order to seize shall become null and void unless upheld by the judge within forty-eight hours at the latest.

(10) Confiscation of periodical and nonperiodical publications shall be forbidden unless the publications are in violation of private life or constitute criminal evidence.

(11) A printing house and its annexes, duly established as a press enterprise under law, and press equipment shall not be seized, confiscated, or barred from operation on the grounds of having been used in a crime.

(12) Individuals and political parties have the right to benefit from mass media channels other than the press in order to guarantee society's rights in conformity with the principles of equity and justice to receive information and to freely form public opinion.

(Proposal of AKP: Individuals and the political parties have the right to benefit from the mass media other than the press owned by the public corporate bodies in conformity with the principles of equity and justice. Related procedures and principles shall be determined by law.)

(13) The principles regarding the profession of journalism shall be regulated by law on the basis of free enjoyment of union rights and freedoms, effective achievement of the freedom of press, and free formation of public opinion.

Reasoning on the Third Paragraph: "Pluralism" referred to in the article is an inclusive term that subsumes the idea of prevention of monopoly in the press.

Reasoning on the Sixth Paragraph: Legal values which are intended to be protected by this article shall be overtly expressed in the reasoning.

(Presumption of innocence, public's right of receiving information, and the problem of effecting the judiciary through media and press.)

Freedom of Association

Article 23: (1) Everyone has the right to form associations, or become a member of an association, or withdraw from membership without prior permission. No one shall be compelled to become or remain a member of an association.

(2) Freedom of association may be restricted for the purposes of public order *(BDP objects to the notion "public order")* and the protection of the rights and freedoms of others.

(3) Associations may be dissolved or suspended from activity by the decision of a judge in cases prescribed by law. However, where it is required for, and a delay constitutes a prejudice to, national security, public order, prevention of commission or continuation of a crime, or an arrest, the public prosecutor may suspend the association from activity. The decision of this authority shall be submitted for the approval of the judge having jurisdiction within twenty-four hours. The judge shall announce his or her decision within forty-eight hours; otherwise, this decision shall be annulled automatically. *(BDP objects to the second and the third sentence of this paragraph as a whole.)*

(4) The internal order, operations, and activities of the associations shall be in accordance with the principles of democracy.

(5) Nongovernmental organizations are one of the essential elements of a democratic societal life.

(6) Provisions of the first paragraph shall not prevent imposition of restrictions on the rights of the Turkish Armed Forces and security forces officials and judges and the public prosecutors to the extent that their duties so require. *(Proposal of BDP: This paragraph is objected to as a whole.)*

Note: Being involved in an association is prohibited for members of the Turkish Armed Forces and security forces, whereas restrictions might be imposed for judges and public prosecutors only to the extent that their duties so require.

(7) The provisions of this article shall also apply to foundations, to the extent that it conforms to their legal characteristics.

Reasoning: 1) Situations that violate the liberal/free basic democratic order (and associations that promote or provoke racist, ethnic, or religious hatred or violence, rancor, or hostility in their activities) shall be considered while an association is dissolved.

2) Judges and public prosecutors benefit from the freedom of association in order to protect and improve their professional and social rights and freedoms. The law shall not impose restrictions that hinder the exercise of this freedom.

3) The legal characteristics of foundations, which rely on being a group/ community of goods that are allocated to realize a purpose, will be taken into consideration.

Note: The third paragraph of this article will be reviewed.

Freedom to Claim Rights and Right to a Fair Trial

Article 25: (1) Everyone has the right to claim rights, access to justice, and right to appear before the judicial organs either as plaintiff or defendant by utilizing legitimate tools and means. Regulations regarding the legal remedies and alternative dispute resolutions shall not be considered contradictory to the right of access to justice.

(2) Everyone has the right to a fair trial within a reasonable time by an independent and impartial tribunal having jurisdiction. Financial and administrative requirements that defuse or hinder access to justice cannot be stipulated.

(3) The trials shall be conducted publicly. However, the trials may be conducted wholly or partially closed, where it is required for the purposes of national security, protection of public morals, and where the interests of juveniles or the protection of the private life, rights, and freedoms of the parties so require.

(4) Everyone charged with a criminal offense has the right to be informed promptly *(Proposal of AKP and CHP: in a language which he or she understands) (Proposal of BDP: in a language which he or she prefers)* and in detail of the nature and causes of the accusation against him or her; to have adequate time and facilities for the preparation of his or her defense, including access to all documents regarding the accusation; to be present in the trial; to defend himself or herself in person or through legal assistance; to show witnesses and to examine witnesses; and to have the free assistance of an interpreter if he or she cannot understand or speak the language used in court. *(MHP objects to the addition of the terms "in a language which she or he understands" or "in a language which he or she prefers" in the Constitution. As "having the right to free assistance of an interpreter if he or she cannot understand or speak the language used in court" is regulated within Criminal Procedure Code, MHP is of the opinion that it is unnecessary to refer to that under this article.)*

(5) The principle of equality of arms shall apply both for the prosecution and the defense in all phases of a trial.

(6) No one shall appear before an institution other than his or her own natural judge. Extraordinary institutions that would result in someone having to appear before an institution other than his or her own natural judge cannot be established.

(7) No court can refuse to proceed on a case that is within its jurisdiction.

(8) Illegally obtained materials cannot be used as evidence. Information and data concerning the private and family life of individuals that are irrelevant for the crime alleged and the ongoing case cannot be used in any judicial procedure.

(9) The decisions of all courts shall be written with a justification.

(10) Trials of children are subject to special provisions determined by law.

Reasoning: What is to be understood from the notions of qualified and effective judiciary will be explained in detail.

Reasoning: The provision regarding "introducing relevant application mechanisms" will be discussed later on (Current Article 129(5)).

National security – espionage [incomplete in the original, TN].

C) Political Rights and Freedoms

Citizenship (AKP and BDP) / Turkish Citizenship (MHP) / Citizenship – Turkish Citizenship (CHP)

Article 29: *(AKP)* (1) *Everyone who is bound to the state with the bond of nationality is a citizen of the Republic of Turkey.*

(2) *A child born to a mother or a father who is the citizen of the Republic of Turkey shall acquire the citizenship by birth.*

(3) *Citizenship shall be acquired in accordance with the conditions prescribed by law and shall be lost only under the circumstances specified by law.*

(4) *No one shall be deprived of citizenship.*

(CHP) (1) *"Turkish citizenship" means that everyone, regardless of language, religion, race, sex, ethnic origin, political opinion, or philosophical belief or sect, is citizen of the Republic of Turkey on the basis of "equality."*

(2) *The principles and the procedures regarding the acquisition and loss of citizenship shall be prescribed by law. No one shall be deprived of citizenship unless there are justifiable reasons absolutely necessitated by the acts incompatible with the loyalty to the motherland.*

(MHP) (1) *Everyone who is bound to the Turkish state with the bond of nationality is Turkish.*

(2) *A child born to a Turkish citizen mother or a Turkish citizen father shall be a Turkish citizen.*

(3) *Citizenship shall be acquired in accordance with the conditions prescribed by law and shall be lost only under the circumstances specified by law.*

(4) *No Turkish person could be deprived of citizenship unless he or she acts in a way that is incompatible with loyalty to the state.*

(5) *Legal remedies cannot be blocked against the decisions and the procedures regarding the loss of citizenship.*

Note: *The subject of the acquisition and loss of citizenship might be reviewed in the upper commission.*

(BDP) (1) *Differences with regard to language, religion, race, ethnic origin, culture or sex, sexual orientation, and the like cannot be taken into consideration for the acquisition, exercise, and loss of the citizenship of Turkey. The principles regarding the citizenship shall be prescribed by law.*

(2) *No one shall be deprived of citizenship against their own will.*

Right to Vote, to Be Elected, and to Engage in Political Activity

Article 30: (1) In conformity with the conditions set forth in law, citizens have the right to vote, to be elected, to engage in political activities independently or in a political party, and to take part in a referendum. Principles that allow Turkish citizens resident in foreign countries to enjoy their right to vote shall be regulated by law.

(2) Elections and referenda shall be held under the direction and supervision of the judiciary, in accordance with the principles of free, equal, secret, direct, general vote, and public counting of the votes.

(3) All citizens *(Proposal of MHP: Turkish citizens)* over eighteen years of age shall have the right to vote in elections and to take part in referenda.

Note: The subject of foreigners' voting in local elections shall be discussed under the article concerning the rights of foreigners.

(4) Privates and corporals at arms, cadets, and convicts in penal execution institutions excluding those convicted of negligent offenses and sentenced to imprisonment less than one year and those who have been deprived of legal capacity shall not vote. *(BDP does not agree with the rest of the paragraph after the term "cadets.")*

(5) *(Proposal of CHP and BDP: Election laws shall be determined in light of the principle of stability in governance, but they shall never hinder the principle of fair representation.)*

(Proposal of AKP and MHP: Election laws shall be determined in a manner that reconciles the principles of stability in governance and fair representation.)

Note of BDP: If the issues of equal representation of men and women and abolishment of electoral thresholds in both local and general elections cannot be regulated in the relevant articles in election laws, BDP will revert to its original proposal: "Election laws shall consider the principle of fair representation, there shall be no local or general electoral thresholds;

specials measures shall be taken in order to ensure fair representation and participation between genders."

(6) Amendments to election laws shall not apply to the elections to be held within one year from the date of the entry into force of amendments.

(7) The Supreme Electoral Council shall execute all the functions to ensure the fair and orderly conduct of elections from the beginning to the end; carry out investigations and make final decisions, during and after the elections, on all irregularities, complaints, and objections concerning the electoral matters; and receive the electoral records of the members of the Turkish Grand National Assembly and presidential elections. No appeal shall be made to any other authority against the decisions of the Supreme Electoral Council.

Note: Changing the statement of "no appeal shall be made to any other authority against the decisions of the Supreme Electoral Council" into "the decisions of the Supreme Electoral Council are final" was proposed. This paragraph will be discussed again in the article regarding the Supreme Electoral Council.

Freedom of Political Parties

Article 31: (1) Political parties are indispensable elements of democratic political life.

(2) *(Proposal of MHP: Turkish)* Citizens holding the right to vote have the right to form political parties and join and withdraw from them without prior permission.

(3) Judges and prosecutors and those considered in this profession, members of the armed forces and security forces, the president and the members of the Court of Accounts, public servants, except for heads of local public administrations, and students in higher education may join political parties.

(4) The state shall provide political parties that had at least one percent of the total valid votes in the last general elections financial assistance in an equitable manner. The principles regarding aid to political parties and incomes and expenses of the parties are regulated by law in accordance with the principle of transparency.

(5) Principles, procedures, and sanctions regarding the incomes and expenditures of parties and candidates and the limits to the donations that they may accept shall be regulated by law in accordance with the principle of transparency.

(6) *(Proposal of AKP: Principles with which political parties shall comply shall not be regulated in a separate paragraph. Reasons for dissolution of*

political parties would imply in a reverse order which principles political parties must follow.)

(Proposal of CHP: Statutes, program, and actions of political parties cannot be in contradiction with principles of pluralist democracy based on human rights, the rule of law, the secular republic, and the integrity of the state and cannot support or promote violence, racism, and incitement to crime.)

(Proposal of MHP: Statutes, program, and actions of political parties cannot be in contradiction with the independence and inseparability of the state with its territory and nation, human rights, the principle of rule of law, and characteristics of a secular republic and cannot promote terror, violence, and hatred.)

(Proposal of BDP: Political parties cannot aim at destruction of the democratic constitutional order based on human rights and the rule of law and cannot advocate warmongering, xenophobia, discrimination, and hatred.)

(7) Internal regulations of political parties cannot be in contradiction with democratic principles. Political parties shall take necessary measures to ensure gender equality in representation. *(Proposal of CHP and BDP: Decision-making bodies of political party organizations shall be established in a manner ensuring fair representation and participation between genders.)* *(Proposal of BDP: Gender quota shall not be less than 40 percent.)*

(8) Political parties cannot conduct commercial activities.

(9) Investigation of incomes and expenditures of political parties shall be conducted in accordance with the special regulations prescribed by law. *(Proposal of AKP and BDP: by the Court of Accounts.)* *(Proposal of CHP and MHP: by the Constitutional Court.)*

(10) Political parties may be dissolved only if they engage in or promote violence. In order to render a decision regarding the dissolution, the political party shall become the center of such actions. The principles regarding becoming the center of such actions shall be prescribed by law in accordance with the requirements of a democratic society. The dissolution of political parties shall be decided by the Constitutional Court with a two-thirds majority of the total number of members on the basis of a case brought to the court with the demand of the Chief Public Prosecutor of the High Court of Appeals, and with permission of three-fifths of the total number of members of the Turkish Grand National Assembly. According to the intensity of the actions brought before the court, the Constitutional Court may decide to issue an administrative fine instead of dissolution.

(11) In cases of violations of the Constitution other than engaging in or promoting violence, the chief public prosecutor shall request from the

Constitutional Court that it issue a warning against political parties. The Constitutional Court shall issue an administrative fine if the political party does not act in compliance with the warning decision. The chief public prosecutor may directly file a lawsuit before the Constitutional Court against a political party that was sentenced to administrative fines twice in the previous three years.

(BDP does not agree with the tenth and eleventh paragraph.)

(Proposal of BDP: When a political party's statute is determined to be in violation of the fourth paragraph or if it is established that the political party consciously, determinedly, and consistently acts in violation of this paragraph, the Constitutional Court shall issue a warning against the party upon the request of the Chief Public Prosecutor of the High Court of Appeals. The Chief Public Prosecutor of the High Court of Appeals shall request a lawsuit to be filed against the political party from the Turkish Grand National Assembly, if the contradictions in the party's statute and program are not eliminated or the actions of the political party that are deemed in violation of the fourth paragraph continue. The Presidency of the Assembly shall establish a commission composed of five members from each political party group represented in the Assembly and headed by the President of the Assembly. The Chief Public Prosecutor of the High Court of Appeals shall file a lawsuit against the political party upon the decision of the commission that is voted on secretly and with a three-fifths majority of the total number of members of the commission. The final decision regarding this lawsuit shall be rendered by the Constitutional Court.)

(Proposal of BDP: In the lawsuits filed by the Chief Public Prosecutor of the High Court of Appeals, the Constitutional Court may rule to temporarily deprive the concerned party of state aid, except for electoral periods, or to temporarily suspend the concerned party's operations.)

Notes: (1) The third paragraph is to be redacted in accordance with the status of the Court of Accounts in the Constitution.

(2) It shall be regulated under the relevant article concerning the Supreme Electoral Council that the competent organ to execute the fifth paragraph is the Supreme Electoral Council.

Reasoning on the Ninth Paragraph: The aims of the political party and the margin of appreciation of the political party regarding the expenditures shall be considered during the investigation of incomes and expenditures.

Right to Enter into Public Service

Article 32: (1) Every *(Proposal of MHP: Turkish)* citizen shall have the right to enter into public service.

Note: The definition of "citizen" agreed under the relevant article shall also apply here.

(2) No distinction shall be made in recruitment to a service other than the qualifications required by the duty,; the principle of equality between genders shall be considered without prejudice to the qualifications required by the duty.

C) Social and Economic Rights

Right to Collective Agreement and Strike

Article 38: (1) Workers and employers have the right to conclude collective agreements in order to reciprocally regulate their economic and social positions and work conditions.

(2) *(Proposal of AKP: Public servants and other public employees may apply to the Public Servants Arbitration Board if disagreement arises during the process of collective agreement. The Public Servants Arbitration Board shall be established on grounds of impartiality and objectivity; the decisions of the Public Servants Arbitration Board shall be final and have the force of a collective agreement.)*

(3) The form, the scope, and the exceptions of the collective agreement; the persons that benefit from the collective agreement; the extension of the provisions of collective agreement to retired persons; and other matters concerning the principles and procedures shall be prescribed by law.

(4) In case a disagreement arises during the process of the conclusion or the application of a collective agreement *(Proposal of AKP: collective labor agreement)*, the employees *(Proposal of AKP: the workers)* have the right to strike.

(5) The right to strike may only be restricted in cases where the strike endangers the life, health, and security of society in part or as a whole due to disruption of a public service and provided that ensuring continuity of the public service is kept to minimum.

(6) In cases where the right to strike is restricted, the dispute shall be settled by the Supreme Arbitration Board upon the mutual request of the parties.

(7) The scope, the exercise, the exceptions, and the other principles and procedures regarding the right to strike shall be prescribed by law.

Note: The legal status of the Supreme Arbitration Board's decisions laid down in the sixth paragraph shall be reviewed (whether they are final or not).

ADDITIONAL PROPOSALS

(Proposal of BDP) Right to Truth

Article 45: (1) *Everyone has the right to access to the truth and the genuine information regarding the historical development of the country and to demand the disclosure of the documents and the information, including the state archives, concerning this history.*

(2) *State is under the duty to establish temporary or permanent institutions in order to ensure the right to truth.*

(3) *Statute of limitations does not apply to genocide and crimes against humanity.*

(AKP and MHP object to the addition of such an article to the Constitution.)

The Right to Marry and Found a Family

Article 46: (1) Men and women of marriageable age have the right to marry and to found a family.

(2) The family *(Proposal of AKP: is the basis of society) (Proposal of MHP: is the basis of Turkish society)* is based upon the principle of equality between the spouses.

(3) Caring, raising, and educating children is the right and duty of the parents. The state shall ensure the achievement of this right and duty. *(BDP rejects the notion of "right" in this paragraph.)*

(4) The state shall ensure the protection of children and women against domestic violence and prevent the early and forced marriage of girls. *(Proposal of CHP: and take necessary measures to provide the teaching and implementation of family planning.)*

Service to the Country

Article 54: (1) Service to the country is every *(Proposal of MHP Turkish)* citizen's right and duty. The fashions to fulfill this duty either in the Armed Forces or in other public services or situations where the service of duty may be considered to be fulfilled shall be prescribed by law.

(Article Proposal of BDP)

Article –: (1) *No one shall be forced to fulfill the duty of military service or to be recruited against their personal conviction. The conditions for the objection to the military service due to conscientious reasons and the principles concerning the alternative public services to be envisaged shall be prescribed by law.*

Duty to Pay Taxes

Article 55: (1) Everyone is under obligation to pay taxes according to his or her financial resources in order to meet public expenditure.

(2) An equitable and balanced distribution of the tax burden is the social objective of fiscal policy.

(3) Taxes, fees, duties, and other such financial obligations shall be imposed, amended, or revoked by law.

(4) The Council of Ministers *(Proposal of AKP: The President)* may be empowered to amend the percentages of exemption, exceptions, and reductions in taxes, fees, duties, and other such financial obligations within the minimum and maximum limits prescribed by law; the elected decision-making organs of local administration may be empowered for those imposed, accrued, and collected by local administrations (*Proposal of BDP: elected regional public administrations*).

(5) The Council of Ministers *(Proposal of AKP: The President)* may be empowered to impose or revoke taxes and other similar economic duties regarding imports, exports, and other foreign transactions for the purpose of the regulation of foreign trade in benefit of the national economy.

Right to Cultural Identity

Article 56: (1) Everyone has the right to develop his or her own identity and culture.

(2) The state recognizes all identities and cultures and ensures everyone's right of free expression, protection, development, and dissemination of their own culture and identity.

(3) The state promotes the development of the culture of tolerance and dialogue between all individuals and groups from different cultures and identities and takes necessary measures in the fields of education, culture, and media to ensure reciprocal respect, understanding, and cooperation.

Note of MHP: *The addition of this article is unnecessary as everyone's right to develop their own material and spiritual well-being is regulated under the Constitution.*

(Proposal of BDP) Right to Use Mother Tongue

Article 57: (1) *Everyone has the right to use their mother tongue. No one shall be deprived of the right to use their mother tongue.*

(2) *Everyone has the freedom to express and disseminate their opinions and ideas in their own mother tongue individually or collectively by using*

all legitimate tools and means. This right includes establishing, operating, and utilizing written, visual, and audial media in their mother tongue.

(3) Everyone has the right to be educated and instructed in their mother tongue provided that the official language is taught and learned. This right applies to all phases of education and instruction.

(4) Everyone has the right to receive public services in their mother tongue and use their mother tongue in their relations with the public administration.

(5) The principles relating to the exercise of this right shall be regulated by law.

LEGISLATIVE POWER

The Composition of the Turkish Grand National Assembly and Representation of the Nation

Article 64: (1) The Turkish Grand National Assembly shall be composed of five hundred fifty deputies elected by universal suffrage.

(Proposal of BDP: The Turkish Grand National Assembly is the highest organ that represents the will of all citizens.)

(2) Four hundred fifty deputies shall be elected from the electoral districts in accordance with proportional representation. *(Proposal of CHP: The electoral threshold cannot be more than five percent.) (Proposal of BDP: There should not be an electoral threshold.)* One hundred deputies, on the other hand, shall be elected *(Proposal of CHP and BDP: with a separate vote)* from the general electoral district in accordance with proportional representation. *(AKP objects to this paragraph.)*

(3) Deputies shall not only represent their own constituencies or constituents but the nation as a whole. *(Proposal of BDP: all citizens.)*

(4) (Proposal of AKP) Candidates who are in the list of deputy candidates in the electoral districts of political parties and who cannot be elected are considered as substitute deputies on the basis of their ranking. Additionally, in general elections political parties shall nominate substitute deputy candidates in proportion to one-fifth of the total number of deputies to be elected, at least one substitute deputy candidate per electoral district, in each electoral district, and independent candidates shall nominate one substitute deputy candidate. In case a seat for a deputy becomes vacant, the vacant memberships shall be initially replaced by substitute deputies who could not be elected in that electoral district. Where all members of the Assembly were elected from the same political party in an electoral district, substitute candidates shall substitute the vacant seat in turn.

If the vacant seat was from one of the independent candidates, the substitute candidate who was shown in the voting ballot of that candidate shall substitute the other. If the substitution did not happen, no rights shall arise for being a deputy.

(5) *(Proposal of BDP: The Grand National Assembly shall be formed in accordance with the principles of equal representation between the genders, pluralism, and proportionate representation.)*

Eligibility to Be a Deputy

Article 65: (1) Every citizen over the age of *(Proposal of AKP and BDP: eighteen) (Proposal of CHP: twenty-one) (Proposal of MHP: twenty-five)* is eligible to be a deputy.

(2) The following cannot become a candidate and cannot be elected as a deputy:

(a) Those who do not read and write in Turkish,
(b) Those who have been deprived of legal capacity,
(c) *(Proposal of CHP: Those who have failed to perform service for the country) (Proposal of MHP: Those who have failed to perform military service),*

(ç) Those who have been sentenced to a prison term totaling two years or more, excluding involuntary offenses; those who have been convicted for dishonorable offenses such as embezzlement, corruption, bribery, theft, fraud, forgery, breach of trust, and fraudulent bankruptcy; crimes against sexual integrity, violence against children and women, torture and crimes against humanity *(Proposal of MHP: involvement in acts of terrorism, or incitement and encouragement of such activities) (Proposal of MHP: even if they have been granted amnesty).*

(3) Candidacy cannot be subjected to resignation from public service. Public officers shall be considered on nonpaid leave if they become candidates in elections.

(4) Judges and prosecutors and those who are considered from that profession, the members of the Armed Forces and general security forces, those who work for the intelligence services, heads of local public administrations, ambassadors, and rectors shall be considered as having resigned from their duties if they become candidates.

Parliamentary Nonaccountability and Immunity

Article 67: (1) Deputies shall not be liable for their votes, statements, and opinions they express during parliamentary proceedings. Acts considered as defamation and disciplinary penalties to be ruled in accordance with the Rules of Procedure shall fall outside the scope of nonaccountability.

(1) *(Proposal of MHP: Deputies shall not be liable for their votes and statements during parliamentary proceedings, for the views they express before the Assembly, or for repeating or revealing these outside the Assembly.)*

Note: *MHP is of the opinion that it is not correct to turn parliamentary nonaccountability into legal nonaccountability with the exception of the acts of defamation. It is paradoxical that acts of defamation are the only exception to the rule of nonaccountability, while much graver crimes, such as praise or incitement of terrorism and violence or promotion of rancor and hatred between individuals, are left outside the scope of the exception.*

(2) A deputy who is alleged to have committed an offense before or after election shall not be detained, interrogated, arrested, or tried unless the Assembly decides otherwise with secret voting. The decision of arrest shall only be taken with a … [text missing in the original, T.N.] majority of the total number of members. In its decision, the Assembly may not authorize some of these competences temporarily or permanently. The decision of the Assembly shall be limited to the accused crime in question. The cases where a member is caught in flagrante delicto with respect to willful homicide shall be outside the scope of immunity. However, the competent organ shall promptly inform the Assembly regarding this case.

(Proposal of MHP: A deputy who is alleged to have committed an offense shall not be detained, searched, or arrested unless the Assembly decides otherwise. The execution of a criminal sentence imposed on a deputy shall be suspended until he or she ceases to be a member; the statute of limitations does not apply during the term of membership. The same rule applies to those who are reelected.

The crimes of terrorism and the crimes when caught in flagrante delicto constitute aggravated criminal felonies fall outside the scope of immunity. However, the competent organ shall promptly inform the Assembly regarding this case.)

(3) *(Proposal of CHP and MHP: The investigation regarding a deputy who is alleged to have committed an offense shall be conducted by the Chief Public Prosecutor of the High Court of Appeals while the prosecution shall be conducted by the High Court of Appeals. The public prosecutors and the members of the courts shall be determined by lot from among the members of criminal chambers. The most senior member shall act as president of the committee. The relevant principles and procedures shall be prescribed by law.) (AKP and BDP are of the opinion that this issue is subject to general regulations.)*

(4) The request for the waiver of immunity shall be considered rejected if it is not decided upon by the Assembly within ninety days.

(5) The execution of a criminal sentence imposed on a deputy either before or after his or her election shall be suspended until he or she ceases to be a member, unless the criminal sentence in question concerns a crime that impedes the eligibility of being a deputy.

(6) The investigation and prosecution of a reelected deputy shall depend on the Assembly's waiving the immunity again.

(7) The statute of limitations does not apply during the term of membership.

(8) Political party groups represented in the Turkish Grand National Assembly shall not hold discussions or make decisions regarding parliamentary immunities.

Oath

Article 70: (1) *The deputies (Proposal of AKP: The President, the Vice President, and the Ministers) shall take the following oath:*

(Proposal of AKP: "I swear by what I hold sacred and honor that I will adhere to human rights, the rule of law, and democracy and I will preserve the independence of the state, the integrity of the country, the unconditional sovereignty of the nation.")

(Proposal of CHP: "Before the Turkish Nation, I swear by my honor that in my capacity as a deputy, I will abide by the Constitution faithfully; I will protect the independence of the Republic of Turkey, the integrity of the country, and the unconditional sovereignty of the nation; I will adhere to the principles of the democratic and secular republic based on human rights and the Reforms of Atatürk; I will never use my status and authority as a deputy to derive personal interest and benefits; I will work for the welfare and well-being of the citizens.")

(Proposal of MHP: The members of the Turkish Grand National Assembly shall swear as follows on the holy book that they believe in when they take the office:

"Before the great Turkish Nation, I swear by what I hold sacred and honor that I will protect the existence and independence of the state, the inseparable integrity of the country and the nation, and the unconditional sovereignty of the nation; I will adhere to the rule of law, the democratic and secular republic, and the principles and reforms of Atatürk; I will abide by the Constitution faithfully.")

Note of Article: The commission did not negotiate the note in parentheses formulated by the AKP as it was about the presidential system, but an explanation has been provided by the person who proposed it.

Convening and Recess

Article 71: (1) The Turkish Grand National Assembly shall convene of its own accord on the first day of October each year.

(2) During adjournment or recess, the Assembly may be summoned directly by the President of the Republic *(Proposal of AKP: The President)* or by the Council of Ministers. The Speaker of the Assembly may also summon the Assembly either on his or her own initiative or at the written request of one-fifth of the members.

(3) The regulations regarding the adjournment or recess shall be determined in the Rules of Procedure.

Note of Article: The commission did not negotiate the note in parentheses formulated by the AKP as it was about the presidential system, but an explanation has been provided by the person who proposed it.

The Rules of Procedure and Political Party Groups

Article 73: (1) The Turkish Grand National Assembly shall carry out its activities in accordance with the provisions of the Rules of Procedure that it draws up.

(2) The provisions of the Rules of Procedure shall be drawn up in a way to ensure the participation of each political party group in all the activities of the Assembly in proportion to its number of members. The special provisions in the Constitution are reserved.

(3) The political party groups shall be composed of at least twenty deputies.

(4) Amendments to the Rules of Procedure shall be made by the decision of at least three-fifths of the total number of members of the Assembly. *(Proposal of AKP: The procedure relating to the amendment of the Rules of Procedure shall be stipulated in the Rules of Procedure. Any decision of the Assembly that is not taken in accordance with the formation procedures of the Rules of Procedure cannot be considered as part of the Rules of Procedure.)*

Quorums and Majority for Decisions

Article 74: (1) The Turkish Grand National Assembly shall convene with at least one-third of the total number of members for all its affairs, including elections it holds. Unless otherwise stipulated in the Constitution, the Grand

National Assembly of Turkey shall make decisions by an absolute majority of those present; however, the majority for a decision can, under no circumstances, be less than one more than a quarter of the total number of members.

(2) Decisions for laws regarding general and local elections, referenda, political parties, local administrations, governance procedures under state of emergency, and concerning the judiciary and the independent administrative boards shall be taken with the absolute majority of the total number of members.

(3) Members of the Council of Ministers may delegate a minister to vote on their behalf in sessions of the Turkish Grand National Assembly that they are unable to attend. However, a minister shall not cast more than two votes including his or her own. In secret voting, votes cannot be delegated.

Note: As AKP proposes the presidential system, it technically rejects the term "Council of Ministers."

The Functions and the Powers of the Turkish Grand National Assembly

Article 76: (1) The duties and powers of the Turkish Grand National Assembly are as follows:

a) To enact, amend, and repeal laws,
b) To scrutinize the Council of Ministers and the ministers,
c) *(Proposal of MHP: To select the President of the Republic,)*
ç) To debate and adopt the budget bills and final account bills,
d) To decide to issue currency,
e) To approve the ratification of international treaties,
f) To decide with the majority of three-fifths of the Turkish Grand National Assembly to proclaim amnesty and pardon, *(BDP objects to envisage a special majority.)*
g) To exercise the powers and carry out the duties envisaged in other articles of the Constitution,
ğ) *(Proposal of BDP: To scrutinize the Armed Forces, security and general forces, intelligence institutions, and their expenditures,)*
h) *(Proposal of BDP: To establish permanent, temporary, or special committees to conduct legislation and supervision procedures.)*

Note: AKP reminds of its determinacy to amend the relevant articles in accordance with the presidential system.

Note: CHP notes that the proposals of AKP concerning the presidential system were not negotiated in the commission.

Introduction and Deliberation of Bills

Article 77: (1) The Council of Ministers and deputies are empowered to introduce bills. *(Proposal of BDP: The party groups and the public with the signature of 300,000 registered voters are also empowered.)*

(2) The principles and procedures regarding the deliberation of government bills and private members' bills in the Turkish Grand National Assembly shall be regulated by the Rules of Procedure in accordance with the understanding of democratic negotiation and the principle of effective opposition. The principles and procedures regarding the consulting of the relevant professional organizations, experts, institutions, and organizations during the commission negotiations in the Turkish Grand National Assembly and submission of these opinions with a special report to the Turkish Grand National Assembly shall be prescribed in the Rules of Procedure.

(3) Provisions relating to issues that are not related to each other in scope and content and amendments to those cannot be regulated with one bill.

(4) Proposals and drafts regarding general and local elections, referenda, political parties, local administrations, governance procedures under state of emergency, and laws concerning the judiciary and the independent administrative boards, and basic laws that would systematically amend a specific legal field partially or wholly cannot be discussed in the initial commission after their distribution. They cannot be discussed in the Turkish Grand General Assembly within a week following the distribution of the report of the initial commission.

(Proposal of AKP: The principles and procedures regarding the deliberation of bills in the Turkish Grand National Assembly shall be regulated by the Rules of Procedure. The Rules of Procedure shall be regulated in accordance with the evaluation of proposals in detail in the expert commissions and general negotiations and voting in the General Assembly through commission reports. Special procedures for legislation may be envisaged by the Rules of Procedure.)

Note of Article: As AKP proposes a presidential system, it did not participate in the negotiations of the term "Council of Ministers" in the first paragraph.

Promulgation of Laws by the President of the Republic
(AKP: The President)

Article 78: (1) The President of the Republic *(AKP: The President)* shall promulgate the laws adopted by the Turkish Grand National Assembly within ten days.

(2) The President of the Republic *(AKP: The President)* shall send the laws, except for the budget bills, that he or she deems, in whole or in part, unsuitable for promulgation, along with the justification, back to the Turkish Grand National Assembly for reconsideration in the same period. In case of being partially deemed unsuitable by the President of the Republic *(AKP: The President)*, the Turkish Grand National Assembly may discuss only those articles. Budget bills cannot be sent back by the President of the Republic *(AKP: The President)*.

(3) If the Turkish Grand National Assembly adopts the law sent back for reconsideration without any amendment, the law shall be promulgated by the President of the Republic *(AKP: The President)* within five days.

(4) The laws that are not sent back by the President of the Republic *(AKP: The President)* and are not promulgated on time shall be promulgated by the Speaker of the Assembly.

Note of Article: The proposals of AKP concerning the presidential system were not negotiated in the commission.

Ratification of International Treaties

Article 79: (1) The ratification of treaties concluded with foreign states and international organizations on behalf of the Republic of Turkey shall be subject to adoption by the Turkish Grand National Assembly by a law approving the ratification.

(2) *(Proposal of MHP and CHP: International treaties shall be reviewed by the Constitutional Court before the Assembly issues the law approving the ratification.)*

(3) Agreements regulating economic, commercial, or technical relations, and covering a period of no more than one year, may be put into effect through promulgation, provided they do not entail any financial commitment by the state and provided they do not interfere with the status of individuals or with the property rights of Turkish citizens abroad. In such cases, these agreements shall be brought to the knowledge of the Turkish Grand National Assembly within one month of their promulgation.

(4) Implementation agreements based on an international treaty, and economic, commercial, technical, or administrative agreements that are concluded depending on the authorization as stated in the law, shall not require approval of the Turkish Grand National Assembly. However, economic and commercial agreements or agreements relating to the rights of individuals concluded under the provision of this paragraph shall not be put into effect unless promulgated.

(5) In cases where there is a reservation to a treaty, the relevant reservation shall be included either in the law approving the ratification or the decree of the Council of Ministers and shall be promulgated with the treaty itself.

(6) Agreements resulting in amendments to Turkish laws *(Proposal of BDP: or creating military duties)* shall be subject to the provisions of the first paragraph.

(7) International agreements duly put into effect have the force of law. No appeal to the Constitutional Court shall be made with regard to these agreements on grounds that they are unconstitutional.

Declarations of State of War and Deployment of the Armed Forces *(Proposal of BDP: Authorization of Use of Force)*

Article 80: (1) The power to authorize the declaration of a state of war, in cases deemed legitimate by international law, and to send the Turkish Armed Forces to foreign countries or to allow foreign armed forces to be stationed in Turkey, except when required by international treaties to which Turkey is a party or by the rules of international courtesy, is vested in the Turkish Grand National Assembly.

(Proposal of BDP: The Turkish Grand National Assembly has the power to authorize the use of force in cases deemed legitimate by international law and when required by international treaties that oblige mutual defense.)

(2) If the country is subjected to sudden armed aggression, while the Turkish Grand National Assembly is adjourned or in recess, and it thus becomes imperative to decide immediately on the use of the armed forces, the President of the Republic *(AKP: the President)* upon the suggestion of the Council of Ministers can decide on the use of the Turkish Armed Forces.

(Proposal of BDP: The principles regarding sending the armed forces to foreign countries shall be determined by law and in compliance with an international treaty that is approved by the Turkish Grand National Assembly. The presence and movement of foreign armed forces in Turkey shall be determined by international treaties that are approved by the Turkish Grand National Assembly and by law. The Turkish Grand National Assembly will take these decisions with qualified majority.)

Note of Article: (CHP) The proposals of AKP concerning the presidential system were not negotiated in the commission.

Election Term of the Turkish Grand National Assembly

Article 81: (1) Elections for the Turkish Grand National Assembly shall be held every four years.

(2) The Assembly or the President of the Republic, under the conditions set forth in the Constitution, may decide to hold a new election before the termination of this period.

(3) In the event of a decision to hold new elections, the powers of the Assembly shall continue until the election of a new Assembly. When it is decided to hold new elections, the elections shall be held within ninety days at the latest; the new Assembly shall convene within five days after the announcement of the final results at the latest.

Note of Article: AKP is satisfied with references made in other articles as it proposes a presidential system. The proposals of AKP concerning the presidential system were not negotiated in the commission.

(Proposal of AKP Regarding the Article) Election Term of the Turkish Grand National Assembly and the President

(1) *Elections for the Turkish Grand National Assembly and presidential elections shall be held every five years and on the same day. If the required majority cannot be obtained in the first ballot of the presidential election, a second ballot shall be held in compliance with the procedure of Article .... [text missing in the original, T.N.]*

(2) *The principles and the procedures regarding the election of the Assembly and the President shall be prescribed by law.*

Deferment of Elections for the Turkish Grand National Assembly *(Proposal of AKP: and the President)* and By-Elections

Article 82: (1) If holding new elections is deemed impossible because of war, the Turkish Grand National Assembly may decide with a three-fifths majority of the total number of members to defer elections for a year. If the grounds do not disappear, the deferment may be repeated in compliance with the procedure for deferment.

(2) By-elections shall be held when vacancies arise in the membership of the Turkish Grand National Assembly. By-elections shall be held once in every election term and cannot be held unless eighteen months elapse after the general election. However, in cases where the number of vacant seats reaches five percent of the total number of seats, by-elections shall be decided to be held within three months. By-elections shall not be held within one year before general elections. *(As the AKP proposes substituent deputyship instead of by-elections, it suggests its proposal to be added as the fourth paragraph to Article 67.)*

Note of Article: AKP is satisfied with references made in other articles as it proposes a presidential system. No elements of the presidential system were negotiated.

Note: The majority for deferring elections in cases of war shall be reviewed.

Proposal of AKP Regarding the Article:

(1) *If holding new elections is deemed impossible because of war, the Grand National Assembly of Turkey* and the Presidency may decide to defer elections for a year. *If the grounds do not disappear, the deferment may be repeated in compliance with the procedure for deferment.)*

(Proposal of CHP and MHP) Authorization to Issue Decrees Having the Force of Law

Article 83: (1) *The Turkish Grand National Assembly may empower the Council of Ministers with the absolute majority of the total number of members to issue decrees having the force of law only in necessary and urgent cases. However, with the exception of governance procedures regarding a state of emergency, the fundamental rights and freedoms, except for social and economic rights that impose positive obligations on the state, shall not be regulated by decrees having the force of law.*

(2) *The empowering law shall define the purpose, scope, and principles of the decree having the force of law, the operative period of the empowering law, and the laws to be repealed. The implementation of decrees having the force of law cannot be made continuous and general by extending the operative period of the empowering law.*

(3) *Decrees having the force of law shall come into force on the day of their publication in the Official Gazette unless a later date is indicated in the decree, and they shall be submitted to the Turkish Grand National Assembly on the same day.*

(4) *Decrees not submitted to the Turkish Grand National Assembly on the day of their publication, decrees that are not negotiated by the Turkish Grand National Assembly at the end of six months from their submission, and decrees rejected by the Turkish Grand National Assembly on the day of publication of the resolution in the Official Gazette shall cease to have effect. The amended provisions of the decrees that are approved as amended shall go into force on the day of their publication in the Official Gazette.*

(5) *The President of the Republic may send the decrees that he or she deem unsuitable for promulgation, along with the justification, back to the Council of Ministers within seven days. If the Council of Ministers adopts the decree sent back without any amendment, the decree shall be promulgated by the President of the Republic within three days. The Council of Ministers shall promulgate the decrees that are not sent back by the President of the Republic or not promulgated by him or her.*

(6) Resignation or removal of the Council of Ministers or expiration of the legislative term shall not cause the termination of the power conferred for the given period.

(7) The provisions regarding decrees having the force of law to be issued by the Council of Ministers in cases of state or emergency shall be reserved.

Note of Article: BDP is against the idea of decrees having the force of law.

Note of Article: AKP did not participate in the negotiations of this article as it proposes a presidential system.

(Proposal of BDP) Public Initiative

Article 84: (1) *Bills and constitutional amendments may be introduced with the signature of three hundred thousand voters that are registered in the electoral register. These proposals of legislation and constitutional amendments shall not be in contradiction with international law, shall not contain provisions that are in contradiction with the achievement of human rights, and shall be in compliance with the basic requirements of the creation of legal norms. The proposals of legislation that do not meet these requirements shall be null and void.*

(2) *The proposal of legislation of the public initiative shall be accepted in the Turkish Grand National Assembly with the absolute majority of the total number of members, while the proposal of constitutional amendments shall be accepted with a two-thirds majority of the total number of members.*

(3) *Those who support the proposals of legislations shall attend the negotiations in the Turkish Grand National Assembly as representatives.*

(4) *In case the Turkish Grand National Assembly does not accept the proposal of legislation, it shall submit it to referendum. If the proposal is accepted, it shall become law.*

Ways of Obtaining Information and Supervision by the Turkish Grand National Assembly

General

Article 85: (1) The Turkish Grand National Assembly shall exercise its power of obtaining information and supervision by means of question, parliamentary inquiry, general debate, censure, parliamentary investigation, and reports. The form of presentation, content, and scope of the motions concerning question, parliamentary inquiry and general debate, and the procedures for answering, debating, and inquiring them shall be regulated by the Rules of Procedure.

Note of Article: As AKP proposes a presidential system, it proposes parliamentary inquiry as the only way of obtaining information. It does not negotiate the proposals concerning a classical parliamentary system.

Question

Article 86: (1) A question is a request for information addressed to the Prime Minister or ministers to be answered orally or in writing on behalf of the Council of Ministers.

(2) In case a motion of question is not answered, the relevant minister shall be invited by the Speaker of the Turkish Grand National Assembly to answer the question in the General Assembly. If the invitation is not complied with, the motion of question shall be promulgated in the Official Gazette and on the official website of the Turkish Grand National Assembly. The deputy who tabled the motion of question shall be given the right to take the floor in the General Assembly for ten minutes.

Note of Article: As AKP proposes a presidential system, it proposes parliamentary inquiry as the only way of obtaining information. It does not negotiate the proposals concerning a classical parliamentary system.

Parliamentary Inquiry

Article 87: (1) A parliamentary inquiry is an examination conducted to obtain information on a specific subject.

(2) An inquiry commission may be established with a decision taken by the General Assembly upon the request of a political party group. However, in case it was requested by the Turkish Grand National Assembly with at least one-third of the total number of members, the establishment of the commission is mandatory. *(AKP did not give consent to this sentence.)*

(3) The parliamentary inquiry commission may request relevant information and documents from public or private institutions and may listen to those concerned. The organizations, individuals, and institutions shall obey the request of the commission.

(Proposal of AKP and BDP: Submission to the judiciary shall not prevent the establishment of a parliamentary inquiry commission on an issue.)

(4) *(Proposal of BDP: Trade and state secrets shall not be claimed as an excuse not to respond to the request of the parliamentary inquiry commission.)*

Note: (CHP and MHP: The scope of the terms "trade secret" and "state secret" shall be determined technically, objectively, and manifestly; the operations of the inquiry commission shall not to be obstructed by contradictory approaches.)

Censure

Article 88: (1) A motion of censure shall be tabled on behalf of a political party group or by the signature of at least twenty deputies.

(2) A motion of censure shall be printed and circulated to members within three days after being tabled; inclusion of a motion of censure on the agenda shall be debated within ten days of its circulation. In this debate, only one of the signatories to the motion, one deputy on behalf of each political party group, and the Prime Minister or one minister on behalf of the Council of Ministers, may take the floor. Inclusion of a motion of censure in the agenda is mandatory if the motion of censure is tabled by at least one-third of the total number of members.

(3) Together with the decision to include the motion of censure in the agenda, the date for debating it shall also be decided; however, the debate on censure shall not take place sooner than two days after the decision to place it on the agenda and shall not be deferred more than seven days.

(4) During the debates on the censure, a motion of no-confidence with a statement of reasons tabled by deputies or party groups or the request for a vote of confidence by the Council of Ministers shall be put to vote only after a full day has elapsed.

(5) In order to unseat the Council of Ministers or a minister, the absolute majority of the total number of members is required in the voting, in which only the votes of no-confidence shall be counted.

(6) Motion of no-confidence that was tabled against the Council of Ministers shall include the name of the Prime Minister candidate. The President of the Republic shall appoint the deputy shown in the motion as the Prime Minister, if the Council of Ministers is unseated with the absolute majority of the total number of members.

Note of Article: As AKP proposes a presidential system, it proposes parliamentary inquiry as the only way of obtaining information. It does not negotiate the proposals concerning a classical parliamentary system.

Parliamentary Investigation

Article 89: (1) Parliamentary investigation may be requested against the Prime Minister or ministers through a motion tabled by at least one-tenth of the total number of members of the Turkish Grand National Assembly. The Assembly shall debate and decide on this request through secret ballot within one month at the latest.

(Proposal of CHP and MHP: In case of rejection of the motion, those who tabled the motion may submit a petition of objection to the Presidency

of the Constitutional Court. A temporary investigation committee that is composed of one member from the Constitutional Court, two members from the penal departments of the High Court of Appeals, one member from civil departments of the High Court of Appeals, and one member from the Council of State who are to be appointed by lot shall review the objections within fifteen days after the decision. The most senior member shall act as president of the committee.)

(2) If a decision to launch an investigation is made, the investigation shall be conducted by a committee of fifteen members, chosen by lot, for each political party in the Assembly, separately from among three times the candidates nominated for each seat reserved for a party group in proportion to its strength. The committee conducts it duties based on the principles of impartiality and secrecy. The committee shall submit its report on the result of the investigation to the Assembly within two months. If the investigation is not completed within the time allotted, the committee shall be granted a further and final period of two months. At the end of this period, the report shall be submitted to the Office of the Speaker of the Turkish Grand National Assembly.

(3) Following its submission to the Office of the Speaker, the report shall be distributed to the members within ten days and debated within ten days after its distribution and, if deemed necessary, a decision may be taken to bring the person involved before the Supreme Court. The decision to bring a person before the Supreme Court shall be taken through a secret ballot only by the absolute majority of the total number of members. A member who is brought before the Supreme Court shall lose his or her duty.

(4) Political party groups in the Assembly shall not hold discussions or make decisions regarding parliamentary investigations.

Note of Article: As AKP proposes a presidential system, it proposes parliamentary inquiry as the only way of obtaining information. It does not negotiate the proposals concerning a classical parliamentary system.

Reasoning: This procedure shall also apply to previous ministers and Prime Ministers since parliamentary investigations are conducted for offenses committed while in office.

Request of Report

Article 90: (1) Political party groups and at least one-tenth of the total number of members of the Turkish Grand National Assembly may request from the Council of Ministers to file a report regarding the application and consequences of the legislation concerning fundamental rights and freedoms.

(2) When it is permitted to send Turkish Armed Forces *(Proposal of BDP: Armed Forces)* to foreign countries or when foreign armed forces are permitted to be stationed in Turkey, the Council of Ministers shall file a report regarding the condition of the armed forces to the Assembly every two months. The procedures for debating these reports in the Plenary shall be regulated by law.

Note of Article: AKP is of the opinion that such supervision is already provided for by the existing supervisory means. Therefore, it finds this article unnecessary.

General Administration and Supervision of Elections

Article 91: (1) Elections and referenda shall be held under the general administration and supervision of the judiciary.

(Proposal of BDP: Elections, referenda, and public initiatives shall be held under the administration and supervision of the judiciary and the Assembly in accordance with the principles of transparency, pluralism, and fair competition. This authority belongs to the Assembly and Electoral Council.)

(2) The Supreme Electoral Council shall execute all functions to ensure the fair and orderly conduct of elections from beginning to end, carry out investigations, and make final decisions during and after the elections on all complaints and objections concerning electoral matters, decide on the annulment of electoral records due to the reasons concerning the eligibility to be a deputy occurred after the elections, receive the electoral records, list the members that are registered and notified by the political parties, and supervise the financing and the expenditures of political parties and candidates for the elections.

(3) The Supreme Electoral Council shall be composed of fifteen members. *(Proposal of AKP: Eleven members of the council shall be determined from among the candidates who are members of the Court of Appeals) (Proposal of CHP and MHP: Six members of the council shall be determined from among the candidates who are members of the High Court of Appeals; five members of the council shall be determined from among the candidates who are members of the Council of State)* by lot and for four years. Four members of the council shall be determined and notified by the four political parties that gained the highest votes in the last elections; these members do not hold the right to vote. The council shall elect one president and one vice president among its members with absolute majority and secret ballot. The members of the Supreme Electoral Council shall carry out their duties permanently and shall not assume other official and private duties, apart from their fundamental duties.

(4) The functions and powers as well as the principles and procedures concerning the election of the members of the Supreme Electoral Council and other electoral boards shall be determined by law.

Reasoning: The membership registrations in political parties shall be carried out by the competent organs of the political parties, and the lists of membership registrations shall be notified to the Supreme Electoral Council by the headquarters of the political parties. The Supreme Electoral Council is authorized to ensure the publicity of the records of memberships and to preserve and disclose these lists to the relevant authorities during party congress periods.

(Article Proposal of BDP) Electoral Council

Article –: (1) *The Electoral Council shall be composed of elected members based on gender equality and in accordance with the principles of pluralism and merit.*

(2) *Some of the members of the Electoral Council shall be elected by the Turkish Grand National Assembly. One person from each political party represented in the Assembly shall take a seat in the Electoral Council. Moreover, three members from among teaching staff working in law or political sciences departments of higher education institutions or lawyers that at least have ten years of experience shall be elected by the Turkish Grand National Assembly with a two-thirds majority of the total number of members and by secret ballot. Two members shall be elected by the General Assembly of the High Court of Appeals, and two members shall be elected by the General Assembly of the Council of State from among their members with the absolute majority of the total number of members and by secret ballot.*

(3) *The members of the Electoral Council shall stay in office for six years. One person cannot be elected more than two times. The members shall elect a president and a vice president from among themselves with the absolute majority of the total number of members and by secret ballot.*

(4) *The members of the Electoral Council cannot assume any other duties apart from their fundamental duties except for those who teach at universities.*

(5) *The decisions of the Electoral Council relating to objections against candidacy and objections raised within the time prescribed by law after the elections, which require the annulment of the records of an electoral district or the records of one or more of those elected and which may affect the results of the elections, shall become final after they are approved by the Turkish Grand*

National Assembly with a two-thirds majority of the total number of members and by secret ballot.

(6) *The operations and organs of the Electoral Council shall be regulated by law.*

ADMINISTRATION AND THE PUBLIC SERVICES

Principles of the Administration

Article 92: (1) The administration forms a whole, with regard to its structure and functions, *(BDP does not agree with this statement)* and shall be regulated by law.

(2) The organization and functions of the administration are based on the principles of centralization and *(Proposal of BDP: democratic)* decentralization.

(3) Public corporate bodies shall be established only by law, or by the authority expressly granted by law.

(4) All activities of the administration shall be based on transparency and accountability *(Proposal of BDP: equality, participation)*. The administration shall give justification for its acts, and it has to introduce the legal means to be used against its acts.

(5) *(Proposal of AKP and BDP: There shall be no discrimination in the performance of the public services.) (Proposal of BDP: The establishment of administrative organs shall be grounded on the principle of gender equality.)*

Reasoning: The term "administrative activity" used in the fourth paragraph shall include administrative acts, actions, and contracts.

Bylaws

Article 93: (1) The Prime Ministry, the ministries, and the public corporate bodies may issue bylaws in order to ensure the implementation of laws relating to their jurisdiction, as long as they are not contrary to these laws and regulations.

(2) Bylaws issued by the Council of Ministers shall be promulgated in the Official Gazette, and which other bylaws are to be published in the Official Gazette shall be designated by law.

Note: AKP does not agree with the terms "The Prime Ministry" and "The Council of Ministers" due to its proposal about the [government, TN] system.

(Article Proposal of BDP) The Regulatory Authorization of the Public Administration

Article –: (1) *Public authorities and public corporate bodies may issue regulatory acts in order to ensure the implementation of laws relating to their* *jurisdiction as long as they are not contrary to these laws and regulations. Which of these regulatory acts are to be published in the Official Gazette shall be designated by law.*

Judicial Review

Article 94: (1) None of the acts and actions of the administration shall be excluded from judicial review. In concession, conditions and contracts concerning public services and national or international arbitration may be suggested to settle the disputes arising from them. Only those disputes involving a foreign element may be submitted to international arbitration.

(2) Judicial power is limited to the review of the legality of administrative actions and acts. *(Proposal of AKP and BDP: The expression "in no case may it be used as a review of expediency" shall be added to this sentence.)* No judicial ruling shall be passed that restricts the exercise of the executive function in accordance with the forms and principles prescribed by law, that has the quality of an administrative action and act, or that removes discretionary powers. *(CHP is of the opinion that only the first sentence of this paragraph shall be in the Constitution.)*

(3) A justified decision regarding the suspension of execution of an administrative act may be issued should its implementation result in damages that are impossible or difficult to compensate for and if, at the same time, the act would be clearly unlawful. *(Proposal of AKP: Making a decision on the suspension of execution may be restricted by law for the purposes of national security, public order, public interest, general health; moreover, in case of a state of emergency, making a decision of suspension of execution relating to the issues that caused the declaration of a state of emergency may be restricted by law.)*

(4) The administration shall be liable to compensate for damages resulting from its actions and acts. *(Proposal of AKP: The law may envisage alternative legal regimes, including civil jurisdiction, concerning these damages.)* Compensation suits concerning damages arising from faults committed by public officials *(Proposal of AKP: personnel)* shall be filed only against the administration in accordance with the procedures and conditions prescribed by law, and provided that the public officials *(Proposal of AKP: personnel)* will be liable to recourse.

Central Administration

Article 95: (1) In terms of central administrative structure, Turkey is divided into provinces on the basis of geographical situation, economic conditions, and public service requirements; provinces are further divided into lower levels of administrative districts.

(2) The administration of the provinces is based on the principle of devolution of powers.

(3) Central administrative organizations comprising several provinces may be established to ensure efficiency and coordination of certain public services. The functions and powers of these organizations shall be regulated by law.

(Article Proposal of BDP) Central Public Administration

Article –: (1) *In terms of central administrative structure, Turkey is divided into regions on the basis of economic conditions, social and cultural characteristics, geographical situation, and public service requirements; regions are further divided into provinces, which are further divided into lower levels of administrative units.*

(2) *The administration of the regions and provinces is based on the principle of devolution of powers.*

(3) *The duties and services that shall be carried out by the central public administration are as follows:*

a) *Duties and services concerning justice, national defense, national security and foreign affairs;*
b) *Duties and services regarding the regulation of exchequer, treasury, foreign trade, customs services, and marketplace;*
c) *In the utilization of financial resources, the principle of financial autonomy shall be applied to the regional public administrations;*
d) *Duties and services to ensure the implementation of program and projects that aim at preparing economic, social, and physical plans on the national level and elimination of development differences between the regions;*
e) *National duties and services that are envisaged by laws to be carried out exclusively by the central administration.*

Local Administrations

Article 96: (1) Local administrations are public corporate bodies established to meet the common local needs of *(Proposal of CHP and MHP: the inhabitants of provinces, municipal districts, and villages) (Proposal of AKP: the local inhabitants)*. Their formation principles, duties, and powers are determined by law and their general decision-making organs are determined in elections. Special governance arrangements may be introduced by law for larger urban centers.

(2) The establishment, duties, powers, ties, and relevance between them and the central administration and the relations to be built between themselves; the principles and procedures for the election of their decision-making organs; the carrying out of the services by the governance unit closest to the citizen and in a manner most convenient for the requirements of the service; and the integrity of the administration shall be regulated by law in accordance with the principles of decentralization and participation.

(3) The elections for local administrations shall be held every five years in accordance with the principles set forth in Article … of the Constitution. However, local elections that are to be held within a year before or after the general elections *(Proposal of CHP and MHP: or by-elections)* for deputies shall be held simultaneously with the general elections or by-elections for deputies. If holding local elections is deemed impossible because of war, the Turkish Grand National Assembly may decide with three-fifths of the total number of members to defer elections for a year. If the grounds do not disappear, the deferment may be extended in compliance with the procedure for deferment.

Note: In compliance with the fundamental regulations regarding the right to vote and to be elected, Articles 67 and 76 of the Constitution in force shall be reviewed to be replaced with the expression "Article … ."

(4) The local elections shall be held under the direction and supervision of the judiciary. The status of the elected organs of the local administrations and the loss of membership to those organs may only be determined by a judicial decision.

(5) As a provisional measure, the Minister of Internal Affairs may remove from office *(Proposal of CHP and MHP: not exceeding a month and for one time only)* those organs of local administration or their members against whom an investigation or prosecution has been initiated on grounds of offenses related to their duties. The judicial organ shall finalize the application launched against such a decision within 30 days at the latest.

(6) *(Proposal of CHP and MHP: Any adjustments regarding the borders of a local administration shall only be made upon a referendum to be held in the relevant local administration.)*

(7) It is essential to advise the local administrations regarding the plans and the decision-making procedures that directly concern the local administration.

(8) The central administration has the power of administrative tutelage over the local administrations in the framework of principles and procedures set forth by law with the objective of ensuring the integrity of the administration and safeguarding the productivity and harmony in services.

(9) The central administration may temporarily suspend the execution of the acts and decisions of the local administration that are manifestly contrary to public interest and where their implementation results in damages that are impossible to compensate for.

(10) These administrative bodies shall be allocated financial resources in proportion to their functions prescribed by law. The decisions, activities, incomes, and expenditures of the local governments shall be made public regularly, in accordance with the principles and procedures prescribed by law.

(Article Proposal of BDP) Local Public Administrations

Article –: (1) *Local administrations are public corporate bodies established to meet the common local needs of the inhabitants of regions, provinces, and other lower levels of administrative units and whose decision-making organs are elected by the public.*

(2) *Elections for the local public administrations shall be held every four years.*

(3) *Supervision regarding the acquisition and loss of status of elected organs of local public administrations shall only be carried out by the judiciary.*

(4) *Laws concerning the local public administrations shall be issued by the Turkish Grand National Assembly with the absolute majority of the total number of members.*

(5) *Principles and procedures regarding the establishment, duties, and powers of the local public administrations and the election of their decision-making organs; establishment of unions and the division of powers, authorities, and incomes between themselves; their relations with international institutions; and their membership to the international local administration institutions shall be regulated by law in accordance with the principle of democratic local governance. Special administrative arrangements may be introduced by law for larger urban centers.*

(Proposal of BDP) Regional Public Administration

Article –: (1) *The borders of the autonomous regional public administrations shall be determined by law considering the historical, cultural, sociological, geographical, and economic features.*

(2) *The Regional Public Administration consists of Regional Assembly and Presidency.*

(3) *The Regional Assembly shall be composed of three times the number of members of the total number of deputies in the provinces within that region.*

(4) *The regulations regarding the activities incompatible with the membership, legislative nonaccountability, legislative immunity, loss of membership, and*

salaries and travel allowances of the members of the Turkish Grand National Assembly shall apply to the members of the Regional Assembly.

(5) *The Regional Assembly shall be authorized to use all powers exclusively except for those left to the Turkish Grand National Assembly or other public administration and the common powers. The Regional Assembly shall be authorized to issue legislative regulations and make decisions. It shall have the authority to budget the resources transferred from the central budget and the local financial resources in accordance with the principle of financial autonomy.*

(6) *The Regional Presidency consists of the President of the Region and the Regional Executive Board. The President of the Region shall be elected by the public from among citizens who are eligible to be deputies. The President of the Region shall be authorized to execute the laws and decisions accepted by the Regional Assembly. The President of the Region shall appoint and, when necessary, discharge the members of the Regional Executive Board that assist him or her in conducting his or her duties from among and outside of the members of the Assembly. A motion of confidence shall be held in the Regional Assembly in the first session after the appointment of the Regional Executive Board by the President of the Region. The number of members of the Regional Executive Board shall not be more than two-fifths of the total number of members of the Regional Assembly.*

(7) *The Regional Public Administration shall carry out its powers and duties based on the principles of territorial integrity and with respect to the powers of provinces and other lower levels of administrative units.*

(Proposal of BDP) Prohibition of Dual Membership to Assemblies

(1) *The members of the Regional Assembly cannot be members of the Turkish Grand National Assembly at the same time.*

(Proposal of BDP) Supervision of the Local Public Administrations

(1) *The President of the Republic and the political parties that are represented in the Regional Assembly shall be authorized to appeal to the Constitutional Court for the annulment of the laws issued and the decisions made by the Regional Assembly on the grounds that they are unconstitutional.*

(2) *Regional local authority and everyone whose interests are violated may apply to administrative judicial organs within the time prescribed by law against the decisions, acts, and actions of the Regional Presidency that are deemed unconstitutional and unlawful.*

Provisions Relating to (Proposal of AKP: Employees) (Proposal of CHP and MHP: Public Servants and Other Public Officials) (Proposal of BDP: Public Employees)

Article 97: (1) *(Proposal of AKP) The duties of the public services that the state and other public corporate bodies are assigned to perform are carried out by employees. The circumstances under which public services will be carried out through service procurement shall be regulated by law.*

(Proposal of CHP and MHP) The fundamental and permanent functions required by the public services that the state, state economic enterprises, and other public corporate bodies are assigned to perform in accordance with principles of general administration shall be carried out by public servants and other public officers.

(Proposal of BDP) The duties of the public services that the public administrations are assigned to perform are carried out by public personnel.

(2) The procedures and principles regarding the promotion of the *(Proposal of AKP: employees) (Proposal of CHP and MHP: public servants and other public officials) (Proposal of BDP: public employees)* in the profession, their duties and powers, their rights and obligations, their salaries and allowances, and other matters related to their status as well as the training of high-ranking administrators shall be regulated by law in accordance with the principle of merit *(Proposal of CHP and MHP: seniority and requirements of service).* However, provisions on collective agreement concerning financial and social rights are reserved.

(3) *(Proposal of AKP: Employees) (Proposal of CHP and MHP: Public servants and other public officials) (Proposal of BDP Public employees)* are obliged to carry out their duties with loyalty to the Constitution and the laws. *(Proposal of CHP and BDP: In performing their duties, they cannot make any distinction between individuals because of their beliefs and thoughts.)*

(4) The initiation of a criminal investigation for alleged offenses committed by *(Proposal of AKP: employees) (Proposal of CHP and MHP: public servants and other public officials) (Proposal of BDP: public employees)* related to their duties shall be subject to the permission of the administrative authority in the cases specified by law. *(Proposal of CHP and BDP: The initiation of a criminal investigation for offenses of murder, deliberate injury, torture, or ill-treatment cannot be subject to permission, in any way.)*

(5) *(Proposal of CHP and MHP: Public servants and other public officials) (Proposal of BDP: Public employees)* and members of public professional organizations or their higher bodies shall not be subjected to disciplinary

penalties without being granted the right of defense; disciplinary decisions cannot be excluded from judicial review. *(Although AKP agrees with the content of this provision, it does not consider the provision as a problem of the Constitution.)*

(6) Disciplinary provisions regarding the members of the *(Proposal of MHP: Turkish)* Armed Forces are reserved. *(BDP opposes this paragraph.)*

(7) *(Proposal of AKP) The term of office of the undersecretary, governor, and general managers shall terminate automatically upon the termination of the duty of the President.*

Article Note: The AKP proposal of paragraph seven has not been negotiated under the principle of postponing the negotiation of the articles on the executive body.

Unlawful Order

Article 98: (1) In case a(n) *(Proposal of AKP: employee) (Proposal of CHP and MHP: public servant and other public official) (Proposal of BDP: public employee)* finds an order given by his or her superior to be contrary to the provisions of law, he or she shall not carry it out and shall inform the person giving the order of this inconsistency. However, if his or her superior renews the order in writing, it shall be executed; in this case, the person executing the order shall not be held responsible.

(2) An order that in itself constitutes an offense *(Proposal of BDP: under national or international law)* shall under no circumstances be executed; the person who executes such an order shall not evade responsibility.

(3) *(Proposal of MHP) Exceptions indicated by law relating to the execution of military duties and the protection of public order or public security in urgent situations are reserved.*

Presidency of Religious Affairs

Article 99: (1) *(Proposal of AKP) The Presidency of Religious Affairs, which is a public corporation, fulfills the duties indicated in the law, in line with the principle of political impartiality.*

(Proposal of CHP) The Presidency of Religious Affairs is within the general administration. It fulfills its duties that are enumerated in the law, in accordance with the principles of the freedom of religion and belief in the Constitution and in accordance with the principle of secularism, provided that it considers the diversity of religions and sects in society.

(Proposal of MHP) The Presidency of Religious Affairs carries out the duties indicated in the law in line with the principles of freedom of religion, conscience and belief, secularism, and political impartiality.

Note: Political parties will try to reconcile their views in line with the principles of the freedom of religion, conscience and belief, secularism, and political impartiality.

Office of Commander-in-Chief and National Defense

Article 100: (1) The Office of Commander-in-Chief belongs to the spiritual existence of the Turkish Grand National Assembly and is represented by the President of the Republic *(Proposal of AKP: The President)*.

(2) The Council of Ministers *(Proposal of AKP: The President)* shall be responsible to the Turkish Grand National Assembly for national security and for the preparation of the armed forces for the defense of the country.

(3) The Chief of the General Staff is the commander of the armed forces and is attached to the Minister of National Defense.

(4) *(Proposal of CHP and MHP) The Chief of the General Staff is appointed by the President of the Republic upon recommendation of the Minister of National Defense and the proposal of the Council of Ministers.*

(5) *(Proposal of BDP) No orders can be given that violate international laws regulating the use of force and that can result in committing crimes against humanity. Preventing peoples from living together in peace and to prepare a war of aggression are against the Constitution.*

Note: The issue of "ensuring national security" negotiated in paragraph two shall be among the duties of the Council of Ministers/the President. BDP will consider this proposal under the heading of Council of Ministers.

Article Note: (CHP) The note that is attached to several other articles and that states that the proposal of a presidential system by AKP is not negotiated could not be attached to this article due to AKP's objection to its attachment.

Extraordinary Administration Procedures

Article 101: (1) The Council of Ministers *(Proposal of AKP: The Turkish Grand National Assembly at the request of the President)* may declare a state of emergency in cases of serious disturbance of public order due to natural or manmade disasters, dangerous epidemic diseases, serious economic crises, the emergence of widespread violence against the constitutional order, or the elimination of fundamental rights and freedoms in one or more regions of or throughout the country for a period not exceeding two months.

(Proposal of MHP) If public order is seriously disturbed due to the emergence of widespread violence against the constitutional order or the elimination of fundamental rights and freedoms, the opinion of the National Security Council may also be requested.

(2) In the event of a declaration of a state of emergency, this decision shall be published in the Official Gazette and shall be immediately submitted to the Turkish Grand National Assembly for approval. *(AKP does not agree with the rest of the sentence after "and.")* If the Turkish Grand National Assembly is in recess, it shall be immediately assembled. The Assembly may extend the duration of the state of emergency period for a maximum of two months each time at the request of the Council of Ministers *(Proposal of AKP: The President)* or may lift the state of emergency.

(3) In extraordinary cases, for each category separately, the restriction or the temporary suspension of fundamental rights and freedoms must be in accordance with the article titled "Suspension of the Exercise of Fundamental Rights and Freedoms" of the Constitution and other principles relating to it; obligations to be introduced to citizens; the nature and execution of measures to be taken in a state of emergency; and the powers to be given to public officials shall be regulated by law.

Note: Shall be reviewed when agreement is reached on the term "public official."

(4) The Turkish Grand National Assembly, upon the request of the Council of Ministers (*Proposal of AKP: The President*), may decide on a state of mobilization or war in the events of war or the emergence of a situation necessitating war.

(Proposal of MHP) The Council of Ministers, after consultation with the National Security Council, may declare martial law in one or more provinces or throughout the country for a period not exceeding four months in the event of widespread acts of violence that are more dangerous than the cases necessitating a state of emergency or an uprising or widespread acts of violence of internal or external origin threatening the indivisibility of the country and the nation. The Turkish Grand National Assembly may extend the duration of the state of martial law period for a maximum of four months each time at the request of the Council of Ministers or may lift the state of martial law. In the event of a state of war and mobilization, the time limit does not apply.

(5) In cases of a state of war or mobilization, the restriction or the temporary cessation of fundamental rights and freedoms must be in accordance with the article titled "Suspension of the Exercise of Fundamental Rights and Freedoms" of the Constitution and other principles relating to it; obligations to be introduced to citizens; the nature and execution of measures to be taken in a state of war or mobilization; the powers to be given to public officials shall be regulated by law.

(6) During the extraordinary administration procedures, the Council of Ministers *(Proposal of AKP: The President)* may issue decrees having the force of law if required by the situation. These decrees shall be published in the Official Gazette and shall be submitted for approval to the Turkish Grand National Assembly on the same day. The Turkish Grand National Assembly shall discuss these decrees with priority and shall approve them either without any amendment or with amendments or reject them within 60 days at the latest. Decrees that are not determined by the Assembly within this period shall be annulled. The procedures and principles regarding the approval of these decrees by the Assembly shall be indicated in the Rules of Procedure.

(7) Decrees issued during extraordinary administrative procedures and those approved and enacted by the Assembly shall be applicable only in the period when the extraordinary administrative procedure is duly in force, and only in places where the extraordinary administrative procedure is duly declared. With the abolition of the extraordinary administrative procedure, these decrees or the ones approved and enacted by the Turkish Grand National Assembly shall be annulled automatically. No amendments to the laws can be made by the decrees issued during extraordinary administrative procedures. The Constitutional Court shall debate the cases filed against these decrees with priority.

Note of BDP: *It is considered unnecessary to grant the Council of Ministers the power to issue decrees having the force of law, in addition to the laws, in the case of a state of emergency, war, and mobilization.*

Universities

Article 102: (1) Universities are established by the state and by law, in accordance with the principles of scientific and academic freedom and institutional and academic *(Proposal of CHP and BDP: and financial)* autonomy. The foundations with sufficient resources exclusively devoted to education, culture, science, and technology can establish nonprofit universities in accordance with the principles and procedures set forth by law in accordance with the principle of scientific freedom.

(2) Universities have juridical personality.

(3) Universities, teaching staff, and other faculty members can freely engage in research, artistic production, publication, explanation, and teaching.

(4) Executive bodies and academic staff of universities cannot be dismissed from their duties for any reason by authorities other than the universities themselves or the Higher Education Regulatory Board.

(5) Academic titles, designation, promotion, and retirement of the teaching staff; education/training of the teaching staff; education levels and duration; introduction to higher education; disciplinary and criminal affairs; financial affairs and other personal rights; learning and teaching in freedom and security and according to the universal requirements of science and technology; and the use of financial resources provided by the state to the universities shall be regulated by law.

(6) Higher education institutions affiliated with the Turkish Armed Forces *(Proposal of BDP: Armed Forces)* and the police are subject to the provisions of universities except for the specific requirements of these institutions.

(7) Reports of the evaluation authority are taken into account in the determination of the share to be allocated to the higher education institutions from state finances and other financial contributions.

Professional Organizations Having the Characteristics of Public Institutions

Article 104: (1) Professional organizations having the characteristics of public institutions and their higher bodies are public corporate bodies established by law, with the objectives of meeting the common needs of the members of a given profession and to ensure that the profession is maintained in accordance with ethical rules and their bodies are elected by their own members in accordance with democratic procedures, under judicial surveillance and supervision. *(Proposal of CHP: Financial audits shall be performed in accordance with the procedures laid down in their constituent law. More than one higher organization cannot be established for the same profession, and membership of the professional organizations to the higher organizations is compulsory.)*

(2) Elected bodies of the professional organizations having the characteristics of public institutions cannot be *(Proposal of CHP: temporarily and)* permanently removed from office without judicial decision, and new organs shall be elected in their place.

(3) *(Proposal of CHP and MHP) In necessary cases explicitly envisaged by law and where delay constitutes a prejudice to national security, (Proposal of MHP: public order, prevention of commission, or continuation of a crime), a judge having jurisdiction may temporarily suspend the operation of professional organizations and their higher bodies from activity within twenty-four hours.*

(4) *(Proposal of CHP) In order to practice the profession, membership in/to the relevant professional organization is compulsory.*

(5) *(Proposal of CHP) The authority to regulate professional principles and to carry out inspections belongs to the professional organizations. Regulatory acts, working principles, and rights and obligations of professional organizations cannot be contrary to democratic principles. No disciplinary proceedings may be carried out, and no disciplinary sanctions may be applied, by any authority other than the relevant professional organization or its higher organization regarding the professional activities of the members of the professional organizations. In disciplinary investigations, the accusation shall be notified clearly and in writing and the right to written defense shall be given.*

(6) *(Proposal of CHP and BDP) The cooperation of the professional organizations with other people or organizations, and their rights to organize meetings and demonstrations, to use legal and judicial means in order to achieve the aims of the professional organizations, and to create public opinion cannot the restricted. (MHP is of the opinion that since the regulation in this paragraph is very obvious in nature, it is unnecessary for it to be included in the Constitution.)*

Reasoning: In the event that a lawsuit is filed against those concerned, the measure in the proceedings shall be assessed in accordance with the general provisions.

Article Note: Since AKP does not find it appropriate to include constitutional administrative bodies and other public corporate bodies under the title of "Executive," it will be reevaluated whether the professional institutions having the characteristics of public institutions will be included in the Constitution.

Ombudsperson

Article 105: (1) Everyone has the right to appeal to the Ombudsperson.

(2) The Institution of the Ombudsperson examines complaints on the functioning of the administration on behalf of the Turkish Grand National Assembly.

(3) The Chief Ombudsperson shall be elected by the Turkish Grand National Assembly for one time and for a term of five years by secret ballot with a two-thirds *(Proposal of AKP: three-fifths)* of the total number of members. The candidates who are distinguished in the field of merit and human rights shall be publicly heard by the relevant commission in the Turkish Grand National Assembly before the election. This commission submits the report to the General Assembly by examining each applicant's application file.

(4) The Chief Ombudsperson fulfills his or her powers and duties in impartiality and independence. The Chief Ombudsperson cannot be held responsible for any statements made in connection with his or her duties.

(5) The Chief Ombudsperson has the authority to investigate and review complaints against the administration for the protection of fundamental rights

and freedoms, to make recommendations to the administration, to mediate between the parties, to file a criminal complaint to the prosecutor's office where necessary, and to apply for a constitutional complaint in exceptional cases indicated by law.

(6) At the beginning of each legislative year, the Chief Ombudsperson submits an annual report to the Assembly on his or her work. Moreover, he or she may also prepare reports, on his or her own initiative, regarding a situation that disturbs public conscience, or upon the request of the Turkish Grand National Assembly, regarding an issue of special importance.

(7) Other matters relating to the Institution of the Ombudsperson are indicated in the Rules of Procedure and the law.

Note: AKP considers the provisions in this article, with the exception of the first two paragraphs and the first sentence of paragraph three, to be subject to the Rules of Procedure.

Reasoning: 1) It will be written that "the Institution of the Ombudsperson will be established to examine, investigate, and make recommendations to all kinds of actions and operations of public administration and their attitudes and behaviors in terms of compliance with human rights, nondiscrimination, law, and equity."

2) The implementation of extraordinary administrative procedures does not prevent the ombudsperson from working.

(Proposal of CHP and MHP: Regulatory and Supervisory Institutions)
Article 106: (1) *Apart from the hierarchy of the central administration, regulatory and supervisory boards that are public corporate bodies may be established by law, in order to protect the basic rights, to ensure the execution of the administrative activities in accordance with fundamental rights and freedoms, and to regulate the economy on a sectoral scale so as to ensure the functioning of the market economy in a healthy manner.*

Note: AKP recognizes the regulatory and supervisory boards as the basic condition of good governance in the exercise of fundamental rights and freedoms and other areas, but treats the issue at the legal and not at the constitutional level.

Radio and Television Corporation of Turkey and Public-Affiliated News Agencies
Article 107: (1) The establishment and operation of the Radio and Television Corporation of Turkey, which is established as a public legal entity, and other state-owned radio and television institutions and news agencies that are

assisted by public corporate bodies, are regulated by law in accordance with the principles of autonomy and impartiality of publication. Publications of these institutions shall be based on science, art, culture, history, and news areas *(Proposal of BDP: and protect cultural pluralism with publications/ broadcasting in mother tongue)*.

Note: AKP states that both the Radio and Television Corporation of Turkey and the Radio and Television Supreme Council can be regulated by law.

Reasoning: The eleventh paragraph of the article concerning the freedom of press, which is as follows, shall be emphasized in the commentary: "Persons and political parties have the right to benefit from nonpress mass communication and broadcasting instruments owned by public corporate bodies in accordance with the principles of equality and justice. The conditions and procedures of this are regulated by law on the basis of the right to receive information and the free formation of public opinion."

Radio and Television Supreme Council

Article 108: (1) The Radio and Television Supreme Council, which is established to regulate and supervise radio and television activities, operates in accordance with the principles of pluralism, autonomy, and impartiality *(Proposal of BDP: and in a way that protects cultural pluralism with publications in mother tongue)*.

Note: MHP does not accept the expression "cultural pluralism" with the concern that it can be interpreted against the integrity of the country.

(2) The Radio and Television Supreme Council is composed of fifteen members *(Proposal of BDP: on the basis of gender equality)*. Nine of these members are elected by the Turkish Grand National Assembly by simple majority from among the candidates who are nominated by the political parties to be represented in proportion to their strength, with each political party group being represented by at least one member. Six members are elected by lot, from among those who are employed in the field of audio-visual media for at least ten years, one of whom is a jurist and the others are members of the relevant professional organization. *(Proposal of BDP: Two of the six members are determined by women's and disabled persons' organizations.)*

(3) The establishment and operation of the Radio and Television Supreme Council, its duties and powers, and other matters related to its election are regulated by law in accordance with the principles of effective use of press freedom and the free formation of public opinion.

Note: AKP states that both the Radio and Television Corporation of Turkey and the Radio and Television Supreme Council can be regulated by law.

Reasoning: The council shall make its decisions on the basis of the freedom of information.

JUDICIARY

Attorneyship and the Bar Associations

Article 113: (1) Defense is one of the founding elements of the judiciary and it is independent.

(2) Attorneyship is a self-employed public service. Representation for claiming rights and defense before the authorities having jurisdiction and the courts shall be ensured through attorneys. The assurances required by the duties of attorneys are regulated by law.

(3) Attorneys have the authority to collect evidence for the cases that they accept. The procedures and principles with regard to this shall be regulated by law.

(4) Depending on the principle of reciprocity, foreign attorneyship institutions can only provide consultation services on foreign law and international law.

(5) The professional organization of attorneys is the bar association. The Bar Association of Turkey shall determine the professional ethical rules.

(6) No audit can be made to damage the financial and administrative autonomy of bar associations. Principles and procedures regarding the financial and administrative transparency of bar associations and the Bar Association of Turkey shall be regulated by law.

Note: AKP considers it sufficient to include the norm "defense is one of the founding elements of the judiciary and it is independent" in the judiciary chapter in the Constitution and, therefore, does not participate in the remaining provisions of the article (paragraphs two through six).

Note: *CHP will reconsider paragraphs four and five after consulting the Bar Association of Turkey.*

Reasoning: Representation by attorneys referred to in the second paragraph shall not be interpreted as preventing the individuals, his or her parents and guardians, and public institutions, in cases where there is a suit filed against them, from claiming their rights and defending themselves on their own.

Military Justice

Article 114: (1) *(Proposal of CHP and MHP) Military justice is composed of military courts and military disciplinary courts. These courts shall have jurisdiction to try military offenses committed by military personnel and offenses committed by military personnel related to military services and duties.*

(2) *(Proposal of CHP and MHP) Nonmilitary persons shall not be tried in military courts, except during a state of war.*

(3) *(Proposal of CHP and MHP) The formation of military justice organs, their functioning, matters relating to the status of military judges, relations between prosecutors, and the military command under which they serve shall be regulated by law in accordance with the principles of the independence of the judiciary and the security of tenure of judges.*

(4) *(Proposal of AKP and BDP) No military courts can be established by law except for disciplinary courts. In the event of war, military courts may be established to deal with offenses committed by the military in relation to their duties.*

Formation of the Constitutional Court

Article 117: (1) The Constitutional Court is composed of twenty-five members.

(AKP) Formation of the Constitutional Court

(2) *The Turkish Grand National Assembly shall elect nine members by secret ballot and with a two-thirds majority of the total number of its members, from among those at least seven of whom are teaching staff in constitutional law, public law, or political science. In case the election cannot be made with two-thirds majority in the first ballot, a second ballot shall be held, and, in this ballot, the absolute majority of the total number of members shall be sought. The President shall elect eight members from among those who are teaching staff in constitutional law, public law, or political science; high-ranking executives; self-employed attorneys; judges and prosecutors who served at least fifteen years in the profession; and rapporteurs of the Constitutional Court who served for at least five years.*

(3) *In order to be elected as a member of the Constitutional Court, it is required to be forty years old; to have higher education in the field of law, social, or political sciences; and to have worked at least fifteen years in his or her profession. These conditions are sought for all candidates.*

(4) *The president and the deputies of the Constitutional Court shall be elected for a period of four years by members from among themselves by secret*

ballot and the absolute majority of the total number of members. The president and deputies may not be elected to these positions more than once.

(5) *The members of the Constitutional Court cannot accept any official or special duties other than their essential duties.*

(6) *Procedures and principles regarding the election of the members shall be regulated by law.*

(CHP) Formation

(2) *Four members from the High Court of Appeals, four members from the Council of State, and four members from the Court of Accounts shall be elected by the plenaries of those, from among their own presidents and members who have been a member for at least three years, by secret ballot, and with the absolute majority of the total number of members.*

One member shall be elected by the High Council of Judges from among first-category judges and public prosecutors by secret ballot and with the absolute majority of the total number of members.

Seven members shall be elected by the Turkish Grand National Assembly. The Assembly shall elect two members from among the law or political sciences professors of the Inter-University Board and two members from among the attorneys nominated by the Bar Association of Turkey, which should be three times the number to be elected. The Turkish Grand National Assembly shall elect three members directly. Prior to the election by the Turkish Grand National Assembly, the candidates shall be heard by a commission in which all political parties having a group in the Assembly are represented in equal numbers. Commission meetings shall be broadcast by the Radio and Television Corporation of Turkey. This commission shall submit the report that it will prepare by examining the application file of each candidate to the Plenary of the General Assembly.

The Turkish Grand National Assembly shall elect the members of the Constitutional Court by secret ballot and with a three-fifths majority of the total number of members. The election of the Turkish Grand National Assembly shall be completed within ninety days from the notification of the candidates to the Bureau of the Assembly.

(3) *In order to be elected as member of the Constitutional Court, it is required to be over the age of forty-five; to have graduated in law, political sciences, economics, or administrative sciences; to have worked in public service for at least fifteen years; to have worked at least fifteen years as teaching staff for those to be elected from among teaching staff; and to have practiced as an attorney for at least fifteen years for those to be elected from among attorneys.*

(4) *The principles and procedures to be applied for nomination and election for the membership of the Constitutional Court shall be regulated by law.*

(5) *The Constitutional Court shall elect a president and two deputy presidents for a period of four years by secret ballot from among its members and by the absolute majority of the total number of its members. Those whose duties have expired can be reelected.*

(6) *The members of the Constitutional Court cannot accept any official or special duties other than their essential duties.*

(MHP) Formation of the Constitutional Court

(1) *The Constitutional Court is composed of thirty-four members and carries out its duties through the Plenary and three chambers.*

(2) *Seven members of the Constitutional Court shall be elected from among professors working in the departments of public law and of political science, seven members shall be elected from among the members of the High Court of Appeals, six members shall be elected from among the members of the Council of State, one member shall be elected from among the members of the Court of Accounts, four members shall be elected from among high-ranking executives working for fifteen years in public service, two members shall be elected from among attorneys registered in a bar association for fifteen years, one member shall be elected from among certified public accountants working in the field for fifteen years, and six members shall be elected from among law graduates who have served as deputies and who are to be nominated by the political parties that received at least ten percent of the valid votes in the last general election by drawing lots before the Constitutional Commission and for an eight-year single term.*

(3) *Candidates over the age of forty-five shall apply to the Constitutional Commission of the Turkish Grand National Assembly in order to participate as a candidate in the election by lot.*

(4) *The Constitutional Court shall elect a president and a deputy president for a period of four years by secret ballot from among its members and by the absolute majority of the total number of its members. The president and the deputy may be elected twice, at most.*

(5) *The members of the Constitutional Court cannot accept any official or special duties other than their essential duties.*

(BDP) Constitutional Court (Constitutional Council)

(1) *The Constitutional Court shall be composed of twenty-one members elected on the condition that they are declared in advance.*

(2) The Turkish Grand National Assembly shall elect nine members to the Constitutional Court. Four of the members are elected from among teaching staff working in the field of public law or political science, three from judges and prosecutors who have the qualifications to be elected to the high courts, and two from among the rapporteurs of the Constitutional Court by two-thirds of the total number of members of the Turkish Grand National Assembly.

(3) Four members from the High Court of Appeals, four members from the Council of State, and two members from the Court of Accounts shall be elected by the plenaries of those, from among their members, by secret ballot, and with the absolute majority of the total number of members.

(4) To be elected as a member of the Constitutional Court, it is required to be forty years old and have at least ten years of professional experience.

(5) The Constitutional Court shall elect a president and three deputy presidents for a period of four years by secret ballot from among its members and by the absolute majority of the total number of its members. The president and the deputies may be elected twice, at most.

(6) The members of the Constitutional Court cannot accept duties other than their primary duties except for lecturing in universities.

(7) The procedures and principles regarding the election of members of the Constitutional Court shall be regulated by law.

(8) The Turkish Grand National Assembly shall elect the members from among the candidates, who shall be three times the number of those to be elected, and shall be nominated by the commission, which will be established on the basis of equal representation of the political parties having a group in the Assembly.

Duties and Powers

Article 119: (1) The Constitutional Court shall examine the constitutionality, in respect to both form and substance *(Proposal of CHP and MHP: Constitutional amendment laws shall be examined only with regard to their form)*, of laws and *(Proposal of AKP: presidential decrees) (Proposal of BDP: laws enacted by the Regional Assemblies) (Proposal of MHP: decrees having the force of law) (Proposal of CHP and MHP: international treaties conditioned to as preliminary review)* the Rules of Procedure of the Turkish Grand National Assembly, and decide on the cases regarding the political parties and on the appeals to constitutional complaint *(Proposal of CHP and MHP: carrying out financial supervision of the political parties). (Proposal of AKP and BDP: Constitutional amendments can neither be examined with regard to form nor with regard to substance.)*

(2) *(Proposal of BDP) The Constitutional Court finally determines the jurisdiction disputes between the central and regional bodies of the state, between the regional bodies themselves, and between the lower units within a region's boundaries.*

(3) *(Proposal of AKP) The Constitutional Court tries the President, the Speaker of the Assembly, and the ministers for offenses related to their duties. The Chief Public Prosecutor of the Court of Appeals shall act as the prosecutor for these cases. Applications for reexamination against the decisions taken in these proceedings shall be decided by the Plenary of the Assembly.*

Procedure of Functioning and Trial

Article 120: (1) The Constitutional Court functions with two chambers and the General Assembly. Commissions can be established for constitutional complaints.

(2) The General Assembly deals with annulment cases and objections to them and with appeals against the decisions regarding the political parties, and it resolves disagreements between the chambers regarding constitutional complaints, upon application of one of the chambers.

(3) The chambers deal with the cases regarding political parties, the appeals to constitutional complaints, and other affairs that are not examined by the General Assembly.

(4) The General Assembly convenes with at least ... members under the chairmanship of the president or the deputy president that he or she determines and makes its decisions with the absolute majority of the participants.

(5) The presidency of each chamber is carried out by a deputy president. Each chamber shall convene with at least ... members and make its decision with the absolute majority of the participants.

(6) In order to decide on the annulment of constitutional amendments with respect to their form, and on the dissolution of political parties or the revocation of state aid when they resort to violence or encourage violence, a two-thirds majority of the participants is required. *(BDP opposes the dissolution of political parties.)*

(7) Priority shall be accorded to annulment cases related to form.

(8) In cases related to political parties, the Constitutional Court shall hear the chairperson of the relevant political party or the deputy who is assigned by him or her after it hears the Chief Public Prosecutor of the High Court of Appeals.

(9) The establishment of the Constitutional Court, judicial procedures, working principles, and disciplinary proceedings of the members shall be regulated by law.

Note: (AKP) The annotation proposed to be added to the second paragraph by AKP, which is as follows: "and to the decisions of the Supreme Court," shall be revised once it is determined whether the task of acting as the Supreme Court is going to be assigned to the Constitutional Court.

Note: The limits of the examination regarding form are going to be determined after the codification of the articles relating to "Duties and Powers of the Constitutional Court" and "Amendments to the Constitution."

Annulment Action

Article 121: (1) The President of the Republic *(Proposal of AKP: The President)*, political parties having a group in the Turkish Grand National Assembly *(Proposal of BDP: and political party groups represented in the Regional Assemblies)*, and one-tenth of the total number of members of the Turkish Grand National Assembly shall have the right to apply for annulment action to the Constitutional Court. *(Proposal of CHP and BDP: Council of Judges, Council of Prosecutors, the High Court of Appeals, the Council of State, and universities regarding issues related to their existence and duties) (Proposal of CHP: also, the metropolitan municipalities and higher bodies of the professional organizations having the characteristics of public institutions.) (Proposal of BDP: local administrations, bars associations, the Court of Accounts) may apply for annulment action directly to the Constitutional Court based on the assertion of the unconstitutionality, in form and in substance, of laws or of certain articles or provisions thereof.*

(Second paragraph Proposal of BDP) The President of the Republic and the president of the Regional Executive Board may have the right to apply for annulment action to the Constitutional Court based on the assertion of the unconstitutionality of the laws enacted by the Turkish Grand National Assembly relating to the duties and powers of the central and regional organs of the state.

(2) The right to apply for annulment to the Constitutional Court shall lapse forty-five days after publication in the Official Gazette of the contested law *(Proposal of AKP: presidential decree)* or the Rules of Procedure.

(3) *(Proposal of BDP) The right to apply for pre-review of the Rules of Procedure shall lapse ten days after the approval of the contested provision by the Plenary of the Assembly.*

(Proposal of CHP) The President of the Republic, political parties having a group in the Turkish Grand National Assembly, and one-tenths of the total number of members of the Turkish Grand National Assembly shall have the right to apply for the review of constitutionality of the law approving the

ratification of the international treaty enacted by the Turkish Grand National Assembly and the international treaty. The right to apply for review shall lapse ten days after the law was sent to the President of the Republic for publication. The Constitutional Court shall decide on the matter within thirty days from the date of the application. The provisions of the international treaty, which the Constitutional Court found unconstitutional, shall not be approved.

Objection Action

Article 122: (1) If a court hearing a case finds that the law *(Proposal of AKP: presidential decrees) (Proposal of CHP and MHP: the decree having the force of law)* to be applied is unconstitutional, or if convinced of the seriousness *(Proposal of BDP: it must be taken into consideration in accordance with the rule of law and democratic state order)* of a claim of unconstitutionality *(Proposal of BDP: or conflict with an international human rights and freedoms treaty duly put into effect)* submitted by one of the parties, it shall postpone the consideration of the case until the Constitutional Court decides on the issue.

(2) If the trial court is not convinced of the seriousness of the claim of unconstitutionality, such a claim, together with the court judgment, shall be decided upon by the competent authority of appeal.

(3) The Constitutional Court shall decide on the matter and declare its justified judgment within six months of receiving the contention. If no decision is reached within this period, the trial court shall conclude the case under legal provisions in force. However, if the trial court receives the decision of the Constitutional Court before the judgment on the merits of the case is rendered final, the trial court is obliged to comply with it.

(4) Nonconstitutionality due to form cannot be invoked by objection action.

High Court of Appeals

Article 125: (1) The High Court of Appeals is the last instance for reviewing decisions and judgments given by civil courts *(Proposal of CHP and MHP: and military courts)* that are not referred by law to other civil judicial authority. It shall also be the first- and last-instance court for dealing with specific cases prescribed by law.

(2) The members of the High Court of Appeals shall be elected in the meeting to be held together with the Council of Judges and Council of Prosecutors from among judicial judges and prosecutors, teaching staff, and attorneys who have actually worked for fifteen years in their profession; by taking the qualities indicated in law, such as merit and

success, into consideration; and by secret ballot with a three-fifths majority of the total number of members for one time and for a nine-year term. Prior to the elections, candidates will be heard publicly by a joint committee to be established by the Council of Judges and the Council of Prosecutors. This commission prepares a report by examining each applicant's application file.

(3) The organization and the functioning of the High Court of Appeals and the qualifications and procedures of the election of its president, deputy presidents, heads of departments, members, chief public prosecutor, and deputy chief public prosecutor shall be regulated by law in accordance with the principles of the independence and impartiality of courts and the security of tenure of judges.

Council of State

Article 126: (1) The Council of State is the last instance for reviewing decisions and judgments given by administrative courts and not referred by law to other administrative courts. It shall also be the first and last instance for dealing with specific cases prescribed by law.

(2) The Council of State also shall give its opinion within two months on the conditions and the contracts under which concessions are granted concerning public services, settle administrative disputes, and discharge other duties as prescribed by law.

(3) Three-fifths of the members of the Council of State shall be elected in a joint meeting to be held by the Council of Judges and the Council of Prosecutors from among administrative judges and prosecutors who have actually worked for fifteen years in their profession and meet the requirements indicated in law and by secret ballot with a three-fifths majority of the total number of members. Two-fifths of the members shall be elected from among four times the candidates to be nominated from attorneys, teaching staff, and high-ranking executives who have actually worked for fifteen years in their profession and by secret ballot with a two-thirds *(Proposal of AKP: three-fifths)* majority of the total number of members of the Turkish Grand National Assembly, for one time and for a nine-year term. In case the election cannot be concluded in three ballots, the election of the members shall be finalized by drawing lots between the two candidates who have received the majority of votes in the last ballot. *(Proposal of AKP: with the absolute majority of the total number of members.)*

(4) High-ranking executives are nominated by the Council of Ministers from among public officials who have served as high-ranking executives for at least two years. The proportion of the high-ranking executives to be elected

shall not exceed one-tenth of the total number of members of the Council of State. The qualifications and nomination procedures of the candidates who are to be elected by the attorneys and teaching staff shall be regulated by law, and in accordance with the democratic, pluralistic, participatory, electoral principles, and the principle of proportional representation. In the elections to be held, everyone shall vote for only one of the candidates.

(5) Before the election that is to be held by the Turkish Grand National Assembly, the candidates shall be heard by a commission in which all political parties are represented in equal numbers. The meetings of the commission shall be broadcast by the Radio and Television Corporation of Turkey. This commission shall examine the application files of each candidate and prepare a report of its review that is submitted to the Plenary of the General Assembly. The Turkish Grand National Assembly shall complete the election within ninety days from the notification of the candidates to the Office of the Speaker of the Assembly. *(AKP opposes this paragraph.)*

(6) The president, chief public prosecutor, deputy presidents, and heads of departments of the Council of State shall be elected by the General Assembly of the Council of State from among its own members for a four-year term by secret ballot and by the absolute majority of the total number of members. They may be reelected at the end of their term of office.

(7) The organization and functioning of the Council of State and the qualifications and procedures of election of its president, chief public prosecutor, deputy presidents, heads of departments, and members shall be regulated by law in accordance with the nature of the administrative judiciary and the principles of the independence of the courts and the security of tenure of judges.

Reasoning: In terms of qualification criteria referred to in the third paragraph, merit and success will be prioritized.

Supreme Court

Article 127: (1) The Supreme Court shall try, for offenses relating to their functions, the President of the Republic, the Speaker of the Turkish Grand National Assembly, members of the Council of Ministers; presidents and chief prosecutors of the Constitutional Court, High Court of Appeals, Council of State; and the president of the Council of Judges *(Proposal of BDP: Presidents of Regions) (Proposal of CHP and MHP: Chief of the General Staff).*

(2) The Supreme Court is composed of ten members. The president of the Supreme Criminal Court is the president of the Criminal Plenary of the High Court of Appeals; six of its members shall be determined from among the

members of the Criminal Plenary of the High Court of Appeals, two of its members shall be determined from among the members of the Constitutional Court, two of its members shall be determined from among the members of the Council of State, by drawing lots before the plenaries of the High Court of Appeals, the Constitutional Court, and the Council of State.

(3) The Criminal Plenary of the High Court of Appeals, except for the members who have served as members of the Supreme Court, shall act as the appeal organ for the judgments of the Supreme Court.

(4) The chief public prosecutor shall act as prosecutor in the Supreme Court.

Note: AKP is of the opinion that the duty of acting as the Supreme Court shall be assigned to the Constitutional Court.

Council of Judges

Article 128: (1) The Council of Judges shall be composed of fifteen members.

(2) The members of the council shall be elected by the Turkish Grand National Assembly, two of them from among the members of the High Court of Appeals; two of them from among the members of the Council of State; two of them from among members of teaching staff who have been working in the fields of law, political science, or public administration at institutions of higher education for at least fifteen years; two of them from among attorneys working in their profession for at least fifteen years; and six of them from among the first-category judges who have been working in their profession for at least fifteen years, through an election with nominees four times the number to be elected. The eligibility criteria and procedures for nomination shall be regulated by law and in accordance with the democratic, pluralistic, participatory electoral principles and the principle of proportional representation. In the elections to be held, everyone shall vote for only one of the candidates.

(3) The Turkish Grand National Assembly shall elect the members of the council separately by secret ballot with a two-thirds majority of the total number of members. In the event that a sufficient majority cannot be obtained in the third ballot, the election of each membership shall be completed by drawing lots among the candidates.

(4) The term of office of the council members is four years. A member whose term of office has expired cannot be reelected.

(5) The council elects a president from among its members with the absolute majority of the total number of members and by secret ballot. The Minister of Justice may attend the meetings and chair the sessions in which he

or she participates (*Proposal of CHP: and chair the sessions in which he or she participates without having the right to vote*), with the exception of the meetings where matters of discipline and personnel affairs are negotiated.

(6) The council executes the appointment, assignment, discipline, and personnel affairs of the judges and carries out other duties indicated by law in accordance with competence, merit, and other principles stipulated by law.

(7) Supervision and investigation of judges shall be carried out by judge inspectors attached to the chairman of the Council of Judges, with the permission of the president of the council.

(8) The council shall decide on the proposals of the Minister of Justice to abolish courts or to amend their jurisdiction.

(9) Council members cannot perform any other special or official duties.

(10) The working procedures and principles of the council and the organizational structure of it shall be regulated by law in accordance with the principles of the independence of the judiciary and the impartiality of judges.

Reasoning: The independence and impartiality of the judiciary includes financial autonomy as well as autonomy of the activities of the council.

Article Note: 1) AKP prefers a three-fifths rather than a two-thirds majority in the third paragraph and does not agree with the method of election by lot.

2) MHP is of the opinion that the number of members of the council shall be increased and the number of members to be elected from among the universities and bar associations shall be decreased, and it opposes the direct election by the Assembly, referred to in the last sentence of the second paragraph. It recommends that teaching staff and attorneys should vote separately for each candidate, and that at least three candidates should be assigned to each vacant seat (i.e., the three persons who receive the majority of votes.). Among these candidates, the Assembly shall elect a member to the Council of Judges with a two-thirds majority of the total number of members and, if such majority cannot be obtained, shall determine a member by lot.

3) CHP, MHP, and BDP are of the opinion that as the exam to be held at the stage of candidacy for the profession is part of the admission procedure, it shall be organized by the council, and it is necessary to evaluate and add this issue under the article relating to "profession and security of tenure of judges."

4) CHP and BDP propose this regulation as they do not agree with the sentence "and chair the sessions in which he or she participates" referred to in the fifth paragraph.

Council of Prosecutors

Article 129: (1) The Council of Prosecutors is composed of seven members and the president of the council shall be the Minister of Justice.

(2) The members of the council shall be elected by the Turkish Grand National Assembly, one of them from among the Plenary of the High Court of Appeals, one of them from among the Plenary of the Council of State, and two of them from among three times the number of those to be elected from prosecutors that have been in the profession for at least fifteen years and based on criteria such as merit and other criteria indicated by law. In the elections to be held in the Plenary of the High Court of Appeals, the Plenary of the Council of State, and among the prosecutors, each member and prosecutor shall vote for only one of the candidates. One member of the council shall be elected directly by the Turkish Grand National Assembly from among teaching staff who have been working in the fields of law or political science at institutions of higher education for at least fifteen years, and one member of the council shall be elected directly by the Turkish Grand National Assembly from among attorneys who have been working in their profession for at least fifteen years.

(3) The Turkish Grand National Assembly shall elect the members of the council separately and by secret ballot with a *two-thirds [CHP and MHP, TN] (AKP and BDP: three-fifths)* majority of the total number of members. In the event that a sufficient majority cannot be achieved in the third ballot, the election shall be completed by drawing lots among the candidates *(AKP: two candidates who receive the majority of votes)* for each membership.

Note: *CHP will internally reevaluate the formation of the Council of Prosecutors. It will declare its view after this evaluation.*

(4) The term of office of the council members is four years. A member whose term of office has expired cannot be reelected.

(5) The council executes the appointment, assignment, discipline, and personnel affairs of the prosecutors and carries out other duties indicated by law in accordance with competence and merit.

(6) Supervision and investigation of prosecutors shall be carried out by prosecutor inspectors attached to the chairman of the Council of Prosecutors, with the permission of the president of the council.

(7) Council members cannot perform any other special or official duties.

(8) The working procedures and principles of the council as well as its organizational structure and other issues shall be regulated by law in

accordance with the principles of the independence and impartiality of the judiciary.

Reasoning: 1) The independence and impartiality of the judiciary also includes financial autonomy as well as autonomy of the activities of the council.

2) "Other issues" referred to in the eighth paragraph means merit and success.

FINANCIAL, ECONOMIC, AND SOCIAL PROVISIONS

Budget and Final Accounts

Article 130: (1) *(Proposal of CHP and BDP) The aim of the budget is meeting public expenditures and ensuring the fair distribution of incomes and wealth in a manner that virtually eliminates inequalities.*

(1) The expenditure of the state, and of public corporate bodies other than state economic enterprises, shall be determined by annual budgets in accordance with the time limits and the procedures indicated by law.

(2) The preparation and implementation of the central government budget shall be regulated by law. No provisions other than those pertaining to the budget shall be included in the Budget Act. *(Proposal of BDP: The budget shall be regulated in accordance with the development plans and in a manner that prevents the presence of secret allowances and funds.)*

(3) The Council of Ministers *(Proposal of AKP: Budget Committee)* shall submit the central government budget bill and the report indicating the national budgetary estimates to the Turkish Grand National Assembly at least before seventy-five days from the beginning of the fiscal year. It shall be debated and adopted by the Turkish Grand National Assembly before the beginning of the fiscal year. *(Proposal of AKP: If the budget law cannot be put into force until the beginning of the fiscal year, the provisions of the budget law of the previous fiscal year shall apply until the budget law is adopted.)*

Note: The establishment of the Budget Committee is assigned to the Commission of Rules of Procedure.

(4) Proposals that entail an increase in expenditure or a decrease in revenue cannot be made while the budget bills are debated in the Plenary.

(5) The appropriation granted by the central government budget shall indicate the limit of expenditure allowed. The Council of Ministers *(Proposal of CHP and MHP: by decrees having the force of law)* cannot amend the budget and cannot make decisions to the effect that the limit of

expenditure may be exceeded. No provision shall be included in the budget law to that effect. *(AKP does not agree with the last two sentences.)* In the amendment bills entailing an increase in appropriations under the budget of the current fiscal year, and bills and motions entailing financial burden in the budgets of the current or following fiscal year, the financial resources to provide the stated expenditure shall be indicated.

(6) The procedures and the principles regarding the negotiation and the adoption of the final accounts bill shall be regulated by the Rules of Procedure.

(Proposal of AKP: Central government final accounts bills shall be submitted to the Turkish Grand National Assembly by the Budget Committee within six months of the end of the relevant fiscal year. The final accounts bill shall be debated and determined with the new year budget bill. The principles and the procedures of the preparation and negotiation of the final accounts bill shall be regulated by law.)

(Proposal of CHP: Final accounts bills shall be submitted to the Turkish Grand National Assembly by the Council of Ministers within seven months of the end of the relevant fiscal year, unless a shorter period is prescribed by law. The Court of Accounts shall submit its statement of general conformity to the Turkish Grand National Assembly within seventy-five days of the submission of the final accounts bill to which it is related.

The final accounts bill shall be placed on the agenda of the Committee on Final Accounts after the approval of the budget bill of the new fiscal year. The president of this committee shall be appointed among the opposition parties.

The submission of the final accounts bills and the statement of general conformity to the Turkish Grand National Assembly shall not preclude the auditing and trial of the accounts for the relevant fiscal year that have not been concluded by the Court of Accounts and shall not mean that a final decision has been taken on these accounts.)

Note of BDP: *(Proposal of BDP) The share allocated to national defense cannot exceed the shares allocated to education, health, and social security provided that they are calculated separately.*

In the allocation of resources from the budget, equality between religions and sects and the principle of positive discrimination shall be taken into consideration.

Development and Regulation of Markets

Article 131: (1) The state shall take measures to ensure and promote the sound and orderly functioning of the markets for money, credit, capital, goods, and services and to protect the consumers; and it shall prevent the formation of monopolies and cartels in the markets that emerge through practice or by agreement.

(2) In favor of the national economy, the Council of Ministers *(Proposal of AKP: The President)* may be empowered by law to introduce additional financial impositions on foreign trade transactions, except taxes and similar impositions, or to lift them.

Note: The first and second paragraphs in the article proposal of CHP will be discussed later.

Supervision of Funds

Article 132: (1) No funds can be established unless their resources are determined by law.

Note: *According to AKP such a constitutional provision is unnecessary considering the fact that public expenditures can only be made through the budget law.*

Court of Accounts

Article 133: (1) For the purposes of ensuring the accountability with respect to acquisition and use of public resources, the Court of Accounts, on behalf of the Turkish Grand National Assembly, shall fulfill its duties of investigating, auditing, and reporting the revenues, expenditures, and assets of public administrations financed by the central government budget, social security institutions, local administrations, public institutions, and corporations whose capital is to more than 50 percent directly or indirectly owned by those mentioned and other public corporate bodies, and of taking final decisions prescribed by law.

(2) Funds cannot be excluded from the audit of the Court of Accounts.

(3) The Court of Accounts acts through audit and judgment chambers.

(4) The concerned parties may appeal to the judgment chambers against the decisions of the audit chambers within fifteen days after the notification. The decisions upon the appeal are final, and no applications for judicial review of such decisions shall be filed in administrative courts. In case of conflict between the decisions of the Council of State and the Court of Accounts regarding taxes or similar financial obligations and duties, the decision of Council of State shall prevail.

(5) The Turkish Grand National Assembly shall appoint the members of the Court of Accounts in accordance with the principle of merit from among teaching staff of universities working in the fields of law, economy, management, finance, or accounting for at least fifteen years, judges of the administrative judiciary, certified public accountants, and high-ranking executives, by secret ballot and with a two-thirds majority of the total

number of members. The candidate who gets the least votes in the first ballot is considered to have withdrawn. If there is not a large enough majority in the third ballot, the election shall be finalized by drawing lots among the candidates.

(6) One of the members of the judgment chambers of the Court of Accounts shall be a judge of the civil judiciary, and the judgment chambers of the Court of Accounts shall be established so that the judge members outnumber other members. The judge candidates shall be determined from among the members of their own profession who are qualified to be a member of the Court of Accounts, with each elector voting for only one of the candidates; the candidates to be nominated from the Court of Accounts, shall be elected by the General Assembly of the Court of Accounts, with each elector voting for only one of the candidates.

(7) The audit chambers of the Court of Accounts shall be established on the basis of the majority of the members being from the profession eligible to be elected to the Court of Accounts, provided that at least one of them works as a financial advisor and one of them works as teaching staff at a university in the fields of law, economy, management, finance, or accounting. The teaching staff candidates shall be determined by the teaching staff from among the members of their own profession who are qualified to be a member of the Court of Accounts, with each elector voting for only one of the candidates; the candidates from the profession eligible to be elected to the Court of Accounts and from financial advisors shall be determined by the General Assembly of the Court of Accounts and by the General Assembly of the financial advisors' profession chamber, with each elector voting for only one of the candidates. The high-ranking executives shall be elected from among four times the candidates nominated by the Council of Ministers for each vacant seat.

(Proposal of AKP for the fifth, sixth, and seventh paragraphs)

The Turkish Grand National Assembly Committee on Plan and Budget shall nominate four times the candidates for the membership of the Court of Accounts audit and judgment chambers from among teaching staff, judges, financial advisors, and members from the Court of Accounts whose qualifications shall be indicated by law, with a two-thirds majority of the total number of members. The Turkish Grand National Assembly Plenary shall determine the members of the audit and judgment chambers from among those candidates with a three-fifths majority of the total number of members.

(8) The establishment, functioning, auditing procedures, appeals to be made against the decisions of the audit chambers, qualifications, appointments, duties and powers, rights and obligations, and other

personnel matters of the members shall be regulated by law in accordance with the principle of tenure of judges.

Reasoning: 1) The issue of grading shall be detailed in the reasoning.

2) The chamber whose decision is appealed will not be represented by more than one member in the General Assembly.

(Proposal of CHP and BDP) Planning

Article 134: (1) *Economic, social, and cultural development shall be carried out according to a plan. The development plans shall aim at ensuring sustainable development, protecting the renewable nature of natural resources and assets, developing sectors and regions in harmony with each other, fair and equitable sharing of incomes and wealth, synchronizing the social and cultural policies with economic policies, and promoting the protection and development of the quality of life and environment, considering the next generations. It is the duty of the state to establish the organization that accomplishes these objectives*

Note: *AKP believes in the necessity of planning, but it does not consider this to be a constitutional issue.*

(Proposal of BDP) The Organization of Central Planning

Article 135: (1) *The Organization of Central Planning shall be established in order to ensure the achievement of planning principles indicated in the Constitution on a scientific basis. The planning organization shall be established as an autonomous institution, considering the principles of proficiency and gender equality.*

(2) *Development projects shall be prepared with the participation of local and regional administrations, civil society, and organizations of workers, women, and professions.*

(3) *The Fund of Central Development shall be established in order to eliminate regional inequalities.*

(4) *Principles regarding the establishment and the duties of the organization of central planning, organization of it on a regional scale, and the prevention of the amendments that result in the destruction of integrity of the development plans shall be regulated with a basic law.*

(Proposal of CHP and BDP) Economic, Social, and Environmental Council

Article 136: (1) *The council is the organ that is responsible for consultation on and compatibility between the fields of economic and social policy as well as environment. It delivers its opinion regarding motions and bills (Proposal of CHP: bills of decrees having the force of law), rules, regulations and* *development plans, and annual plans concerning these issues to the Turkish Grand National Assembly or the Council of Ministers upon their request or on its own initiative. The council shall submit its reports to the Turkish Grand National Assembly, the Council of Ministers, and the public.*

(2) *The council, as well as the participation of local administrations, employee and employer organizations and relevant ministries, workers' unions, professional organizations, environmental organizations, organizations of the youth and disabled persons, and the local and regional representatives in the council, shall be regulated by law.*

(3) *The establishment and operation procedures of the Council shall be regulated by law and in accordance with the principles of transparency and autonomy.*

(Proposal of CHP and BDP) The Principles of Public Finance

Article 137: (1) *(Proposal of CHP and BDP) The collection of public incomes and the public expenditures shall be based on the principles of efficiency, utility, and accountability. All sorts of incomes collected and expenditures made on behalf of the public shall be open to the knowledge of the public and the supervision of the Turkish Grand National Assembly.*

(2) *(Proposal of BDP) The management of public finance aims at ensuring financial discipline; the equivalence of incomes and expenditures in line with the objects indicated in plans and development program; increasing the standards of social welfare and life in accordance with the principle of actual equality; developing the conditions for sustainable economic development; and promoting employment.*

(3) *(Proposal of BDP) Economic and social development shall be planned democratically; the state shall take necessary measures in order to develop participation and supervision of the public in the management of the country's economy. The state shall implement a scientific and technological policy that ensures and promotes the planned development.*

(4) *(Proposal of BDP) The development of the country through industrial policies on the basis of science and new technologies that are not exploiting natural resources; welfare of the society; fair sharing of income and wealth; elimination of poverty; protection of the environment; allocation of incomes appropriate to the basic necessities of society, such as education, health, social security, housing, and alternative energy sources; the ensuring of social justice and equal opportunity; exclusion of inequality in wealth and incomes; and the implementation of an energy policy protecting ecological balance shall be taken into consideration while the economy is planned.*

(5) *(Proposal of BDP) Management of the economy shall be based on the elimination of inequalities between regions and developing the economic status of women and those who are discriminated against.*

Note: *Consultants will work.*

(Proposal of BDP) Turkish Statistical Institute

Article 138: (1) *The provision of independent, reliable, and scientific information for enabling the productive and fair operation of the economic and financial system shall be carried out by the Turkish Statistical Institute.*

The Institute shall be independent from the political authority, and it shall be autonomous in its operation and administrative structure.

The President of the Turkish Statistical Institute shall be elected by the Turkish Grand National Assembly with a qualified majority and appointed by the President of the Republic. The term of the President is nine years. A person cannot be elected as President twice.

(Proposal of BDP) Central Bank of the Republic of Turkey

Article 139: (1) *The Central Bank of the Republic of Turkey shall be structured autonomously. Independently from the political authority, it shall carry out the function of establishing and implementing the monetary policy on behalf of the public and in accordance with international rules.*

The President of the Central Bank of the Republic of Turkey cannot become a member of a political party and cannot carry out public activities that are incompatible with the dignity of the position. Provisions regarding the candidacy of the President of the Central Bank of the Republic of Turkey and the election, appointment, and powers and duties of him or her shall be regulated by law, in accordance with the principles of autonomy and merit.

(Proposal of BDP) Institutions Regulating the Financial System

Article 140: (1) *The law shall regulate the autonomy of the Competition Authority, the Stock Exchange, the Capital Markets Board, and the Energy Market Regulatory Board.*

(Proposal of BDP) Supervision

Article 141: (1) *The Turkish Grand National Assembly shall audit the budget through the final accounts law and the statements of general conformity that are prepared by the Court of Accounts.*

(Proposal of BDP) Energy Policies

Article 142: (1) *An energy policy that aims at production and utilization of clean, sustainable, affordable, convenient, and renewable energy sources shall be pursued. The protection of the natural and historical assets shall be taken into consideration while the energy production is planned.*

(Proposal of BDP) Cooperatives

Article 143: (1) *The state shall recognize the social functions of cooperatives and unions and shall ensure those to be established in accordance with the principles and criteria of international cooperatives and support their activities. It shall determine the budgets and financial aids that cooperatives and unions shall utilize and the conditions for using credit and technical aids. It shall provide the necessary conditions for the protection and development of handcrafts. It shall support the establishment of manufacturing, sale, processing, and service cooperatives as well as the creation of unions.*

(Proposal of BDP) Supervision of Decentralized Organs

Article 144: (1) *The supervision of the decentralized organs shall be conducted by the supervisory units of the Court of Accounts, which are established and organized on a regional scale in order to achieve the principles of financial transparency and accountability. Local administrations, associations established by local governments, corporations, and all institutions that receive money from the local government budget are subject to audit.*

(Proposal of BDP) Financial Supervision of the Security and Defense Sector and the Military and Security Forces

Article 145: (1) *All security expenditures shall be transparent and open to public supervision. The supervision of productivity, legitimacy, and efficiency that is required for the security and intelligence institutions to perform in accordance with the international standards shall be conducted by the Court of Accounts.*

(2) *All institutions that serve in the field of security shall prepare a strategic plan and a program of performance, determine targets and indicators of performance, and disclose those to the public. The properties, expenditures and budgets, and planning of public institutions that serve in the fields of security and defense cannot be left outside the scope of the supervision of the Court of Accounts due to confidentiality and security reasons.*

The balance between the principles of accountability and transparency and the subjects of intelligence that assuredly require confidentiality and the protection of military security systems shall be taken into consideration.

The democratic supervision of the security institutions by the Assembly and the Court of Accounts's authority to audit the security institutions and services, and affiliated companies and their expenditures, shall be regulated by law in accordance with international standards. The results of the supervision shall be submitted to the Bureau of the Turkish Grand National Assembly in order to be reviewed in the relevant commission.

(3) *The procedures regarding supervision shall be determined by the Court of Accounts and shall be open to the public. The supervision reports and results regarding the institutions of defense, security, and intelligence shall be shared with the public in accordance with international standards. Issues regarding the publication of the reports shall be regulated by the Court of Accounts by taking the opinion of the relevant security and intelligence institution into consideration.*

Note: *(BDP) This proposal shall be negotiated under the chapter on financial and economic provisions.*

FINAL PROVISIONS

Amending the Constitution

Article 146: (1) Amendment to the Constitution shall be proposed in written form by at least one-third of the total number of members of the Turkish Grand National Assembly. Bills to amend the Constitution shall be debated twice in the Plenary and be accepted by secret ballot.

(2) A constitutional amendment law adopted at least by a two-thirds majority of the total number of members of the Turkish Grand National Assembly shall be published in the Official Gazette by the President of the Republic *(Proposal of AKP: President)*, unless the Assembly decides to submit it to referendum with at least a two-thirds majority.

(3) The President of the Republic *(Proposal of AKP: President)* may either send the constitutional amendment law back or submit it to referendum in case the constitutional amendment law is approved by a three-fifths majority of the total number of members of the Turkish Grand National Assembly. If the Assembly readopts the law sent back without any amendment with at least a three-fifths majority of the total number of members, it may be submitted to referendum upon a decision taken with a three-fifths majority of the total number of members of the Assembly; otherwise, the law shall be considered as accepted. If the law is

accepted by the Assembly with at least a two-thirds majority of the total number of members without any amendment, the President of the Republic *(Proposal of AKP: President)* shall approve the law and publish it in the Official Gazette. In any event, it may submit the law to referendum with a decision taken with a two-thirds majority of the total number of members of the Assembly.

(4) Approval of the constitutional amendment law submitted to referendum shall require the affirmative vote of more than half of the valid votes cast. The constitutional amendment law accepted in the referendum shall enter into force with its publication in the Official Gazette.

(5) The Turkish Grand National Assembly shall decide which provisions shall be submitted to referendum together and which shall be submitted individually, in case the law is submitted to referendum. Apart from cases of amendment of the entire Constitution *(Proposal of CHP and MHP: amendments that alter the systemic integrity of the Constitution)*, the voters shall also be provided with the opportunity to vote separately on provisions not related to each other.

(6) Negotiation and approval of bills to amend the Constitution shall be subject to the provisions regarding negotiation and approval of laws, with the exception of the conditions laid down under this article.

Reasoning: MHP considers the expression "the amendment of the entire Constitution" unnecessary. Because in this case there will be no Constitution to be amended.

Preamble and Headings of Articles

Article 147: (1) *(Proposal of AKP and BDP: The preamble and the heading of the articles shall not be regarded as part of the text of the Constitution.) (Proposal of CHP and MHP: The preamble, which states the fundamental concepts and principles the Constitution is based upon, shall form an integral part of the Constitution.)*

(2) The headings of the articles shall not be regarded as part of the text of the Constitution.

Note: This article will be renegotiated when the preamble is debated.

PREAMBLE, GENERAL PROVISIONS, AND FUNDAMENTAL PRINCIPLES

Preamble

(Proposal of AKP)

We, the Turkish Nation, who reject all kinds of discrimination with the belief that everyone has universal rights and freedoms arising from human dignity;

acting with the desire to live together around our common history and values by respecting our ethnic and religious differences that are the source of our cultural wealth, we recognize and declare this Constitution, based on democracy, human rights, and the rule of law, as an expression of our sovereign will.

(Proposal of CHP)

***The Community of the Republic of Turkey**, who is the successor of the **ancient civilizations** that breaded the earth, built the civilization, lived in amity for thousands of years since **Çatalhöyük**; who met in Anatolia coming from the Balkans, the Caucasus, Central Asia, and Mesopotamia;*

*With the name of the "**Turkish Nation**" who shouted the "**Epic of Independency**" to the whole world in Çanakkale, in Sakarya, and in Afyon; who guided the oppressed nations; who, under **the leadership of the Mustafa Kemal Atatürk**, objected to all sorts of discrimination with an understanding of **equality** that takes into consideration differences and cultural pluralism, in line with the understanding of **national integrity**, as the source of the cultural richness;*

***Have created this Constitution with its common will**; which regulates the foundations and institutions of the **secular Republic** based on the understandings of human dignity, human rights, the rule of law, social justice, and pluralist democracy, and aims at protecting and maintaining our historical and cultural heritage and the environmental values;*

*As the generations who considered this beautiful country called "**Turkey**" as our **motherland**, without making any distinction on the grounds of origin, language, gender, or belief;*

*Under the flag with "**the star and crescent**";*

*As an expression to our commitment to the "**target of contemporary civilization**" **and** "**the ideal of lasting peace**" set forth by **Mustafa Kemal Atatürk**, the founder of our Republic and our sovereign will,*

*Accept this Constitution, together with our **elected representatives**, in the light of progressive science, in accordance with the requirements of the ever-changing world, with an understanding of **solidarity** and **voluntary unity** among citizens;*

For the freedom, prosperity, and happiness of future generations;

*Entrust and submit this Constitution to the future generations with the belief that they will protect it and they will exercise their **right to resistance** against everyone that has lost their legitimacy.*

(Proposal of MHP)

This Constitution, which was built on the principles of the eternal existence, independence, and indivisible integrity of the Turkish State, which was established by the Independence War under the leadership of Gazi Mustafa Kemal Atatürk; the Turkish Nation, which has been free from time immemorial and the Hallow Turkish Motherland and the principle of sovereignty, belongs to the nation without any restriction or condition;

Confirms the fundamental rights and freedoms of Turkish citizens based on human dignity and honor, the equality of everyone before the law and the fact that no one can be discriminated against for any reason, in accordance with the requirements of the rule of law and a democratic society.

This Constitution is interpreted and applied together with its essence and word.

This Constitution is entrusted to the future generations of the Turkish Nation, which contributes to the universal values of humanity and the values of culture and civilization it has built, with the sense of national unity and fraternity and faithfulness.

(Proposal of BDP)

We, the people of Turkey, composed of Turks, Kurds, Arabs, Circassians, Lazes, Armenians, and all other ethnic, religious, and linguistic identities;

We believe that all individuals and peoples have universal human rights and freedoms. We recognize that everyone is equal without discriminating on any grounds such as race, language, religion, sect, gender, sexual orientation, ethnic origin, and the like. All different identities, cultures, languages, and beliefs living in Turkey are under the protection of this Constitution. We see our differences as the cement of our social cohesion. We consider it the basic duty of the state to ensure justice in all its actions and to guarantee the rights and freedoms of people in every situation. As individuals and communities carrying the ideal of eternal peace, we refuse war and the use of force against the freedom of other peoples except for reasons of legitimate self-defense.

We are determined to establish a democratic order based on human dignity, the rule of law, freedom, and equality that considers the harmonious relationship with nature by protecting the balance of nature and aims at the well-being of everyone. We accept and confirm this Constitution as a document that proves our loyalty to these values and will to live together.

Characteristics of the Republic

Article 149: *(Proposal of AKP: The Republic of Turkey is a democratic, secular, and social state based on human rights.)*

(Proposal of CHP: The Republic of Turkey is a democratic, secular, and social state governed by the rule of law; embedded in an understanding of public peace, national solidarity, and justice; respecting human rights; loyal to the nationalism of Atatürk; and based on the fundamental tenets set forth in the preamble.)

Note: CHP is of the opinion that the first four articles of the Constitution shall be kept intact, as the four parties could not agree whether to keep Article 4. Hence, there should not be any amendments strengthening the principles in the first three articles.

(Proposal of MHP: The Republic of Turkey is a democratic, secular, and social state governed by the rule of law; embedded in an understanding of public peace, national solidarity, and justice; respecting human rights; loyal to the nationalism of Atatürk; and based on the fundamental tenets set forth in the preamble.)

Note: MHP opposes any amendments to the first three articles that represent the founding philosophy of the republic and Turkey, and to Article 4 which protects those three.

(Proposal of BDP: (1) *The Republic of Turkey is a democratic, secular, and social state based on human rights.*

(2) *The state recognizes the pluralism of ideologies, religions, beliefs, and lifestyles and remains neutral toward the pluralist structure of society. No ideology, religion, belief, or lifestyle can be prioritized by or taken under guardianship of the state.*

(3) *The administrative structure of the state is regulated on the basis of the decentralized system. The territorial integrity of the state is inviolable.)*

Integrity, Official Language, Flag, National Anthem, and Capital of the State

Article 150: (1) The Turkish state, with its territory and nation, is an indivisible entity.

(2) Its language is Turkish.

(3) Its flag, the form of which is prescribed by the relevant law, is composed of a white crescent and a star on a red background.

(4) Its national anthem is the "Independence March."

(5) Its capital is Ankara.

(Article Proposal of BDP)

Symbols of the State
Article –: (1) *The flag of the state, the form of which is prescribed by the relevant law, is composed of a white crescent and a star on a red background. Its national anthem is the "Independence March." Its capital is Ankara.*

The Official Language of the State
(1) *The official language of the state is Turkish. Every citizen has the right and duty to learn the official language.*

The other languages used by the society of Turkey may be used as the second official language with the decision of the regional assemblies.

(2) *Everyone has the right to use his or her mother tongue as well as the official language in his private life and in his relations with public authorities.*

(3) *The state is obliged to respect all languages that make up the common cultural heritage of the country, to protect languages, and to ensure the use and development of languages.*

Irrevocable Provisions
Article 151: *(Proposal of CHP: The provision of Article 1 regarding the form of the state being a Republic, the characteristics of the Republic in Article 2, and the provisions of Article 3 shall not be amended, nor shall their amendment be proposed.)*

(Proposal of MHP: The provision of Article 1 regarding the form of the state being a Republic, the characteristics of the Republic in Article 2, and the provisions of Article 3 shall not be amended, nor shall their amendment be proposed.)

Note: AKP does not propose any irrevocable provision in the Constitution.

Note: BDP rejects the inclusion of irrevocable provisions in the Constitution.

Fundamental Aims and Duties of the State
Article 152: (1) The fundamental aims and duties of the state are to protect human dignity; to guarantee fundamental rights and freedoms; to eliminate political, economic, and social barriers incompatible with the principle of social justice; to prepare the necessary conditions for the development of the individual material and spiritual existence; to ensure peace, prosperity, and security; and to protect the integrity of the *(Proposal of MHP: Turkish)* Nation, indivisibility of the country *(BDP considers these two notions unnecessary here. The integrity of the country is referred to in Article 2)*,

cultural pluralism *(MHP opposes the term "cultural pluralism" in virtue of the possibility that it could become a collective ethnic right)*, the Republic, and democracy.

Sovereignty

Article 153: (1) Sovereignty belongs to the Nation without any restriction or condition. *(Proposal of BDP: The society of Turkey is the only source of power.)*

(2) *(Proposal of AKP: The Turkish Nation shall exercise its sovereignty through its elected representatives and through referendum.)*

(Proposal of CHP and MHP: The Turkish Nation shall exercise its sovereignty through the authorized organs, as prescribed by the principles set forth in the Constitution.)

(Proposal of BDP: The people use their power through elections, popular voting, and the public initiative, which are regulated by law.)

(3) The exercise of sovereignty shall not be delegated by any means to any individual, group, or class.

(4) No person or organ shall exercise any state authority that does not emanate from the Constitution. *(Proposal of AKP: In virtue of the principle laid down under the first paragraph, we consider the other powers as derivative powers.)*

(5) *(Proposal of CHP and BDP: The provisions of international treaties that require membership in institutions with supranational powers are reserved.)*

Legislative Power

Article 154: (1) Legislative power is vested in the Turkish Grand National Assembly *(Proposal of BDP: in the Turkish Grand National Assembly and in the Regional Assemblies) (Proposal of CHP and MHP: on behalf of the Turkish Nation). (Proposal of CHP and MHP: This power shall not be delegated.)*

Executive Function *(Proposal of AKP and MHP: and Power)*

Article 155: (1) Executive function *(Proposal of AKP and MHP: and power)* shall be carried out by the President of the Republic *(Proposal of AKP: The President)* and the Council of Ministers *(Proposal of BDP: and the Presidency of Regions)* in conformity with the laws *(Proposal of BDP: in accordance with the principles of decentralization)*.

Judicial Function and Power *(Proposal of BDP: Judicial Function)*

Article 156: (1) Judicial power and function *(BDP only agrees with the term "function")* shall be exercised by independent courts *(Proposal of CHP and MHP: on behalf of the Turkish Nation.)*

(Proposal of BDP) Measures for Determination and Compensation of War Damages

Article 158: (1) *A parliamentary commission shall be established for the determination of war damages, for the return and economic support of displaced persons, for the rehabilitation of destroyed habitats and mined agricultural lands, and for reparation and compensation of damages.*

(2) *The operation, establishment, participation of civil society, compensation and restitution methods, and the funds to be allocated from the budget are regulated by law.*

(Proposal of BDP) The Provision Regarding Minority Foundations, Their Property Rights, and the Restitution of Property

Article 159: (1) *The state is under the obligation to make and implement necessary legal regulations regarding the return of immovable properties of minority foundations registered in the name of the Treasury and Foundations General Directorate and the retroactive reimbursement and compensation for goods sold or merged with third parties, and to regulate juridical personalities and their property rights in accordance with international law.*

(Proposal of BDP) Special Measures for Romani People

Article 160: (1) *Increasing the living standards of Romani citizens, erasing the traces of discrimination in the social, cultural, and economic spheres, and the measures to be taken regarding housing, education, health, and employment in accordance with Romani culture and lifestyle are determined by law.*

THE EXECUTIVE POWER

The President of the Republic (AKP: The President)

Qualifications and Impartiality

Article 161: (1) The President of the Republic shall be elected by *(Proposal of CHP and MHP: The Turkish Grand National Assembly) (Proposal of BDP: the public)* from among *(Proposal of CHP and BDP: the citizens of the Republic of Turkey) (Proposal of MHP: Turkish citizens)* who are over forty years of age, eligible to be deputies *(Proposal of CHP and MHP: and have completed higher education; BDP does not require the higher education criterion)* for one *(Proposal of CHP and MHP: seven-year) (Proposal of BDP: five-year)* term. *(Proposal of BDP: The President of the Republic's term of office shall be five years. A person may be elected as President of the Republic for two terms at most. No one can be elected as President of the Republic twice in a row.)*

(2) *(Proposal of CHP and MHP) Nomination of a candidate for the presidency from among the members of the Turkish Grand National Assembly or from outside of the Assembly shall require a written proposal of ten percent of the total number of members of the Turkish Grand National Assembly. (Proposal of MHP: may be nominated as a joint candidate by the political parties that received more than ten percent of the valid votes in the latest parliamentary election and upon application of two percent of the number of registered voters in the latest parliamentary District Election.) (Proposal of BDP: The President of the Republic shall be nominated by the written proposal of ten deputies or at least one hundred thousand voters.)*

(3) *(Proposal of CHP and BDP: The President shall be impartial in carrying out all his or her duties and powers.)* The President of the Republic's relationship with his or her party shall be severed and his or her membership in the Turkish Grand National Assembly shall cease.

(4) *(Proposal of BDP: The Prime Minister and the members of the Council of Ministers, who are candidates for the Presidency of the Republic, shall resign and cannot return to the office if they are not elected. Other public duties that fall within the scope of this law shall be determined by law.)*

(5) *(Proposal of BDP: The duties and powers of the Presidency of the Republic shall be determined by enumeration in the Constitution.)*

(6) *(Proposal of BDP: Candidates shall declare their property prior to the election and the declarations shall be published in the Official Gazette. The donations and grants received by the candidates are supervised by the Electoral Council and the Court of Accounts according to the principles of transparency and honesty.)*

(7) *(Proposal of BDP: Deputies and ministers about whom a summary of proceedings regarding crimes that fall outside of the scope of immunity exists cannot be a candidate before these cases are concluded.)*

(8) *(Proposal of BDP: The other issues regarding the candidacy and election of the President of the Republic shall be regulated by law.)*

(Proposal of AKP) Eligibility of the Presidency and the Candidacy

(1) *The President shall be elected by the public from among the citizens over forty years of age who are eligible to be a deputy and have completed higher education.*

(2) *The President's term of office shall be five years. A person may be elected as the President for two terms at most.*

(3) *The President may be nominated by political parties that received at least five percent of valid votes in the latest parliamentary election or by at least one hundred thousand voters.*

(4) The President-elect's membership in the Turkish Grand National Assembly shall cease.

Election

Article 162: (1) *(Proposal of CHP and MHP) The presidential election is initiated thirty days before the end of the President of the Republic's term of office, or ten days after the presidential office is vacant, and the election is finalized within twenty days of the date of election. In the first ten days of this period, the candidates are announced to the Bureau of the Turkish Grand National Assembly. In the remaining twenty days the election is completed.*

(Proposal of BDP) The election of the President of the Republic shall be completed within sixty days prior to the expiry of the term of office of the President of the Republic or within sixty days following the vacancy of the office for any reason.

(Proposal of BDP) The election of the Presidency shall be made in accordance with the principles of transparency, honesty, equality, and fair competition under the administration and supervision of the Electoral Council.

(2) *(Proposal of CHP) The President of the Republic shall be elected by a two-thirds majority of the total number of members of the Turkish Grand National Assembly. If no candidate can obtain this majority after three ballots within forty-eight hours, the Presidential Election Board shall be formed immediately. The number of members of the board is twice the number of members of the Turkish Grand National Assembly. The Presidential Election Board is composed of members of the Turkish Grand National Assembly and members of the provincial assembly of each province. Each province is represented in the board with its population ratio and at least one representative. The procedures and principles regarding the establishment and the election of the Presidential Election Board shall be indicated by law. The Presidential Election Board elects the President of the Republic by the absolute majority of the total number of members from among the two candidates with the highest number of votes in the last vote held in the Turkish Grand National Assembly.*

(Proposal of MHP) If a majority of two-thirds of the total number of members is not obtained in the first two ballots that are held within a minimum of two days, a third vote shall be held; the candidate who obtains the absolute majority of the total number of members in the third ballot shall be elected as the President of the Republic. If the absolute majority of the total number of members is not obtained in this ballot, the fourth ballot shall be held between the two candidates who have received the majority of votes in the third ballot. If the President of the Republic cannot be elected with the absolute majority of the

total number of members in this ballot either, elections to the Turkish Grand National Assembly shall be renewed immediately.

(Proposal of BDP) In the election to be held by a general vote, the candidate who receives the absolute majority of the valid votes is elected as the President of the Republic. In case this majority cannot be achieved in the first ballot, a second ballot shall be held on the next second Sunday following this vote. The two candidates with the highest number of votes shall participate in this ballot and the candidate who receives the majority of the valid votes is elected as the President of the Republic.

(3) The term of office of the incumbent President of the Republic shall continue until the President-elect takes office.

(4) *(Proposal of BDP) Presidential elections shall not be held ninety days before and after general elections. In this case, the term of office of the incumbent President shall extend automatically for a sufficient period of time.*

(5) *(Proposal of BDP) In the event of death of any candidate or if an obstruction occurs regarding him or her fulfilling his or her duty as the President of the Republic, the election process shall restart under the conditions determined by law.*

(Article Proposal of AKP) (1) In presidential elections conducted based on universal suffrage, the candidate who receives the absolute majority of the valid votes shall be elected as the President. In case this majority cannot be obtained in the first ballot, a second ballot shall be held on the next second Sunday following this vote. The two candidates with the highest number of votes shall participate in this ballot and the candidate who receives the majority of the valid votes is elected as the President.

(2) *In the event that one of the candidates eligible for the second ballot is unable to participate in the election for any reason, the second ballot shall be conducted by substituting the vacant candidacy in conformity with the ranking in the first ballot. If only one candidate remains for the second ballot, this ballot shall be conducted as a referendum. If the candidate receives the majority of the valid votes, he or she shall be elected as the President.*

Duties and Powers

Article 163: (1) The President of the Republic is the head of the state. In this capacity, he or she shall represent the Republic of Turkey and the unity of *(Proposal of CHP: the nation) (Proposal of MHP: the Turkish Nation) (Proposal of BDP: the citizens). (Proposal of CHP: The President of the Republic shall ensure the implementation of the Constitution, and the orderly and harmonious functioning of the organs of the state.)*

(2) The President of the Republic shall exercise the following powers by himself or herself:

a) To deliver, if he or she deems it necessary, the opening speech of the Turkish Grand National Assembly on the first day of the legislative year,
b) *(Proposal of CHP and BDP) To preside over the Council of Ministers whenever he or she deems it necessary, (Proposal of BDP: The President of the Republic shall not have a right to vote,)*
c) To promulgate laws *(Proposal of CHP and MHP: and decrees having the force of law)*,
ç) To send laws back to the Turkish Grand National Assembly to be reconsidered *(Proposal of CHP and MHP: and decrees having the force of law to the Council of Ministers)*,
d) To appeal to the Constitutional Court for the annulment *(Proposal of MHP: of laws, decrees having the force of law, and the Rules of Procedure of the Turkish Grand National Assembly on the grounds that they are unconstitutional in form or in content)*,
e) To decide to renew elections for the Turkish Grand National Assembly and appoint the Council of Ministers temporarily,
f) To appoint the Prime Minister and to accept his or her resignation. *(Proposal of BDP: The candidate who is nominated by the Assembly as Prime Minister in accordance with the provisions of the Constitution regulating the censure shall be appointed by the President of the Republic.)*
Note: This proposal shall be evaluated within the scope of censure and the constructive vote of no-confidence.
g) *(Proposal of CHP and MHP) To remit or commute sentences imposed on certain individuals on grounds of chronic illness, disability, or old age.*

(Proposal of BDP)

The Power of Amnesty of the President of the Republic
(1) *The President of the Republic may remit or commute sentences imposed on certain individuals.*

(2) *Crimes against humanity and cases of ministers handled in the Supreme Court are outside the scope of this power.*

(3) *The President of the Republic shall exercise his or her power of amnesty with the counter-signature of the Minister of Justice.*

h) To accredit representatives of the Turkish state to foreign states and to receive the representatives of foreign states appointed to the Republic of Turkey.

Note: This paragraph proposal shall be removed in case it is enumerated under the powers subject to counter-signature.

ı) *(Proposal of MHP) To appoint and dismiss ministers on the proposal of the Prime Minister,*
i) *(Proposal of MHP) To ratify and promulgate international treaties,*
j) *(Proposal of MHP) To decide on the use of the Turkish Armed Forces,*
k) *(Proposal of MHP) To represent the Office of Commander-in-Chief of the Turkish Armed Forces on behalf of the Turkish Grand National Assembly.*

(Article Proposal of AKP)

Article –: (1) *The President is the Head of State. The executive power shall be vested in the President.*

(2) *The President in his or her capacity as the Head of State shall represent the Republic of Turkey and the unity of the Turkish Nation, and he or she shall ensure the implementation of the Constitution and the orderly and harmonious functioning of the organs of the state.*

(3) *The President executes general politics.*

(4) *The duties and powers of the President are as follows:*

a) *To deliver, if he or she deems it necessary, the opening speech of the Turkish Grand National Assembly on the first day of the legislative year,*
b) *To annually give a message to the Assembly regarding domestic and foreign policies of the country,*
c) *To approve the laws,*
ç) *To veto the laws,*
d) *To appeal to the Constitutional Court for the annulment of laws on the grounds that they are unconstitutional,*
e) *To appoint and dismiss the ministers,*
f) *To issue presidential decrees,*
g) *To accredit representatives of the Turkish state to foreign states and to receive the representatives of foreign states appointed to the Republic of Turkey,*
ğ) *To adopt and promulgate international treaties,*
h) *To represent the Office of the Commander-in-Chief of the Turkish Armed Forces,*

1) *To decide on the use of the Turkish Armed Forces,*
i) *To appoint and dismiss high-ranking executives,*
j) *To request from the Assembly to declare a state of emergency,*
k) *To remit or commute sentences imposed on certain individuals, on grounds of chronic illness, disability, or old age.*

(5) *The President of the Republic shall also exercise powers of election and appointment and perform other duties conferred on him or her by the Constitution.*

Presidential Decree

Article –: (1) *The President of the Republic may issue presidential decrees on matters he or she deems necessary for the execution of general politics. In order for a presidential decree to be issued on a matter, there shall be no applicable explicit provisions regulating that matter in the laws. The rights and freedoms of individuals and the political rights and freedoms cannot be regulated by a decree. In case there are different provisions on the same subject in the laws and decrees, the provisions of the laws shall apply.*

(2) *The President may issue regulations in order to ensure the implementation of the laws and to provide that they are not contrary to them.*

(3) *Decrees and regulations shall enter into force on the day of publication in the Official Gazette, unless a date after the publication is determined.*

Article Note: (CHP) AKP's proposal for the presidential system was not negotiated as it envisages a different system.

Accountability

Article 164: (1) The President of the Republic is not responsible for the acts that he or she performs alone. The Prime Minister and the ministers concerned shall be accountable for the acts and the decisions of the President of the Republic that are signed by the Prime Minister and the ministers.

(2) The President is subject to the provisions on legislative nonaccountability and immunity.

(3) The President of the Republic shall be referred to the Supreme Court solely on the basis of high treason *(Proposal of BDP: and the crime of deliberate violation of the Constitution and crimes against humanity)* and upon a motion of at least one-third of the total number of members of the Turkish Grand National Assembly and with a decision of at least a *(Proposal of CHP and BDP: three-fourths) (Proposal of MHP: two-thirds)* majority of the total number of

members. The President's duty shall be terminated upon the decision to refer him or her to the Supreme Court. *(Proposal of CHP and BDP: The acts to be considered as high treason shall be indicated by law.)*

(Proposal of BDP) The Circumstances Terminating the Duty
Article –: (1) *The President's term of office shall be terminated when he or she resigns, is referred to the Supreme Court, cannot perform his or her duty due to a permanent mental or physical illness, or dies. The Constitutional Court decides the state of being absolutely unable to perform the duties due to physical or mental illness upon application of the government.*

(Article Proposal of AKP) Criminal Liability of the President
Article –: (1) *At least a two-thirds majority of the total number of members of the Turkish Grand National Assembly may table a motion requesting that the President is to be investigated on allegations of a crime. The Turkish Grand National Assembly shall debate the motion in one month at the latest and decide on it by secret ballot.*

(2) *If an investigation is decided to be launched, it shall be conducted by a committee of fifteen members, chosen by lot, from each political party in the Assembly, separately from among three times the candidates nominated for each seat reserved to party groups in proportion to their strength. The committee shall submit its report on the conclusion of the investigation to the Assembly within two months. If the investigation is not completed within the time allotted, the committee shall be granted a further and final period of two months. It is mandatory to submit the report to the Office of the Speaker within this period.*

(3) *The report shall be distributed within ten days from the date of its submission to the Office of the Speaker, it shall be debated in the Plenary within ten days following its distribution, and, if it is deemed necessary, it shall be decided to refer the concerned person to the Supreme Court. The decision to refer the report to the Supreme Court shall be taken with a two-thirds majority of the total number of members and by secret ballot. The duty of the President who is convicted by the Supreme Court for a crime that prevents him or her from being elected shall be terminated.*

Article Note: (CHP) AKP's proposal for the presidential system was not negotiated as it envisages a different system.

Acting for the President
Article 165: (1) *(Proposal of CHP and BDP) In the event of a temporary absence of the President of the Republic, until the President of the Republic resumes his*

or her functions, and in the event that the Presidency falls vacant, until the election of a new President of the Republic the Speaker of the Turkish Grand National Assembly shall serve as Acting President of the Republic and exercise the powers of the President of the Republic.

(Proposal of MHP) In the events of a temporary absence of the President of the Republic and that the Presidency falls vacant, the Speaker of the Turkish Grand National Assembly shall serve as Acting President of the Republic.

(Article Proposal of AKP) Deputy of the President and Acting for the President

Article –: (1) *The person who is appointed as the deputy presidential candidate in the ballot of the President shall be elected as the Deputy President at the time that the President is elected. In order to be nominated as Deputy President, it is required to have the eligibility to be elected as a deputy.*

(2) *In case the presidential office becomes vacant for any reason, the Deputy President shall act as and exercise the powers of the President until the election. In the event that the Office of the Deputy President becomes vacant for any reason, the person who will act in this period until the election shall be determined by the Turkish Grand National Assembly from among three candidates to be nominated by the President.*

(3) *In the event that the President leaves the office temporarily due to reasons such as illness and going abroad, the Deputy President shall act as and exercise the powers of the President until he or she returns to duty.*

(4) *The Deputy President shall be subject to the same legal status as deputies and shall enjoy the provisions of deputies concerning nonaccountability and immunity.*

Article Note: (CHP) AKP's proposal for the presidential system was not negotiated as it envisages a different system.

The Council of Ministers

Article 166: (1) The Council of Ministers shall consist of the Prime Minister and the ministers.

(2) The Prime Minister shall be appointed by the President of the Republic from among the members of the Turkish Grand National Assembly.

(3) The ministers shall be appointed by the President of the Republic *(Proposal of BDP: based on the principles of gender equality and merit)* upon the proposal of the Prime Minister from among the members of the Turkish Grand National Assembly *(Proposal of CHP and MHP: from among those*

eligible to be elected as deputies). (Proposal of CHP and MHP: They can be dismissed by the President of the Republic upon the proposal of the Prime Minister when deemed necessary.)

(4) *(Proposal of CHP and MHP) The members of the Council of Ministers who are not deputies shall take oath before the Plenary of the Assembly. (Proposal of MHP: and they shall be subject to the same status as the deputies.) (Proposal of CHP: and as long as they hold this status, they enjoy the rights of deputies, including legislative immunity, and are subject to responsibilities of deputies.)*

(5) A minister who is brought before the Supreme Court by decision of the Turkish Grand National Assembly shall lose his or her ministerial status. In case the Prime Minister is brought before the Supreme Court, the government shall be considered to have resigned.

(6) If a ministerial position becomes vacant for any reason, a new appointment shall be made within ten days at the latest.

(7) A minister may temporarily act for another if a ministerial position becomes vacant or if the minister is on leave or excused. However, a minister shall not act for more than one minister.

(8) The formation, abolition, functions, powers, and responsibilities of the ministries shall be regulated by law.

(Article Proposal of AKP) Ministers

Article –: (1) *The ministers shall be appointed and removed from office by the President. The ministers shall be eligible to be a deputy. The current members of the Turkish Grand National Assembly cannot be appointed as ministers even if their status is terminated.*

(2) *Each minister shall be responsible to the President.*

(3) *Ministers shall be subject to the same legal status as deputies and enjoy the provisions of deputies concerning nonaccountability and immunity.*

(4) *A minister may temporarily act for another if a ministerial position becomes vacant or if the minister is on leave or excused.*

(5) *The formation, abolition, functions and powers, and the organizational structure of the ministries shall be regulated by presidential decree.*

Article Note: (CHP) AKP's proposal for the presidential system was not negotiated as it envisages a different system.

Vote of Confidence

Article 167: (1) The complete list of the Council of Ministers shall be submitted to the Turkish Grand National Assembly. If the Turkish Grand National Assembly is in recess, it shall be summoned.

(2) The program of the Council of Ministers shall be read out by the Prime Minister or by one of the ministers before the Turkish Grand National Assembly within one week, at the latest, of the formation of the Council of Ministers, and a vote of confidence shall be held. Debate on the vote of confidence shall begin after two complete days elapse from the date the program is read out, and the vote shall be held after one complete day elapses from the end of the debate.

(3) When the number of those having voted for confidence is greater than the number of those having voted for no-confidence, the Council of Ministers shall be considered as having received the vote of confidence.

Article Note: *As AKP proposes a presidential system, it does not propose an article regarding the "Vote of Confidence."*

Vote of Confidence While in Office

Article 168: (1) If the Prime Minister deems it necessary, he or she may ask for a vote of confidence in the Turkish Grand National Assembly after discussing the matter in the Council of Ministers.

(2) The request for a vote of confidence shall not be debated before one complete day elapses from the time of its submission to the Turkish Grand National Assembly and shall not be put to a vote until one complete day elapses after the debate.

(3) A request for a vote of confidence shall be rejected only by the absolute majority of the total number of members.

Article Note: *As AKP proposes a presidential system, it does not propose an article regarding "Vote of Confidence While in Office."*

Functions and Political Responsibilities

Article 169: (1) The Prime Minister shall ensure cooperation among the ministries and supervise the implementation of the government's general policy, the ministers' fulfillment of their duties in accordance with the Constitution and laws, and take necessary corrective measures. The Council of Ministers has collective responsibility for the implementation of the government's general policy.

(2) Each minister shall be responsible to the Prime Minister for the conduct of affairs under his or her jurisdiction and for the acts and activities of his or her subordinates.

Article Note: *As AKP proposes a presidential system, it does not propose an article regarding "Functions and Political Responsibilities."*

Provisional Council of Ministers During Elections

Article 170: (1) When elections are renewed by the President of the Republic in accordance with the Constitution, the current Council of Ministers shall resign, and the President of the Republic shall appoint a Prime Minister to establish a provisional Council of Ministers.

(2) The members of the Provisional Council of Ministers shall be chosen from the political party groups in proportion to their representation in the parliament.

(3) The Provisional Council of Ministers shall be established within five days of the date of the announcement of the renewal decision in the Official Gazette.

(4) The vote of confidence does not apply to the Provisional Council of Ministers.

Article Note: *As AKP proposes a presidential system, it does not propose an article regarding "Provisional Council of Ministers During Elections."*

Renewal of Elections to the Turkish Grand National Assembly by the President of the Republic

Article 171: (1) When the Council of Ministers falls by a vote of no-confidence, if a new Council of Ministers cannot be formed within forty-five days or fails to receive a vote of confidence, the President of the Republic, in consultation with the Speaker of the Turkish Grand National Assembly, may decide to renew elections. If a new Council of Ministers cannot be formed within forty-five days of the resignation of the Prime Minister, or within forty-five days of elections to the Bureau of the Speaker of the newly elected Turkish Grand National Assembly, the President of the Republic may likewise, in consultation with the Speaker of the Turkish Grand National Assembly, decide to renew elections.

(2) The decision on the renewal of elections shall be published in the Official Gazette and the election shall be held.

(Article Proposal of AKP) The Turkish Grand National Assembly and the Decision of the President Regarding the Renewal of Elections

(1) *The Turkish Grand National Assembly or the President, alone, may decide to renew the elections of both bodies together. If the Assembly decides to renew the elections during the second term of the President, the President may once again be a candidate.*

(2) *The powers of the Assembly and the President whose elections are decided to be renewed together shall continue until election of these organs.*

(3) *The term of office of the Assembly and the President elected in this manner shall also be five years.*

Article Note: (CHP) AKP's proposal for the presidential system was not negotiated as it envisages a different system.

(Article Proposal of MHP) National Security Council

Article 172: (1) *The National Security Council shall be composed of the Prime Minister; deputy prime ministers; ministers of Justice, National Defense, Internal Affairs, and Foreign Affairs; the Chief of the General Staff; and the commanders of the Land, Naval and Air Forces under the chairmanship of the President of the Republic.*

(2) *Depending on the particulars of the agenda, ministers and other persons concerned may be invited to meetings of the Council.*

(3) *The National Security Council submits its views to the Council of Ministers to assist in the decision-making and coordination of national security.*

(4) *The agenda of the National Security Council shall be drawn up by the Prime Minister taking into account the proposals of the Chief of the General Staff.*

Index

Abdülhamit (sultan), 88–89, 93, 116
Adalet Partisi. *See* Justice Party
Adalet ve Kalkınma Partisi. *See* Justice and Development Party
Akan, Murat, 50
AKP. *See* Justice and Development Party
Akser, Murat, 124
Akyıldız, Ali, 279
Albayrak, Berat, 124–125
Albert, Richard, 249–250, 263
All-Party Accord Commission, 77
Altaylı, Fatih, 138–139
amendment culture, 254–255
amendment rate, 254–256
amendment-making rules, 249–250, 251–252, 253–254, 255, 264
  1921, 1924 Constitutions and, 256, 257, 258–259, 261–267
  under 1961 Constitution, 257–259, 261
  under 1982 Constitution, 251, 258–259, 260, 261–262, 269, 270–273, 280
  1987 amendment of, 259, 260, 261–263, 265, 266–267, 269, 270–273, 274–276, 280–281
  2007 proposal for, AKP and, 274
  AUK, 249, 250–251, 267, 272, 273–281
  AUK, 1982 rules and, 251, 269, 270–273, 280
  AUK, AKP on, 269–272, 274–279
  AUK, BDP on, 269, 270, 273, 274–275
  AUK, CHP on, 269, 270, 272, 274–275, 276–278, 279
  AUK, MHP on, 269, 270, 272–273, 274, 276–277, 278–279
  constituent power and, 268–269
  flexibility, rigidity, and, 249, 251–256, 269, 270, 272–273, 276, 277, 280–281
  in Turkish constitutional history, 251, 256–259, 261–267
amendments, referendums on, 259–263, 265, 266–267
ANAP. *See* Motherland Party
Anavatan Partisi. *See* Motherland Party
Anayasa Mahkemesi. *See* Constitutional Court, Turkish
Anayasa Uzlaşma Komisyonu (Constitutional Conciliation Commission) (AUK). *See specific topics*
Anti-Terror Law, 125–126
AP. *See* Justice Party *(Adalet Partisi)*
Arato, Andrew, 25–26, 27–28, 104–106, 171
  on constitution making, post-sovereign, 66–67
  on constitutional referendums, 265, 266
  Lefort and, 65–66, 67, 83
Arsel, Ilhan, 70
Arslan, Zühtü, 156
Aşık, Ozan, 127–128
Assembly, National *(Meclis-i Mebusan)* (MM), 87–91
Association for the Defense of National Rights *(Müdafaa-i Hukuk Cemiyeti)*, 34
Ata, Ayla Akat, 191, 197–198
Atar, Yavuz, 165, 167–168, 178–179, 203
  on amendment-making rules, 275, 278–279
  on presidential system, 173–174
Atatürk. *See* Kemal, Mustafa
AUK (Constitutional Conciliation Commission) *(Anayasa Uzlaşma Komisyonu)*. *See specific topics*

authoritarianism, Turkish, 59–61, 71, 104, 219
1924 Constitution and, 71–72, 80, 83, 85–86
1961 Constitution and, 75–76, 85–86, 99, 102, 160–161
1982 Constitution and, 61, 76–77, 84–85, 102–103, 151, 188–189
of 2017 amendments, 111–112, 149, 181–182, 263
AKP, 13, 60, 67, 104, 110–111, 115, 116, 117, 188, 190, 217, 266, 281
embodiment claim and, 62–63, 67, 77–78, 80, 83
hegemonic-totalitarian logic of, 62–63, 71–72, 77–78, 81–82, 83
phases of, 84–86, 87–90, 93, 95–96, 97, 99, 101, 102, 105, 110–111, 115–117
autocratic legalism, 266
AYM. *See* Constitutional Court, Turkish

Bagehot, Walter, 155
Bakıner, Onur, 60
Bal, Faruk, 41, 42, 168, 178, 199–200, 204–205, 214–215
on amendment-making rules, 276–277, 278–279
on consultants, 211–212, 278–279
on coup mentality, 218
on parliamentarianism, presidentialism, 145, 173–175
Balyoz (Sledgehammer) investigation, 125–126
Barın, Taylan, 192
Barış ve Demokrasi Partisi. *See* Peace and Democracy Party
Batum, Süheyl, 173–174, 203–204, 211, 278
Bayar, Yeşim, 80
Baybars-Hawks, Banu, 124
BDP. *See* Peace and Democracy Party
Belge, Ceren, 223
Beştaş, Meral Danış, 167–168, 178, 204, 233
Bickel, Alexander, 221
Blount, Justin, 23–24, 29
body, constitution-making, 24–28
Bölükbaşı, Osman, 97
by law clauses, 188, 212–214, 215–216

Cairo Declaration on Human Rights in Islam (1943), 199
Çalı, Başak, 190–191
censorship, 128–129, 139–141
center-periphery narrative, 59–63, 81, 83
Charter of Alliance *(Sened-i İttifak)* (1808), 33
Cheibub, José, 110
Chernykh, Svitlana, 185–186
CHP. *See* Republican People's Party
Çiçek, Cemil, 38–39, 55, 133–134, 137, 267
drafting, AUK, and, 129, 195–197, 210
on media coverage, AUK, 130–131, 132, 141
citizenship, Turkish, 50–51, 53–54, 106
civilian authorship, 61–62, 83
coalition building, 54–55, 180–181
competitive politics, 95–97, 100–101, 103–104
Congleton, Roger, 251
constituent assembly, 21, 25–28, 29–31
AUK and, 146, 195–196, 267–269
in Turkish constitutional history, 35, 73, 76, 91–92, 93–94, 98, 102, 156
constitutional borrowing, 184–185, 186–187, 189–190, 192
from Convention, 186, 200–202, 204–205, 206–209, 216
from ECtHR, 177, 186, 187–188, 204–205, 208–209
of fundamental rights and freedoms, 184, 187–188, 192–193, 200
horizontal, 184–185, 187–188, 195–200, 204–206, 207–208, 209, 216
of human dignity, 187–188, 194, 197–199, 216
non-borrowing and, 184–185, 201–202, 203–204, 205–206, 216
vertical, 184–185, 187–188, 200–209, 216
Constitutional Conciliation Commission *(Anayasa Uzlaşma Komisyonu)* (AUK). *See specific topics*
Constitutional Court, Turkish *(Anayasa Mahkemesi)* (AYM), 36, 60, 103–104, 153–154, 161–162
under 1961 Constitution, 99–100, 156, 158–159, 228, 257, 258
under 1982 Constitution, 157, 158–159, 228, 246, 258
2017 amendments and, 114, 115, 248
AKP and, 37–38, 78, 104–105, 108–109, 228–230, 263
AUK on, 173, 175–176, 177–179, 220, 241–247
as countermajoritarian institution, 218–219, 220, 223, 228–230, 231–232
on fundamental rights and freedoms, 190–191, 215, 216
on law, rule of, 157–158, 159–161
parties shut down by, 150, 160–161, 202, 219, 243
statist approach of, 156, 159–161

constitutional history, Turkish, 33–34, 62–63, 84–86, 115–117, 147–148
amendment-making rules in, 251, 256–259, 261–267
authoritarian phases and, 84–86, 87–90, 93, 95–96, 97, 99, 101, 102, 105, 110–111, 115–117
constituent assembly in, 35, 73, 76, 91–92, 93–94, 98, 102, 156
constitutional borrowing in, 200
democratic phases and, 80, 84–85, 86, 87–90, 91–92, 96–97, 101, 105–106, 116–117
Ottoman, 33–34
public participation absent in, 82–83
republican era, 34–37
constitutional non-borrowing, 184–185, 201–202, 203–204, 205–206, 216
constitutional stickiness, 191, 274–275
consultants, 211–212, 215–216, 278–279
Convention. *See* European Convention on Human Rights
conventions, 25–26
Council of Higher Education *(Yükseköğretim Kurulu)* (YÖK), 218–219, 223, 225–227, 231, 247
under 1982 Constitution, 225–226, 227, 234–235, 239–240
AUK on reforming, 233–236, 246–247
MGK in, 226, 227
countermajoritarian institutions, 75, 218–223, 230–232, 247–248
before 2011, 224–232
AYM as, 218–219, 220, 223, 228–230, 231–232
HSYK as, 218–219, 220, 223, 227–228, 231, 236–241, 246–247
MGK as, 218–219, 220, 223, 224–225, 230–231, 232–233
military and, 218–220, 223, 224–225, 248
YÖK as, 218–219, 223, 225–227, 231, 247
coups, 218. *See also* 2016 military coup attempt
1960, 35, 37, 73, 75, 83, 97–100, 116, 122–123, 154, 265
1971, 75–76, 101, 116, 154, 161–162
1980, 35, 37, 61, 76, 83, 101–103, 104–105, 116, 123, 150–151, 225–226, 235, 258, 265
courts, special security, 161–162, 176
Cumhuriyet Halk Partisi. *See* Republican People's Party

deadline, AUK, 55, 56
decision costs, 212
Demirkent, Dinçer, 68–71
democracy, 24, 65–67, 79
1961,1982 Constitutions and, 152–153, 154–155, 157
AKP and, 77, 82–83, 170
in AUK, contested, 163, 164, 169–171, 180
as empty signifier, 152, 163, 180
indeterminacy of, 153–154
Lefort on, 62–63, 64–65
media in, 119
state action justified through, 154–155
Turkish, phases of, 80, 84–85, 86, 87–90, 91–92, 96–97, 101, 105–106, 116–117
Democratic Party, Turkish *(Demokrat Parti)* (DP), 62–63, 72, 73, 77–78
after 1960 coup, 98–99, 100
rule of, 96–98, 104, 116, 122
Demokrat Parti. *See* Democratic Party, Turkish
divided societies
Lerner on, 52–53, 54, 168, 179, 180, 195, 198, 209–210
Turkey as, 105, 168, 179–180, 198
Dixon, Rosalind, 212, 252
Diyanet *(Diyanet İşleri Başkanlığı)*. *See* Presidency of Religious Affairs
Doğan Group, 124, 126, 140–141
DP. *See* Democratic Party, Turkish
drafting, 195, 214–216
of 1921 and 1924 Constitutions, 34
AUK, 21, 43–45, 47–48, 53–54, 55, 129, 183, 188, 195–197, 209–210
AUK, media covering, 133–138
in Icelandic constitution-making process, 30–31
public participation and, 29, 31–32, 47
drafting, deferral in, 209–210, 216
by law clauses for, 212–214, 215–216
to subcommissions and consultants, 210–212, 215–216
Dündar, Can, 126–127

ECtHR. *See* European Court of Human Rights
EEC. *See* European Economic Community
1876 Constitution. *See* Ottoman Constitution
Elkins, Zachary, 23–24, 29, 110, 185–186
Elster, Jon, 25, 28–29, 131, 166, 254
embodiment claim, 62–63, 64–66, 67, 72, 80
AKP and, 63, 77–78, 79, 81–82, 83
of military, 74–78, 83
empty signifiers, 147–148, 152, 163, 180
epistemic community, AUK, 201
Erbal, Ayda, 198, 199

Erdoğan, Recep Tayyip, 78–79, 81–82, 111, 281
 AUK and, 55, 120–121, 136–137
 media and, 120–121, 124–125, 129–130, 138–140
Ergenekon investigations, 125–126
Esen, Selin, 208–209, 278, 279
EU accession, Turkish. *See* European Union
European Convention on Human Rights (Convention), 187–188, 202, 203–204, 207
 1982 Constitution, amendments to, and, 189–190
 AUK borrowing from, 186, 200–202, 204–205, 206–209, 216
European Court of Human Rights (ECtHR), 37
 AUK and influence of, 177, 186, 187–188, 198–199, 201–206, 208–209
 party closure cases before, 202–203
European Economic Community (EEC), 259, 262
European Union (EU), Turkish accession to, 162
 1982 constitution, amendments to, and, 37, 77, 78, 104–105, 224–225, 263–265
 countermajoritarian institutions, reform of, and, 219, 224–225
Evren, Kenan, 102–103, 258

failure, AUK, 21, 45–49, 56, 80, 182
 AKP and, 21, 49–50, 80–81, 83, 181–182, 265–266
 authoritarianism rising after, 217, 219
 constitutional referendums following, 265–266
 contested issues and, 22–23, 49–54, 106, 110–111, 147, 163–165, 180–181, 198
 deadline and, 55
 by design, 80–81, 116–117
 MHP and, 49–50, 181–182
 unanimity rule in, 54–55
failure, of Icelandic constitution-making process, 31
feedback loops, 32
Ferejohn, John, 255
Final Provisions, AUK, 267
flexibility, constitutional, 249, 251–256
 of 1921 and 1924 Constitutions, 256, 257, 258–259, 266–267
 AUK amendment-making and, 251, 269, 272–273, 276, 280–281
France, constitution of, 24–25, 29–30, 92
Free Republican Party *(Serbest Cumhuriyet Fırkası)* (SCF), 95
fundamental rights and freedoms, 101, 115–116, 190–191, 215
 under 1982 Constitution, 37, 104, 187–195, 206–208, 212
 in AUK, 44, 183–184, 187–188, 191–195, 200, 206–211, 212, 215–217
 constitutional borrowing and, 184, 187–188, 192–193, 200

Gargarella, Roberto, 53–54
Gençkaya, Faruk, 37–38, 75–76, 155
German Basic Law, 200
 human dignity in, 187–188, 192, 197–198, 199, 216
 parliamentary system of, 99
Germany, 1918 constitution-making process in, 29–30
Gezi protests, 128–129, 138–139, 217
Ginsburg, Tom, 23–24, 25, 29, 185–186, 212
 on amendment culture, 254–255
 on hyper-presidentialism and pure presidentialism, 110
Goderis, Benedikt, 185–186
Göral, Özgür Sevgi, 174, 192, 194
Gören, Zafer, 268
Göztepe, Ece, 229
Grand National Assembly, Turkish *(Türkiye Büyük Millet Meclisi)* (TBMM), 41, 90, 108–110, 115–116, 146
 1921, 1924 Constitutions and, 34, 71, 91–93, 150, 155
 under 1961 Constitution, 100–101, 150
 1980 coup and, 76
 1982 Constitution and, 102–103, 114, 150, 156–157
 in 2017 amendments, 112–115
 in AUK, debated, 172, 175–176
 in AUK, parties from, 38–39
 AYM and, 229–230, 231–232
 constituent power of, 39, 195–196, 267–269
 under DP rule, 96–97
 first, ministers in, 92–93
 with Ottoman Assembly, continuity of, 90–91
 second, 71, 93–95
Gül, Abdullah, 78, 104–105
Gülen, Fethullah, 125, 133, 138, 139, 140, 247
Gylfason, Thorvaldur, 31

Hâkimler ve Savcılar Yüksek Kurulu. *See* High Council of Judges and Prosecutors
Halkların Demokratik Partisi. *See* Peoples' Democratic Party
HDP. *See* Peoples' Democratic Party
headscarf ban, 78, 159–160, 204–205, 219, 226
hegemonic-totalitarian logic, 62–63, 67, 77–78, 83
  in 1924 Constitution, 71–72
  of AKP, 63, 81–82, 83
High Council of Judges and Prosecutors *(Hâkimler ve Savcılar Yüksek Kurulu)* (HSYK), 218–219, 223, 227–228, 247, 248
  under 1982 Constitution, 227, 234–235, 239–240
  2010 reform of, 228–229, 231, 239–240
  in AUK, proposed reform of, 220, 236–241, 246–248
Higher Education Coordination Council *(Yükseköğretim Düzenleme Kurulu)* (YDK), 235–236
Holmes, Stephen, 253
HSYK. *See* High Council of Judges and Prosecutors
human dignity, 197
  AUK on, 187–188, 192–193, 194, 197–200, 208, 216
  in German Basic Law, 187–188, 192, 197–198, 199, 216

Iceland, constitution-making process in, 30–31
IDEA. *See* Institute for Democracy and Electoral Assistance
incrementalist constitution, 52–53, 180
indeterminacy, 153–154, 159–160, 176–177
Institute for Democracy and Electoral Assistance (IDEA), 195
Inter-Party Constitutional Committee *(Partilerarası Uzlaşma Komisyonu)* (PUK), 263–265
Inter-University Council *(Üniversitelerarası Kurul)* (ÜAK), 226, 234–235, 247
Isiksel, Turkuler, 160
Islam, 88, 151–152, 189. *See also* religion
  1921 Constitution and majoritarianism of, 70–71
  2017 amendments and, 112
  AKP and, 127–128, 217
  human dignity and, 199
  nationalist, ideological shift to, 121–122
Istanbul Convention, 205–206
İttihat ve Terakki Partisi (İTP). *See* Union and Progress Party
Iyimaya, Ahmet, 174, 203–204, 211, 214–215, 233
  on amendment-making rules, 249, 272, 277, 278
  on national sovereignty, 167, 168

journalism, 122, 123–124
  after 1960 coup, 122–123, 154
  under AKP, persecution of, 124, 125–127, 138–140
  AUK coverage, 120–121, 132, 133–134, 135–136, 141
  partisan, constitution making and, 118–119
Justice and Development Party *(Adalet ve Kalkınma Partisi)* (AKP), 147–148, 248. *See also* 2017 amendments
  1982 Constitution, amendments to, and, 37–38, 78, 81–82, 84, 104–105, 263–264
  on 1982 Constitution, in AUK, 197–198
  2007 and 2010 amendments under, 250–251, 260, 263–266, 278–279, 280–281
  2010 referendum and, 78–79, 263–265
  amendment-making proposal, 2007, and, 274
  on amendment-making rules, AUK, 269–272, 274–279
  AUK, establishment of, and, 79–80, 105
  AUK, failure of, and, 21, 49–50, 80–81, 83, 181–182, 265–266
  in AUK, 38–39, 42, 44, 46–48, 54–55, 129
  authoritarianism of, 13, 60, 63, 67, 81–82, 83, 104, 110–111, 115, 116, 117, 170, 188, 190, 217, 266, 281
  AYM and, 37–38, 78, 104–105, 108–109, 263
  AYM and HSYK reform of, 2010, 228–230, 231, 239–240
  on AYM reform, in AUK, 177–178, 241–242, 243, 244–247
  center-periphery narrative and, 60–62, 81, 83
  on citizenship, in AUK, 51
  corporatist–clientelist media under, 124–125, 127–128, 140–141
  corruption scandal of, 2013, 138–139
  countermajoritarian reforms, AUK, obstructed by, 220, 246–247
  democracy contested by, in AUK, 169–171
  democratic demands and, 77, 82–83
  Diyanet contested by, in AUK, 50
  on ECtHR, in AUK, 203–204

embodiment claim and, 63, 77–78, 79, 81–82, 83
Erdoğan of, 55, 78–79, 81–82, 111, 120–121, 124–125, 129–130, 136–137, 138–140, 281
on freedom, in AUK, 187–188
heavy penal courts under, 162
as hegemonic party, 111, 117
on HSYK reform, AUK, 236–237, 238–241, 246–248
on human dignity, in AUK, 197–198, 199–200
Islamism of, 127–128, 217
journalists persecuted under, 124, 125–127, 138–140
Kurds and, 123–124, 126, 129–130, 181–182
on laicism, in AUK, 135, 164–167, 180–181
on law, rule of, in AUK, 175–176, 177–179
majoritarianism of, 104–105, 241–242, 265–266, 281
media and, 111, 119–122, 124–130, 133–135, 137–138, 139–142
national sovereignty contested by, in AUK, 167–169, 180–181
party closure and, 202, 203–204
people, will of, claimed by, 46–47, 79–80, 81–82, 170–171, 180
populist political strategy of, 78–79
power, empty place of, and, 62–63
powers, separation of, violated by, 163–164
presidential system advocated by, 51–52, 53, 81–82, 84, 107, 108–111, 112, 115, 116–117, 121, 136–137, 146–147, 163–164, 171–172, 174–175, 180–181, 244–245, 270–271
Şentop of, 53, 55, 165–166, 169–170, 171, 177, 178, 198–200, 203–205, 277
on sexual identity and orientation, in AUK, 205–206
state organization contested by, in AUK, 171–172, 173–175, 180–181
unanimity rule, AUK, and, 106
on YÖK, in AUK, 234–235
Justice Party *(Adalet Partisi)* (AP), 99, 100, 101

Kantorowicz, Ernst, 63–64
Kars Kaynar, Ayşegül, 224, 225
Kart, Atilla, 165–166, 178, 197–198
Katılımcı Demokrasi Partisi. See Participatory Democracy Party
Kemal, Mustafa, 70, 90, 122, 178–179, 223
1921 Constitution and, 69
TBMM and, 93, 94
Kemalism, 50, 75, 77–79, 217
1924 Constitution and, 71–72
1961 Constitution and, 74–76
center-periphery narrative and, 59–61, 62–63
raison d'état and, 148
second TBMM dominated by, 93–94
Kili, Suna, 73–74
King, two bodies of, 63–64
Köker, Levent, 70
Kurdistan Workers' Party *(Partiya Karkerên Kurdistan)* (PKK), 123–124, 129–130, 139–140
Kurds, 126–127, 130–131, 139–140, 189
AKP and, 123–124, 126, 129–130, 181–182
AUK and issues of, 45, 80, 129–130, 168–169, 174, 177, 180–181, 199–200, 213
party closure of, 150, 219

Laclau, Ernesto, 147
laicism, 50
of 1924 and 1961 Constitutions, 151–152
in AUK, contested, 135, 163, 164–167, 180–181, 182
law, rule of, 157–162
in 1921 and 1924 Constitutions, 158–159, 162–163
under 1961 Constitution, 158–159, 160–161, 162–163
under 1982 Constitution, 158–159, 162–163, 176
AUK on, 157–158, 163, 175–179, 180
Lefort, Claude, 63–64
Arato and, 65–66, 67, 83
on power, empty place of, 62–65, 79
legitimacy, 25–26, 32
of 1921 and 1924 Constitutions, 34–35
1960–1961 process lacking, 35–36
1980–1982 process lacking, 35–37, 61
AUK and, 45, 48–49
input, 31, 34, 35, 48–49
output, 31, 34–35, 36–37, 48–49
throughput, 31, 34, 35–36, 48–49
weak, of Turkish constitutions, 33–34
Lerner, Hanna, 195
on divided societies, 52–53, 54, 168, 179, 180, 195, 198, 209–210
on incrementalist constitution, 52–53, 180

Lijphart, Arend, 253, 274–275
limitation, rights, 101, 115–116, 158, 160–161, 162, 207
  under 1982 Constitution, 76–77, 161, 176–177, 188–190, 206–208
  AUK on, 176–177, 179, 187–188, 206–209
Lippmann, Walter, 142
Loewenstein, Karl, 23
Lord, Ceren, 67, 70–71, 81–82
lots, drawing of, 234, 247–248
Lutz, Donald, 253–254, 255

majoritarianism
  of 1921 and 1924 Constitutions, 70–71, 73–74, 81–82, 85–86, 93–94, 95, 96
  of 1961 Constitution, 74–75, 99
  AKP, 104–105, 241–242, 265–266, 281
majority imposition
  of 2017 amendments, 145–146, 181–182, 250–251
  in popular constitution making, potential, 118
Mardin, Şerif, 59, 60
maximum conditions, for popular constitution making, 21, 22, 31–32. *See also* minimum conditions, for popular constitution making
  AUK and meeting, 37, 48–49
  in Iceland, 2010 to 2013, 30–31
Meclis-i Mebusan. *See* Assembly, National
media, 118–120
  after 1960 coup, mass, 122–123
  AUK coverage of, 129–138, 141
  AUK polarization and, 120–121, 128–129, 132–133, 134–135, 136–138, 141–142
  AUK seeking media limitations on, 130, 131–132
  Gezi protests and repression of, 138–139
  Kurdish, 126, 130–131
  social, 138–141
  Turkish, polarized pluralistic model of, 123–124
media, illiberal
  under AKP, 119–120, 121–122, 124–129, 141–142
  Turkish history of, 121–124
media, mainstream
  as corporatist–clientelist, 124–125, 127–128, 140–141
  Gezi protests covered by, 138
  Kurdish issues in, 123–124, 126–127
media, opposition, 128, 132, 134–135, 137–138
media control, 111, 128–129, 140–141
media independence, 119, 120–121
  AKP curtailing, 124–128, 129–130
  AUK and, 135–136
Melton, James, 254–255
MGK. *See* National Security Council, Turkish
MHP. *See* Nationalist Movement Party
military, Turkish, 59–61, 78–79
  1960 coup of, 35, 37, 73, 75, 83, 97–100, 116, 122–123, 154, 265
  1961 Constitution and, 22, 35–37, 73–76, 98, 99–100, 101, 102–103, 116, 265
  1971 coup of, 75–76, 101, 116, 154, 161–162
  1980 coup of, 35–37, 61, 76, 83, 101–103, 104–105, 116, 123, 150–151, 225–226, 235, 258, 265
  1982 Constitution and, 22, 35–37, 61, 75–77, 102–103, 265
  countermajoritarian institutions and, 218–220, 223, 224–225, 248
  embodiment claim of, 74–78, 83
military tutelary regime, Turkey as, 218, 219–220, 223, 248
Milli Güvenlik Kurulu. *See* National Security Council, Turkish
Milliyetçi Hareket Partisi. *See* Nationalist Movement Party
minimum conditions, for popular constitution making, 21, 22, 29–30, 31, 37
Missak-ı Milli. *See* National Oath
MM. *See* Assembly, National
mother tongue, AUK on, 106, 133–134, 187–188
Motherland Party *(Anavatan Partisi)* (ANAP), 103, 259–263, 265, 271
MPNP. *See* Multi-Party Negotiating Process
Müdafaa-i Hukuk Cemiyeti (Association for the Defense of National Rights), 34
Multi-Party Negotiating Process (MPNP) (South Africa), 26–27
Murphy, Walter, 25, 28–29

narratives, 119
  of AKP, Islamist-nationalist, 127–128
  AUK, 120–121, 132–133, 142
  center-periphery, 59–63, 81, 83
  state, journalism influenced by, 123–124
National Oath *(Missak-ı Milli)*, 90
National Security Council, Turkish *(Milli Güvenlik Kurulu)* (MGK), 60, 102, 218–219, 223, 224–225
  in 1961 Constitution, 36, 99–100, 224

1982 Constitution and, 76, 102–103, 224–225, 232–233
in 2017 amendments, 247
reforming, 220, 224–225, 230–231, 232–233, 246–247
in YÖK, 226, 227
national sovereignty, 148, 151–152, 182
in 1921 and 1924 Constitutions, 67–68, 69–70, 149–150
in AUK, contested, 163, 164, 167–169, 180–181, 196–197
Nationalist Movement Party (*Milliyetçi Hareket Partisi*) (MHP), 38–39, 41, 42, 47–48, 79–80, 217
2017 amendments and, 81–82, 112, 113, 115, 145–146, 148, 181–182, 247–248, 250–251, 266
on amendment-making rules, AUK, 269, 270, 272–273, 274, 276–277, 278–279
in AUK coalitions, 54–55
on AYM reform, in AUK, 177–178, 241, 243, 244, 245–247
Bal of, 41, 145, 168, 173–175, 178, 199–200, 204–205, 211–212, 218, 276–277, 278–279
on citizenship, in AUK, 50–51
democracy contested by, in AUK, 169–170
Diyanet contested by, in AUK, 50
failure, AUK, and, 49–50, 181–182
on HSYK reform, in AUK, 236, 238–241, 246–248
on human dignity, in AUK, 197–198, 199–200
laicism contested by, in AUK, 164–167, 180–181, 182
on law, rule of, in AUK, 175–176, 177–178
MGK and, in AUK, 220, 232–233, 246–247
on national sovereignty, in AUK, 167–169, 180–181, 196–197
on presidential and parliamentary systems, in AUK, 46, 51–52, 107–108, 174–175, 180–181
on sexual identity and orientation, in AUK, 205–206
state organization contested by, in AUK, 171–172, 173–175, 180–181, 196–197
on YÖK, in AUK, 234–236
nationality, Turkish, 50–51, 148
news reporting. *See* journalism
1921 Constitution, Turkish, 91–92, 116, 150
1924 Constitution compared with, 67–70, 71, 257
flexibility of, 256, 258–259, 266–267
law, rule of, in, 158, 162–163
legitimacy of, 34–35
national sovereignty in, 67–68, 69–70, 149–150
pluralism of, 69, 70–71
TBMM and, 34, 71, 91–93, 150, 155
1924 Constitution, Turkish, 37, 95, 116, 150, 256
1921 Constitution compared with, 67–70, 71, 257
1961 Constitution and, 73–74, 99–100
amendment-making rules under, 257, 258–259, 261
authoritarianism and, 71–72, 80, 83, 85–86
CHP dominant under, 95–96
competitive politics under, 95–97
DP rule under, 96–97
flexibility, rigidity of, 257, 258–259, 266–267
Kemalism and, 71–72
laicism of, 151–152
law, rule of, in, 158–159, 162–163
legitimacy of, 34–35
majoritarianism of, 73–74, 81–82, 85–86, 93–94, 95, 96
national sovereignty in, 67–68, 149–150
parliamentary system of, 94–95, 96, 150, 155
TBMM and, 34, 71, 93–95
1961 Constitution, Turkish, 74–76, 98, 101–102, 116
1924 Constitution and, 73–74, 99–100
1960 coup and, 35, 37, 73, 75, 83, 97–100
1982 Constitution and, 37, 75, 76–77, 102–103, 188–189
after 1971 coup, amendments to, 75–76, 101, 154, 161–162
amendment-making rules under, 257–259, 261
AUK and, 52
authoritarianism and, 75–76, 85–86, 99, 102, 160–161
AYM under, 99–100, 156, 158–159, 228, 257, 258
CHP and, 74, 100
constitutional borrowing of, 200
constitution-making process of, 35–37, 50, 98–99, 151–152
democracy in, 152–153, 154–155
HSYK in, 227
laicism in, 50, 151–152
law, rule of, under, 158–159, 160–161, 162–163
legitimacy lacking for, 35–36
as majoritarian, 74–75, 99

1961 Constitution, Turkish, (cont.)
mass media and, 122–123
MGK in, 36, 99–100, 224
military and, 22, 35–37, 73–76, 98, 99–100, 101, 102–103, 265
parliamentary system of, 52, 99–101, 150, 155–156, 172
pluralism and, 74, 75–76, 151
powers, separation of, in, 155–156
referendum adopting, 257, 265, 266–267
representation in, 150, 151, 154–155
rigidity of, 258–259, 266–267
1982 Constitution, Turkish, 102–103, 116
1961 Constitution and, 37, 75, 76–77, 102–103, 188–189
1980 coup and, 35, 37, 61, 76, 83, 258, 265
amendment-making rules under, 251, 258–259, 260, 261–262, 269, 270–273, 280
amendment-making rules under, 1987 amendment of, 103–104, 259, 260, 261–263, 265, 266–267, 269, 270–273, 274–276, 280–281
amendments to, 1995 and 2001, 37–38, 86, 104, 188–190, 224–225
amendments to, 2007 and 2010, 37–38, 104–105, 193, 250–251, 260, 263–266, 278–279, 280–281
amendments to, AKP and, 37–38, 78, 81–82, 84, 104–105, 263–264
amendments to, democratic, 37–38, 86, 103–104, 116, 263–265
amendments to, EU accession and, 37, 77, 78, 104–105, 224–225, 263–265
AUK and, 41, 43, 44, 52, 103, 184, 187, 191–196, 197–198, 199, 206–208, 213, 216, 267–269
authoritarianism and, 61, 76–77, 84–85, 102–103, 151, 188–189
AYM under, 157, 158–159, 228, 246, 258
center-periphery narrative and, 61
competitive politics under, 103–104
democracy and, 152–153, 154, 157
embodiment claim of, 76–77
fundamental rights and freedoms under, 37, 104, 187–195, 206–208
HSYK under, 227, 234–235, 239–240
law, rule of, and, 158–159, 162–163, 176–177
legitimacy lacking for, 35–37, 61
MGK and, 76, 102–103, 224–225, 232–233
military and, 22, 35–37, 61, 75–77, 102–103, 265
parliamentary system of, 103–104, 109–110, 150, 156–157, 172, 174
political parties in, 184
powers, separation of, and, 156–157
referendum adopting, 258, 265
representation in, 150, 151, 154–155
rights, limitation of, under, 76–77, 161, 176–177, 188–190, 206–208
rigidity of, 258–259, 266–267
state security courts under, 162
TBMM and, 102–103, 114, 150, 156–157
YÖK under, 225–226, 227, 234–235, 239–240
norms, 186–187
hierarchization of, 186, 200–206
international, 184–185, 186, 187–188, 198–199, 200, 203–204, 216
vernacularization of, 186–187

Oder, Bertil Emrah, 196, 214–215, 259, 264
Ólafsson, Jón, 30, 31
Önder, Sırrı Süreyya, 198–199, 205–206
Örücü, Esin, 200
Ottoman Constitution (1876), 33–34, 87–88, 90, 93, 116, 256
amendment-making rule in, 256, 261
sovereignty in, 149–150
Ottoman Empire, 33–34, 50–51, 86–88, 96
Assembly in, 87–91
special courts in, 161–162
Özal, Turgut, 259–260, 262, 265, 271
Özbudun, Ergun, 37–38, 74, 75–76, 260
on 1924 Constitution, 72, 257
on powers, fusion of, 155
Öztürk, Oktay, 211, 276–277

Panizza, Francisco, 66
parliamentarianism, 146
of 1924 Constitution, 94–95, 96, 150, 155
1961 Constitution and, 52, 99–100, 101, 150, 155–156, 172
1982 Constitution and, 103–104, 109–110, 150, 156–157, 172, 174
in AUK, contested, 51–52, 106–108, 146–147, 174, 180–181
participation, public, 23–24, 29, 82–83
in AUK, 23–24, 38, 42–43, 45–50, 80–81, 131, 145–147, 267–268
direct, in Iceland, 30–31
media and difficulties of, 118–119, 120

Participatory Democracy Party *(Katılımcı Demokrasi Partisi)* (KADEP), 45
parties, political, 150, 154–155, 183–184
hegemonic, 111, 116, 117
polarization and system of, 100–101
Partilerarası Uzlaşma Komisyonu. See Inter-Party Constitutional Committee
Partiya Karkerên Kurdistan. See Kurdistan Workers' Party
party closure, 202–204
AKP and, 202, 203–204
by AYM, 150, 160–161, 202, 219, 243
Kurdish, 150, 219
path dependency, 67, 80, 161–162, 184
constitutional stickiness as, 191
of state organization, 147, 148–149, 164, 182
Peace and Democracy Party *(Barış ve Demokrasi Partisi)* (BDP), 38–39, 42, 44, 47–48, 79–80, 213
amendment-making proposal, AUK, of, 269, 270, 273, 274–275
in AUK, issues proposed by, 133–134
in AUK coalitions, 54–55
on AYM reform, AUK, 177–178, 241, 243–244, 245–247
on citizenship, in AUK, 51
democracy contested by, in AUK, 169–171
Diyanet contested by, in AUK, 50
on fundamental rights and freedoms, in AUK, 191, 192–193, 194
on HSYK reform, AUK, 236, 238–240, 246–247
on human dignity, in AUK, 197–199
laicism opposed by, in AUK, 164–167, 180–181
on law, rule of, in AUK, 175–176, 177–179
on mother tongue issue, in AUK, 133–134
national sovereignty contested by, in AUK, 167–169, 180–181
party closure and, 202
on presidential and parliamentary systems, in AUK, 46, 51–52, 107–108, 180–181
on sexual orientation, in AUK, 205–206
state organization contested by, in AUK, 171–172, 173–175, 180–181
on YÖK, in AUK, 234, 235
people, the
in 1921 Constitution, 149–150
AKP claiming will of, 46–47, 79–80, 81–82, 170–171, 180
AUK on, 163, 167–169, 170–171
ethnic and civic definitions of, 167
will of, 46–47, 62–63, 76, 79–82, 87–88, 167, 170–171, 180
Peoples' Democratic Party *(Halkların Demokratik Partisi)* (HDP), 111
PKK. *See* Kurdistan Workers' Party
pluralism
of 1921 Constitution, 69, 70–71
1961 Constitution and, 74, 75–76, 151
media, polarized, 123–124
representational, obstruction of, 150–151, 159–160, 162–163
pluralist-democratic logic, 62–63
polarization, 187–188
AUK, media coverage and, 120–121, 128–129, 132–133, 134–135, 137–138, 141–142
of party system, 100–101
pluralistic, media, 123–124
populism, 63, 65–66, 78–79, 83
power, constituent, 66–67, 83
in AUK, question of, 39, 195–196, 267–269
military appropriating, 74–75, 76
power, empty place of, 64–66, 67, 74–76
Lefort on, 62–65, 79
performative closing, opening of, 62–63, 66–67, 75, 83
powers, fusion of, 155
powers, separation of, 115–116, 145–146, 155–157
in AUK, contested, 163–164, 171–175, 180–181
fusion contrasted with, 155
A Practical Guide to Constitution-Making (IDEA), 195
predrafting agreements, 195
Presidency of Religious Affairs *(Diyanet İşleri Başkanlığı)* (Diyanet), 50
presidentialism, 112–114
in 2017 amendments, 81–82, 84, 112–115, 140, 250–251, 263–265
AKP advocating, 51–52, 53, 81–82, 84, 107, 108–111, 112, 115, 116–117, 121, 136–137, 146–147, 163–164, 171–172, 174–175, 180–181, 244–245, 270–271
in AUK, contested, 46, 51–52, 53–54, 106–111, 112, 116–117, 120–121, 145, 146–147, 163–164, 171–172, 173–175, 180–181
DP rule and, 96
hyper-presidentialism and pure presidentialism, 110
public opinion on, 146, 180–181
principles, constitutional, 195, 199
process, constitution-making, 28–29, 166

Progressive Republican Party *(Terkakkiperver Cumhuriyet Fırkası)* (TCF), 95
publicity, 118, 128, 131–133
PUK. *See* Inter-Party Constitutional Committee

raison d'état, 147–149, 156
Rawls, John, 25
reasoning-writing, 188, 214–216
Refah Partisi. *See* Welfare Party
referendums, 266, 281
  1961 Constitution and, 257, 265, 266–267
  1982 Constitution and, 258, 265
  in 1987 amendment, 269
  2010, 78–79, 265–266
  on 2017 amendments, 260, 265–266
  amendment-making, 259–263, 265, 266–267, 269, 270–273, 281
religion
  center-periphery duality and, 59–61
  freedom of, 204–205
representation, 24, 150
  pluralist, obstruction of, 150–151, 159–160, 162–163
  political party, 150, 154–155
Republican People's Party *(Cumhuriyet Halk Partisi)* (CHP), 71, 96–97, 98, 223
  1921,1924 Constitutions and, 34, 95–96
  1961 Constitution and, 74, 100
  2007 election and, 78
  on amendment-making rules, AUK, 269, 270, 272, 274–275, 276–278, 279
  in AUK, 38–39, 42, 44, 46–48, 79–80
  in AUK, on constitution, vision for, 196–197
  in AUK coalitions, 54–55
  authoritarian turn of, 104
  on AYM reform, AUK, 177–178, 241, 242–243, 244, 245–247
  on citizenship, in AUK, 51
  democracy contested by, in AUK, 169–171
  on ECtHR, in AUK, 203–204
  embodiment claim of, 72, 83
  on fundamental rights and freedoms, in AUK, 187–188, 192–193, 194
  on HSYK reform, AUK, 236, 237–240, 246–247
  on human dignity, in AUK, 197–198
  journalism and rule of, 122
  laicism contested by, in AUK, 135, 164–167, 180–181
  on law, rule of, in AUK, 175–176, 177–179
  national sovereignty contested by, in AUK, 167–168, 180–181
  on party closure, in AUK, 202–203
  on presidential and parliamentary systems, in AUK, 51–52, 53, 107–108, 180–181
  in second TBMM, precursors of, 93
  on sexual orientation, in AUK, 205–206
  in single-party period, 71–72, 116, 122
  state organization contested by, in AUK, 171–172, 173–175, 180–181
  Türmen of, 166, 167, 169–170, 187–188, 198–199, 201–203, 204–206, 214, 215, 276–278, 279
  on YÖK, in AUK, 234–235
rigidity, constitutional, 254, 255–256, 257, 258–259, 266–267
  AUK amendment-making and, 251, 269, 272–273, 276, 277, 280–281
  flexibility and, 249, 251–256, 269, 280–281
Rosanvallon, Pierre, 64–65
roundtable, 25–28
Rousseau, Jean-Jacques, 92

Şahin, Mehmet Ali, 205–206
Sancak, Ethem, 124–125
Sartori, Giovanni, 100–101
Saving Deposit Insurance Fund *(Tasarruf Mevduatı Sigorta Fonu)* (TMSF), 124–125
SCF. *See* Free Republican Party
Schudson, Michael, 119, 141
Scotti, Valentina, 200
secrecy, 28–29, 131
secularism. *See* laicism
Sened-i İttifak (Charter of Alliance) (1808), 33
Şentop, Mustafa, 53, 55, 165–166, 177, 178, 204–205
  in amendment-making debate, 277
  on democracy, 169–170, 171
  on ECtHR, 203–204
  on human dignity, 198–200
Serbest Cumhuriyet Fırkası. *See* Free Republican Party
sexual orientation and identity, 205–206
Sledgehammer. *See* Balyoz investigation
snap elections, 2015, 111, 139–140
social media, 138–141
Sosyal, Mümtaz, 95

South Africa, 26–28, 195, 199
spectrum, popular constitution making, 29–33
Stasavage, David, 132
state organization, 146, 147–148, 163, 167–169, 179–180
  2017 amendments reconstructing, 147–148
  in AUK, contested, 51–52, 106–108, 146–148, 163, 171–175, 180–182, 196–197
  failure, AUK, and, 147, 163–165, 180–181
  path dependency of, 147, 148–149, 164, 182
statism, 148–149, 151–152, 170, 198, 216
  2017 amendments and return to, 181–182
  of AYM, 156, 159–161
Strøm, Kaare, 95
subcommissions, 210, 215–216
Sweet, Alec Stone, 220–221

Tan, Altan, 166, 168
Tanör, Bülent, 69, 74
Tasarruf Mevduatı Sigorta Fonu. *See* Saving Deposit Insurance Fund
TBMM. *See* Grand National Assembly, Turkish
TCF. *See* Progressive Republican Party
television, 122–123
Terkakkiperver Cumhuriyet Fırkası. *See* Progressive Republican Party
territorial integrity, 151–152, 182
Thatcher, Mark, 220–221
TMSF. *See* Saving Deposit Insurance Fund
totalitarianism, 63, 65
  embodiment claim and, 65–66
  hegemonic-totalitarian logic, 62–63, 67, 71–72, 77–78, 81–82, 83
transparency, 28–29, 120, 131
  1980–1982 process lacking, 35–36
  of AUK, 40, 131–133, 141–142
TRT. *See* Turkish Radio and Broadcasting Corporation
Tsebelis, George, 255–256
Turkish Radio and Broadcasting Corporation *(Türkiye Radyo Televizyon Kurumu)* (TRT), 122–123, 138–139
Türkiye Büyük Millet Meclisi. *See* Grand National Assembly, Turkish
Türkiye Radyo Televizyon Kurumu. *See* Turkish Radio and Broadcasting Corporation
Türmen, Rıza, 166, 167, 169–170, 205–206
  on amendment-making rules, 276–278, 279
  ECtHR and, 187–188, 198–199, 201–203, 204–205
  reasoning-writing and, 214, 215
Twitter, 138–141
2007 election, 78, 104–105
2011–2013 constitution-making process. *See specific topics*
2011 elections, 128
2016 military coup attempt, 111, 112, 188
  AKP referendums following, 266, 281
  Gülen and, 140, 247
2017 amendments, 111–115, 116, 117, 260, 265–266
  AUK and, 181–182
  authoritarianism of, 111–112, 149, 181–182, 263
  AYM and, 114, 115, 248
  censored coverage of, 140
  HSYK in, 247–248
  as majority imposition, 145–146, 181–182, 250–251
  MGK in, 247
  MHP and, 81–82, 112, 113, 115, 145–146, 148, 181–182, 247–248, 250–251, 266
  presidential system in, 81–82, 84, 112–115, 140, 250–251, 263–265
  state organization reconstructed by, 147–148
  TBMM in, 112–115
  YÖK and, 247

ÜAK. *See* Inter-University Council
unanimity rule, AUK. *See* working principles, AUK
Union and Progress Party *(İttihat ve Terakki Partisi)* (İTP), 89–90, 93, 104, 116
United States (U.S.)
  constitution of, 24–25, 29–30, 119
  Supreme Court of, 222
Üniversitelerarası Kurul. *See* Inter-University Council

Vahdettin (sultan), 90–91
Varol, Ozan, 191, 274–275
Venice Commission, 203–205
Versteeg, Mila, 185–186
viewpoint diversity, 119–120

website, AUK, 130, 131–132
Welfare Party *(Refah Partisi)*, 202–203
women, 22, 34–35, 91, 194
working principles, AUK, 22–23, 39–41, 42, 53, 267, 278
  transparency, 40
  unanimity rule, 22, 39–40, 41–42, 43, 54–55, 56, 79–81, 105–106, 129, 196–197

YDK. *See* Higher Education Coordination Council
Yeğen, Mesut, 50–51
Yeşil, Bilge, 124, 126–127
YÖK. *See* Council of Higher Education
Yükseköğretim Düzenleme Kurulu. *See* Higher Education Coordination Council
Yükseköğretim Kurulu. *See* Council of Higher Education